Mr. Cheap's
San Francisco

Mark Waldstein

Contributing Editors
Tami Monahan
Hiyaguha Cohen

Editorial Assistant
Alanna Kelleher

BOB ADAMS, INC.
Holbrook, Massachusetts

ACKNOWLEDGEMENTS

A heartfelt thank you goes out to all the people who helped make Mr Cheap's first West Coast foray a reality. Thanks to Susan Manning, Angie Rando, and Jan Altman. Thanks also to Liza Zenni at Theater Bay Area for all sorts of useful information about the arts scene. Back home, thanks to Erica Jorgensen and Kim Camlet for additional research contributions.

From Tami: Thanks to Ali Woolwich and Karen Bennett and all their friends for showing me around the Castro and Noe Valley and giving me a home away from home. I'd also like to thank the many people I met in The City who were only too happy to offer suggestions of the "best" cheap places in town. Lastly, much thanks to Mom, Dad, and Preston for their endless supply of support and encouragement.

Published by Bob Adams, Inc.
260 Center Street, Holbrook, MA 02343

ISBN: 1-55850-388-9

Printed in the United States of America

A   B   C   D   E   F   G   H   I   J

Library of Congress Cataloging-in-Publication Data
    Waldstein, Mark.
    Mr. Cheap's San Francisco : bargains, factory outlets, off-price stores, deep discount stores,
cheap eats, cheap places to stay, and cheap fun things to do / Mark Waldstein.
        p.   cm.
    Includes index.
    ISBN: 1-55850-388-9
    1. San Francisco (Calif.)—Guidebooks. I. Title.
    F869.S33W35   1994
    917.94'610453—dc20   94-16132
                                                                  CIP

This publication is designed to provide accurate and authoritative information with regard to the subject matter covered. It is sold with the understanding that the publisher is not engaged in rendering legal, accounting, or other professional advice. If legal advice or other expert assistance is required, the services of a qualified professional person should be sought.
    — From a *Declaration of Principles* jointly adopted by a Committee of the American Bar Association and a Committee of Publishers and Associations.

This book is available at quantity discounts for bulk purchases.
For information, call 1-800-872-5627.

CONTENTS

A Few (Carefully Chosen) Words from Mr. Cheap

SHOPPING

A FEW (CAREFULLY CHOSEN) WORDS
FROM MR. CHEAP

About this "cheap" business. I'll admit, there are more elegant ways to put the idea.

Lots of folks want to save money, especially in these tough times. When it comes to low *prices*, few people know as many good places as I do. But, strictly speaking, that doesn't make these stores and restaurants "cheap." Nor does it make anyone who uses this book a "cheapskate." I think *thrifty* would be a better word. Or perhaps *frugal*.

After all, a cheap person, in my mind, is someone who has plenty of money to burn, and refuses to touch it; a thrifty person would probably spend the cash if he or she had it—expecially for something of good value. Most of us fall into the latter category, don't we?

Anyway, everyone loves a bargain, and it's my pleasure to pass these tips along. This whole idea grew out of my own personal experience, from years of living on the financial edge as a "starving artist." My background is in theater and writing; and, as most people know, actors don't make any money—even with steady work. I learned to live "cheaply" out of necesssity, and developed my first book (*Mr. Cheap's Boston*) as a way to put this knowledge to good use, helping out folks in similar straits. That book wound up on the *Boston Globe* bestseller list; *Mr. Cheap's New York* soon followed. Suddenly, I discovered myself on a mission!

There is, by now, a research technique behind these books, but "cheaping" is hardly an exact science. Prices change all the time. Stores come and go. Restaurants change their menus. So, you won't find the exact same items on the shelves tomorrow that I found during my travels; but the descriptions in this book are sure to help you track down just about anything you may be looking for, at the lowest possible price.

A few words of caution: "You gets what you pays for." It's been said many times, and it's generally true. With new merchandise in particular, prices are always discounted for a reason. It may be that the item is simply a leftover from last year, yet still perfectly good; in other cases, if the price is low, the quality may not be far behind. I have tried to point out, wherever I could, items that are cheap because they are less well made, or because they are irregular or damaged. Even these "IR" goods may be useful to the reader who only needs them to last for a short time—students furnishing a dorm room, for example—or, to shoppers who happen to be handy with a hammer, or a needle and thread. Sometimes, the "truly cheap" is all you need.

I fully expect to hear from readers who insist I've left out their favorite diner, or some resale boutique they love. To these fellow bargain hunters, I say, Mr. C can't be *everywhere*; but I encourage you to please pass along the information, and I'll be happy to scout your suggestions out for our next edition. The address is:

Mr. Cheap
c/o Bob Adams, Inc.
260 Center St.
Holbrook, MA 02343

So, get ready to use the book—but be careful how you use the name! As you see, "cheap" can mean many things. And when you tell your friends that you paid only $45 for your designer outfit, nobody will be laughing. They'll just want to know how you did it.

On to the goodies!

Mark Waldstein
a.k.a. Mr. Cheap

SHOPPING

The hundreds of stores in this section are all places which will save you money in some way. They actually cover a broad spectrum of discount shopping, from the latest designer clothing to thrift shops, new furniture and used, major brands and second-rate imitations. Mr. Cheap wants to cover it all, giving his readers as many options as possible for saving cash.

Whenever it's appropriate, Mr. C points out *why* an item is marked down—whether it's discontinued, second-quality (imperfect), or just plain cheap stuff. Thus informed, it is up to you to decide which stores are right for you.

The prices quoted, again, are based upon items Mr. C found at the time of his research. You shouldn't expect to find the same items, at the same prices, when you shop; these prices are just examples which are similar to what you may find. Even as prices go up overall, you should still find the book completely useful in comparing one place against another, since all the research was done around the same time.

Many stores which sell several kinds of merchandise have been cross-referenced for you, appearing in each appropriate chapter; but remember to consult "Discount Department Stores" and "Flea Markets and Emporia" for many of the same items which have their own chapters. Similarly, the "General Markets" portion of the "Food Shops" chapter gives you more places to look for individual kinds of foods.

Finally, you won't see much here in the way of "superstores" and big national chains. It's not that there's anything wrong with such places; they certainly offer good prices in general, and special sales which few independent stores can match. But Mr. C figures you already know about these mega-stores, with their huge advertising budgets. He prefers to save costly ink for those unique, out-of-the-way "discoveries" that hardcore shopping fans love.

Okay, enough talking—*Go to it!*

A SHOPPING NOTE
FROM MR. CHEAP

Among its many bargain opportunities, San Francisco has two shopping centers packed with large and small discount shops. Both are found in SoMa: The Six-Sixty Center, located at 660 Third Street, and the Yerba Buena Center, at 899 Howard Street. Most of these are clothing shops, although some other kinds are mixed in.

Several of these are described in this book's "Clothing—New" chapter. Mr. C has culled their names below, just to give you a handy list. You may want to check them off as you work your way through!

The Six-Sixty Center:
Dress Market
Glassware International
Kidswear Center
Kris Alyssa Michele
Kyda Trading Company
Madelles
The Newport Trading Co.
The Outerwear Co.
Sister Sister

Yerba Buena Center:
Bright Blue Limited
$5 and $10 Store
Malson's Ragsmatazz
Multiple Choice$ Outlet
Salina Fashion
Shoe Pavilion

APPLIANCES

There are lots of places to save money on appliances and electronics in the Bay Area. Some, unfortunately, are as far below repute as they are below retail. With merchandise that is imported from foreign countries, there is a greater possibility of shady deals, or shoddy quality. Mr. C says this not out of any kind of prejudice, but because he wants you to be careful.

One of the best ways to protect yourself, if you have doubts as to *any* store's reliability, is to ask about their guarantee policy; make sure the item you want carries an American warranty. Since some stores deal directly with manufacturers in the Far East, their merchandise many carry a foreign warranty instead. Even for identical products, a foreign warranty can make repairs a hassle—unless you don't mind paying the postage to Japan! Remember, you are perfectly within your rights to inquire about this in the store.

ABC Appliance
- 2048 Taraval St. (31st Ave.), San Francisco; (415) 564-8166

This Parkside store is your classic, longtime neighborhood appliance business. But, if it looks sleepier than those bright, glitzy superstores, don't be fooled—you can get good deals here on the same current models, for kitchen and laundry. ABC is an authorized dealer for several major brands, including KitchenAid, Maytag, Whirlpool, Admiral, and more. And they're all here, jammed into two small showrooms with not a millimeter between them.

But who needs in-store amenities, when you can get deals like a Hotpoint large capacity washing machine, listed at $420, selling here for $349? Mr. C also saw an Admiral steel-top gas range, with a self-cleaning oven, reduced from $780 to just $519. And a Whirlpool 21 cubic-foot side-by-side refrigerator and freezer, with an in-door ice dispenser, was nearly $200 off at $1,039.

Some of these are end-of-year closeouts, mixed right in with newer models, for even better deals. All are fully warrantied by the manufacturers. Financing is available through the store; so is delivery, for an extra fee. Open Mondays through Saturdays from 9 a.m. to 4 p.m., and Sundays from 10-2 only.

C.G. Electric Appliance
- 6422 Mission St. (Daly Blvd.), Daly City; (415) 756-3931

Just over the line into Daly City (at the "Top of the Hill"), C.G. has been offering good deals on all major appliances for nearly forty years. As a member of a large buying group, the store is able to get low prices directly from the manufacturers, and thus keep its own prices down. This is a factory authorized dealer and repair center for most major brands, including several lesser-known European brands, like Bosch and Asko. These makers tend to use higher-quality materials (how about an all-stainless steel dishwasher); but here, they are priced to compete with the American lines.

There are always lots of in-store specials and closeout deals, along with good prices on current models. A year-end deal on a Magic Chef dishwasher, for example, could save you $150 at a sale price of $399. Another Magic Chef item, a twenty-pound capacity dryer (yes, they make these too), was recently on sale for just $199. And, would you believe: A Jenn-Air 23.6 cubic-foot refrigerator-freezer, side-by-side with an ice and water dispenser in the door—all for $999? That's a huge machine, at huge savings. On the smaller side, you can get microwave ovens from as low as $89 and up.

C.G. is also a member store in the Electric-Gas Industry Association, which means that it honors the full range (sorry, no pun intended) of rebates offered on new machines by P.G. & E. The store also has extra discounts for contractors and landlords. Free financing is available, along with free delivery on certain models. Open weekdays from 9 a.m. to 6 p.m., and Saturdays from 10-5.

Related to C.G., but right in town, is **Bob's Supply** at 1665 Mission Street (near 12th Street); telephone (415) 626-6246. This store focuses more upon those high-end and imported brands; but again, offers competitive prices.

Cherin's Discount Appliances
• 727 Valencia St. (18th St.), San Francisco; (415) 864-2111
Don't come into Cherin's Discount looking for, well, a discount. This longtime neighborhood store in the Mission doesn't exactly mark anything down; it's the way they mark *up* their merchandise which attracts Mr. C's attention. Unlike many bargain stores which advertise the percentage they take off the retail list price, Cherin's has one standard pricing policy. They start from their wholesale cost, and add a miniscule 8% on top. That's not much in the business world!

Cherin's carries all of the top name brands, including Frigidaire, General Electric, Maytag, Whirlpool, and more—in refrigerators, stoves, dishwashers, and other major appliances. They are highly service oriented, and will take all the time you need to consult with you and get you the right equipment. As for the price, you can rest assured that it's a good deal.

Cherin's is open Monday through Friday from 9:30 a.m. to 5:30 p.m., and on Saturday from 10 a.m. to 5 p.m.

Goodman Lumber
• 445 Bayshore Blvd. (Waterloo St.), San Francisco; (415) 285-2800
Appliances at a lumber store? Ah, but Goodman aspires to be so much more than that. It's really like the general stores of old, also selling a bit of this 'n that—hardware, lighting, furniture, plants, and yes, home appliances.

The selection is not vast, but you can find some neat deals, especially on closeouts. Mr. C noted a Caloric gas range with a 30" top, recently on sale for $199—exactly $100 off its regular selling price. A Gibson 17-cubic foot refrigerator/freezer, frost-free, was also seen for a cool $569. And a Tappan dishwasher in the store's "scratch and dent" area actually showed few scratches—but there were enough to scratch the price down from $359 to $159. What the heck, it's worth a look if you're in the market for appliances. Open seven days a week.

Hoover Factory Store
• 3628 Geary Blvd. (Arguello Blvd.), San Francisco; (415) 668-5101
Wanna clean up on vacuums? This is one place to try. It's a genuine Hoover store, providing sales, repairs and supplies to neat-freaks in the Richmond area and beyond. The deals Mr. C found here were on discontinued models and reconditioned trade-ins. In fact, before going on to describe some of these, it should be noted that you can trade in any model of vacuum cleaner—by any brand, not just Hoover—for a discount on any new model in the store. That's a good deal already.

But then, you have the trade-ins for purchase. There are usually only a handful on display at any given time in this small store, but some of the machines Mr. C found on his visit included a "Quik-Broom" upright for $40, and a Scrub 'n Vac shampoo polisher, originally $200, on sale for

$140. Among the non-used manufacturer closeouts, there was a self-propelled Powermax upright vacuum reduced from a list price of $350 to just $220.

A tiny, neighborhood kind of shop, the friendly folks in here do expert repairs (you'll need to drop your machine off) and can also sell you all the bags, belts, foams and other accessories you could possibly need. Open weekdays from 8 a.m. to 6 p.m., and Saturdays until 5.

Nappcor Appliance Bargain Center

- 7404 Mission St. (San Pedro Rd.), Daly City; (415) 755-6740 or 755-5958

Also known as Primer's Maytag, this store is located just above the Colma line—and right underneath the Town and Country Billiards parlor. The latter fact makes for rather interesting noises coming steadily through the ceiling. But it's worth it, since you can definitely get bargain-basement prices on used and closeout appliances.

The folks here (it's a family operation, in fact) estimate that about 80% of the stock is used; the other 20% are good deals on new units. It's pretty hard to tell the difference. Mr. C found a Caloric gas range for $299, absolutely like new; and a Frigidaire top-mounted refrigerator-freezer for $479. Other, more used-looking washers and dryers start as low as $75 and up; all the big names are here, including Maytag, Kenmore, Tappan, and so on.

Mr. C was also told that there is a bit of bargaining room in some of these prices; if you're a good haggler, give it a shot. All sales, meanwhile, are "as is" and final; however, reconditioned appliances do come with a guarantee of thirty days on labor, ninety days on parts. Open Monday-Saturday, 9 a.m. to 6 p.m.

Sam's Appliances

- 569 Valencia St. (17th St.), San Francisco; (415) 861-5890

Sam's fills three large storefronts in the North Mission district—about

---

MR. CHEAP'S PICKS
Appliances

✔ **Cherin's Discount Appliances**—Neighborhood store in the Mission with low markup on big-ticket items. Nearby, **Sam's Appliances** can get you reconditioned appliances for pennies on the dollar.

✔ **Nappcor Appliance Bargain Center**—In Daly City, great deals on new and used appliances, all guaranteed.

---

half the block—with a vast quantity of big-ticket appliances, both new and used. On one side, you'll find good prices on shiny, new units for the kitchen and laundry room; some of these are "slightly imperfects" and floor models, all of which still carry the full manufacturer's warranty. Mr. C found a good closeout deal on a 20 cubic-foot Magic Chef side-by-side refrigerator-freezer, with a built-in water-ice dispenser on the door (enough hyphens for ya?), all for $1,150—and a Kelvinator 15 cubic-foot frost-free model for just $450. A Tappan gas stove, with a self-cleaning oven below, was priced well at $599; and, for $699, you could recently get a Frigidaire combination washer and dryer.

Meanwhile, the other half of the store is filled with secondhand versions of the same things—a great way to save even more money. There is usually a large stock on hand, allowing you to choose the size and quality you want (some of these are fairly recent models; some are older, at lower prices). Need a fridge? Some cost as little as $75 (for those half-size, apartment or dorm numbers). If you want a newer, frost-free model, these start at $150 and go up to $250 or so. Dishwashers are about $165 and up; washing machines and dryers are about $125 each and up. Mr. C saw a Maytag washer/dryer unit in here for $325.

These used appliances have been restored to good working order by a trained repair staff on the premises; their work is warantied for three months, parts and labor—as good a guarantee as you'll ever get on such items. Given these options, the store is ideally suited to its working-class neighborhood—as well as students, first-time apartment renters, or anyone else looking to save big. Closed on Sundays.

Down the street a couple of blocks, you may also want to check out **King's Refrigeration** at 659 Valencia Street; telephone (415) 431-0255. This smaller storefront operation buys and sells used appliances of all kinds, not just refrigerators; although Mr. C did find, believe it or not, a Frigidaire 21 cubic-foot frost-free for a cool $200 (sorry, it's probably gone by now). You can also get washers and dryers in here for about $150 each. All appliances are repaired in the store, and again carry a 90-day warranty. Also closed on Sundays.

BOOKS

You can save extra money on books by shopping for *used* titles. San Francisco, Oakland and Berkeley are blessed with enough of these to give the hungriest bookworm indigestion; several are mixed into the listings below. Save even more by bringing in books that you no longer want. Most stores will give you a choice of cash or in-store credit; you'll usually get a higher figure by choosing the credit. It's a good, cheap way to check out new authors—and to keep your library lean.

Abandoned Planet Bookstore
● 518 Valencia St. (16th St.), San Francisco; (415) 861-4695

For an Abandoned Planet, this store feels a lot like home—with a sunny skylight and pillow-strewn window seats, not to mention the requisite cat strolling about. It's a comfortable, laid-back place where you'll find a great selection of used books at excellent prices.

The biggest savings are on hardcover books. Some recent bargains included *Where is Joe Merchant?* by Jimmy Buffet, cover price $19.95, selling here for $6; and *Beloved* by Toni Morrison, originally $18.95, here $6.50. Savings on paperbacks are smaller, but still good. A paperback edition of Hemingway's *A Farewell to Arms*, originally $4.95, was priced at just $3.

In addition to their huge selection of used books, Abandoned Planet Bookstore has occasional literary readings and other cultural events. Recently, they sponsored a Sunday evening in-store performance of the play *Talk to Me Like the Rain and Let Me Listen* by Tennessee Williams. For more information about these readings, stop in or call them at the number above.

Abandoned Planet Bookstore is open Monday through Thursday from noon to 11 p.m., Friday from noon to midnight; Saturday from 10 a.m. to midnight; and Sunday from 10 a.m. to 11 p.m.

A few doors down, check out **Maelstrom** at 572 Valencia Street; telephone (415) 863-9933. It's another Mission venue for buying, selling, and trading books. They also have a titles search service. They're open Monday through Friday from 10 a.m. to 8 p.m., Saturday and Sunday from 11 a.m. to 7 p.m.

A Clean, Well-Lighted Place For Books

- 601 Van Ness Ave. (Golden Gate Ave.), San Francisco; (415) 441-6670
  And other suburban locations

Hemingway lives! Whether he would frequent this ritzy shopping/dining plaza is another matter. Anyway, he would doubtless approve of this well-lighted (and well-stocked) bookstore. Oh, do they have books. It's a huge store, with tall, neatly arranged sections and an extremely helpful staff.

Like many of the big chain stores, Clean, Well-Lighted Place gives you a 30% discount off *New York Times* bestsellers in hardcover. So you can save, say, $7.50 on a book with a list price of $24.95. Further, they give you 20% off their own "Buyer's Choice" selections, which often include major titles and hot authors.

As if all that weren't enough, they give you 10% off *everything* over $50. This store is also a great place to go for readings; they have a huge space for it (see listing under "Entertainment: Poetry and Literary Readings"). Pick up a calendar of upcoming events by the cash register. They're open seven days a week from 10 a.m. to 11 p.m., until midnight on Friday and Saturday.

Around The World

- 1346 Polk St. (Pine St.), San Francisco; (415) 474-5568

In how many places can you find records by such diverse artists as James Taylor, Ozzy Osbourne, Anita Baker, and the Temptations, for as little as $1? Well, this is one—but in fact, the big thing here is books. They're crammed into every possible crevice, and they're all very cheap.

If you're looking for a bit of light reading, you may enjoy *The Philosophy of Kant* for $6.50, in hardcover. Want something a little more up-to-date? How about *The Official Guide to the Prodigy Service* for just $10,

softcover; or *The Mac Revealed*, with a cover price of $24.95, selling here for $18. Indeed, the store has quite a good selection of computer books.

Among recent bestsellers, Mr. C found *Tough Guys Don't Dance* by Norman Mailer for $15, and *Dream Girl: My Life as a Supreme* by Mary Wilson for $12. Mystery buffs may detect *The Mousetrap and Other Stories* by Agatha Christie for $8.50.

Paperbacks, of course, are even cheaper. A Calvin and Hobbes collection, *Something Under the Bed is Drooling*, was seen for $4.50; Anne Rice's *Belinda* went for $3; and a beat-up copy of *The Catcher in the Rye* was just $2.50. Plus a wide range of classic authors, from Shakespeare to George Bernard Shaw. Oh, and Jackie Collins—again, it takes all kinds to make a world. Around the World is open seven days a week.

Blue Sky Books
West Side Records

- 1819 Polk St. (Washington St.), San Francisco; (415) 441-4519

By sharing storefront space, and splitting the rent, Blue Sky Books and West Side Records are able to keep their costs down and pass the savings on to their customers. Both stores buy, sell, and trade their wares, so you can find used books and records cheap or you can sell off your collections to make a little dough.

At Blue Sky Books, you'll find bestselling hardcovers as low as $2.95. Titles seen at this astonishingly low price include *The Doomsday Conspiracy* by Sidney Sheldon and *Curtain* by Michael Korda. Prices on paperbacks vary, from $5.50 for *Acquired Tastes* by Peter Mayle to $2.95 for *The Art of the Deal* by Donald Trump. A paperback edition of the much-talked about *Vox* by Nicholson Baker was $3.95. The selection is highly specialized; they even have sections on "War" and "Ships and Sea."

Blue Sky Books and West Side Records are both open seven days, but it's important to note that the owners are not always available. So, if you're looking to sell or trade in your books or records, you should call ahead to find out the buying hours of each establishment.

Book Bay

● Fort Mason Center (Marina Blvd. at Buchanan St.), Building C, San Francisco; (415) 771-1076

Perfectly complementing the various artistic organizations housed at the Fort Mason Center, Book Bay is a quiet, cozy little bookstore crammed with bargains in used books. In their "Next-To-New" section, Mr. C found Irving Wallace's recent *The Second Guest* reduced from a cover price of $18.95 to just $5.50; plus a variety of Danielle Steel ditties, all $4-$6. The arts are particularly well-represented here, of course; that includes back issues of Architectural Digest for a dollar each. And a separate "Bargain Books" area is filled with paperback novels and non-fiction, from Frank Herbert's *Dune* to Dr. Herbert Benson's *The Relaxation Response*. These all go at four for a dollar; drop in on Sundays from 2-5 p.m., and they're *eight* for a dollar.

The store is open Wednesdays through Sundays only, from 11 a.m. to 5 p.m. (Thursday evenings until 8). Donations are always welcome; sales profits benefit the Friends of the San Francisco Public Library.

Books etc.

● 538 Castro St. (18th St.), San Francisco; (415) 621-8631

Books etc. is crammed with used books, in dozens of categories, appealing to even the most finicky reader. Since these are all used, you can save bundles on bundles. For example, Terry McMillan's smash novel *Waiting to Exhale*, in hardcover, was seen here for just $13.50. New, it sold for $22. The hardcover edition of *Thinking Out Loud*, by Pulitzer Prize-winner and *New York Times* columnist Anna Quindlen, was seen for $13.20. It, too, had been priced at $22 new.

The store has hundreds of paperbacks, and most are sold at half-off the cover price. Jay McInerney's ever-

popular *Bright Lights, Big City*, originally $5.95, was seen for just $3. They also have a bargain bin, in the front of the store, filled with all kinds of paperbacks for $1 each.

Like many used bookshops, you can sell off your old books for cash or credit here. You'll get more in trade; 10 percent more, to be exact. Books etc. will pay you 20 percent of their selling price in cash or 30 percent in trade. The store is open daily.

Book Warehouse Outlet

● 21 Westlake Mall, Daly City; (415) 755-4848

In this large Parkside shopping center, The Book Warehouse Outlet is not the sort of mall bookstore you'd expect; it offers a good selection of new books, mostly hardcover, all at discount prices. Recent bestsellers are sold at 10% off the cover price; remainders and overstocks, including more top titles, are anywhere from 40% to 90% off; and all computer books are at least 40% off.

How can bestsellers go so cheap? Well, once a popular title comes out in paperback, the publishers want to get rid of the remaining hardcover versions. So, in many cases, you can get the hardcover book for little more than the current paperback.

Some of the bargains found here recently include Norman Mailer's *Harlot's Ghost*, originally $30, here just $4.99. Stephen King's *Needful Things*, which came out at $24.95, was seen for $8.99, and Alice Hoffman's *Turtle Moon*, originally $22.95, for $5.99. *Cruel Doubt* by Joe McGuiness sold well at $25; but you'd much rather pay only $5.99, wouldn't you? Mr. C also spotted a copy of *Mapplethorpe*, an oversized photo book highlighting the late artist's work, half-price at $24.99.

Special interest books run the gamut from cooking, like TV chef Martin Yan's *Everybody's Wokking*, half-price, $6.99—to computing, with the popular *DOS for Dummies*, $5 off at $11.99. Speaking of computers, an unusual find here is the bin of shareware disks, all kinds of public domain software programs at $3 each, or two for $5. Plus books on audiocassette tape, and lots of classical cassettes and compact discs for $4.99 and $7.99, respectively.

They do have a wonderful selection of kids' books: *Where's Waldo?*, originally $12.95, was found (get it?) for just $7.99 and a Bugs Bunny Book and Tape, originally $9.95 was just $3.99. A book on dinosaurs with color illustrations, originally $13.95, was just $4.99. You'll also see plenty of Sesame Street and Peter Rabbit books. Open seven days.

Carroll's Books
- 1193 Church St. (24th St.), San Francisco; (415) 647-3020

Carroll's Books is not just a great place to find inexpensive used books; it's a neat place to hang out. The store is huge, with a large and varied selection, yet it manages to feel cozy—thanks to an arrangement of overstuffed chairs and comfortable lighting. It's nice and quiet in here, except for the birds chirping merrily in a large cage in the middle of the main section. And with the cats roaming about, you'll feel more like you're in the library of a large mansion than a book store.

Secondhand hardcovers usually sell here for nearly half of the original cover price. Stephen King's *It*, listed at $22.95, was just $12; same prices for Tracy Kidder's acclaimed *Old Friends*. Some titles get even better discounts, such as *The Hearsts: Father and Son* by William Randolph Hearst, Jr., reduced from $29.95 to $7; or *American Star* by Jackie Collins, regularly $23, seen here for $10. If you're particularly lucky, you may find very recent books selling at these great low prices. Mr. C saw *The Robber Bride* by Margaret Atwood, which was still enjoying hardcover retail success at the time of his visit, for just $12.

Carroll's Books also tons of paperbacks at very low prices. Recent choices included *The Prince of Tides* by Pat Conroy for $1.75 and Ernest Hemingway's *To Have and To Have*

MR. CHEAP'S PICKS
Books

✔ **Green Apple Books**—An absolute treasure trove in the Richmond, crammed with new and used bargains.

✔ **Half Price Books**—No need to read deeply into this name—most of the books here are half-off their original cover prices.

✔ **Moe's**—A four-floor tower in the heart of Berkeley, open until midnight.

✔ **O'Neil Book Company Warehouse**—In the Berkeley outlets area, this store specializes in remainders and bargain books.

Not for $3. At that price, you can definitely have!

Carroll's Books is open from 10 a.m. to 10 p.m. daily.

Columbus Books
- 540 Broadway (Columbus St.), San Francisco; (415) 986-3872

Don't be put off by the adult bookstores and entertainment establishments that surround Columbus Books, in that honky-tonk area between North Beach and Chinatown. This store is rated G (well, maybe PG), and is filled with an eclectic mix of new and used books at low prices.

Used books predominate. A hardcover edition of Katharine Hepburn's autobiography, *Me*, originally $25, was glimpsed for $12.98. Like-new paperback copies of the Armistead Maupin canon—*Further Tales of the City*, *Significant Others*, and *Sure of You*—were reduced from $12 each to $10. You'll find pocket paperbacks even cheaper.

Parents will find a good selection of children's books, including titles by Dr. Seuss and Walt Disney. *The Cat in the Hat* came back for $4.98, while *101 Dalmatians* was $2.98. A variety of kids' learning workbooks were all priced at five books for five bucks.

Columbus does have a small selection of new books, many of which are reviewer's copies. *I'll Be Seeing You* by Mary Higgins Clark was originally $23; here, not long after its release, it was just $11.50. The much-ballyhooed new tome by David Halberstam, *The Fifties*, regularly $27.50, was available here for $19.98 with a bonus: The publisher's press release was still tucked inside. Naomi Wolf's *Fire With Fire*, originally $21, was still hot when it was seen here for $14.98.

To quote the store's owner, "It's a most unusual collection." They have sections of military books and drama books. *There's* a pair of genres you won't often hear in the same breath. They have a collection of sheet music, Broadway scores, and songbooks. You'll find a section of English as a Second Language books, as well as books in Spanish, Chinese, Slavic, and Laotian, and many others. Columbus Books is open late, seven days a week.

Green Apple Bookstore
- 506 Clement St. (Sixth Ave.), San Francisco; (415) 387-2272

In a bustling area of the Richmond better known for ethnic restaurants, Green Apple is an unexpected oasis of book bargains—the sort you'd expect to find in Berkeley. Two huge floors (plus mezzanines) are jam-packed with new and used books, nearly all at discount. It's been a literary landmark for over 25 years.

The adventure begins before you even enter the store, as tables brimming with near-giveaway books and magazines flank the entrance. Most are priced from 75¢ to $1.50. Inside on the main floor, you'll find selected new hardcovers selling at 20% off the cover prices. Remainders offer great deals, too. But the real fun starts as you work your way up-stairs—first through a mezzanine loaded with used fiction paperbacks, like Robin Cook's *Vital Signs* for just $3.50, or *London Fields* by Martin Amis, reduced from $11 to $7.

Continuing up the creaky wooden staircase, with more books displayed on each landing, you eventually reach the second floor. Here are sections for every reader: history, movies, travel, sports, computers, art, you name it. All are at discounts of some sort. There are even unusual items, like collectible science fiction pulps from the 1950s. Plus cards, maps, calendars, blank books, and books on audiocassette.

The place just rambles on and on. You can get lost in here for hours; but alas, you must confine yourself to 10-10 Sunday through Thursday, and 10 a.m. to midnight on Friday and Saturday.

Half Price Books
- 2525 Telegraph Ave. (Dwight Way), Berkeley; (510) 843-6412
- 1849 Solano Ave. (The Alameda), Berkeley; (510) 526-6080

Half Price Books is a new-and-used books chain with close to fifty stores in eight states. The have a huge selection of new and used books, most of which are marked at half of the cover price—and some even less. They also pay cash for books, CDs, LPs, magazines, and other printed or recorded material.

As Mr. C browsed the shelves, he came across such hardcover new bargains as *The Client* by John Grisham; originally $23.50, here it was available for just $7.98. The large-sized Grateful Dead Family Album, originally $29.95, was just $9.98, and *The Dog Lover's Literary Companion*, regularly $16.95, was $5.98. Used hardcovers included Amy Tan's "The Joy Luck Club" for $6.98. Most paperbacks are, again, half of the cover price, like *The Beauty Myth* by Naomi Wolf, originally $11, for $5.50. They also have shelves and racks of used paperbacks priced at 50¢ each, including lots of pulp novels, romance, and science fiction.

Half Price Books is a big advocate for getting young people to read, and so they have a great collection of kids' books. These recently included stories like *Babar's Battle*, originally $10, for $4.98. The also have a "Frequent Reader" program for children under 15, and a 10% discount for teachers and librarians.

HPB's art and theater sections are exceptionally well-stocked. The computer section has lots to see, but most of it is rather old and out of date. Of course, that only takes about a week in the computer world. Meanwhile, if your computer is old and out of date, you may be in luck!

Used records are priced at $2 to $5 each, and used cassette tapes from $3 to $5. Mr. C didn't run across too much in the way of CDs. This is really a store for books, anyway. Half Price Books is open from 10 a.m. to 10 p.m., daily.

Moe's
- 2476 Telegraph Ave. (Dwight Way), Berkeley; (510) 849-2087

Four incredible floors of books make this off-campus store an academic landmark. Moe's deals in new and used books of every kind, from recent paperbacks to antiquarian rarities. All new titles are sold at a 10% discount off the cover price; there is also a large selection of recent remainders. Mr. C browsed and found *The General in His Labyrinth*, by Gabriel Garcia Marquez, reduced from $19.95 to just $8.

Among used books, he saw *1001 Word for Windows Tips*, marked down from $40 to $24 (tons of computer books here); as well as lots of paperback novels at half their cover prices.

Moe's claims to pay some of the highest prices for your used books. This is also a great place to search for sheet music books, a world of magazines (including alternative press), cards, and more. Open seven days and evenings a week; until 11:00 p.m. Sunday to Thursday, and to midnight on weekends.

And right across the street, don't miss **Shakespeare & Co. Books** at 2499 Telegraph Avenue; telephone (510) 841-8916. It's yet another example of Berkeley's embarrassment of literary riches, featuring new and used books, specializing in (but not limited to) the classics.

O'Neil Book Company Warehouse Outlet
- 1150 Sixth St. (Harrison St.), Berkeley; (510) 527-9883

You may feel like you've stepped into a fantasy novel here, especially with the castle mural painted on the wall. And when you check the prices on these books, you'll really think you're fantasizing! These are all new books, mostly remainders, all sold at a discount.

During his visit, Mr. C saw cartoonist Matt Groening's *Greetings from Hell* postcard book, originally $7.95, for just $3.99. In the fiction section, a hardcover edition of *Cat's Eye* by Margaret Atwood was just $5.99. Gilda Radner's autobiographical *It's Always Something*, with a cover price of $18.95, was seen here for just $6.99.

O'Neil has lots of books for special interests as well. A varied selection of Clymer's automobile shop manuals were just $5.99 each. Greg LaMond's *Complete Book of Bicycling*, originally $10.95, was just $3.99. A bunch of *New York Times Crossword Puzzles* books, regularly $7, were just $2.99 each. Lots of children's books, too. A hardcover edition of *The Velveteen Rabbit*, originally $12.95, was just $6.49.

The store has a true warehouse feel, with plenty of space and lots of display tables comfortably spread out. O'Neil Book Co. is open daily from 9 a.m. to 7 p.m.

Not far away, also in Berkeley, check out the **Nolo Outlet Bookstore** at 950 Parker Street (Ninth St.); telephone (510) 549-1976. This shop specializes in self-help, legal, and business books at good discounts. They're open Monday through Friday from 9 a.m. to 6 p.m., Saturday from 10 a.m. to 5 p.m., and Sunday from 11 a.m. to 4 p.m.

The Other Change of Hobbit
* 2020 Shattuck Ave. (University
  Ave.), Berkeley; (510) 848-0413

Along with a cute name, this bookstore has everything you could imagine in science fiction and fantasy literature. Some of their stock is new, and not discounted, but they also have a good selection of used books at really great prices. For the most part, used books, both hardcover and paperback, are half-off the original cover price. So, a paperback edition of *Interview With a Vampire* by Anne Rice would be just $2.98. Also seen here was a book club paperback edition of Margaret Atwood's *Cat's Eye* for just $5. A hardcover edition of *The Great and Secret Show* by Clive Barker, which sold new for $19.95, was seen here for $10.

OCH also stocks some remainders—brand-new editions which had not sold at full price. Stephen King's *Four Past Midnight*, originally $22.95, was recently spotted for just $12. The selection of books, particularly the used titles, changes often; stop in regularly and check out the shelf of recent arrivals. They're open Monday through Saturday from 11 a.m. to 8 p.m. and Sunday from noon to 6 p.m.

Phoenix Books and Records
* 3850 24th St. (Sanchez St.), San
  Francisco; (415) 821-3477

If you feel burned by high retail book and music prices, you'll arise again when you step into Phoenix Books and Records. This store has a wide selection of new and used books, along with some CDs, records, and tapes.

You'll obviously find low prices by perusing the used book section. Among hardcovers, Harvey Penick's *And If You Play Golf You're My Friend*, originally $20, was just $9.98 here. A paperback edition of *The Good Times* by New York Times columnist Russell Baker, regularly $8.95, was seen for $5.40. The selection of used paperbacks is extensive, including such popular titles as Milan Kundera's *The Unbearable Lightness of Being*, Amy Tan's *The Joy Luck*

Club, and more.

You can also find a good selection of remainders and other new books that are discounted for various reasons. For instance, they recently had a reviewer's copy (complete with press release!) of the much-ballyhooed *Mad As Hell: Revolt at the Ballot Box, 1992* by Jack Germond and Jules Witcover. Originally $24.95, it was just $14.98 here—and of course, used only slightly if at all.

Their music selection, while smaller, is also well-priced. Mr. C found a copy of Living Colour's *Time's Up* on compact disc for $7.98. In the tape section, which holds the most of the store's offerings, he saw titles like Madonna's *Erotica* for $5.98 and many others for even less. Phoenix Books and Records is open daily from 10 a.m. to 10 p.m.

Russian Hill Bookstore
* 2234 Polk St. (Vallejo St.), San
  Francisco; (415) 929-0997

Russian Hill Bookstore carries new and used books (naturally, you'll save the most money by buying used). Browsing through the used paperbacks, Mr. C found such titles as Danielle Steel's *Thurston House* for $2.50, and *The High Cost of Living* by Marge Piercy for $3; as well as used hardcovers like that ubiquitous *The Bridges of Madison County* for $10 and *The Illustrated Dictionary of English* for $15.95. A hardcover edition of *The Essential Wordsworth* looked like new, and was only $6.98.

Indeed, most of the used books here are in very good condition. Russian Hill Bookstore also buys and trades books, so if you need to pare down your library, come here. They're open every day from 10 a.m. to 10 p.m.

Walden Pond Books
* 3316 Grand Ave. (Mandana St.),
  Oakland; (510) 832-4438

Walden Pond Books is a bright, attractive bookstore with a good selection of new and used books. Their new books aren't discounted, but their used stock is very well-priced. They have lots of hardcovers, including *The Complete Notebooks of Henry James*, originally $30, for just $18; and the ever-present *Joy Luck Club* by Amy Tan, originally $18.95, for just $10.50. Their paperbacks are also inexpensive, like Saul Bellow's *More Die of Heartbreak* for $2.60. Walden Pond Books also has a great selection of stationery, blank books, and postcards. This is a fun place to browse.

Writer's Bookstore

- 2848 Webster St. (Union St.), San Francisco; (415) 921-2620

Believe it or not, Mr. C has found you a book bargain in Pacific Heights. This is a small, cozy, neighborhood shop which has been here

since 1967—filled with all kinds of new and used titles at terrific prices; it's hard to walk out of here without *something* in hand.

Among the deals here are reviewer's copies of current bestsellers, as much as ten bucks off the cover price; these are available in very limited, hit-or-miss quantities, but you never know. Then, there are the used paperbacks—fiction, mystery, sci-fi—all at half the cover prices. Other individual titles, new and used, hardcover and paperback, are individually priced. The shop is open seven days a week, but only on an informal schedule of afternoons and evenings.

CAMERAS

There are lots of places to save money on appliances and electronics in the Bay Area. Some, unfortunately, are as far below repute as they are below retail. With merchandise that is imported from foreign countries, there is a greater possibility of shady deals, or shoddy quality. Mr. C says this not out of any kind of prejudice, but because he wants you to be careful.

One of the best ways to protect yourself, if you have doubts as to *any* store's reliability, is to ask about their guarantee policy; make sure the item you want carries an American warranty. Since some stores deal directly with manufacturers in the Far East, their merchandise many carry a foreign warranty instead. Even for identical products, a foreign warranty can make repairs a hassle—unless you don't mind paying the postage to Japan! Remember, you are perfectly within your rights to inquire about this in the store.

Adolph Gasser

- 181 Second St. (Howard St.), San Francisco; (415) 495-3852
- 5733 Geary Blvd. (21st Ave.), San Francisco; (415) 751-0145
- 750 Bryant St. (Fifth St.), San Francisco; (415) 543-3438

This is one of The City's many longtime, established camera dealers, offering good discounts on a full range (no pun intended, camera buffs) of photographic equipment for professionals and amateurs. They are an

authorized dealer for such brands as Leica, Minolta, and Vivitar.

Point-and-shoot cameras start as low as $69; 35mm SLR cameras from around $175 and up. Mr. C found a Pentax "IQ Zoom 280" selling for a reasonable $400; as well as a closeout deal on a Yashica auto-focus "Sensation" kit—including a panorama adapter, film and batteries—marked down from an original $175 to just $99.

Gasser also carries video camcorders and related equipment; you can get a basic Sony 8mm model for $699. Plus tons of accessories, from lenses, bags, and tripods to lighting, photo albums, educational books, and more.

And there's another way to get even better deals here. Gasser buys and sells used equipment, sometimes on consignment; cameras, after all, are built to last for years (just like cars; all they need is a little maintainance). So, you can find a Konica T-4 35mm camera, with auto-winder, for just $200, far below its original retail value; or a Sony Hi-8 video camera, which sold for $1,500 new, for just $799. Since Gasser also rents cameras, they sometimes sell their rental models off at similar discounts. There is no warranty, but these are generally high-end cameras in good shape. The stores are open Monday through Saturday from 9 a.m. to 6 p.m.

Alpha Photo Products
- 985 Third St. (Filbert St.), Oakland; (510) 893-1436

Right off I-880, along Oakland's waterfront, Alpha makes a fine "first" stop when it comes to cameras and photographic supplies. Their large warehouse/store carries just about anything you could possibly need, at competitive prices; in fact, in this age of superstores, they've been consolidating their operation and cutting their overhead costs so that they can continue to offer good deals on hundreds of product lines. And *unlike* superstores, the folks behind these counters are experts behind the camera; Alpha has been around since 1947.

They do a lot of business with commercial clients, and the general public can come in and get the same low prices. Snap up a Polaroid "Spectra" auto-focus camera for $130, a savings of $36 off the list price; at the high end, a Nikon N8008s, with a retail price of $915, was recently seen here for $669. Add accessories like a LowePro "Elite" carry bag, $15 below retail at $60; a Quantum

"1+" battery pack, reduced from $195 to $169; plus lighting, graphic arts, computer imaging, video equipment, and more.

Many varieties of film and photographic paper are always available at discount here. Alpha also carries printing and enlarging equipment, and other needs for the darkroom. They also have reasonable rates on all kinds of rentals, offer technical seminars, and even make film-to-video transfers. They've got it all. Take a look, Mondays through Saturdays from 9 a.m. to 5:30 p.m.

Camera Bug
- 2560 Ocean Ave. (J. Serra Blvd.), San Francisco; (415) 585-3099

Meeting the demands of cash-starved students is the driving force behind the low prices at the Camera Bug. Not that you have to be a poor college student to take advantage of these low prices. The store carries a number of top camera brands, including Olympus, Minolta, Nikon, and Pentax, all at discounts of 10% to 20% off list prices.

Even better deals abound here on the large selection of darkroom supplies, along with camera bags and accessories, amateur grade-film, and more, all 25% off list price! They carry all the popular names, like Kodak, Ilford, and Fuji. The Camera Bug is open Tuesday through Saturday, from 10 a.m. to 6 p.m.

Cameras Unlimited
- 15 Kearny St. (Geary St.), San Francisco; (415) 392-2400

Cameras Unlimited offers competitive prices, coupled with exceptional knowledge and service. The store has been in the business for years, and the sales staff is happy to give advice and help you solve those pesky pix problems. They specialize in 35mm models; prices range from about $25 for a very basic point-and-shoot model to thousands of dollars for professional cameras with all the latest bells and whistles.

Better-quality auto-focus cameras start nice and low, around $100; for something with a little more ooomph, you can get a Pentax K1000 for about $225 (body and lens). The suggested retail price on this particular setup was about $350. Of course, *nobody* ever pays those suggested retail prices, but this is about as good an everyday discount as you're likely to find.

Now, if it's video equipment you want, you've still come to the right place. CU has a great selection of top-name VCRs, camcorders, and more, at good prices. Recent bargains included a Fuji 122 video camera (list price $1,400) selling here for about $700. It features automatic fade-in/fade-out, ultra-low-light capability, a remote control, and a color viewfinder—the latest hot feature. A more advanced camcorder, a Sony V-101, which lists for $1,900 and sells at many area stores for $1,600, was seen here for $1,400.

A few doors down the block, you'll also find **San Francisco Discount Camera**, 33 Kearny Street; telephone (415) 392-1100. Though these stores are in competition with each other, they are in fact owned by members of the same family—and carry many of the same brands at similarly low prices.

Fireside Camera
- 2117 Chestnut St. (Steiner St.), San Francisco; (415) 567-8131

Even on a ritzy street like this one in the Marina, there are bargains to be found. Fireside has been in business for over forty years, a small storefront shop dedicated to good prices and service. Mr. C was assured of this even before he went inside; newspaper articles posted in the window help caution shoppers to be aware of the price gouging some stores engage in.

All film sold here is marked at 20% off the list price; if you do a lot of shooting, buy your film in "brick" quantities and you'll save another 5% on top of that. On cameras themselves, the folks at Fireside actually don't mark their prices down from retail; they mark them up from wholesale, often a measly 10% above cost.

MR. CHEAP'S PICKS
Cameras

- ✔ **Alpha Photo**—A vast Oakland warehouse with competitive prices on absolutely everything for the professional.
- ✔ **Cameras Unlimited**—The selection does seem unlimited, but the prices are strictly rationed. You'll save money, and they have a knowledgeable sales staff.

That goes for everything from little point-and-shoot cameras to high-quality 35mm models.

The same holds true for video camcorders by all the major brands—in VHS, VHS-C, 8mm, and Hi-8 formats. Some of these started from just $700 at the time of Mr. C's visit. Of course, camcorder prices have begun falling a bit, so perhaps by the time you read this, that won't sound too spectacular; but for an independent store to rival department store prices, as this one does, is no small feat.

Fireside also carries binoculars (from just $35) and telescopes, offers portrait services, and is a just-plain-friendly place. Open Monday through Saturday from 9 a.m. to 6 p.m.

San Francisco Camera
- 1066 Market St. (Seventh St.), San Francisco; (415) 431-4461
- 1472 California St. (Larkin St.), San Francisco; (415) 775-6436

San Francisco Camera ships film and equipment all over the country, and their local shops are well-frequented by professionals—two signs of a good business indeed. This tip is borne out by the prices found therein: decent point-and-shoot models start around $69. They carry some of the top names in the business, from Canon and Nikon right up to Hassel-bad, Gitzo, and Leica.

S.F. Camera also carries used models. Cameras that originally cost $500 to $600 can often be found here, used but in perfect working condition, for about $250. The salespeople chose not to give specific examples, since used stock changes constantly; but

you get the idea. And, if you ever do have a problem with your camera, new or used, they do minor repair work on the premises. Another bargain bonus: you can purchase film at the wholesale price if you buy 20 or more rolls. Now you know why the pros shop here.

CARPETING AND RUGS

A & M Carpets
• 98 Twelfth St. (Van Ness Ave.), San Francisco; (415) 863-1410

For some 25 years, this family operation has been quietly offering great deals on all kinds of carpeting and rugs. There is a surprisingly large selection for what appears from the outside to be a small, neighborhood shop. They carry such brands as Philadelphia, Cabin Crafts, Diamond, Coronet (residential and commercial), and others. You can always find all-nylon broadlooms as low as $6.99 and $7.99 per square yard; stair runners from $2.99 per linear foot; plus lots of rugs and remnants.

Orientals, both in handmade wool styles and machine-made synthetics, range from $59 (for a 6' x 9' synthetic) to hundreds of dollars; but even these are bargains. Mr. C saw a handsome woolen Oriental rug, 5' x 8', reduced from a list price of $289 to a more reasonable $180. And remnants, many in huge rolls, start around $10 per yard.

Installation and padding are available, though extra; a drop in the bucket after you've saved so much on the carpeting itself. A & M is proud of its attention to service: "No job is too small," they say, and they even offer free measurement in your home. Open Monday through Saturday from 9 a.m. to 5:30 p.m.

Carpet Center
• 1065 Ashby Ave. (San Pablo Ave.), Berkeley; (510) 549-1100

Carpet Center has been in business in

Berkeley for almost fifty years, selling brand name carpets, tile, wood, linoleum, and other floor coverings. The big news for the budget-minded here is: Remnants. The store sells brand name remnants from makers like Bigelow and Royalweave, in wool and wool blends, for 30% to 60% below their retail value. So, if you find a remnant for $15, the actual worth is probably closer to $30 or $40. The drawback, of course, is that you can't get a custom size or color, what you see is what you get. But many pieces are large enough to be trimmed to fit a full room; or, the edges can be bound to make a like-new rug.

Carpet Center's regular rugs are pretty reasonably priced, too. Most are cheaper by $3 to $4 per yard than major department stores. They also use the Trustmark labeling system, which rates rugs for durability, price, etc., so you can be sure you're getting the best value for your needs and budget. CC offers a ten-year wear guarantee on most of its rugs, as well as a 30-day trial period. If you don't like the color, they will replace the carpet; you'll still be charged for labor, but this unusual feature certainly allows you more purchasing flexibility. Call them for more details on these warranties.

Carpet Center is open Monday through Saturday from 8 a.m. to 6 p.m., and Sunday from 11 a.m. to 5 p.m.

Carpet Connection

- 390 Bayshore Blvd. (Oakdale Ave.), San Francisco; (415) 550-7125

A block up from the venerable Floorcraft (see listing below), Carpet Connection is a no-frills warehouse which deals primarily with commercial clients—offices, landlords, and the like. You can go in and get the same low prices, though; these tend to be about 25% to 35% above wholesale cost, a fairly low markup.

These are just your basic styles: mostly synthetics in solid colors, both tight-weaves and plush piles (just think of any office or apartment building you've ever been in). There's not much in the way of fancy floorcoverings here, but then, these could be perfect for your basement, rec room, or your own office. Many of these large rolls are discontinued and closeout patterns, though nothing seemed particularly *un*desirable to Mr. C; meanwhile, most of them cost just $14 per square yard, installed. These could easily go for $20 a yard retail.

There are lots of remnants, most large enough to cover one or two rooms. And, in the very basic styles, commercial carpeting costs as little as $10.50 per square yard, installed. By the way, you can order higher grades and fancier styles, if you wish, at the same great discounts—they have plenty of sample books to look through.

Carpet Connection employs its own crews, always a good and reputable sign; they will even do custom bordering, inlays, and binding. Their merchandise is guaranteed for the life of the carpet. The store is open seven days a week, as well as weeknights until 7 p.m. (Fridays until 6).

Floorcraft

- 470 Bayshore Blvd. (Industrial St.), San Francisco; (415) 824-4056

This large store has been flooring the Bay Area for over fifty years. They offer plenty of selection in carpeting—not to mention tile, linoleum, and other coverings—all at reasonable prices. The store is a member of

MR. CHEAP'S PICKS
Carpeting and Rugs

✔ **A & M Carpets**— Neighborhood shop near the Civic Center only looks small from the outside.

✔ **Carpet Connection**—You can get commercial prices on basic commercial carpeting, even if you're not a business client.

✔ **Orient Express Rug Company**—These rugs may cost thousands of dollars, but they *could* cost thousands more elsewhere.

Carpet One, a buying consortium whose combined volume of business leads to lower costs for each member store. Several major name brands are combined into the Carpet One private label, which carries a very strong price and quality guarantee—including a promise to beat any price for the same item from any other store, and replacement of any carpeting found to be defective in manufacture or installation.

You can find stain-resistant wool berber as low as $10.99 per square yard, installed; and wool blends from $21.99 installed. There are frequent in-store specials, such as two rooms' worth of carpet, fully installed with padding, for $449. They have some Oriental rugs too; all-wool handmade rugs can be found around $300 for a 6' x 9' size ($150 for synthetics).

As with so many carpeting stores, remnants offer even better deals— and Floorcraft has lots of 'em. Mr. C was shown a 25-square yard piece of plush, 100% wool berber for $259. That's about $10 per yard, for carpeting worth about $30 per yard. You get the idea—and there are usually plenty of small sizes and large bolts to check out. Open seven days a week.

MMM Carpets
- 375 Gellert Blvd. (Hickey Blvd.), Daly City; (415) 994-4000

And other suburban locations

Here's a good place to check out for inexpensive residential broadloom. With a lot to choose from in the $20-$30 per square yard price range, you can find many well-known brands like Du Pont, Shaw, and Philadelphia, at reasonable prices. Of greater interest to cheapsters, however, will be the selection of all-nylon rolls under the $10 mark—some starting as low as $7.99 per square yard. Now, that's cheap! Some of these are even protected with Stainmaster.

Now, these prices don't include installation, of course; but the store sometimes offers special deals in which you get free padding and installation thrown in. Other sales may knock 50% off the price of the carpeting itself. At those rates, you can afford to pay for the installation, even on a tight budget!

Orient Express Rug Company
- 377 Geary St. (Mason St.), San Francisco; (415) 421-1969

Orient Express Rug Company has a beautiful selection of handmade Oriental rugs in wool and silk from China, Iran, Afghan, Pakistan, India, Turkey, and Russia. What's even more beautiful is that their prices are generally 20% below department store *sale* prices. Many of these are still very expensive, of course; they're cheaper, but not at all cheap. You may not consider a 9' x 12' rug for $4,995 to be a bargain—but the same rug could cost up to $10,000 in other stores. We're talking *serious* rugs!

But you don't have to be an expert. These guys won't try to pull the wool (ha ha) over your eyes. They're very helpful, and they are happy to discuss quality and price with you. And they do have less expensive designs, starting from a down-to-earth $125 and up. You can find a good quality 6' x 9' area rug for $1,000. Mr. C was shown a 4' x 6' rug from China, of the heaviest quality. Elsewhere, it would sell for $1,200; here, they had priced it at $475.

It's not hard to see why this company has customers all over the world. They will deliver your rug free of charge (locally, that is), or help you arrange to have it shipped anywhere. Open from Tuesday through Saturday from 10 a.m. to 7 p.m. and Sunday noon to 5 p.m.

CDS, RECORDS, TAPES, AND VIDEO

You can save extra money on music by shopping for used recordings. Like used book shops, many of the stores below will allow you to trade in music you no longer want. Alas, they won't take just anything; most used LPs, in particular, have become less marketable. Most stores will give you a choice of cash or in-store credit; you'll usually get a higher figure by choosing the credit. It's a good, cheap way to check out artists you might not take a chance on at full price.

Amoeba Music
- 2455 Telegraph Ave. (Haste St.), Berkeley; (510) 549-1125

Amoeba Music has so many bargains it almost defies science. In fact, of all the music stores Mr. C found, this is one of the few that has *new* CDs at low prices. Most record stores charge around $15.99 or more for a new disc. But here, *Become What You Are* by the Juliana Hatfield Three and *Ring* by the Connells were seen for just $12.98 each as new releases.

But true cheapsters know that new is not the way to go with CDs. Amoeba Music has a huge selection of used CDs in a number of price ranges. Most discs in the "pretty new/barely used" category run $8 to $10. Madonna's *Erotica*, for example, was seen for $9.95. And then there are the clearance CDs, where stuff like *9* by Public Image Ltd. was seen for just $4.95. And check out the super clearance section with CDs under $3!

There's more than just CDs to be found here. Used tapes average $2 to $4; Buffalo Tom's *big red letter day* was seen for $4.95. Clearance cassettes are a mere 50¢ to $1; Mr. C saw Robert Plant's *Now and Zen* for $1. The large selection of used records included *Made in the Shade* by the Rolling Stones for $2.95.

Not into music? Like your entertainment visual? Amoeba can change its shape to suit your format needs. They have a great selection of used movies on videocassette, including such titles as *Bob Roberts* for $14.95. *Batman* was seen in the clearance video box for just $2.95. Holy cheapness! Good place to shop for used laserdiscs, too.

At Amoeba, everything priced over $1 is guaranteed from defects for seven days. Further, there is the Amoeba insurance policy: you can return any item priced over $2 (with receipt) and get 75% of the purchase price in store credit. That certainly makes trying new sounds a lot less risky. They also buy and trade music, so bring in all those old discs you don't listen to anymore. With Amoeba's huge selection, you should have no problem refilling your own CD rack.

Bay Area Records and Tapes
• 1409 Polk St. (California St.), San Francisco; (415) 441-9697
Welcome to BART! No, not Bay Area Rapid Transit, but in this case, Bay Area Records and Tapes. And, while this store won't take you across the Bay, they will buy, sell, and trade

tapes, CDs, and videos. You can find used CDs for as little as $4.98. Of course, these at the bottom of the scale won't be the most popular ones, but you'll see titles by Marilyn McCoo, Monie Love, and Kenny Loggins.

More CDs go for $7.98, like releases by the Dead Kennedys and Jello Biafra; while the most popular artists, like New Order, the Pet Shop Boys, and Madonna, go for just $9.98. That still beats the department stores. You can also find used cassette tapes for $3 to $4.

BART's selection is huge, with over 12,000 new and used CDs and some 5,000 new and used tapes. Shouldn't have any trouble finding something you like. The store is open Monday through Saturday, 10 a.m. to 11 p.m., and Sunday 11 a.m. to 11 p.m.

Blue Sky Books
West Side Records
• 1819 Polk St. (Washington St.), San Francisco; (415) 441-4519
By sharing storefront space, and splitting the rent, Blue Sky Books and West Side Records are able to keep their costs down and pass the savings on to their customers. Both stores buy, sell, and trade their wares, so you can find used books and records cheap or you can sell off your collections to make a little dough.

West Side Records specializes in collectors' LPs—meaning that many of their records are not necessarily cheap. Mr. C saw titles like *The Sonny Side of Cher* for $7, and Judy Garland's *That's Entertainment* for $8. But, you'll find plenty of great old records for $5 and under, like *Where is My Man* by Eartha Kitt for $3.50, *The George Carlin Collection* for $4.50, and the same price for artists from Kris Kristofferson to the Borderlords to Ella Fitzgerald.

Blue Sky Books and West Side Records are both open seven days, but it's important to note that the owners are not always available. So, if you're looking to sell or trade in your books or records, you should call ahead to find out the buying hours of each establishment.

The Musical Offering
- 2430 Bancroft Way (Telegraph Ave.), Berkeley; (510) 849-0211

Mr. C is cheating a bit by putting this store in the book, but they have such an interesting and unique discount program that he felt compelled to tell you about it. First, you should know that they only sell classical music and opera; most are new releases, not much cheaper than anywhere else. But, here's the fun part: If you buy a tape or disc on the anniversary of the composer's birth, you get 10% off. Don't worry if you're not up on the birthdates of dead composers (though they do it for living ones, too); they have a sign at the cash register telling you whose birthday it is that day.

Other than this program their aren't too many bargains here, though they do have a small selection of used discs. They're all $9.98, unless otherwise marked. Mr. C found a used copy of Beethoven's Symphony Number 9 for $4.99.

The Musical Offering doubles as a cafe, with a menu of soups, sandwiches, salads, and, of course, the *de rigeur* espresso and cappuccino. The cafe is not super-cheap, but the prices are reasonable and the atmosphere is delightful. The Musical Offering is open Monday through Saturday from 10 a.m. to 9 p.m. and Sunday from 11:30 a.m. to 5 p.m.

Neurotic
- 1126 Folsom St. (Seventh St.), San Francisco; (415) 552-8069

Here's an unusual combination, even in SoMa: Used clothing plus new and used CDs, tapes, and records. You'll spot the funkiness of this place from the street; the store looks to be permanently under construction. Once inside, you can't miss that "aren't-we-such-cool-minimalists" style, with merchandise spread on planks laid over sawhorses, and CDs displayed in wooden boxes hung from the ceiling.

You'll have to hunt a bit to find clothing that is both cheap and enticing, but it can be found. Recent bargains included a black slip dress for $5, a red mohair sweater for $6, and a ton of grunge-look flannel shirts from $5 to $9. You'll find some rather unusaul dresses, like a lace dress from the 1960s for $6 and a beaded velvet dress for $14. Then there are those items that are difficult to find any adjectives for—like a black robe with ostrich feather sleeves for $20. They also have a few shoes and bags.

Their music selection leans toward heavy sounds; rock, alternative, punk, and progressive. Flip through the used CDs and find stuff like *Don't Tell a Soul* by The Replacements for $10, and *Dreamland* by Black Box for $8. A word of caution: Do not be fooled by CD singles, priced at $3 to $4, mixed in with the regular full-length selections.

Tapes are generally $3 to $5, used. Examples include the Meat Puppets with *Huevos* for $6 and Public Enemy's *Fear of A Black Planet* for $4. The store also has a good selection of cheap used records. Mr. C found the Clash's *Combat Rock* for $3 and, for the same price, the Cure's *Boys Don't Cry*. And, don't leave without checking out the table of kitschy items, like old lunch boxes and board games. Some of these are cheap, some aren't, but it's fun just to browse through. Neurotic is open Monday and Tuesday from 11 a.m. to 7 p.m., Wednesday through Saturday from 11 a.m. to 9 p.m., Sun 11 a.m. to 6 p.m.

Phoenix Books and Records
- 3850 24th St. (Dolores St.), San Francisco; (415) 821-3477

If you feel burned by high retail book and music prices, you'll arise again when you step into Phoenix Books and Records. This store has a wide selection of new and used books, along with some CDs, records, and tapes.

You'll obviously find low prices by perusing the used book section. Among hardcovers, Harvey Penick's *And If You Play Golf You're My Friend*, originally $20, was just $9.98

here. A paperback edition of *The Good Times* by New York Times columnist Russell Baker, regularly $8.95, was seen for $5.40. The selection of used paperbacks is extensive, including such popular titles as Milan Kundera's *The Unbearable Lightness of Being*, Amy Tan's *The Joy Luck Club*, and more.

You can also find a good selection of remainders and other new books that are discounted for various reasons. For instance, they recently had a reviewer's copy (complete with press release!) of the much-bally-hooed *Mad As Hell: Revolt at the Ballot Box, 1992* by Jack Germond and Jules Witcover. Originally $24.95, it was just $14.98 here—and of course, used only slightly if at all.

Their music selection, while smaller, is also well-priced. Mr. C found a copy of Living Colour's *Time's Up* on compact disc for $7.98. In the tape section, which holds the most of the store's offerings, he saw titles like Madonna's *Erotica* for $5.98 and many others for even less. Phoenix Books and Records is open daily from 10 a.m. to 10 p.m.

Reckless Records
- 1401 Haight St. (Masonic St.), San Francisco; (415) 431-3434

With stores stretching from California to London, Reckless Records leans toward alternative and punk sounds. They also carry interesting stuff like imports, avant-garde bands, and interview discs. Most of their vast selection of used CDs are priced at $9.99. This includes discs by The Jesus and Mary Chain, Phil Collins, Spyro Gyra, Bell Biv Devoe, Depeche Mode, and even recent releases by bands like Porno for Pyros and the Best Kissers in the World. Some used CDs go for even less, $2.99 to $5.99, including titles by lesser-known bands and discs marked "scuffed but guaranteed." In fact, everything over $1.50 is guaranteed for seven days (with a receipt, of course).

Reckless Records also carries used records for those of you who still believe in vinyl. Used records are rated

MR. CHEAP'S PICKS
CDs, Records, Tapes, and Video

──────

✔ **Amoeba Music**—A huge selection of reasonably priced new (and super-cheap used) CDs, records, tapes, and videos for the rock crowd.

✔ **Reckless Records**— "Interesting" and "eclectic" characterize the selection here; "cheap" describes the prices.

as good, very good, or mint, and are priced between $2.99 and $8.99. Prices on used cassettes, $4.99 and under, are some of the lowest Mr. C has seen. Recent bargains included albums by Love and Rockets, Pat Benatar, and Elton John. Oldies, like *The Best of Gerry and the Pacemakers* go for as little as $1.99.

They also carry posters, T-shirts, blacklites, and some videos, though all of these are full retail price, unless there is a sale. Hours are 10 a.m. to 10 p.m. Monday through Saturday and 10 a.m. to 9 p.m. on Sunday.

Recycled Records
- 1377 Haight St. (Masonic St.), San Francisco; (415) 626-4075

True to its name, Recycled Records has used records—lots of 'em. Hundreds. Maybe thousands. While prices can range wildly, from $1.50 for Springsteen's *Born in the U.S.A.* to $15 for a mint copy of the Rolling Stones' *Aftermath*, most are priced at $6 to $7. They have records in just about every category imaginable, including rock, soul, blues, jazz, zydeco, world beat, and more. Recent finds include Janet Jackson's *Rhythm Nation* ($7.50), John Lennon's *Imagine* ($7.50), and Peter Gabriel's *So* ($4.50).

They also have some used CDs,

most priced from $7 to $10. You'll find some good stuff, like *What You See Is What You Sweat* by Aretha Franklin for $7, and Billy Joel's *Storm Front* for $8. What's more, they'll hold a CD, tape, or record for you for up to four days, so you don't have to try and hide a disc you can't pay for at the moment. In a sense, they'll hide it for you.

RR also has a small selection of used books, mostly music related, of course. The store is open from 10 a.m. to 10 p.m. every day of the week.

Rough Trade
- 1529 Haight St. (Ashbury St.), San Francisco; (415) 621-4395

Rough Trade has a small but interesting collection of used CDs at good prices. Some are a little on the high side, but considering the price you'd pay new, they're still a good deal. For example, Nirvana's *in utero* was seen for just $10.99; and *Pocketful of Kryptonite* by the Spin Doctors was just $9.99. A disc by the Steve Miller Band was just $3.99. All used CDs are guaranteed for seven days.

The real bargains, though, are in the vinyl bin—where you can find records for as low as 99¢. What could one possibly find at this ridiculously low price? How about Sting's *Dream of the Blue Turtles*. Keep in mind, of course, that the condition of a 99¢ record is probably not as good as, say, a $4.99 record. But, of course, less is sometimes more. A Peter Gabriel record marked "excellent condition" was just $3.49. Look for "Big Deal" stickers, records that have them are half-off the sticker price.

You can also pick up singles, such as Madonna's *Like a Virgin* for $2.49 and Wham!'s *Wake Me Up* for a measly 49¢ (dontcha miss the 1980s?). Rough Trade also has imports and independent labels, seven-inch singles, new and used tapes, and posters. They're open 10 a.m. to 11 p.m., Monday through Saturday and 10 a.m. to 8 p.m. on Sunday.

Streetlight Records
- 3979 24th St. (Sanchez St.), San Francisco; (415) 282-3550
- 2350 Market St. (Castro St.), San Francisco; (415) 282-8000
And other suburban locations

Streetlight Records has a huge selection of new and used records, tapes, CDs, and video discs. And, as you have probably already guessed, the bargains are in the used bins. Where else could you find the Spin Doctors' *Pocketful of Kryptonite* or *Nevermind* by Nirvana, each just $9.95? Titles by George Harrison, the Red Hot Chili Peppers, and many more were seen for just $8.95 apiece.

Great deals, all—but Mr. C is here to tell you about even better bargains. Streetlight has CD bargain bins filled with used discs at astonishingly low prices. The prices on these CDs are so low because they do not look perfect: they may have scuffed or damaged cases, but they are likely to play perfectly well. In fact, they are *guaranteed* to play perfectly; if you do get a defective disc, you can return it within seven days (be sure to keep your receipt). Anyway, since you want to listen to the disc, not look at it, this is a great way to get save a bundle on new tunes. Mr. C saw the Bangles' *Everything*, and *X* by INXS for an incredible $3.95 each. Depeche Mode's *Music for the Masses* was just $4.95 and *The Immaculate Collection* by Madonna could be added to your collection for just $5.95.

What's that you say, you don't own a CD player? Don't despair, Streetlight has great deals on used tapes and vinyl too. If it's tapes you want, Mr. C saw bunches, including *So* by Peter Gabriel and David Byrne's *Rei Momo*, each just $2.95. Used records reaped the biggest savings, especially in the bargain bin filled with records for $1 (sorry, no returns on dollar records). Why, for a measly four quarters you could have picked up such classics as Duran Duran's self-titled debut album, Culture Club's *Color by Numbers*, or Billy Joel's *The Stranger*.

Stop at the Streetlight on Monday through Saturday 10a.m. to 10p.m. and Sunday 10:30 a.m. to 8:30p.m.

The Wherehouse

- 1303 Van Ness Ave. (Sutter St.), San Francisco, (415) 346-1978
- 1300 Ninth Ave. (Irving St.), San Francisco, (415) 564-5600
- 3301 Geary Blvd. (Parker St.), San Francisco, (415) 751-3711
- 165 Kearny St. (Sutter St.), San Francisco, (415) 249-0871
- 2083 Union St. (Webster St.), San Francisco, (415) 346-0944

And other suburban locations

The Wherehouse is a local chain that carries a wide selection of used CDs for $3.99 to $6.99 (most of them at the more expensive end). Discs priced at $6.99 include *Best of Dark Horse* by George Harrison, *Upfront* by jazzman David Sanborn, Van Halen's *OU812*, and many others. Discs by artists from Robert Palmer to Dizzy Gillespie were seen for $3.99. Wherehouse is also a great place to sell or trade in your CDs; they'll give up to $6 credit for used CDs. They even have listening stations, so you can audition discs before you buy them; and they carry accessories like CD and tape holders, CD cleaners, and such.

There are used videos here, as well. Most are about $12.95, with titles like *Mr. Saturday Night*, *Sister Act*, and *Passenger 57*. Check out the section of videos under $10, which on a recent visit included the Steve Martin/Lily Tomlin comedy *All of Me* and *Educating Rita* with Michael Caine. Some videos are very cheap indeed: *Necessary Roughness* and *Wayne's World* were seen for $4.95. That's almost the price of a rental! Speaking of which—they also rent videos, and sell new releases at reasonable prices. This is a total entertainment store. Hours vary for each store, but they're all open seven days.

CLOTHING—NEW

Know what you're buying! Clothes, like anything else, are sold at discount for many reasons. Let's quickly go over some basic terms.

With new merchandise, "First-quality" means perfect clothing—it has no flaws of any kind, just as you would find in any full-price store. Such items may be reduced in price as a sales promotion, because they are left over from a past season, or because too many were made. Some stores are able to discount first-quality clothing simply through high-volume selling and good connections with wholesalers. "Discontinued" styles are self-explanatory; again, these are usually new and still perfectly good.

"Second-quality," sometimes called "irregulars," "seconds," or "IRs," are new clothes which have some slight mistakes in their manufacture, or which have been damaged in shipping. Often, these blemishes are hard to find. Still, a reputable store will call your attention to the spot, either with a sign, or a piece of masking tape directly on the the clothing item.

If you're not sure whether you're looking at a first or a second, always ask!

MEN'S AND WOMEN'S WEAR—GENERAL

AHC Apparel Outlet Store
- 625 Second St. (Brannan St.), San Francisco; (415) 957-1983

AHC Apparel Outlet Store sells off overruns by Go Silk, a maker of fine clothes in all-natural fabrics—including wool, linen, cotton, and of course, lots of silk. These are very high-quality clothes made of high-quality fabrics, so they don't come cheaply, even here; but AHC's discounts will certainly take the sting out of some of the price tags. For example, a silk jacket, originally $320, was seen here for $192; silk pants, regularly $198, were reduced to $119; and a silk parka, regularly $460, was on sale for $276. A beautiful 100% silk sweater, originally $270, was just $162. In linen, you'll find great buys like a smart-looking jacket, regularly $260, selling for $156. They do have a small selection of menswear, like men's fancy linen shirts, regularly $360 (!) for just $185.

Don't leave without checking out the clearance rack where, at least during Mr. C's visit, *everything* was $35, including pants, skirts, shorts, and some tops. And be on the lookout for special sales. On the day Mr. C stopped in everything in the store was further reduced by 30% off—including clearance items. Those savings sure add up. Open Monday through Saturday from 10 a.m. to 5 p.m.

Christine Foley Knitwear
- 430 Ninth St. (Harrison St.), San Francisco; (415) 621-8126

The selection here is rather limited, but Mr. C feels the store is worth a mention since these are handmade, 100% cotton sweaters selling at about half off retail prices. Most of these are discontinued styles, with a few samples and irregulars thrown in. Seconds are clearly marked as such; everything else is first-quality. Adult sweaters average $130 and children's sweaters are about $68. Pricey still, but far less than they can be in department stores.

Christine Foley sweaters feature brightly colored designs, of very high quality; these are heavy, well-made sweaters that will last you through many a season. When you stop in, be sure to put your name on their mailing list—the store occasionally has special warehouse sales, when you can *really* save big.

Cut Loose Factory Outlet
- 690 Third St. (Townsend St.), San Francisco; (415) 495-4581

Cut Loose manufactures high-quality cotton casual clothes, and sells off its first-quality past season overruns and current season seconds at this outlet. These are mostly weekend-type clothes that can best be described by adjectives like *soft*, *moveable*, *comfortable*, and, of course, *loose*. And the prices are just as comfortable. Mr. C saw ribbed cotton turtlenecks for $8, cotton leggings for $8, and cotton skirts for $4. Many items were as much as 50% off their original retail prices, like a cotton flannel nightshirt, regularly $24, for just $12; workshirts, originally $30, for $15; and a $75 corduroy coat, in lots of colors, for just $35. Some items offer even bigger discounts, like a $60 sweater for just $15.

They also have a line of velour pieces, including tops, pants, and skirts, for $15 to $20. That's more than 50% off retail, and you'll find lots of different colors. The same is true for their line of crinkled rayon wear. All of the merchandise here is top-quality in fabric and construction. Hours are 10 a.m. to 5:30 p.m., Monday through Saturday.

Déjà Vu á Paris
- 400 Brannan St. (Third St.), San Francisco; (415) 541-9177

Déjà Vu á Paris is a step beyond outlets. It's the workshop of a Parisian designer who uses the space to sell off past-season fashions at a discount. Some of the merchandise is *way* past-season, and you won't find anything current since he doesn't want to compete with his retail accounts. But many of the pieces here are classics, and don't look the least bit dated. For example, a basic black jacket, originally priced at $315, was seen for just $149; and a pair of navy pants, originally $159, were *trés* affordable at $55. A silk and linen blazer, originally $299, was reduced to $149, and a 100% wool skirt, originally $98, was just $55.

When you do see some trendier pieces, they tend to be even cheaper. A pink and white jacket, originally $299, was marked down to a mere $39, while a pink tank dress, initially priced at $199, was just $29. All of these clothes are of exceptionally high quality, and most are crafted from natural fabrics, like silk, linen, cotton, and wool. You will find some casual clothes, but mostly this is a place to look for sophisticated career basics.

Hours at Déjà Vu á Paris vary. Generally, you can count on Fridays from 11 a.m. to 5 p.m., and Saturdays from 10:30 a.m. to 5 p.m.; for other weekdays, or just to be sure anytime, call ahead.

Designer's Co-op
- 625 Third St. (Brannan St.), San Francisco; (415) 777-3570

Designer's Co-op offers men's, women's, and kids' clothes by famous and trendy makers at discount prices. Shoppers will find career wear, casual duds, and dressy evening looks. And the prices? Well, you may find an $86 silk and cotton blouse for $29.99, a $200 dress for only $69.99, or a $240 cotton sweater for $89.99. Designer shirts for men, some in silk, were seen for as little as $14.99, and silk jackets were just $27.99. A $350 leather jacket was marked down by half, to $175!

Ski bums will be eager to hit the slopes after they pick up a ski jacket ($39.99) and pants ($19.99). Snowsuits, with retail prices as high as $300, were seen here for just $69.99. You'll also find a great selection of shoes; Sam & Libby work shoes, for instance, were just $29.99.

In the super-affordable sections you'll find designer jeans as low as $14.99 for women's styles, with

men's from $29.99 to $39.99. Sweatshirts by B.U.M. Equipment were just $19.99. Cotton and linen shorts were a steal at $9.99. And, don't miss the clearance racks where you'll find merchandise at super-reduced prices.

Kids' stuff is more limited, but the prices are still great. Jumpsuits, regularly $37.50, were just $16.99 and a bin of cotton jumpsuits by Trumpette were just $12.99. Infants will stay warm and snuggly in a reversible bunting for just $40. If you're looking for funky kids' clothes, not the usual ballerina pink and baseball player blue, this is definitely the place to try. They recently had a white cotton jumper, infant-sized, with black letters that proclaimed "Tax Deduction." Decidedly offbeat.

Designer's Co-op is open 10 a.m. to 6 p.m. Monday through Saturday, 11 a.m. to 5 p.m. on Sunday.

Designers' Outlet
- 300 Brannan St (Second St.), #102, San Francisco; (415) 957-5978

During his visit to this SoMa store, Mr. C did not see any designer names, at least none that the average shopper would recognize. What he did see, however, were men's and women's clothes, including pieces in silk and cotton, at great low prices. Silk jackets in loads of colors were just $19, washable silk pants and skirts were $15, and men's washable silk shirts were $12.

Some prices were astonishingly low, like silk tanks and shorts for $8 each (two for $15), print camisoles and bike shorts for $2, decorated T-shirts for $10, and boxes of sweaters for just $5. You'll find great career and basic clothes, including dresses and suits for $30, pantsuits for $30, sweaters for $24 and palazzo pants for $18. Just about any wardrobe will be complimented by a bright beaded vest for $20. Designers' Outlet also has a small selection of jewelry, including earrings as low as $3. They're open Monday through Friday from 10 a.m. to 5:30 p.m., Saturday from 9:30 a.m. to 5:30 p.m., and Sunday from 11 a.m. to 5 p.m.

Dress Market
- 660 Third St. (Townsend St.), #102, San Francisco; (415) 495-6768

Part of the off-price mecca that is the Six-Sixty Center, the Dress Market sells quality fashions at discount prices. During a recent visit Mr. C spied cotton dresses, originally $80, selling here for $40—plus an *additional* 20% discount. A two-piece ivory pantsuit, regularly $185, was just $90, also reduced 20% further. Dress Market also has a $25 rack, where you may find goodies like a denim dress or a brightly colored rayon suit. Fancier duds included a black beaded lace dress for $64. Or, how about a mauve rayon dress with matching jacket for $75?

This is actually two stores in one: the second side is called Cotton Candy. Here are the *really* casual clothes, like jogging suits for $39.99; leggings and stirrup pants, in lots of colors, for $9.99; and skirts for $9.99. Cotton Candy also has discount perfumes. They asked not to have names or prices quoted, since the stock and its discounts vary widely depending on availability; but suffice it to say, the names are big and the discounts are noteworthy.

East West Concepts
- 625 Second St. (Brannan St.), San Francisco; (415) 777-5918

East West Concepts is a designer's outlet. You may not recognize the names on the labels, but you'll definitely recognize the good quality of these garments. Most of the clothes here are made of natural fabrics, the sort you'd expect from a store with this name. For instance, you may find silk pants ($18.99), silk tops, ($15.99), cotton sweaters ($14.99), or beaded sweaters of angora and lambswool ($19.99). At these fantastic prices, who can resist? Silk jackets are a steal at $34.99 and you'll certainly want to fill your closets with long skirts in cotton and rayon for just $10.99 each. You won't need a special occasion to buy a special occasion dress of velvet, satin, lace, se-

quins, etc., for just $39.99.

There are some casual clothes, catering to the latest fashion whims: bell bottom jeans for $20.99, and pastel coatdresses for $34.99. Plus lots of separates under $15, like flowered denim shorts ($7.99), stirrup leggings in lots of colors ($8.99), and silk shorts ($11.99).

East West Concepts is open 10 a.m. to 5 p.m., Monday through Saturday.

Eileen West Outlet
- 2915 Sacramento St. (Divisadero St.), San Francisco; (415) 563-0113

Eileen West specializes in manufacturing fine-quality sleepwear for women. At this outlet store on a quiet corner in Pacific Heights, overstocks and samples are sold at a considerable discount. Not all of the merchandise is marked with the original retail price, but if you poke around on the racks, you'll get a pretty good feel for the kinds of savings they offer. Of course, many of the store's regular shoppers know this already.

Among the recent bargains were a 100% cotton flannel bathrobe, originally $79, selling here for $47.40; a cotton nightshirt with pink candy stripes, originally $44, for just $10; and a cotton terry robe, meant to sell for $137.50, here a more relaxing $82.50. They usually offer a selection of samples too, including cotton gowns or pajamas for $32.

Eileen West occasionally fills out its store by getting in some daytime clothes which are also sold at a discount. A long rayon dress, originally $160, was seen for $46.20 here. Even though some of these fashions can get a bit pricey, the discounts here will certainly bring them into many women's price range. The store is open from 10 a.m. to 6 p.m., Monday through Saturday and Sunday from noon to 5 p.m.

Esprit Factory Outlet
- 499 Illinois St. (16th St.), San Francisco; (415) 957-2500

Those who love Esprit clothes and shoes will think they've found heaven here. The Esprit Factory Outlet sells all of their most popular fashions at discounts that range from unimpressive to phenomenal—all in a modernized warehouse building that's big and bright, complete with a cafe, along the industrial waterfront.

Gals may find jeans, normally $48, for just $20; and cotton sweaters in lots of colors, regularly $60, for $29. A wool/silk sweater, regularly $110, was recently seen for $49, while a purple mohair and acrylic sweater, originally $58, was just $15. You'll also find plenty of cheap basics, like sweatshirts for $19 and long sleeve cotton T-shirts for $10.

Most of the stuff here is standard-issue Esprit; but there is also a good selection from their Susie Tompkins line of dressier styles and career-appropriate clothing. Recent specials among these included a navy jacket, regularly $222, for $105—and matching pants, originally $138, for $59. Ribbed cotton sweaters fit into any wardrobe and when they're just $38, down from the regular $64, who can pass 'em up? These styles are anything but boring, even though they are classic in style and have a high-quality construction so they will last many seasons.

Esprit shoes are always popular, and the outlet has a ton. Suede strap-style shoes, in five different colors, were marked down from $42 to $20; and hip-looking heels in black and brown suede, originally $42, were just $15. The ever-versatile black leather shoe, regularly $50, was just $20.

There are aisles and aisles of clothes for the younger set. Teens can pick up a pair of denim shorts, usually $32, for just $10; and kids will love the colorful overalls, usually $34, for $15. During Mr. C's visit, the store featured a rack of kids' samples, all for $10. You'll find even bigger savings in the bargain section, where there are always lots of bins marked "$5 and up" or "$10 and up." Get on Esprit's mailing list to find out about special sales and promotions.

The Esprit Factory Outlet is open Monday through Friday from 10 a.m.

MR. CHEAP'S PICKS
Men's and Women's
Wear—General

✔ **Déjà Vu á Paris**—Step into this designer's workshop and rifle through the racks of past-season *couture*. The quality is high, the prices are low; you may have found heaven.

✔ **Designer's Co-op**—If you lean more toward youthful styles that are trendy or offbeat, this is your place.

✔ **The Fashion Center Sample Sales**—Pre-season fashions at past-season prices. How? These are the salespeople's samples, and they need to get rid of them before the new selling season begins.

✔ **Jeanne Marc Downs**—This famed SoMa outlet is where designer Jeanne Marc gets rid of what didn't move on Sutter Street.

✔ **Spaccio**—Spending $1,200 on an Italian suit may have been okay in the '80s, but this is the '90s and saving money is as "in" as a good cut. Here, you can get the same suit for 50% off.

✔ **Vogue Alley**—Beautiful clothes in sumptuous natural fabrics like wool, cashmere, silk, and leather, at prices that are way below retail.

to 8 p.m.; Saturday from 10 a.m. to 7 p.m.; and Sunday from 11 a.m. to 5 p.m.

$5 and $10 Store
● 899 Howard St. (Fifth St.), San Francisco; no phone
This store in the Yerba Buena Square center lives up to its name: Everything here costs either $5 or $10.

Makes Mr. C's job pretty easy! Most of the stuff falls into the $10 category, except for accessories, jewelry, and T-shirts. But hey, even ten bucks is a good price for all these casual, junior-oriented styles: Cotton/ramie sweaters in lots of colors, cotton pants, cotton/poly ribbed turtlenecks, rayon dresses, raw silk blouses, rayon shirts, and more.

You may also see a small selection of children's clothes for $4 to $5. This stuff is not very high-quality, but it's not junk either—and for young girls who will grow tired of them soon enough anyway, these will fit easily into their wardrobe and your budget.

The Fashion Center Sample Sales
• 699 Eighth St. (Townsend St.), San Francisco; (415) 864-1561

Samples are the clothes that sales representatives bring to retail buyers to show off the latest fashions and take in orders. At the end of the selling season (but before the buying season), the reps are done with these samples, and need to get rid of them. Five times a year, the Fashion Center in SoMa opens its doors to the public, for a $3 admission fee, and you can take advantage of huge savings on current looks. Three hundred booths fill an exhibition hall with men's and women's wear, children's clothes, beauty supplies, fashion accessories, gift items, and more. You'll find some brand names: Levi's and B.U.M. Equipment make regular appearances. But a lot of the stuff here is from independent designers, mostly from San Francisco and other parts of California.

You should realize that since these are samples, the size selection may be limited. These rarely favor people toward the extremes. And you may not see every color that would be available in a retail store. What you see is what they've got. Just remember that these are *pre-season* fashions; they haven't even reached the stores yet. You are getting up-to-the-second fashions at below-retail prices. Keep a lighthearted attitude,

take a chance, and you may be surprised.

The best way to find out about these two-day events (they generally run on Fridays from 3 to 7 p.m. and Saturdays from 10 a.m. to 4 p.m.) is to get on the Fashion Center mailing list. You can do this by calling them at the number above or sending them a postcard with your name and address (the ZIP code is 94103). They will then send you notices of upcoming sales, often with extra discount flyers and such.

Frank et Gertie
• 1020 Harrison St. (Sixth St.), San Francisco; (415) 255-6099

You won't find Frank here, or Gertie. They are a Parisian couple, "*citoyens du monde*," in an old photograph. Instead, you will find designers Eric Schultz and Byron Furuya, since this SoMa address houses their offices and retail store. Their ultra-contemporary casual fashions, meanwhile, can be found in such upscale men's clothiers as Barney's of New York; here, you can get the same clothes without the department store markup.

That doesn't make these clothes cheap, just less expensive; this store isn't really an outlet per se—though you can sometimes find end-of-season reductions. A loose-fitting, large-button shirt made to sell for $135 in stores may be found here for $79; a cotton-lycra pullover that would be $110 can go for $65. These are very handsome separates, designed "with a Japanese/European sensibility," in superior fabrics ("densely woven microcotton"). Earth tones make up the color palette, and spare natural wood decor makes up the store's atmosphere.

Some of the other clothes seen here on Mr. C's visit included a pair of corduroy pants, double-lined, selling for $85 (that's $100 below retail, folks) and a reversible, waterproof, hooded jacket—in brushed cotton with a soft, peach-fuzz finish. Made to sell for $275, it was seen here for a more reasonable $145. Jackets and fashions in leather and lambswool are usually found here as well.

As you can guess, this isn't a store for everybody; however, Frank and Gertie—er, Eric and Byron—consider these fashions to be "modern sportswear for men that looks great on women too." Open Mondays through Saturdays from 11-5:30.

Georgiou
- 925 Bryant St. (Seventh St.), San Francisco; (415) 554-0150

Georgiou is a manufacturer of high-quality (read: high-priced) women's fashions. But, here at their outlet store, you can find many of the same looks at huge discounts. You'll find wonderful pieces in natural fabrics including wool, silk, linen, cashmere, and cotton—in career, dress, and casual styles. And the savings are tremendous; most items are half of their original prices. A pair of gray silk and cotton pants, originally $75, was seen here for $37.50; a matching blazer, regularly $135, was just $67. A raw silk dress, originally $155, was just $77.50; and a 100% silk blouse, initially $75, was very affordable at $37.50.

But these only scratch the surface of the bargains to be found. During Mr. C's visit, a sale rack featured items all marked at $5. This included cotton pants and skirts that were originally $45, raw silk pants originally $80, a raw silk dress originally $155, and wool pants originally $95. They also had a special occasion dress in ivory-on-ivory silk, once $155, now a mere slip of a price at $10!

You'll also find fancy accessories (like silk scarves, originally $38 and up, from $20). Georgiou Factory Outlet definitely has that warehouse feel, with cavernous ceilings and concrete floors; but the private dressing rooms, well-organized racks, and helpful and attentive staff will make you feel completely pampered.

Most of the merchandise here is past-season or overstock, and thus in perfectly good condition. But, since this is an outlet, there may be the occasional blemish, so do check items carefully before your purchase.

Good Byes
- 3464 Sacramento St. (Laurel St.), San Francisco; (415) 346-6388

See listing under "Clothing—Used: Consignment Shops."

House of Blue Jeans
- 979 Market St. (Sixth St.), San Francisco; (415) 252-2929
- 1029 Market St. (Seventh St.), San Francisco; (415) 255-7699
- 1059 Market St. (Seventh St.), San Francisco; (415) 255-0575

You don't have to be a genius to figure out what they sell at House of Blue Jeans. You'll find a number of different brands of jeans, all at discounted prices. The discounts vary greatly, and many aren't that spectacular—but even a few dollars off these fashionable staples is always worthy of note.

Recent bargains included Levi's 550s (their semi-new loose fitting jeans), regularly $58, seen here for just $34. The 901 series of stretch jeans for women, regularly $55, were $47 here. If you're looking to throw a little color into your denim wardrobe, they had a 501s in various colors, usually $60, here $52. A selection of fancy denim jackets were all ten bucks off at $73.

As you can see, they specialize in Levi's, but you can also find other popular brands at similar discounts. Lee relaxed-fit jeans, regularly $42, were going for $36. Lee Easy Riders, regularly $38, were just $31. HBJ has a great selection of children's styles, too. Kids' 501s, list price $38, sell here for $32.

And keep an eye out for special deals. During Mr. C's visit they had Guess? jeans for men—$60 elsewhere, usually $56 here—marked down to $39. They also had a table full of Lee jeans at $19 each. This is also a great place to look for other non-jean type casual wear, as well. You might find Fruit of the Loom sweatshirts, regularly $20, for $16, or Levi's T-shirts, originally $22, for $17.

HBJ is open everyday from 9:30 a.m. to 6:30 p.m.

J & G European Fashion

• 2029 Fillmore St. (California St.),
  San Francisco; (415) 921-2987

I & G European Fashion carries a great selection of men's apparel and furnishings at hugely discounted prices. Be forewarned: Most items will still be quite pricey, because of the high quality here. For example, men's blazers with a retail price of $459 can be found here for $220. Savings? Yes. "Cheap"? No.

A cotton/wool raincoat by John Weitz, originally $350, was just $175. Two-piece wool suits made in Italy, list price $499, were seen for $259 here. If you prefer silk, how about trousers, regularly $87, for just $39—and the matching jacket, originally $198, for just $79. Cotton and polyester dress shirts by Next Original, meant to sell for $69, were just $29 and dress shirts by Bosa, originally $69, were just $21.

They also have leather coats and jackets at similar discounts. A black leather jacket, normally $549, was just $249. A gorgeous leather coat, originally selling for $799, was just $399. You'll find a good selection of non-leather outerwear, as well. I & G European Fashion is open daily from 11 a.m. to 7 p.m.

Jeanne Marc Downs

• 508 Third St. (Brannan St.), San
  Francisco; (415) 243-4396

Don't ya love a good pun—"marc downs," get it? Jeanne Marc manufactures and sells a line of designer clothes which are found in many chichi department and specialty stores, as well as in JM's own posh Sutter Street digs. But this outlet store in SoMa features a small selection of past-season overruns selling for much less, sometimes hundreds of dollars less, than their uptown counterparts. Some of the stock here is rather old, since they don't want to compete with their retail branch; but if you're more interested in high-quality clothing at a discount than you are in being up-to-the-minute, then you'll be in heaven.

So, what exactly, will you find here? Well, it varies, of course, but shoppers might find things like a pair of classic wide leg pants in black, originally $178, for $89. Multi-color jumpsuits, meant to sell for $238, were $149, and a pair of turquoise and gold pants, originally $238, were just $69!

The clearance racks yielded the absolute best bargains. Mr. C saw a dress meant to sell for $408, priced at $69. A pair of red and gold pants, originally $238, were just $29. A short, full skirt, in cinnamon or blue, regularly $248, was just $29. Needless to say, such bargains do not hang around for long. Put your name on their mailing list if you want to be the first in line for their big sales and end-of-season purges.

They also sell the fabric they use in their designs, although these materials aren't particularly cheap at $8 to $12 per yard. They're open Monday through Saturday from 11 a.m. to 5 p.m.

Not far down the block at 592 Third Street is **TJ's Factory Store,** telephone (415) 974-1760. They didn't want Mr. C to mention brands or prices, but they do have a significant selection of designer merchandise at really great prices. They have an especially large selection of women's career wear and special occasion dresses. TJ's is open 10 a.m. to 4:30 p.m., Monday through Saturday.

KM Wear

• 625 Second St. (Brannan St.), San
  Francisco; (415) 546-7331

At KM Wear, you can find a variety of high-quality cotton casual clothes for 50% or more below retail prices. A ribbed cotton top that originally sold for $40 was seen here for $20; matching leggings, originally $50, were just $20. Why are they so low? Well, this is the past season stuff. But, with styles and colors that are so versatile and classic, unless you're a slave to up-to-the-second fashions, you probably won't even notice.

You'll find a vast selection of tops, leggings, and dresses. They also have great jackets; one, with a cinched waist in several colors, was originally $150 but selling here for just $75. Sweaters and cardigans will help round out your wardrobe. These clothes are made of heavy, high-quality fabrics and solid construction—you'll really get a lot for your money. Get on their mailing list so you can be notified of special sales. KM Wear is open Monday through Saturday, 10 a.m. to 5 p.m.

Kris Alyssa Michele

- 660 Third St. (Townsend St.), #210, San Francisco; (415) 882-4628

Part of the Six-Sixty Center off-price mall, Kris Alyssa Michele sells quality separates at low prices. Here, shoppers may find angora and lambswool sweaters for $24, silk jackets for $19, and embroidered sweaters for $24. A rack of rayon and cotton skirts were selling for $11 each (or any two for $20). There's great stuff for women who love rayon: long dresses for $40 and jumpsuits for $60. Their washable silk collection includes pants and skirts for $15 and shirts for $12.

Accessories include things like $5 earrings. Men aren't left out, by the way. Men's silk shirts, in lots of colors, were just $12 apiece. Kris Alyssa Michele is a small store, but the selection is good. Definitely worth checking out.

Kyda Trading Company

- 660 Third St. (Townsend St.), #108, San Francisco, (415) 495-2383

You won't find fur pelts or glass beads at this trading post. What you will find are contemporary women's fashions, in dressy and casual styles, all at discounted prices. Kyda Trading Company is one of the many small, interesting stores in that discount metropolis, the Six-Sixty Center.

Here you'll find great stuff like silk "poet" blouses (y'know, frilly cuffs and all) for $19.99; or a two-piece suit ensemble for $75. Some of the merchandise will tell you the original retail price so you can really

see how much you're saving, like a cotton T-shirt and legging set, elsewhere $35.99, here just $28.99. Often, the sale clerks will inform you that certain items are discounted further off the reduced tag price. For example, a sequined dress, originally $360, was $239, but became an even better deal at 25% off. A three-piece rayon pantsuit, originally $95, was already a bargain at $79.99, but was a little better at 10% off.

They occasionally have stuff for men, too, like printed silk shirts, originally $18.99, for just $16.15; but this place is primarily for the gals.

Lilli Ann Outlet

- 2701 Sixteenth St. (Harrison St.), San Francisco; (415) 863-2720

The Lilli Ann Outlet sells off this manufacturer's irregular, past-season, and discontinued styles at significantly discounted prices. These are beautiful, if conservative, career styles and coordinated separates for women only. Merchandise will vary from one visit to another, depending on whatever season has just ended, though many of these styles are permanent basics. Recently, these included items like a beige wool blazer, with a retail price of $264.50, selling for just $97.50; and matching slacks, list price $142, for $52.50. Other finds included silk blouses marked down from $89.50 to $36.75, and silk skirts marked down from $112.50 to $41.25.

The clearance racks also yield fantastic bargains. Polyester blouses in blue, red, and purple, regularly $45, were seen for $20; acrylic cable-knit sweaters, originally $34, were $25 each. Also seen on the clearance racks were some flashier items, like wide-leg slacks in gold lamé for just $19. Look for occasional "two-for-one" specials in the clearance section.

Days of operation tend to vary; generally, they're open every Saturday, plus a few Thursday and Friday afternoons. Mr. C suggests you definitely call ahead before making a special trip.

Loehmann's

- 222 Sutter St. (Kearny St.), San Francisco; (415) 982-3215
- 75 Westlake Mall, Daly City; (415) 755-2424

Loehmann's means low prices on fancy women's clothing and shoes, plain and simple. These folks practically *invented* the designer closeout store years ago in New York; suave Manhattanites still shlep out to Brooklyn for their famous deals.

Mr. C found a rayon pantsuit by Karen Miller, which retails for $190, selling here for just $90; and a Gillian wool coatdress, list price $270, here just $150. Two-ply cashmere sweaters were just $100, but get to the store early if these are advertised, because they sell out *fast.*

Don't miss the better-name designer suits and eveningwear in the now-famous Back Room. Here, a Bill Blass silk plaid dress with pleated skirt was slashed from an original $390 to an amazing $60; and a Bob Mackie silk blouse was just $80, less than half-price. Calvin Klein fashions can usually be found here too, like a pure cashmere sweater listed at $750 but reduced to $400.

At the time of Mr. C's visit, Loehmann's was running a special sale, offering a selection of suits at a ridiculously low *two* for $199. These were originally valued at $225 to $300 each, made by designers like Kasper for A.S.L. and Oleg Cassini.

Note also that petites can do very well for themselves here—with plenty of suits, dresses, and pants to choose from. A petite dress by Depeche was seen for $299, almost $400 off the retail price. Open from 8 a.m. to 8 p.m. Monday through Friday, from 9:30 a.m. to 7 p.m. on Saturday, and Sunday from 11 a.m. to 6 p.m.

Madelles

- 660 Third St. (Townsend St.), #110, San Francisco; (415) 495-5254

Madelles is part of SoMa's off-price mall, Six-Sixty Center, and they sell women's career clothes along with a small selection of casual clothes. Cotton turtlenecks in several colors were just $9.99. Washable silk blouses, originally $40, were just $14.99. Dresses meant to retail for $40 to $120 can be found here as low as $14.99 to $19.99. Office-appropriate pantsuits, originally $100, were seen for just $49.99; and two-piece micro-pleat pants sets, originally $60, were just $20.

Frequently, Madelles will take further markdowns to move their merchandise. White cotton blouses, originally at $21.99, were already a bargain at $14.99. But, at $14.99, who can resist? You'll also find some great weekend clothes, like hooded fleece shirts that sell in retail stores for $22.50 to $30, priced here at $14.99-$19.99. A Mickey Mouse sweatshirt, originally $52.80, was seen for just $41.99.

If you're looking for similar merchandise that's more junior-oriented, try **The Fashion Bin** nearby at 615 Third Street; telephone (415) 495-2264. They have a large selection of career and casual fashions for teens and young women. The quality isn't always the highest, but they have fun pieces that will fit well into just about any wardrobe. The Fashion Bin is open Monday through Saturday from 10 a.m. to 5 p.m.

Major's Manufacturer's Outlet

- 65 Geary St. (Grant St.), San Francisco; (415) 391-3965

Major's makes clothing for some of the top department stores and boutiques in The City. What they can't get rid of they sell off here at deep discounts—sometimes below cost. These are fun, youth-oriented clothes of good, basic quality; not quite junior styles, they lean more toward the "club kid" look. Of course, that's this week. Fashion moves at lightspeed.

Anyway, recent specials included ribbed mock turtlenecks, regularly $48, for $19.50; a flirty polka dot dress, regularly $98, for $29.50; and a patchwork blazer, regularly $179, just $39.50. Bodysuits, all the rage at the time of this writing, normally sell for as much as $48. Here they were seen for just $19.

During Mr. C's visit, the store was having a special on all velvet clothes, another up-to-the-minute look. Everything in velvet was $15.50 or less, including long-sleeve dresses (originally $108!), hot pants, spaghetti-strap dresses, short skirts, and more—in black, blue, and cranberry.

They also sell off some of their fabrics at low prices, so if you're handy with a needle and thread you can make your own coordinating fashions. Major's Outlet is open Monday through Saturday from 9:30 a.m. to 7 p.m.

Malson's Ragsmatazz
- 899 Howard St. (Fifth St.), #104, San Francisco; (415) 495-5037
- 622 Clement St. (Seventh Ave.), San Francisco; (415) 221-2854
- 2021 Broadway (21st St.), Oakland; (510) 763-3735

Ragsmatazz sells a big selection of brand name, junior-style clothes for women at big discounts. Recent specials included an Esprit mohair sweater, regularly $75, for $24.75; a Gunne Sax floral print dress, originally $75, for $19.75, and a microfiber jacket by Susie Tompkins for Esprit, originally $250, for a mere $39.75.

Most of the styles you'll find here are casual—like Esprit jeans, originally $45, for $14.75, or cotton sweaters by Best American Clothing Co., regularly $75, for $24.75. A rack of silk blouses in a bunch of colors, which normally sell for $45, were just $19.75 each; while cotton skirts, same list price, were $14.75.

You will find some dressy styles, however, such as rayon and polyester floral dresses, regularly $75, for just $29.75; and a ruffled blouse from the Limited, usually $60, for just $19.75. And, don't leave without checking the $5 table. At these prices, who can't afford a little indulgence?

If you're looking for clothes that are a little less faddish, try **Salina Fashion**, telephone (415) 777-3089,

or **Bright Blue Limited**, telephone (415) 243-8898, both nearby in Yerba Buena Square (899 Howard Street). Each sells mid-quality women's fashions and accessories are great low prices.

The Men's Wearhouse
- 27 Drumm St. (Sacramento St.), San Francisco; (415) 788-6363
- 601 Market St. (Third St.), San Francisco; (415) 896-0871
- 47 Colma Blvd. (280 Metro Center), Colma; (415) 992-6767

Buying in BIG lots for its 200 stores nationwide lets the Men's Wearhouse sell top names like Yves St. Laurent, Ralph Lauren, Oscar de la Renta, and Givenchy at fractions of their retail list prices. The vast tie selection alone is worth a trip from just about anywhere.

These are first-quality, current fashions, at literally hundreds of dollars off retail. A Ralph Lauren "Polo" suit, listed at $750 (ouch!) might be a more comfortable $350 here. Other suits begin at $119 and $129, and an Oleg Cassini tuxedo was seen for $199. The suits lean toward conservative, classic styles. There's not a heck of a lot of choice for smaller sized or "big and tall" men; but if you're of an average size, the stock is tremendous.

Mr. C found out that the lesser-known Vito Rufolo brand sold here is made by the same company that makes clothing for Perry Ellis. VR dress shirts, with retail prices of $55, are just $35 here. The only difference that Mr. C could find between these shirts and Perry's is that the stripes on the Rufolo shirts aren't aligned as sharply on the collar, noticeable only at the very tips. But who's complaining, if it saves you $20 or more?

Shirts from brands like Damon, Adolfo, John Clarendon, and Pattinni are also priced in the $20-$30 range. So are those ties, in 100% silk, by Italian and American manufacturers; same price range for lizard-skin belts. Kenneth Cole socks are always $5 off retail. Open seven days a week.

Moray California Outlet
- 2109 University Ave. (Shattuck Ave.), Berkeley; (510) 548-7400

Moray Outlet carries a nice selection of mix-and-match budget fashions, mostly synthetics, at wholesale prices. Shoppers will find rayon jumpsuits as low as $28, and rayon pants for just $23. The store recently featured a rack of beautiful beaded vests for just $31; similar styles sell in catalogs and department stores for $60 or more. They also have bargain clearance racks on a regular basis. They're open 7 days a week.

Multiple Choice$ Outlet
- 899 Howard St. (Fifth St.), #301, San Francisco; (415) 495-2628

Here's a quick quiz: This store is called Multiple Choice$ Outlet because they carry so many different brand names in clothes for A) kids, B) teens, C) adults, D) all of the above. If you guessed "D," go to the head of the class. Better yet, go to the store—for a huge selection of casual clothes cheap. For the kids: Guess? jeans, normally $24, are just $17.99 here. Jordache overalls, regularly $36, are just $22, and Buster Brown jumpsuits, regularly $27, are only $20.99. Even when you don't see a brand name tag, you'll still see savings. A variety of frilly party dresses for little girls, usually $32 and up, were seen for just $15.99, and novelty T-shirts, usually $13, for $9.99.

If you're looking for stuff for bigger kids (i.e., adults), they have plenty. Hooded sweatshirts by No Fear, regularly $40, were just $29.99; and Levi's relaxed denim jackets, regularly $110, were spied for just $79.99. The store also carries some irregulars, like Levi's 501 jeans for $24.99 and 550s for just $9.99 (!) You'll save on accessories, too, like nylon tote bags, reduced from $36.99 to just $9.99.

New West
- 426 Brannan St. (Third St.), San Francisco; (415) 882-4929

New West sells a line of high-quality contemporary clothing, very similar to what you might see in the Gap or the Limited. Much of this can still be expensive, but it's much lower than retail prices. Ladies' blouses meant to sell for $99 can be found here for $49. You may find dressy, career fashions like silk pants ($54), women's jackets ($59), men's dress shirts ($19), and men's wool jackets ($39). They have a great selection of dresses for $29 to $49. Jeans start as low as $19, though most are about $39.

Check out their clearance racks! They recently had ribbed cotton turtlenecks, in lots of colors, for $9. A rack of cotton knits, including tops, pants, and dresses, was all one price at $19. Plus cotton tops for $9, men's shorts for $19, and more. Be aware, however, that some clearance items were damaged—so check merchandise carefully.

New West is open Monday through Saturday from 10 a.m. to 5 p.m. and Sunday noon to 5 p.m.

The Newport Trading Co.
- 660 Third St. (Brannan St.), #111, San Francisco; (415)764-1668

Part of the SoMa off-price mall, the Six-Sixty Center, The Newport Trading Co. outlet store carries a whole line of quality silk clothes at astonishingly low prices. A recent visit by Mr. C found blazers for $29, shirts for $16.50, pleated skirts for $29, and pantsuits for $35. A simple silk shell was just $8.50 and a beautiful silk and cotton corduroy blazer was just $54.99.

Clearance bins were filled with short-sleeve blouses and tank tops for $4.99 (do look at these carefully, though; some were stained). There were lots of colors in each style making it easy to mix and match coordinating outfits.

Nordstrom Rack
- 280 Metro Center, 81 Colma Blvd., Colma; (415) 755-1444
- 1285 Marina Blvd., San Leandro; (510) 641-1742

In olden times, "send him to the rack" was a kind of torture. When it comes to Nordstrom's clothing, going to this Rack is a delight—since it means relief from this otherwise-expensive store's prices. Men, women, and kids alike can find fantastic closeout bargains on designer clothing and accessories. And when the Rack holds extra special sales, advertised in the papers, look out.

Gals may find things like a Donna Karan black dress, originally retailing for $650, and selling here for $189; a lined, all-weather Calvin Klein overcoat, reduced from $690 to $350; or a pair of 9 & Co. boots, once $55, here $35. Not to mention lots of workout gear, like Danskin leotards for $19.97 and Ryka aerobics sneakers, marked down from $75 to $36.90.

For the guys (c'mon, you love this stuff too), Mr. C found wool/cashmere blazers by Joseph Abboud reduced from $395 to $197; a Ralph Lauren "Polo" handknit wool sweater, once $325, now $160; Adolfo leather tassel loafers for $69; and denim shorts by Marithé and François Girbaud, marked down from $40 to $26.97.

Not to mention basics, underwear, outerwear, and clothing for children—like kids' Jordache jeans for $19.97 and OshKosh overalls for $12.97. All sales at Nordstrom Rack stores are "as is" and final; but even if you go for something that's slightly damaged and have it tailored, you'll probably still come out ahead financially. Open seven days a week.

The North Face Factory Outlet
- 1325 Howard St. (Ninth St.), San Francisco; (415) 626-6444
- 1238 Fifth St., Berkeley; (510) 526-3530

The North Face sells high-quality, upscale (read: expensive) lines of sportswear and sporting gear. If you love their stuff, but can't afford it (because you also enjoy little things like, oh, *eating*), don't despair. They have not one, but two outlets in the Bay Area where you can find end-of-season closeouts and second-quality goods at varying discounts.

Of course, most of the merchandise still won't be cheap *per se*, but you will save a pile off their regular prices. For example, a Gore-Tex jumpsuit, listed at $890, was seen here for $499.99. A Goldwin Sierra down parka, originally $170, was $79.99. Camping equipment includes things like pup tents, reduced from $445 to a somewhat cozier $389.

There is clothing here for everyone, whether you're into rock climbing or a member of the Olympic Couch Potato Team. Mr. C found men's casual pants, regularly $54, for $19.99; and a lightweight flight jacket, regularly $89, selling for $49.99. They carry a large selection of sweaters, T-shirts, khakis, and outdoorsy stuff, alongside serious gear for camping, hiking, etc. They also have a huge selection of hiking boots and backpacks.

Watch for specially-priced items. Recent in-store specials included a windbreaker marked down from $70 to $24.99—plus an additional 25% off! Similar deal for a pair of women's ski pants, regularly $175, selling here for $69.99, plus an additional 30% off. Don't leave without checking out the clearance rack for even bigger bargains.

An important note: None of the outlet merchandise is warrantied. This may not matter very much if you're buying a ski parka; but if you're in the market for a tent or other heavy-duty equipment, it may not be worth the savings. You decide.

The North Face Outlet is open Monday through Saturday 10 a.m. to 6 p.m., until 7 p.m. on Thursday.

Outback
- 2517 Sacramento St. (Blake St.), Berkeley; (510) 548-4183

This fun and funky shop makes and wholesales its own fashions for women; these are high-end, unique designs, meant to be eye-catching and comfortable at the same time. The store itself is also one-of-a-kind, with splashily painted decor—a sort of psychedelic look with a 90s sensibility. Signs on the walls implore you to "Be Fearless—Choose Love!" And owner/designer Devi Jacobs is often found here herself, lending a personal touch to the friendly service.

Some of the fashions seen here recently included a glamorous black velvet column gown, sleeveless, and well-priced at $108. Cotton woven separates had a casual, southwestern look, with tops for $22 and skirts for $28. In addition to its own lines, Outback also snaps up clothing returns from other retailers; you may find things like embroidered vests from We Be Bop for $40, London Jean denims for $28, or a green velvet dress by Moda Intl. (these latter two items are brands found in a famous British catalog and store chain) reduced to just $60. Another long, flowing ribbed dress—made of 100% organic cotton, in a natural off-white tone—was seen for $36.

Some of these have been returned because of slight defects; they are clearly marked, so keep an eye out. In addition, Outback offers its own "recycled clothing"—in other words, used—in good shape, with many items priced from $1-$10. You can also find jewelry and accessories here, as well as some children's clothing in these same colorful styles. Open seven days a week.

Rock Express Store
- 100 Harrison St. (Spear St.), San Francisco; (415) 597-9861

Hey, man, like, what happens to all those unsold rock concert souvenirs—T-shirts, programs, y'know, memorabilia—when the show is over? They wind up at this store, selling at prices substantially lower than those foisted upon captive audiences at the actual concerts. T-shirts, of course, are the biggest item at concerts, often priced anywhere from $12 to $25 a pop. Here, Mr. C saw tees from big shows like Michael Bolton, Madonna, the Divinyls, and Melissa Etheridge, for just $6 each. Sweatshirts, emblazoned with Madonna or Kenny G, were just $10.

Not everything here is rock-related. Winterland Productions, the distributor for which this store is a sort of clearance outlet, makes similar items for a number of organizations and corporations, including Green-

peace, the Sierra Club, Esprit, and the Hard Rock Cafe. Mr. C saw T-shirts from the *Coneheads* and other movies, as well as logo shirts from Levis and other brand names, for just $8. There are lots of other cheap goodies here too, like blank tees for $5, caps for $2, and posters for $1. Programs for artists ranging from Anita Baker to the Beastie Boys go for just $1 here; these usually cost $10 or so at the shows. You'll also find bags, notepads, pins, cards, and more. It's a fun store just to browse in—for music fans, it feels more like a candy store.

Ross Dress for Less
- 5200 Geary Blvd. (16th Ave.), San Francisco; (415) 386-7677
- 4949 Junipero Serra Blvd., Colma, San Francisco; (415) 997-3337
- 799 Market St. (Fourth St.), San Francisco; (415) 957-9222

And other suburban locations

Dress for Less is an off-price retailer selling all kinds of clothes—many of which are well-known brand names and designer labels—for much less than their intended prices. Recent bargains included cotton sweaters by Pierre Cardin, listed at $68, seen here for $29.99; same price for khaki pants by Liz Claiborne, originally $58. Also found here were silk jackets, regularly $138, here just $69.99.

Men aren't left out: Perry Ellis dress shirts were recently on sale for $19.99. These go for up to $39.50 in full-price stores. And both men and women will find the jeans of their dreams at Ross. Men's jeans by B.U.M. Equipment, list price $38, were $19.99; while women's jeans by Lee, regularly $32, were just $16.99. In the children's department, $38 dresses were selling for $22.99 and trendy vests, regularly $30, were just $19.99.

Ross also carries shoes, including athletic styles (women's Reeboks were seen for just $34.99), as well as some housewares and accessories. Tags indicate whether merchandise is first-quality or irregulars. Most of the stuff, including all the examples given here, are first-quality.

Royal Robbins Factory Outlet
- 841-A Gilman St. (Sixth St.), Berkeley; (510) 527-1961

The Royal Robbins Company was started by acclaimed rock climbers Liz and Royal Robbins. Their goal: to create clothing that would look good, yet stand up to the punishment that a sport like rock climbing dishes out. Their emphasis is on function and quality. These are clothes that are designed and constructed to last, on the rock face and off. Of course, this all comes at a high price; RR fashions are, for the most part, pretty expensive duds. But don't despair! Like many manufacturers, Royal Robbins has an outlet store where they sell off past-season and discontinued merchandise at substantial discounts.

How substantial? Well, that depends on the item, but this isn't one of those phony outlets full of regularly-priced merchandise with a few dollars knocked off. You'll find honest savings. Mr. C saw a Wyoming bomber, a great jacket which had originally retailed for $130, selling here for just $39! A selection of windbreakers, originally selling for $98, were just $59 each, and $18 T-shirts were marked down to $5.

For those seeking weekend casual wear, how about denim jeans—originally $50—for just $35, and soft flannel shirts, originally $46, for $28. Even bigger savings were seen on a rack of women's shorts that had a retail price of $44: these were marked down to just $15. There is also a clearance table with shirts and shorts for just $5. For people who seek adventure, or just want to look like they do, Royal Robbins has the clothes for it and their outlet has them at prices that are easy to scale.

San Francisco City Lights Factory Outlet
- 333 Ninth St. (Harrison St.), San Francisco; (415) 861-6063

San Francisco City Lights is a leading maker of activewear and casual clothes. Here at their clearance outlet, you can get these great clothes at "light" prices. Most of the stock here

consists of irregulars, and these are marked as such; but on most items the problem isn't even detectable. Mr. C found cotton sweaters for $27 to $37, and T-shirts for $8 to $12. There was also a small selection of samples in the men's department, including cotton wrestling suits for $6. They also have a good selection of stuff for kids, including leggings for $5, shorts for $5-$8, T-shirts for $4, and sweatshirts for $10. And don't leave without checking the bargain bin, which recently included kids sweatshirts and pants for $5.

Not everything here is made by SFCL. During his visit, Mr. C came across a rack of discontinued leggings by Moda Int'l. (the brand that Victoria's Secret sells through their catalog) at three pairs for $30. Vicki sold 'em for $23 each. The store is open Monday through Saturday from 10a.m. to 6p.m.

Sandra Ingrish Outlet
- 1000 Brannan St. (Ninth St.), San Francisco; (415) 864-5545

Sandra Ingrish designs great sportswear and career separates, which you can buy here at near-wholesale prices. With knit shorts for just $4, cotton stirrup pants in gingham for $14, and rayon print tops for $11, you can easily afford to stock up on the basics. Of course, if you're looking to splurge a little, they can happily accommodate you there as well: 100% cotton dress shirts for $38, and chambray shirts for a modest $40, are a few of the higher-end items. Please note that all sales are final.

Simply Cotton
- 610 Third St. (Brannan St.), San Francisco; (415) 543-2058

It's simply amazing how many different pieces you can get for under $10 here. On any given day, shoppers may choose from leggings for $6.99, V-neck tee-shirts for $4.99, jeans for $6.99, or cotton cardigans for $8.99. Most of the merchandise here is mid- to good-quality cotton casual wear. Frequently, the already-low prices are discounted further to move merchandise out the door. Short-sleeved elastic-waist dresses for $36 were recently marked at 50% off. The same for $45 long-sleeve, drop-waist dresses and $24 short jumpers. Cotton vests at $22 were marked an additional 10% off.

There are some pricier items too, like heavy-knit, wide leg pants for $54 and heavyweight cotton sweaters for $48. The majority of the stock, however, is very inexpensive. They do carry some children's clothes, as well—like racks of kids' tee-shirts for $3.99 each. Simply Cotton is open Monday through Saturday from 10 a.m. to 5 p.m. and Sunday noon to 5 p.m.

In Berkeley, folks can get similar buys on quality cotton clothing at **The Cotton Outlet**, 2322 Fifth Street at Bancroft Way; telephone (510) 849-0492. They're open Wednesday through Saturday from 11 a.m. to 5 p.m. and they sell clearance cotton clothing at prices below wholesale.

Sister Sister
- 660 Third St. (Brannan St.), #105, San Francisco; (415) 243-4392

Part of the Six Sixty Center bargain hub, Sister Sister is an off-price store for plus-size women. Now, it's difficult enough to find stylish fashions in larger sizes at regular (read: outrageous) retail prices; it can be impossible to find them at a discount. That's where Sister Sister comes to the rescue. Here, you'll find a great selection of contemporary, high-quality fashions at low prices. The merchandise here consists mainly of factory overruns, many of which are in-season, while some are a bit older.

You'll find lots of career separates and casual clothes, along with a few dressy, evening styles as well. Some of the name brands you'll recognize, some you won't. Pants by August Max were seen for just $21.75, and Cherokee jeans, regularly $24.99, were just $12.99. Other bargains included a purple rayon dress for $35.99, and a floral print long dress for $46.99. In their eveningwear section, they had a sequin print top for $39.99 and the same price for the matching skirt. Open from 10 a.m. to 5:30 p.m. Monday through Saturday. They are open occasionally on Sunday; call ahead to be sure.

Spaccio
- 645 Howard St. (Third St.), San Francisco; (415) 777-9797
- 1840 Union St. (Laguna St.), San Francisco; (415) 923-0131
- 2030 Union St. (Buchanan St.), San Francisco; (415) 777-2221

Spaccio carries quality menswear from a factory in Italy that manufactures clothing for some twenty different labels. These aren't well-known names, but if you're looking for BIG names, look elsewhere. If you're looking for good-quality European styled menswear at fifty percent off retail, then you've come to the right place.

Suits, of 100% wool, range in price from $299 to $599. This may not strike you as cheap, and it isn't, but the same suits would cost at least twice as much in department and specialty stores. There are plenty of separates, too—wool blazers from $189 to $369, and wool slacks from $85 to $145. Complete the look with cotton dress shirts, at $45 to $69, and silk ties, from $16.99. They also carry Italian all-leather shoes, priced from $59 to $129. Overcoats, made of wool-cashmere blends, are just $349. Again, you can find such coats at lower prices, but not of this craftsmanship.

The selection here is very large, with a good variety of colors and styles in each section. It doesn't feel like a warehouse; it's clean, well-lit, and there are private dressing rooms. Alterations are available, at an additional charge.

Spare Changes
- 695 Third St. (Townsend St.), San Francisco, (415) 896-0577

Spare Changes carries overruns by many manufacturers which don't have their own outlets; this is actually more an off-price store than an outlet. The advantage is that they have greater variety of styles. The disadvantage is that since you're not buying directly from the manufacturer the savings aren't as big. But, the prices are still terrific; you won't see these clothes much cheaper.

Women will find a great selection of career styles and a lesser selection of casual clothes. A red dress in rayon by Karen Alexander, originally $250, was selling for half-price at $125; and a two-piece black suit, also by Karen Alexander, was reduced from $230 to $120. Vests by Joan Walters were just $17.50. The always versatile Oxford shirt, in cotton, regularly $56, was just $28.

But, it's at the clearance racks where you'll really clean up. Here, find merchandise at big discounts, like a green evening coat, originally $230, marked all the way down to $69.50. A sleeveless rayon jumpsuit, regularly $110, was just $17.50; a Harvé Benard sweater, once $180, was only $19.50.

They also have a good selection of kids' clothes, particularly play stuff. Two-piece casual sets by Spumoni were just $19. There was also a rack of playsets for just $10, and a bin of kids' pants for just $5. Spare Changes is open Monday through Friday from 9:30 a.m. to 5:30 p.m. and Saturday from 9:30 a.m. to 5 p.m. They also have a store in San Mateo.

Tight End

● 434 Ninth St. (Harrison St.), San Francisco; (415) 255-8881

Tight End designs and manufactures high-quality, coordinated activewear for women. You've probably seen their stuff in department stores and specialty shops. Here at their SoMa outlet, they sell first-quality overstocks and past-season lines at wholesale prices.

During Mr. C's visit, the company's newest items included a "thermal wear" line. The sales clerk showed Mr. C an ad for it in a national magazine. But forget those fancy prices—they had many of the same pieces right there in the outlet at wholesale, like a nifty hooded sweatshirt for $25.

Other bargains included a baseball-style shortsleeve shirt for $24. You'll find lots of T-shirts and bike shorts for just $9, and bunches of leotards and leggings for $12. Unitards, which sell in department stores for $40 or more, are a bargain at $15.

All of Tight End's stuff is made in San Francisco, mostly of the very comfortable cotton/Lycra blend. The outlet has a good selection, in lots of prints and colors. They're open Monday through Friday from 8:30 a.m. to 3:30 p.m. only.

Van Heusen Factory Store

● 601 Mission St., (Third St.), San Francisco; (415) 243-0750

This longtime manufacturer has more to offer than plain ol' men's dress shirts. These, along with casual contemporary fashions for men and women, are available at discount at this SoMa location.

Those dress shirts, in traditional business pastels, are sold here for $9.99 and $12.99. A true factory pipeline, the store has tons of these, in every conceivable combination of neck/sleeve size and color. All are first quality, unless you find them on special tables or the "Less than Perfect" rack, further reduced. Silk ties to go with these are $8.99—seemingly hundreds of 'em. Plenty of basic cotton/poly dress slacks, too, reduced from a list price of $28.99 down to $17.99.

But even VH knows there's more to life than the office. There's the golf course, for when you want to get away from the office. Van Heusen's own "Players" line of golf separates include things like colorful pullover knit shirts, marked down from $40 to a below-par $25.99. Along with these, a recent winter clearance sale featured Shaker-style sweaters, half-price at $14.99. And good-looking suede jackets, originally $140, were on sale for $89.99.

Meanwhile, let's not leave out "Van Heusen for Her"—with cotton slacks reduced from $38 to $21.99 and again to $16.99. Cotton skirts, in navy blue, khaki, and white, were seen for nearly half-price at $19.99.

And a rack of elegant-looking cardigan sweaters, hand-knit in a cotton-ramie blend, were down from $98 all the way to $39.99.

Vogue Alley

- 432 Sutter St. (Powell St.), San Francisco; (415) 362-7200

And other suburban locations

Vogue Alley snaps up overstocks, overruns, and past season merchandise from quality manufacturers and then sells them at prices that are way below retail. These are designer-quality fashions and the discounts are substantial. For example, a black silk jacket that would retail $198 was seen here for $78. Another silk jacket, in green, originally $238, was just $78—with matching pants for just $68.

As you may have noticed, the clothes here are not cheap, even at discount. But the quality is consistently high, and you'll see career separates, evening clothes, and some casual wear in natural fabrics like cashmere, silk, wool, leather, and cotton. A red cardigan, 100% cashmere, had a retail price of $256 and sold here for just $88. A wine-colored turtleneck sweater, in 100% wool, originally $110, was just $33.60. Shoppers may find great bargains like buttery-soft black leather pants for $128 (originally $328), a black wool coat dress for $98 (originally $398), and a natural-color cotton sweater for $58 (originally $198). Vogue Alley is open Monday through Saturday from 9:30 a.m. to 6:30 p.m.

Warm Things Factory Outlet

- 3063 Fillmore St. (Union St.), San Francisco; (415) 931-1660
- 6011 College Ave. (Claremont Ave.), Oakland; (510) 428-9329

And other suburban locations

At its factory in San Rafael, Warm Things manufactures its own...er, warm things. These range from the kind you wear, like down jackets, to the kind you have around the house, like pillows and comforters. Either way, these products are made to exacting standards, including genuine goose down and high thread-count

fabrics. And, by shopping at these outlet stores instead of through their mail-order catalog, you can save 25% to 65% off list prices—enough to give you a very warm feeling indeed.

Want to feel completely pampered on a cool morning? Slip on a down-filled bathrobe, originally $160, but reduced to $89 at a recent clearance. They even make matching down *slippers*, reduced from $38 a pair to $22. And there are over a dozen styles of ski jackets and 3/4-length coats, many available with such features as removable hoods, zip-out sleeves, elastic waists, and so on. On sale, models which normally would cost between $100 and $150 can be found here for $59-$79. They're all filled with 100% genuine goose down.

Warm Things guarantees the workmanship and materials of its products; these are definitely made to last, making a good-value investment at any price. Those tightly woven fabrics, for example, make sure that feather ends won't poke through to annoy you. Comforters are "baffled" on the inside, to make sure they stay evenly filled. These folks have been making warm things for over twenty years; they know what they're doing. Open seven days a week.

Weaver's World

- 587 Castro St. (19th St.), San Francisco; (415) 487-9050
- 2570 Bancroft Way (Telegraph Ave.), Berkeley; (510) 540-5901

Once upon a time, not too long ago, this store was called the Weaver's Factory Outlet; and they were, as the name suggested, an outlet for Weaver's, a company that made casual cotton clothing. Well, as luck would have it, Weaver's went out of business. That fact did not deter this outlet, however, which had already begun selling used clothes and other closeouts, anyway. So, they changed their name, opened a new branch in the Castro, and they plan to continue to sell clothing that is discontinued, past-season, irregular, used, or otherwise discounted.

The styles here are still hip and

casual, with some workout wear thrown in for good measure; all that "California lifestyle" stuff. Recent bargains on new clothes included long sleeve cotton T-shirts for $12, marked down from $15; organic cotton long sleeve tees, originally $27, for $15; and organic cotton sweatshirts, originally $44, for just $18. Other sweatshirts were as low as $8, and new jeans started at just $12.

Weaver's World's selection of used clothing is also quite plentiful. These are, of course, meant as high fashion; many of the shirts, for example, are dress shirts which have been dyed in trendy colors. Though Mr. C was a tad put off by used Levi's for $20, he was reassured by racks of used business suit vests for $6-$8 and used khaki workpants for $5 and $10. WW also has occasional specials; during Mr. C's visit, used flannel shirts were a mere two for $5. Such a deal!

We Be Bop
• 1380 Tenth St. (Gilman St.), Berkeley; (510) 528-0761

We Be Bop designs and manufactures a full line of funky fashions, including tunics, vests, harem pants, caftans, and more—in soft, fluid fabrics like cotton and rayon. These high-quality pieces are bright and colorful and fun to wear. Unfortunately, they're also quite expensive, especially when purchased in chi-chi department stores and upscale specialty shops. Here at their outlet, though, you'll find overstocks and past-season merchandise at discounts that range from Lilliputian to gigantic.

The freshest stock is still close to the retail price, though discounted slightly. In the main racks you may see things like a beautiful beaded vest for $48; a sleeveless, button-front shift dress, in rayon, for $44; and rayon wide leg pants for $46.

Still too pricey? The big secret here is the $10 rack. These pieces are well past-season, and occasionally you'll run across something that's been damaged (do check everything over carefully), but the prices are impossible to beat. On this rack, Mr. C saw a beaded top and a pair of emerald green rayon pants. They also have a bargain rack where items are a little newer, but also not quite as cheap. An oversized shirt in red, originally $46.50, was just $20 on this rack.

We Be Bop also has a great children's section. You may find a rayon skirt and top set, with an abstract print and lots of beads, for $35; or a rayon jacket at $30. A sale box is filled with infant and toddler clothes, including dresses and jumpers for just $15. The children's section, too, has sale racks of its own.

We Be Bop is also just a very pleasant store to shop in; the merchandise is well-presented and they have private dressing rooms. Open from 10 a.m. to 5 p.m. Monday through Friday and from noon to 5 p.m. Saturday and Sunday.

Weston Wear
• 900 Alabama St. (21st St.), San Francisco; (415) 550-8869

Designer Julienne Weston began her career as a dancer, branching into costume design for that very particular field. As you might guess, these needed to be clothes that were meant to attract attention, yet be incredibly light and easy to move in. A dozen years ago, she branched further into designing similar clothes for the retail market; now her fashions are sold in boutiques and major department stores throughout the country, and across the Pacific as well.

Using stretchy fabrics like chiffon, gauzy fishnet, and good ol' cotton/lycra, the dance influence is easy to see. These are wild, fun, and downright sexy dresses and separates, along with more practical sweatshirts, bike pants, and leggings that are perfect for the aerobic lifestyle. Other pieces are most definitely "special occasion." All of them are less expensive in this second-floor factory shop than in those boutiques; what's more, there are always racks filled with past-season closeouts.

These, of course, are the real bargains. Oh sure, you can do very well with a glittery, gauzy black dress—

one that sweeps around, nearly reaching the floor, as you walk—for $64; at certain times, you may even find it reduced here to $45. And there are plenty of other frilly, whimsical dresses in that range. But, on the clearance racks, items are priced to move in more ways than one: most are $10, $12, $15, and $20. There is a good variety of styles and colors, making for plenty of fun browsing. Plus a $5 rack of slightly damaged pieces, which you may still find useable. Same price, by the way, for

long, colorful, gauze scarves and stretch headbands.

The store is only open on Fridays (from 12:30 to 5:00 p.m.) and Saturdays (11:00 a.m. to 3:00 p.m.), except for holidays; in general, calling ahead is always a good idea, just to be sure. Better yet, get on the Weston Wear mailing list, so that you'll receive postcards with the exact dates and information about special sales. By the way, parking in this industrial/residential Potrero neighborhood is not easy! Allow yourself extra time.

LEATHER AND OUTERWEAR

D & K Leathers
- 93 Jefferson St. (Mason St.), San Francisco; (415) 433-9320
- 133 Powell St. (O'Farrell St.), San Francisco; (415) 399-9148

D & K Leathers carries a good selection of leather apparel at reasonable prices. Nothing here is going to blow you away, but you will find a consistent selection of top-quality merchandise. The Jefferson Street location, near Fisherman's Wharf, is very small; thus, the selection is limited, and geared more toward tourists. You're better off at the downtown location.

Either way, there are plenty of jackets in the $79 to $99 price range, like black leather motocycle jackets for $99. You'll also find vests for $59 and $69. The majority of the women's jackets are $129 to $139; for men, they range from $139 to $189.

Full-length leather coats start at just $189. If you really want to splurge, go for something in lambskin, starting as low as $219. For really extravagant items, check out fur-lined jackets for $800 to $900. But, at the other end of the spectrum, the store does have belts and wallets starting at $10.

D & K Leathers is open everyday from 9 a.m. to 9 p.m.

Leather Etc.
- 1201 Folsom St. (Eighth St.), San Francisco; (415) 864-7558

This SoMa store is an outlet for a manufacturer of leather goods, mostly jackets, pants, and such. Whatever they don't sell through their regular retail accounts comes back here, to be sold at heavily discounted prices. So, you can get leather motorcycle jackets for $69 and vests from $39. Some of the nicer jackets go for $139 and up, potentially hundreds of dollars below list prices.

Mostly, the merchandise here is on the tougher side of the leather styles. It leans toward biker-types, so along with the jackets you'll find pants, chaps, etc., all at a discount. Don't let some of the hardcore leather-and-metal paraphernalia scare you; the staff is friendly and helpful. They're open Monday through Friday 10:30 a.m. to 7 p.m., Saturday from 11 a.m. to 6 p.m., and Sunday from noon to 5p.m.

Leather to Go
- 200 Potrero Ave. (15th St.), 2nd Floor, San Francisco; (415) 863-6171

Golden Bear Sportswear is a company manufacturing men's leather jackets; or, as they refer to it, "rugged outerwear." They've been doing so for about seventy years. Major department stores and mail-order catalogs from around the country buy these up wholesale, and put their own names on them—along with some rather rugged price tags. Well, upstairs on the second floor of this industrial building (actually, the entrance is around the corner on 15th Street), a small retail shop gives you a chance to buy these same products direct from the factory, at remarkable savings.

Mr. C was asked not to mention the names of the catalog houses, but trust him—they are some of the biggest names to be found stuffed through any door slot. Meanwhile, by coming to the source, a man's field coat of genuine lambskin—which can cost up to $400 retail—will only cost $225 instead. A bomber jacket which would also be $300-$400 elsewhere can be found here for $200. And baseball-style jackets, with wool bodies and leather sleeves, were seen reduced from $135 to $99.

With prices that are still "upscale" at discount, you can see that these are high-quality coats—as Mr. C did on his visit. The materials are top-notch, the styles are current, and the construction is sturdy. You can even see them being made; only glass windows separate the small store from the factory. Other items seen here may include motorcycle jackets, hip-length hunting coats, and some occasional women's items. The stock, and styles, change through the seasons.

Be sure to check out the rack of factory seconds and returns too, where some of these coats are priced as low as $50. Now, *that* leather *really* goes. The store takes major credit cards, and is open weekdays from 9-5, and Saturdays from 10 a.m. to 2 p.m.

The Outerwear Co.
- 660 Third St. (Brannan St.), San Francisco; (415) 777-4220

As the name would suggest, this store sells a selection of outerwear, including raincoats and leather jackets, at discounted prices. You may find a Misty Harbor raincoat, originally $225, marked down first to $159 and then put on sale for $139; or a tan silk jacket, originally $99, marked down to $69, and again to just $49. In wool blazers, you may find several choices for $59 each (or two for $99).

Their selection of leather goods is extensive and well-priced. Black

MR. CHEAP'S PICKS
Leather and Outerwear

✔ **The Raincoat Outlet**—This is an actual factory, so the surroundings will look nothing like the chi-chi boutiques where the merchandise ends up. But then, the prices don't look the same, either.

✔ **Sauvage**—A classic, black motorcycle jacket for $69? That and more at this leather manufacturer and retailer.

leather motorcycle jackets, with retail prices up to $300, sell here for just $89 to $179. A brown leather jacket, originally $339, was clearance-priced at $169; and a long jacket in tan, regularly $450, was on sale for $279. They also carry skirts in leather and suede, ordinarily $89, for just $29.

The Raincoat Outlet
- 543 Howard St. (First St.), 2nd Floor, San Francisco; (415) 362-2626

The Raincoat Outlet is probably unlike any outlet you've ever been in. And, the owner, Marguerite, is probably unlike any salesperson you've ever run across. The outlet is the actual factory for this line of raincoats, capes, vests, and more; and Marguerite is very eager to tell you all about them. She will happily point out which of her functional fashions have been sent off to various presidents and first ladies. She even has an autographed picture of President Bush wearing a jacket with a map of the world emblazoned on it; not three feet away is the actual item, ready for you to buy. Does that make the purchase a New World Order?

There aren't any tags on anything, so if you see something you like you'll have to ask how much it is. These are not cheap, in the standard sense of the word. Marguerite showed Mr. C a gold and black velvet jacket that has been sold for $300 in a certain chi-chi boutique. But here, she'll sell it directly to you for $135. It's *cheaper*, but this is top-notch stuff.

You will find plenty of raincoats here of course, but the store also has beautiful capes, vests in lots of fabrics from cotton to velvet, and jackets. Check out the huge selection of reversible vests with unusual loop buttons. Marguerite will tell you in no uncertain terms what you can and can't touch. Also note that since this is merchandise that she is sending to stores, you should treat it carefully.

There's someone at the factory most of the time, but that isn't always true of the outlet itself. The store doesn't have set hours, so it's best to call ahead.

Sauvage
● 17 Stockton St. (O'Farrell St.), San Francisco; (415) 693-9983

This store isn't exactly an outlet, since it's the *only* place Sauvage sells its designs, but, since you're buying directly from the manufacturer, you do get outlet-like prices. Classic black motorcycle jackets go for $69; in fact, you'll find dozens of different jackets from $49 to $69. These are high-quality, heavy leather jackets in up-to-date styles—another plus over "past-season" outlets. A suede baseball jacket with knit cuffs and waistband was just $69, while a jacket in black suede was seen for $59.

You will also find some more expensive (but still discounted) deals. A black three-quarter length jacket, this year's look, is a bargain at $99. Another three-quarter length, in lambskin, was just $199. And, lest you think that coats are the only stock in trade here, the store does carry other items. A pair of women's lambskin pants, meant to sell for $495, were found here for just $139. Skirts, listing for $295, were just $99; same deal for vests. You'll also find a great selection of leather bags, some as low as $32.

BRIDAL AND FORMAL WEAR

Bridal Veil Outlet
● 124 Spear St. (Howard St.), San Francisco; (415) 777-9531

The people at the Bridal Veil Outlet want to make it very clear that what they sell here are *bridal accessories*; they do not have wedding gowns, at any price. All you will find here are veils and their accoutrements, in a multitude of styles, at up to 50 percent off retail. Mr. C saw one veil which had retailed for $200, selling here for $100; and another, originally priced at $240, for just $110. In addition, the folks here do custom work and alterations, including some dyeing, at reasonable prices.

Accessories include a small selection of floral headpieces, for bridesmaids or flower girls, available here for $25 to $35. A bridal hat of white satin, originally $104, was reduced to just $38! There is also a clearance box full of pre-dyed hairpieces, barrettes, combs, etc., for just $10 apiece. Among the other wedding necessities found here were a guest book, with a retail price of $40, selling for just $29, and a "Memories" book, marked down from $56 to $40. These bargains could be happy memories in themselves. And, for the bride who needs "something blue," garters in a variety of styles are just $8 each.

Do you have a little girl who likes to play dress-up? Mr. C saw a basket of "costume veils" for just $15. The store also carries a selection of first communion necessities. They're open Tuesdays through Saturdays from 10 a.m. to 4 p.m.

The Discount Bridal Store
● 300 Brannan St. (Second St.), San Francisco; (415) 495-7922

The Discount Bridal Store has hundreds of wedding gowns, bridesmaid dresses, prom dresses, and more, at great savings. The wonderful thing about this store is that it offers the best of both worlds: You can order designer dresses, two to three months in advance, or, if you need it *now*, you can pull something right off the rack and take it home (the store does not offer alterations). They can order from over a dozen well-known designers, in sizes from 4 to 44. Gowns start as low as $190, but the average price is $300 to $500—very reasonable indeed.

One of the styles Mr. C noted was meant to sell for $780, but available here for just $450. Formal evening dresses can be found for $125 to $150, and a black lace style was seen for $89. You'll also find a selection of discontinued gowns; these are automatically half off the already-discounted tag price. Discontinued gowns, obviously, cannot be ordered; what you see is what you can choose from. The store has a no-frills outlet atmosphere, but not the service—the staff is friendly and helpful. With a little patience, you'll have no trouble finding the gown of your dreams, and your dream will be even sweeter at these prices.

Open Monday through Saturday 10 a.m. to 5 p.m., Sunday 11 a.m. to 5 p.m.

Gunne Sax Discount Outlet Store

- 35 Stanford St. (Second St.), San Francisco; (415) 495-3326

The Gunne Sax Outlet is an institution around here; people come from all around to get great buys on gowns and special occasion dresses. For the uninitiated, Gunne Sax designs and manufactures several lines of wedding gowns, bridesmaids dresses, prom gowns, and other fancy duds. Here at their outlet, you can get many of these at huge discounts.

The big item here for many women is, of course, wedding gowns. During Mr. C's visit there were a couple of racks with brand-new gowns priced at $276, and a couple more racks for $150. You don't have to be

MR. CHEAP'S PICK
Bridal and Formal Wear

✔ **Gunne Sax Discount Outlet Store**—People travel from miles around to come to this outlet. You'll find racks of dreamy bridal gowns, fun prom dresses, and more, at unbelievable savings.

a genius to figure out that the $150 gowns are more likely to be damaged; there are no returns allowed here, so check every piece of merchandise very carefully. Meanwhile, some blemishes are easily corrected, and even with tailoring costs, you can still come out way ahead on the deal. Some dresses may only need a good cleaning (again, be sure it will come clean).

Cautions aside, Gunne Sax recently had a beautiful white lace wedding gown, with the original $900 price tag still on it, sitting on the $276 rack. You save $624! They also had bridesmaid gowns as low as $90, and cute flower girl dresses as low as $50.

This store is a huge warehouse just filled with bargains. A gorgeous black velvet evening dress, originally $350, was seen here for just $103; and an ivory lace dress with a matching bolero jacket, regularly $325, was just $108. Clearance racks have dresses that originally sold for as much as $280, now as low as $20. Three racks of dresses, originally $68 and up, were all marked $15. Plus christening gowns for $75 and christening suits for $25; racks of spring dresses were $39 (sizes 4X to 6X), $64 (sizes 7 to 14, girls), and $75 (sizes 6 to 14, juniors).

Watch for occasional special sales. During Mr. C's visit, they had cotton dresses for $5, special occasion dresses for $10, and bridesmaid gowns for $15. These were located in the back of the adjoining Gunne Sax Fabric Outlet (see listing under "Sewing and Fabrics") and there were hundreds of each style, making it easy to do that oft-dreaded bridesmaid shopping. The good selection included long, short, formal, and informal styles.

The Gunne Sax Outlet is open Monday through Saturday from 9 a.m. to 5:30 p.m.; and Sunday from 11 a.m. to 5 p.m.

CHILDREN'S AND JUNIORS' WEAR

Fritzi Outlet Store
• 218 Fremont St. (Folsom St.), San Francisco; (415) 979-1399

This store is an outlet for the Fritzi, My Michelle, and You Babes labels. These are teen-oriented budget brands, meaning that they are very trendy looking, though not always of the highest quality. But at these rock-bottom prices, who can resist? Here you'll find racks of short dresses, in a number of colors and styles, priced at just $6 each. For the same price, you may find short velvet dresses in green, red, brown, and black. In fact, the most expensive dresses in the store were only $25. Fritzi also carries separates, such as velvet tops for $8, lace skirts for $6, and unlined blazers for $10. Clothes for smaller children were seen for $4 to $8.

Fritzi has a no-frills warehouse atmosphere, with cavernous ceilings and communal dressing rooms. Certain sizes can be difficult to find, though it is worth noting that they do have racks dedicated to plus sizes. The store is open Monday through Saturday until 5 p.m. Of course, shoppers-in-the-know stop in on Friday mornings from 8 a.m. to 10 a.m. when Fritzi offers its special early bird sale. Check it out.

And while you're in the neighborhood, drop in next door to the **Wyn Factory Outlet** at 224 Fremont St.; telephone (415) 882-9368. This store too carries a good variety of lesser-quality sportswear for teens and young adults at significantly low prices.

The Kids Outlet
• 625 Second St. (Brannan St.), #201, San Francisco; (415) 495-6659

Amidst this outlet-laden section of SoMa, Mr. C likes the Kids Outlet, filled with high-quality children's clothes at low prices. Mostly what you'll see here are playclothes. Reversible fleece pants (seen here for $18) and reversible fleece jackets ($40) will go through many hours of play without quitting. Cotton pants, splashed with fun abstract designs, were a steal at $10—and they paired up nicely with cotton shortsleeve tops for $6.50.

You'll also find some really ingenious stuff here. Mr. C found brightly-colored toddlers' shorts made with velcro at the waist, so they can be adjusted to last through several summers at the beach, for just $5! The store itself has some interesting, kid-friendly touches like mirrors set on the floors so little customers can see how good they look in their new duds.

The Kids Outlet is open Monday through Saturday, 10 a.m. to 5 p.m.

Kidswear Center
• 660 Third St. (Townsend St.), #109, San Francisco; (415) 543-4355
• 843 Gilman St. (Sixth St.), Berkeley; (510) 528-9810

No matter which side of the bay you call home, you'll find a Kidswear Center to outfit the whole brood in style, without breaking the bank. Kidswear Center carries brand name kids' clothes at a discount, along with some lower-quality stuff that is very inexpensive indeed.

Discounts vary, and merchandise is ever-changing. But you can expect to find things like playsuits by Baby B.U.M., regularly $29, for just $22.99; Osh Kosh jumpers, regularly

$22, for $16.99; and Guess? jeans, in the 24-month size, originally $20, for $15.99. Frilly dresses by L.A. Touch, regularly $26, were just $19.99; and a little girl's dress coat, by French Toast, regularly $50, was also just $19.99.

Plenty of basics here, too. Turtlenecks were $3.99 to $4.99, cotton pants were just $9.99, jogsuits were as low as $6.99. Plus novelty stuff, like glow-in-the-dark sweatshirts with pictures of dinosaurs, sharks, dolphins, and more. Originally $19 each, these were recently on sale at two for $13.

You will find a small selection of toys, like a bag of plastic dinos for $1.99 and wooden panda train for $9.99. Both stores are open seven days.2

Mousefeathers
- 1003 Camelia St. (Gilman St.), Berkeley; (415) 526-4900

If you're looking for frilly dresses for your little angel, Mousefeathers makes a beautiful collection of dresses for young girls. Unfortunately, the price tags on these creations tend to be equally fancy. This branch, however, is their outlet store—where they sell off merchandise that is irregular, discontinued, or past-season.

Recent deals here included a plaid flannel dress, originally $76, marked down to $49.50, and a beautiful blue velvet dress, once $95, now just $65. On the irregulars rack, a full-length dress meant to sell for $110 was shortened (the price, not the hem) to just $68.75. When you stop in, get on their mailing list and they'll notify you of upcoming special sales like the one that was in progress during Mr. C's visit—in which everything in the store was further reduced by

ACCESSORIES

Bridal Veil Outlet
- 124 Spear St. (Howard St.), San Francisco; (415) 777-9531

See listing under "Bridal and Formal Wear," above.

MR. CHEAP'S PICKS
Children's and Juniors' Wear

✔ **Mousefeathers** and **Sweet Potatoes Factory Outlet**—A pair of Berkeley shops carrying upscale kids' clothes at down-to-earth prices.

50%. Open Tuesday through Saturday from 9a.m. to 5p.m.

Sweet Potatoes Factory Outlet
- 1716 Fourth St. (Virginia St.), Berkeley; (510) 527-5852

Sweet Potatoes sells better-name kids clothes, for all ages from infants on up to young teens, at discount prices. Doting parents may find cotton playsuits by Marimekko for $10.25, or jeans by S.P.udz for $18 (do you love that name, or what?). They also carry some frilly and fancy stuff like a cotton taffeta party dress—perfect for all those cotton taffeta parties—for $25.50. Simpler styles, like cotton pants for $18.75 and cotton long sleeve shirts for $13.75, are colorful as well as plentiful. Sweet Potatoes is also a good place to search for the unique and offbeat, things like an infant boy's S.P.udz football shirt with matching football pants for just $18.25.

The selection here is limited, but definitely worth checking out. The store is open Monday through Friday 10a.m. to 6p.m., Saturday 10 a.m. to 5p.m., and Sunday 12p.m. to 5p.m.

Griffco Leather Factory Outlet
- 204 Martin Luther King Jr. Way (Second St.), Oakland; (510) 444-3800

For over twenty years, Griffco

MR. CHEAP'S PICK
Accessories

✔ **Griffco Leather Factory Outlet**—Griffco handcrafts leather bags and other accessories. The workmanship is magnificent and, since you buy at the source, there is little markup.

Leather Factory has been making quality leather bags. Originally, they wholesaled these to retail stores, but gradually they began selling directly to the public—and now they only sell their bags through their store here in Oakland, and by mail order.

These are high-quality leather bags—still at wholesale prices. Because you buy directly from the manufacturer, you save a bundle (pardon the pun). Most bags are priced from $25 to $35. You can get a huge shopping bag for $30 or a small clutch for $10. They even make leather fanny packs for $18.50 and shaving bags for $13.50. Always popular are their soft-sided briefcases, priced from $44 to $52. A medium-sized duffel bag is a fabulous deal at $46.50. Plus carry-on bags, backpacks, and more.

You'll also find a good selection of useful small accessories, like coin purses for $2.25, luggage tags for $1.50, snap key chains for $1.50, men's trifold wallets for $6.50, and women's credit card cases for $3.

All of Griffco's merchandise is made of top grain leather in a variety of colors. Furthermore, their materials and workmanship are guaranteed for life! If you have a problem, just bring it in and they'll repair it free—clearly, they know they won't have to do this too often. This doesn't cover accidental damage or zipper replacements, but it's only a nominal charge to fix those. And, unlike many outlets, you can return anything within fifteen days for a refund or exchange.

Griffco Leather Factory Outlet is open from 9 a.m. to 5 p.m. Monday through Friday, and from 9 a.m. to 4:30 p.m. on Saturday.

Sven Design
• 2301 Fourth St. (Bancroft Way), Berkeley; (510) 848-7836

For over twenty years, Sven Design has been making fine-quality leather handbags for sale in chic boutiques all over town; Mr. C always prefers going to the source, and that's exactly what you can do at their Berkeley factory. Here, a small outlet store offers the same bags at substantial discounts; current styles are sold at 20% off the retail price, while older, discontinued models go for up to half off the original prices.

There's a lot to choose from, in a variety of colors, sizes, and shapes; many are around $50 and under, but even the bags priced from $60 and up are good deals—considering their stylishness and the obvious quality of construction. These babies are going to last for years, you can feel it. In addition to handbags, there are many other small leather goods, like checkbook cases and tote bags.

The store is open weekdays from 9 a.m.to 5 p.m., and Saturdays from 11-5.

CLOTHING—USED

Used clothing is another great way to save lots of money—and don't turn up your nose at the idea. Recycling doesn't just mean bottles and cans, y'know. In these recessionary times, people are taking this approach to nearly everything, and it makes a lot of sense. There is a wide range of options, from trashy stuff to designer labels. Again, a few terms:

"Consignment" and "resale" shops are all the rage these days. Most sell what they call "gently used" clothing—the original owner wore the article only a few times, then decided to resell it. Often, these are fancy outfits in which such people don't *dare* to be seen twice. Fine! This is how you can get these high fashion clothes at super low prices. Since they still look new, your friends will never know the secret (unless, of course, you want to brag about your bargain-hunting prowess).

You can also sell things from your own closets at these shops, if they are recent and in good shape; the store owners will split the cash with you.

"Vintage" clothing is usually older and more worn-looking, often the flashiest duds from past decades. Sometimes these can cost more than you'd expect for used clothing, depending on which "retro" period is back in style at the moment.

Finally, "thrift shops" sell used clothing that has *definitely* seen better days. These items have generally been donated to the stores, most of which are run by charity organizations; in such places, you can often find great bargains, and help out a worthy cause at the same time.

CONSIGNMENT AND RESALE SHOPS

Abbe's
● 1420 & 1431 Clement St. (15th Ave.), San Francisco; (415) 751-4567

This women's consignment store is so packed, it takes up two stores! Located across the street from each other, Abbe's divides into one shop for fancy attire (that's at 1420) and one for sportswear, separates, and more casual items (at 1431, obviously).

On the fancy side of the street, Mr. C found such lovely things as a cream-colored short blazer by Anne Klein II, selling for $32; a Carolyn Roehm cocktail party dress, in black velvet, for $80; and a suede skirt by Vakko (for Saks Fifth Avenue) for $50. Also an Henri Bendel raincoat with a racoon collar and lining, a good deal at $220; and, if you'd prefer to stay warm for less cold cash, a merino wool cardigan from Nordstrom's for $36.

This store also has high-end accessories, like Judith Leiber handbags—which can go for as much as $800 new, but sell here for more like $450—and costume jewelry by Chanel.

Meanwhile, at the other store, you can get a pair of Ann Taylor wool slacks for $25, or a pair by Valentino for $80. Jeans from Levis, the Gap and such, are priced between $12 and $16. Plus bathing suits, some lingerie, activewear, and other separates, all similarly well-priced. All sales are final; both stores are open Tuesdays through Saturdays from 11 a.m. to 5 p.m. only.

Carousel Consignment Shop
● 1955 Shattuck Ave. (University Ave.), Berkeley; (510) 845-9044

Carousel Consignment Shop accepts merchandise that is stylish, in season, and in good condition. What this means for you is great-looking, quality clothing at great prices. Have you always craved cashmere, but couldn't warm up to the price? Carousel recently had a mocha-colored cashmere turtleneck selling for just $16. And a pair of lizard-skin western boots, originally $300, were seen here for just $80 (sorry, these are certain to be gone by now).

They carry a lot of clothing in natural fabrics, like a burgundy wool sweater from Benetton for just $16. They also tend to get in plenty of designer and brand-name clothes, like a two-piece gray pantsuit by Yves St. Laurent for just $22. During Mr. C's visit they had a large selection of outerwear on display, such as a down jacket for $22 and a black leather jacket for $60. You may find anything from career basics like gray wool pants for $14 to basic basics like Gap jeans for just $12. Plus accessories, including scarves and jewelry (sterling silver earrings, $10). Carousel's is open Tuesday through Saturday from 11 a.m. to 5:30 p.m.

Charlene's on 2
* 41 Sutter St. (Montgomery St.), Suite 215, San Francisco; (415) 989-0644

Hidden inside an otherwise staid office building is a boutique that carries the best of used designer clothes. Trouble is, the place is so well-hidden, you won't find it unless you already know about it. That's why Charlene's offers you a 10% discount everytime you bring in a new friend. So spread the word, pile up the savings, and tell 'em Mr. C sent you.

And what are you saving on? Great clothes from great makers. Charlene's carries used clothing on consignment, as well as a selection of department store returns. Recent items seen here included a two-piece Anne Klein suit for $85, a red jacket from I. Magnin for $38, and a gray wool skirt by Ralph Lauren for $34. Caught out in the rain without a jacket? Mr. C found a British Mist raincoat for just $58. And there are shoes also, such as a pair of Calvin Klein suede pumps, in like-new condition, for $36.

You will see the BIG names here: Donna Karan, Perry Ellis, the Kleins (Anne and Calvin), as well as the BIG department store labels. Mr. C

was asked not to mention the store names, but you'll know them when you see them. The selection is small, but the merchandise changes daily, so it's a good idea to stop in often. Charlene's is open Monday through Friday 'til 6 p.m. and Saturday by appointment. They're closed Sunday.

Clothesport Consignment
* 3702 Grand Ave. (Weldon Ave.), Oakland; (510) 893-8194

Opened for business in 1970, Clothesport lays claim to being the oldest consignment shop in the Bay Area. This narrow storefront is crammed with a blend of designer labels and more generic donations, all for women. The atmosphere is quiet and pleasant, with fitting rooms and very friendly service.

Among the well-known names being dropped here during Mr. C's visit, a Perry Ellis pantsuit was seen for $60; a navy skirt and blazer by Evan-Picone for Saks Fifth Avenue was just $38. Shoes are in decent shape, like a pair of leather basket-weave Bandolino sandals for $10.

And you can check out Clothesport for special occasion wear, from a Peyton-Marcus mink stole ($150) to a stunning red velvet full-length evening gown ($68). CC also has a half-price clearance rack, where you may find things that are in good shape, but a bit out of date. A Guess denim jacket and jeans set was a find at $28, but this may be due to the fact that the acid-washed look is not exactly *au courant* anymore. Still, it's always fun to look!

All purchases benefit the Women's American Organization for Rehabilitation through Training (ORT), which supports vocational schools around the world. Open Tuesdays through Saturdays only, from 11 a.m. to 4 p.m.

Cris
* 2056 Polk St. (Broadway), San Francisco; (415) 474-1191

Cris is an upscale consignment shop where you will find high-quality used clothes. You will find some of the best labels around in this store and the clothes are in great shape; some have never even been worn. Mr. C saw a pair of Gap jeans, still bearing the original tag ($58!), selling here for just $23. Other casual looks included a denim skirt by Giorgio Armani for $25 and black velvet jeans by Liz Claiborne for $22. Most of what you'll find here are dressy apparel and lots of professional clothes.

Career looks seen here included a wool/cashmere dress by Anne Klein for $99. A dark gray Evan-Picone pantsuit was a steal at 50% off the already low price of $98. You'll also find a good selection of separates like a Christian Dior blazer for $59, a gray blazer from Neiman Marcus for $75, or an ivory skirt by Ann Taylor for $29. Every so often, you'll run across something a little out of the ordinary, like a black leather skirt with a 100% silk lining by Chanel for $99 or a blue fox jacket, from Neiman Marcus, for $275.

If you're looking for something very dressy, they have that, too. An ivory lace dress by Scott McClintock was just $45. Another beautiful dress in black velvet was only $68. Cris' selection of special occasion dresses truly is special. Shop from noon to 6 p.m. Monday through Saturday, and noon to 5 p.m. on Sunday.

Dresses & Tresses
- 147 Clement St. (Third Ave.), San Francisco; (415) 386-4025

Well, here's a new one on Mr. C: Consignment clothing and a hair salon, all at one address. As Nola, one of the owners, puts it, they are uniquely qualified to "make you look good from head to toe."

For years, there was only a "tresses" part here, and quite a large one; but, as business fell off, someone had the idea to sell some accessories and clothing at the front of the store. It started with simple stuff, and became fancier; now, the "dresses" part takes up the front half, usually spilling out onto sidewalk racks, and may offer anything up to fur coats.

Some of the fashions Mr. C saw here included new sweaters by Magnolia, in wool with beaded applique

MR. CHEAP'S PICKS
Consignment and Resale
Shops

─────

✔ **Abbe's**—So many women's fashions, it takes two shops across the street from each other to hold them all!

✔ **Cris**—A very choice collection of well-cared-for, top-label clothing at realistic prices.

✔ **Good Byes**—A large selection of new *and* used fancy duds, run by one of the pioneers in the resale business.

✔ **Joy Boutique**—These fashions are still somewhat pricey—but imagine what they would cost new. Stop in regularly, as the best stuff goes quickly.

✔ **Rockridge Rags**—Would you believe—used clothes for women *and* men, a maternity section, and more? It's true.

designs, selling for $55; other new items on consignment included Italian leather handbags by Castello, and replicas of designer jewelry. All new items sell here for much less than they would at department stores.

In secondhand clothing, there were some low-priced separates (many $5-$10), as well as those furs. A white mink, three-quarter length coat, in decent shape, was seen for $280. They even had a stock of used wedding dresses, all dry-cleaned and ready for another walk down the aisle, ranging in price from $250 to $400. The store is open weekdays from 10 a.m. to 7 p.m., and weekends from 10-6.

Good Byes
- 3464 Sacramento St. (Laurel St.), San Francisco; (415) 346-6388

Way up in Presidio Heights, Margaret

Hensley (who calls herself the "soul proprietor") has created a wonderful clothing shop. Its two long rooms are filled with designer fashions, both new and used, for men and women. Some fifteen years ago, b.c. (before consignments), she founded a similar business in Dallas; judging by the popularity of such shops these days, she was clearly ahead of her time.

Good Byes, her latest venture, is about three years old. In it, Margaret combines secondhand labels with some unused clothing as well. These are samples, closeouts, and a few seconds; there is a goodly amount of these, although they are in the minority. The stock changes all the time, depending on what her sources make available, but Mr. C loved a pile of denim shirts—by a manufacturer who sells his private label to a very big department store in the area—priced here at just $15. And a rack full of power ties, by an English maker, was reduced from the range of $65-$85 (that's *each!*) to a more sensible $24-$32. Not too much new stuff for women, at least on this visit.

In the recycled department, however, it's another story. Ladies can while away many a happy hour among these racks, perhaps finding an Anne Klein II coat—of lined wool, full length—for $175; a DKNY black-and-gray plaid blazer for $150; a Moschino blazer, originally priced at $1,200, here just $165; or a lambswool sweater by Calvin Klein, in navy blue, for just $12. Lots of shoes, too, in good to great condition. One pair of Escada heels, in red suede, looked absolutely like new at $85 (sorry, they're probably gone by now). Another pair of Ferragamo heels was a mere $18.

Back to the men: There are some incredible deals on used fine-maker suits, by such names as Armani, Ralph Lauren, and more. A trendy, olive green all-wool suit by Oxford, a British label—with hand-finished construction, and an original retail price of $1,500—was seen here for $400. Also, a more conservative Brooks Brothers pinstripe for $125,

and a wild aqua plaid suit by Hugo Boss for just $65. There is a smaller selection of shoes than for women (we just walk 'em into the ground, don't we, guys); by the way, all shoes are reduced if they don't sell in their first thirty days.

Everything taken in to be sold here is in very good shape. In fact, one customer was overheard to say, "I can't tell the used from the new!" Folks seem to leave here quite satisfied, indeed, with the service as well as the clothing. Open seven days a week.

Heather's Boutique
*   2249 Clement St. (23rd Ave.), San Francisco; (415) 751-5511

This women's shop differentiates itself somewhat by catering particularly to professionals, ladies who are looking for very high quality clothing by top American and European designers. Most of these are separates, with some formal wear mixed in. Everything is in excellent condition, or it's not accepted for resale; nothing is more than two years old, and if it hasn't sold in 90 days (even on the half-price racks), it's returned to the consigner.

Mr. C saw a number of smart-looking blazers, from a Jean Muir design which originally cost $800, and was selling here for $160, to a new Bebe for $95. Another, by DKNY, was $75; same price for a pair of DKNY heels to go with it. In between, you may go for an Ellen Tracy wool skirt, just $22. And, for something dramatic over it all, how about a cape? A flowing creation by Laise Adzer, which might have cost $200 or more originally, was seen here for $84.

In sweaters, you could choose between a cashmere number from Harrod's of London, and one in fleece wool by Ferragamo, each $95 and, again, in great condition. Mr. C also saw a black two-piece jogging suit by Sonia Rykiel for $98. Lots of similarly unusual pieces in here, always sure to be an interesting browse. Very helpful, low-key service, too. Heather's is open Tuesdays through Saturdays from 11 a.m. to 5 p.m. only.

Joy Boutique
- 456 Montgomery St. (Sacramento St.), San Francisco; (415) 434-4848

Tucked into the "Garden Court" level of a chi-chi downtown plaza, the Joy Boutique sells what are commonly referred to as "pre-owned" designer clothes. Be warned though: Cheap is a relative term, and the clothes here are still *very* expensive. Just look at the neighborhood. If, however, you crave clothes from designers like Armani, Chanel, Christian Dior, Jean Paul Gaultier, Matsuda, Versace, Yves St. Laurent, and more—and you can't afford them new—this may be just what you need.

The selection here is small, but it changes constantly as merchandise comes in from those aforementioned fashion plates; so it's a good idea to stop in often. Mr. C saw a raincoat by Anne Klein for $70, black leather pants by Montana for $140, a buttery soft black leather jacket by Alaia for $280, and an Escada jacket for $175. The selection of shoes is very small, but what they do have is in great shape. A pair of Alaia pumps looked like new, and were just $100.

Men are not left out at Joy Boutique. While most of the merchandise here is for women, there is a limited selection of men's designer wear. Mr. C saw a handsome blazer by Matsuda for $210, and a sweater by Emporio Armani for $105—way below what it must have sold for when new.

The Joy Boutique is open from 10 a.m. to 6 p.m. Monday through Friday. They do have hours by appointment on Saturday; call for more info.

Mariana's
- 1425 Grant St. (Green St.), San Francisco; (415) 433-7503

Mr. C has decided to file Mariana's under used clothing because the majority of her merchandise, about two-thirds of it, is quality used clothing. You may find stuff like a wool skirt by I.B. Diffusion for $24, or a jumpsuit by Liz Claiborne for $28. Mr. C also saw inexpensive silk separates, including a skirt for $16 and silk pants from the Limited for $20.

But Mariana's also has an interesting secret: the rest of her merchandise consists of her own original designs, and she sells them for the same prices as the used stuff. Would Mr. C lie to you?

In fact, her designed pieces range from the ridiculously cheap, like a $25 blue and gold cocktail party dress, to the amazingly inexpensive, as in a gorgeous red fringe dress for just $55. Mariana has a variety of skirts for $38; and check out what she does with blue jeans. Hours are 11:30 a.m. to 8 p.m. Monday through Thursday, noon to 11 p.m. on Friday and Saturday, and noon to 8 p.m. on Sundays.

Mary's Exchange
- 1302 Castro St. (24th St.), San Francisco; (415) 282-6955

Mary's Exchange sells used clothing on consignment, along with some samples and irregulars, including designer and brand-name merchandise. Be forewarned: not everything here is cheap. There are enough bargains, however, to keep even the most parsimonious shopper content. Recent finds included a white angora sweater for $28, trousers by Calvin Klein for $48, and a black blazer from Nordstrom's for $25. Mr. C also spied an Esprit rain jacket for $32; and a selection of jeans, including Levi's, for just $15.

Mary's Exchange also carries used shoes in varying conditions. Loafers by Ferragamo were seen for just $35, while a pair of red pumps by 9 West were just $30. The observant shopper will see merchandise from Benetton, Liz Claiborne, and more. Mary's Exchange is open Monday through Saturday, noon to 6 p.m.

Michelle's Boutique
- 24 Clement St. (Arguello Blvd.), San Francisco; (415) 221-4717

You can do a "resale crawl" along the entire length of Clement, starting here on its first block; this end is bouncing back after years of being in decline. Michelle Cassar has some of the fanciest clothing of the bunch, with a good mix of new fashions for women bought directly from major manufacturers, along with great used clothing as well. These range from clothing for the office to dazzling looks for a big night out.

New fashions come from such designers as Liz Claiborne, Anne Klein, Christian Dior, Cathy Hardwick, and others. These can often be found here at half the prices seen in department stores. One Dior suit, which would list at $600, was recently seen here for only $200. And an Essay blazer and slacks set, which would cost about $90 elsewhere, was going for $45 here.

Among used clothing, the deals are even better. How about a Laura Ashley skirt for $12...? These racks have suits and separates by Evan-Picone, Ann Taylor, and many other classic names, all for just a few bucks.

Michelle stocks a limited selection of shoes and boots to go with these; she also sells lots of interesting accessories, like hats and jewelry by local artisans who have no shops of their own. She showed Mr. C a variety of sterling silver pieces dotted with such stones as lapis, garnet, and onyx; most rings were about $20, with earrings in the $15-$25 range. Plus costume jewelry, like bracelets for $4 to $10. The store is open Tuesdays through Saturdays, from 11:00 a.m. to 6:00 p.m.

Recycled Stuff!
- 2423 Clement St. (25th Ave.), San Francisco; (415) 379-9453 (WILD)

At Recycled Stuff! the fliers promise "snazzy stuff" for "cheapo prices." Well, they certainly live up to their billing. Some of the "snazzy" merchandise recently seen here included a tuxedo jacket by Pierre Cardin for $18, a trench coat from Burberry's for $30, and a gorgeous green gown in velvet and taffeta for just $24. Also spotted was a women's two-piece suit by Outback Red, which used to be *the* line at The Limited, for $14. Wow! Recycled also carries simpler items, like jeans by Esprit for as little as $8 or Levis for just $10. Mr. C saw lots of vests, the trend of

the moment as of this writing, for just $8 to $12.

For those who are looking for pieces with more staying power, a sweater by the venerable Brooks Brothers was seen for just $8. And an item that is never completely "in" or "out" on the fashion barometer, the Hawaiian shirt, can be found here for a balmy $4. The store is small and funky; recycled stuff is truly stuffed into every corner and crevice. They're open Tuesday through Saturday until 6 p.m.

Rockridge Rags
- 5711 College Ave. (Miles Ave.), Oakland; (510) 655-2289

In this upscale neighborhood of Oakland, near the Berkeley line, Rockridge deals in fine used designer fashions. It's really two stores connected on the inside; one for men and one for women—and you'll rarely find such a large selection of secondhand mens' stuff (we're not into cleaning out our closets, are we, guys?) as this store offers.

Everything on display here is less than two years old. Among the fancier finds on Mr. C's visit was a Perry Ellis Portfolio suit—a grey pinstripe with a few thin lines of color blended in—for $50. A classic denim shirt by Calvin Klein Sport was $12. And a pair of tooled black cowboy boots was $35.

For women, Mr. C's companion found a pair of black rayon pants by Liz Claiborne for $16. In the store's maternity section, a biege skirt suit by Liz was $48; never used, it still had the original tags on it. Other great looks included a black dress by Henri Bendel for $24, and a blue angora sweater dress for just $18. A Kikit cotton sweater was seen for $12.

Plus racks and racks of basics for everyone, from shirts to socks. Everything is very clearly tagged with the price, brand name, and date the item went on sale. Check the colors of those tags, too—each week, a different color gets an extra 50% off at the register. Also, one month after the date on the tag, the price is automatically dropped by 30% to keep the stock moving; a week later, if it's still around, the price goes to 50% off.

The store is open seven days a week, including Thursdays until 8:00 p.m.

Scanlon's
- 540 Van Ness Ave. (McAllister St.), San Francisco; (415) 255-9283

Scanlon's is a tiny shop filled with quality used clothes and some housewares at very reasonable prices. On his visit, Mr. C found a silk shell for $4.95, a linen shirt by Perry Ellis for $6.25, and a sport jacket by Calvin Klein for $11.25. Most of the merchandise consists of brand name and designer clothes and, though the selection is small, they get new items in every week. Further, the merchandise here is in great shape; it's difficult to tell that some of this stuff is used.

Casual clothes seen here included women's cotton shorts by Generra for $3.98, white denim shorts from the Gap for $3.98, and a silk camp-style shirt for $2.95. Mr. C did see a few things for guys, including dress shirts from Macy's for $11.90 and a couple of men's sportcoats for $24.90. They have a good selection of ties for $6, or two for $10.

You'll also see some really interesting and unusual housewares here. On Mr. C's visit, these included a handcrafted, one-of-a-kind picnic basket for $18.95, a pair of decorated silvertone candlesticks with candles for $12, and a set of four silver and brass goblets, originally $60, for just $35. Plus lots of memorabilia—notably 49ers and Beatles collectibles and old lunch boxes—but these are not necessarily cheap. Scanlon's is open from 10 a.m. to 6 p.m. Monday through Saturday.

Sophisticated Lady
- 4020 Piedmont Ave. (Glen Ave.), Oakland; (510) 654-1718

Sophisticated Lady is an upscale consignment shop in which you can find quality clothing, including classic fashions, for hundreds of dollars less than their original selling prices. Things like a gray wool suit from Harrod's of London, which Mr. C noted here for a mere $35, and a navy pantsuit by Larry Levine for just $55. Yow!

No need to fret about the condition, either. Sophisticated Lady only consigns high-quality clothing that is in excellent shape, and less than two years old. They only deal in clothing made from natural fabrics, such as cotton, linen, silk, or wool, and quality synthetic blends. Some of the items consigned here have never been worn. Mr. C saw a purple taffeta gown by Gunne Sax, still bearing its original tag of $165, selling here for just $55. Shoppers may also find a selection of samples—unused clothes which salespeople have used to market their collections to department and specialty stores.

In all, the selection is huge. Shoppers will find everything here, from a basic blouse by Anne Klein for $10 to a blue velvet and gold lamé evening gown for $53. You never know what you'll find among these racks, whether it's a full-length blue fox coat for $500 to a variety of 501's (Levi's, that is) for $12. You may find wardrobe basics like unlined wool pants in navy and green plaid from the Gap for $20, or a gray wool sweater from the Limited for $18. This is also a great place to pick up fun, if less practical, items—like purple suede pumps by Anne Klein for $16.

Serious shoppers should cruise through here regularly, if they can, for two reasons: one, new merchandise comes in all the time, and two, SL's automatic markdowns. Clothes that don't sell within a month are reduced by 25%, and clothes that don't sell within 60 days are discounted 40%. Markdown dates are written right on the tags, so it's easy to keep track of the savings.

CHILDREN'S RESALE SHOPS

Baby Boom
- 1601 Irving St. (17th St.), San Francisco; (415) 564-2666

Just below Golden Gate Park, this tiny Sunset shop is nevertheless packed so tightly with new and used children's items that it's hard to move around inside. Unlike many other such shops, BB actually sells more furniture and accessories than clothing, though there's a good amount of everything.

In clothes, a recent visit found things like a boys' London Fog fleece jacket for $15; same price for a girls' two-piece "Baby Duckies" ensemble—a cotton floral print top and drawstring pants. And a size 2 pair of Fisher Price sneakers, in an electric blue "high-top" style, was seen for just $5. There's also a half-price rack, filled with ridiculously cheap stuff: A Minnie Mouse jumpsuit for a 24 month-old, originally selling here for $8.50, was further reduced to $4.25.

New cribs, baby furniture, and all kinds of strollers (for those who like to jog, as well as those who walk) are on display at very good prices indeed. A Century carriage, list priced at $130, was selling here for $89 instead. And a Graco "Deluxe" high chair was $30 off at $49. There are secondhand versions of many similar items, usually lined up on the sidewalk in front of the store. Where else could they put them? Mr. C saw a used Graco "Swingomatic" swing chair, battery-powered for non-stop amusement, for just $45, and lots of good strollers from as low as $20. Open daily from 10 a.m. to 6 p.m., and Sundays from 12-5.

Jazzirob Kids Corner
- 3704 Grand Ave. (Weldon Ave.), Oakland; (510) 834-2226

Next door to Clothesport, a consignment shop for grownups (see listing above), Jazzirob does exactly the same thing for children—used, quality brand clothing, in good condition, for much lower prices than new.

This packed little store is literally bursting with bargains, like a good selection of party dresses in sizes 2T-4T for around $13. You know, red plaid decorated with bows, that sort. Add a pair of shiny black patent leather Mary Janes for $10. For slightly older kids, Mr. C found a size 12 winter jacket by Rothschild for $18, and a Guess denim jacket (yup, they start 'em early nowadays), never worn, for $39.

The store also has lots of toys and practical items, from a Li'l Chef bakery mixer (new, still in its original box) for $8.50, and a Graco twin baby stroller in great shape for $60. Other, generic-brand strollers—with umbrellas attached—were just $8-$12 each.

Jazzirob is open Tuesdays through Saturdays from 10 a.m. to 6 p.m., and Sundays from 11-5. Closed Mondays—and for occasional short breaks during weekdays when the owner steps out to pick up his kids from school.

Peek-a-bootique
- 1306 Castro St. (24th St.), San Francisco; (415) 641-6192

Peek-a-bootique carries quality used children's clothes, as well as toys and equipment, at really great prices. You may find anything from a winter jacket for $10 to a 100% cotton running suit for $7.75. You'll also find brand names, like kids' jeans from Macy's, or Nike sneakers (size 2), each seen for $6.95; and overalls by Osh Kosh for just $5.50. Mr. C saw receiving blankets for $1.50 and $2, and infant-size T-shirts for 50¢ to 75¢.

Peek-a-bootique has a great selection, though most of it is for infants and very small children; the selection for bigger kids is more limited. But the prices are just as good for bigger sizes when you find them: a running suit, size 10/12, was spotted for just $17.50.

Their selection of baby equipment is also pretty small, but definitely worth noting. Mr. C saw a used cradle for $32 and a stroller for just $49. The store also has lots of toys and books. They do have some new items, mostly small accessories like outlet covers, pacifiers, training cups, and such.

This is also a great place to get rid of clothes and equipment that your kids have outgrown. As with most places, you'll get more in store credit than in cash. They're open seven days a week, but buying hours are limited, so call ahead first.

Tiddly Winks
• 1302 Gilman St. (Curtis St.), Berkeley; (510) 527-5025

For ten years, this bright, pleasant shop just north of the main outlets area in Berkeley has been reselling slightly used children's clothing, toys, and accessories. Unlike many similar stores, Tiddly Winks is rather large, and everything is as nicely spread out as any boutique would be.

Although a fair amount of the clothes Mr. C looked at were well-worn, everything is clearly tagged with current prices, and these are accordingly low. A size 14 pair of girl's jeans by Guess, for example, was seen for just $6; a one-piece snowsuit, size 8, was $25. A Polly Flinders party dress, size 6, was spotted for $5.50. Meanwhile, a pair of denim overalls by OshKosh (for an 18 month-old) was a mere $4.50—cheap enough that you won't mind how fast your tyke outgrows them.

TW also stocks a lot of new items, like pink Danskin leotards for your

VINTAGE SHOPS

Aaardvark's Odd Ark
• 1501 Haight St. (Ashbury St.), San Francisco; (415) 621-3141

This ark certainly is odd—they don't even know how to spell "aardvark." But, they do know how to *sell* interesting and unusual vintage clothes at low prices. Mr. C found terrific sweaters, including some in wool and angora, for $10 each. Definitely "odd" (in such a store) was a blue suede jacket with an I. Magnin label. It was a real find for only $20, though it needed cleaning. A rack of men's two-piece suits was $15 to $30. If you're

---

MR. CHEAP'S PICK
Children's Resale Shops

✔ **Peek-a-bootique**—Kids generally grow out of their clothes before they wear out, so why not "go used"? You can also trade in Junior's old clothes for a spiffy new wardrobe.

---

little ballerina, just $10; lace-up leather ankle shoes for $15, and handmade fleece booties for infants, $6 a pair. And there are bins filled with assorted mittens, slippers, undies, and other essentials—each just a buck or two.

Kids will love the toys, of course; the ever-popular Playskool "Busy Box" was seen here for $7, and a brand-new stuffed brown bear was $9. On the transportation front, a large Graco stroller was available for $38 during Mr. C's visit.

When you stop in, ask about their "Frequent Buyer Card," entitling you to further discounts. The store is open seven days a week—another rarity among consignment stores.

looking for something even dressier, Mr. C saw an After Six tux jacket for $40—and you could even top it off with a black top hat for just $20. On the basics side, Aaardvark's had a rack of white dress shirts from $6-$8.

Women can choose from racks of dresses, the likes of which you probably won't see at the mall. A green taffeta dress with matching jacket was just $30, and a maroon dress with an ivory lace collar, circa 1940, was just $10. It was not in the best of shape, however, and thus was marked "as is." Mr. C also saw a two-piece cashmere suit, with a skirt, for $50, and a full-length green velvet cape with gold satin lining for $75. The selection is, in a word, eclectic.

Of course, this wouldn't be a good vintage store if they didn't have used jeans. At Aaardvark's you can get three pairs of well-broken-in Levi's for $50. Individually, used Levi's sell for about $20 each. They also had a rack of vests from $12 to $20 and flannel shirts for $6 to $12. Denim jackets start at just $30. They do carry some of the more expensive vintage clothes, but there's plenty of regular (cheap!) used clothes to keep any bargain hunter happy. Set sail on Aaardvark's Odd Ark everyday from 11 a.m. to 7 p.m.

American Rag Company Cie

- 1305 Van Ness Ave. (Sutter St.), San Francisco; (415) 474-5214

While not everything in this store fits Mr. C's definition of cheap, this store is so much fun, and there are enough good buys, that he felt it should be included. Need a little black dress? They've got a whole rack of 'em, in plenty of styles, priced as low as $14.95. If you want something really fancy, you'll also find items like a black velvet and satin dress for just $24.95.

You'll find some very high-quality clothes, like a pure wool turtleneck sweater in ivory for $9.95. Don't bother with the used jeans; they are way too expensive. Flannel shirts are available for under $15, though. Even better is the selection of trench coats priced from $29.95 to $39.95. Mr. C also saw a white pima cotton dress shirt with French cuffs for a mere $4.95. Not to mention a rack of sport coats, each priced under $30.

Don't leave without checking the sale racks, where you may find some of the clothes you've been coveting—at much lower prices. American Rag Company is open Monday through Wednesday from 10 a.m. to 9 p.m., Thursday through Saturday from 10 a.m. to 10:30 p.m., and Sunday from noon to 7 p.m.

Clothes Contact

- 473 Valencia St. (16th St.), San Francisco; (415) 621-3212

Clothes Contact is one fun store. Let Mr. C say right up front: You're not going to find the best quality used clothing—frankly, most of it's just above the quality of the Salvation Army. But it's all *way* cheap, just a few dollars for most items. Besides, this is where you come to find clothes to paint in (or paint on), clothes to make costumes out of, and just general fun stuff.

The store tends to have "one price" racks. For instance, they had a rack of pants, all priced at $6 each. Some were even leather, though they were pretty worn and, in some cases, damaged. A rack of flannel shirts, ever-popular with the grunge set, were just $5, while another rack had plain shirts for just $3. Several racks of dresses, arranged by color, were only $5 each.

A rack of outerwear ranged in price from $10 to $15, including a London Fog raincoat for just $12. Mr. C saw leather jackets for $8 and $10, but they were beyond "broken-in". Used Levi's go for $10, same price for denim overalls. You can find men's two-piece suits for $25 and dress shirts to go with them for just $4 each. Ties, at $1 each or 3 for $2, complete the look.

Keep an eye out for specials, like sportcoats for $6—buy one, get one free! They also sell fabrics by the pound. These are mostly remnants of mid- to low-quality material, but at just $3 per pound, it may be perfect for craft projects or costumes.

Please check all merchandise very carefully since all sales are final. You can get close at Clothes Contact Monday through Saturday, 11 a.m. to 7 p.m., Sunday and holidays noon to 6 p.m.

Crossroads Trading Company

- 1901 Fillmore St. (Bush St.), San Francisco; (415) 775-8885
- 2231 Market St. (Noe St.), San Francisco; (415) 626-8989
  And other suburban locations

Here's a store for the wild and wacky clothes horse. Crossroads features mostly vintage clothing, along with some mainstream designer labels, all with a definite urban beat. The sixties definitely live on here, whether genuine or recent retro. Women will love things like a Joseph Magnin sleeveless minidress, seen for $13.50; or a flowery rayon blouse from Perry Ellis America for $9. Plenty of jeans (some of which may well have been around way back when) for men and women, most priced between $9 and $13. Broken-in leather jackets for $30. Add a pair of blue suede platform clogs by Euro Club, or for guys, a pair of Doc Marten-style boots, both $18.

You will also find more up-to-date items, like a jacket from the Limited for just $18. A shirt from Forenza was just $7. Women's casual shirts go for as little as $2.50. During Mr. C's visit, the store was having a "half off sweaters" sale. So, the sweater for Express marked $10 was only $5 and a sample sweater from DKNY marked $15 was only $7.50!

You'll also find a really fun selection of special occasion dresses. There are plenty in velvet, like a green full-length with long sleeves for $18. A vintage dress from Gunne Sax was just $15. These can make fun, and different, prom gowns. In these, as with all the merchandise here, you're bound to find blemishes and some occasional damage. Check items carefully, and weigh the cost of repairs against the savings; you can still come out way ahead.

Among accessories, Crossroads has lots of fun hats, like a velvet print cloche by Haberdashery, a Seattle maker, seen for $12.50. Some of these items are new, including some of the shoes. The stores have spacious fitting rooms. They're open seven days a week.

Held Over

- 1543 Haight St. (Ashbury), San Francisco; (415) 864-0818

When Mr. C walked into Held Over, the first thing he noticed was a rack of raincoats for $10. A great deal any-

---

MR. CHEAP'S PICKS
Vintage Shops

✔ **Aaardvark's Odd Ark**—The ark may be odd (and they don't know how to spell), but it's also filled with funky cheap clothes and accessories.

✔ **Crossroads**—Where old meets new, mostly used, all cheap.

✔ **The Wasteland**—Fun and funky sum up these stores— where else could you find a bright orange halter dress, at *any* price??

✔ **Worn Out West**—Not worn-out, worn-in! The extensive selection of used cowboy boots is a big draw, but don't overlook the jeans, shirts, and jackets.

---

time, these coats seemed to be an even sweeter deal since it was raining outside. Fact is, you'll find plenty of bargains at Held Over, even if you visit on a sunny day. They have velvet skirts in numerous colors for $7.99. Men's white dress shirts are as low as $9.99. Men's black dress pants are $19.99 to $22.99. If you're looking for dress-up costumes, this is a good place to check out—with a variety of gowns for $30 and up.

Come in here for Haight-trendy items like flannel shirts ($8.99), military jackets ($19.99-$34.99), and combat boots ($25). Used Levi's can be had for $19.99 to $24.99, with overdyeds at the higher end. Denim overalls were just $24.99.

You can find lots of *really* cheap stuff here, too. Check out the box labeled "Junk $1", filled with baubles and beads of various sorts. Ties, from tasteful to tacky, are just $3, five for $10. Fishnet stockings can be found for just $5. And don't miss kitschy items like mood rings for $5.99 and sunglasses for $8.99.

Choose your purchases carefully, though; Held Over does not offer refunds or exchanges. They're open 11 a.m. to 6 p.m., Monday through Thursday and 11 a.m. to 7 p.m. on weekends.

Crave more true vintage clothing? Try **La Rosa**, nearby at 1711 Haight Street; telephone (415) 668-3744. Their prices are higher (a blue silk velvet, full-length gown from the 1930s, selling for $290), but so is the quality. Each piece of clothing has a tag with the approximate year of the garment's manufacture, plus fabric, condition, and care instructions—a nice touch.

Now & Again
• 473A Haight St. (Webster St.), San Francisco; (415) 621-1679

Now & Again is an interesting thrift store filled with clothes and furniture of varying quality and prices. They have a great selection of theatrical costumes and fancy dress outfits which can be rented for $10 to $30; you can buy them if you wish, but they're generally not inexpensive that way.

This is not the case for the rest of their clothing, however. You can find used black leather motorcycle jackets for around $40, men's pants from $6.95 to $12.95, winter coats for $29.95 and even less, and flannel shirts as low as $8.95. A lined raincoat was seen for just $16.95, and a red Izod sweater for $6.95. Unusual items, like a blue taffeta skirt for $16.95, abound. And just for fun, check out the $1 clothes rack.

Now & Again has one of the larger selections of furniture Mr. C has seen in thrift stores, but most of it is pretty worn-out. Some pieces worth noting included a couch and chair set for $125, a recliner for $25, a pair of director's chairs for $30, and a sectional couch for $60. Worth a look.

Old Vogue
• 1412 Grant Ave. (Green St.), San Francisco; (415) 392-1522

Old Vogue is a great place to find funky, trendy clothes without paying a fortune. And the fashions aren't even that old. You can find used Levi's here for just $20. In fact, for used jeans this may well be your best bet because their selection is huge. They have racks and tables piled high with denim in every shape, size, and color.

But, that's not all you'll find here. they also have a great selection of vests, most about $25, and Hawaiian shirts (remember Magnum P.I.?), from $25 to $40. Mr. C also saw a white cropped tuxedo jacket for $60, in fact they had a number of tuxedo jackets, many as low as $80. Need something to go under your new old tuxedo jacket? Don't worry, they have dress shirts for $18 each.

Like so many of the now-trendy vintage shops, prices here are not always the lowest—though they're not outrageous. Old Vogue carries a lot of great vintage hats, which can get pretty expensive, but are undoubtedly worth the price. Even among these, you can find bargains, like berets, *de rigueur* for the North Beach cafe set, just $10 each. Maybe you can have your hipness and afford to eat, too.

Sharks
• 2505 Telegraph Ave. (Dwight Way), Berkeley; (510) 841-8736

Sharks is a funky used clothing store where you can find used Levi's for $15 to $18, denim overalls for $17 and less, and Hawaiian shirts for $10 to $12. Those in the know, however, shop here on Tuesdays—when everything in the store is sold at 20% off the tagged price. When you consider how low everything is to begin with, Tuesdays become real red-letter days.

You'll find more than just denim and Hawaiian shirts here, of course. For those of you who are into the "grunge" look, used flannel shirts sell for $10 and under, and they had a whole rack of 'em. More into the artsy, café scene? Pick up a beret for $7. After all, Berkeley *could* be considered the Left Bank of the Bay Area....One-of-a-kind items seen recently included a green satin dress with black fringe for $18, a red

lambswool and angora sweater for
$12, and even a navy blue tuxedo for
$60. Sharks also features a half-price
rack, as well as a "$5 and under" bin.
Remember: it's not a true find unless
you have to dig for it.

If you like Sharks, visit their new
store, **Tiki Town**, at 1579A Solano
Avenue, in Richmond; telephone
(510) 559-TIKI. Both locations are
open seven days.

The Wasteland
- 1660 Haight St. (Cole St.), San
  Francisco; (415) 863-3150
- 2398 Telegraph Ave. (Channing
  Way), Berkeley; (510) 843-6711

The Wasteland is kind of like a hip
Salvation Army shop. And, unlike
many similar stores, Wasteland does
not try to cash in on the "old + used
= markup" equation by charging
more for used clothes than you'd
pay for new. Jeans are a good illus-
tration: Most of the jeans here are
priced at $15 to $18. There are exceptions, of course—Mr. C saw a
pair for $50—but most are quite a
bargain.

Not that anyone comes here just
for jeans. When you need a pair of
black vinyl hot pants ($8.50), a long,
orange halter dress (Cher, circa 1974,
$20), or a purple leather mini-skirt
($16.50), this is the place. Not every-
thing is so completely outrageous,
though. You can find more practical
items like a maroon wool sweater by
Benetton for $18. Denim shirts from
$10 to $18. Raincoats were seen for
$8 to $12, with heavier winter coats
from $30 to $40. Leather jackets
were worth a look at $100 and up,
but many were very worn. Shoes,
alas, yielded few gems, but worth
checking out. You may also see interesting housewares like a "vintage"
toaster for just $35.

Besides all the great bargains,
Wasteland has got to have some of
the funkiest window displays in the
Bay Area. They also buy and trade

clothes, so if you need to empty out
your closets, do it here. They'll give
you 40% of the selling price in cash
or 60% in trade. Wasteland is open
Monday through Saturday 11 a.m. to 7
p.m. and Sunday from noon to 6 p.m.

Worn Out West
- 582 Castro St. (18th St.), San
  Francisco; (415) 431-6020

This is one of the best places around
if you're in the market to lasso a pair
of used cowboy boots—a great way
to save on an expensive wardrobe
item. WOW has a huge selection in a
variety of styles, colors, and prices.
Mr. C saw one pair selling for just
$15! The average price is $30 to $40,
and they certainly have some more
expensive ones, as well. The store
also carries used leather jackets, as
low as $30 to $45.

But great prices on used leather
and boots are not the only reasons
to come here. Worn Out West offers
a great selection of used Levi's,
worn but not worn out; and the $8
to $12 price tags are among the low-
est Mr. C has seen *anywhere*. You
can pick up a men's blazer for $25
or less. And what to put under your
new blazer? Well, choose your
look—either a button-down shirt for
$6-$10, or a plain T-shirt for $3.
Sift through a basket of tees and
sweats, all for a dollar each, or take
a spin through a rack of jeans all
marked $5. Mr. C saw denim jack-
ets, shirts, and sweaters in this section. Hunt a bit and you may even
find some names, like pants by
Perry Ellis for $14 or a coat by Lon-
don Fog for $40. Yep, there's gold
in them thar hills!

Upstairs, the store has new leather
goods, including chaps and such, as
well as police and military uniforms,
along with the used cowboy boots.
Go on up—the staff is extremely
friendly and they're glad to help you
whether you're looking for something mild or wild.

THRIFT SHOPS

Bear-ly New
• 1752 Fillmore St. (Sutter St.), San Francisco; (415) 921-2789

You'll feel good knowing that this Pacific Heights shop benefits the UC/SF Medical Center Auxiliary. But you'll *really* want to shop here because you can find high-quality used clothes at great prices. During a recent visit, Mr. C found a Limited Express cotton shirt for $4, DKNY jeans for $12.50, Perry Ellis pants for $5, and a women's red two-piece suit by Larry Levine for $22.50. A knit dress by Adrienne Vittadini, for Neiman Marcus, was just $17.50. A Talbots sweater for $6 and a pair of Esprit khakis for $5 are two more examples of the basics that can be found here. They also have a good selection of menswear and children's clothes.

Speaking of kiddies, there is a small selection of well-used toys. Their selection of housewares is also limited, yielding some interesting bargains like a Rubbermaid coffee mug wrap for $1.50 and a variety of coffee mugs to go with it for just 50¢. A baby stroller, in good condition, was definitely a bargain at $30. They didn't have too many books, and nothing that is well-known, but they were in excellent condition. Bear-ly New is open Monday through Saturday from 11 a.m. to 4 p.m.

Buffalo Exchange
• 1800 Polk St. (Washington St.), San Francisco, (415) 346-5726
• 1555 Haight St. (Ashbury St.), San Francisco; (415) 431-7733
• 2512 Telegraph Ave. (Dwight Way), Berkeley; (510) 644-9202

Buffalo Exchange is a chain of used clothing stores with locations in Arizona, New Mexico, Southern California, and Nevada. Since the majority of their inventory, some 85%, is bought directly from customers, each store is a unique shopping experience. A small percentage of their merchandise is new, but it's all stuff they were able to get inexpensively—all the prices here are kept low.

You can find used jeans here for $9 or $10. Velvet leggings, *trés* trendy, were seen for $7. From fun stuff like funky platform shoes ($7.50) to more sensible items like gray tailored trousers ($12), you'll lots of looks here. You'll also find great brand name and designer clothes, like a red 100% wool dress from Saks Fifth Avenue for $10; a velvet and satin gown by Jessica McClintock for Gunne Sax, just $22.50; and a Gucci purse for $13.50.

Sometimes these heavy-hitters are mixed in with everything else, so it pays to poke through all the racks. Remember, it's not a true find unless you work for it! Of course, some items are a bargain even without a chi-chi label. Mr. C saw a grey wool cardigan for $6.50, a cotton/ramie sweater for $18.50, and a lambswool and angora sweater for $8.

Check merchandise over carefully—Mr. C did notice some damaged items. Buffalo Exchange is open from 11 a.m. to 7 p.m. Monday through Saturday and noon to 6 p.m. on Sunday.

Community Hospice Thrift Shop
• 1173 Sutter St. (Polk St.), San Francisco; (415) 673-3030

Community Hospice Thrift Shop is crammed with clothes, housewares, and books. Some of the stuff here is pretty worn, but there always seem to be a few real gems mixed in. Most items are priced with color-coded tags: Pink tags are $1, yellow tags are $2.88, purple tags are $3.98. Don't get much cheaper than this, folks.

Jump into blue jeans (well broken-in, of course) for as little as $3.50, sweaters for $3-$5, and men's or women's wool suits from $10-$20. You're search may turn up some name items, like a green wool sweater from Yves St. Laurent for $5, a purple cotton/linen sweater from Banana Republic for $3.98, or a terry cloth robe from Nordstroms for $7.

Like most stores of this type, the selection of furniture is slim, but worth a look. Mr. C found a set of four tray tables with a cart for $18. A glass top end table was pretty worn, but definitely priced right at $16.95. They have some toys and games, but most appear to have been played out. Housewares included a drip coffeemaker for $5.50, plus coffee mugs for $1 to $2. Samsonite suitcases for $12 and $15. Records and books for 25¢ to $1.50.

Proceeds benefit Hospice by the Bay. The Community Hospice Thrift Shop is open Monday through Saturday from 9 a.m. to 5 p.m.

Departures From The Past

* 2028 Fillmore St. (California St.), San Francisco; (415) 885-3377

Departures From The Past is also a departure from high-priced vintage clothing. The stuff here is terrific, and the prices will make you feel like you've somehow made a departure from the present. Mr. C saw a mohair cardigan for $19.95. You'd pay twice that for a new one in cotton! A red velvet dress was seen for $36.99 and vintage prom gowns were priced at $39 and less. They also had lots of great stuff for guys, including coats for $49.95 and less; pants under $30; raincoats for $17.95-$19.95; and dress shirts as low as $6.95. And don't miss the bin of $1 ties.

A sure tip-off that this is Mr. Cheap's kind of store: used jeans for under $10. Wow. You'll find everything from the practical—like white cotton nightgowns ($19.95) and black velvet skirts ($19.99)—to the whimsical, like feather boas ($15) and mood rings ($5). You'll even find some funky housewares. Check the merchandise carefully; all sales are final. They're open daily until 7 p.m., Sundays until 6 p.m.

Gabardine's

* 531 Haight St. (Fillmore St.), San Francisco; (415) 864-7143

This thrift shop in the lower Haight offers a small selection of very interesting clothes, at prices that haven't been inflated to jump on the "thrifty is trendy" bandwagon. That's especially noteworthy in this area where

---

MR. CHEAP'S PICKS
Thrift Shops

✔ **Buffalo Exchange**—A used clothing chain, with everything from $10 jeans to well-worn designer names.

✔ **Pacific Heights thrift district**—Several stores clustered into three blocks carry big-deal used clothing to benefit big-time causes, including **Next-To-New, Repeat Performance, Seconds-To-Go,** and **Victorian House.**

✔ **Thrift Town**—More like a department store than a thrift shop—except for the prices. Clothing, housewares, toys, exercise bikes, you name it.

---

so many other thrift stores have gone in that direction.

You'll find used Levi's at a reasonable $18 to $25 each. Men's dress pants, most sized 24 to 38, were seen for just $16. They even had bell bottoms—back in the height of fashion—for only $12. Lots of dresses are $24 and under, like a red velvet and taffeta long-sleeve number. If you're looking for outerwear, you'll find that here, too. A raincoat from Saks Fifth Avenue was seen for just $32, and a variety of denim jackets were $42 and under. For dressier occasions, try something like a blue velvet coat for just $38. They did have a half-price rack, but it didn't yield anything noteworthy.

Gabardine's is open seven days a week from 11 a.m. until 7 p.m.

The Goodwill Store

* 3801 Third St. (Evans St.), San Francisco; (415) 641-4470
* 820 Clement St. (Ninth St.), San Francisco; (415) 668-3635

- 1700 Fillmore St. (Post St.), San Francisco; (415) 441-2159
- 822 Geary St. (Hyde St.), San Francisco; (415) 922-0405
- 241 Tenth St. (Howard St.), San Francisco; (415) 252-1677
- 1700 Haight St. (Cole St.), San Francisco; (415) 387-1192
- 2279 Mission St. (19th St.), San Francisco; (415) 826-5759
- 2058 University Ave. (Shattuck Ave.), Berkeley; (510) 649-1287
- 6624 San Pablo Ave. (66th St.), Oakland; (510) 428-4911
- 2925 East 14th St. (29th St.), Oakland; (510) 534-3037

San Francisco boasts some of the best Goodwill stores Mr. C has ever seen. They are bright, clean, well-organized, and filled with truly nice merchandise. Some even have neon signs adorning each department, like any other boutique. Of course, it's still a thrift store, and some of the stuff here is a bit shabby; but the majority is well worth a look.

Mr. C found T-shirts for $2.50, sweaters for $5.95, neckties for $3, dresses for $9.95, and winter coats for $15.95 to $19.95. Poke through the racks yourself, and you'll find brand name merchandise mixed in. Recent finds included L.L. Bean denims for $5.95, a 100% silk blouse from Talbots also for $5.95, a short sleeve cotton blouse from the Gap for $3.50, and a nightshirt from Victoria's Secret for $7.95. You'll even see the occasional designer name, like a gray skirt suit by Larry Levine for $24.90 and men's gray wool trousers by Pierre Cardin for $5.95. You'll also find a few new items, like no-name pantyhose for $1.

They do have shoes, but these are pretty worn out. Men's shoes start around $8.95; women's shoes are $3.95 to $6.95. Again, you will see brand and designer names in the shoe department, like a pair of Ferragamo open toe pumps in taupe for $6.95. They also have a great selection of kids' clothes starting at $1.95.

Don't leave without checking out the housewares department. Stock up on glassware, as low as 60¢ apiece.

You'll find coffee mugs for $1 and cup and saucer sets for $1.80. There tends not to be much in the way of furniture, but usually you can find some decent electronics and small appliances. Mr. C saw a color television set for $70. They also have a great selection of books at super-low prices, with plenty of bestsellers on the shelves for a few bucks each. Paperbacks are, for the most part, 75¢. All stores are open seven days; specific branch hours vary.

Next-To-New
- 2226 Fillmore St. (Sacramento St.), San Francisco; (415) 567-1627

Within a few blocks of Fillmore in fashionable Pacific Heights, there are no less than four thrift shops which give new meaning to the term. These stores (including Repeat Performance, Seconds-To-Go, and Victorian House, all listed below) definitely don't look or feel like traditional thrifts, with piles of clothing that have reached the end of the line. No, these four fit right in with the neighborhood—in every way but price. And that's great news for the bargain shopper who wants to look wealthy.

Next-To-New is one of the best around, filled with lots of designer name clothing in great condition for men and women. Mr. C saw a classic navy blue pinstripe men's suit by Adolfo, made for Saks Fifth Avenue, selling here for only $55. Throw a trench-style raincoat, by Rafael of Italy, over it for $35, or go casual with a Polo cotton knit sportshirt, looking like new for just $15.

Women may find things like a bright white Jantzen cable sweater, far below its original price at $30; or a John Meyer herringbone wool skirt for a mere $6.50. Add a pair of Selby navy pumps, with bows, for $8.50. And there are racks and racks of children's clothes, like little boys' Wrangler jeans for $2.50. Plus lots of books and housewares.

The store is open weekdays from 10:00 a.m. to 5:00 p.m., and Saturdays from 10-4. Proceeds benefit the San Francisco chapter of the Junior

League, an organization of women who volunteer their services to a wide range of causes such as cancer, child abuse, and homelessness. These activities have been aided by this store since 1927; it's one of the most successful Junior League benefit stores in the country.

Purple Heart Veterans Thrift Shop

• 1855 Mission St. (14th St.), San Francisco; (415) 621-2581

Purple Heart Veterans Thrift Shop is huge, with a large selection of used clothes, along with some furniture, books, and housewares. Unfortunately, most of the stuff here is very old and worn, but there are always a few gems to be unearthed. Lots of artsy Mission-types cruise the aisles here for the latest in anti-fashion chic, along with good ol' local folks.

You will come across the occasional brand name, although this does not guarantee that they are in better shape than anything else. Recent finds included a preppy all-wool sweater by Boston Traders for $3.99, and a cotton Oxford shirt to go with it for $3.99. A black denim dress by Calvin Klein was $5.99, and plaid flannel pants from Talbots for $2.99.

Their used jeans are priced very nicely indeed, from just $3.99 to $9.99. You may find women's two-piece suits as low as $5.99, and men's as low as $9.99. A satin prom gown was seen for just $7.99. They also had some well-worn fur jackets for $89.99.

Shoppers will find an interesting collection of housewares, including glassware, dishes, and linens. They have a small selection of toys, but they are not in very good condition. Plus rows and rows of books, records, cassettes, and even some 8-track tapes (EEK!). Open from 9 a.m. to 8 p.m. Monday through Friday, from 10-8 on Saturday, and from 10-6 on Sunday.

Raphael House Thrift Store

• 1065 Sutter St. (Hyde St.), San Francisco; (415) 474-4621

This Nob Hill thrift store is filled with good-quality used clothing, along with some housewares and furniture. It's located inside the Raphael House, which has provided shelter for homeless families since 1971. Bargains become all the more satisfying when you can help other people out at the same time.

In many cases, the pricing seems to be as random as the merchandise is varied. You may find a blue silk blouse for $8, and a silk dress by Liz Claiborne for the same price. Designers and brand names are tucked in all over the place, like a red wool sweater by Halston III, a Lands' End sweater in yellow, and a gray wool and angora sweater from Liz Claiborne, all priced at just $3 each.

You'll find a huge selection of lesser-brand clothing, including plenty of skirts and pants for $3 to $4 and shirts for $2 to $3. Shoes here are pretty worn, but they are unquestionably cheap. Via Spiga pumps were seen for $5 and black Esprit shoes for $10, though both pair had walked quite a few miles. Skip them and go take a gander through the rack of winter coats priced from $8 to $15, and ties for $1.

You'll find plenty of non-clothing items, too. Mr C found curling irons for $2.50, air popcorn poppers for $3 to $4, and glassware as low as 50¢. They had some small toys for a quarter and children's books were four for a dollar. Plus books for grown-ups, such as paperbacks for 50¢. These recently included *The Firm* by John Grisham, *Rising Sun* by Michael Crichton, and that children's classic, *Anne of Green Gables*.

Raphael House Thrift Store is open Thursday, Friday, and Saturday from 10 a.m. to 4 p.m.

Repeat Performance

• 2223 Fillmore St. (Sacramento St.), San Francisco; (415) 563-3123

Most thrift shops are charities for schools, hospitals, and the like; at the cleverly named Repeat Performance, the sales of secondhand clothing and housewares benefit the San Francisco Symphony. Indeed, classical music plays in the store, which is one of several "upscale" thrifts (no pun intended) in a three-block stretch of fashionable Pacific Heights. When well-to-do patrons of the arts clean out their closets, you can put some pretty nice things into your own for very little money.

Take a look first at the "Designs of Note" rack (get it?) near the counter. Here, you may find things like a red wool dress by Ellen Tracy for $65, or a Raul Blanco black silk blazer and skirt set for $95. No doubt, some of these glittery fashions have been worn to various opening night galas, and are still in shape for more. But, since society folks don't dare to be seen in the same dress twice, why shouldn't you take advantage?

Elsewhere around the shop, you may find more everyday looks, from a pair of Calvin Klein khaki pants ($8.50) to a tailored wool/polyester skirt by Jaeger ($22). Add a pair of Bandolino pumps for $25, looking practically like new. There is a more limited selection for men, which recently yielded a tweed blazer by Aquascutum of London—one of the highest of the high-note labels—for just $35. The store also has books, handbags and scarves, furniture, and some housewares. Be sure to check out RP's big annual furniture sale, held every March.

Everything sold here is carefully chosen for good quality and condition; donations which don't meet these standards are handed on to the Salvation Army instead. Repeat Performance is open every day but Sunday, from 10 a.m. to 4 p.m. (Tuesdays and Fridays until 6:00); and Tuesdays are senior citizen discount days, when an extra 20% is taken off the total sale.

Savers
- 2840 Geneva Ave. (Rio Verde St.), Daly City; (415) 468-0646
  And other suburban locations

Wow. Savers is like a thrift department store. Part of a huge national chain, each branch is well-stocked with secondhand clothes, furniture, and

toys, books, and small appliances and electronics. It's all definitely used, but much of this stuff still has plenty of life left—and the prices, well, they just couldn't be any lower if they tried.

Clothing is separated into large sections for men, women, and kids. Mr. C found items like a Halston suede sportcoat for $5.99, a conservative blazer from the Emporium for $17.98, and even a Ralph Lauren Polo cashmere cardigan for just $7.99. A friend, meanwhile, was busy perusing the women's section. Now, not only did she find a simple black cotton dress by Esprit selling for a slim $1.99; but, when she got to the register, she was told that, because of the tag color, the dress was half-price that day!

You'll always find plenty of outerwear, from raincoats (London Fog, $3.99) to kids' stuff (a boy's Jordache denim jacket, $5.99); not to mention special items, like fur, leather, and suede jackets ranging from $10-$20. Plus racks and racks of shoes and boots, though most of these have walked quite a few miles. Lots of older fashions here, by the way, for you "retro" fans.

Housewares include things for the kitchen, like stoneware coffee mugs for 69 cents; chairs, toasters, televisions, cameras (a genuine, old Kodak "Brownie" for $7.99!), golf clubs, and toys, including stuffed dinosaurs for $1.99.

Savers offers lots of amenities not often found in thrift shops. There are dressing rooms, for example, as well as a seven-day return policy (for exchange only). You can even pay by check, or credit card. And while senior citizens get an automatic 20% discount off their total purchase anytime, this deal is extended to the general public on Sundays. Needless to say, the store is open seven days a week.

St. Vincent De Paul Society Thrift Shop
- 1745 Folsom St. (14th St.), San Francisco; (415) 626-1515

- 1519 Haight St. (Ashbury St.), San Francisco; (415) 626-1515
- 186 West Portal Ave., San Francisco; (415) 626-1515

Like most charity thrift stores, this trio collects and sells a variety of goods including clothing, shoes, books, and furniture. Most of the clothes here cost only a few dollars, but a lot of the stuff is pretty well-worn. Observant shoppers will find a few name labels mixed in: Mr. C found a pair of Guess jeans and a Land's End sweater, each for $6. Winter overcoats are under $20, and one by Larry Levine was seen for $15. Shoes are a little bit more difficult. A pair of Gap loafers was seen for $7, but they didn't have a lot of miles left in them. A pair of leather pumps in taupe were in better shape and still just $8.

Housewares are abundant. They have the usual things like glassware for 50¢ to $1 and towels for $2 apiece. Again, there are usually some brand name goods, like a Braun coffee maker ($15), a Rival crockpot ($20), and a Proctor-Silex two-slice toaster ($7.50). Furniture is only in fair to good condition. Mr. C did see some interesting pieces including a five-piece dining room set for $85 and a six-drawer chest for $65. St. Vincent De Paul Society thrift stores, benefitting this organization's charity programs, are open Monday through Friday from 9:30 a.m. to 4:30 p.m. and Saturday from 9 a.m. to 4:30 p.m.

Seconds-To-Go Resale Shop

- 2252 Fillmore St. (Sacramento St.), San Francisco; (415) 563-7806

Up the street a bit from Repeat Performance, S-T-G is another storefront thrift stocked with good quality clothing—this time, benefitting the scholarship funds of the Schools of the Sacred Heart. You won't find as many "big names" here, but Mr. C did notice a LizWear black leather skirt—like new—for $65, and a sweater dress of lambswool and angora for $28; the men's racks included a Perry Ellis pinstripe suit for $80, and a cricket-style cardigan

from the Gap for $12. Now, that *is* good cricket, eh what?

You can also find jeans for $8, tons of shirts and blouses; plus a good amount of toys and sporting goods. In fact, Seconds-To-Go has one of the better selections of children's clothes and toys, probably because of their school affiliation.

And they do have one of the better selections of books, in both hardcover and paperback. Mr. C saw *Millie's Book* (remember that silly book Barbara Bush wrote and gave her dog Millie all the credit for?) for just $3; the original list price was $24.95. Most hardcovers are $1, like *I'll Take Manhattan* by Judith Krantz. Paperbacks are generally 50¢ and they have a good selection with bestsellers like *Hunt for Red October* by Tom Clancy, and *Rising Sun* by Michael Crichton. They have some housewares and glassware at very good prices. They carry some jewelry and antiques, but these won't necessarily be cheap.

Seconds-To-Go is open Monday 10 a.m. to 4 p.m. and Tuesday through Saturday 10 a.m. to 5 p.m.

The Street Shop

- 2045 Divisadero St. (California St.), San Francisco; (415) 931-4382

The Street Shop, one of the many upscale thrift stores in Pacific Heights, carries a large selection of designer and brand name clothes for men and women. You won't have to look very hard to find bargains like a jacket by Giorgio Armani for $65, an Anne Klein II silk and wool sweater for $10, or a man's dress shirt by Land's End for $3.50. Mr. C. spied a nylon rain jacket by Eddie Bauer for $10 and Forenza jeans for $7. Black corduroys and classic pants from Talbots will fit into any wardrobe, and budget, nicely.

They have a good selection of books, including fairly current hits like *Patriot Games* by Tom Clancy for just 25¢ in paperback. Their small housewares selection included some glassware and even brand names like a Rival crockpot for $15. You'll have fun poking around this shop. They're open Tuesday through Friday 10:30 a.m. to 4:30 p.m. and Saturday 11 a.m. to 3 p.m.

Thrift Town
- 2101 Mission St. (17th St.), San Francisco; (415) 861-1132

This is quite simply one of the largest thrift stores Mr. C has seen anywhere. Since 1973, this store—which, unlike most thrifts, is a commercial business and does *not* benefit charities—has packed tons of clothing, furniture, and houseware items into two big floors. As they say themselves, "It's like a garage sale every day of the week."

The main selling floor divides pretty neatly down the middle into women's clothing on the left, and men's clothing on the right. Again, new stock pours in each week; but a recent visit found such things as an evening dress in black velvet and satin by Gunne Sax, studded with rhinestones, for $24.95, and a Pierre Cardin skirt suit for $15.95. Among more casual women's stuff, Gap jeans and a pair of Liz Claiborne cotton slacks were both seen for $5.95. At the rear of the store, you'll find racks of shoes, most rather well-worn, for $5-$10 a pair, plus bins of handbags. There is even a selection of real and fake fur coats, most in decent condition, ranging from $20-$70.

On the men's side, Mr. C noted a good Harris Tweed sportcoat for $14.95, an Yves St. Laurent pinstripe vest for $3.95, Levi's jeans for $7.95, and a camelhair topcoat by Abercrombie and Fitch for just $39.95. Plus a whole rack of Hawaiian shirts, most $9.95.

Also in that rear area, is a section filled with clothes for children, like an Osh Kosh girl's (size 4) pink corduroy winter jacket for $7.95, or a pair of boy's Reeboks for $3.95. This is also where you'll see rows and rows of housewares, from a handmade ceramic pitcher ($1.95) to wine glasses (95¢ a stem) to pots, pans, and cutlery.

But wait, there's more! Head upstairs to the mezzanine, and check out the used furniture and appliances section. Mr. C found a genuine leather sofa, still looking quite comfy, for $79.95; also a swivel-rocker easy chair, in corduroy, for $39.95. There is usually a good selection of exercise bicycles and such, well-pumped but far from finished; one rowing machine was $19.95. At that price, you won't feel so guilty about not using it.

Also up here are small appliances—toasters, coffee makers, popcorn poppers, you name it—complete with electrical outlets so that you can plug them in and test them in the store. A Black & Decker toaster oven was seen for $9.95. Then, there are the walls lined with used books and magazines, from children's books to computer manuals (aren't they the same thing nowadays?) to hardcover novels, all from a quarter to about three bucks. Nearby is the real kiddie stuff—car seats for $4.95, strollers for $9.95. Whew!

Back at the front counters, by the way, you can look at lots of finer items, from costume jewelry to fancier creations in silver and crystal. There are comfortable, well-lit fitting rooms up here too. Thrift Town is open seven days a week, including weeknights until 8:00. Look for periodic sales, often geared to holidays—just like full-price department stores!

Town School Clothes Closet
- 3325 Sacramento St. (Presidio Ave.), San Francisco; (415) 929-8019

Among the many thrifts in Pacific Heights, this store offers lots of brand names and variety—and the merchandise is in very good condition. Mr. C found plenty of jeans for $10 and under, a pair of women's grey wool pants for $8, an Esprit cotton shirt for $9, and a blouse by Oleg Cassini for $15.

TSCC has a great selection of dress and career apparel for women; you may find items like a gray wool dress by Liz Claiborne for $30, or a silk and wool dress from Saks Fifth Avenue for $80. Some of these may seem rather pricey for a thrift shop; but when you consider the quality and the condition, they're usually a good deal. Mr. C also saw a fur cape, in good condition indeed, for $100; same price for a pair of black suede slacks by Ann Taylor. A jacket by Emporio Armani for $60 was the bargain of the visit that day.

Traipse over to the clearance rack, too, where you may see a Brooks Brothers sweater in emerald green for a mere $3. The store also offers the standard selection of glassware, books, shoes, and assorted bric-a-brac. Sales benefit the Town School for Boys. They're open Monday through Friday from 9 a.m. to 5 p.m., and Saturday 10 a.m. to 5 p.m.

Victorian House Thrift Shop

- 2318 Fillmore St. (Washington St.), San Francisco; (415) 923-3237

The furthest north of the upscale Fillmore thrift shops, Victorian House is another fine example of the sort of place where you can save big bucks on fancy clothing—and help out charities at the same time. Like its

neighbors (listed above), VH is a thrift that feels more like a boutique.

Wander through its two floors of bargains, and you may find a Laura Ashley dress or an Evan-Picone linen blazer and skirt set, both of which were recently seen for $28; add a pair of black strap heels by John Weitz for $12, still in fine condition. Or, perhaps a down-filled ski parka for $15. Downstairs is where you'll find men's stuff, including racks of sportcoats—mostly conservative—for $20 each. Also lots of jeans for about $10 a pair.

Back up on the street level, VH also has a better-than-most selection of housewares; Mr. C found a microwave oven—an older model, but shiny and clean as new—selling for $75. Plus shelves and shelves of glasses, dishware, cutlery, and the like; and lots of magazines for a quarter, paperbacks for fifty cents, and hardcovers for a dollar. Open Mondays from 11 a.m. to 4 p.m., Tuesdays through Saturdays from 10-5.

COSMETICS AND PERFUMES

Bare Necessities

- 421 Castro St. (Market St.), San Francisco; (415) 626-5859

This small shop is packed from floor to ceiling with all manner of fancy hair and skin care products at what they call "the lowest prices in the Castro." That's as much a mixed blessing as it sounds: These are high-toned products being purveyed in an expensive neighborhood—which makes the prices very reasonable indeed.

On what? Top national brands like Kiss My Face (a twelve-ounce bottle of moisture shave lotion, $5.95), Tom's of Maine (a four-ounce tube of baking soda toothpaste, $3.69), and Nature's Gate Rainwater Shampoo (eighteen ounces for $4.50). Other

items are locally made, some right in San Francisco—like a selection of handmade soaps, chamomile and such, for $2.49 each.

Meanwhile, everything here is all-natural, and cruelty-free. A selection of herbal vegetable hair colorings, for instance, has no ammonia or peroxide; a variety of colors are available at $12.59 for a four-ounce bottle.

And here's an extra money-saver: Buy two or more of any product in the store, and you'll get an extra 10% off. Open seven days and evenings a week.

Cash and Carry Beauty Supply

- 1605 Church St. (28th St.), San Francisco; (415) 285-4110

This small Noe Valley store is absolutely crammed with stuff. Every-

MR. CHEAP'S PICKS
Cosmetics and Perfumes

✔ **Cash and Carry Beauty Supply**—Good prices on name brand hair and skin care products, plus lesser-known brands in bulk sizes at huge savings.

✔ **New York Cosmetics and Fragrance**—They manufacture a line of high-quality cosmetics costing much less than department store counterparts. Brand name beauty products and fragrances at a discount, too!

✔ **Perfumania**—Part of a national chain, whose buying power saves you up to 60% off retail on all the big-name fragrances.

where you turn, you'll find products to help make you beautiful (at least that's what they all claim). C & C's prices are very good, and an extra feature is that they carry bulk sizes of lesser-known brands at very low prices. Stock up and save big.

You will find some name brands here, too. Nexus Botanical Treatment Shampoo was seen for just $8.50 for a 17-ounce bottle. Fifteen ounces of Roux rinse, used by professional hairdressers, was just $4.50. Other neat products include things like a pack of twelve spiral perm rods for just $4.95; or sixteen ounces of non-acetone nail polish remover, perfect for artificial nails, just $2.95. In addition, you'll find brushes, combs, nail polish, and more.

Cash and Carry is open open five days a week until 5:30 p.m.

New York Cosmetics and Fragrance
• 318 Brannan St. (Second St.), San Francisco; (415) 543-3880
New York Cosmetics and Fragrance

sells brand name hair care products and fragrances at a discount, along with its own line of inexpensive makeup. For instance, you'll find the popular KMS and Focus 21 brand products at a couple of bucks below salon prices.

On the "Fragrance" side, the store offers good deals on brand name and designer perfumes. Discounts vary depending on the deals they can get. You may find such names as Drakkar, regularly $45, for $36.99. An eau de toilette from Gucci, normally $39, was seen for just $29.99, while one from Opium was reduced from $55 down to $45.99.

NYC & F also distributes its own line of high-quality makeup at low prices. Lipsticks are just $2.99, or three for $7.50; blush and eye shadow go for $2.79 each, three for $7.50. Their own blend of water-based foundation is just $4.99 and loose translucent powder is $5.99. Mascara and liquid eyeliner are $2.99 each; buy three, and you'll get one free. They have a great selection of colors, and the sales staff gives you all the service of a fancy department store cosmetics counter.

In addition, you'll also find sponges, bath accessories, brushes, makeup applicators, and more. They're open Monday through Friday from 11 a.m. to 5:30 p.m, Saturday 10 a.m. to 5 p.m., Sunday 12 noon to 5 p.m.

Perfumania
• 40 Serramonte Center, Daly City; (415) 994-7145
Perfumania is a national chain of 150 stores (and growing); their vast buying power enables them to sell top-name designer perfumes for men and women at cut-rate prices. You can save big on names like Elizabeth Taylor's "Passion" and Cher's "Uninhibited," as well as colognes by Alfred Sung, Paco Rabanne, Ralph Lauren, Paloma Picasso, Halston, and many others. Price tags are color-coded to show you which bottles are selling at 20%, 40%, and 60% off.

Sample as many of these as you

like; the staff is extremely knowledge-able and relaxed. The scents are sprayed onto special papers, which are then labeled for you with the respective brand; this way, you don't walk out of the store wearing ten contrasting fragrances.

The store also specializes in boxed gift sets; again, at up to half-off or more. In many cases, you can get a cologne set, with extras like matching lotion, shower gel (or whatever), for the same price as the perfume alone. Some even come pre-wrapped! There are some cosmetic gift sets as well, such as eye shadow color kits. And you can always find a good selection of gifts here for under $10. Open seven days a week.

Rainbow Grocery
- 1899 Mission St. (15th St.), San Francisco; (415) 863-0620

This is the kind of place people mean when they talk about, like, classic California-style shopping, y'know? Walk into the Rainbow Grocery, and it's like a time warp back to the 1960s. Folks in Birkenstocks and tie-dyes wander around, browsing bulk food bins, organic fruits, and all-natural hair care products. In many parts of the country, this has come to be fashionable (and expensive); not under the Rainbow.

Inside the "General Store" section, you can take the bulk approach to all sorts of cosmetics, household cleaning products, vitamins, herbs, and books; bring your own recycled containers, or buy them here. For just 20¢ per liquid ounce, you can get 100% real aloe gel, Jason biotin shampoo, or Naturade hand lotion; for 10¢ an ounce, try a jug of Granny's Old Fashioned Laundry Liquid (in your wash, that is). Of course, you'll find many of the same products in the traditional pre-packaged method; for example, Mr. C found a 17-ounce container of Jason jojoba shampoo for $4.

Rainbow Grocery is open seven days a week until 8:30 p.m.

DISCOUNT DEPARTMENT STORES

J.J. Newberry's
- 2036 Shattuck Ave. (Addison St.), Berkeley; (510) 845-6353

The perfect off-campus necessity store, J.J Newberry's is filled with all sorts of goodies, including housewares, health and beauty aids, clothing, and more. Some of this is good stuff, some of it is junk, and all of it is cheap.

During Mr. C's visit, the store had a whole slew of Betty Crocker kitchen appliances, perfectly sized for a small living space. You could choose between an electric can opener or a two-slice toaster, each just $9.99. They also had a six-piece steak knife set, regularly $5.99, for $2.99. They always have plenty of dishware and cookware, too. Mr. C found a 24-piece porcelain dinner-ware set, regularly $29.99, here $14.99; and a seven-piece enamel-on-steel cookware set, same price.

This is a good place to stock up on health and beauty aids, like a bottle of Listerine, elsewhere $5.29, here $4.19; or three-bar packs of Zest, Safeguard, or Coast soap, regularly $2.49, for $1.88. You'll also find plenty of cleaning supplies really cheap, too, like a large angle broom for $3.24. Get 22 ounces of Windex for $1.24 or 32 ounces of Liquid Plumr for $1.34. You can find no-name brands of cleaning supplies even cheaper.

Newberry's also stocks some food items, mostly packaged, processed goods. They had boxes of sugar wafer cookies or pretzel rods, two for a dollar; and individual envelopes of mi-

MR. CHEAP'S PICKS
Discount Department Stores

✔ **J.J. Newberry's**—From kitchen appliances to soap, you'll find all of life's basic necessities here. And, you won't have to shell out your life's savings to afford them.

✔ **Whole Earth Access**—A little bit of everything under the sun, at discount.

crowave popcorn at four for a dollar.

Their downstairs section yields more great buys, especially in the back area where everything is 99¢. These are mostly cleaning supplies, plasticware, and some food items. Good place to look for stuff if you're having a big party.

National Discount
- 929 Market St. (Fifth St.), San Francisco; (415) 546-3828
- 660 Broadway (Stockton St.), San Francisco; (415) 362-7533
- 1633 Fillmore St. (Post St.), San Francisco; (415) 346-5310
- 2610 Mission St. (22nd St.), San Francisco; (415) 282-2057
- 3618 East 14th St. (36th Ave.), Oakland; (510) 532-5298
- 108 Eastmont Mall, Bancroft Way (73rd St.), Oakland; (510) 562-1240

And other suburban locations
National is your basic place to stock up on basics. An affordable department store since before you were born, they carry a little bit of everything, mostly in budget brands you've never heard of. Still, for college students or families on a tight budget, much of this merchandise will do fine.

Mr. C did find sets of Cannon towels, most likely salvage closeouts, on sale at $2.88 for bath size and $1.88

for hand towels. You may also find things like sofa throws for $14.99, turtleneck shirts for $5, boys' corduroy jeans for $7.88, cheap vinyl handbags for $8.88, or a set of four coffee mugs for $3.88. Plus underwear, toys, budget-brand bikes and tricycles, and all sorts of household gadgets.

Whole Earth Access
- 401 Bayshore Blvd. (Cortland Ave.), San Francisco; (415) 285-5244
- 2990 Seventh St. (Ashby Ave.), Berkeley; (510) 845-3000

And other suburban locations
These stores certainly do give you access to bargains on, seemingly, everything under the sun. From power ties to power tools, you name it, they've got it—or something close—at a discount. And, you lucky Bay Area cheapsters, the San Francisco and Berkeley stores are known to get first dibs on the best merchandise (sorry, suburbanites), though all branches are packed with interesting stuff.

During Mr. C's recent visit, these included a Mitsubishi television monitor with a 26" screen and stereo sound; a demo model, it was reduced from a list price of $598 to a sharper $449. Elsewhere among appliances, there is usually a good choice of refrigerators, stoves, and microwave ovens. A KitchenAid 14-cubic foot frost-free refrigerator/freezer was recently on sale for just $849, easily a hundred bucks below retail.

There are always plenty of electronics to see here as well, including cameras (and film), boomboxes and personal stereo, and even desktop and notebook computer systems. Along with small appliances like food processors and teapots, you'll find kitchen gadgets, cooking utensils, flatware, dishes and glasses, and cookbooks.

In the clothing department, Whole Earth has a lot to see in contemporary fashions for men and women. You may find an Eileen Fisher camelhair/wool blazer, originally meant to retail for $248, selling here for $148; or Columbia ski parkas, once $154, reduced to $119—and again, to a final $72. Plus jeans, underwear, shoes and sneakers (a recent sale offered Reeboks at 40% below retail, all styles), and the rest. Not to mention a luggage section, small but serviceable, of bags to put these clothes into when vacation time rolls around. These may include Samsonite suitcases at 30% off list price, garment bags, carry-ons, etc.

You don't find the vast selection of a full department store here; just the models they can get deals on—often closeouts. Usually, this is still enough to merit regular visits. Store hours are 10 a.m. to 6 p.m., seven days. Their open until 8 p.m. Thursday and Friday.

ELECTRONICS

There are lots of places to save money on appliances and electronics in the Bay Area. Some, unfortunately, are as far below repute as they are below retail. With merchandise that is imported from foreign countries, there is a greater possibility of shady deals, or shoddy quality. Mr. C says this not out of any kind of prejudice, but because he wants you to be careful.

One of the best ways to protect yourself, if you have doubts as to *any* store's reliability, is to ask about their guarantee policy; make sure the item you want carries an American warranty. Since some stores deal directly with manufacturers in the Far East, their merchandise many carry a foreign warranty instead. Even for identical products, a foreign warranty can make repairs a hassle—unless you don't mind paying the postage to Japan! Remember, you are perfectly within your rights to inquire about this in the store.

AUDIO AND VIDEO EQUIPMENT

Macy's Furniture Liquidation Center
• 1556 El Camino Real (Hickey Blvd.), South San Francisco; (415) 878-0802

Electronics bargains in a furniture store? Wait, hear Mr. C out. Macy's has recently shifted the focus of its longtime furniture clearance store, adding other kinds of closeout deals to make it more like a discount version of its entire department store. That means, along with markdowns on mattresses, you can now find a decent selection of audio and video equipment and accessories.

On an early visit, these included unusual items like a Philips CD-Inter-active 910 player, reduced from a list price of $699 to just $249—dozens of 'em, brand new, still in their original boxes. Of course, this may have been due to the fact that CD-I remains a technology in search of an audience.

More everyday choices ranged from a Sony rack system, with a tuner, EQ, and dual cassette recorder, half-price at $149; an Onkyo TA-203 cassette deck, reduced from $399 to a mere $99; and smaller gadgets, like the "VCR-Plus" programmer (you know, the gizmo that uses those long numbers on the TV page to set your VCR); originally $59.95, it was seen here for the smaller number of $29.95.

Accessories, like wires and cables,

can be found here; so can tapes, both blank and pre-recorded. A three-video "Billy Crystal" package (*City Slickers, When Harry Met Sally..., The Princess Bride*) was half its original retail price, just $29.95 for the set. Furthermore, a phalanx of phones included a Panasonic "Auto-Logic" telephone/answering machine for $89.

Knowing that many of these are leftovers, returns, and other varieties of poor cousin, Macy's allows you to bring back any defective items for a refund or exchange within two weeks. Video equipment sold here also carries the same "Video Doctor" in-store repair warranty found in the regular Macy's. The clearance center's hours are Wednesday through Sunday only, from 11 a.m. to 6 p.m.

Sound & Alarm, Inc.
- 1161 Mission St. (Eighth St.), San Francisco; (415) 626-6382
- 6444 Mission St. (Daly Blvd.), Daly City; (415) 991-4448

This is the sort of electronics store you'd expect to find in a city just across the big pond from Japan and the Far East. Not only does it carry many of the big-name brands at low-markup prices, but it also specializes in 220-volt products. That's the voltage used in many foreign countries, but *not* in the United States (where electric outlets give out 110 volts); if you frequently travel overseas, this is a good place to get adapters to run your American appliances, or to get units that are designed to run over there. In particular, S & A offers larger appliances, like refrigerators, in 220-volt versions only.

For stereo and video, however, there is a good selection of equipment intended for use right here in the good ol' U.S. of A. Some of these are closeout bargains on last year's models; Mr. C found a Toshiba 20" TV monitor, cable-ready with stereo sound and remote control, for $299. Also by Toshiba, a four-head VCR (better picture, especially in search mode) with a new automatic head-cleaning feature, was on sale for $259—good prices, both.

On the audio side of things, Mr. C found a good variety of basic and high-end models. A Pioneer VSX-3700S receiver, meant for serious audiophiles, with a built-in equalizer and television sound reception as well as radio (all at a powerful 65 watts per channel), was well-priced at $389. Meanwhile, a Sanyo compact rack system—CD player, double cassette deck, AM-FM receiver, and speakers, all molded together into one piece—was seen for just $229.

Sound & Alarm also offers car stereo units, along with an installation service in their adjacent garage. A Toshiba AM-FM-cassette player, with 50 watts of power per channel and a detachable faceplate (to help you foil would-be thieves) was recently on sale for $129.95. Installation, of course, is extra.

Everything here carries an American warranty (even the 220-volt units), which will help you in case of defective merchandise. Financing is available for big-ticket items. S & A also sells plenty of smaller things, from boomboxes and "personal stereo" to all the different kinds of blank audio and video tape you could need. Open from 10 a.m. to 6 p.m., every day but Sunday.

Sound Well
- 1718 University Ave. (McGee Ave.), Berkeley; (510) 549-2126

Saving money on audio equipment certainly sounds well to Mr. C, and that's just what you can do at this store near the Cal campus. They specialize in used stereo components, a great way to save; in fact, the only new items in the whole store are the speakers which they assemble in their own shop. You won't find car systems, boom boxes, or walkpersons. What you will find is high-quality brand name components for home stereo systems. They deal in quality brand names like Pioneer, Kenwood, and Sony—the kinds of models which, with this kind of maintenance, can last for years. Best of all, most items are guaranteed on parts and labor for six months, one of the best store warranties Mr. C has found in any city. Some pieces are not guaranteed, and these are clearly labeled "as is." Sound Well has been in business for almost twenty years, so you know this isn't a fly-by-night operation. They preferred not to quote prices, since their stock is always different; but you can bet on paying about half of the original price for these components.

Of course, Sound Well also buys and sells equipment (it has to come from somewhere, right?). Trading-in can be a great way to upgrade your system. Or, you may be able to sell your gear in the store on consignment, usually with more expensive items (so you can both make a profit). You'll get more cash by consigning—but only if and when it sells.

Sound Well is open Tuesday through Saturday, from 9:30 a.m. to 5:30 p.m.

Video Only

- 1199 Van Ness Ave. (Geary St.), San Francisco; (415) 563-5200
  And other suburban locations

This Seattle-based regional chain puts an interesting twist on the strategy used by some superstores—which often spring up near small neighborhood shops and try to put them out of the picture. Well, Video Only put *its* downtown branch directly across the street from Circuit City. Why? To save money on advertising. Shoppers are attracted to the high-profile superstore, notice a competitor nearby, and stop in there, too. Video Only gets the same shoppers without running full-page newspaper ads; this saves the store money, and keeps prices low. Circuit City may hit rock bottom on selected sale items, but Video Only's everyday prices tend to be lower overall.

What should you make of these high-tech pretzel-cart wars? Take advantage by checking them both out! In fact, VO maintains a file box at the counter, filled with competitors' ads. You'll generally find that prices here are already better; you're sure to find a bigger selection here, since

MR. CHEAP'S PICKS
Audio and Video Equipment

✔ **Sound Well**—Savings here sure sound well to Mr. C! They specialize in reconditioned equipment, so you can get high-quality gear at low-end prices.
✔ **Video Only**—Bravely taking on the superstores, one camcorder deal at a time.

Video Only doesn't bother with vacuum cleaners, compact discs, microwave ovens, and all that jazz. Just VCRs, TVs, and camcorders, (there are some audio products as well—those designed for use with large projection TVs, in what has come to be known as "home theater").

All of the major brands are here: Sony, JVC, Canon, and more. Sometimes, you can save more money by going with a lesser-known brand of equal quality—like Quasar, which is actually made by Panasonic. A Quasar four-head VCR was recently selling here for $229, a price more commonly found among two-head models.

In large-screen TVs, prices average about $200 below those at competing stores. A Toshiba "Cinema Series" TV, with a 35-inch screen, was recently seen for $2,299 elsewhere; Video Only had it for $1,999. An RCA 8mm camcorder, with a 10:1 zoom lens, was found here for a nice, compact $699. Mr. C was even told that some prices still have a bit of room for some good ol' fashioned haggling! Give it a try—can't hurt.

Just like the superstores, everything here is up and running; you can play with these gizmos to your heart's content. And, *unlike* the megachains, the salespeople at VO are highly trained and truly know how to demonstrate each item or answer your electronics questions. The staff also makes deliveries on larger units, and will do all the hookups for you, taking the time to make sure you

know how to run everything yourself. And, the store offers a liberal refund/exchange policy. Open seven days a week, including weeknights until 9:00 p.m.

COMPUTERS

LCI Computers

• 467 Pine St. (Montgomery St.), San Francisco; (415) 981-6666

LCI Computers prides itself on a knowledgeable and friendly staff who will help assess your computer needs and find the right system for you at a low price. Personal support is part of the package when you buy at LCI; they also do upgrades and repairs in shop, as well as training and consulting.

Prices change so quickly, of course, that it's worthless to list them here; suffice it to say, they are indeed have very competitive at LCI. That covers a full range of the latest IBM-style desktop systems, which can be "made to order" in any configuration of sizes and features. Good prices on notebook computers too, by Toshiba and Texas Instruments.

Currrently, if you're looking for a very basic (and cheap) system, these folks can can set you up with a 386 computer for under $1,000. They also carry software at competitive, and sometimes discounted, prices. They carry Softkey software, including Database Plus, Publisher, and Accounting, for just $24.95 each. LCI computers is open Monday through Friday 9 a.m. to 6 p.m. Closed weekends.

Mac

• 2156A University Ave. (Shattuck Ave.), Berkeley; (510) 644-0500 or (800) BUY-A-MAC

This store specializes in—what else?—Macintosh. It's all they carry. They have some of the best service and support around, and their prices on new Macs are very competitive. They showed Mr. C a Quadro 610 system, which they were selling for $1,699—while a major superstore

was selling the same computer for $1,859. Good prices on PowerBooks, too. The PowerBook 180C, at the top-of-the-line (with 4 megs of RAM, an 80 megabyte hard drive, and an active-matrix color screen) was recently seen for a very reasonable $2,499. They sell used machines, as well, but they didn't want Mr. C to quote prices, since the stock changes so rapidly; suffice it to say there are incredible bargains to be found by going this route.

Mac also carries a complete line of books, accessories, peripherals, and software. Again, prices change all the time, but at the beginning of '94, "Quicken" was selling here for $49.95 and "MacWrite Pro" for $189.95. This is also a great place to go for Mac repairs. They do component-level repairs which they say saves a lot of money. Finally, they also rent Macs, so if you need a computer for a short-term project, or you just want to give one a spin, this can be another money-saving option. The store is open 10 a.m. to 6 p.m., Monday through Saturday.

MACadam Computers

• 1062 Folsom St. (Sixth St.), San Francisco; (415) 863-6498

Guess what brand of computers they sell here? You got it, mac. This spacious SoMa shop (say that three times fast) is an authorized Apple reseller, whose large quantity purchasing keeps prices low. It also means frequent rebate specials direct from the manufacturer; one recent deal offered $100 to $700 back on a selection of Radius "Color Pivot" monitors. And that's not all! You can even save a little more on these already-good prices, not by purchasing in quantity, but in cash. These extra discounts range from 3% on equipment to about 10% on lots of software packages and books.

Though computer prices never stand still for more than a nanosecond, some of the bargains found at the beginning of 1994 included an Apple Macintosh Powerbook 165 (with 4 megs of RAM and an 80mb hard drive) for $1,675—a good price indeed, including an extra $50 off just for paying without a credit card. Use it toward some Microsoft Excel software, and save another $10 on that!

Among printers, Mr. C found several in-store deals—like an Apple Stylewriter II selling for just $299, and an Apple Color Printer capable of using 11" x 17" paper for $575. According to the folks here, this closeout originally retailed for over $2,000.

Interested in the newest Apple creation, the Newton MessagePad? (Especially now that many of the bugs seem to have been worked out. . .) Play with one here at the large sales display. Several Mac workstations are also available for rental use in the store. MACadam does its own servicing on the premises, honoring full manufacturers' warranties. The store is open weekdays from 10:00 a.m. to 7 p.m., Saturdays from 10-5, and Sundays from 11-4.

Software Etc.
• 217 Sutter St. (Kearny St.), San Francisco; (415) 986-8157
Software Etc. sells IBM and Macintosh software at discounted prices. These discounts can be small, especially on lower-priced items, or quite substantial, in the case of more expensive packages. A program like Quickbooks for Windows, regularly $159.95, was seen here for just $99.99; and the Quicken/TurboTax bundle, regularly $139.90, for just $64.99. On the Macintosh side of things, you may find Aldus SuperPaint, originally $199, for $99.99— or Claris MacWrite Pro, regularly $249.99, for $189.99.

Of course, all work and no play makes Mr. C a dull boy. Games like

MR. CHEAP'S PICKS
Computers

✔ **Software Etc.**—Distressed by the high price of computer software packages? Try here, where you can find discounts on some of the most popular programs for both IBM and Macintosh.

✔ **The Used Computer Store**—Buy yesterday's top-of-the-line today, and save big bucks. This Berkeley store has a mega-capacity of used computers and parts in every price range.

"Prince of Persia" for Macintosh, regularly $49.95, sell here for $39.99 (Mac) or $29.99 (IBM). The "Etc." includes accessories, like diskettes, mousepads, and so on; plus books and magazines, though these are not discounted. Hours are 9 a.m. to 6 p.m. on weekdays, Saturday 10 a.m. to 5:30 p.m., and Sunday 12 noon to 5:30 p.m.

The Used Computer Store
• 2440 Shattuck Ave. (Haste St.), Berkeley; (510) 548-8686
Finding bargains in the computer market is tricky. Buying used equipment is one way to save money. Similar to the concept of buying used cars, computers lose value quickly as newer and faster models with more bells and whistles come along, even though they're still in great condition. And just like buying a used car, it's also important to find a reputable dealer. The Used Computer Store in Berkeley is such a place. They buy and sell all kinds of machines, including IBM, Apple, Compaq, and Macintosh, and do their own repairs. These carry a three-month store warranty, as much as you'll ever get on used electronics—a definite sign of an

aboveboard operation.

So what can you find here? It varies constantly, but they generally have lots of used 386 PCs for $400-$500; fourteen-inch SVGA color monitors can be added for as little as $200, making it possible to get a complete 386 system for $600 or so! Mac fans aren't left out, either. The store recently had a Mac IIsi with a 12" color monitor for $799 complete, and a Mac Plus with a built-in monitor *and* an Imagewriter II printer for just $599! That should set any student up nicely.

Used printers start from under $100. Recent deals included a 24-pin dot-matrix Toshiba for $119, and an Apple Imagewriter for $159. Laser printers are available, too, like a Hewlett Packard LaserJet I for $299. On all of this equipment, Mr. C has

listed the least expensive examples; of course, if you have a little more money to spend, you can get good deals on more recent models too.

The Used Computer Store also has used software. Be forewarned that there is no refund or exchange on used software, but there are still great deals to be had. For IBM, Mr. C found programs like Microsoft Chart for $49.95. In Mac, he found Excel 3.0 for $149.95 and Adobe Type Manager for $19.95. A lot of the used software is no-name stuff, which may or may not be useful to you. At these ridiculously low prices, though, these are worth a shot!

The Used Computer Store is open Monday through Saturday from 10 a.m. to 7 p.m., and Sunday from noon to 5 p.m.

FLEA MARKETS AND EMPORIA

Berkeley Flea Market
- 1937 Ashby Ave., Berkeley; (510) 644-0744

Every Saturday and Sunday from 8:00 a.m. to 7:30 p.m., the Ashby BART station parking lot transforms itself into the home of one of the Bay Area's biggest outdoor flea markets. Some three hundred vendors deal in all manner of trinkets, from clothing to jewelry to books, with lots of gift ideas as well. Naturally, lots of this stuff is good and cheap; some of it is cheap in all senses of the word, but it's always fun to poke around. In the words of one of the women who run it all, the market basically sells "everything but food." Admission is free.

Cost Plus Imports
- 2552 Taylor St. (Bay St.), San Francisco; (415) 928-6200
- 201 Clay St. (Market St.), Oakland; (510) 834-4440
- 785 Serramonte Blvd. (El Camino Real), Colma; (415) 994-7090

Much like the national chain Pier 1 Imports, Cost Plus Imports sells an eclectic assortment of merchandise from around the world. And they can do this at considerably low prices. In some cases, the prices are so low because the quality is not far behind; but most of the merchandise is fine, fun, and attractive.

Cost Plus is a great place for housewares, especially dishes and glassware. Mr. C found porcelain mugs from China for $3.99 each. Blue Willow dinnerware from England, no match for Wedgwood but handsome nonetheless, was just $17.26 for a four-piece place setting. You'll also find baskets by the hundreds, like a large woven picnic basket for $24.99. Tons of baskets go for under a dollar.

Cost Plus imports some food items, too. A box of Twinings Darjeeling tea was just $1.99. There's a very good selection of teas, and tea accessories to go with them. Imported gourmet cakes, in flavors like orange and kiwi, were also seen for $1.99 recently, and a liter of extra virgin olive oil from Italy was just $5.99—an incredible price anywhere.

Decorating your home? You'll find lots of nice things here. Mr. C found a colorful cotton 6' x 9' rug for $89.99. The always-popular papasan chair was just $99, twin size, with cushion. Also, there's lots of framed art starting as low as $19.99.

Cost Plus also carries clothes, jewelry, and all kinds of international bric-a-brac. Recently, they had a selection of Moroccan jewelry as low as $19.99 and sterling silver and turquoise earrings for $14.99. Plus straw hats for $5.99, colorful rayon skirts for $12.48, and more. Open seven days.

Geneva Swap Meet
- 607 Carter St. (Geneva Ave.), Daly City; (415) 587-2884

Every Saturday and Sunday from 8:00 a.m. to 4:00 p.m., the parking lot of the Geneva Drive-In movie theater becomes a gigantic outdoor flea market. There is a nominal entrance fee.

Roam around the sprawling set-up from vendor to vendor, and you may find anything from Avon Skin-So-Soft to used power tools. Perhaps you'll pick up ten pounds of fresh oranges for $3, or a pair of simulated zebra-skin car seat covers for $24. Not to mention secondhand books, new cassettes and CDs, clothing, jewelry, and other assorted junk. Some folks deal from fully outfitted booths; others from blankets spread out on the asphalt. In any case, it can be fun to wander through.

Markus Square International Marketplace
- 301 Jefferson St. (Third St.), Oakland; (510) 832-6525

Markus Square International Marketplace can best be described as a cross between a flea market, a mall, and a fair. It is filled with booths rented by various retailers who sell a wide variety of merchandise, including clothes, jewelry, furniture, luggage, and housewares. Because they share

---

MR. CHEAP'S PICKS
Flea Markets and Emporia

- ✔ **Berkeley Flea Market**—About 300 vendors, and about as much fun as you can have for free—unless you buy something, of course.
- ✔ **Markus Square International Marketplace**—This indoor bazaar in Oakland offers better quality than a flea market, and lower prices than a mall. Plus free entertainment on weekends!

---

the overhead costs, these enterprises can often afford to discount their wares, so you get better deals than at retail stores, and better quality than at a flea market. Some of the booths are occupied by businesses that have regular stores elsewhere in the city.

Mr. C saw lots of clothing here, with bargains that included men's casual slacks for $23.50, silk blouses for $9.99, young children's sweatsuits for $3.99, and athletic T-shirts for $4. One booth specialized in leather cowboy boots, starting at just $90. A jewelry booth offered a sterling silver bangle bracelet for $20. Another booth filled with electronics had a Sharp boom box with CD player, regularly $150, for $130. And Mr. C has always found these bazaars to be havens for haggling.

In addition to retail booths, Markus Square International Marketplace has a snack bar; what's more, the Bay Area Blues Society sponsors free concerts here every Friday, Saturday, and Sunday at noon. Keep your eye out for more entertainment options as this place continues to grow and expand.

Paul's Stores
- 465 Pine St. (Kearny St.), San Francisco; (415) 989-6884
- 390 Grand Ave. (Miller St.), South San Francisco; (415) 589-1537

Paul's Stores are very similar to the "All for a Dollar" stores that are popping up all over; their merchandise and prices, though, are a little more varied. Their stock is mostly salvaged goods, liquidation merchandise, etc. from other stores. You'll find some great stuff, and plenty that is, quite frankly, junk. It's still a fun store to poke around in, at any rate.

The mix is eclectic and ever-changing. On any give day you might find neon shoelaces for 29¢, two-liter bottles of Canada Dry lemon ginger ale for 79¢ each, or wooden wine racks for $2.99. They sometimes have clothes or shoes, like kids' T-shirts for $1.99; but this is more a place for housewares, personal care products, and general bric-a-brac. You'll find lots of things for under $1, like drinking mugs for 99¢ and bottles of hairspray, also 99¢. Need to jazz up your couch? How about some throw pillows for $3.99 each, or two for $7?

You just never know what's going to be here. Paul's Stores are open Monday through Friday.

Plentyoff
• 1803 Polk St. (Washington St.), San Francisco; (415) 673-5256

What's in a name? In this case, everything. Plentyoff is a small store, but it's filled with all sorts of household items and bric-a-brac that you can pick up cheap. You'll find big sponges at three for $1, "genuine crystal" tumblers for $2.99 each, and frying pans for $1.99. As you can probably guess, this stuff is not of the highest quality and some of it is downright junk. But, for some people, this parade of paraphernalia may yield just the right thing, at just the right price.

They have lots of low-grade luggage, like a small canvas duffel bag for $8.50—you can even get an entire set of black canvas luggage for $24.50. Elsewhere around this eclectic store, Mr. C found a jumprope for $3.25, a lamp (without shade) for $19.95, vacuum cleaner bags for $1.99, and light bulbs, in a variety of

colors, for $1.59. Plus toys, picture frames, and more. Do be careful; some of this stuff is scuffed or scratched. Definitely worth looking around, though.

South Van Ness/Mission Street Flea Market
• Mission St. (Twelfth St.), San Francisco; no phone

True to its name, this little flea market can be found in the "Gateway Center" parking lot at the junction of South Van Ness Avenue and Mission Street. It takes place every weekend, Saturdays and Sundays, from a bright and early 6:30 a.m. to 4:00 p.m., with free admission.

The vendors, who mainly work from folding tables, display a variety of useable and useless stuff. Mr. C found a rack of brand-new jeans from Limited Express, still bearing store tags of $38 each; here, they were selling for $20. Another guy had all kinds of sports collectibles, from baseball cards to Giants switchplates for your wall. There is usually someone selling fresh produce at from-the-farm prices; plus the standard assortment of old silverware, some furniture, and other bric-a-brac.

Union Street Flea Market
• 1611 Jackson St. (Polk St.), San Francisco; (415) 771-2574

If you only think of flea markets as those traditional parking lots filled with booths selling everything from electronics to hubcaps, then you may be in for a surprise here. Union Street Flea Market is a proper store filled with collectibles, furniture, clothes, books, and more—an eclectic mix of merchandise at low prices.

They have a vast displays of cobalt glass, 1940s and 1950s costume jewelry, and all kinds of glassware and dishware. You might find wineglasses or mugs for $1 each. Mr. C saw a full 30-piece china set for just $15. Their selection of furniture is smaller, though it's of very high quality. A solid-wood Baker coffee table sold for just $272; new, it would easily cost $800 to $900. A handsome dining room set was just $225, and a coffee table and lamp table were sold together for just $100.

They also have low-priced books, like a hardcover edition of *Gone With The Wind* for $5. You'll also find all kinds of clothes, like sweaters for $8. They have jewelry, including marcasite, Baltic amber, and Oriental

styles. Earrings start as low as $10 a pair.

Come in and poke around; you never know what you'll find. They're open Wednesday through Saturday from 1 p.m. to 6 p.m., and Sunday from 1 p.m. to 4 p.m.

FLOWERS AND PLANTS

The Biggest Little Flower Shop in the World
* 1919 Fourth St. (University Ave.), Berkeley; (510) 845-4365

It's a cute name, and owner Dick Hoeflein isn't kidding. This isn't even a shop, but rather a stand in front of the popular Spenger's Fish Grotto store and restaurant in Berkeley's outlet district.

Meanwhile, he's got a decent selection of cut flowers and small plants. And, since it's all cash (or check!)-and-carry, you definitely save money—just don't brag about it to the person who's getting the flowers. Would you believe two dozen roses for ten bucks? Okay, they're not the fanciest you've ever seen—all packed together into a bunch, with no extra foliage or box. Hey, what do you expect at these prices?

They are available in various colors and stem lengths. You can also get a single red rose for $2, or a bunch of tulips for $8. Plus a limited selection of small potted cacti and house plants, ready to go (with note cards) as quick gifts. Open seven days a week from 8 a.m. to 10 p.m.

Cost Plus Nursery
* 2633 Taylor St. (North Point), San Francisco; (415) 885-5100

From the same folks who brought you Cost Plus Imports and Cost Plus Wines, comes the Cost Plus Nursery, right across the street—bringing the same overwhelming approach to cut flowers, silk flowers, house plants, and everything you need to care for them.

Tulips are $4.99 a bunch here, and a dozen roses are $7.99. Pots of chrysanthemums were going for $3.49 during Mr. C's visit. A wide variety of houseplants in four-inch containers are just $1.99 each, while six-inch hanging planters are $6.99.

Want to plant out some herbs in your garden? Choose from all kinds of starters at $1.59 apiece. Or, get a small jasmine tree in a one-gallon pot for $6.99. Back on the indoor front, a recent sale offered a braided ficus tree (young, in an eight-inch pot) for $14.99. Meanwhile, a full-grown six-footer was seen for $69. Open seven days a week.

Elmwood Florists
* 2636 Ashby St. (College Ave.), Berkeley; (510) 848-6199

Some stores tell you how much they've marked their merchandise below retail list prices; At Elmwood Florists, they take the opposite approach. Everything they sell is marked up just 15% above the wholesale price—a well-pruned profit margin indeed. This includes a wide selection of cut flowers and plants; a dozen long-stem roses, for example, are just $17.50.

If you really want to save, come into the shop and take your flowers with you, saving delivery costs. This option keeps them from having to build these expenses into the prices. If you have money to burn, of course, delivery is available on orders of $25 or more. For addresses in Berkeley, the charge is a reasonable $5; it's more for other parts of the Bay area.

Plants and blooms are similarly low-priced. Get a fiddle-leaf fig for $28, or an orchid for $35. They also do arrangements for all occasions, including weddings. Hours are Monday through Saturday from 9 a.m. to 7 p.m. and Sunday from 10 a.m. to 6 p.m.

Flowers Faire

• 360 Bayshore Blvd. (Oakdale Ave.), San Francisco; (415) 641-7054

"No-frills flowers" may sound like a contradiction in terms, but that's the phrase that came to Mr. C's mind in this warehouse-type store. Don't expect much in the way of amenities here; but then, when you're buying a dozen roses for $5.99, could you complain? These are not long-stemmed or boxed, of course; they're wrapped in cellophane and otherwise unadorned. In fact, for $9.99, you can get a bunch of 25—count 'em, 25—roses.

Inside the walk-in cooler (walk in yourself—remember, this is no-frills), you can also pick out gladiola at $3.99 a stem, or two for $4.99; miniature carnations at $3.99 a bunch; or "Bird of Paradise" at $1.49 per stem (five for $6.99).

There are lots of houseplants to choose from as well; buy three or more, and get a dollar off the price of each one. That's just one of several discount deals available here; you can even get a sort of "frequent flower" card, allowing you a half-price item after every three purchases. The store also has tons of decorative additions, like baskets, mylar balloons, and hand-painted signs. Open seven days a week, including evenings.

Just down the street, check out two other places for flower and plant bargains—although they're better known for other things. **Goodman Lumber** at 445 Bayshore Blvd., telephone (415) 285-2800; and **Floorcraft Garden Center** at 550 Bayshore Blvd., telephone (415) 824-1900, may have gained longstanding reputations for things like hardware and carpeting, but they also have lots to see in the way of flora. They're

particularly strong in the area of outdoor plants, trees, and shrubs, as well as industrial-size bags of soil, peat moss, and other supplies. Both stores are open seven days a week.

Plant Warehouse

• 1355 Bush St. (Polk St.), San Francisco; (415) 885-1515

Walking into this shop is like finding yourself in the middle of a jungle. These folks specialize in selling (and renting) "the large and unusual," meaning things like corn plants ($6.95), cacti of all kinds (from $1 and $3 up to $60), jade plants ($15.95 for a two-foot size), plus rubber trees, ficus trees, and more.

They have indoor "starters," in four-inch pots, of flowering plants like impatiens, ivy, and begonias, all $1.95 apiece; geraniums and tulips in four-inch pots for $3.95 each; and deep, rich violets for $2.95 a pot.

The store is open seven days a week, from 10 a.m. to 6 p.m.; you can also visit their greenhouses, located in Half Moon Bay; telephone (415) 726-0129, which do sell foliage plants directly to the public.

ROSExpress

• 643 Seventh St. (Townsend St.), San Francisco; (415) 864-7600

Here's a flower deal that may not seem cheap in price—or in style. That's why it's a bargain. For $29.95, you can buy a dozen three-foot long-stemmed roses, boxed and gift wrapped; that's already a decent price. But, for an additional $3, you can then have these delivered by a driver dressed to the nines in a full tuxedo. For areas of The City further than downtown, including the East Bay and Marin County, the rate is only $5. When you figure this all together, it's a way to really impress someone without going into debt.

Part of a nationwide chain, ROSExpress specializes in high-quality gifts and service. Their roses are flown in daily, directly from growers in Central and South America. Over a dozen color varieties are available, from Royalty red to Sterling Silver lavender to Cream Ariana white. You can also order a single red rose ($5), a bud vase with one rose ($8), or a chocolate rose ($3.50 each, $36.00 a dozen).

The company is pioneering the delivery side of the business in other ways, too. They offer guaranteed delivery, within 24 hours, of a dozen roses anywhere in the country for $49.99; these are shipped in special boxes, lined by hand with styrofoam to keep the flowers fresh. Oh yes, and they even have a "Frequent Flower" credit program. Gotta love it.

Though they do some walk-up business, this is primarily a telephone service; call anytime from 8 a.m. to 6 p.m. Monday through Friday, and from 10 a.m. to 4 p.m. on Saturday.

Silver Terrace Nurseries
• 625 Brannan St. (Sixth St.), San Francisco; (415) 543-4443

One of the largest of the Flower Market growers, you are as welcome to shop here as the florists themselves. They seem to have just about every kind of flower, plant, foliage, and supplies you could want, all at near-wholesale prices to the public. Expert service, too.

There are all kinds of flowering plants, like hyacinth in a six-inch pot for $4.50, tulips for $3, and chrysanthemums for $2.50 (three for $6). And long, elegant single cala lilies in a pot for $8.25. Among foliage, Mr. C found a four-foot-tall potted palm tree for $22.50, and a six-foot ficus for $75, as full and lush as any he's ever seen.

They have cut flowers here too, such as pre-packaged (but healthy) roses from $16 to $22—per *two* dozen. Miniature carnations are $4 ($5 in red) for a bunch of 25. Plus tulips, irises, orchids, and more. Several varieties of mixed bouquets cost just $6.50 each.

Roam around upstairs on their mezzanine, and you can rummage through a bazaar of vases, pots and baskets in every size and shape imaginable; you may see wicker baskets from $6, and blue glass vases from $8.

The hours here are irregular, with

MR. CHEAP'S PICKS
Flowers and Plants

✔ **Elmwood Florists**—Rather than mark down their wares, this florist only takes a small markup. A rose by any other price couldn't smell as sweet.

✔ **ROSExpress**—Fine, long-stemmed roses delivered by a tuxedo-clad driver, for less than some stores charge just for the flowers.

✔ **Silver Terrace Nurseries**—This large Flower Market wholesaler also sells to the public at certain hours.

---

certain times devoted to the florist trade only. The store is open to the public from 9 a.m to 3 p.m. on Mondays, Wednesdays and Fridays; and from 6:30 a.m. to 3 p.m. on Tuesdays and Thursdays.

Spring Fever Flowers
• 5711 College Ave. (Miles Ave.), Oakland; (510) 655-2289

Don't go looking for a store bearing this name. For over a dozen years, Jill Koenigsdorf has operated her florist business from a covered spot on College Avenue in Oakland. It's right in front of Rockridge Rags Clothing (described elsewhere in this book), giving new meaning to the term "storefront shop." Along a tiered display platform, in buckets on the sidewalk, and hanging from the awning, are her well-cultivated blooms. Naturally, this no-frills operation (apart from the flowers, of course) means very low prices to you.

A dozen red roses costs $12 here; a half-dozen large, gorgeous tulips, in a palette of colors, is only $7. Pluck a half-dozen baby gladiola for $6.50, or white narcissus at five for a dollar (or 25¢ a stem.) Jill also makes lovely arrangements of dried flowers;

most bouquets are $5-$10 each, depending on the size and contents. She tends to have a greater variety during the summer months.

Spring Fever Flowers is open (or should that be "present"?) year-round from 12 noon to 6 p.m., Wednesdays to Saturdays only. Here's an extra tip

from Mr. C: If you can, stop by around 4:30 on Saturdays, when Jill needs to clear out the decks for the week. That's when she puts many remaining bouquets out at $10 apiece, with any purchase of $25 worth of flowers. Move quickly, though; these are usually gone by 5.

FOOD SHOPS

Quoting prices on fresh food is about as dependable as quoting politicians on *their* promises. Neither seems to keep very long. Many food costs are also subject to seasonal ups and downs. The prices mentioned in this chapter, like everything else in this book, are simply examples which should give you some idea of each store's general pricing.

However, it's worth noting that the shops below were all visited at the same time of year; because of this, you can certainly use these descriptions for comparison with each other.

Finally, remember that many of the foods listed under individual categories can also be found at stores in the "General Markets" section of this chapter.

BAKERIES

Entenmann's Bakery Outlet
- 1798 Bryant St. (17th St.), San Francisco; (415) 863-4773
- 264 South Spruce Ave. (El Camino Real), South San Francisco; (415) 761-2714

And other suburban locations
Here's a great way to save on those wonderful sweet treats. Each time Entenmann's puts fresh packages of its pastries on supermarket shelves all over The City, the unsold ones come off—and go instead to their outlets. These packages, though, have not yet reached their expiration date; they're perfectly good for a few more days, and here, they cost a lot less than in the supermarkets.

So, you'll find deals like an apple cinnamon twist danish, originally $3.89, here $1.89; same price for a box of chocolate chip cookies, even though they were meant to sell for $2.49. The stores also sell some prod-

ucts by other bakeries: Oroweat whole-grain breads for as little as 79¢ a loaf, Boboli pizzas from $1.25, and various snack foods. Open Mondays through Saturdays.

House of Bagels
- 5030 Geary Blvd. (14th Ave.), San Francisco; (415) 752-6000

People (usually transplanted Easterners) often lament that you can't get a decent bagel in California. This little Richmond discovery is worth a try, says Mr. C—a native Bostonian himself. It's a true, no-frills, bakery with a storefront counter; here, bagels aren't a fashion statement, they're bagels. And they're 50¢ each, or $5.75 for a dozen. Bialys are 55¢; crusty loaves of Polish-style corn rye bread are $1.75, and pumpernickle is $1.65. You can also find some pastries here, like marble cakes for $3.50. Plus a day-old shelf, where any of these that are leftover at the end of the day go on sale for half-price. Now, *that's* a bargain! It's not exactly the Lower East Side, but out here, it'll do nicely.

Italian French Baking Company of San Francisco

- 1501 Grant Ave. (Union St.), San Francisco; (415) 421-3796

The Italian French Baking Company holds court in the heart of North Beach, where they sell their delicious breads, rolls, muffins, and other homemade yummies. Pick up some homemade biscotti, in a variety of flavors, for $5.65 a pound—a remarkable price, when you consider that any cafe worth its latte sells these for at least a dollar *each*. Soft sourdough rolls are just 30¢ apiece, and whole wheat baguettes are just 85¢. Bags of broken grissini—you know, those ultra-long, ultra-skinny, ultra-chic breadsticks—are just $1.85 each. And, if you're in the area around breakfast time, stop in for a blueberry muffin. They're only $1.50 and they're so big, one may well last you straight through lunch!

The Italian French Baking Company is open Monday thru Saturday 7am-6pm, Sundays 7am-2:30pm.

Kilpatrick's Bakery Store

- 1990 Folsom St. (16th St.), San Francisco; (415) 986-5348

Kilpatrick's is a direct retail outlet from its bakery in the same building. Like the Entenmann's store (above), packaged breads and pastries which have come back from supermarkets—but haven't reached their expiration dates—can be purchased here at a fraction of their supermarket prices.

These may include things like Kilpatrick's English muffins, normally about $1.50 retail, selling here at three packages for $1.99. A two-pound bag of Rainbo sugar cookies goes for just $2.39.

Unlike Entenmann's, you can also find some fancier brands here. Country Hearth Honey Wheat Berry Loaf, which retails for $1.99, goes for 79¢ here (or three for $2.35). Same prices for French sourdough loaves from Earth Grains, normally $1.95 each.

The store accepts food stamps; it's

MR. CHEAP'S PICKS
Bakeries

✔ **Entenmann's Bakery Outlet**—You may not save calories, but you can save up to half the cost on these popular sweets at their store.

✔ **Italian French Baking Company of San Francisco**—North Beach source of great biscotti found in cafes all over The City—plus muffins, cookies, and bread.

open Monday through Saturday, from 9 a.m. to 6 p.m.

Your Black Muslim Bakery

- 5832 San Pablo Ave. (Stanford St.), Oakland; (510) 658-7080
- 365 17th St. (Webster St.), Oakland; (510) 839-1313
- 7200 Bancroft Ave. (73rd Ave.), Oakland; (510) 568-6024
- 3404 MacArthur Blvd. (35th Ave.), Oakland; (510) 531-1258
- 160 Eddy St. (Mason St.), San Francisco; (415) 929-7082
- 609 Cole St. (Haight St.), San Francisco; (415) 387-6384

You don't have to be black, or a Muslim, to shop at these bakeries, which specialize in all-natural breads and pastries. The San Pablo branch is the main bakery, but all of these shops are considered "outlets" for their goodies, which are also sold in stores all over California. Depending on the item, you can save a dollar or so by going directly to YBMB's outlets.

Try such delights as blueberry cheese pies, honey carrot cakes, carob cookies, and whole wheat breads. No preservatives or additives are used. Wherever you purchase them, a portion of the proceeds are donated to charity—for the creation of jobs, housing, and education. Store hours vary by location.

CHEESE

Castro Cheesery
- 427 Castro St. (Market St.), San Francisco; (415) 552-6676

If you've ever attended a movie at the Castro Theater, then you've probably noticed this tiny, yet bustling little storefront shop next door. Though there seems to be no place to put it all, the store actually sells hundreds of pounds of fresh cheese (and coffee beans) every week—all at below-retail prices.

The selection and prices are nothing less than amazing. A letter board over the refrigerator case runs to five columns of cheeses—there are twelve varieties of cheddar alone. You can find Italian reggiano parmesan for $9 a pound; some stores sell this for up to $12. French brie goes for $4.50 a pound; same price for Fontina. Jarlsberg starts as low as $3.98, and fresh mozzarella is just $1.45 a pound.

Sip a cappuccino and nibble biscotti in the store while you wait; you can also have stuff shipped anywhere in the country. This incredible shop is open seven days a week, including weeknights and Saturdays until 10 p.m. (Sundays until 8 p.m.)

Country Cheese Company
- 415 Divisadero St. (Fell St.), San Francisco; (415) 621-8130
- 2101 San Pablo Ave. (Addison St.), Berkeley; (510) 841-0752

This no-frills wholesale/retail operation offers bulk quantities (and prices) on many kinds of cheeses, as well as grains, nuts, and dried pastas. Get an eight-ounce package of smoked fresh mozzarella for $2.75; French brie for $4.25 a pound; Canadian cheddar for $3.69; or Gouda for $3.89.

Open barrels are filled with things like oat bran granola for $2.05 a pound, or naturally dried apples for $3.49 a pound; roasted sunflower seeds ($1.49), cashew nuts ($4.35), carob raisins ($2.69), yogurt almonds($3.59), pinto beans (69¢), and lots more.

Plus spinach fettucine for $1.15 a pound, as well as fresh baguettes, smoked meats and sausages...you get the idea. Now, go get the food. Open every day but Sunday, from 10 a.m. to 6 p.m.

COFFEE AND TEA

Castro Cheesery
- 427 Castro St. (Market St.), San Francisco; (415) 552-6676

From very humble beginnings, owner Ken Khoury has built up this tiny storefront next to the Castro Theater into a little dynamo. At first, Ken sold 900 pounds of coffee a month; he now sells 3,500 pounds *a week.* Talk about a caffeine rush. You can see them, in large sacks piled up against the wall—and right up to the ceiling. The prices are the clear reason why: Dozens of varieties are available here, starting under $3 a pound for three different grades of French Roast. Many others (including Sumatra, Zimbabwe Dark, Espresso Roast, "Morning Rush," and more) are just above that incredible

$3. Flavored beans, like Irish Cream and Hawaiian Kona Macadamia, as well as several types of Swiss water decafs, are all around $4 a pound. Flavored decafs top out the menu at $6. How can he do it? Volume!

Similar bargains in cheese abound here as well (see listing above). Sip a cappuccino and nibble biscotti in the store while you wait; you can also have stuff shipped anywhere in the country. This incredible shop is open seven days a week, including weeknights and Saturdays until 10 p.m. (Sundays until 8 p.m.)

Peerless Coffee Company
- 260 Oak St. (Third St.), Oakland; (510) 763-1763

Is this coffee truly without peer? Perhaps not as much in these caffeine-crazed days as it was in 1924, when the company was founded by an eastern European immigrant. Still, any doubts will be washed away by the delicious aroma that greets you as soon as you enter the small shop at the front of the Peerless factory along Oakland's Embarcadero.

In fact, you can watch the beans being roasted through the windows behind the cash register. In the shop, you can sip any of several varieties, brewed up fresh and served for 75¢ per 12-ounce cup. The prices for these beans are not all the lowest around, but many are quite reasonable, starting at $4.95 a pound for the Columbian Cafe Blend. Several are priced around $5.50, including Brazilian Fancy, French Roast, Viennese Blend, and New Orleans Blend (flavored with chicory).

If you're very budget-minded, many of these are available in two-ounce vacuum-sealed packs for just 99¢ each—a great way to try out new flavors without being wasteful.

Peerless also sells loose teas from all over the world, starting at $1.45 per half-pound for Broken Leaf Black. Many others fall into the $2-$4 range. And they also load peanuts into those roasters, turning out fresh warm peanuts for just $1.99 a pound.

Meanwhile, if you desire, you can also buy other specialty items here, from cheeses to preserves to chocolates—plus coffee makers, tea infusers, Melitta filters, and a wealth of Peerless logo items from mugs to shirts. These, of course, are not so cheap.

San Francisco Herb Company
• 250 Fourteenth St. (Mission St.), San Francisco; (415) 861-3018

Cooking fans, take note! Here's your one-stop bargain spot for every kind of spice under the sun. Primarily a mail-order company, this tiny store

GENERAL MARKETS

Canned Foods Grocery Outlet
• 1717 Harrison Ave. (14th St.), San Francisco; (415) 552-9680

MR. CHEAP'S PICKS
Coffee and Tea

✔ **Castro Cheesery**—Talk about a caffeine rush. This tiny storefront moves 3,500 pounds of beans *a week*! Could it be due to prices starting under $3 a pound?

✔ **San Francisco Herb Company**—National mail-order business, run from a house in the Mission. Soothing prices on all kinds of loose teas.

---

packs a world of spices into its barrels and shelves, all at bulk prices. Most are sold in one-pound bags; these include three-inch cinnamon sticks for $3.85, garlic granules for $3.45, and nutmeg for $2.75.

SFHC also makes up its own blends of things like curry powder, barbecue spices, taco seasoning, and more. Plus a wide variety of potpourri blends, for as little as 25¢ and 50¢ a bag. Special blends in both of these categories are made for the holidays; whether you're looking to put something in your stocking or in your cider, this is the place.

Finally, speaking of hot drinks, there are the store's "Tasty Teas." From plain ol' Chinese black tea ($2.50/lb.) to English Breakfast ($4.25/lb.) and Jamaican Rum Royal ($5.90/lb.), there are enough familiar and unusual flavors to keep you coming back for more. Check out the "15% Off" table for extra deals. The store is open weekdays from 10 a.m. to 4 p.m. only.

• 2000 Fifth St. (University Ave.), Berkeley; (510) 845-1771

The Canned Foods Grocery Outlet

looks like any other supermarket—but there's a big difference. They grab up inventory imbalances, dented packages, discontinued items and more, selling them to you at huge discounts. Maybe some bread is close to (but not past) its freshness expiration date. Maybe a manufacturer has changed its packaging, and wants to sell off the old style; it could simply be a new color on the label. The store also has a lot of bulk-size quantities, always a money-saver. Of course, you should exercise some care as you look at these items, but it's all above-board—often at fantastic savings.

Among the shelves, Mr. C found things like Kellogg's stuffing mix—regularly $1.39 a box—here, two for a dollar. Kellogg's Corn Pops cereal, normally $4.09, was seen for $2.69; and Kraft grated Parmesan cheese, regularly $2.99, was just $1.99. Sara Lee gourmet English muffins were close to their expiration date, but still perfectly good, and a bargain at 99¢. A six-pack of Coke, in 8-ounce glass bottles decorated with Santa for a Christmas promotion, were $3.99 during Yule—and just $1.99 here a month later.

If you have room to store bulk items, you'll be in luck here. Big families may be able to use a six-pound restaurant size can of La Choy bean sprouts for $1.89; perhaps more realistic, a gallon of olive oil imported from Italy, originally $12.99, was just $8.99.

You will find a small selection of packaged meats, like Louis Rich Polska Kielbasa, $2.99 elsewhere, here $1.69. They also have a section of California wines—call it "factory-direct"—most of which are $2.99. These have retail values of up to $7.99 and more. Health and beauty aids are another big draw here; Mr. C found ten-ounce bottles of Permasoft shampoo and conditioner, regularly $2.99, selling for 99¢ and Revlon Flex & Go shampoo, regularly $2.59, for $1.49. Open seven days a week.

CGF Cash and Carry

- 455 Toland St. (Oakdale Ave.), San Francisco; (415) 285-9333

If you don't mind the rumble of trucks and the bumpy streets of this industrial area, you can shop at this wholesale food supplier just like the grocery store owners do. It also helps, of course, if you can use industrial sizes, like soda by the case. If so, you'll certainly enjoy taking the Pepsi challenge when Coke and Pepsi are just $5.89 for 24 cans. Why, that's just a quarter a pop (sorry about the pun). If you do a lot of cooking, you may be able to use a three-liter can of extra virgin olive oil, for an incredible $11.19. Similar deals abound on canned goods, packaged breads, cheeses, and meats, as well as paper supplies. Definitely a good place to shop for a big party! CGF is open seven days a week.

Rainbow Grocery

See listing under "Health Food and Vitamins," below.

San Francisco Farmers' Market

- 100 Alemany Blvd. (Crescent Ave.), San Francisco; (415) 647-9423

Since 1943, this has been The City's largest and most constant farmers' market, offering the general public a chance to shop at "direct from the farm" prices. Even now, in the shadows of Freeways 101 and 280, this is a bit of the old world style of selling. Nearly two hundred dealers (less during winter months, of course) set up shop in the semi-enclosed structures here, selling fruits, vegetables, nuts, honey, and some prepared foods.

During the summer, the market operates from Tuesdays through Saturdays, dawn to dusk; in winter, Saturdays are really the only days with any activity. Given this informality, Mr. C suggests you call ahead to find out the current schedule.

Smart & Final

- 170 South Van Ness Ave. (13th St.), San Franciso; (415) 864-8240
- 355 Bayshore Blvd. (Army St.), San Francisco; (415) 642-0499

- 1941 San Pablo Ave. (Hearst Ave.), San Francisco; (415) 649-2381

The name of the game at Smart & Final is: BULK. And you're sure to bulk up just carrying some of these packages to your car. Almost everything here is sold in massive quantities; but is why the savings are tremendous. For those who have large families, or if you're having a big party, this place is perfect. Pick up picante sauce by the gallon for $6.69, add five pounds of tortilla chips for $3.99, and invite everyone you've ever met over to the house.

You can keep an army of rug rats happy with two pounds of Krispy crackers for $2.49, or two pounds of potato chips for $3.49. Many of the perishable items, including meats, poultry and fish, are frozen; so if you have a large freezer they make great deals. Non-perishable items are always a good bet; you can get your mornings going for months with a 100-envelope package of Maxwell House instant coffee for $8.09. Do the math: That's eight cents a cup.

Even more than most supermarkets, S & F offers lots of ways to clean up on household cleaning supplies and paper products. Pick up a gallon of Mr. Clean for $9.49 or four 25-ounce cans of Comet for $2.95. What you wipe it all up with? Why, six rolls of Brawny paper towels for

---

MR. CHEAP'S PICKS
General Markets

- ✔ **Canned Foods Grocery Outlet**—If you don't mind dented cans or outdated packages, this supermarket will save you lots of dough.
- ✔ **Rainbow Grocery**—Classic earthy market in the Mission, filled with organic foods and all-natural health products at bargain rates.
- ✔ **Smart & Final**—Bulk is the name of the game here. If you have a huge freezer or lots of storage space, here's the place to stock up.

$4.79, of course.

Some of the stuff at Smart & Final is just too big for most average shoppers; many items are sold in institutional sizes. But then, these are definite bargains, especially for those who have lots of storage space—like an extra garage. Just something to think about. Stores are open seven days a week.

HEALTH FOOD AND VITAMINS

Rainbow Grocery
- 1899 Mission St. (15th St.), San Francisco; (415) 863-0620

This is the kind of place people mean when they talk about, like, classic California-style shopping, y'know? Walk into the Rainbow Grocery, and it's like a time warp back to the 1960s. Folks in Birkenstocks and tie-dyes wander around, browsing bulk food bins, organic fruits, and all-natural hair care products. In many parts of the country, this has come to be fashionable (and expensive); not under the Rainbow.

Here, you can find dairy-free To-

futti frozen snacks, as low as $1.99 a pint; fresh pecans for $4.99 a pound; organically grown oranges, 49¢ a pound; bulk dried pastas from 80¢ a pound; and extra virgin olive oil for $4.49 a pound. Plus weekly savings on an ever-changing variety of premium brands, like R.W. Knudsen, Arrowhead Mills, Hain, and more.

Other bulk goodies range from coffee to sun-dried tomatoes, not to mention beans, rices, and spring water. Bring your own recycled containers, or purchase them in the store. Even on fancy items like these, this system can save you lots of money.

Inside the "General Store" section, you can take the same approach to all sorts of cosmetics, household cleaning products, vitamins, herbs, and books. For just 20¢ per liquid ounce, you can get 100% real aloe gel, Jason biotin shampoo, or Naturade hand lotion; for 10¢ an ounce, try a jug of Granny's Old Fashioned Laundry Liquid (in your wash, that is). Of course, you'll find many of the same products in the traditional pre-packaged method; for example, Mr. C found a 17-ounce container of Jason jojoba shampoo for $4.

Rainbow Grocery is open seven days a week until 8:30 p.m.

Vitamin Express
- 1425 Irving St. (15th Ave.), San Francisco; (415) 564-8160
- 1400 Shattuck Ave. (Rose), Berkeley; (510) 841-1798

Health-food fans who don't already know about these shops will want to check them out for all their supplemental needs. Vitamins are all they sell here—which by no means limits the stock! There's a wide variety of compounds, strengths, and name brands to choose from, all at discounted prices.

Recently on sale were such goodies as GAIA Golden Seal Echinacea, reduced from $9.50 for a one-ounce size to $6.85; ThermoGenics supplements, in the 60-capsule bottle, ten dollars off retail at $19.95; Alacer "Emergen-C", marked down from $12.65 to $7.50; and New Chapter "Everywoman" supplements, 180 tablets, slimmed down from a whopping $53.15 per bottle to $36.95.

The Sunset store is closed on Sundays; the Berkeley store is open seven days a week.

MEAT AND FISH

Golden Bay Seafood Center
- 125 Hickey Blvd. (El Camino Real), South San Francisco; (415) 991-9298

This large store, in a suburban shopping center, seems to have been transplanted directly from Chinatown. Talk about a fish out of water....Anyway, they have a vast selection of fresh seafood at rock-bottom prices. Live crabs, bouncing around in a tank, are just $2.49 a pound; live oysters go for 49¢ each. Jumbo white shrimp were recently caught for $4.99 a pound, while red snapper were $1.69. Sea bass and halibut steaks were each $3.99 a pound; there are also more exotic fin finds, like Ecuador pompano.

Meanwhile, this is actually a full supermarket—with an Asian flavor, of course. Next to the seafood counter, a nice array of fresh meats are available at similarly low prices. Meaty pork ribs may go for as little as $1.79 a pound; several grades of ground beef start from just 99¢ a pound, and chicken leg/thigh pieces from 59¢ a pound.

And, along with basic produce and packaged foods, you can find exotic goods like teas, ginger candy, Oriental fish sauces, sacks of rice, and more. Open seven days a week, including evenings until 8.

Lo-Cost Market
- 498 Haight St. (Fillmore St.), San Francisco; (415) 621-4338

This Asian market specializes in meats and seafood, all of which look fresh and wonderful. It's a cash-only, low-rent kind of operation, which is what helps keep the prices low; here, you may find red snapper for $1.50 a pound, or frozen crabmeat for $1.99; boneless short ribs for $2.49 a pound, top sirloin steak for $3 a pound, plus many other cuts of beef, lamb, pork, and veal. There are usually a few other items as well, such as a dozen eggs for 99 cents.

Nikko Fish
- 699 Illinois St. (18th St.), San Francisco; (415) 864-5261

Mr. C has covered the waterfront, searching for fresh fish bargains right off the pier; at Pier 66, he caught a live one. Nikko Fish, also known as the "Fish Club," you may find fresh bay scallops for $5.95 a pound, live or cooked crab for $2.95 a pound, or salmon steaks for $6.95 a pound. There are even more exotic varieties, such as mahi mahi and jumbo tiger shrimp, as well as local halibut, and more. Nothing is ever frozen; it's all fresh as the new day.

Become a member, and you'll receive further discounts, like coupons for future purchases. And do ask for your free fish recipes, available with any purchase. Open Monday through Saturday until 6:15 p.m.

Spenger's Fish Grotto
- 1919 Fourth St. (University Ave.), Berkeley; (510) 845-7771

Part of a sprawling restaurant and store complex right next to the University offramp from I-880, Spenger's is a well-known landmark for anyone who shops the Berkeley outlets. Step inside this turn-of-the-century wooden structure, and you'll find fresh seafood at good, if not al-

---

MR. CHEAP'S PICK
Meat and Fish

✔ **Golden Bay Seafood Center**—Worth a trip to South San Francisco for low prices on both meat and fish.

---

ways spectacular, prices. You may find mussels for $2.25 a pound, smoked salmon for $3.50, or salmon steaks for $5.75. Baby shrimp go for as little as $4.50 a pound.

You can also get Spenger's house blends of seafood sauces, as well as prepared foods to go—including fried clams, chowder, catfish "burgers", and fish 'n chips. Open seven days a week, from 6 a.m. (for breakfast) until 10 p.m.

PASTA

Lucca Ravioli
- 1100 Valencia St. (22nd St.), San Francisco; (415) 647-5581

From its headquarters in the Mission, the Lucca family sells its own varieties of pastas right on the premises—leading to incredible deals on incredible homemade foods. Pick up a box of 54 (yes, 54) frozen cheese or spinach ravioli for just $3.75; it'll keep you going for days. Or, for purists who won't even allow their pasta to be frozen, try fresh egg pasta for $1.99 a pound—or garlic basil pasta for $2.59. You can't do better unless

you make it yourself.

Lucca also makes fresh focaccia bread; get a half-sheet, topped with diced tomatoes, for $2.75. And their sweet anise sausage is just $2.98 a pound. They also carry all kinds of imported specialty goods, like Havarti cheese ($3.98 a pound), extra virgin olive oil ($3.98 for a 17-ounce container), Italian table wines, and those wonderful Amaretti di Saronno cookies. The tiny store tends to be as crowded with customers as with food; it's open Monday through Sunday from 9 a.m. to 6 p.m.

PRODUCE

Berkeley Farmers' Market
- Various locations, Berkeley; (510) 548-3333

Berkeley is blessed with several city-run farmers' markets, bringing you fresh produce at direct-from-the-

growers prices. The sites vary just as the merchandise does, by season. The main location is at the junction of Center Street and Martin Luther King, Jr. Way, held from 10 a.m. to 2 p.m. every Saturday through the year.

MR. CHEAP'S PICK
Produce

✔ **United Nations Plaza Farmers' Market**—A veritable bazaar of fruit, vegetables, nuts, and more. Merchants fill the plaza, selling their wares at dirt-cheap prices.

In addition, a market is also held at the intersection of MLK and Derby Street; it takes place from 2-7 p.m. on Tuesdays during the summer months, and from 1 p.m. to dusk during the winter. Finally, another market can be found on Haste Street, between Telegraph Avenue and Bowditch Street, from 11 a.m. to 3 p.m. every Sunday from May to November.

El Chico Produce Market
• 2214 Clement St. (23rd Ave.), San Francisco; (415) 752-7372

The Richmond, that ethnic melting pot, is laced with great fruit and vegetable stores like this one. Prices vary with the seasons, but you're sure to find good deals like flats of twenty jumbo eggs for $1.89, oranges for 18¢ a pound, Romaine lettuce for 49¢ a head, five pounds of sweet potatoes for a dollar, and more—on apples, bananas, mushrooms, sacks of rice, bok choy, tofu, etc. Open every day, into the evening.

Another similar shop nearby is the **18th and Geary Produce Market** at 5350 Geary Blvd., telephone (415) 751-1177. Or, wander around the neighborhood; you're sure to stumble upon another one.

Old Oakland Farmers' Market
• Broadway and Ninth St., Oakland; (510) 452-3276

Every Friday, all year long, this block of downtown Oakland is transformed into an open-air marketplace. Over sixty vendors gather to sell not only fresh fruits and vegetables, but also flowers, organic foods, and even prepared foods—many of which you can sample before buying.

There are lots of arts and crafts too, making this a fun outing for the family. The market runs from 8 a.m. to 2 p.m., each Friday.

Parkside Farmers' Market
• 555 Taraval St. (16th Ave.), San Francisco; (415) 681-5563

Not an outdoor farmers' market, this is actually another one of those great neighborhood produce shops like those in the Richmond; this one, obviously, is in the Parkside. Again, prices are ever-fluctuating, but you may nab seven pounds of navel oranges for a buck, or four pounds of white zucchini for that same dollar. Bet you didn't even know there *was* such a a thing as white zucchini.

In fact, Parkside has lots of exotic produce, including things like sun-dried organic walnuts, pommelos, and a variety of Middle Eastern spices. Plus a limited selection of fresh coffee beans for $4.99 a pound. Open seven days a week.

United Nations Plaza Farmers' Market
• Market St. (bet. Seventh St. and Eighth St.), San Francisco; no phone

Every Wednesday and Sunday from 7 a.m. to 5 p.m. in the Civic Center, the United Nations Plaza turns into one huge farmer's market. Here, you can find fruits, vegetables, nuts, plants, honey, and more, being sold at from-the-grower-to-you prices. Take your time strolling through; with so many vendors, price comparison is a breeze. Mr. C saw some amazing values, including sweet oranges at 50¢ a pound, or three pounds for a dollar; cabbage, five pounds for $1; kiwi fruit, two pounds for $1.25; huge carrots, four pounds for $1. At any time you might see stands selling dried fruits, bonsai trees, eggs, and even fish. Mostly, you'll see lots of fresh produce at really great prices. Talk about international flavor!

FURNITURE

This chapter combines stores selling furniture for the home as well as for the office. Many major retailers operate clearance centers, where you can find leftovers and slightly-damaged models at drastic savings—if you're patient.

A caveat to the cash-conscious: Be very careful when you're shopping for any leather products. The quality of leather used in making sofas can vary widely, and this can determine how durable your sofa will be in the long run. If you see lots of very obvious flaws in the grain of the leather, think twice before buying.

HOME FURNITURE AND BEDS

Ambiente International Furniture
● 390 Kansas St. (17th St.), San Francisco; (415) 863-9700

Ambiente specializes in modern-styled furniture for the living room, home office, dining room, and bedroom. Whether your taste runs to "Techline" modular desks or maple-frame beds "inspired by the designs of Frank Lloyd Wright," you'll find lots to choose from here at good prices. Join their mailing list (by purchasing something, of course), and you'll get early notification of special sales with even better savings.

One recent clearance sale featured such goodies as a mahogany bookcase for $199 ($50 off); Japanese-styled dining chairs reduced from $129 to a closeout price of $29; a burgundy-colored leather sofa reduced by $300 to $1,399; and a marble-top "bistro" table for just $69. Many of these were one-of-a-kind pieces, but the sale offered lots to choose from at up to 75% discounts. The store is open seven days a week.

American Mattress and Furniture
● 300 Jefferson St. (Third St.), Oakland; (510) 444-1990

AMF is one of the Bay Area's largest independent mattress stores; from this one shop, owner Ted Matthews sells brand-new furnishings for the living room and bedroom at insider prices. This includes current models from Simmons, Serta, Stratolounger, and more—for which he is an authorized dealer and clearance center. Some items here are seasonal closeouts; many are one-of-a-kind pieces. Ted keeps the prices low by running the place himself, by using his contacts, and by not advertising. And, since he and his staff don't work on commission, you can get honest deals with a minimum of sales hassle.

During Mr. C's visit, he saw a Simmons loveseat/sofabed; a floor demo model, it was marked down from a list price of $639 to just $399. A plush leather Stratolounger chair was reduced from $999 to $549, and still available in several colors. In fact, on many of the newer items, you can get discount prices even with specially-ordered fabrics.

Toward the rear of the large showroom, you'll find the bedding area. Mr. C saw a whole row of Simmons Beautyrest closeouts; the full-size "Royalty" set, with a 15-year warranty, was $420—about 40% below department store prices. A queen-size Beautyrest set—factory seconds, merely because of mismatched fabrics—was an incredible $299 complete. Once you put the sheets on, who will know?

You get the idea. Come on in, have a cup of coffee, and check out the bargains—*these* certainly won't lose you any sleep. The store is open seven days a week.

Angelus Furniture Warehouse

• 55 Fourth St. (Oak St.), Oakland; (510) 268-0265

Along Oakland's waterfront shopping outlet area (did you even know they have one?), Angelus is a goldmine of contemporary furniture bargains for the living room, dining room, and bedroom. It's a 15,000-square foot warehouse filled with big names like Bernhardt, Stearns and Foster, Bassett, Lexington, and many others. The out-of-the-way location means low overhead and low prices, on first-quality furniture in the latest styles.

A Highland House sofa, for example, with a list price of $1,700, could be gotten here for $1,169—except that, when Mr. C found it, it was on sale for $999. And you can order it in your choice of fabric. A Stanley five-piece dinette set of solid maple, seen for $1,599 at a certain department store, was only $1,369 at Angelus; the chairs were slightly different, but the name and quality were the same.

The store sometimes gets samples and closeouts directly from manufacturers. Mr. C was shown a gorgeous sofa with a retail price of $3,299. It had been ordered for someone at a department store, but shipped in the wrong fabric; and so, here it was, for only $1,999—literally, at cost. In a similar deal, a Bassett oak bed frame was not $1,165, but $549.

"We're trying to save money for people who can spend a bit on really nice merchandise," says Micki Turner, one of the folks who's been running this store for over ten years. She clearly knows what she's doing; this is one of the most stylish warehouses you'll ever see. Open Wednesday through Sunday only, from 10 a.m. to 5:30 p.m.

Beds and Bedding

• 5036 Geary Blvd. (14th Ave.), San Francisco; (415) 387-1684

Here's a smart idea: A bed shop located in a charming woodframe Victorian house in the Richmond. Makes you comfy the minute you walk in. So does the friendly, laid-back staff.

B & B (another pun!) sells high-quality mattresses and frames only; but they have something for every budget, from student-level on up to fancy fashions. The house specialty is the Restonic brand, one of the nation's fastest-growing; yet, being less famous than its competitors, prices are lower. And they make just as many grades of firmness as the other major brands.

You can save on other varieties of bedding here, too. Get a complete waterbed set for as little as $239; these include a 14-year warranty. And futon mattresses begin as low as $180, complete with basic pine frames. Low service rates on delivery and assembly as well, if you wish them. Beds and Bedding is open seven days a week.

Bob's Discount Wood Furniture

• 2078 San Pablo Ave. (University Ave.), Berkeley; (510) 848-6662

Bob's Discount Wood Furniture has carved a niche for itself (sorry, couldn't resist) as "The Bookcase Specialist." Bob certainly has plenty of them, in a range of prices, from very cheap particle board models to custom-made cases in solid oak, pine, and alder.

The back of the store is their "economy section," which is filled mostly with bookcases and other furnishings made from particle board. These are cheap, in both price *and* quality, but they may be perfect for a dorm room or first apartment. Depending on size, these cases range in price from $14 to $24, and you can add drawers to some for about $6.50 to $8 per drawer. You'll also find desks and tables; a 30" particle board table is $33, and a free-standing desk is $40.

Of better quality, yet still inexpensive, are the pieces in unfinished solid pine. A bookcase of this material costs $96 for a 36" x 60" model, while a 24" x 24" one goes for $49. If you'd like something a little nicer, but can't quite afford solid wood, go with a veneer. They have some beautiful oak veneer bookcases for as low as $76, for an 18" x 24" model.

Meanwhile, if you *can* afford a little more, this is a good place for custom-built furnishings—the kind of pieces that can become family heirlooms. A solid oak hutch will cost about $960, but it will last a lifetime, and then some. A dining table in solid pine, oak, or alder was only $275, very reasonable indeed. Bob occasionally sells floor samples at a discount. A corner bookcase that had been a floor sample was selling for $100, as is; it did have a few scuffs, but it was still in great condition and definitely a bargain. Open seven days a week.

Busvan for Bargains
- 244 Clement St. (Fourth Ave.), San Francisco; (415) 752-5353
- 900 Battery St. (Broadway), San Francisco; (415) 981-1405

If you've ever shopped for inexpensive furniture, you probably know something about Busvan for Bargains. After all, this quirky but comprehensive dealer has been around since 1946. Much of the stock is comprised of manufacturers' closeouts from all over the country, for which this store is a sort of clearance outlet. If you've never ventured in, give it a shot—and prepare to be overwhelmed.

The Richmond location, in particular, is gigantic; it actually takes up seven storefronts, or most of its block of Clement. Room leads to room leads to room, each loaded with a different type of furniture (couches, dinette sets, armoires...). Plus a mezzanine level which winds around, overlooking the main floor, as well as a clearance section in the basement. Whew!

B for B sells a wide range of quality, too. Famous makers are mixed in with no-name budget brands—many

of which may be perfectly acceptable if, for example, you're setting up your first apartment. Wandering around this maze, you may encounter things like a striped cloth sofa and matching loveseat for $499.50 combined; an assembly-required five-drawer chest, in a white laminate finish, for $90; or a solid maple kitchen table with white ceramic tile inlays, plus four maple chairs, reduced from $489 to $369. Even Oriental rugs range from synthetic throw rugs at $19 right on up to full-size wool blends for $500.

Fashions on the big-ticket pieces include both contemporary and traditional. All of the accessories to go beside them are here too, like halogen torch lamps (from $30) and Japanese folding *shoji* screens (marked down from $79 to $59). Office furniture is well stocked, with lots of computer desk units and ergonomic chairs. Moving up in style, an Edwardian-style genuine leather banker's chair, orignally $899, was seen for $499.

Along with bedroom sets, there is a decent selection of mattresses; most of these are closeouts, complete with full manufacturer's warranties. A recent sale featured deals on Sealy sets, beginning as low as $199.50 for a "Classic Rest" twin-size set. High-end "Medalist Posturepedic" sets ranged from $399.50 twin to $799.50 king.

Five-piece bedroom furniture ensembles to go with these, meanwhile, were seen for as little as $350 (in fake wood with laminated veneer). Also on sale was a six-foot futon sofa, with a black metal frame and a basic 7' futon mattress, reduced from a list price of $350 to just $199.50. Lots of furnishings for kids rooms, too.

The "Bargain Basement" area offers floor samples, scratched pieces, and other leftovers at further reductions. Among the items worth mentioning, Mr. C saw a smoked glass console/table for $99.50; a white-finish writing desk for $39; and a cherry and brass coat tree, reduced from $70 to $30. These, of course, are sold "as is."

Both stores are open from 9:30 a.m. to 6:00 p.m., Mondays through Saturdays, and from noon to six on Sundays. The downtown store offers validated parking on weekdays. Layaway and 90-day no-interest charges are available; all sales are final.

Butler Furniture
- 814 Clement St. (Ninth Ave.), San Francisco; (415) 387-7550

This craftsman's shop and store in the Richmond district specializes in custom ordered furniture, mostly of solid oak or pine. These can be sold untreated, or given a natural, hand-rubbed finish. It's a no-frills, all-business kind of shop; furniture is stacked up everywhere, representing Butler's 100 styles and configurations of dressers, bookcases, and tables. Sketches of further patterns are taped onto the walls.

You can get a 30" x 48" farmhouse-style finished dinette table, with four Windsor chairs, for $199; a ten-drawer double dresser for $350; or a tall, narrow, seven-drawer lingerie chest for $69. At the same price, Mr. C noticed a handsome hardwood rocking chair. An oak bookcase, five feet tall and two feet wide, sells for $99; in pine, it goes for $49.

Some items are reproductions of styles from the past (cheap antiques?), such as an 1890s "jelly cupboard" hutch. The cabinet's doors are fitted with punched tin panels, as was the look back then. This was selling here for $250; the genuine article, if you could find one, would doubtless cost two or three times as much!

Like everything in the store, these are made to order, with a waiting period of ten to twenty days for most items. Butler's is closed on Sundays.

Cottage Table Company
- 550 18th St. (Illinois St.), San Francisco; (415) 957-1760

If you want to save money, you've got to go to the source. All the way down near the waterfront on 18th Street, this unassuming building consists of two rooms. In one room, they make tables; in the other room, they sell them. Can't get more "factory-direct" than that.

Now, these aren't just *any* tables. These are simple, gorgeous wooden tables that are elegantly stylish, yet would look right at home in a 19th century farmhouse. They are made from solid maple, ash, cherry, walnut, and other woods, including rare, exotic woods like bubinga. They are hand-rubbed and finished with up to four coats of polyurethane, but so lightly that the tops are durable without looking plastic-coated. And, although there are a dozen examples to look at, your purchase is made to order and may well be unique.

Owner Tony Cowan is not from Ireland, but he began his business there over a decade ago; now, he's got shops both here and over there. He and his crew are true artisans, creating large-surface tables from basic to ornate. There's really no textbook name for his style—it's evolved over the years, with diverse elements mixing together based upon his whims and customers' requests. Want an oval top instead of a rectangle? Like the legs tapered? Need a drawer built into the side? Choose the wood, the size, and the features—and Tony will construct it for you in six to eight weeks. Not only do you get a good deal on a custom order, but your name and the date of your purchase will be stamped into the underside for future generations to see.

Yes, you can save a lot of money by buying at Cottage, but these creations are not exactly cheap, in price or quality. Standard prices start around $1,200, going up to about $5,000. Ah, but think of how much more they would cost in some fashionable boutique! A $2,000 table here is comparable to one costing as much as $8,000 elsewhere—*and* it'll be made to your specifications. Tony must be doing something right; the walls of his office are lined with personal letters from delighted customers. The showroom is open Monday through Saturday, from 1-5 p.m. only, with free parking on the premises.

Country Living
- 1033 Clement St. (12th Ave.), San Francisco; (415) 751-1276

A few blocks down from Butler (above), Country Living—as its name suggests—also features furniture for the natural, wholesome crowd, but in a wider variety of fashions. It's all solid wood, strong and sturdy; the styles range from your basic unfinished pine to fancy oak pieces. Prices are competitive, as marked; however, the clerk told Mr. C that just about everything here is always discounted by another 10% to 15% off the tag. Sort of like an unofficial, continuous sale. Why not just tag 'em with those lower prices in the first place? Who knows.

Anyway, a good prowl around the shop's two large floors could definitely land you good deals on pieces that can become family heirlooms. Things like a solid oak dining table with two center leaves (extending to a total length of eight feet), listed at $895, but selling for $699; or a walnut coffee table, with oak "herringbone" inlay, for $225.

Those raw pine bookcases come in lots of sizes and shapes. A 29" high by 24" wide, three-shelf model goes for $50. A completely finished pine rolltop desk, meanwhile, is quite handsome at $450. Mr. C also saw a solid pine bunk bed for $189.95. Open seven days, with a young, friendly staff to serve you.

Discount Depot
- 520 Haight St. (Steiner St.), San Francisco; (415) 552-1474
- 2020 San Pablo Ave. (University St.), Berkeley; (510) 549-1478

Discount Depot has some of the best prices around on futons, mattresses, furniture, and linens. They claim to have the lowest rates on the Serta Perfect Sleeper, saying that department stores charge about twice as much. Their price, for the mattress and box spring, is $599 full or $699 queen. They also offer to beat any competitor's price, no matter what it may be, on anything they carry.

Futon frames, each with a six-inch

MR. CHEAP'S PICKS
Home Furniture and Beds

- ✔ **American Mattress and Furniture**—Closeout and current deals on basics for living room and bedroom.
- ✔ **Angelus Furniture**—15,000 square foot Oakland warehouse filled with current lines of high-fashion furniture, well below department store prices.
- ✔ **Busvan for Bargains**—Seven storefronts strung together in the Richmond (downtown, too), jam-packed with good, cheap stuff for the younger crowd.
- ✔ **Macy's Furniture Clearance Center**—The name says it all, no?
- ✔ **Manor House Associates**—Fancy furniture, including lots of country and European styles, all half-price.
- ✔ **Vogue Interiors**—The latest lines in contemporary fashions for the home, at contractor's rates to the public.

---

thick futon, sell for $259 twin, $279 full, and $299 queen (an okay deal at the small end, great at the big end). Add linens, like towels, pillows, futon covers, sheets, and more: Duvet covers sell for $29 twin, $39 full and queen, and $49 king. Basic kitchen tables were selling for just $129 (or $199 with four upholstered chairs). You'll also find a small selection of unfinished pine furniture, like student desks for $129.

Miscellaneous pieces include things like adjustable bookshelves in black or white laminate for $59; a three-panel shoji screen for $69; and occasional clearance items, like 24-inch stools for $24.95. Most of the merchandise is made in California.

The sales staff is very laid-back, with no high-pressure selling; but they have plenty of information if you need assistance. Hours are from 11 a.m. to 7 p.m. weekdays, and from 10 a.m. to 6 p.m. on weekends.

Furniture Express Outlet
- 667 Folsom St. (Third St.), San Francisco; (415) 495-2848

In the summer of '92, Bob McCullough took his department store experience and opened up his own shop. Beginning small, but making use of his furn biz contacts, he's steadily built up what has become a major store with a vast inventory of home furnishings which can truly be described as "good and cheap." That means, in most cases, pieces of the assemble-it-yourself variety, but trendy and high-quality ones. Still, nothing is priced over $300.

An ultra-modern executive's desk, made only of heavy black metal wire with a glass top, redefines the word minimal; so does its price, at $150. You'll certainly never have any trouble moving it around. Adjustable shelving by Professional's Choice (more Euro-techno-style) is sold in sets priced from $80-$100; in specialty shops, the same products can cost $30 to $50 more.

For the home, you may find things like a solid pine storage trunk (of unfinished wood) for just $79.99; or a 36" X 60" dinette table of solid beechwood for $99, with matching Windsor chairs at $30 apiece. There are lots of Scandinavian-style bedroom and living room items, in that bright white laminated finish (no pun intended), such as an eight-level tower bookshelf for $50. Plus computer and television stands, CD racks from $20, microwave carts, and more. Lots of quickie convenience things, like those brightly colored fabric-and-foam "chairs" that fold out into a narrow futon mattress.

Delivery and assembly services are available, for a fee; otherwise, they'll help you load up your car. The store continues to grow and add new lines, plainly geared toward the city's young, yuppie apartment dwellers. Meanwhile, McCullough's SoMa location keeps overhead costs (thus, his prices) easily within most anyone's reach. Open seven days a week.

The Futon Shop
- 1011 25th St. (Tennessee St.), San Francisco; (415) 920-6801
- 810 Van Ness Ave. (Eddy St.), San Francisco; (415) 563-8866
- 3545 Geary Blvd. (Stanyan St.), San Francisco; (415) 752-9908
  And other suburban locations

The Potrero branch of this popular chain, near the Army Street Terminal, is in fact the main factory and national headquarters. Thus, in addition to good discounts on a wide variety of futons and frames, you can also save even more by checking out the floor samples and demo models on sale here.

On Mr. C's visit, these included a double-length couch frame in Mission-style solid teak wood for just $250; a "Sonoma" oak armchair for $185; and a full-size "Brazilia" maple tri-fold frame for $150. A double-size "Oregon" couch/bed, in black lacquered oak, was reduced from $675 to a mere $330, with just a scratch or two.

Meanwhile, you can add high-quality futon mattresses for as little as $92 in twin-size, up to $190 king-size, in the "economy" grade; and you can go on to the "super deluxe" grade, made with 18 layers of cotton, for just about $20 more per size. All of these futons are made with 100% cotton, and all of these prices reflect a 40% savings off the suggested retail prices. That should help you rest easier. The top-grade double-size futon, for instance, has a list price of $264; at any Futon Shop, you can get it for $159.

The main store also sells reduced-price accessories, like designer futon covers in attractive floral prints (full-size, $35.95), as well as decorative throw pillows for $5 apiece.

Save a few extra bucks by picking the merchandise up yourself; the folks here will help load it onto your car. If you prefer, delivery is available for a reasonable fee. All stores are open seven days a week.

Giorgi Brothers
• 212 Baden Ave. (Linden Ave.), South San Francisco; (415) 588-4621

For over sixty years, this big-time furniture dealer has been a Peninsula landmark. In their closeout center, directly across the street from their main showroom, two floors are filled with bargains on name-brand items for every room in the house.

These are samples, floor models, and leftovers, mostly in traditional styles; many offer good prices on very fancy looks indeed. You may find a Century oak dining table—with a chevron inlay top—and eight highback chairs, selling for $1,295 complete; originally, the chairs alone had been $1,640, and the table $699. Or a Berkline sofa with built-in "Wall-away" recliners at each end, reduced from $775 to $499. Mr. C also saw a handsome six foot-tall oak curio cabinet, with glass shelves and a mirrored interior, well-priced at $575.

Other items include bunk beds, brass headboards, rolltop desks, coffee tables, and more, from such manufacturers as Bassett, Kimball, Lane, Hooker, Bernhardt, and Stanley. The store is open Mondays through Saturdays from 9 a.m. to 6 p.m., and Friday evenings until 9.

Home Furniture Outlet
• 1099 Ashby Ave. (San Pablo Ave.), Berkeley; (510) 486-8016

This huge store in a remote area of Berkeley offers big-time bargains on all kinds of contemporary furniture and bedding. It's all solid wood, of quality construction; you can find full room ensembles or individual accent pieces. Whether you want Mission-style bookcases (available in any size and configuration) or halogen lamps, this store is filled with manufacturer's overstocks, closeouts, and floor models.

Many items here are one-of-a-kind. Mr. C was ready to dive into a gorgeous wooden sleigh bed; with a list price of $549, it was on sale here for $299. Add a matching dresser for $349. An oak coffee table, with cross-hatched oak inlays, was reduced from $399 to $259. And a butcher-block maple kitchen table with four white-finish Windsor chairs was just $299 complete. Klausner living room chairs, in the latest fabrics, were also $299—down from a list price of $699.

In bedding, the folks here snap up great factory-direct deals from Simmons, Restonic, and other brands. A Simmons Beautyrest "Aristocrat" mattress and boxspring, in queen-size, was marked down from $999 to $699 for the set. And there's always a lot to choose from. A Sealy sofabed, in a linen weave finish, was seen for $600 off at $899. The store is open seven days a week, including Thursday evenings until 8 p.m.

Hoot Judkins
• 1142 Sutter St. (Polk St.), San Francisco; (415) 673-5454
And other suburban locations

For over thirty years, Hoot Judkins has been selling high-quality wood furniture at discounts of 20% to 50 % off retail. While some of the items here are discounted because they're samples or discontinued models, most are first-quality new merchandise. Hoot Judkins is able to discount all of these because, with three stores, they can buy in volume and pass the savings on to you.

The store is huge, so you'll have plenty to choose from. A handy VCR/entertainment cart with wheels, list price $169.95, was seen here for $99.95. Another good deal was a huge solid wood entertainment center, regularly $725, here just $450. And how about a 30" square solid oak dining table for just $159.95, and matching chairs for $49.95 each. Or, save $100 on an upholstered leather arm chair. Mr. C even found unusual things like fabric pieces for director's chairs, in discontinued colors, reduced from $12.95 to $9.95.

Check out the huge selection of unfinished furniture, mostly in pine and maple, too—you can save a good deal of money by doing your own staining and varnishing. An unfinished pine computer desk, with three drawers and a keyboard tray, was seen for just $289.95. Lots of stuff for kids, too, like solid wood high chairs for $78.95 or a child-size table for $69.95.

With over 10,000 pieces of furniture and some 50,000 pieces available on order, Hoot Judkins is bound to have the piece you're looking for. If you don't see it, the friendly and knowledgeable sales staff can probably help you find it. The downtown store is open Monday through Friday from 9:30 a.m. to 6 p.m., Saturday from 8:30 a.m. to 5 p.m., and Sunday from noon to 5 p.m.

J. Gorman & Son, Inc.
• 2599 Telegraph Ave. (Parker St.), Berkeley; (510) 848-6094

There are a number of different ways to save money at J. Gorman & Son. For starters, head straight to the economy section in the back. Here, you may find pieces like a solid pine loft bed for just $201.75 or a solid oak wall unit for $279.95. The economy section is jammed with all kinds of furniture, most of it unfinished, from a pine student's desk ($81) with matching chair ($31.75) to a hardwood high chair ($74.50) or a rubberwood Boston rocker ($82.95). Pine bookcases are also a bargain, from just $48.75 for a 12" x 36" model.

Most of the furniture at J. Gorman & Son is unfinished; you can arrange to have it stained and lacquered in the store, but as you probably know, you'll save a bundle by finishing it yourself. For example, you can get an unfinished Shaker table for $144.50. The same table would cost $276.50 finished. That's a savings of $132— far more than the cost of a can of varnish and a few sheets of sandpaper.

J. Gorman & Son also carries a line of particle board storage units that are very cheap indeed. These aren't exactly heirloom-quality (not even close); they're made of pre-cut particle board that you have to assemble yourself. But, for a playroom, workroom, or, that four-year experience many of you know as the college dorm, this may be just the thing. You can get a ten-inch deep shelf unit, measuring 36" x 36", for just $12.50 (!) or a 32" by 32" by 12" deep cabinet for just $18.25. You can put together some stacking cubes, 32" x 16" x 16" deep, for just $16.75 each.

There is a charge for delivery, anywhere from $10 for some parts of Berkeley to $35 for San Francisco. J. Gorman & Son is open Monday through Saturday 9a.m.-5:30p.m. and Thursdays.9a.m.-8p.m.

Macy's Furniture Clearance Center
• 1556 El Camino Real (Hickey Blvd.), South San Francisco; (415) 397-3333

When you want to save money off of department store prices, where better to go than a department store outlet? From this large warehouse (with plenty of parking!), Macy's sells off its remainders, overstocks, and slightly damaged pieces at hundreds of dollars off. The selection always varies, but Mr. C found a Lexington colonial oak side table, in fine condition; originally $875, it was on sale for $349. A plush sofa by Ralph Lauren, in a floral print fabric with a solid maple frame, once $2,352 (gulp) was reduced here to $1,399. Yes, one arm was loose; but it certainly couldn't cost a thousand bucks to repair, could it?

Indeed, these are all sold "as is," meaning what you see is what you get, with no warranties. Again, if you're willing to put a little fix-up into some pieces, you'll still come out way ahead.

A solid oak kitchen table, with a white tile top surface (all the rage these days) and six matching chairs, meant to sell for up to $1,680, was seen for $699. A Bassett white pine chest of five drawers was reduced from $690 to 349. And a china cabinet by Stanley, made of cherry and maple wood, with glass doors and a mirrored back, was reduced from $2,480 to $899. Plus mattress sets, rugs, entertainment centers, and more.

As you can see, some of these items get pretty fancy; for many folks, this clearance center may bring such pieces into the range of possibility. The store has also expanded into clearance items from other departments, such as luggage and stereo (see listing under "Shopping: Electronics"). It's open Wednesday through Sunday only, from 11 a.m. to 6 p.m.

Manor House Associates
- 200 Kansas St. (15th St.), San Francisco; (415) 621-6442

Here's one of the more unusual finds in the furniture design district of Potrero Hill. Manor House stocks closeouts and discontinued fancy furnishings from over 250 manufacturers, selling them all at half of the retail prices, period. These are assembled from showrooms all over the Bay Area, and then displayed in Manor House's rather tight but elegant exposed brick quarters.

The merchandise varies all the time, but you may find a Broyhill country dining table and chairs marked down from $800 to $400; Hitchcock side chairs, reduced from $300 each to $150; or a Flexsteel leather recliner, not $1,710, but a cozy $855. Some items are seconds and samples, on consignment. A few have been refinished, selling for even less.

Many of the looks here are very fancy indeed. Imported French provincial chairs by Provost, of cherry wood and leather upholstery, are $400 each even at half-price. Torchiere lamps and chandeliers are on display. And the shop can also order many lines of carpeting and wallpapers at 40% off retail. Though this is a new location in a hot area, Manor House has been doing this for over 35 years; when you're looking for something elegant without an elegant price tag, this is the place. Open weekdays from 9 a.m. to 5 p.m., weekends 10-4.

National Furniture Liquidators
- 1177 Mission St. (Seventh St.), San Francisco; (415) 863-7160
- 2719 Telegraph Ave. (27th St.), Oakland; (510) 251-2222

National Furniture Liquidators is just what the name implies, snapping up manufacturer overruns, discontinued items, and demos from around the country. They carry a huge selection of new furniture at discounted prices, along with a good selection of used furniture. You'll see a few brand names, but the majority of the merchandise here is mid- to low-grade stuff. Still, it may be perfect for that first apartment.

Some recent bargains included a foam-filled sleeper sofa, list priced at $185, selling for $125; a better-grade sofa and loveseat pair, regularly $800, here were $499.95; and a three-piece glass and brass table set, regularly $200, was $139.95. You'll find good deals on bedroom ensembles, too, like a five-piece set including dresser, mirror, two night stands, and a full- or queen-size headboard, regularly $575, for just $379.95. Some pieces get marked down further off their already low price; a sofa and loveseat, originally $700, was already a deal at $499.95, but was further reduced to $399.95.

Among brand name items, Mr. C found a Simmons Queen Sleeper sofa with a deluxe innerspring mattress, retail price $1,000, here $499.95. They also had a Jenny Lind crib, in natural maple or white finish, complete with a foam mattress. It was reduced from $250 to $179.95.

National also sells used furniture, and you can find some really terrific deals—like an oak desk, which would have cost $600 new, for $145. You'll find a lot of used office furniture too; office desks for $40, a four drawer file cabinet for $95, a metal desk for $25, an eight-foot conference table for $75. The condition of their used furniture runs from very good to really worn out. Check merchandise over carefully and evaluate your needs.

Their store on Mission Street is

open Monday through Saturday from 10 a.m. to 6 p.m. and Sunday from noon to 5 p.m. The Oakland store is open Monday through Thursday from 10 a.m. to 6 p.m., Friday from 10 a.m. to 7 p.m., and Saturday 10 a.m. to 6 p.m. The Oakland store is closed on Sunday.

Next...Express
● 1315 Howard St. (Ninth St.), San Francisco; (415) 255-1311

This SoMa shop functions as the clearance center for Next Interiors, which offers high-end artsy furnishings for the home and office nearby at 50 Van Ness Avenue; telephone (415) 255-7662. Meanwhile, here at Next...Express, you can check out samples and closeouts for 30% to 60% below retail prices. Mr. C found things like a large, hardwood frame "Big Sur" sofa—available in several discontinued fabrics—for $299; rattan bar stools, imported from the Philippines, reduced from $300 to $150 each; and a black round dinette table with four chairs, marked down from $755 to just $280 complete.

Not everything in this branch is a closeout; many are budget-oriented lines of sofas, beds, and more. This means you can get decent prices and still be able to order from a variety of fabrics and finishes. But the store only purchases what they feel to be high-quality merchandise, even at the budget level. Good place to browse for yups on the way up. Open Monday through Saturday from 10 a.m. to 6 p.m. and Sunday from 11 a.m. to 6 p.m.

North American Warehouse Furniture
● 102 E. Grand Ave., South San Francisco; (415) 877-0848

Just east of the Bayshore Freeway, near the airport, this large, cavernous warehouse offers low prices on budget furniture for the living room, dining room and bedroom. By that, Mr. C means that this furniture is not exactly heirloom quality; laminated wood assembly-required dressers, couches filled with hard foam, and the like. But if you're furnishing a

home or apartment from scratch on a limited budget, or perhaps for a temporary period of time, the price is right.

After all, for just $599, you could get a floral print sofa and matching loveseat, with a coffee table and two end tables of smoked glass and brass; or a similarly styled dinette table with four chairs for $298. The same price can get you a simulated wood-finish dresser, mirror, bedframe and headboard.

Speaking of beds, this is a good place for inexpensive mattresses. Most of what you'll find here are knockoff brands, like a Posturamic super-firm set, reduced from a list price of $189 per full-size piece to just $94 per piece. Though it's not a famous brand, it does carry a twenty-year manufacturer's warranty. There's a good selection on hand, ranging down to the most basic of foam mattresses from a mere $29 per piece. Hey, could be okay for the kids, or a rarely used guest room, right?

Everything sold here is new, but all sales are final. NAW buys in bulk, ensuring the low prices, and distributes to other stores from this central warehouse; it's only open to the public Monday, Tuesdays and Fridays from 10 a.m. to 8 p.m., Saturdays from 10-6, and Sundays from 11-5. Free layaway is available. They will deliver to your home for a nominal fee, or load up your car for you at no charge.

Ortho Sleep Centers
● 2950 Geary Blvd. (Wood St.), San Francisco; (415) 668-2255
And other suburban locations

Here's a good place to shop for basic mattress sets and frames. Ortho manufactures its own line of bedding, and at their retail stores, you can get these at factory-direct prices. In the most basic of models, these can start as low as $59 per piece in twin-size. This was during a recent clearance sale; but their everyday prices are definitely budget-oriented. The full-size version of that basic model was normally $134 per piece, reduced to $119 on sale. Either way, not a bad deal.

Other sale items included a contemporary-style daybed for $139; metal bunk beds in bright colors for the kiddies, from $169; and more. One advantage here: Ortho doesn't force you to buy mattresses in sets only. If you just want to replace a boxspring, for instance, you can do so—and still get a discounted price. Open seven days a week.

Vogue Interior Design

- 300 Kansas St. (16th St.), San Francisco; (415) 626-8100

Located in the heart of the furniture design area of Potrero Hill, Vogue is a home furnishing showroom meant primarily for other merchants and interior designers; but they sell to the public at the same wholesale prices. Everything is out on display in this fashionable store, tagged with both the suggested retail price and the wholesale price (about 30% less).

What's more, these are not closeouts or leftovers. You can get big discounts on current lines of contemporary furniture and bedding, and if you prefer a different fabric or wood finish, you can order it at the same low price. Service is key here; the staff consists of professional decorators, who are ready to consult with you on any design issue.

And the bargains themselves? Mr. C loved an oval mahogany dining table, extendable from 72 inches to 89 inches, with a high-gloss surface; it had a list price of (gulp) $2,100, but was available at Vogue for $1,470. Matching chairs were marked down from $639 to $447 each. Cheaper, but definitely not cheap in any sense!

Some items are marked down from the already-reduced prices. A six-piece Portofino bedroom ensemble, in a low, modular European style, was recently on sale; list priced at $3,865, it normally sells for $1,900—and was chopped again to $1,399. That included the headboard, pedestal bed platform, two nightstands, corner storage unit, and double dresser. Add a queen-size Restonic "ChiroTonic" mattress for $420, saving an additional $180.

The shop is also filled with decorative items and accent pieces. An art deco halogen torchiere lamp, in your choice of enameled pastel colors, was marked down from $450 to $199. Open seven days a week.

Just up the block, check out **Interior Resources** at 350 Kansas Street, telephone (415) 864-2232, for more artsy contemporary furniture. This is another trade showroom that's open to the public, filled with fancy looks from local designers. Be sure to catch their end-of-season sample sales, held in January and July, for extra bargains; the store even holds free design seminars, open to the public, to show off new arrivals. Call for more info.

OFFICE FURNITURE

Big Mouth Office Furniture

- 1129 Airport Blvd. (Linden Ave.), South San Francisco; (415) 588-2444

Mr. Cheap has to love a bargain place that has a sense of humor about itself. As you would guess from the name, there's nothing pretentious about Big Mouth. The big deal is used and freight-damaged office furniture of all kinds, jammed into a small roadside store with a hippopotamus stretching open its wide jaws to greet you.

If you can squeeze your way through the narrow aisles inside, you'll find lots of interesting pieces for the office—like a Kimball mahogany executive's desk, worth $1,445 new, selling here for $595 *like* new. A four-drawer file cabinet by Hon, one of the big names in filing, was reduced from its original $280 to a mere $69. And you can grab a handful of plastic stacking chairs, perfect for big meetings, at ten bucks each.

There are some unused items from

time to time, including things like assemble-it-yourself bookcases. And even though this store looks tiny, there are two more warehouses filled with stuff. If you don't see something you're looking for, just ask. They can even order new items from many manufacturers at discount prices! Hey, it's all in who ya know. Especially when you know someone with a big mouth. Open weekdays from 9 a.m. to 5:30 p.m., and Saturdays from 10 a.m. to 2 p.m. only.

Office Furniture King

- 325 East Grand Ave., South San Francisco; (415) 952-2822

Here's one king that truly deserves its crown. For over sixteen years, Office Furniture King has been making great deals on new and used furniture for everyone from the largest business to the in-home entrepreneur. Longtime loyal customers and word-of-mouth business allows this company to save money on advertising; its out-of-the-way location, amidst a modern industrial park, also contribute to the low prices. But once you walk through the unassuming front door, you'll find yourself in a gigantic warehouse absolutely packed with furnishings of all kinds.

Many of the new items are manufacturer's overruns and closeouts, such as a Vogel Peterson ergonomic chair reduced from a list price of $489 to $319; or a double pedestal desk by Hon, in a walnut veneer finish, marked down from $783 to $469. OFK also specializes in office design, with good deals on partition systems and wall units, computer workstations, and the like.

Head over toward the right and you'll find the used stuff. These can range from vinyl conference room chairs for $14 apiece to secretary's desks (you know the type, black metal base with simulated woodgrain top) priced at $99 each. They've got rows and rows of 'em. Computer workstands go for around $69, Steelmaster file cabinets for $89, and scratched-up executive's desks for just $59—invest a little capital into

restoring one of these, and you'll wind up with an incredible bargain.

Unlike the new items, which are clearly tagged, many of the used pieces are stacked up and unmarked. Yes, the helpful staff here are willing to negotiate a bit on the prices—especially if you're buying in any kind of quantity. Office Furniture King is open on weekdays only, from 8 a.m. to 5:30 p.m.

Office Furniture Warehouse Sales

- 228 First St. (Howard St.), San Francisco; (415) 979-0477

This SoMa warehouse offers savings as big as its humongous inventory—that's because all of this furniture has been in offices before yours. No matter how low your budget, you can probably find something here. Got ten bucks? You can get a nice coat rack. Got $40? You can afford some decent file cabinets. Got $100? Cart off a really great used desk. Plus tables, chairs, shelf units, and more. Better still, the owner is willing to bargain on his used inventory; he's got so much stuff, he just wants to get rid of it.

Some of the bargains Mr. C saw include a 30" x 60" laminate desk for $125 and a used Herman Miller ergonomic chair with arms for $175—easily less than half its original price. If you're lucky, you may find a floor model on sale, such as the La-Z-Boy executive chair Mr. C found. Originally retailing for $900, it was still like new and just $399.

OFWS also has very competitive prices on new furniture, too; they import directly from several manufacturers. The used areas, meanwhile, are absolutely crammed with stuff. You may get the feeling that these folks would sell you the desk they're working from (make 'em an offer...), but the staff is extremely friendly and helpful. Open from Monday through Friday 9a.m.-5:30p.m.; Saturdays 10a.m.-4p.m.

Rucker Fuller Office Furniture

- 601 Brannan St. (Sixth St.), San Francisco; (415) 495-6895

In the business interiors business for over 120 years, Rucker Fuller is truly a giant. In their 42,000-square foot showroom near the Flower Market, you can stroll through aisle after aisle of new and used office furniture, all at great discounts. You know the old phrase: "How do they do it? Volume!"

RF is a distributor for such makers as Steelcase, Kimball, Superior, Office Master, and more. In many cases, the store is also the Bay Area clearance outlet for these companies, selling off discontinued items at 30% off list prices. And, when mistakes are made, the savings go as high as 70%. What kind of mistakes? Things like a shipment of Steelcase ergonomic chairs that were sent with the wrong color of fabric. Y'know, mistakes anyone else could live with—especially when it means they can get a $700 chair for $300.

Among the used furniture sections, Mr. C found file cabinets by major brands at up to 75% off the original prices; a Gunlocke task chair, once $299, here $119; tons of basic metal desks, reduced from $600 to just $129 each; even conference tables and chairs. Often, these items come from RF's long-term rental operation—and they still have plenty of mileage left. The store does lease and rent furniture, but only uses quality brands that will last (no "assembly required" stuff). They can also make workstations and partitioned spaces to fit your needs.

Meanwhile, with all their connections, they can also order just about anything in the office furniture world, and have it delivered to your office tomorrow (there is a fee for delivery). In summary, ladies and gentlemen, let Mr. C conclude that you should see this place for yourselves. It's open weekdays from 8 a.m. to 5 p.m. only; free parking is available.

MR. CHEAP'S PICKS
Office Furniture

- ✔ **Office Furniture King**—Huge warehouse in South San Francisco filled with new and used deals.
- ✔ **Office Furniture Warehouse Sales**—These guys just might sell you the chair out from under them. Big inventory of used furniture, and plenty of room to bargain.
- ✔ **Rucker Fuller**—42,000 square feet of used furniture, closeout deals on new stuff, and next-day service.

HOME FURNISHINGS

Bayshore Lights
- 55 Waterloo St. (Bayshore Blvd.), San Francisco; (415) 826-3278

It sounds kind of funny to describe a discount lighting store as having a low overhead, but that's exactly the story at this small, no-frills shop next to Goodman Lumber. Low overhead means low prices on ceiling fixtures, lamps, reading lights, wall sconces, and more; there's not as much to see here as at most other lighting stores, but Bayshore has all the catalogs, and can order any line at similarly discounted prices.

Mr. C saw a three-arm chandelier by Progress, with satin-finished etched globes, carrying a retail price of $268; here, it was selling for $188. A white-finish halogen torch floor lamp, with a swing-arm top, was on sale for $59, marked down from

$119. And a Granrich halogen desk lamp, seen for up to $100 elsewhere, was $60 here.

Budget wall and ceiling fixtures start under ten dollars; you can also get things like individual halogen lamp units for track lighting, from $7.50 each. Case discounts on bulbs are offered, too. Major brands can be found here as well, including Halo, Juno, Lightolier, and others; remember, if you don't see it, you can probably order it. Bayshore promises to meet anyone else's advertised price, and has its own 30-day "110% price guarantee." The store is open from 8-5 Mondays through Saturdays, and from 9-3 on Sundays.

The Bed & Bath Superstore
● 555 Ninth St. (Brannan St.), San Francisco; (415) 252-0490

The Bed & Bath Superstore is a mecca for all that is housewares. This store is gigantic—on two floors—and they carry just about every designer and brand name in the business. You'll find anything you could possibly need here, including sheets, pillows, rugs, frames, towels, dishes, glasses, lamps, storage units, and much, much more.

Queen-size sheet sets by Springmaid are priced at $59.99 here, and full-size cotton flannel sheets by Martex are $39.99. A Wamsutta 3-piece twin sheet set was on sale for $17.99. Another great bargain seen recently was in down comforters, just $59.99 for twin, $89.99 queen, and $99.99 king, with sturdy 200-thread-count covers. If it's designer looks you crave, B & B has 'em. Laura Ashley comforters, in full/queen, just $159.99. The same size comforter by Bill Blass could be had for $299.99. Not cheap, but cheaper than in many department stores!

This is also a great place for kitchen stuff. They carry dozens of brands of china and crystal, from Corning to Baccarat. You'll find great gift-type items, too, like marble salt and pepper shakers for $14.99 a set. There is a small selection of furniture: mostly chairs, small tables, TV

carts, and such. A solid wood utility cart—with wheels, shelves, a cutting board, and knife holders—was just $89.99. You can also get materials to remodel your home, including Levolor blinds. And, don't miss the kids department with toys, games, and fun furnishings. Bed & Bath Superstore is open Monday through Saturday 9:30 a.m. to 9 p.m. and Sunday 10:30 a.m. to 7 p.m.

Cheap Pete's Frame Factory Outlet
● 4720 Geary Blvd. (11th Ave.), San Francisco; (415) 221-4720

Whether you're looking for a picture to spruce up your home, or you're looking for a frame to spruce up a picture to spruce up your home, you'll find what you need at Cheap Pete's Frame Factory Outlet. This store has a dual purpose: They are an outlet store for Frame-O-Rama, which is located at 1940 Polk Street; telephone (415) 441-3636. They also acquire overstocks and seconds from other companies, and sell them at a discount. When they get a deal—say a factory goes out of business—they snap up the stock and pass the savings right along to you. Their selection of styles ranges from contemporary to traditional, from plain to ornate.

During Mr. C's visit, he saw a wheelbarrow filled with small photo frames for just $3.99 each. Wood and glass collage-style photo frames (you know, your whole life in a square foot), were reduced from $19.99 to just $8.99. Solid wood and glass 16" x 20" frames, ready to fill, were just $12.99. And if you don't even want to work *that* hard, a variety of framed pictures, originally $79, were just $49.

Don't forget to check out the bargain bins, where Mr. C found ready-made 20" x 20" wall frames with some minor scuffs, originally $52.50, marked down to $24.99—then further reduced to just $14.99. You might call it the framework of a frame price. Plus bins of less-than-perfect and odd sized frames that may be just right for your particular needs.

The staff can do custom framing for you; and though this can be costly, their labor rates are kept lower than many other places. If you prefer, they will do all the prep work for you, cutting the matte and frame, etc.; then you can take it home and put it together yourself. This saves on labor charges considerably. The staff is very friendly and they're more than happy to help you out.

Cheap Pete's is open Monday through Saturday from 10 a.m. to 6:30 p.m., 'til 8 p.m. on Wednesday and Thursday, and Sunday from 12 noon to 5 p.m.

Chef's Cordon Bleu
- 28 Westlake Mall, Daly City; (415) 756-0200
- 926 Broadway St., Redwood City; (415) 364-3604

An unbelievable treasure trove for anyone who likes to cook—or even just to serve with style—Chef's Cordon Bleu combines great deals on cookware and appliances with bargains on its own line of stoneware and porcelain.

Roam around this vast store, and you may find an eight-quart stainless steel double boiler, list priced at $60, selling for $48. Or a Krups espresso/cappuccino maker, retail $230, here $168. A Maverick juice extractor, squeezed from $178 to a juicy $90. Or a fancy 18-inch shiny metal serving tray, once $25, now just $9.99. Many of these are closeouts and specials; the selection changes frequently, but there is always a lot to see.

There is also a wide range of cookbooks, all 10% off the cover price, as well as enough knicknacks, doodads and gadgets to make any kitchen magician happy for hours. Now, what to serve your creations on? Cordon Bleu International makes elegant dishware in a variety of patterns and sizes to meet every need, selling them through mail and retail stores. Here in their own store, you can stock up on overruns and discontinued pat-

terns, most at 50% off the original prices. A porcelain two-quart casserole, whimsically decorated with colorful fruits and vegetables on the sides, was thus reduced from $30 to $15. A matching sauce boat (speaking of reducing), was marked down from $34 to $17. And a large buffet plate, once $21, was seen for $10.50. Meanwhile, a boxed set of stoneware dishes, twenty pieces in all, was just $10. And there are discount prices on linen napkins and placemats, candles and candleholders, aprons, earthenware mugs, and much more—even some gourmet packaged foods. Open seven days a week.

China Bazaar
- 826-832 Grant Ave. (Clay St.), San Francisco; (415) 982-9847

Two words could not more accurately

describe any store. China Bazaar is two huge floors of imported Asian goods, from clothing to kitchenware to ornate decorative pieces.

The street level has clothing and home furnishings, all rather touristy; but Mr. C recommends that you head downstairs to the basement. Here, tall shelves are stacked from floor to ceiling with (a sign says) 10,000 items— and that looks about right. Find rice paper lampshades from $6.99, dishes, soup bowls, and porcelain teacups (two for 80¢), not to mention all kinds of exotic teas to put in them. You can buy a box of 100 jasmine tea bags for a mere $2.99—hard to beat in any supermarket. Around a corner, you'll find larger decorative pieces, like four-panel black lacquered folding screens from $150. Plus shelves of "as is" items at reductions of 50% to 90% off their original prices; Mr. C liked a handsomely carved wooden jewelry chest, once $25.95, now $10.95—with, seemingly, no defects.

A few blocks south, you can browse another packed emporium, **Bargain Bazaar** at 667 Grant Avenue, (415) 391-6369. Along with more kitchen goods (a 20-piece dinnerware set, $29.95, and the ever-popular bamboo steamer, $7.99), this store deals more in clothing, including a "bargain attic" with racks of silk-look rayon robes. Plus electronics, like Panasonic boom boxes and Casio calculators, as well as jewelry, carved ivory figures, and tons of cheap (truly) toys.

Crate & Barrel Outlet Store
- 1785 Fourth St. (Hearst St.), Berkeley; (510) 528-5500

Anyone who loves the look of Crate & Barrel housewares, but doesn't love the prices, should head immediately to the Crate & Barrel Outlet Store where you'll find a selection of seconds, past-season, and over-stocked items. Mostly what you'll find here is kitchenware, glassware, and other home stuff. All seconds are clearly marked, as reputable stores will do; meanwhile, most blemishes are barely discernable.

Savings can vary widely depending on the item. A twenty-piece set of porcelain tableware, originally $39.95, was available here for $33.95; another twenty-piece set yielded a bigger savings, reduced from $59.95 to $34.95. A Salton coffeemaker, listed at $69.95, was ground down to $34.95. You'll find a few things here that are manufactured just for the outlet—like a picnic basket with a set of chic plasticware for four, at $29.95. These items tend to be of slightly lower quality than the lines C & B sells in its regular stores; they are to housewares what ready-to-wear is to *haute couture*. There's a place for each.

You will find a small selection of Crate & Barrel furniture, mostly smaller pieces like chairs, tables, and the like. The ever-popular Adirondack chair, in hunter green of course, regularly sells for $84.95; here, it was just $59.95. During Mr. C's visit they also had some children's furniture, like a tiny rocking chair, regularly $36.95, for just $17.95; and a small picnic table, originally $64.95, for just $32.95.

Beyond these, there are always plenty of odds and ends, like a halogen desk lamp, originally $158, for just $79.95; and a canvas briefcase, regularly $99.95, for just $29.95. This can also be a good place to come across unusual accessories, such as replacement fabric for those wacky canvas "butterfly" chairs, regularly $26.95, here only $12.

The Crate & Barrel Outlet Store is open seven days a week, nightly until 6:00 p.m.

Glassware International
- 660 Third St. (Townsend St.), #116, San Francisco; (415) 495-3140

Glassware International, located at the Six-Sixty Center discount mall in SoMa, carries a large selection of housewares at good prices. These include cake platters, storage jars, serving bowls, mugs, glasses, and more, at 20% to 70% off retail prices. Mr. C found sets of four drinking glasses, retailing for $11.95 to $15.95, selling here for just $5. An elegant set of six glass cups and saucers from France, regularly $23.95, was just $18.95. Matching plates, bowls, and the like were also available at similar discounts.

If you're into crystal (the decorative kind), GI recently had a beautiful 9" crystal bud vase; list price $7.95, here normally $5.95, but on sale for $3.25! Mr. C also saw a 13" serving platter reduced from $19.95 to just $5.95, and a 12" hors d'oeuvre tray, regularly $9.95, for just $5.95.

Not all the savings are so substantial; some things are only $1 or so off retail. But this place is generally cheaper than department stores, and there are always a few big bargains to make it worth the trip.

Heritage House, Inc.

- 2190 Palou Ave. (Industrial St.), San Francisco, (415) 285-1331

Bridal registry is the main business at Heritage House, and if you're looking to keep those whopping costs down, this is certainly one of the best places to go in the Bay Area. But there's no reason why *anyone* shopping for great values in china, crystal, and silverware can't buy here as well.

Heritage House displays one of the largest selections around, stocking over 1,500 patterns in all, at prices that range anywhere from 10% to 40% below retail. Thanks to high-volume sales, even lines by manufacturers who do not traditionally offer discounts to dealers can be gotten here at up to 25% off. And, the greater the quantity of your purchase, the higher the discounts can be.

A handsome Wedgwood "Amherst" five-piece china setting, which currently lists for $120, would cost $72 here—or less, depending on how many settings you buy. That's just one of the many examples Mr. C found here, among designs by Lenox, Christian Dior, Royal Doulton, Noritake, and more; in crystal, the names include Baccarat, Waterford, Orrefors, and Spode, along with flatware by Oneida, Georg Jensen, Mikasa,

and many others. In short, all the biggies.

Most of the patterns shown here are traditional ones, although just about any line can be ordered; there are some contemporary designs on view as well, like "Asymetria" china by Rosenthal of Germany, and "Mosaic Tile" patterns by Dansk. There are also lots of interesting gift items on hand, such as clocks, decanters, and more.

If you *are* looking for a place to have your bridal registry, Heritage House can meet your needs beautifully. They can provide gifts to fit any budget; give you mailing cards to notify all of your guests about the store; allow them to shop in the store or by phone; and keep track of every purchase on computer.

Other important features of note to value-conscious shoppers: HH does sell individual pieces, for those of you looking to restore a set without purchasing a whole new one. They have a matching service for discontinued patterns in sterling silver. There is also a "Club Plan" which entitles you to further discounts up to 50%, especially if you refer another customer to the store. Best of all, if you buy any crystal or china here and later break a piece, HH will replace it for you at half-price—no questions asked.

Well, you'd hardly expect to find all this fancy stuff in such a bustling, Mack truck-jammed, industrial warehouse section of the Bayview area—but it's true. After all, lower rents mean lower prices! The store is located right in the "V" formed by the junction of Routes 101 and 280 (take the "Industrial Street" exit from Bayshore Boulevard). Once you get inside, though, the showroom is as elegant as any you'd find in town. So is the service (no pun intended); the patient and pleasant sales staff will sit with you for as long as you wish, showing you one dazzling design after another, until you find exactly the right one. Hours are Monday through Friday from 10 a.m. to 6 p.m., plus Saturdays by appointment.

Lamps Plus
- 4700 Geary Blvd., (12th Ave.), San Francisco; (415) 386-0933

And other suburban locations

Lamps Plus is a lighting superstore, with a huge inventory and selection to prove it. Because they have over thirty stores and buy in such huge volume, they can offer low prices as well as a wide range of styles. You'll find everything from contemporary to traditional looks. You'll also find every conceivable *kind* of lighting, from floor and table lamps to chandeliers and track lighting.

Like everything else, the prices vary widely as well, but they're all discounted. Mr. C saw a budget-brand halogen floor lamp reduced from $69.99 to $39.99; another halogen torch model, list priced at $1,200, was selling here for $799.99. And, if you *really* want to spend a mint, they can accommodate you with a crystal chandelier by Strass for $3,999.99. Yes, this is still a "bargain"; the suggested list price is $5,999.99.

All right, so maybe you're looking for something a little less stratospheric. Lamps Plus always carries a great selection of contemporary table lamps, some as low as $19.95. Save $100 on a brass table lamp by Stiffel. A beautiful brass floor lamp, built into a glass-top table, was just $79.99. Another floor lamp by Pacific Coast which regularly sells for $329.99 was on sale here for $219.99. LP also stocks outdoor lighting and lampshades by the hundreds. They're open seven days a week.

The Light Palace
- 2060 Polk St. (Broadway), San Francisco; (415) 474-3673

The Light Palace may seem more like a humble abode, but the large selection of beautiful lamps at discount prices will definitely make you feel like royalty. A floor lamp that normally sells for $165 can be found here for $105, for instance; and a table lamp, usually $49.99, would be just about $34.99. You'll find desk lamps, originally $24.99, for just $16.99.

The big thing in lamps these days are halogens, and the Light Palace has plenty. Mr. C saw a black halogen light with frosted glass, list price $99.99, here $59.99. You'll see great contemporary styles, along with traditional styles and lots of stuff in between.

Big selection of shades too, starting at just $20, as well as bulbs. They sell three-ways for $2.99 and regular bulbs are two for $2. Decorators shop here because of the great prices and the wonderful service: Lamps can be returned for refund or exchange within four days (exchanges only on shades).

The Light Palace is open from 11 a.m. to 5:30 p.m., Tuesday through Saturday.

Lighting Warehouse
- 701 16th St. (Kansas St.), San Francisco; (415) 252-0797

This Potrero shop sells better-quality lamps and lighting at 20% to 30% below regular retail prices. You'll even find some items priced as much as half-off retail, like a table lamp that normally sells for $120, seen for just $60 here. Many of these are designer brand names, too. A George Kovacs desk lamp, normally $240, was just $144; a black and glass table lamp by Frederick Raymond, originally $516, was just $300; and a black Dansk wall light, regularly $126, was just $63. The more expensive items have the higher discounts, but even inexpensive items are well below retail.

The store also carries styles for the children's rooms, not to mention chandeliers, track and recessed lighting, and more. The Lighting Warehouse is open 8:30 a.m. to 5:30 p.m., Monday through Friday, and 10 a.m. to 4 p.m. on Saturday.

The Linen Factory Outlet
- 475 Ninth St. (Harrison St.), San Francisco; (415) 861-1511

The Linen Factory Outlet is an outlet for Western Linen, Inc., a manufacturer, distributor, and importer of custom home textiles. Mr. C should warn you up front that this stuff is not, strictly-speaking, cheap. But at 40% to 60% below suggested retail prices, you will definitely save a ton on very high-quality tablecloths, napkins, placemats, sheets, blankets, pillows, and more.

They carry some great brand names. Reversible duvets by Palms & Pomegranates were seen here for just $75 in full/queen-size and $80 for king-size. Cannon bath towels were available for $7 each and bath sheets were $12. They also had cotton blankets by Early's of Witney for just $30 and, for those who want to truly indulge, full-size merino wool blankets for $126.

This is also a great place for all kinds of fashionable aprons; they sure have a lot of 'em. Some styles, meant to sell for $18, were seen for just $7.20. Also in the wearables department, cozy cotton/poly nightgowns—listing at $94—were reduced to $56. That'll help you sleep a little better. And don't worry, there are less pricey items available here: tablecloths as low as $10, cotton flannel sheets for $10 each, and handpainted cotton placemats for $3 each, or $8 for a set of four.

The Linen Factory Outlet is open Wednesday through Friday from noon to 4 p.m. and Saturday 10 a.m. to 4 p.m. only.

Moss Lighting
- 1026 Mission St. (Sixth St.), San Francisco; (415) 863-2400

For traditional, decorative styles, Moss Lighting has become something of a tradition in itself (a fixture, one might say). For over sixty years, this family-owned business has been offering discounted prices on everything from bathroom fixtures to Tiffany lamps.

The high-end pieces are a specialty here, including designs in crystal (available in three grades), brass, and iron. These may be *cheaper* here, but they are by no means cheap: A Schonbek 24-light crystal chandelier, which retails for $3,600, was recently seen here selling for $1,800. Mr. C also saw a Tiffany shaded floor lamp,

with a list price of $1,300, on sale for $600. And an iron verde green chandelier, a more rustic style currently in vogue, was reduced from $1,800 to $899.

If these are still a bit rich for you, not to worry. Lately, Moss has begun adding more contemporary, casual styles in with its showier pieces. There are table lamps from $50 and up; one, with a large, ceramic pottery-style base and an oversized white linen shade was seen for $99, marked down from a list price of $185. And there are lots of wall units. In a mix of old and new, an art deco three-light strip with frosted semi-circle shades, fitted with halogen bulbs, was reduced from $435 to $225.

Service is expert and friendly. The store is open Mondays through Saturdays from 9:00 a.m. to 5:30 p.m.

Ritch Street Outlet
- 688 Third St. (Townsend St.); San Francisco; (415) 546-1908

At one time the Ritch Street Outlet, which sells kitchen, dining, and gift items at wholesale prices, was on Ritch Street; hence the name. They've moved, however, to Third Street. So now, while the name may not make sense, the savings still do. You'll find linens, potholders, tablecloths, ceramic cookware, mugs, and more. Mr. C saw aprons, some each for cooking and for gardening, at just $2.98 each. Placemats ($2.50) and napkins ($1.50) are plentiful, though it may be difficult to find enough of each style and color to set a table. With a little creativity, however, different combinations should yield table settings fit for a queen or, at least, the average dinner guest. You'll also find plenty of dishtowels ($1.10) and oven mitts ($2.75).

Ritch Street Outlet also carries kitchenware and some cuisine cookware. A variety of plastic utensils were available for just 80¢ each and a garlic press was just $4. Mugs, in a number of different styles and patterns, were just $3.95 each, $19.75 for six or $36 for twelve. Again, it may be difficult to find a matching set, by for everyday use these should do you just fine. Ritch Street Outlet is open Monday through Friday, 10 a.m. to 5:30 p.m., Saturday 10 a.m. to 5 p.m., and Sunday noon to 5 p.m.

Seng Son Pottery Company
- 1659 San Pablo Ave. (Virgina St.), Berkeley; (510) 525-1357

Seng Son Pottery Company is a fun place to poke around and find interesting housewares in various Oriental motifs. All of which, meanwhile, is well-removed from the crazed hustle and bustle of similar shops in Chinatown. They have a variety of teapots for $6.75; soup bowls for $2.99 each; and a complete six piece tea set with gold leaf trim for $29.99.

What you will find in the greatest abundance, perhaps, is large-sized planters, the kind that are big enough to hold small trees, and large vases. These are obviously more expensive than cups and bowls, but they are still quite reasonable and very beautiful. Many of these are priced around $25 and up.

Seng Son Pottery Company is open Monday through Saturday from 10 a.m. to 5 p.m., and Sunday from noon to 5 p.m.

Ssilkss
- 635 Brannan St. (Sixth St.), San Francisco; (415) 777-1353

No, that's not a typo. Perhaps this sssibilance is meant to sssymbolize the sssmooth way these "flowers" impersonate the real thing. Ssilkss imports and distributes silk flowers, silk trees, and foliage; plus baskets, ceramic vases, and more. You can buy any of these at the same wholesale rates the decorating trade gets; and if you purchase in quantity, you'll get an additional 10% off.

This faux flora includes very natural-looking roses for $1.75 each, foxglove "blooms" for $9.50 each, and plastic cactus for $17. Some of the finer-quality stems can be even more expensive, though not always. Mr. C found paper gladiolas, regularly $3 each, marked down in-store to $2 each.

The larger silk plants and trees are

what really draws people in. You'll find hanging ivy for $30; a seven-foot ficus tree with a real birch trunk for $110; or a ten-foot cherry blossom tree for $210. For something a little different, they have seven-foot dracena palm trees for $100.

The best thing about all of these? None of them have to watered! Ssilkss is open seven days a week, from 8 a.m. to 5 p.m.

For related home furnishings, visit the **SPI Clearance Center** nearby at 530 Brannan Street; telephone (415) 777-5222. They carry a large selection of discounted housewares, including frames, mugs, brassware, ceramics, and more.

Smith & Hawken
- 1330 10th St. (Gilman St.), Berkeley; (510) 527-1076

Walk into this store, and you'll almost feel like you're back outside—in a setting far more attractive than the actual, industrial, Berkeley surroundings. Smith & Hawken is a Kentucky-based catalog company specializing in things for the home and garden, along with casual fashions to match. This retail store, with its skylights, indoor trees, and natural wood walls, feels like someone's very fancy backyard; it divides between straight catalog sales in one half, and a clearance outlet in the other.

In the outlet, you can save money two ways: on first-quality discontinued items, and second-quality irregulars. These seconds are identified with yellow price tags, and usually have the defect pointed out. For your own backyard, you can get things like first-quality Adirondack porch chairs, in green of course, reduced from $225 to $175 each; or big 18-inch wide terra cotta pots reduced from $37 to $25. A discontinued Newport chaise lounge, originally $695 in the catalog, was seen for $450 here.

Clothing bargains on Mr. C's visit included heavy corduroy work shirts (in S & H's own label), once a pricey $62, now a well-pruned $39. Irregular, but still very handsome, thick wool sweaters were reduced from $125 to $65. And straw gardening hats, perfectly good, were marked down from $24 to $18. There are even Smith & Hawken seeds—both flowers and vegetables—which go for $2.00 a pack in the catalog, yours for the picking at 50¢ apiece.

And finally, the outlet offers discounts on imported decorative items, like a Dartington crystal bud vase (once $45, now $32), Mexican water pitchers of cobalt blue glass ($22 down to $15, plus goblets to match), and hand-painted and glazed clay flower pots ($15 down to $10). It's a beautiful store to browse through, not only for its oasis-like atmosphere, but for the diversity of its merchandise. Open every day, from 10 a.m. to 6 p.m.

Warm Things Factory Outlet
- 3063 Fillmore St. (Union St.), San Francisco; (415) 931-1660
- 6011 College Ave. (Claremont Ave.), Oakland; (510) 428-9329
  And other suburban locations

At its factory in San Rafael, Warm Things manufactures its own...er, warm things. These range from the kind you wear, like down jackets, to the kind you have around the house, like pillows and comforters. Either way, these products are made to exacting standards, including genuine goose down and high thread-count

fabrics. And, by shopping at these outlet stores instead of through their mail-order catalog, you can save 25% to 65% off list prices—enough to give you a very warm feeling indeed.

Goose down comforters are made in several grades of filling, weight, and construction; some here are as low as an amazing $69, about half their catalog price. Or, go for a premium, 270-thread-count cotton, box-stitch version for $299 in queen size—again, half its original cost. Warm Things also imports a variety of zip-on covers in contemporary fashions, as well as wool mattress pads, and even real feather beds—a sort of plush futon. Oh, and of course, goose down pillows. Again, there are several grades of pillow, starting as low as two for $25 on sale; these standard-sizers were made to sell at $49 each.

Warm Things guarantees the workmanship and materials of its products; these are definitely made to last, making a good-value investment at any price. Those tightly woven fabrics, for example, make sure that feather ends won't poke through to annoy you. Comforters are "baffled" on the inside, to make sure they stay evenly filled. These folks have been making warm things for over twenty years; they know what they're doing. Open seven days a week.

JEWELRY

Leo Hamel & Company
- 209 Post St., Suite 902, San Francisco; (415) 398-5531

Quoting jewelry prices is always a tricky business. As you may know, fine jewelry comes in a variety of quality ratings which determine market values. Diamonds, for example, are rated by cut, color, clarity, and carat weight. Unless you're an expert, it's very difficult to determine the actual worth of a stone. Add to all

that the huge fluctuations in the value of gold from week to week, and it becomes nearly impossible to determine a true bargain in jewelry.

Having made that huge disclaimer, Mr. C would like to point you toward Leo Hamel & Company. This shop deals in jewelry and fine watches, both new and used, at prices that are far below the traditional jewelry mark-up. Leo puts out a monthly newsletter of sorts, listing in-store specials, sales, and so on. Mr. C is going to give you some examples of the kinds of pieces you may find (it gets a bit technical), along with Leo's estimate of the full retail value; but please be reminded of all the disclaimers above and remember that these are just examples.

A 14K gold engagement solitaire, with a .91-carat round brilliant diamond might cost up to $3,200 elsewhere; here it was $2,100. A 14K gold wedding band with a .45-ct. diamond would cost $2,300; here it was only $1,250. For the woman who has almost everything, how about a tennis bracelet with 3.50 cts. of superior quality diamonds? It could cost $4,500 at another jewelry or department store, but here it's just $2,450.

Do you prefer the simplicity and elegance of pearls? Leo showed a string of 7.5mm cultured pearls in an 18" necklace that would cost $2,100 elsewhere, but here they were just $1,200. Don't despair if you don't have thousands to spend. The store has a selection of 14K gold hoop earrings, in a number of popular styles, starting at just $50.

The store also sells estate jewelry. That's another word for secondhand, but these aren't the kind of pieces you're going to find at the corner thrift shop. These are very high quality, often expensive, items that people sell or consign for any number of reasons. For example, a 10-ct. (total weight) diamond and platinum brooch, which sold new for $20,000, could recently be found here for $8,000. And there are plenty to see in a more moderate price range. For instance, a 14K white gold ring set with a .85-ct. diamond was originally $1,700—here it was just $750. Of course, like any used merchandise, estate jewelry is subject to fluctuations in availability. Hamel's is committed to service, and the knowledgeable staff will try to help you find what you're looking for.

Leo Hamel & Company is also well-known for its wonderful selection of watches, specifically better-quality watches like Rolex, Kriëger,

Patek Phillipe, Cartier, and many more. There is less room for them to discount on new watches, because of their relationships with the buyers; but again, they have a huge inventory of pre-owned watches, in those same fine brands, at really great prices. These are completely reconditioned and, most importantly, guaranteed. One recent deal was a Rolex Datejust in 18K gold and steel; it would have cost $4,500 new, and was selling for just $2,650. Another Rolex was priced at a timelessly low $750!

Leo Hamel & Company is open Monday through Friday from 10 a.m. to 6 p.m.

Lloyd's Jewelry

- 118 Old County Rd. (Bayshore Blvd.), Brisbane; (415) 467-7375

Tom Lloyd is literally sitting on a goldmine, tucked into a sleepy shopping center just off Bayshore Boulevard. For over ten years, he has been making his own jewelry—in gold, diamonds and colored gemstones—and selling these at prices that are easily half as expensive as you'd find in a fancy downtown boutique (with fancy downtown rent and overhead). A certified gemologist, Tom buys his stones directly from the cutters at wholesale prices; he gives them sturdy mounts, and can even make jewelry to order—including wedding band sets.

Among the gorgeous creations he showed Mr. C and a friend were a tennis bracelet in 14-karat gold, with two carats total weight in diamonds; elsewhere, it might cost up to $1,350, but here, you could get it for $900. That's a third off. A citrine and diamond ring, probably $300 anywhere else, was selling for $135 here. And there are plenty of less expensive items, like sapphire earrings in 14K gold mounts priced from $20 to $50.

Gold chain starts at $16.50 per gram; it's weighed and priced for you on the spot (Tom encourages you to shop around and educate yourself on the price range in other stores). He only uses strong, rope-style chains, which aren't prone to kinking and tangling. A 22-karat gold bracelet, hand-made in Thailand with a screw-in clasp, sells here for $430; anywhere else, it could cost twice as much.

Given his expertise, Tom also does expert jewelry repair. Service is a major priority here; he even tells the story of a Las Vegas woman who comes in to do her Christmas shopping each year. Tom actually picks her up at the airport, brings her to the shop, helps her pick out gifts, and takes her back to SFO. You'll probably have to provide your own transportation, but then, you're probably not coming from such a distance; in any case, it'll be worth it.

Lloyd's Jewelry is open Monday through Friday from 11 a.m. to 6 p.m. and Saturday from 10 a.m. to 4:30 p.m.

Vy's Art and Jewelry
- 544 Grant Ave. (Pine St.), San Francisco; (415) 982-2717

Wandering through the maze of Chinatown shops in search of bargains? Not sure who's for real and who's not? Mr. C has found a good place for you to check out. Vy's specializes in fresh water pearls imported directly from growers in Japan and China; these include Biwa, South Sea, cultured, and seeded varieties, all at wholesale prices. Indeed, there are more pearls here than a pirate could shake a scabbard at.

Small strands begin at just 99¢ each; in some department stores, even these can cost up to $5 or $6. Necklaces with three strands braided in rope-style start around $12. Strands with larger pearls, seen for up to $15 in departments stores, cost as little as $2.99 here. And even at these prices, the pearls have a lustered finish; many lower-priced pearls do not. Check and see!

Mr. C was also told that, on higher quality pearls such as the Biwa varieties, prices can be negotiable. Vy's is open seven days a week, from 9:30 a.m. to 6:30 p.m.

Zwillinger and Company
- 760 Market St. (Grant Ave.), Suite 800, San Francisco; (415) 392-4086

Upstairs on the eighth floor of this

MR. CHEAP'S PICKS
Jewelry

✔ **Lloyd's Jewelry**—Head south of the city to Brisbane—yes, Brisbane—for serious deals on gold and diamonds.

✔ **Zwillinger & Company**—Few things here are "cheap," but this upstairs shop sells high-quality jewelry and watches, new and used, at substantial savings.

downtown office building, Zwillinger has been a jewelry landmark for over forty years. The company itself has been around for 75 years; though in fact, owner Mel Wasserman bought it out about five years ago. He has worked to maintain the longstanding reputation associated with the name; this is borne out by endorsements from the Better Business Bureau and the California State Employees Association—which recommends only two jewelers in the entire state to its members (don't bother to look; the other one's in L.A.).

Zwillinger sells fine-quality diamonds, gold, pearls, semi-precious stones,and watches, all at actual wholesale book values—anywhere from 20% to 35% below retail.. You can walk right in and get the same prices that another jewelry merchant would get; not only that, but you'll get private, personal service into the bargain. Wedding and engagement rings, for example, are sold by individual piece: Choose the stone first, then the setting, so that you can mix and match to stay within any budget. Some rings start as low as $250. A diamond anniversary ring, seen for about $1,000 in Macy's, sells for $675 here.

Mel pays close attention to detail; diamond tennis bracelets are made with carefully selected stones, not "promotional quality" stuff. Name brand watches feature some of *the* fanciest names (which Mr. C was asked not to print), also below retail. Select gold and colored stone earrings are imported from Europe.

Mel calls the store "a sort of fine jewelry Price Club." Meanwhile, even at wholesale prices, there is a certified GIA gemologist on the premises, to keep appraisals honest. Little

advertising and large volume help keep the overhead costs down. The store even offers a 30-day money-back guarantee on all but custom-made pieces; and if you buy a diamond here, you can use it to trade up in the future. You'll always get at least your original cost back in trade. Zwillinger and Company is open Tuesday through Saturday only, from 9:30 a.m. to 5:00 p.m.

LIQUOR AND BEVERAGES

Cost Plus Wine Shop

• 2598 Taylor St. (Bay St.), San Francisco: (415) 928-2030

Right next door to the venerable Cost Plus Imports, this full-service liquor shop brings CPI's buying power to booze. Wines are a particular specialty here, although the store is not limited to them; you're just as likely to find good deals on beers from around the world, by the pack or case. Different brands go on sale each week, like a six-pack of Holsten for $3.99. Mr. C saw everything from Canada's Moosehead to Razor Edge Beer from Tasmania (yup). Cost Plus puts many of these into its own ten-pack variety samplers for $9.99.

Back to the wines: There is a large selection of local and international vintages, all very clearly labeled and described in detail. The extremely courteous staff really knows its stuff too, able to uncork gallons of information on the spot; they are happy to walk around with you and make recommendations. As one example, Mr. C found a bottle of Blackstone Napa Valley Merlot '92; seen for more than $12 in other stores, it was available here for $6.99. Not all the savings are as dramatic, but they're quite good indeed. Open seven days a week until 9 p.m. (Sundays until 8 p.m.)

D & M Wine & Liquor

• 2200 Fillmore St. (Sacramento St.), San Francisco; (415) 346-1325

Wine bargains in Pacific Heights? Well, yes, if you're looking for deals on champagne in particular, and are willing to pay in cash. D & M has long been a San Francisco favorite for such deals, and justifiably so. They stock dozens of well-known and not-so-well-known labels of champagnes (as well as wines and other liquors, but without the cash incentives), and sell them on a two-tiered price structure.

For starters, the prices are already competitive and often lower than many other specialty wine shops (the sort in which you're likely to find such a vast selection). Charge your purchase, and you get a decent discount. Buy your bubbly in cold, hard greenbacks, and you'll do even better. Thus, a 1985 Perrier Jouet Fleur de Champagne, which might sell elsewhere for as much as $89.99, goes for $73.99 here if you charge it—and $69.99 in cash. Or, if that's still a bit, er, rich for your tastes, you can find a bottle of Mumm Brut Prestige, meant to sell for $16.99, for $10.99 (credit) or $9.99 (cash).

You get the idea. Other vineyards well-represented at D & M, from California and around the world, include Piper, Iron Horse, Chandon, Bollinger, Schramsburg, and many others. Plus an impressive collection of rare, older vintage champagnes, along with weekly in-store wine specials, too. The store itself could be considered "vintage," in business since 1935. And perhaps best of all, they offer validated parking with your purchase—a valuable commodity in this busy area.

The Jug Shop

- 1567 Pacific Ave. (Polk St.), San Francisco; (415) 885-2922

The Jug Shop is well-known around the city for carrying a huge selection of beer, wine, and liquor at low prices. And what if you find a lower price elsewhere? They'll match it.

Naturally, California wines are nice and cheap here. A recent special offered a red table wine from Marlstone Vineyards for $12.99—the suggested retail price was $21.99. The Jug Shop also tries to find ways for you to enjoy finer tastes, without paying finer prices. A French label, La Forest pinot noir, was seen here for $7.99; it's comparable to wines costing $15 or more. And there is a wide variety of wines in the $6.99 to $10.99 range. They also carry hard-to-find imports; you'll see wines from Greece, Chile, Australia, and other countries not well-known for their vineyards. Many of these wines are highly respected by reviewers, and yet are lower in price than comparable bottles from France or Italy.

The Jug Shop holds wine tastings on Fridays and Saturdays, and occasionally on Thursdays. There is a nominal charge for each glass; and the wines being sampled are discounted $3 to $4 per bottle.

But wine isn't all there is to taste here. The store stocks some two hundred varieties of beer, at good prices. A six-pack of Samuel Adams Boston Lager (the Anchor Steam of the East Coast) is just $5.99. Hard liquors won't be hard on your wallet either. You can find a 750ml bottle of Absolut Vodka for $14.99, and the same size of Bailey's Irish Cream for $25.99. Open seven days a week.

Mr. Liquor

- 250 Taraval St. (Funston Ave.), San Francisco; (415) 731-6222

Yes, folks, it's the matchup you've been waiting for: Mr. Cheap meets

---

MR. CHEAP'S PICKS
Liquor and Beverages

✔ **D & M Wines**—Pacific Heights shop is the place for deals on champagnes.

✔ **The Jug Shop**—Would you believe over 200 varieties of beer? Wines from around the world? All at prices that will intoxicate you.

✔ **The Wine Club**—No, it's not a group of people who sit around and complain all day. Big bargains on local and international wines, thanks to no-frills setup.

Mr. Liquor! Does this result in anything more than a cheap joke? Yes, actually. This comfortable Parkside shop discounts all of its prices by 25% to 35% off retail. Markups on some wines are as little as 6%; you MBAs know how rare that is. And yet, with these super-low prices, you still get top-quality service in a well-stocked neighborhood shop.

Mr. L specializes in California wines, as well as French burgundies, bordeaux, and Rhone wines. If it's in here, you can bet it's a good value— keeping the stock moving is obviously a key to the low prices. Among some recently-spotted examples: A 1990 Caymus cabernet sauvignon, selling in most stores for around $20 (according to a magazine review posted on the wall beside it) was selling here for a tasty $12.85. And a 1991 Sanford Barrel Select chardonnay, another Napa Valley product, was seen here not for $30 a bottle, but a mere $19.85.

A small bar in the corner offers wines for the tasting during the week; pay by the glass, on the honor system. On weekends, this activity picks up with wine experts visiting to lead you through tastings of fancier labels. There is a fee for these events, usually held on Fridays and Saturdays from 2-6 p.m.

Mr. Liquor also has a deep selection of single-malt scotches, also at bargain prices; a bottle of Glenlivet, which might cost up to $30 in some stores, goes down more smoothly at $19.99 here—and sometimes, on special, for as little as $16.99. Other hard liquors are also discounted; recent specials included Gordon's gin at $12.99 for a 1.75 liter bottle, and a one-liter size of Bacardi for $9.98. Clearly, though, wines offer the best deals overall (including 10% off by the case). The shop is open seven days a week.

The Wine Club
• 953 Harrison St. (Sixth St.), San Francisco; (415) 512-9086

Well, it's like a warehouse club, especially the prices; the only difference is that you don't have to join anything to shop here. Just show up and save. The Wine Club works out near-steal deals with vineyards, both domestic and foreign, and keeps its own overhead costs as low as possible. One look around the store will confirm this. But hey, what do you care—you're not going to drink the stuff here!

Markup is low too; sometimes as low as 5% above cost. They're quite honest about all this, as you can read in their extremely informative newsletter, available in the store or by mailing list. Its thirty pages details hundreds of bottled bargains, indexed by type—Bordeaux, cabernets, etc. These are often accompanied by articles describing why they've chosen to sell these particular wines. A listing for Dow's Vintage Port '91, for instance, not only describes the fla-

vor (as far as words can), but tells you that only 6,500 cases of this label were made that year; it even suggests that "cellaring until 2010 or 2015 will make it a real beauty." Whether or not you'd wait that long, you certainly should jump at the chance to buy a bottle when it's reduced from a list price of $33 down to $21.59.

So, whether you want to save $30 off a $105 bottle of '90 Chateau Lafite Rothschild Bordeaux, or you just want a good value on a California chardonnay—say, $4.59 for a '92 Cotes de Sonoma, rated a "Best Buy" in the *Wine Spectator*—you'll find lots of good prices (and lots of help) here.

How cost-conscious is the Wine Club? They even encourage you to "recycle" styrofoam shipping cartons (they do a lot of phone/mail orders). Bring 'em in, and these folks will credit $4 toward your next purchase for each useable foam package. The store also offers a few wine-related bargains, including books, caviar, roses for Valentine's Day, cooking ingredients, and even "Wine Design" boxer shorts (!) created by Nicole Miller. There is also a wine tasting bar in the store; and free special events are held regularly, such as tasting lectures by nationally known experts.

This is the second branch of the Wine Club, which is based in Santa Ana; the San Francisco outpost has only been around since summer of '92, but based on the weekday crowd Mr. C witnessed, that's already proving to be a very good vintage indeed. Open seven days a week, including evenings until 7:00 and Sundays from 12-5 p.m.

LUGGAGE

AAA Luggage
- 585 Howard St. (Second St.), San Francisco; (415) 781-5007

In the same SoMa location (and the same family) since 1946, AAA Luggage has been a full-service store and repair center offering discounts on top name brands like Samsonite, Andiamo, Delsey, Travelpro, and more; plus National attaché cases and Zero Haliburton steel cases. Save 20% to 50% off retail prices, from folks who really know their stuff. Mr. C saw a Samsonite 26" soft-sided "EZ Packer" suitcase, with a retail price of $215, reduced to a light $144. A Travelpro 747 carry-on, with wheels, was reduced from $240 to $180. And a handsome saddle-leather attaché by National, with a list price of $498, was seen for just $298 here.

Often, AAA gets second-quality luggage, and sells these at even greater discounts. They even restore and sell pieces from airline lost-and-found departments. In fact, they are an authorized repair center for most major brands; no discounts on this service, but you can certainly save a bundle on your trundles by keeping them fixed up. These folks work on over 100 pieces each week, so they advise you to make arrangements well in advance of your next trip. Open weekdays from 8 a.m. to 5 p.m., and Saturdays from 9-3.

Leather Fetish
- 15 Westlake Mall (Daly Blvd.), Daly City; (415) 992-4464

Don't be scared off by the racy name of this shop in the Westlake Mall Shopping Center. They carry a good selection of suitcases, handbags, and clothing, all at 50% to 60% off retail prices. And none of it is adorned with metal studs or spikes.

Actually, this is sort of direct outlet; the owner formerly worked at a leather clothing factory in Los Angeles, and has parlayed those connections into good prices for you. Women's 3/4-length black lambskin coats, with retail prices of $380, sell here for $199. Even in department stores, they can sell for up to $300. A men's full-length lambskin trenchcoat was reduced from $499 to $280. At the lower end of the price scale, suede skirts sell here for as little as $19.95.

Luggage comes in from other sources, but also at discount. A Samsonite "Piggyback" suitcase with a suggested retail of $310 would sell for $250 in other stores; here, it's $199. And the shop carries all sizes of suitcases, up to the mammoth 34-inchers—which you often cannot find in department stores at all. Among budget brands, a 32" soft-sided suitcase by Locomotor was seen for a mere $49.

The store also has leather backpacks, briefcases (hard and soft-sided), and gift items. Open seven days a week.

The Luggage Center
- 828 Mission St. (Fourth St.), San Francisco; (415) 543-3771
- 2221 Shattuck Ave. (Allston Way), Berkeley; (510) 843-3385

  And other suburban locations

The Luggage Center is a luggage superstore, with over a dozen locations statewide. This means they can buy in large volume, and pass the discounts on to you. Thus, you can get something like a sturdy Samsonite suitcase on wheels for just $139.49, a substantial savings from the $205 list price. A soft-sider version, also with wheels, was just $143, originally $215.

Luggage Center carries more than just suitcases, of course. This is also a great place to pick up a nice brief-

MR. CHEAP'S PICK
Luggage

✔ **AAA Luggage**—Carry out some fine discounts on name-brand travel gear. Expert repairs, too.

case. Leather briefcases listing for, say, $270, may sell here for $180. A Lark nylon garment bag was over $100 off at $250. Hey, students, need a backpack? Luggage Center has a great selection, including Eastpaks as low as $29. If you're looking for something a little nicer, a shoulder-style book bag, regularly $75, was recently seen for $49. They also have lots of duffel bags and they're a great source for travel accessories like locks, money belts, and the like.

Luggage Center stores are open Monday through Saturday 10a.m. to 6p.m.and Sundays 11a.m. to 5p.m.

Mr. H Luggage and Gifts
- 55 Serramonte Center, Daly City; (415) 997-3111

Mr. C met Mr. H in this shopping mall just south of The City, and was pleased to make his acquaintance. Mr. H sells name brand luggage, briefcases, day planners, fountain pens, and other business accouterments at below-retail prices. He also claims to meet any advertised price you bring into the store.

Among the names you'll find here are Boyt, Toomey, Samsonite, Delsey, Orient Express, and others. Mr. C liked a Travelpro budget-grade carry-on; meant to sell for $180, it was on sale for $100 here. This is also a good place to look for backpacks, duffels, and leather handbags. With a second store in the Tanforan Center in San Bruno, Mr. H has been in business for over thirty years; both stores are open from 10 a.m. to 9 p.m. daily.

MUSICAL INSTRUMENTS

Here's another category in which you can save money by "going used"—though many instruments actually increase in value as they age. Often, a top-quality used instrument which can repaired is a better investment than a cheaper, newer version. It will sound better and last longer.

Black Market Music
- 1016 Howard St. (Sixth St.), San Francisco; (415) 252-1055
- 1354 N. Main St., Walnut Creek; (510) 944-0910

Black Market Music claims to be the largest dealer of used musical instruments on the West Coast. But don't just take their word for it; come in and see the thousands of used instruments on display and in stock at any given time. The majority of these are priced at about half of their original, new value. Some items will be above

or below that mark, depending on how old, how used, and how rare they are. There is also a good selection of collectors' vintage guitars and amps; these are definitely *not* cheap.

Black Market has tons of guitars, both electric and acoustic, starting as low as a mere $50. They also have plenty of amps, keyboards, and drums. Keyboards start around just $75; drum sets range from $250 to $400 and up.

Black Market Music buys and trades instruments; and they will arrange to sell your axe on consignment, if you wish. They will also rent instruments on a daily or weekly basis. The San Francisco store is open Monday through Saturday from 11 a.m. to 8 p.m. and Sunday from 11 a.m. to 6 p.m. The Walnut Creek branch is open Tuesday through Saturday from noon to 7 p.m. and Sunday from noon to 5 p.m.

Blue Note Music
* 2556 Telegraph Ave. (Dwight Way), Berkeley; (510) 644-2583

Blue Note Music sells new and used instruments—mostly for rock bands, as you'd expect in this student-filled area—along with accessories, amplifiers, and more. One big bargain here is Martin guitar strings for $1.75 a set, electric or acoustic; these usually sell for $6 or $7 elsewhere. Furthermore, they sell other brands of strings for up to 50% off retail.

The folks at Blue Note were hesitant to let Mr. C list examples of used instruments, since inventory changes so frequently; but you can almost always find good acoustic guitars from about $100 or so. New guitars are discounted 25% to 40% off list prices. One model of an electric guitar, list priced at $599, was selling here for just $325. The store offers repairs done on the premises, including guitar tune-ups at very reasonable rates.

Blue Note Music is open Monday through Saturday from 12 noon to 7:30 p.m.

Guitar Center
* 1321 Mission St. (Ninth St.), San Francisco; (415) 626-0362
* 3271 Adeline St. (Alcatraz.), Berkeley; (510) 652-6104

And other suburban locations

You'll find more than just guitars here. Guitar Center carries drums, keyboards, professional audio equipment—oh, and a huge selection of guitars. Because they have over a dozen stores, their buying power allows them to discount heavily.

How much? Well, GC has Squire Stratocasters for $179—the list price for these is $319.99. Keeping in mind that no one sells at list price, this is

still a clear bargain. A classical acoustic guitar, regularly $299.99, was seen for just $150. If it's drums that make your heart go boom-boom, you can find an beginner-level Pearl drum kit, complete with drums, cymbals, hardware, a stool, and pedals, for $1,048. The list price for the same set would total $2,249. The markdowns on keyboards include top names like Kawai and Korg; models that list for $450 to $1,950, sell here for $199 to $1,600.

Guitar Center does have some used gear, mostly stuff they take in as trade-ins, but it's not as extensive as some of the other shops around. You can try out all merchandise before you buy (as evidenced by the *sound* volume in the store), and they have a satisfaction guarantee: If you're not satisfied with your purchase—for any reason—return it in its original condition within 30 days, and you'll get your money back. Don't forget to bring in *all* receipts, manuals, and original packaging. Their are a few exceptions to this guarantee, but they'll explain these, if any, at the time of purchase. Guitar Center is open seven days a week.

Haight-Ashbury Music Center
* 1540 Haight St. (Ashbury St.), San Francisco; (415) 863-7327

Given its location, you'd be right in guessing that this store is mainly geared toward rock 'n roll, and it is—though there are other kinds of instruments and supplies to see. Still, guitars and electric keyboards—the very sound that put Haight on the map all those years ago—are the primary traffic here.

In fact, some 500 guitars are on display here at any given time; the folks here boast of having the largest selection of Stratocasters and Les Pauls in the Bay Area, and it certainly looks that way. The store carries bargains in both new and used instruments. New acoustic guitars begin around $139 and up; that price can get you something like a Hohner steel-stringed model. Electric guitars start a bit higher up, but you can get a basic model for about $150. Add a Fender amplifier for another $160 or so.

Used axes can go for as little as $99, depending on what has come into the store; all used instruments carry a 90-day warranty against defects which the repair department may have missed (it doesn't happen often). In addition, there is a wide selection of Korg and Roland keyboards, along with amps, drum kits, microphones, and PA systems. Not to mention strings, sticks, sheet music, instructional videos, and more.

For the less raucous, HAMC also stocks wind and brass instruments, along with a fascinating and diverse range of ethnic instruments from around the world. Pick up a set of maracas for just eight bucks, or try your hand at a Russian balalaika. If you're in search of the exotic, this is a great place to look. In fact, the store does a brisk mail-order business with customers all over the world. They've been doing so for over fourteen years. Open seven days a week.

K & K Music Super Store
- 1222 Sutter St. (Polk St.), San Francisco; (415) 928-1233
  And other suburban locations
Super is right. K & K Music Super Store has brand-new guitars, drums, audio equipment, and more, most at 20% to 30% below retail prices. Here, you can pick up a new Yamaha acoustic guitar for $449 or Latin percussion drums, with a retail price of $500, for $379. You'll find great prices on professional audio equipment and music-related electronics: Mr. C saw a DJ-70 Sampler, regularly $3,500, for just $975 and a dual CD player, normally $1,700, for $1,299. The store sometimes offers special promotions, as well. One recent sale featured a Tascam DA-88 digital 8-track recorder, meant to sell for $4,495, available for just $2,195 with a trade-in.

K & K also has a small selection of used equipment. The used gear is ever-changing, so they were reluctant to quote specific prices. They give you about a week's warranty on used

stuff, but it's important to make sure you are clear on the terms of any guarantee before you leave the store. They do minor repairs, as well. Open from 11 a.m. to 8 p.m. Monday through Friday and Saturday from 11 a.m. to 6 p.m.

Noe Valley Music
- 3914-A 24th St. (Sanchez St.), San Francisco; (415) 821-6644
Noe Valley Music sells new, used, and vintage instruments all at competitive prices. Now, many of the items here are still going to be expensive, especially the vintage and custom-made instruments; but that doesn't mean you aren't saving money. The folks here showed Mr. C a custom handmade electric bass guitar for $850. That may seem very expensive, but it is worth at least twice as much—especially in music, where the right "feel" is invaluable.

Those of you who are just starting out or who don't have a bunch a money to throw around for a custom instrument, don't despair. Noe Valley does have good-quality new and used instruments at bass-clef prices. Acoustic guitars can be found for as little as $100 to $150, for decent used models or beginner's quality new ones. Similar types of electric guitars start under $200.

The sales people at Noe Valley Music are very friendly; stop in and they'll be more than happy to help you figure out which guitar will best suit your needs and your budget. Open Monday through Saturday from 11 a.m. to 7 p.m. and Sunday from 11 a.m. to 5 p.m.

Piano Care Company
- 2011 Divisadero St. (California St.), San Francisco; (415) 567-1800
Piano Care Company offers what it calls "honest deals" on used pianos. The owner will readily admit that you can find *cheaper* pianos elsewhere, but what he is selling is quality at a good price. All of the instruments that come into the store are completely refurbished, restored, and reconditioned; they are so confi-

dent in their work that they guarantee it. They don't call it a "lifetime guarantee," Mr. C was told, but they stand behind their work and there is no set limit on the warranty or any fine print. This is business "the old-fashioned way"—call it a gentlemen's agreement. In any case, there is clearly room for a bit of maneuvering; but, if you have particular concerns, the store will give you a warranty in writing.

Pianos here range in price from just over a thousand dollars to several thousands. You can easily find a good piano in the affordable range of $1,300 to $1,700. These include major brand names like Yamaha, Steinway, Baldwin, and Wurlitzer—most at anywhere from one-half to one-third off their original retail prices. This standard doesn't apply to all of their wares, of course. They carry a lot of rare and antique pianos that are worth *more* today than they were when they were new. Just because something is old, though, doesn't mean it's necessarily expensive; Mr. C noticed a 1927 Fisher piano for a very reasonable $1,745.

The staff here is very friendly and knowledgeable, and they will be happy to assist you in finding a piano that fits into your lifestyle and your budget. Piano Care Company is open Monday through Friday from 11 a.m. to 7 p.m., Saturday from 10 a.m. to 6 p.m., and Sunday from 11 a.m. to 6 p.m.

Piedmont Piano Company

- 4382 Piedmont Ave.(Pleasant Valley Ave.), Oakland; (510) 547-8188

Along with competitive prices on new pianos, both new and electronic, Piedmont has one of the largest selections of used pianos in the Bay Area. In fact, they have not one, but two separate warehouses filled with a varying selection of uprights, baby grands, and spinets.

Owner Jim Callahan reminds his customers that "a fifty-year-old piano can be just as good as a new one," and that this is often the way to a terrific deal. Used uprights, merely in

---

MR. CHEAP'S PICKS
Musical Instruments

✔ **Haight-Ashbury Music Center**—Good prices on guitars and keyboards, right from the unofficial heart of the rock music world.

✔ **Piano Care Company**—These folks restore and recondition used pianos. Their experienced staff can help you find just what you need, on virtually any budget.

"working" condition, start as low as $1,000 apiece or less; fully restored, the same instruments are mostly priced from $1,500 to $3,000. Considering the fact that budget models of brand-new pianos also start around $3,000, you can come out way ahead by going with a used piano of a higher grade.

As an example, Callahan mentioned a Steinway upright of 1890s vintage (still a baby, by music world standards). It was available, "as is," for $3,000; fully reconditioned by his staff, including a ten-year warranty, it would sell between $7,000 and $8,000; but, if you were to buy the same type of Steinway new, that would probably go for about $15,000. The savings are big—though, of course, it's all relative.

In the main showroom, there is another cost-saving option: electronic, or digital, pianos. Perhaps you've seen them already; with improvements in digital technology, these keyboards now sound just like acoustic pianos. Yet, most models are priced in the $1,500-$3,000 range, far less than the "real" thing. Plus, they never need tuning. Callahan even gets the occasional used digital, though these don't stick around for long.

Piedmont Piano has been in business for over fifteen years, with regular clientele of loyal customers. Many wait for the three or four occasions a year when Callahan puts all Yamaha pianos on special sale. The store is open seven days a week.

Sam Adato's Drum Shop
- 283 Ninth St. (Folsom St.), San Francisco; (415) 863-DRUM

Sam Adato's Drum Shop carries a good selection of used and vintage drums. Vintage drums, being valuable collector's items, are not cheap. But, this is not the case for used drums (no pun intended); going this route can save you hundreds of dollars. Since it's the drum heads that take the pounding, and these are replaceable, used drums can be almost as good as new for a lot less.

You can set yourself up with a good beginner's kit for about $300 to $400. The same set would easily cost $1,000 to $2,000 new. All used sets are clean, and in very good condition. And, if you're looking to move up to a bigger and better set of drums, you can sell or trade in your old ones here. As with any such buy-sell-trade business, you'll get more value in trade. Sam's does minor repairs on the premises, also, and they have drums for rent on a daily basis. Open from Monday through Saturday 11a.m. to 7p.m.

PARTY SUPPLIES

CGF Cash and Carry
- 455 Toland St. (Oakdale Ave.), San Francisco; (415) 285-9333

If you don't mind the rumble of trucks and the bumpy streets of this industrial area, you can shop at this wholesale food supplier just like the grocery store owners do. It also helps, of course, if you can use industrial sizes, like soda by the case. If so, you'll certainly enjoy taking the Pepsi challenge when Coke and Pepsi are just $5.89 for 24 cans. Why, that's just a quarter a pop (sorry about the pun.) If you do a lot of cooking, you may be able to use a three- liter can of extra virgin olive oil, for an incredible $11.19. Similar deals abound on canned goods, packaged breads, cheeses, and meats, as well as paper supplies. Definitely a good place to shop for a big party! CGF is open seven days a week.

Fantastico
- 559 Sixth St. (Brannan St.), San Francisco; (415) 982-0680

In addition to selling perhaps the world's largest collection of silk flowers, Fantastico (sounds like the name of a bad magician, doesn't it?) is also a wholesaler of every kind of party supply from kiddie paper plates to wedding cake decorations. Get a 25-pack of Duraplate 7" deep plastic dishes for $4.20, in a choice of colors; then add the matching cups, napkins, placemats, and tablecloths. For those children's parties, there are posters, plates, and loot bags adorned with the likes of Batman, Mickey Mouse, or Ren and Stimpy (Mr. C's choice).

If it's prom time, 500-foot rolls of crepe paper cost $2.65 each; get a matching 24" fold-out tissue paper globe for $3.25. In fact, there are banners for almost any theme, straight or comic: "Happy 21st Birthday," "Over the Hill," "Still Perfect After All These Years," etc. Plus tons of stuff for any holiday, as each one approaches.

Bride and groom wedding cake decorations—the serious kind—start from $20 and up; Fantastico also offers an invitation printing service at reasonable prices, along with lots of other wedding accessories. Bring cash or a check; you can really go wild in here, and they don't take

credit cards—one of the ways stores
keep prices low.

Paper Plus Outlet
- 2924 College Ave., (Ashby)
  Berkeley; (510) 540-4836
- 1643 San Pablo Ave., Berkeley;
  (510) 525-1799

Paper Plus Outlet is a great place to
pick up small-sized packages of party
goodies like plates, cups, and so on—
at 10% to 75% below retail prices. A
24-pack of paper plates, in an assortment of colors, regularly $7.10, sells
here for just $4.95. Two-dozen cups,
meanwhile, were marked down from
$4.75 to $2.50; and a twelve-piece
box of plastic forks, knives, or
spoons, go for almost half the list
price at $1. Coordinate an entire table
for under $15! Decorated plates are
priced at $1.70 to $2.85 a pack, depending on size. And, if it's a birthday shabang you're planning, don't
forget the candles, at 65¢ a box.

PP has many other kinds of paper
and non-paper products as well, including wrapping paper, cards, frames, and
rubber stamps. Hardcover blank books
are priced at $5.95 (do these save you
money because the words have been
left out?), and a 29-foot roll of tissue
paper was just $1.50.

This store is absolutely crammed
with stuff, much of it being sold right
out of the shipping cartons; it can be
tricky to navigate past all the boxes
and whatnot in the aisles, but that is
clearly part of the fun. Paper Plus
Outlet is open Monday through Saturday, 10 a.m. to 6 p.m. and Sunday,
noon to 5 p.m.

The Party Warehouse
- 2121 Harrison St. (17th St.), San
  Francisco; (415) 863-0912
- 65 Southgate (Lake Merced Blvd.),
  Daly City; (415) 992-5570
- 221 Oak St. (Third St.), Oakland;
  (510) 893-1951

MR. CHEAP'S PICK
Party Supplies

✔ **Fantastico**—Part of the Flower
Market area, this huge
warehouse sells silk flowers,
party goods, and everything for
any kind of bash—at wholesale
prices.

And other suburban locations
Party Warehouse is one of those
mega-stores, carrying every kind of
party favor, supply, and decoration
imaginable, all at discount. Possibly
even a few you didn't imagine. Need
a cake pan in the shape of a dino-
saur? Or a baseball player? They've
got 'em here for $9.99 each, less a
10% markdown. They have candles,
from tapers to votive, plus simple
glass holders to go with them; mylar
balloons with all kinds of splashy or
cute patterns, to be filled with he-
lium; you can even make your own
silver mylar banner, with any kind of
saying on it.

Needless to say, Party Warehouse
is ready to outfit you completely for
any kind of theme party, be it a holiday, a "Teenage Mutant Ninja Turtles" birthday party, a baby shower, a
wedding, or what have you. They
also have an invitation printing service in each store. In addition, all
greeting cards and wrapping paper is
always sold at 50% off the list price.

And Mr. C hasn't even mentioned
the basics—plates, napkins, cups,
plasticware, tablecloths. You get the
idea. All Party Warehouse stores are
open seven days a week.

PET SUPPLIES

These are some of the best places to buy pet foods and supplies around the Bay area. Mr. C also suggests that you check out some of The City's many "dollar" stores, since many of them sell reduced-price canned food, and sometimes even leashes, collars, and doggie and kitty toys.

Animal Farm
- 1531 San Pablo Ave. (Cedar St.) Berkeley; (510) 526-2993

All pet stores are created equal, says Orwell, but some are more equal than others. With everyday low prices on pet food and supplies, Animal Farm is about as egalitarian as you can get.

The shop has great prices on bulk quantities of the most popular premium dog and cat foods. You can get Iams cat food for $14.99 a case. For dogs, get an eight pound bag of Eukanuba for $10.49. Science Diet dry dog food is just $9.89 for a ten-pound bag, and the cans are just $25.19 a case.

You'll also find good prices on various pet supplies. A medium-sized, airline-approved carrier cage was just $36.99. Is Fluffy getting a little frisky with the furniture? Get a small scratching post for just $29.99. Fish fans can find a ten-gallon aquarium, with all the necessary accessories, for as low as $39.99.

Animal Farm is open Monday through Friday from 10 a.m. to 6:30 p.m., Saturday from 9:30 a.m. to 6 p.m., and Sunday from 11 a.m. to 5 p.m.

By The Pound Pet Supplies
- 1677 Washington St. (Polk St.), San Francisco; (415) 563-2226

The name of this store is taken from the store owner's pets, who came to him "by the pound." For you, this pun means you can find pet foods in large quantities—by the pound or by the case—at competitive prices. These include such high-end brands

as Iams, Sheba, and others, for dogs, cats, birds, and more.

They also have a good selection of pet accessories at competitive prices. Hamster balls were seen for $7.69; large, sturdy food bowls were $3.89, and an assortment of cat and dog toys were selling for just $2.58 apiece.

By The Pound is open by the week: Monday through Friday from 10 a.m. to 7 p.m., Saturday from 9:30 a.m. to 6:30 p.m., and Sunday from 12 noon to 6 p.m.

Cal's Discount Pet Supply
- 5950 California St. (21st Ave.), San Francisco; (415) 386-1720

Catering to canines (and others) in the Richmond, Cal's is a classic neighborhood shop—big on service, low on prices. They won't bother trying to sell you things you don't need. In fact, they won't bother you at all, unless of course you ask for assistance.

The store has all kinds of dog and cat food at discount prices, including high-quality brands like Iams, Nutro, and Science Diet. They also have barrels filled with bulk food for birds (with different mixes of seeds specially made for each kind of bird), as well as for rabbits and guinea pigs. Many of these cost just a dollar a pound, or less.

The store also offers percentage discounts to senior citizens, and schoolteachers (you all remember the pet hamster you had at the back of the room in fourth grade, don't you?). Open seven days a week, into the early evening.

Pet Food Express

- 1798 19th Ave. (Noriega St.), San Francisco; (415) 759-7777
- 371 West Portal Ave. (15th Ave.), San Francisco; (415) 759-1400
- 2655 Shattuck Ave. (Derby St.), Berkeley; (510) 540-7777
- 5144 Broadway (51st St.), Oakland; (510) 654-8888
  And other suburban locations

At this local chain of stores, you'll find some terrific prices on all kinds of pet foods and acccessories. In addition to their already discounted rates on brands like Nutro, Iams, Eukanuba, Avo-Derm, and good ol' Purina. They also have some of the best prices around on accessories like grooming trimmers, medicated baths, collars, scratching posts, and all the rest.

PFE runs special sales periodically—like 20% off all S.A.M. bird cages and hamster products. They also offer coupon books for extra savings ($2 off a bag of Jonny Cat litter, $25 off a professional dog training program, etc.); a recent edition offered $350 in savings, with the $5 purchase price donated to pet adoption causes.

All stores are open seven days a week, often into the early evenings for all you working pet parents.

Petcetera

- 2226 Taraval St. (32nd Ave.), San Francisco, (415) 661-4236

Along with a cute name, Petcetera has great prices on large quantities of premium brands of pet food including Iams, Eukanuba, and Science Diet. Pet owners already know it's generally cheapest to buy in bulk; Petcetera has plenty, such as bulk dog biscuits for $1.09 a pound. While the name brands aren't as cheap, it's still less expensive to buy in large bags or cases. Here you can get six-ounce cans of Iams cat food for $14.99 a case of 24. A case of Friskies six-ounce cans is $8.64. You can get dry food cheap, too. Science Diet dry puppy formula is just $18.99 for twenty pounds, and Eukanuba dry original formula is $18.49 for the

MR. CHEAP'S PICKS
Pet Supplies

✔ **Cal's Discount**—This shop in the Richmond makes feeding your pet as inexpensive as all those Richmond cheap-eats places for us humans.

✔ **Sammy's Pet World**—Pet supply bargains abound in this recently-expanded Mission store; if you adopt from the shelter next door, you get extra discounts.

---

twenty pound bag. Petcetera also has a frequent buyer card for premium food, so if you buy a lot you can save even more.

Petcetera is not just for dog and cat lovers, however. You can buy rodent, bird, and even primate food in bulk. Prices range from 39¢ a pound for "pigeon popcorn" to $1.29 a pound for primate chow.

You'll also find a wide selection of accessories, including toys, food bowls, cages, and so on, but these aren't always cheap. Mr. C saw some pretty unusual items; a glow-in-the-dark runabout for a hamster or gerbil was just $5.99.

Petcetera is open Monday through Friday from 10 a.m. to 7 p.m., Saturday from 9:30 a.m. to 6:30 p.m., and Sunday 11 a.m. to 6 p.m.

Sammy's Pet World

- 2404 16th St. (Bryant St.), San Francisco; (415) 863-1840

Is it too much of a pun to say that this place is so wildly popular, they've just moved into a larger space? Co-owners Brian and Sam (no, not *the* Sam—he's a pet, sort of the store mascot) have literally doubled their square footage, and it's a good thing, too. The old place was just bulging with pets and supplies of every kind.

All foods are marked up very little above cost, in order to compete with the new wave of mall superstores (they're managing just fine, obviously); the store also has things like bulk food for birds and small animals, as well as cat litter. Does your dog tear through rawhide treats? Buy ten or more, and get 15% off.

In fact, there are all kinds of discount opportunities here. Buy $100 worth of food (not unheard of), and you'll get a $10 credit on accessories. The store is located right next to the S.P.A., and these guys are experts on adoption. So, if you adopt a pet through them, you'll get a 10% discount card, good on all non-food items. The store also offers grooming services.

Sam and Brian will do just about anything to help pet owners out. They even accept ATM cards as a method of payment. And, they're just plain fun guys. Open seven days a week, including weeknights until 7 p.m.

SEWING AND CRAFT SUPPLIES

Coast Wholesale Florist, Inc.
- 149 Morris St. (Fifth St.), San Francisco; (415) 781-3034 or (800) 562-3681

Coast Wholesale Florist sells their dried flowers and foliage to manufacturers, gift sellers, designers, and decorators. These are raw materials used for arrangements, wreaths, gift baskets, and home or office decor. At this store, you can purchase these materials for your own crafts and hobbies at the same wholesale prices that manufacturers and decorators enjoy.

It's just a fun place to shop, too. Coast is basically a huge warehouse in the Flower Market district, filled with dried flowers, baskets, spices, and more. Take a moment to look up at the ceiling and you'll see hundreds of bunches of flowers hanging upside down as part of the drying process.

Their prices are just as artfully withered. You'll find a three-ounce package of basil for $4.50, cinnamon sticks for $5 a pound, small gourds for $4, grapevines at $7 a dozen, and chilies, very much a part of Southwestern decor, for just $4.50 each. While most items can be purchased in reasonably small quantities, some items are only sold in bulk amounts. For those things, you may want to consider going in with a friend or two and splitting the costs. For example, spray rosebuds are $13.25 per bag; each bag contains approximately 800 rosebuds.

Coast Florists also has potpourri at $6.75 for an eight-ounce bag, and potpourri oils at $2.75 for a quarter-ounce. You'll find a whole range of products and materials to help you with any project. Coast carries baskets in every size, shape, and color imaginable, from very large ones for $13 to little, teeny, tiny ones for 60¢. They have floral tape for $2 a pack and glue sticks for $4.50 a pound, not to mention every manner of ribbon and wire available. You'll occasionally run across instruction books at a discount, too. Mr. C found *The Book of Potpourri*, $4 off its cover price at $18.50. Coast is your one-stop floral craft center.

Elsewhere in the Flower Market area, check out **Fantastico** at 559 Sixth Street; telephone (415) 982-0680. This is another gigantic warehouse filled with all manner of dried and fake flowers, as well as party supplies, wedding cake decorations, engraving services, and more, all at wholesale prices to the public.

Discount Fabrics
- 4556 Mission St. (Ocean Ave.), San Francisco; (415) 586-8045

- 2315 Irving St. (24th Ave.), San Francisco; (415) 564-7333
- 1432 Haight St. (Masonic St.), San Francisco; (415) 621-5584

Bargain hunters, take note: There are two stores called Discount Fabrics in San Francisco. They are not related, except by name. *This* Discount Fabrics is Mr. C's choice, and it has three locations: In the Mission District, in Sunset, and in Haight-Ashbury. And, while it looks like most fabric stores you may be familiar with, there's a distinct difference.

Not all of their fabrics have the regular retail prices marked, so you can't always tell exactly how much you're saving—but avid sewing fans know a bargain when they see one. You'll find things like sandwashed rayon (with a drape like silk, only easier to care for) for $12.99 a yard; cotton/polyester blend calicos for $1.98 to $4.98 a yard; and satins for $4.98 to $5.98 a yard. Mr. C found purple handwoven silk, at least $16 a yard elsewhere, for just $9.98 a yard here. Solid 100% cotton sheetings, in colors galore, were reduced from $4.75 a yard to $3.59, and again to $2.98 a yard.

True cheapsters don't stop there, however. The bargain bins, in the back, are where the real treasures are buried. You may find materials like 100% cotton sail cloth, regularly $5.98 a yard, for $2.98 a yard; indigo denim, regularly $6.29 a yard, for $3.98 a yard; and 100% wool in teddy bear brown, regularly $29 a yard, for just $5.98 a yard! They also had muslin for 99¢ a yard, sold "as is."

Speaking of which, a word of caution: When buying remnants, check the material over carefully, as it usually cannot be returned. The bargain bins also had upholstery fabrics, lace, and lots of great materials for costumes. Discount Fabrics also has a great selection of notions and patterns. All three stores are open Monday through Saturday from 9:30 a.m. to 6 p.m. The Mission and Haight-Ashbury stores are also open on Sunday.

MR. CHEAP'S PICKS
Sewing and Craft Supplies

✔ **Coast Wholesale Florist, Inc.**—This warehouse is filled with dried plants and flowers of all varieties. The raw materials for many a craft and hobby, these can be bought here at wholesale prices.

✔ **Discount Fabrics** and **Discount Fabrics**—Don't let two separately-owned stores with the same name confuse you—both offer extraordinary prices on a large selection of fabrics and notions.

✔ **Gunne Sax Fabric Outlet**—Here you can find the fabrics that Jessica McClintock, et al., use to make their heavenly creations, at a fraction of their value.

Discount Fabrics

- 501 Third St. (Bryant St.), San Francisco; (415) 495-4201

Okay, here's the other Discount Fabrics. It's on Third Street in SoMa, within walking distance of a slew of other bargain outlets, and has only one branch. It's a warehouse-style, no-frills shopping experience, but the sales staff is extremely helpful and there are hundreds of fabrics to choose from.

What you'll find here is yards and yards of great fabrics at discounted prices. Some fabrics are available at an even greater discount if you buy the whole bolt. For example, denim, with a retail price of $6.98 a yard, sells for just $2.25 a yard—or $1.75 a yard for the roll. Rayons, in a huge variety of colors and prints, were $7.98 retail, just $4 a yard here or $3.20 a yard for the roll; and 100% poplin prints, in polka dots, stripes, gingham, and more, regularly $6.99, were just $3.59 a yard or $2.40 a yard by the bolt. You'll find lots of cottons, in prints and solids, for $3 a yard.

Discount Fabrics carries lots of better-quality fabrics at low prices. Mr. C found silk, handwoven in India, regularly $24 a yard, for just $9 a yard. If you're looking for fabrics to make wedding, bridesmaid's, or prom gowns, look no further. Lavender satin, regularly $6.98, was just $4.98. White taffeta was just $4.50 a yard and white lace, regularly $6.99, was just $3.98. Mr. C also spied some taffeta seconds as low as 99¢ a yard, but be careful with these since they are sold "as is."

Other quality fabrics include heavyweight velvets, in lots of colors, regularly $14 a yard, here just $10 a yard; and chiffon in black or beige, regularly $5.98 a yard, here $3.49 a yard. They also carry plenty of career-fashion fabrics, like 100% wool jersey, half of retail at $7.50 a yard; angora and wool blends, regularly $10.95 a yard, here $5.98 a yard; and linen florals, great for a spring suit, regularly $8.98 a yard, here only $3.99 a yard. Poke around in here for specialty materials, too—like upholstery fabrics, normally $10.95 a yard, for just $3.98 a yard. Again, most of these offer lower "by the bolt" rates.

Discount Fabrics also carries a small selection of notions, also at discounted prices. Recently they had 200-yard spools of thread, regularly 59¢ each, for 25¢ each (or five for 99¢); and zippers, in lots of colors, regularly $1.40 each, selling for just 20¢ each (or ten for $1).

Discount Fabrics on Third is open Monday through Friday from 10:30 a.m. to 5:30 p.m., and Saturday from 10:30 a.m. to 3:30 p.m.

Fabric Factory Outlet
• 101 Clement St. (Second Ave.), San Francisco; (415) 387-3936
It's not really an outlet for any textile mill in particular, but this small, clean, and bright corner storefront in the Richmond is absolutely crammed

with fabrics. Most are of the already-inexpensive variety, like rayons and cottons, but there are so many patterns to see! In fact, the highest price in the whole shop is $3.39 a yard, for rayon prints that would cost about twice that in other stores.

Beyond that, there are—get ready—20,000 fabrics priced at $1.99 a yard, and another 4,000 fabrics priced at just 99¢ a yard. Plus bargain bins of lace trims at 25¢ a yard, zippers at 25¢ each, and bags filled with faux fancy-looking buttons for a dollar. Worth a look-see; open every day from 10 a.m. to 6 p.m.

Gunne Sax Fabric Outlet
• 35 Stanford St. (Second St.), San Francisco; (415) 495-3326
Gunne Sax uses a whole lot of fabric in making its popular lines of fancy dresses and wedding gowns. Whatever they have left over, they sell off here. You may find lace for $5 a yard; taffeta, in lots of colors, for $4 to $5 a yard; satin for $3 a yard; or black velvet for $8 a yard.

Since these are some of the same materials they use for their garments, this is the obvious place to look for the necessities to alter or repair that bargain you found in the adjoining Gunne Sax dress outlet (see listing under "Clothing: New"). Like those dresses, fabrics here are sold "as is," so shop carefully.

Not all of the fabrics here are frilly satins, taffetas, and lace. You'll find rayons for $3.50 a yard, or wool/silk blends, regularly $50 a yard, for $10 a yard. You'll also find various necessities like trim for $1 to $2 a yard, buttons for 50¢ a bag, and even satin-covered hangers for $1. They also carry a line of Simplicity patterns. And don't leave without snooping in the $1-a-yard bin!

The Gunne Sax Fabric Outlet is open Monday through Saturday from 9 a.m. to 5:30 p.m., and Sunday from 11 a.m. to 5 p.m.

M.I. Discount
• 2026 Shattuck Ave. (University Ave.), Berkeley; (510) 704-8834
M.I. Discount has a huge selection of

fabrics, all 60% off retail prices. You read right: *everything* in the store is 60% off, period. This means you can get cotton/polyester blends for $4.99 a yard, decorator's fabrics for $12.99 a yard, and ivory lace for $14.99 a yard. Mr. C saw coral taffeta for just $7.50 a yard. Designer screen prints, in 100% cotton, list for $9.99 to $14.99; they were seen here for $4 to $6 per yard. Signs posted on the walls show you all of the sale prices, along with their 60% higher counterparts—so you can see how much you are saving.

What M.I. Discount does not have a lot of is the sewing notions that accompany these fabrics in most other stores. The reason? M.I. can't discount them at (say it with Mr. C, everyone) 60%. For this reason, they are considering staggering the discounts so they can offer a more complete line of products in the near future—perhaps by the time you've read this! Please note that all sales here are final.

New York Fabrics
- 170 Columbus Ave. (Kearny St.), San Francisco; (415) 398-2223
- 969 Market St. (Sixth St.), San Francisco; (415) 543-4345
- 2109 Mission St. (21st St.), San Francisco; (415) 552-4525
  And other suburban locations

New York Fabrics has a huge selection of sewing materials and accessories at low prices. Head straight to the bargain area where you may find nylon cloth, the sort of material used for windbreakers and such, on sale for $2.88 a yard—marked down from $4.59. Also seen in the bargain area were a variety of cotton prints for $3.88 a yard.

But, the prices on all their fabrics are terrific. Shoppers will find cotton plisse, in several pastel shades, for just $3.99 a yard; or polyester and rayon challis, in dozens of colors, for just $6.99 a yard. If you need bridal fabrics they have plenty, including party taffeta for $4.29 a yard. For career wear, try rayon and polyester suiting for $8.49 a yard or wool blends as low as $8.99 a yard.

New York Fabrics also has a great selection of notions and patterns. Their hours are 10 a.m. to 6 p.m. Monday through Saturday, noon to 5 p.m. Sunday.

SHOES AND SNEAKERS

Footwear First Outlet
- 2301 Fourth St. (Bancroft Way), Berkeley; (510) 848-8585

With four retail stores in the Bay Area, this warehouse along the Berkeley outlet stretch is a fine source for men's and women's boots, as well as some other lines of artsy Euro-style women's shoes. Much of the large stock here consists of first-quality leftovers from the other branches; during Mr. C's visit, these included lots of Nocona western boots—a spinoff of Justin Boots. Regularly $225, Nocona bullhide boots were on sale here for $149; Nocona's lizard-skin boots were marked down from $345 to $199, and their pigskin boots were a smart $99 a pair. Now, these may be "past season," but hey—cowboy boots have been in style for years, basically unchanged. Just because newer ones have come in from the factory, why shouldn't you check these out? No reason at all.

Among the dress shoes, heels by American Eagle were selling for just $29—copies of a $300 design by Ferragamo. You decide. Azaleia colored leather sandals from Brazil, patterned after French designs costing $160, were seen here for $48. The store is open Wednesdays through Sundays from 11 a.m. to 6 p.m.

Maraolo

- 404 Sutter St. (Stockton St.), San Francisco; (415) 781-0895

Maraolo is an Italian manufacturer which makes shoes for famous designers like Donna Karan and Giorgio Armani. They also sell their shoes directly through various retail stores all over the country. San Franciscans are particularly blessed, though; this store has become Maraolo's outlet.

You may, for example, find a funky pair of black pumps, originally sold in department and specialty stores for $130, selling here for $99. Even discounted, a lot of this merchandise is still very expensive; like a pair of lizard-skin pumps in brown or black for $295. But, when you consider the fact that these had an original retail price of $590, you'll see that this place is indeed a bargain.

So, what's wrong with the shoes, you're asking? Well, there are some seconds, and they're marked as such, but most are just discontinued or past-season stocks. You'll see a great variety of styles (daytime and evening) and colors—whether you're looking for wardrobe basics or something more trendy. And keep your eyes peeled for special sales. Maraolo recently had a pair of tan lace-up boots, originally $240, marked down once to $168, and then again to a final $120. A pair of woven leather shoes, in brown or black, were reduced from $215 to $125 to $108. The savings just go on and on! Maraolo is open Monday through Saturday, 10 a.m. to 6 p.m.

Shoe Depot

- 280 Metro Center, 43 Colma Blvd., Colma; (415) 755-0556

Here's a throwback to days of old—of neighborhood shops selling basics for average folks, low on prices and high on service. So, what's a place like that doing in a suburban shopping mall? Keeping up with the times. Shoe Depot specializes in "shoes for the working man," i.e., workboots, casual shoes, and sneakers. In business for over forty years, the store lays claim to being the Bay Area's only independent seller of men's work shoes; and man, do they have a lot. All of these are sold at discounts of about 20% off retail.

Work boots by Georgia Boot, meant to sell for $135, go for $119 here. Wolverine boots, listed at $119, sell for $80. Some lines start as low as $29.99. In casual styles, you can find Hush Puppies reduced from $87 to $69; dress styles include Florsheim leather shoes, reduced from $85 to $69. Plus Durango cowboy boots, Reebok cross-trainers, and many more. Need extra-wide widths? You'll find 'em here. Shoe Depot is as big on service as on selection; legions of loyal customers prove it. Open seven days a week.

Shoe Loft

- 225 Front St. (California St.), 2nd Floor, San Francisco; (415) 956-4648

Up in the Shoe Loft, you'll find high-quality brand name and designer shoes at substantial discounts. They carry a wonderful range of styles from the very practical, like navy leather pumps, reduced from $50 to $29.90, all the way to the whimsical, like red leather flats by Nina, reduced from $60 to just $15. At these great prices, who can resist? Shoe Loft's merchandise consists of past-season styles and overstocks from the country's top manufacturers. Discounts vary widely, depending on the deals they can make, but everything is below retail prices.

Mr. C saw navy leather flats by Versani, regularly $115, for $49.90 and white leather pumps by Anne Klein, regularly $135, for $54.90. Other really great deals included off-white leather pumps by Via Spiga ($30), white leather jazz shoes by Joan & David ($30), black suede pumps by Kenneth Cole ($39.90), and Dr. Marten's classic black boots ($49.90).

With a location so convenient to downtown, many women make this a regular lunchtime stop. The store is open Monday through Friday from 10 a.m. to 6 p.m., and Saturday from 11 a.m. to 5 p.m.

Shoe Pavilion

- 899 Howard St. (Fifth St.), San Francisco; (415) 974-1821
- 340 Sansome St. (Sacramento St.), San Francisco; (415) 397-8024
  And other suburban locations

If you love shoes, you will love this store. Why? Because you'll find great brand name and designer shoes, in styles from classic to trendy, at discounts of as much as 50% or more! A recent special offered leather cowboy boots by Vittorio Ricci in black and brown, originally $105, for just $39.99. Flats by Papagallo, in five colors, were reduced from $59.95 to just $29.99, while others by Bandolino, in black, were marked down from $79.95 to the same price.

Looking for pumps? They have 'em by the dozens. Black patent leathers by Evan-Picone, regularly $102.95, may sell for $59.99; Anne Klein models in white or navy, originally $140.95, for just $49.99. And pumps with leather soles by Enrico Gerbi, regularly $115.69, were an incredible $39.99!

The Shoe Pavilion has not forgotten the guys, either. They have a great selection of brand name shoes for men at similar discounts. Loafers by David & Joan (the flip side of Joan & David), regularly $149.99, were just $79.99; boots by R.J. Colt, regularly $84.95, were just $69.99; and brown wingtips by Florsheim, usually $102.95, were just $79.99. Run, don't walk, to Shoe Pavilion.

The Shoe Works

- 280 Metro Center, 51 Colma Blvd., Colma; (415) 756-3413

At the Shoe Works you can pick up a couple of pairs of cool leather shoes for the same price you'd pay for just *one* pair in some chi-chi department

---

MR. CHEAP'S PICKS
Shoes and Sneakers

✔ **Maraolo**—This Italian manufacturer makes shoes for DKNY, Giorgio Armani, and others. This store has become their outlet, selling past-seasons and overstocks at a discount.

✔ **Shoe Loft**—Brand name and designer shoes at discount prices right in the middle of the Financial District. An ideal store to cruise through during lunch break.

✔ **Shoe Pavilion**—Prices are reduced 50% or more on brand name and designer shoes, for women and men.

---

store. Please note that these are not necessarily the highest-quality shoes, with some name brands mixed into a rather generic bunch; but these are real leather and with a little care should wear well. Pumps and flats, in neutral shades, were just $19.98 and $16.98, respectively. Also priced at $19.98 were leather sandals by Candies. The store also carries a good selection of bridal shoes and leather bags.

Be on the lookout for sales. Mr. C saw a pair of *trés* trendy black boots, regularly $49.98, on sale for just $25. Also, be sure to check out the clearance racks, where Mr. C saw more leather boots for as little as $11 (!) and navy flats for $13.

SPORTING GOODS

Big 5 Sporting Goods
- 2159 Chestnut St. (Pierce St.), San Francisco; (415) 474-8670
- 1533 Sloat Blvd. (Lakeshore Plaza), San Francisco; (415) 681-4593
- 314 Gellert Blvd. (Serramonte Center), Daly City; (415) 994-3688
And other suburban locations

This major West Coast chain has a little bit of everything, for the most solitary exercise nut or any size of team. The prices storewide are, well, competitive; better yet, items in every department are reduced in weekly sales. You're sure to find something you need here.

One such sale recently featured 30% off on all skiwear in stock, and during the height of the skiing season, no less. At the same time, city-bound daredevils could save $80 on Ultra-Wheels "Zephyr" in-line skates. Tennis enthusiasts, meanwhile, could find a Wilson "Cobra 95" graphite racquet marked down from $110 to just $49.99.

Big 5 has plenty of home fitness equipment, from Everlast training bags to Weider home gym systems to electronic stairclimbers by Voit and others. Plus savings on golf, baseball, camping, basketball...not to mention the appropriate clothing and footwear for all of these activities. Save anywhere from $10 to $40 on select models of Reebok, Nike, Asics, Pony, Saucony, and many others.

Play ball at all branches seven days a week, open every night until 9:00 (except Sundays, until 6:00).

Fry's Warehouse Sports
- 164 Marco Way (So. Airport Blvd.), South San Francisco; (415) 583-5034
And other suburban locations

At the end of this short sidestreet, around the corner from Windsurf Bicycle Warehouse (see listing above), Fry's has two more sports covered: golf and tennis. Golf is the bigger deal here, with all lines of pro clubs discounted all the time. These reductions can range from 20% to 80% off list prices, especially on closeout models. A set of eight Ping "Zing" irons (that's the name, folks), with steel shafts, lists for $680; here, it sells for $499. A closeout selection of drivers, with original values up to $250, were recently on sale for just $39.95 each.

There are similar discounts on golf balls, bags by Bennington, Sun Mountain, and Hot-Z, golf bag carts, shoes by Foot-Joy, Mizuno, and Dexter, and clothing. Ladies' waterproof nylon windbreakers by Duckster, listing at $65, sell for $39.95. And there's a practice tee area set up for you to try out various clubs.

On the tennis side, Mr. C found rackets like a Prince "Synergy" model, which might cost up to $225 in other stores, selling here for $179. A Wilson 3.0 "Profile" was a recent closeout special, reduced from an original $180 down to a swifter $79. Cans of Wilson tennis balls (well, they're really plastic, now) are always $1.99 each, with no limit on quantities. Shoes by Nike, Adidas, and all the rest are here at good discounts. The store also offers a racquet stringing service. Open seven days a week.

Golf Mart
- 1200 Sixth St. (Channel St.), San Francisco; (415) 703-6190
- 4937 Junipero Serra Blvd. (Serra Shopping Center), Colma; (415) 994-4653
And other suburban locations

With four stores in the Bay Area, Golf Mart has the buying power to get low prices on all of the big names in clubs and related golf equipment. The selection is huge—there are several different ways to save money here.

New clubs are substantially discounted below the manufacturers' list prices. A set of eight Wilson 1200 irons, for instance, was listed at $425; recently, it was selling here for $280. A Yonex ADX set of three woods for ladies was over $100 off at $230. And, southpaws take note— Golf Mart claims to have one of the best selections anywhere of left-handed clubs (if you'll excuse the baseball reference).

All equipment carries a 30-day guarantee, during which time clubs can be returned for store credit. Of course, you can test these without even leaving the store, at one of their practice tees.

Another, far greater cost-saving option is GM's big selection of used clubs; Mr. C saw a set of three Spalding "Lite" woods selling for $69.99. But wait, there's more! Trade *your* old clubs in, and you'll receive store credit toward your purchase. Why, you can even trade used clubs for used clubs, and hardly spend a thing!

Now, all you need is something to hit. Golf Mart sells several brands of balls, all at a very low markup. Sort of an enticement, really. All varieties of Titleist balls sell for $19.99 a dozen; and again, you can save more with used balls (they call them "Experienced"), which go for $14.99 a dozen. Perfect makes for practice.

All this, plus bags from $69.99, pull carts, clothing, and shoes. Men's Foot-Joy "Contemporary Lites" were recently seen for $54.99 a pair, and Nike "Air Golf" shoes for $99.99. All stores are open seven days, including most weeknights until 7 p.m. The downtown location, in the nether world between SoMa and Potrero Hill, can be tricky to find; it's located at the Mission Bay Driving Range. If *you're* driving, call the store for detailed directions.

Pacific Bicycle
- 4329 Geary Blvd. (Eighth Ave.), San Francisco; (415) 666-3377

Pacific Bicycle is a good-sized neighborhood shop in the Richmond district, offering competitive prices and full service. Cannondale and Specialized are their primary brands—good ones indeed. Bikes start around $260, for a mountain bike by Specialized; there is a good selection of children's bikes too, starting around $150.

There are always sales of some sort going on. Early in the year, all bicycles under $500 get a further discount; toward the end of the year, you can get special deals on manufacturers' closeouts. Lots of clothing and helmets here too; and repairs are done on the premises. Open seven days a week, including weeknights until 7:00 (8:00 in the summer).

Play It Again Sports
- 1212 El Camino Real (Sneeth Lane), San Bruno; (415) 952-6882
- 55 Bellam Blvd. (East Francisco Blvd.), San Rafael; (415) 453-7223

From humble beginnings in Minneapolis, this has grown into a national chain of some 400 stores—all buying, selling, and trading new and used sports equipment. The merchandise gets swapped around between stores, insuring a large, balanced selection in every store. Located north and south of The City, it's worth a drive from wherever you play.

PIAS gets good deals on new items that have been discontinued (but hey, how much can a baseball glove change?). Among these, Mr. C saw an Alpine Tracker exercise machine, reduced from $160 retail to a *svelte* $99.95. A pair of Ultra Wheels in-line skates was $25 off at $150. And a Mizuno baseball mitt, worth over $100, was selling here for $59.

About 60% of the stock consists of used equipment. Seen recently were a boy's mountain bike for $69.95, a pair of K2 downhill skis for $89.95, billiard cues from $11.95, and a set of Tommy Armour .845s golf irons, valued at $1,000, selling for $399. Plus hockey sticks, basketballs, baseball bats, footballs, shoulder pads for linebackers of all ages, tennis racquets, and lots more. Best of all, you can trade in your old stuff toward anything in the store—even new items.

Open seven days a week.

REI
- 1338 San Pablo Ave. (Gilman St.), Berkeley; (510) 527-4140
And other suburban locations

To answer your first question, it stands for Recreational Equipment, Incorporated. This is a rather unusual sporting goods store, focusing not on team sports, but outdoor activities—bicycling, running, skiing, rock climbing, camping, and more. It's also unusual in that it's actually a membership cooperative; anyone can shop here, but if you become a member, you'll get all kinds of extra discounts and benefits.

Membership costs a one-time-only fee of $15. That gets you early notification of special sales, some of which are for members only, as well as discounts on equipment rentals and repairs. It also means that you're involved in company profit sharing, which includes an annual dividend—around 10% of whatever amount you've spent during the year. The stores also offer free clinics and demonstrations in various sports.

Meanwhile, about the merchandise itself: REI carries only what it considers to be high-quality stock—brands like Patagonia, Woolrich, Helly-Hansen, Specialized bicycles, and others. These are all competitively priced, even before the dividend you get back. And there is a special "Clearance Corner" section, where you can get big discounts on closeout items. Mr. C found a pair of Nike bicycling shorts reduced from $65 to $45, and Oxford-style leather casual shoes by Rockport marked down from $135 to $99. They even offer bridal registry! Open seven days a week.

Wilderness Exchange, too...
- 1730 San Pablo Ave. (Delaware St.), Berkeley; (510) 528-7756

With the high cost of camping and hiking equipment, it makes sense to consider used gear. Wilderness Exchange, too... buys, sells, and trades skiing equipment, sleeping bags, tents, backpacks, and more. There are evidently a lot of people out there who update their gear on a regular basis; much of what Mr. C saw here hasn't been heavily used, and since they are expensive items, people tend to take good care of them.

The Exchange has lots of used sleeping bags, like a snug EMS model for $64.95 and a down one from The North Face for $119.95. The store also does repairs, so you can continue to keep your gear in good shape. You can return merchandise here, but you have to do so within two days, so it's a good idea to check everything over carefully first.

Wilderness Exchange, too... does have some new stuff, too, at discounted prices. Mr. C saw ski jackets for $29.95 and backpacks, like one with a retail price of $22.50, selling here for $16.95.

Naturally, this is a great place to update your equipment or just get rid of stuff you no longer use. Like most exchange places, you'll get more in trade than in cash; how much you get varies widely depending on the condition and relative demand. They also offer rentals—not a bad idea, especially if you've never set foot outside The City and you suddenly want to live out that Grizzly Adams fantasy. Open from 11 a.m. to 6 p.m. Sunday through Wednesday, from 11 a.m. to 8 p.m. on Thursday and Friday, and Saturday from 10 a.m. to 6 p.m.

Windsurf Bicycle Warehouse
- 428 So. Airport Blvd. (Marco Way), South San Francisco; (415) 588-1714

"We're a destination store," says sales manager Tom Chantler. "If people are going to drive all this way to get here, you've got to offer them something good." And this large, busy store delivers the goods, packed with equipment and accessories for bicycling, windsurfing, roller blading and even snowboarding. All are by top-line makers, at very competitive prices. Chantler urges shoppers to call around; WBW guarantees that its prices are the lowest.

Certainly, the high-ceilinged store is in a low-overhead location, off of the Bayshore Freeway. That helps keep prices low. And, the folks here really are big on customer service. All bicycles come with one full year of free tuneups and simple repairs—they even tell you to "mark your calendar for 11 months" from your purchase, to get in that one last free tuneup. And, with a large, well-trained repair staff on the premises, no appointment is necessary. Their work area is open and visible at the rear of the store, so that you can watch and learn from the repairs if you wish.

Bicycles are the main part of the business, with a large selection of high-end brands in all sizes and styles. About 80% of these are mountain bikes, based on customer demand; they include such makers as Slingshot, Trek, Diamondback, Bianchi, Barracuda, Boulder, and others. Most models sell at $20 to $50 below list prices during the height of the season, and these discounts can increase up to $100 later in the year on remaining models. Prices start around $300 for good bicycles in all varieties; this includes, for example, the Trek 820 mountain bike.

The end of the year also brings more deals in closeout models, which of course are as good as any new bike, and fully guaranteed; in January of '94, Mr. C found such deals as $400 off a Trek 9800 all-carbon body mountain bike, while a midrange model like the Trek 7000 was reduced from $650 to $515.

WBW has all the top-quality accessories to go with these; in fact, when you purchase a bicycle here, you'll be given 20% off the prices of safety helmets—*for life*. They carry six major brands of car racks—quite a choice—and won't let you leave until they've shown you the proper way to attach them to your car. Plus a big selection of shocks, hubs, lightweight carbon wheel spokes, and all the rest.

The service staff, like the sales staff, are low-key; they prefer to give you all the information you need to make informed choices on your own. They believe that it's better for everyone involved if you're happy with your purchase, and get just the right fit (there's a parking lot where you can do a "test drive," unlike some in-city shops), so that you'll keep coming back. "We're interested in long-term customers," says Chantler, "even at the expense of bigger profits on each sale." Open seven days a week, including Thursday and Friday evenings until 8:00.

MR. CHEAP'S PICKS
Sporting Goods

- ✔ **Play It Again Sports**—New and used bargains on equipment for every sport; trade in your old stuff, and save even more.

- ✔ **Wilderness Exchange, too...**—Used equipment is a great way to try out camping without breaking the bank. Great selection of outdoor gear in a range of prices.

- ✔ **Windsurf Bicycle Warehouse**—Low-rent location near the airport makes for low prices on high-end bikes and high-quality service. Nearby, **Fry's Golf and Tennis** does the same for those sports.

STATIONERY, OFFICE, AND ART SUPPLIES

Academy Art Supply Store
* 79 New Montgomery St. (Mission St.), San Francisco; (415) 274-8641

This is the affiliated store of the Academy of Art College, but you don't have to be enrolled there—or even a student at all—to shop here and get the same volume discounts. These may include closeout deals like a Koh-I-Noor "Rapidograph" set of seven technical ink pens, originally listed at $117, seen here recently for $39.95. Or, a set of six Liquitex "Basics" acrylic paints, reduced from $27.50 to $19.95. You can save 30% on Arches watercolor paper, or 40% on Canson recycled newsprint sketch pads.

Also on sale recently were NSM vinyl portfolios, reduced from $46 down to $34.50; and a Studio drafting table, once $180, here $130. The store also sells photographic supplies, including film, at discount; and it offers framing services as well. Open weekdays from 8 a.m. to 7 p.m., and Saturdays from 9-5.

Amsterdam Art Supplies
* 5221 Geary Blvd. (16th Ave.), San Francisco; (415) 387-5354
* 1013 University Ave. (10th St.), Berkeley; (510) 649-4800
* 198 Eleventh St. (Jackson St.), Oakland; (510) 893-3467
* 1279 Boulevard Way, Walnut Creek; (510) 946-9333

One of the Bay Area's leaders in discount art and office supplies, Amsterdam has a large selection and low prices to boot. You may find major brands of oil paints at 40% below list, or Amsterdam's own comparable brand. Nylon/leather portfolio cases reduced from $41 to $37. Bienfang 18" x 24" newsprint sketch pads for $1.99 (and, sometimes, 2-for-1 pad specials). Closeouts on Letraset transfer lettering, marked down from

$6.95 to $1.50 a sheet.

Among larger items, Mr. C found easels on sale for half-price, as well as drafting chairs reduced from a list price of $160 to just $96 (and some as low as $30). Save big on drafting tables, too, as well as flat storage files. Schoolteachers can get a special card, allowing them an extra 30% off all purchases except framing and canvas. All stores are open seven days a week.

Arvey Paper and Office Products
* 2275 Alameda St. (Potrero Ave.), San Francisco; (415) 863-3664
* 330 Brush St. (Third St.), Oakland; (510) 839-8863

And other suburban locations

This growing national chain easily rivals the mega-superstores like Office Depot for discounts and selection. From accordian files to zip code directories, they've got just about anything you could possibly need—for your office at home, or a Fortune 500 company. In fact, if you can buy by the case, you'll often save even more money.

You may find Hammermill copier paper as low as $3.95 a ream; boxes of 500 white woven business envelopes for $6; Avery mailing labels for computer printers, from $7.29; and, speaking of which, good prices on all kinds of computer supplies, including diskettes, dust covers, glare filters, and the like. Not to mention desk calculators, the desks to put them on, and the chairs to put at the desks.

You get the idea. Also, be sure to check out the small-but-you-never-know clearance area, where Mr. C recently found such goodies as a cordless computer mouse, reduced from $89 to $59. Open from 8 a.m. to 5:30 p.m. Monday through Friday and from 9 a.m. to 5 p.m. on Saturday.

Mad Hatter's Outlet
- 228 Townsend St. (Third St.), San Francisco; (415) 512-8487

You'll find plenty of bargains to flip your lid over at Mad Hatter's Outlet. Shoppers will find recycled paper notebooks, originally $3.98, for $1 each; recycled sketchpads, regularly $6, here only $2; and Pop-up greeting cards, originally $4.50, for $2.25. Need to catch up with old friends? At Mad Hatter's you'll find 16-sheet stationery sets with matching envelopes for $4.75, packages of notecards from $2.95, and individual sheets of decorated stationery and envelopes for 15¢ each. If you're a person of few words, you'll prefer artsy postcards for 35¢ each.

This store has quite a mish-mash of gift items and paper goods. Mr. C saw musical bridal cake tops, originally $79.95, clearance priced at $20. Scripto highlighters, usually $1.79, were seen for $1 and hardcover blank books were just $4.95. Binder-style address books were a real bargain at $4.95. You'll find rubber stamps, pic-

---

MR. CHEAP'S PICKS
Stationery, Office, and Art Supplies

- ✔ **Academy Art Supplies**—You don't have to be a student at the Academy of Art to get the same discounts on paints, paper, and even film.
- ✔ **Mad Hatter's Outlet**—No one here is angry, and they don't wear hats. What they do have is an extensive selection of stationery, cards, wrapping paper, and more, all at a discount.

---

ture frames, bows, wrapping paper, teddy bears, and more. Stop in Monday through Friday 11 a.m. to 5:30 p.m. and Saturday 11 a.m. to 5 p.m.

UNUSUAL GIFTS

This is Mr. C's "catch-all" chapter, in which he's put some of the stores which just don't fit anywhere else in the book. Many of the shops below are places to find truly nice gifts, while others fall more into the realm of the fun and decidedly offbeat.

Basic Brown Bear Factory
- 444 De Haro St. (Mariposa St.), San Francisco; (415) 626-0781 or (800) 554-1910
- 2801 Leavenworth St. (Bay St.), San Francisco; (415) 931-6670

What's a childhood without a teddy bear? Basic Brown Bear Factory sells their menagerie of plush pals at rates that are easily a third of what you'd pay in retail outlets. In fact, BBB Factory has stopped selling to the chi-chi retail stores like Macy's and Nordstroms, and now only sells through their own stores

and through mail order.

Most bears are priced in the $20 to $50 range, with many types to choose from toward the lower end. The 18" high Basic Brown Bear goes for $24; you can dress him up in a number of outfits for $6 to $8 each. Rusty, a 9" bear with brown shaggy fur is just $12.75!' Scooter, a cuddly cub, is $40 and small 6" bears dressed as airplane pilots are just $20. Two moveable-jointed bears, Stanley and Jeanette, are just $38 each. A jointed panda is just $42; the larger jointed bears go as high as $66.

But this safari encounters more than just bears. Take home Mother Goose for $36. A fluffy white cat named Purrsia, with a moveable head, is $24. Koalas go for $28, and the 26" high Chocolate Moose (dont ya love that?) costs $52.

You can also take a tour of their Potrero Hill factory and stuff your own bear (see listing under "Entertainment: Children's Activities"). Call them for more information. Basic Brown Bear Factory is open Monday through Saturday from 10 a.m. to 5 p.m., and Sunday from 1-5 p.m.

China Bazaar
• 826-832 Grant Ave. (Clay St.), San Francisco; (415) 982-9847

Two words could not more accurately describe any store. China Bazaar is two huge floors of imported Asian goods, from clothing to kitchenware to ornate decorative pieces.

The street level has clothing and home furnishings, all rather touristy; but Mr. C recommends that you head downstairs to the basement. Here, tall shelves are stacked from floor to ceiling with (a sign says) 10,000 items—and that looks about right. Find rice paper lampshades from $6.99, dishes, soup bowls, and porcelain teacups (two for 80¢), not to mention all kinds of exotic teas to put in them. You can buy a box of 100 jasmine tea bags for a mere $2.99—hard to beat in any supermarket. Around a corner, you'll find larger decorative pieces, like four-panel black lacquered folding screens from $150. Plus shelves of "as is" items at reductions of 50% to 90% off their original prices; Mr. C liked a handsomely carved wooden jewelry chest, once $25.95, now $10.95—with, seemingly, no defects.

A few blocks south, you can browse another packed emporium, **Bargain Bazaar** at 667 Grant Avenue, (415) 391-6369. Along with more kitchen goods (a 20-piece dinnerware set, $29.95, and the ever-popular bamboo steamer, $7.99), this store deals more in clothing, including a "bargain attic" with racks of silk-look rayon robes. Plus electron-

ics, like Panasonic boom boxes and Casio calculators, as well as jewelry, carved ivory figures, and tons of cheap (truly) toys.

Collage
• 1345 18th St. (Missouri St.), San Francisco; (415) 282-4401

At the top of Potrero Hill, in an area where homes give way to a small but delightful cluster of restaurants, cafes and shops, an artist named Delisa runs this studio gallery. It's packed from floor to ceiling with paintings and crafts by about 75 of her fellow artists, who have yet to break into the more established galleries in town. From what Mr. C saw, they are certainly deserving of wider attention. Collage has an eye-catching, eclectic display of sculptures, jewelry, painted furniture, designs in silk, and lots of other fun items.

Most are for sale, and make offbeat, not overly expensive gifts. One artisan takes liquid rubber, in a variety of bright colors, and molds it into useable necklaces and ties. Another makes fake "flagstone" floor mats, which you can place outside your front door instead of the real thing—they even have lizards painted on. Delisa's own works are on display too—beautiful vases and urns, handmade from layers of paper and painted with Oriental designs. They look like ceramics, yet are light as air. Delisa also notes that this makes them "earthquake proof."

Collage is open Thursdays and Fridays from 12 noon to 8 p.m., Saturdays from 12-6, and by appointment. Workshops are offered at reasonable rates, too.

Corazon del Pueblo
• 811 Washington St. (Eighth St.), Oakland; (510) 832-2609

This lovely shop, inexplicably wedged between Ratto's Italian grocery and Oakland's Chinatown, is filled with handmade crafts and folk art from Mexico and Central America. These can make fine gifts, or just something to spruce up your own home.

The shop displays things like colorful pillow covers, woven in Guatemala, for only $10; terra cotta candle holders, handpainted with pictures of parrots and fire-glazed, for $9; not to mention lightweight wooden handpainted parrot earrings for just $2 a pair. An assortment of tiny, handmade toys ranges from 25¢ to $2.

You may also find unframed Frida Kahlo prints for $9 or $10 each; and there's a bargain table at the back of the store, where handpainted gourds were seen reduced from $18 to $10.

House of Magic
- 2025 Chestnut St. (Webster St.), San Francisco; (415) 346-2218

Yes folks, it's your basic joke shop. Maybe it's just Mr. C's wacked-out sense of humor, but when you're looking for just the right gift for that certain pal, well—sometimes, only an atomic buzzer will do. They've got 'em here, along with all the other classics: chattering teeth ($6.95), nose glasses ($3.98), rubber chickens ($10), and more. For $5.95, you can even get stick-on stars for your bedroom ceiling that glow in the dark.

They also have what seems to be the latest thing, various electronic gadgets that make some sort of noise when you walk past them, from screams to evil laughter (Vincent Price lives!). Plus dribble glasses, fake ice cubes with bugs in them, and you know, naughty stuff.

House of Magic also sells magic— at least, the kind you can buy—many of which are simple enough tricks to learn easily and have fun with. And, when Halloween rolls around, this is *the* place for masks and costumes of all kinds.

Quantity Postcards
- 1441 Grant Ave. (Union St.), San Francisco; (415) 986-8866

Postcards as gifts? Well, they can be, when they come from this unique store filled with enough cards to pack several post offices. There are literally thousands of designs to see, from wacky contemporary cards (most are 75¢ each) to actual "vintage" cards— some of which are used! These range in price from a dime or quarter up to

---

MR. CHEAP'S PICKS
Unusual Gifts

✔ **Basic Brown Bear Factory**—Buy one of their fuzzy creations, or stuff-your-own. Either way, you're getting top-quality teddy bears at factory-direct prices. Tour the factory with your kids, too!

✔ **Collage**—Fun and funky gallery at the top of Potrero Hill.

✔ **Corazon del Pueblo**—Oakland gallery filled with delightful crafts from Mexico and Central America.

✔ **Smile Gallery**—Whimsical jewelry, clocks, ceramics, puppets, and more—right in downtown San Fran.

---

about $2-$3, depending on the rarity.

Postcards are actually filed by subject, in bins which line the store, marked by labeled dividers. You can look up any city or country in the world; themes, like baseball or movies; and even such esoteric subjects as "Dams." Yup, if anyone's ever snapped a postcard, it's probably in here. There's even a kind of voyeuristic thrill to reading some of the "used" cards.

You'll find unusual items here too, like "Kopper Kards" ($1.95 each), embossed into a thin sheet of copper; as well as lots of cool T-shirts ("Bowl Your Cares Away") for $15. Open seven days and nights a week.

Rock Express Store
- 100 Harrison St. (Spear St.), San Francisco; (415) 597-9861

Hey, man, like, what happens to all those unsold rock concert souvenirs— T-shirts, programs, y'know, memorabilia—when the show is over? They wind up at this store, selling at prices substantially lower than those foisted upon captive audiences at the actual concerts. T-shirts, of course, are the biggest item at concerts, often priced anywhere from $12 to $25 a pop. Here, Mr. C saw tees from big shows like Michael Bolton, Madonna, the Divinyls, and Melissa Etheridge, for just $6 each. Sweatshirts, emblazoned with Madonna or Kenny G, were just $10.

Not everything here is rock-related. Winterland Productions, the distributor for which this store is a sort of clearance outlet, makes similar items for a number of organizations and corporations, including Greenpeace, the Sierra Club, Esprit, and the Hard Rock Cafe. Mr. C saw T-shirts from the *Coneheads* and other movies, as well as logo shirts from Levis and other brand names, for just $8. There are lots of other cheap goodies here too, like blank tees for $5, caps for $2, and posters for $1. Programs for artists ranging from Anita Baker to the Beastie Boys go for just $1 here; these usually cost $10 or so at the shows. You'll also find bags, notepads, pins, cards, and more. It's a fun store just to browse

in—for music fans, it feels more like a candy store.

Smile Gallery
- 500 Sutter St. (Powell St.), San Francisco; (415) 362-3436

After gallery-hopping for a few hours, perhaps watching upper-crust patrons actually *buy* art, you may start to feel like a destitute outsider. Time to head over to Smile Gallery, where *anyone* can become a collector.

Here you'll find only whimsical, silly, and amusing art—mostly crafts—with price tags starting at a plebeian $10 (and ranging up to the thousands, but you can find lots of nice stuff for under $50). Smile Gallery carries one-of-a-kind mobiles, sculpture, paintings, puppets, dolls, clocks, jewelry, mirrors, ceramics, and more.

Look for life-size soft sculptures of butlers, story people by Brian Andreas, and hundreds of other truly unique, fun items. Hours are Monday through Saturday from 9:30 a.m. to 5:30 p.m., and Sunday from noon to 4:00 p.m.

ENTERTAINMENT

The Bay Area has so much to see and do, and it seems like there is more coming along all the time. Lots of this entertainment is inexpensive, and often free. Movies, concerts, theater, museums, nightclubs . . . you name it, there's a way to enjoy it on the cheap.

Nearly everything in this section of the book is free, or only a few bucks; in some cases, Mr. C has found activities that are normally a bit more expensive, but discounted from their full prices. Hey, there is no reason why a limited budget should keep anyone from the arts.

There are also several telephone numbers that can help you get up-to-date recorded information about many of the attractions and events described in this book.

San Francisco Events Hotline: (415) 391-2001

Berkeley Visitor Information Hotline: (510) 549-8710

Oakland Entertainment Hotline: (510) 835-ARTS (2787)

ART GALLERIES

Art galleries prove that cheap entertainment doesn't have to be seedy! Share upper-crust pleasures with the well-to-do by gallery hopping—for free. Many galleries stock museum-quality pieces, which you can ogle without even paying museum admission.

The downtown/Union Square area has San Francisco's highest concentration of art galleries. Here, you'll find many older, established dealers displaying art you'd have to win the lottery to afford. Don't fear that you'll be tossed out because your annual income is less than that of, say, Ross Perot; go on in! After all, the richer people are, the less they have to care about their appearance. For all the gallery owners know, you could be some rich eccentric in tattered jeans. So have some wine and cheese, dahling, and enjoy. Oh, and be sure to sneer at one or two paintings, as if you *would* buy them "if they were any good. . ."

Is alternative, more cutting-edge art your speed? Then mosey down to the Hayes Valley area or to West Berkeley. You'll find lots of small galleries showing crafts along with the paintings and sculpture, not to mention cheap food and java joints where you can revive yourself. Also check the SoMa area for more gritty, experimental work.

Here are just a few of the more interesting galleries in these and other areas.

Art and Consciousness Gallery
- 360 Camino Pablo, Orinda; (510) 254-0105

For a far out experience (in more ways than one), head over to the Art and Consciousness Gallery, on the campus of J.F.K. University in Orinda (take Route 24 east out of Berkeley). Here, you'll find paintings, drawings, sculpture and multimedia work—all exploring the relationship between art and spirituality. Themes range from mystical experience to personal expression, with a generous showing of mandalas, medicine wheels, and the like. Graduate students from the J.F.K. School of Holistic Studies contribute about 25% of the work on display; the rest comes from other Bay Area artists.

Recent exhibits included sculptures embodying mythic energies, Sharon Siskin's paintings on AIDS, and a fibre-art show exploring connections between fibre and spiritual pursuits. Shows change monthly. Try to catch an opening reception on the first or second Friday of the month, from 7:00 to 9:00 p.m.; it may you a chance to talk with the artist and learn more about the meanings behind the work. Regular gallery hours are Monday through Thursday from 10:00 a.m. until 6:00 p.m., and Friday from 9-5.

Art Warehouse
- 3654 Sacramento St. (Spruce St.), San Francisco; (415) 474-9999

The Art Warehouse—which opened its doors in November of 1993—claims to be the city's only "art gallery collective." Here at this Presidio Heights location, you'll find exhibits of work representing ten different established galleries throughout the Bay area. Displays include paintings in oil and watercolor by international artists, prints, mixed media work, sculpture, and even art furniture.

Exhibitions and artists change on a frequent basis. The Art Warehouse is open seven days a week, from 10:30 a.m. to 5:30 p.m.

Center for the Arts at Yerba Buena

- 701 Mission St. (Third St.), San Francisco; (415) 978-2787 (ARTS)

See listing under "Multicultural Centers" for information about the three galleries at this location.

Circle Gallery of Animation & Cartoon Art

- 140 Maiden Lane (Stockton St.), San Francisco; (415) 989-2100
- 900 North Point (Ghirardelli Square), San Francisco; (415) 776-2370

Here's one gallery where *anyone* can feel completely at ease, safe in the knowledge that no one will sneer at your interest in the pictures in these frames. After all, who would ridicule your intimate knowledge of Bugs Bunny, the Peanuts gang, or Walt Disney? Only a Grinch, perhaps. Animation art has gained popularity and acceptance as a serious art form in recent years; it's been dubbed the "collector's art of the '90s."

Circle Gallery has been around, in fact, since the 1970s. They have direct connections with film studios and artists, allowing them to fill these galleries with the *creme de la creme* of cartoons. The artwork you see here generally consists of production cels, limited edition cels, and some sketches and lithographs. "Cels," by the way, is short for "celluloids," the clear plastic sheets on which animators draw and paint. You'll find all your favorite characters here, including the Berenstain Bears, Garfield, Mickey and Minnie, Cinderella, Donald Duck, and Goofy. Several decades of cartooning are represented, from the early days of Betty Boop to those most recent cultural icons, the Simpsons. This is really a fun gallery, and it's one the whole family can enjoy.

All of these are for sale, but Mr. C

should tell you that cartoon art is not cheap, *per se*; however, relative to other art investments, it is quite affordable. While some limited edition "cels" "sell" for thousands, there are plenty of others which go for only a few hundred dollars. The price usually depends on the popularity of the characters shown. Staff at the Circle Gallery are clearly caught up in the fun, and are happy to advise you if you're thinking of becoming an animation art collector.

Collage

- 1345 18th St. (Missouri St.), San Francisco; (415) 282-4401

At the top of Potrero Hill, in an area where homes give way to a small but delightful cluster of restaurants, cafes and shops, an artist named Delisa runs this studio gallery. It's packed from floor to ceiling with paintings and crafts by about 75 of her fellow artists, who have yet to break into the more established galleries in town. From what Mr. C saw, they are certainly deserving of wider attention. Collage has an eye-catching, eclectic display of sculptures, jewelry, painted furniture, designs in silk, and lots of other fun items.

Most are for sale, and make offbeat, not overly expensive gifts. One artisan takes liquid rubber, in a variety of bright colors, and molds it into useable necklaces and ties. Another makes fake "flagstone" floor mats, which you can place outside your front door instead of the real thing— they even have lizards painted on. Delisa's own works are on display too—beautiful vases and urns, handmade from layers of paper and painted with Oriental designs. They look like ceramics, yet are light as air. Delisa also notes that this makes them "earthquake proof."

Collage is open Thursdays and Fridays from 12 noon to 8 p.m., Saturdays from 12-6, and by appointment. Workshops are offered at reasonable rates, too.

Contemporary Realist

- 23 Grant Ave. (O'Farrell St.), 6th Floor, San Francisco; (415) 362-7152

In the heart of downtown, this claims to be San Francisco's only gallery specializing in contemporary realist art. "We show the very best of contemporary American realist painting and sculpture, from both new and known artists," Mr. C was told. Subject matter ranges from still-lifes to loose gestural landscapes; big-name artists shown here have included Robert Birmelen, Robert Schwartz, Jeanne Duval, and Terry St. John.

The gallery boasts that it's an unsnobby place. "Our prices range from $600 to $50,000, so we see *all* kinds of people," noted the assistant. Heck, even Mr. C can pass for a $600 patron on his better days. In fact, the gallery really is quite user-friendly; it hosts the "Art and Jazz" festival in April, and even welcomes frequent tours by school groups. The Contemporary Realist is open Tuesday through Friday, from 10:30 a.m. to 5:30 p.m., and Saturdays from noon to 5:00 p.m.

Creative Arts Gallery

- 833 Bancroft Way (Sixth St.), Berkeley; (510) 848-4777

Don Ellis opened this gallery downstairs from the publishing company he owns, after he took up painting a few years back. "I knew nobody would show my work, so I decided to open a gallery to show my own," he says. The ploy worked, and now the gallery has expanded to represent an eclectic array of local artists—including graphic designer Michael Cronan, abstract oil painter Charles Fuhrman, painter and calligrapher Sandy Diamond, photographer Daniel David (who also makes unique sculptural lamps), and of course, Don Ellis himself.

You'll find crafts and jewelry along with the paintings. A recent exhibit featured masks by local artists in clay, metal, wood, papier maché, and cloth; another featured art in neon. In the adjacent studio, you can view works-in-progress; or, if you enjoy intellectual as well as visual pursuits, catch a free reading at the gallery by one of the authors Don Ellis publishes.

Recent readings have showcased Barry Gifford, author of *Wild at Heart,* and Al Young, author of *Sitting Pretty.* Call the gallery for a schedule of events. Creative Arts Gallery is open Wednesday through Friday, noon to 5:00 p.m., and Saturday from 10:00 a.m. to 5:00 p.m. (check for expanded summer hours).

Creative Growth Arts Center

- 355 24th Street (Valdez St.), Oakland; (510) 836-2340

This unique, non-profit gallery features extraordinary work by over one hundred disabled artists. Here you'll find everything from drawings, paintings, and sculpture to fiber arts and ceramics. If you fall prey to stereotypes about such people, you're sure to be amazed at the beauty and creativity on display. As Mr. C was told at a similar gallery in Boston, such works "represent the abilities of people with disabilities."

Resident artists take classes in the studio next door; and the gallery hosts symposia on topics relating to art and the disabled, as well as ten different shows a year. Call for an exhibition schedule. Gallery hours are Monday through Friday, 10 a.m. to 4:00 p.m.

Erika Meyerovich Gallery

- 231 Grant Avenue (Post St.), San Francisco; (415) 421-9997

This gallery features artists that even Mr. C has heard of—Chagall, Picasso, Matisse, Frank Stella, David Hockney, and others. "We show fine prints on paper by modern and contemporary masters," the gallery representative said with a distinctly aristocratic tone. "We have ongoing inventory, and rarely need to have shows."

Well. This may be true, but the gallery is still open to one and all, free of charge. Put on your haughtiest face, and stroll in to view some really fine artwork. Hours are Monday through Friday from 9:30 a.m. to 6 p.m., and Saturday 10:00 a.m. to 5:30 p.m.

Galerie Lassen

- 747 Beach St. (Hyde St.), San Francisco; (415) 292-1900

This waterfront gallery specializes in the work of artist Christian Lassen. The paintings and sculptures on view here portray natural subjects, animals, forests, oceans, and more. Lassen's work, especially, is filled with colorful fish, playful dolphins, and textured coral. His techniques are varied and include oil on board, which, says the gallery director, makes the brushstroke "faster." The Galerie Lassen also features bronze sculptures, mostly of dolphins, whales, other majestic creatures. What better place to enjoy this artwork than at a gallery just steps from the bay?

In the same area, check out the **Dyansen Gallery** at 799 Beach Street, telephone (415) 928-0596. With galleries in several major cities, the Dyansen is an elegant studio which features a large collection of works by Erté, one of this century's most famous art deco designers. Prints, bronze statues, and carved crystal all attest to Erté's ability to capture the strength and beauty of the female form.

Harcourt's Modern and Contemporary Art

- 460 Bush St. (Grant Ave.), San Francisco; (415) 421-3428

Right in the heart of the downtown blue-chip gallery row, Harcourt's boasts two floors of pricey art in a historic landmark building—one of the city's original fire stations! The downstairs gallery displays frequently changing exhibitions of contemporary American and European art by such notables as Richard Debecart, Roland Peterson, and David Park. Upstairs, you can gawk at historical works ranging from the French Impressionists to pre-World-War II American modern canvases.

This is a good place to browse if you can't decide whether you're in the mood for traditional art, or more

MR. CHEAP'S PICKS
Art Galleries

- ✔ **Creative Arts Gallery**—Worth the trip just to talk to offbeat owner/artist Don Ellis, who also runs the small publishing company upstairs. Interesting shows from neon art to masks, plus occasional readings by the authors Mr. Ellis publishes.
- ✔ **49 Geary Street Building**—Seven high-toned galleries at a single Union Square address.
- ✔ **Smile Gallery**—Fun and frivolous arts and crafts, some even at affordable prices. Now *that's* something to smile about!
- ✔ **Turn-of-the-Century Fine Arts**—This place knows how to treat its patrons. There's a coffee/pastry shop right in the store, and a sculpture garden with tables out back.
- ✔ **Vision Gallery**—For photography fans, this is *the* place. Three floors display everything from traditional prints to the wildly avant-garde.

contemporary work. Harcourt's has it all. The gallery is open from 10:00 a.m. to 5:30 p.m. Tuesday through Saturday; closed Sundays, Mondays, and major holidays.

Morphos

- 544 Hayes St. (Octavia St.), San Francisco; (415) 626-1936

Located in the gritty (yet gentrifying) Hayes Valley area, Morphos specializes in cutting edge art. The socially conscious gallery takes itself very seriously: This is no place to wear a fur coat (not that Mr. C could afford one). You'll find painting, drawing, sculpture, and photography—all offering some kind of sociological commentary.

Recent shows included Charles Gatewood's photography documenting American subcultures; and a Scott Siedman show of sexually and religiously explicit work. "The censors tried to stop us from sending out invitations to the Siedman show, but we don't censor anything," a gallery representative boasted. Who those censors were is unclear, but you certainly get the idea. You needn't worry about bumping into Jesse Helms in here.

Morphos represents male and female artists equally, and tries to keep a balance of artists from diverse cultures and ethnic groups. The gallery is open Tuesday through Saturday from 12 noon until 7:00 p.m., and Sunday from 11:00 a.m. to 6:00 p.m.

Olga Dollar Gallery

- 210 Post St. (Grant Ave.), 2nd Floor, San Francisco; (415) 398-2297

Don't let the name fool you: This Nob Hill gallery doesn't sell *anything* for a dollar. It does, however, show quite unusual work by about 175 contemporary and emerging American artists, primarily from the Bay Area. All the work at Olga Dollar has a surreal or hyper-realistic feel to it, reflecting artists' innermost visions. Paintings, sculptures, and prints represent a vast range of subject matter—all with strong emotional impact.

Shows change every four to six weeks, and have recently included a display of three-dimensional stage designs by San Francisco Opera designer Gerard Holland, still-lifes by women artists, and a David Durnen exhibit. Olga Dollar is open Tuesday through Saturday, 10:30 a.m. to 5:30 p.m.

Plate and Palette

- 2121 San Pablo Ave. (Cowper St.), West Berkeley; (510) 549-2235

Sounds like a restaurant, but Plate and Palette satisfies only aesthetic appetites. Here you'll in fact find two galleries: one featuring changing exhibitions of paintings, drawings, and sculptures—in styles from folk art to contemporary—and the other showcasing unique, handcrafted furniture,

ceramics, textiles, glass, and upholstery from seventy different countries.

Recent shows focused on artists' interpretations of fairy tales, unique light fixtures, metal sculptures, and the works of five local photographers exploring the camera's relationship with light. Hours are Monday through Saturday from 10:00 a.m. to 5:30 p.m., and Sunday noon to 5:00.

San Francisco Art Exchange

- 458 Geary St. (Taylor St.), San Francisco; (415) 441-8840

The San Francisco Art Exchange is an exciting gallery filled with art from famous and important artists. They feature works that are as varied as they are beautiful. You'll see the "beyond realism" paintings of Charles Becker, rich with color, light, and detail. You'll see charcoal sketchings by Ron Wood (better-known for his work as a guitarist with a certain British rock band). You'll also see the amazingly detailed watercolors of Alberto Vargas, famous for his wartime paintings of voluptuous women, appearing regularly in *Esquire* magazine; these pin-up ladies soon became known as the "Varga Girls." In addition to having much of his *oeuvre* on display, Art Exchange is the exclusive publisher of limited-edition prints of these paintings.

Smile Gallery

- 500 Sutter St. (Powell St.), San Francisco; (415) 362-3436

After gallery-hopping for a few hours, perhaps watching upper-crust patrons actually *buy* art, you may start to feel like a destitute outsider. Time to head over to Smile Gallery, where *anyone* can become a collector.

Here you'll find only whimsical, silly, and amusing art—mostly crafts—with price tags starting at a plebeian $10 (and ranging up to the thousands, but you can find lots of nice stuff for under $50). Smile Gallery carries one-of-a-kind mobiles, sculpture, paintings, puppets, dolls, clocks, jewelry, mirrors, ceramics, and more.

Look for life-size soft sculptures of butlers, story people by Brian Andreas, and hundreds of other truly unique, fun items. Hours are Monday through Saturday from 9:30 a.m. to 5:30 p.m., and Sunday from noon to 4:00 p.m.

Steven Wirtz Gallery
- 49 Geary St. (Kearny St.), 3rd Floor, San Francisco; (415) 433-6879

You don't need to walk all over town to see good art. Why wear down your shoes or (heaven forbid) pay cab fare going from gallery to gallery, when you can see so much at the 49 Geary Street Building, which houses no less than seven well-regarded gallery dealers. All right in fashionable Union Square.

Steven Wirtz Gallery handles abstract and figurative work in all media, representing some thirty major and emerging-name artists. There is a distinct emphasis on recognized artists from the Bay Area, but the gallery also showcases selected works by national and international talent. Recent exhibits have included photography by Michael Kenna, works by Japanese sculptor Katsura Funakoshi, and paintings by Raymond Saunders.

Elsewhere inside 49 Geary Street, you'll find three photography studios: **Robert Koch Gallery, Scott Nichols Gallery,** and **Fraenkel Gallery.** Other fine arts dealers in the building include **Haines Gallery, Ebert Gallery,** and **Daniel Wineberg Gallery.**

Turn of the Century Fine Arts
- 2520 San Pablo Ave. (Dwight Way), Berkeley; (510) 849-0950

This special place offers ambience along with art. View contemporary works by local artists in all media: paintings, drawings, ceramics, sculpture, custom furniture, and a variety of crafts. Then saunter over to the gallery's little coffee shop for a cup of espresso and a bit of pastry. The goodies aren't free, but even we frugal types can cut loose for an occasional, artsy cup of java, right? An added bonus is the gallery's sculpture garden out back, where you can sit at a table and sip your brew when the weather's fine.

This gallery changes its exhibits every six weeks or so. Recent shows included realism drawings by local artists, and a sampler of works by the Glass Arts Society. Turn of the Century Fine Arts is open Mondays from 8:00 a.m. until noon, Tuesdays through Fridays from 8:00 a.m. until 5:00 p.m., and Saturdays from noon to 5:00.

Vision Gallery
- 1155 Mission St. (Seventh St.), San Francisco; (415) 621-2107

People come from all over the world to see the impressive collection of vintage and contemporary photographs at this gallery. One of the largest photography galleries in the world, Vision occupies three floors, housing four main galleries plus a frame shop. You'll find work here by such luminaries as Ansel Adams, Edward Westin, and Robert Mapplethorpe, as well as works by up-and-coming artists. The gallery focuses (no pun intended) largely on local work along with those big names; 18th-and 19-century photographers from Europe, South America, and the United States are also regularly on display.

In all, just about every branch of photographic art can be seen here, from digitally-altered images to platinum flash palladian prints. Shows change every six weeks; one recently featured pictures of dance groups in meadow and woodland settings by Philip Traeger, while another offered prints by James Balog exploring the relationship between humans and chimpanzees. Vision Gallery is open Monday through Saturday from 9:00 a.m. to 6:00 p.m.

Vorpal Gallery
- 393 Grove St. (Gough St.), San Francisco; (415) 397-9200

At this huge (20,000 square feet) Hayes Valley gallery, you'll find contemporary canvases and sculptures by local talent, as well as work from major international artists representing thirty countries. Although most of these pieces fall into the "break it and you'll spend your life in debtor's prison" category (lots of M.C. Escher and printmaker Yozo Hamaguchi, for instance), Vorpal also carries some work by emerging artists.

A large, open room on the second floor houses changing exhibits. A recent show featured Goya paintings; another, Picasso graphics. If all this doesn't sate your need for highbrow culture, take in one of the frequent concerts or lectures in the upstairs gallery: some of these are even free of charge. Check with Vorpal for a schedule of events. The gallery, next door to the Library for the Performing Arts, is open Tuesday through Saturday, 11:00 a.m. to 6:00 p.m.

Zonal Gallery
- 568 Hayes St. (Laguna St.), San Francisco; (415) 255-9307

If you hate to throw anything away, you'll love this Hayes Valley joint.

Zonal specializes in art from salvaged and recycled materials. You'll find turn-of-the-century iron beds, moldings, columns, and wrought-iron fencing. Some of the stuff looks pretty beat up; ah, but that just makes it more beautiful to the folks here at Zonal. New objects lack character, after all, while things that are old and worn have a history, a story behind them. The gallery also carries oil paintings, prints, wooden crafts, and original metal-work.

Zonal's unique approach to art has earned it prominent coverage in *House and Garden* and *Newsweek* magazines. Fame hasn't corrupted the place: it maintains a relaxed, low-key atmosphere. Open Tuesday through Saturday from 11 a.m. to 7 p.m. and Sunday 11 a.m. to 5 p.m.

CHILDREN'S ACTIVITIES

Be sure to also check out the "Museums" and "Outdoors" chapters for listings on zoos and other activities for families.

The Basic Brown Bear Factory
- 444 DeHaro St. (Mariposa St.), San Francisco; (415) 626-0781

Did you ever wonder how your cherished stuffed bear got the name "Teddy"? Find out by taking a free tour of the Basic Brown Bear Factory on Potrero Hill. You'll view the cutting and sewing rooms, learn how eyeballs get installed (sounds gruesome, but it's not), and watch as they are stuffed and showered. Finally, these cuddly bears get dressed up right before your eyes.

After the tour, if you wish, you can pick out a bear "skin" and create your own Teddy—with help from the staff. Although the tour costs nothing, the bears start at $8.50 for the 13-inch size, and most kids will pine for one. It's still a bargain—consider it "factory direct" toy shopping—and lots of fun too. Tours are offered

Monday through Friday at 1:00 p.m., Saturday at 11:00 a.m. and 2:00 p.m., and Sunday at 3:00 p.m. You don't even need to make reservations.

Bay Area Discovery Museum
- 557 East Fort Baker, Sausalito; (415) 552-6090

This "please touch" museum focuses primarily on the San Francisco area itself. At the "Port of San Francisco" exhibit, you and your kids can take out a life-size fishing boat, chart a course, and go fishing—then crawl below the surface in the Underwater Sea Tunnel and check out the living salt marsh. The architecture exhibit demonstrates how bridges operate; or, work on a high-rise at a construction site.

Special exhibits change frequently. The recent "About Disabilities" exhibit enabled children to experience blindness, deafness, and other handicaps. The "Soapbox Derby" displayed real soapbox cars made by kids from the Bay Area. "Muppets, Monsters, and Magic" gave the inside scoop on Grover, Kermit, and pals, with accompanying workshops on puppet-making—as well as performances by renowned puppeteers.

At least twice a week, the museum offers special workshops and events, usually for a small fee. Choose from nature hikes, ceramics classes, and a wide array of arts and crafts activities. On the other hand, if you want to enjoy the museum without the little ones tugging at your sleeves, drop them off at "Tot Spot," a free two-hour program for pre-schoolers held every Wednesday, Thursday, and Friday from 10:00 a.m. to noon.

Admission is $4 for all ages—kids and adults alike. Not bad; but wait. You can get everyone in for free, on the first Thursday of every month. Open 10:00 a.m. to 5:00 p.m. Wednesdays through Sundays during the school year, and 10:00 a.m. to 5:00 p.m. Tuesdays through Sundays in the summer.

Berkeley Summer Programs
- Various locations; Information, (510) 644-6530

For two months every summer, mid-June through mid-August, the City of Berkeley Recreation Department offers an extensive variety of activities for children of all ages. These range from a free, supervised "Summer Playground Program" (for Berkeley residents only) to youth baseball leagues and youth/adult tennis lessons. "Kids Summer Fun Camps," for ages 5-12, fill their days with games, arts and crafts, nature studies, and special trips. The "Summer Teen Club" is a program of sports, horseback riding, and camp-outs for kids ages 12-14. Aquatics are offered for "Parents and Tots," getting children as young as nine months acquainted with the water; formal lessons and recreational swimming for all ages are also offered.

These all take place at various sites in and around Berkeley; while some programs are free and limited to city residents, others are more open and charge varying fees. Call the number above in early spring for more detailed information.

Charlotte's Web Children's Bookstore
- 2278 Union St. (Fillmore St.), San Francisco; (415) 441-4700

Tired of reading the same old stories to your insatiable toddler? Well, you *should* do some. However, every Tuesday and Thursday at 9:00 a.m., Charlotte's Web can take over for you, at their free storytime hours for pre-schoolers. Regular appearances by authors and illustrators of children's books are announced in the store's free newsletter. CWCB also offers $5 gift certificates to kids if they come in during their birthday month.

Joe, the store's resident canine (a chocolate-brown labrador), greets you as you enter. If you come in September, you can catch the week-long celebration for *his* birthday. A real party animal, Joe hosts the festivites in his party hat and jacket. Have your picture taken with him, get discounts on pet-related books, and have a piece of cake. Naturally, there's cake for doggies too.

Charlotte's is open 10:00 a.m. to 6:00 p.m. Monday through Saturday, 10:00 a.m. to 5:00 on Sundays. By the way, if you want to actually drop a few bucks on books, this store carries a large selection of lower-priced paperbacks.

Children's Fairyland
- Grand and Bellevue Avenues, Oakland; (510) 832-3609

Need to get on Junior's good side after trying to get him to eat tofu instead of pizza? Take him (or her) to Children's Fairyland, In Oakland's Lakeside Park. This is the kind of place that evokes magic sparkles in young eyes. It all begins when you enter the park by climbing through a shoe. Once on the other side, you'll find the Three Little Pigs' House, where a three-dimensional wolf threatens three live pigs. These guys are actually there for petting; then, move on to Peter Pan's Corner, where you can jump aboard a pirate ship and let your kids take out their aggressions on Captain Hook. At each exhibit, children are given a special key which they insert into boxes to hear a song and a story.

Other special features include daily puppet shows, at no extra charge. In fact, Fairyland has one of the premier puppet theaters in the world (Frank Oz of the Muppets started out here). There's also a petting zoo, a duck pond, and kiddie rides all on the premises; and, on a more idealistic note, a Children's Chapel of Peace.

Even older tykes can participate in the goings-on at Fairyland: The park uses kids, ages 8-12, as "Fairytale Personalities." Talent scouts have been known to recruit from among these young hams for roles on television shows.

Admission costs only $3 for adults, and $2.50 for kids age eight and under. Not bad, for the place that gave Walt Disney the inspiration to build Disneyland (evidently, he got the inspiration for his prices somewhere else). Open from 10:00 a.m. to 4:30 p.m. on weekends and holidays in winter. Call for summer hours.

Exploratorium
- 3601 Lyon St. (Bay St.), San Francisco; (415) 563-7337

This is the numero uno, happeningest kid's spot in the city—and it's bigtime fun for adults, too. Inside the former Palace of Fine Arts, you'll find more than 650 hands-on science exhibits, including "The Tactile Gallery," where you enter total darkness and use only your sense of touch to guide you through a long tunnel; and "Discernability," which lets you scramble your own television image. The "Light" exhibits let you play with prisms and filters. At "Waves and Resonance," you can move a 400-pound pendulum using only a tiny magnet; while "Weather" lets you play with swirling air and water, or

walk through a cloud.

Everywhere you turn, something is spinning, swinging, lighting up, or making a noise. You can even watch museum technicians constructing the Exploratorium's own exhibits, at the Machine Shop. And, each weekend, new and unusual short films are shown in the McBean Theater, which is free with admission.

Recent additions include displays on virtual reality, computer art, and fun with CD-ROM devices. Also new in '94, the museum has opened "Playspace," a permanent and enclosed activity area for children age four and under with their parents.

Now, with all this to offer, just about any admission price would be a bargain. As it is, admission is $8 for adults, $6 for seniors and students, $4 for kids age six to seventeen, and free for ages five and under. But wait, it gets better. Visit on the first Wednesday of each month, and you can get the whole gang in absolutely free. Hours are Tuesdays through Sundays, 10:00 a.m. to 5:00 p.m. (plus Wednesday evenings until 9:30). The phone number listed above is for speaking to live people; you can also call 561-0360 for recorded information.

Golden Gate Park Children's Playground
- Bowling Green Drive, Golden Gate Park, San Francisco; (415) 666-7107

Located at the eastern end of the park near Kezar Stadium, the Children's Playground is a haven for children of all ages and sizes. From the simplest tire swinging from a heavy rope, to the most elaborate jungle gym, to a genuine merry-go-round from the turn of the century, you and your kids can run yourselves ragged and have a delightful time in the open air. There is no admission charge, and the playground is open every day (the carousel is open weekends only).

Kidshows San Francisco
- Various locations; Information, (510) 527-4977

If you have a tyke in tow, you can give them professional entertainment for a pittance at a Kidshow perform-ance. Don't expect rinky-dink, so-bad-you-want-to-barf-but-your-kid-likes-it entertainment: Recent performances have included the Berkeley Ballet Theater's adaptation of *Alice in Wonderland*, the San Francisco Mime Troupe, the Chinese Folk Dancers, singer Gary Lapow, Japanese Taiko Drumming, and much more.

Kidshows offers as many as forty different performances annually, at four locations throughout the Bay Area:

> The Julia Morgan Theater, Berkeley
> The Cowell Theater at Fort Mason Arts Center, San Francisco
> The Marin Center, San Rafael
> The Regional Center for the Arts, Walnut Creek

Expect to pay between $5 and $7 per ticket; and you can save on these already-low prices by purchasing a multi-show pass. Call the above number for performance schedules and de-tailed ticket information.

Lawrence Hall of Science
- Centennial Dr. (Grizzly Peak Blvd.), University of California, Berkeley; (510) 642-5132

It's on the pricey end of cheap for a museum, but you sure get a lot for your money at this hands-on scien-tific funhouse. Hundreds of interac-tive exhibits let you explore everything from dinosaurs to space-travel to lasers.

At the Biology Lab, play with live frogs, rabbits, and even tarantulas (aw, they're friendly!). The Wizard Lab, meanwhile, lets you create your own experiments with magnets, elec-tricity, and sound. If you get tired of all this interactive stuff and want to just veg out, catch the live "Science Discovery" performance, which blends comedy, music, and audience participation into a fun and educa-tional show. You can always hide in the back, behind some tall teenager.

Other high points include interac-tive planetarium shows (for an addi-

---

MR. CHEAP'S PICKS
Children's Activities

- ✔ **Children's Fairyland**—This is the place young kids would pick if Mr. C let them do the choosing. Dozens of imaginative fairy-tale structures kids can wander inside of, around, on top of, and through—plus one of the country's finest puppet theaters.

- ✔ **Exploratorium**—One of the best "please touch" museums anywhere. Parents and kids alike can get lost for hours amidst all these scientific gizmos, gadgets and geegaws. Free once a month.

- ✔ **San Francisco Maritime National Historic Park**—A full day of nautical fun that's free the first Tuesday of the month. Four real ships to explore, plus kid's activities and a museum. Nearby, aboard the **U.S.S. Pampanito**, kids love exploring the cubbys and passageways inside this WWII submarine.

---

tional fee of $1.50). At one recent show, the audience was given star maps—and everyone learned how to tell time by looking up at the night sky! Outside the museum, the little ones can burn off some energy by climbing on a life-size model of whale, a DNA model, or on a cross-section of a redwood tree.

Up on a hill, the Lawrence has a spectacular view of the Bay Area; if you want to really cut budget cor-ners, you can always just drive up to the parking lot, and enjoy the vista for free. Otherwise, admission is $5 for adults, $4 for kids 7-18, and $2 for kids 3-6. Open 10:00 a.m. to 5:00 p.m. daily.

Museum of Children's Art (MOCHA)

- 560 Second Street (Clay St.), Oakland; (510) 465-8770

Here's one art museum that your kids won't find "bor-ing"—or get you kicked out of with unruly behavior. That's because MOCHA shows only work by kids. Exhibits change each month, and have recently included art by Indonesian children, Japanese children, a papermaking show, "art for peace," and shows by local children.

But this is not just a museum for looking at. After viewing the works on display, kids can head over to the studio and create their own masterpieces—for free. The museum supplies materials for painting, drawing, and a variety of crafts.

MOCHA also sponsors intriguing special workshops, such as "Photography Without Cameras," "Lion-Dance Sculptures" (in celebration of the Chinese new year), "Tie-Dying," and so on. These do involve extra fees; call for a schedule and detailed information.

Admission to MOCHA is free, but donations are appreciated (c'mon now, don't be *too* cheap). All proceeds support the Museum's art-in-the-schools programs. Open Mondays through Fridays from 10:00 a.m. to 5:00 p.m.; Saturdays and Sundays from 10-2 only.

The Nature Company

- 900 North Point (Ghirardelli Square), San Francisco; (415) 776-0724
- 1999 El Dorado Ave. (Sutter St.), Berkeley; (510) 524-6336
- 740 Hearst St. (Fourth St.), Berkeley; (510) 524-9052

And other suburban locations

You probably already know of the Nature Company, that trendy place to buy interesting and unusual items that help children and adults explore the natural world. Actually, for Mr. C, it's more a shop for *playing* with these beautiful toys, gems, and telescopes—and then putting them back on the shelves. But did you know that several of the Nature Company

branches (pardon the pun) also host special educational activities for kids? Well, they do—and they're free!

Some of these are offered on a regular basis. "Terrific Tales," a story hour featuring talks about animals, plants, flowers, and more, currently take place every Saturday at 11 a.m. and every Tuesday at 4 p.m. Their slate covers a wide range of topics, including "Bay Area Bat Encounter," designed to disspell some of the myths about bats; "Mysterious Magical Minerals," showing minerals that glow under ultraviolet light; and "Crack-Me-Up," demonstrating the safe way to crack open a geode rock to expose the crystals inside. There are also lots of hands-on workshops, like "Quilting With Nature" and "Paper from Pulp." The store has even sponsored a "Poems for the Earth Contest."

Not all events are offered at all locations; but you can pick up a calendar of events in any store which will tell you about all programs—what's happening, where, and when. Generally, reservations are required, as space is limited.

Palo Alto Children's Theater (PACT)

- Lucy Stern Community Center, 1305 Middlefield Road, Palo Alto; (415) 329-2216

The oldest children's theater in the country at 60 years young, PACT puts on as many as 25 major productions a year—all featuring a cast of kids from ages 8 to 18. In spite of the age level and bargain-basement ticket prices, PACT shows are *not* your typical "sure it's exruciatingly bad, but I'll go because my little Johnny is in it" pageants. Each show uses professional costumers, scenery designers, directors and musicians.

The material is just as ambitious. Recent choices have included full-scale productions of *Aladdin, Annie,* and *Peter Pan*. Tickets cost $4 for adults and $2 for kids. Shows are usually 7:30 p.m. Fridays and Saturdays and 2:30 p.m. on Sundays. Call for a schedule.

Your kids can try out for PACT shows too, at open auditions held throughout the school year. During the summer, they can also attend PACT's own theater school, for which fees are involved—call for more info.

Pier 39
- The Embarcadero (Beach St.), San Francisco; (415) 981-PIER (7437)

From its Venetian double-decker carousel to the latest in video arcade games, kids can never get enough of the fun at Pier 39. Adding to the carnival atmosphere are street musicians, magicians, jugglers, and the like. Nearby, sea lions by the hundreds make their homes on pontoons floating in the harbor. It's all open every day, and admission is free. Of course, the pinball and video games at "Cyberstation" can cost as much as $2 a pop—for a state-of-the-art, computer generated, three-dimensional battle game. Good luck getting your little space cadets out of here. The arcade closes at 10 p.m. Sunday through Thursday nights, and at midnight on weekends; this may be your only hope.

Quinby's Bookstore
- 3411 California St. (Laurel St.), San Francisco; (415) 751-7727

When bills and traffic and other grownup headaches make you long for a return to the simpler days of childhood, grab your kids and head over to Quinby's Bookstore. Every Wednesday at 10:30 a.m., you can sit on the floor with the rest of the little ones and have a story read to you, for free.

In addition, the store hosts special events throughout the year. These range from readings by black authors during Black History Month to a variety of free crafts workshops. There's also a summer crafts program for kids, which does require a small fee. Call for a schedule of upcoming events, and fee information.

Randall Museum
- 199 Museum Way (Carona Heights Playground), San Francisco; (415) 554-9600

This small, charming, and free (which makes it even more charming, right?) museum really helps kids learn about the world around them—in a very active way. What better place to do that than at the top of one of The City's taller hills? The Carona Heights Playground rises high above the Castro, next to another prime peak, Buena Vista Park.

A major part of the Randall centers around its animal room; this houses more than one hundred small creatures, most of which are native to the area, and includes a petting corral. There's also an "Endangered Species" section, among other special exhibits.

Elsewhere, the Randall ventures into the mechanical world. Always fun for all ages is their large, working exhibit of model trains (only running on Saturday afternoons). There is an array of incredibly cheap crafts and science classes, geared to ages three and up. Choose from puppet-making (eight weeks for $37), clay magic ($22 for eight weeks), woodworking, and more.

Or, drop in any Saturday at 1:00 for the "Craft of the Day" activity, which is usually free of charge. These have recently included the making of shadow-boxes, pop-up valentines, T-shirts decorated with animal footprints, and fun with magnets. There's also a darkroom, a lapidary workshop, a woodworking shop, and a ceramics room on the premises. Call for a schedule of upcoming events. Open Tuesdays through Saturdays, from 10:00 a.m. to 5:00 p.m.

San Francisco Maritime National Historical Park
- Hyde St. Pier (Fisherman's Wharf), San Francisco; (415) 929-0202

For a full day of bargain-basement entertainment, put on your Navy bellbottoms and take the kids to Maritime Park. It's located at the western end of Fisherman's Wharf. Here, four big ships are permanently moored, waiting to be explored—a square-rigger, a pair of 19th-century three-masted schooners, and a friendly old ferry boat. Play around on the poop deck, explore the galleys, turn the wheels, and actually raise the sails, with help from the National Park Service Rangers on board. You can even join in the sea shanty sing-alongs.

On Saturdays, there are puppet shows featuring sailor puppets and rap music (how ship-shape is hip-hop?). Elsewhere in the park, at the end of Polk Street, is the National Maritime Museum, though that's not usually the draw for the typical young Popeye. Mom and Dad will certainly enjoy it, though, with its historical exhibits offering plenty of nautical color.

Admission is free on the first Tuesday of each month, and also during the annual "Festival of the Sea," held in late summer. Otherwise, get on board for $3 adults, and $1 for ages 12-17. Kids 11 and under get in free anytime. Open 9:30 a.m. to 5:00 p.m. in winter, 10:00 a.m. to 6:00 p.m. in summer.

San Francisco Public Library
- Civic Center (Larkin and McAllister Sts.), San Francisco; (415) 557-4554

True cheapsters never spend a penny on books or magazines—not when they can get them for free at the library. Well, here's some more good news: The San Francisco Library system also offers an amazing wealth of kids entertainment, also free.

The main branch, located downtown in the Civic Center, hosts a storytelling hour every Saturday morning at 10:30. On the third Wednesday and Thursday of each month, they show movies for young people, with different series geared to ages from pre-kindergarten through sixth grade. For somewhat older kids, the Junior Chess Club (ages 6 to 18) meets from 3-6 p.m. every Friday afternoon. You don't have to be like that little fellow who was searching for Bobby Fischer to attend; librarians provide instruction, along with a dozen or so types of other

games and puzzles.

In fact, you don't even have to leave your house to enjoy the library's bounty. Call their toll-free (within San Francisco), 24-hour story line. Your kids can hear a tale told in English, Spanish, or Cantonese—such stories as Hans Christian Andersen's "The Princess and the Pea," as well as traditional stories which are native to the culture of each language. The numbers to call are: 626-6516 (English), 552-0535 (Spanish), and 552-0534 (Cantonese).

The SFPL has 25 other branches located all over town, and many host regular children's activities and special events of their own. On any day of the week, you can find a storytelling hour or a movie; or perhaps a special happening such as a puppet show, a dance performance, a magic show, or a concert. Call your branch library for hours and a schedule of events, or call the system's general information line at (415) 557-4400.

U.S.S. Pampanito
- Pier 45 (Fisherman's Wharf), San Francisco; (415) 929-0202

This fully restored World War II submarine provides more entertainment than Nintendo—in considerably more lifelike fashion. Scramble up and down ladders, crawl through tiny tunnels that parents can barely fit through, turn dials and push instrument-panel buttons and levers—it's a kid's paradise. You can view the captain's quarters, see real torpedos, and check out the operational radio room and engine. This is a self-guided tour; the audio program tells the sub's history and describes true stories of its wartime adventures.

Admission is $4 for adults; $2 for kids age 12-17; and $1 for kids under 12, seniors, and military personnel. The Pampanito is open 365 days a year—from 9:00 a.m. to 6:00 p.m. in winter, and 9-9 in summer. Call for information about new overnight programs for kids, which were "coming soon" at the time of this writing.

COLLEGE ARTS

The college campuses of the Bay Area offer a wealth of music, dance, theater, and films which don't require much personal wealth to attend (unlike the colleges themselves). Many events are free to students, of course (don't forget your ID!); but most are also open to the general public, also for free or a very small charge. If you want to put culture into your life on a regular basis, this is a great way to do it.

Mills College
- 5000 MacArthur Blvd. (Seminary St.), Oakland; (510) 430-3308

Mills College, an independent liberal arts school for women, produces some thought-provoking, ambitious theater productions. Shows in the past have included such original creations as *The Legacy of Malcolm X Revisited*, based upon two of the man's speeches—"Message to the Grassroots" and "The Ballot or the Bullet." Spanish playwright Federico Garcia Lorca's rarely-seen tragedy, *The House of Bernarda Alba*, was also presented recently.

The theater department does offer plenty of entertainment on the lighter side as well, such as original musical revues and other student-directed productions. Prices are $7 for general admission; $5 for students, seniors, and the Mills community; and $4 for children age 12 and under. And you can save yourself a dollar on admission if you order your tickets in advance instead of buying them at the door.

San Francisco Art Institute
- 800 Chestnut St. (Jones St.), San Francisco; (415) 749-4588

The San Francisco Art Institute is the oldest and the most renowned cultural institution in San Francisco, with programs focusing exclusively on the fine arts. The institute boasts quite a number of graduates who've gone on to prominence in the art world, including Clyfford Still, Mark Rothko, Ad Reinhardt, Hassel Smith and Frank Lobdell. It was here that

Ansel Adams created the nation's first academic photography department. Instructors over the years have included Minor White, Imogen Cunningham, Dorothea Lange, and Edward Weston.

Oh, Mr. C could go on listing the famous artists who have worked here, but you get the idea. Today, the Art Institute continues to set the pace with its current students and faculty, whose work is continually on display. The Walter/McBean Gallery gives exposure to experimental works by both well-known and unknown professional artists. The Diego Rivera Gallery, named after the Mexican muralist, not only features works by current SFAI students, but it is student-curated as well. Admission to both galleries is free at all times.

The school sponsors many public events, including performances, films, and open lectures. Movie lovers will enjoy the Institute's **Cinemathéque** series, billed as "the Bay Area's premier showcase for avant-garde cinema." Films from around the world are screened every Thursday and Sunday evening. General admission is $6, but students and members only pay $3—and you don't have to be the former to join the latter! Call for schedules and membership information.

San Francisco Conservatory of Music
- 1201 Ortega St. (19th Ave.), San Francisco; (415) 564-8086

Hello, music lovers, wherever you

MR. CHEAP'S PICKS
College Arts

✔ **The San Francisco Art Institute**—New, old, famous, and unknown artwork—this place has it all, plus avant-garde movies, performances, and lectures.

✔ **University of California at Berkeley**—The music, drama, and fine art departments offer a wide variety of performances and exhibits at very low cost.

---

are. . .Enjoy beautiful sounds every night from September to May at the San Francisco Conservatory of Music, located in the Sunset District. For starters, there is a full slate of concerts by student and faculty ensembles, as well as professional guest artists. In addition, the conservatory also presents six orchestra concerts annually; one opera production, in the spring; and other special events through the year.

Play a mean tune yourself? Master classes, in which a professional educator and musician will critique and provide help with your music, are available on occasion. Depending on the guest, the cost for participating in these seminars ranges from free to $5.

All student ensemble performances and recitals are free and open to the public. Tickets for faculty performances and special events are usually $10 general admission, and $6 for students (from any institution), seniors, conservatory members, and the disabled.

Stanford University
• Braun Music Center, 300 Pasteur Dr., Stanford; (415) 723-2300
Sure, you've all heard of Stanford University. After all, it is one of the most prestigious institutions in the Bay Area. But, even in the midst of

their lofty intellectual pursuits, these students take time out for the arts.

The university's **Music Department** offers many public concerts by faculty and student ensembles throughout the year, all at very affordable prices. Recent concerts have included a J.S. Bach Organ Series, performed by The Organ Consortium at Stanford; performances by the Chamber Chorale and University Singers; the Guild Faculty Jazz Showcase, highlighting the development of big band swing music, among other styles; a "Pied Piper Concert" of *Hansel and Gretel*, performed by the Music Guild; the Stanford Symphony Orchestra and Chorus...and other delightful presentations.

Admission prices for the 1993-94 season are $7 general admission and $4 for students. In addition, there is a regular schedule of student recitals, which are free and open to all. Contact the department at (415) 723-2300 for a schedule.

The Stanford **Drama Department** has exciting productions running throughout the academic year. These have included *An Evening of Beckett: Beckett On Air/Beckett On Stage*; Diderot's *Rameau's Nephew*; plus other classics, ranging from Shakespeare's *Othello* to Brecht's *In the Jungle of the Cities*. Tickets for most of these performances are usually $9 general, and $5 for students and seniors; some performances, though, offer admission for free or by donation. Call (415) 723-2576 for a season schedule.

Finally, Stanford's **Art Department** sponsors a lecture series which runs throughout the year, generally offering about twelve programs. Learn from prominent art historians and visiting artists, such as Edward Ruscha and Elizabeth Johns. Once a year, the department features the Christensen Lecture, which is given by an outstanding art historian and honoree. In addition, a graduate student symposium is held each year. The art depart ment's number is (415) 723-3404.

University of California at Berkeley
- University of California at Berkeley, Berkeley; (510) 642-4864

Over forty years in existence, Berkeley's **Department of Music** sponsors a well-attended series of student and faculty ensemble performances. Admission to these events, presented in glorious Hertz Hall, is free and open to all—as are many of the performances given there. Concerts featuring the University Symphony Orchestra generally cost $6; but there is a half-price discount for Berkeley students, and $2 off for any other students, seniors, and UC faculty and staff. For tickets and schedules, call (510) 642-9988.

The university's **Department of Art** has a full palette of delights for art lovers. The Worth Ryder Art Gallery presents student exhibitions throughout the year, both by undergraduates and MFA candidates; admission to all of these are free. The department also hosts a "Visiting Artist Noon Lecture Series," which presents artists, curators, critics, and scholars. The lectures are free as well. Call the department at (510) 642-2582 to find out what's coming up.

The **Dramatic Arts Department** presents a wide variety of shows in Zellerbach Hall/Playhouse—for practically nothing. Talk about dramatic savings! With plays ranging from classics to contemporary, prices tend to be a mere $5 for general admission and $3 for students and senior citizens. Other performances can be more expensive, but it still beats downtown theater prices. For more information call (510) 642-9988.

COMEDY

Whatever happened to all the comedy clubs in San Francisco? Once, The City was a laff mecca with a dozen or more clubs, but now only a handful remain—with a few more in far-flung suburbs. "We don't need comic relief around here," one staffer remarked to Mr. C, "because we're already happy. We don't have snow and sub-zero temperatures like they do everywhere else." Another person added: "Everybody stays home and catches good comedy on the tube. Why go out?"

Well, how about social interaction, for one thing. You *can* still catch good comedy at reasonable prices in the clubs; the joints listed below feature top-notch local talent, as well as big-name national stars. And if you don't mind driving—or if you already live in that timeless source of comic material, suburbia—you can always find a good show at one of the venues outside of town.

Bay Area Theatresports
- Bayfront Theater (Fort Mason Center, Bldg. B), San Francisco; (415) 824-8220

This wacky improvisational ensemble turns comedy into a sports event. The troupe divides into teams; the audience suggests scenes; and a group of judges award points (and penalties), in classic Olympic fashion. And if you want to, like, actualize your inner ham, you can even join in when the performers ask for audience volunteers (but hey, no pressure).

It all makes for a wild and wooly evening. It's a real bargain too, with tickets at $7 (except during the big playoffs, when they rise to $10—but it's a lot easier to get in than Candlestick in October). You can also park for free, and you don't have to buy drinks or food if you really want to economize. Shows (or should that be "matches"?) take place every Monday night at 8:00 p.m.

Bonkers Comedy Cellar
* 1010 Northgate Dr., San Rafael; (415) 472-0314

Billing itself as Marin's only comedy club, Bonkers features national and local headliners every Friday and Saturday starting at 9:00 p.m. Comics seen here recently include Will Durst, Monica Piper, and Bruce Baum. Most shows present two acts in addition to the big-name star. You pay a laughably reasonable $8 admission on Fridays, and $9 on Saturdays. Furthermore, there is no drink minimum—a big plus on the comedy club circuit—though the club is outfitted with a full bar.

Bonkers only holds about 100 people in it's intimate, cabaret-style room. Seating is at tables, and munchies like pizza and nachos are also available.

Cobb's Comedy Club
* 2801 Leavenworth St. (in the Cannery), San Francisco; (415) 928-4320

"Best yuk for the buck," says the *Chronicle* about Monday night shows at this upscale club in a touristy location. For only $5 (plus a two-drink minimum), you can catch this weekly extravaganza featuring no less than *fourteen* acts—all local, professional talent, and no amateurs. That comes to a mere 35¢ per comedian, or just pennies per laugh, depending on your bookkeeping method. The show starts at 8:00 p.m. and runs as much as three hours.

Not only that, it's clean. If smutty and insulting humor turns you off, this is the place for you. Cobb's avoids racist, sexist, and homophobic comics—again, no doubt because of its high-profile location. "We feature cutting edge, smart comedy for smart people," says the management. Sound too high-brow? Nah. Believe it or not, kids, there was a time when comedy was actually just plain fun.

You can also start with dinner at the full-service Italian restaurant adjoining the club, and get guaranteed reserved seating at the show. Entree prices hover in the $8-$11 range—a bit over Mr. C's usual, but not unreasonable—with portions big enough to keep your tummy from growling and drowning out the jokes.

Tuesday through Sunday evening shows start at 9:00 p.m., and feature the best of well-known national and local acts. Admission is $8 (plus two drinks) Sunday through Thursday; $10 plus drinks Friday and Saturday. The nearby Anchorage Garage lets you park free for three hours with a validated ticket.

Coffee Cantata Deli
* 1980 Union St. (Buchanan St.), San Francisco; (415) 563-7274

Every Saturday night at 9:00 p.m., the Coffee Cantata Deli adds a three- to four-hour improv comedy show to its menu, with no cover charge. Just buy two drinks, and you can laugh all night. Who would expect such a bargain in this upscale neighborhood?

The Deli also offers food that's good enough to avoid being the brunt of any jokes. You can nibble your way through large salads and sandwiches during the show, or dine on entrees in the $6 to $10 range. There's also a full coffee bar for java fiends. A neat bonus: The deli's gazebo ceiling opens up to the elements in good weather, adding a pleasant touch of outdoor ambience to the evening.

Giggles
* 1380 Industrial Rd. (Howard Ave.), San Carlos; (415) 595-3319

This huge club (350 seats!) plays host to national-circuit talent only—performers like Mark Roberts of *WKRP in Cincinnati*, Paul Kozak, David Straussman, and more. Now, regular weekend admission is $10, but here's the deal: If you go on Sunday evenings, or during the week, tickets go down to a more comfortable $6. Giggles also has a two-*item* minimum—which means you can substitute food (appetizers or entrees) for drinks if you want to stay sober enough to catch the jokes. For cost-conscious comedy fans, nightclub food is always a better value than the drinks anyway.

Show lineups change every Tuesday night, and usually feature three comedians. Performances are at 8:00 p.m., with an added 10:30 p.m. show on Fridays and Saturdays.

Josie's
* 3583 16th Street (Market St.), San Francisco; (415) 861-7933

This vegetarian-cafe-by-day becomes a gay and lesbian comedy club every night at 8:00 p.m. The kitchen stays open during the show; you can sup on such goodies as tofu stir-fry and pasta dishes for around $5. Once the comedy begins, the kitchen still serves a more limited menu of quiches and soups, along with coffee drinks, beer, and wine.

Local and national headliners recently on the bill have included comics like Margo Gomez, Kate Bornstein, Mark Davis, and Scott Cuporo. Monday is the cheapest night here, with an open-mike program and a $5 cover. Other nights, admission hovers in the $8 to $12 range, with no drink minimum. There's an additional 10 p.m. show on weekends.

Josie's also shows local artwork, usually photography and paintings, in exhibits which change monthly. Some evenings offer performance art instead of the comedy on its stage; the place seats about 100 folks comfortably.

The Punch Line
* 444 Battery St. (Clay St.), San Francisco; (415) 397-4337

This is the *grand dame* of the comedy club circuit—it's been around since 1978 (can you remember back to an ancient time when it was considered bad form to have one comedian follow another?). Even so, The Punch Line remains on the cutting edge of comedy, featuring top-name shows as well as innovative special performances.

Sundays and Mondays are the true cheapster nights, with an admission price of only $5. For this pittance, you'll enjoy high-quality local talent,

MR. CHEAP'S PICKS
Comedy

✔ **Bay Area Theatresports**—Comedy as a competitive sport?? You won't believe it until you see it. You can even get in on the act—all for less than most nightclubs.

✔ **Cobb's Comedy Club**—Imagine, 14 professional acts for only $5 every Monday night. Pound for pound, the best comedic bargain in town.

✔ **Coffee Cantata Deli**—Good food, open-air dining, and a free improv show every Saturday night—on Union Street, yet. No joke.

perhaps an improv troupe, or an open-mike show. Some Mondays occasionally feature experimental theme shows, with titles like *A Comical Look at Rush Limbaugh* (isn't that redundant?), or the *No-Alcohol 12-Step Show.*

Like most clubs, the Punch Line also serves food. There is plenty of the Mexican/Italian appetizer variety, plus entrees ranging from a very reasonable $6 to $8. Showtime is an early 6:00 p.m. on Mondays, a nice work-week alternative; the rest of the week, shows begin at 9:00 p.m., with an added 11:00 p.m. show on Fridays and Saturdays. Admission is $8 on weekdays (other than that Monday show), and $12 on weekends, for big-name performers. The club also requires you to buy two drinks. But then, if you go on a weekend, you'll need those two drinks to calm yourself down after paying the comparatively high price of admission.

The Punch Line also has branch outposts in Walnut Creek and Sacramento.

Rooster T. Feathers
- 157 West El Camino (Matilda), Sunnyvale; (408) 736-0921

Do you know the way to San José? Well, along that route—about halfway between SJ and Palo Alto—this club with a goofy name gets top-line national performers, like Detective Tommy Sledge, George Lopez, and Craig Shoemaker. Most shows generally include three such acts. Weekend admission costs $10; catch a bargain, though, on Tuesdays through Thursdays—when ticket prices drop to $7 plus two drinks.

Shows start at 8:30 p.m. Tuesday through Sunday, with an added 10:30 p.m. show on Friday and Saturday. Although the large club boasts 280 seats, only people over the age of 21 can sit in them. If you can't remember your age, you're probably safe.

Sunshine Saloon
- 1807 Santa Rita Rd. (Valley Pleasant Shopping Center), Pleasanton; (510) 846-6108

What happens if you pay the admission price for a comedy club and the performer bombs? You lose big time! This is less likely to happen at the Sunshine Saloon, where shows are FREE (Mr. C's favorite word!) every Tuesday and Thursday, with no drink minimum. Even on Saturdays, admission is a low $5.

For these bargain prices, you'll enjoy sets by two local comedians. Don't be put off by the absence of national talent here. As the proprietor

points out: "Jay Leno performed here before he was *Jay Leno*, Sinbad performed here before he was *Sinbad,* and Paul Peterson played here before he hit the big time on *Laugh-In*." Well, two outta three ain't bad.

Even if the show does strike out (which can happen anywhere, after all), the evening is not lost. The Saloon offers a DJ and dancing after the show, along with billiards, darts, and pool tables. And if your tummy starts to growl, you can order food off the grill menu. All in all, it's as hard to go wrong here as it is to spend a lot of cash.

Tommy T's
- 2410 San Ramon Valley Blvd., San Ramon; (510) 743-1500

Thursday is Ladies' Night at this far-suburban club outside of Danville, when women get in to see the show—featuring several top-notch local and national comedians—for only $4. Regular admission price is $8 per person, going up to $10 on weekends. You must order two items from the menu—any two, either drinks or food. If you opt for some chow, you can choose from sandwiches, salads, or dinner entrees, all in the $5 to $14 range.

This club doubles as a sports bar, so you can always watch wide-screen TV before or after the show. Weeknights and Sundays, showtime is 8:00 p.m.; Fridays and Saturdays, sets begin at 8:30 and 10:00 p.m.

DANCE

In many cities, it costs more to buy a pair of ballet tickets than to put yourself through grad school. Not so in San Francisco, where even the premier venues offer tickets for as little as five bucks. Dance fans in the know say that the San Francisco scene ranks second only to New York; for experimental, cutting-edge work in particular, this is often *the* place to be. From "The Nutcracker" to the left-most edge of alternative choreography, the Bay Area offers a rich array of superb dance at reasonable cost.

Bay Area Dance Series

- Laney College Theatre, 900 Fallon St. (Ninth St.), Oakland; (510) 464-3540

The Bay Area Dance Series offers multi-cultural, multi-ethnic, and multi-style dance performances over a twelve-week period each spring (February through April). Sometimes, several different dance companies are presented in one weekend. Performances all take place at the Laney College Theatre, reputed to have the best stage for dance in the Bay Area. Recent shows have featured the San Francisco Ballet, the Diamano Coura West African Dance Company, the Abhinaya Dance Company (East Indian Dance), the Savage Jazz Dance Company, and Elaina Marie Ashe Afro-Cuban Modern Dance Company, and even an amazing troupe consisting of disabled artists.

Regular tickets cost $14 at the door, but students and seniors (with ID) can get in for $7-$10; children's matinees cost only $2. If you buy a four-show subscription, tickets go down to $9 each. Performances take place on Fridays and Saturdays at 8:00 p.m., with a 3:00 p.m. Sunday family matinee. Call for schedule and ticket information.

Cowell Theatre

- Fort Mason Center, Marina Blvd. (Buchanan St.), San Francisco; (415) 441-5706

The Cowell Theatre—built primarily for dance—boasts excellent visibility and state-of-the-art sound and light systems. It's part of the Fort Mason Center, which aims to provide cultural events at afforable prices to all Bay Area residents. Performers pay only a minimal amount for stage rental; that means *you* pay less for tickets.

The theatre presents some fifteen or so dance companies a year, ranging from local to international troupes. Recent shows have included the "Asian Dance Festival," and the "Celebration of the Black Dance and Music Experience," each of which featured several different groups; world-acclaimed companies such as

the Ralph Lemon Company and the experimental Pilobilus Dance Group have also performed here. For children, the Berkeley Ballet Theater recently presented its version of *Alice in Wonderland.*

Ticket prices average $5-$20, with reduced prices for many Wednesday and Thursday performances, student and senior discounts, and free admission for children available. Call for more detailed schedule and ticket info. In addition, two art galleries— the Cowell Theater Lobby and the Bayfront Gallery—are open before, during, and after performances, with free admission.

Dancers' Group/Footwork

- 3221 22nd St. (Mission St.), San Francisco; (415) 824-5044

This 65-seat theater in the Mission District—outfitted with full light and sound capabilities—presents modern and experimental dance performances at affordable prices. Many weekends, local choreographers use the theater to try out new works, which you can view for $7. Now, don't let the low admission price delude you into thinking you'll see a half-baked performance; all potential troupes compete at open auditions before acceptance. In fact, you may just catch a top choreographer trying out his or her latest piece.

The studio also sponsors special events, such as the ongoing Bread and Butter Dance Series, which presents works by local dance groups on weekend evenings. The annual EDGE Festival brings in national artists, who perform highly experimental works around a specific theme. Tickets for these shows range from $10 to $12, although the studio has a sliding scale policy—and pledges that it won't turn anyone away for lack of funds.

This theater actually runs "specials"—like two tickets for the price of one on some opening nights, or free tickets for students. An added extra: The theater has an on-site art gallery showing exhibits that fit in with the theme of the current dance offering. This place is truly artist-friendly! Call for a schedule of upcoming performances.

848 Community Space
- 848 Divisadero St. (McAllister St.), San Francisco; (415) 885-2003

Almost anything goes at 848, from alternative dance to theater to visual art. This multi-use performance space offers dancers one of the lowest-cost places in the city to produce their own work. As a result, some highly innovative and original work is seen here.

It's a small space, with seating in risers or on the floor. This is clearly a place for people who just love dance in its purest, raw form. The prominent new dance company Contraband has its home base here, as does The Knee Jerk Dance Project. Performances take place Friday and Saturday evenings. Other frequent events at 848 include performance art, improvisational jazz, world music bands, and theatrical monologues done with visual elements. A recent example, entitled "FTN," was a monologue by a male-to-female transsexual about his/her experience.

Before or after the show, you can check out the on-site art gallery, featuring works by local artists. Recent exhibits include theme shows on political topics, one-of-a-kind art books by feminist artists, mixed-media installations, and erotic art. Tickets for shows generally cost $5 to $10, but 848 applies a sliding scale based on your ability to pay—and never turns anyone away for lack of funds.

8th Street Studio
- 2525 Eighth St. (Dwight Way), Berkeley; (510) 653-2699

Here's another downscale, alternative space to see vital modern dance. Every Sunday in April and May, the studio presents its "Works in the Works" series. Six choreographers get 15 minutes each to present a new piece; the audience then discusses each work and gives feedback to the performers. You don't have to talk if you don't want to or if you have laryngitis, but the artists welcome comments from everyone—and you can certainly learn a lot about dance just by attending. Tickets cost only $5 apiece. Not bad for a series that has won the local Isadora Duncan award for its work.

Other shows offered include special presentations by The Choreographers' Performance Alliance, which has its headquarters here. Most of these shows cost $10, for which you are sure to see something intriguing. For instance, many performances incorporate aerial work with trapezes, since the studio happens to be outfitted with the requisite equipment. The nationally-known AXIS Dance Troupe, comprised of both disabled and fully able performers, is another troupe based here, and frequently performs as well. Call for schedule and ticket information.

New Performance Gallery
- 3153 17th St. (Shotwell St.), San Francisco; (415) 863-9830

This Mission District studio houses two top-notch dance companies: the Oberlin Dance Collective, and the Margaret Jenkins Dance Company. Although both groups have moved up to larger, more elite venues and rarely perform at this space anymore, they do rehearse here and offer frequent lecture-demonstrations with free admission to the general public. Now, that's a great deal!

New Performance Gallery has a 200-seat theater (not exactly a shoebox itself), used by visiting dance companies and protégés of the resident dancers. For $10 or less, you can see student performances featuring the best of up-and-coming new talent. Now, don't expect to see toddlers in tutus. We're talking college-age students, aspiring professionals all. Admission prices to other performances can vary, but the studio has a sliding scale policy making it affordable to all.

Oakland Ballet
- Paramount Theatre, 2024 Broadway (21st St.), Oakland; (510) 465-6400

Few cities offer two excellent ballet

companies in close proximity, but the Bay Area is blessed with both the Oakland Ballet *and* San Francisco Ballet companies (see listing below), just a bridge apart. Don't bite your nails worrying about which group to see: Oakland Ballet performs only in the fall, and the San Francisco Ballet only in spring. Both companies also present the traditional Christmas offering, "The Nutcracker," during December.

Now in its 29th season, the Oakland Ballet also tours constantly; it is, in fact, the largest touring dance company in the United States. It's best known for doing historical reconstructions of works from earlier in the century; the group recently won national attention for reviving a series of works by the master choreographer Sergei Diaghilev.

Tickets cost as much as $32, but they start as low as just $5 apiece for the cheap seats. You can often get better seats with half-price student, senior, and rush tickets at the door; this usually involves waiting in line an hour or two before the show—call the box office for current policy. Starting in the fall of 1994, the troupe also plans to present special community matinees, with all tickets priced at $8, making the best seats accessible to all. Bravo!

San Francisco Ballet

- War Memorial Opera House, 301 Van Ness Ave. (Grove St.), San Francisco; (415) 703-9400

Like its cousin across the bay, a mere $5 enables you to sit high in the balcony and see a full performance by the San Francisco Ballet—one of America's foremost dance companies. It's a tremendous bargain, considering that the aristocrats in the orchestra seats below will have paid anywhere from $35 to $75 to see the same show. Of course, the performers will appear rather small from your rooftop perch, but at least the theater has no obstructions, and your high position will let you easily see the entire "stage picture."

If high seats scare you more than

MR. CHEAP'S PICKS
Dance

✔ **Bay Area Dance Series**—A three-month celebration of every type of dance—from ballet to West African—at the area's best dance venue. Students and seniors get in for as little as $7, but even the most expensive tix cost only $14.

✔ **San Francisco Ballet**—For a mere $5, you can settle into a balcony seat with a perfectly good view and watch some of America's best ballerinas. Or, attend one of the special matinees, when *all* seats in the house go for $5 to $15.

✔ **Theater Artaud**—Check out the Summer Performance Marathon, when a potpourri of top-notch dance companies perform for 14 hours straight. Tickets cost only $5.

---

high prices, wait for one of the five special matinees given each year when all seats in the house cost between $5 and $15. Why, you may even score a budget-priced front-row seat or a private box! Don't wait until the last minute, though—these bargain performances always sell out months ahead of time. Reserve for "The Nutcracker" by September, for example or all you'll get is that infamous lump of coal in your stocking.

Other deals offered regularly include half-price student and senior discounts, and series tickets at subscription discounts. In addition, the SFB gives free performances at the annual Stern Grove Summer Festival (see listing under "Festivals").

The ballet season proper runs from February through April, with Nutcracker performances throughout December. By the way, did you know? This is the oldest ballet company in the United States, begun in 1933. During its history, the troupe has frequently hosted such illustrious choreographers as George Balanchine and Jerome Robbins.

South Bay Dance Companies

• Various suburban locations; Information, (408) 255-4055

Well south of the city, a world of great dance flourishes. You may have to drive for an hour or so to see one of these performances, but dance *aficianados* know that the trek is worth it. Leading dance companies in the area include:

> Gary Palmer Dance Company, San Jose, (408) 280-1436
> Jan Lyn Dance Company, (408) 255-4055 (modern dance and shows for young audiences)
> Margaret Wingrove Dance Company, San Jose Stage, (408) 993-9233
> Nouveau Performance Troupe, Nouveau Theatre, San Jose, (408) 275-0615
> San Jose/Cleveland Ballet Company, San Jose Performing Arts Center, (408) 288-2820 (offering joint performances with the Cleveland Ballet)

For performance schedules and ticket prices, as well as directions, call any of these box office numbers. You'll find admission to most shows running $8 to $15, with tickets slightly higher at the San Jose/Cleveland Ballet.

Theater Artaud

• 450 Florida St. (17th St.), San Francisco; (415) 621-7797

This is *the* elite theater for avant-garde dance, as known for its huge stage and extremely flexible space as for its wide-ranging work. "Our mission is to present adventurous and innovative artists who represent diverse disciplines and cultures," Mr. C was told. You'll see top local and national performers here; yet, tickets can actually cost less than the price of a pizza (no comparison intended).

Recent performances have showcased such major troupes from the national circuit as the American Ballet Theater, the Joe Goode Performance Group, the Donald Byrd Dance Company, and the Margaret Jenkins Dance Company. Each week can bring a different group to town.

The best bargain of all is the "Summer Performance Marathon," featuring 14 hours of back-to-back performances by dance companies scheduled for the coming year. Tickets to this extravaganza cost a mere $5. Normal admission prices, meanwhile, range from $6 to $18, with a $2 discount for students and seniors (with ID). The theater also offers frequent student matinees at half-price; call the box office to see what's coming up.

FESTIVALS

If you like outdoor festivals, you belong in the Bay Area. Few other cities offer as much year-round partying as San Francisco. Mr. C lists only performing arts festivals, but San Francisco also has great street fairs year-round. The **Haight-Ashbury Street Fair** usually takes place in June, while the **Castro** hosts one in October (of course, many would argue that these boulevards are *permanent* street festivals). Also in June are the three-day **Festival of the Viewing of the Moon** in Japantown; and the **North Beach Festival**, with Italian food, arts, and music. February brings the famous celebration of the **Chinese New Year,** where else but in Chinatown; and in April, there's the **Cherry Blossom Festival** (you thought Washington D.C. had this market cornered) and the **International Street Performers Festival**. May means it's time for the **Brazilian Carnaval** in the Mission district. There are many others, too; watch for announcements on posters and in the newspapers.

Blues and Arts on Polk
- Polk Street (from Bush to Pacific), San Francisco; (415) 346-4446

The "thrill isn't gone" at this two-day street festival in mid-July, featuring a chance to hear great blues without sitting in smoke-filled bars. A total of about twenty groups perform on two outdoor stages, with stand-outs like John Lee Hooker making occasional appearances. Like any good street festival, this one accompanies the music with a potpourri of yummy foods, plus displays of works by local artists.

Broadway in the Park
- Golden Gate Park, at Liberty Tree Meadow; (415) 554-9523

See local productions of classic Broadway musicals like *West Side Story* or *Fiddler on the Roof* for free, when The Young People's Teen Musical Company presents these shows in Golden Gate Park. Performances run during the last week in July and the first week in August. These are matinees, with showtimes at 1:00 p.m. Saturday and Sunday at the Liberty Tree Meadow stage.

Comedy Celebration Day
- Golden Gate Park Stadium; (415) 777-7120

Tired of the same old "knock-knock" jokes? Get some new material at this free event, which is generally held on the last Sunday in July from noon until 5:00 p.m. You can picnic on the lawn, or buy snacks at the array of food stands. Meanwhile, top area comedians spend the day working the crowd. In fact, comic stars such as Whoopi Goldberg and Robin Williams have been a part of the yukfest in years past. This is a highly popular event (10,000 people attended in 1993), so arrive early to snag a good spot.

Free Shakespeare in the Parks
- Various locations; Information, (415) 666-2222

"A rose by any name" smells even sweeter when it costs nothing, and that's the deal at this annual summer series of Shakespeare plays. Throughout July and early August, performances take place on weekend afternoons at the Duck Pond Meadow of Oakland's Lakeside Park. In September, shows move across the bay to the Liberty Tree Meadow in Golden Gate Park. Call for this year's schedule.

Jazz and All that Art on Fillmore
- Fillmore Street (between Post and Jackson Sts.), San Francisco; (415) 346-4446

Enjoy great jazz and food at this free, eight-block street party that runs for three days in July. Sample souvenir glasses of California wines and brews at six cafes, listen to the music, and ogle juried works by over 350 artists. The main music stage is at California Street.

San Francisco Folk Music Club Folk Festival
- John Adams Community College, 1860 Hayes St., San Francisco; (415) 661-2217

This free two-day festival happens every year on the first or second weekend in June. Over sixty acoustic/folk musicians come together to do their thing, each delivering a 15-minute set. You won't find any big names on the program, but many of the up-and-coming locals who perform have major talent. Lots of seminars for players, too. See listing under "Music—Folk" for more information.

MR. CHEAP'S PICKS
Festivals

✔ **Comedy Celebration Day**—A full day of free jokes out on the lawn at Golden Gate Park, shared with the other 10,000 happy folks in attendance. Alumni include Whoopi Goldberg and Robin Williams.

✔ **Free Shakespeare in the Park**—The first two words say it all: "Free" and "Shakespeare." How can you go wrong?

✔ **Stern Grove Festival**—Free concerts every Sunday in summer by performers who normally charge enough to land you in debtor's prison—the San Francisco Ballet, Isaac Stern, the Duke Ellington Orchestra, and so on. All outside on a lovely lawn surrounded by redwoods and eucalyptus trees.

San Francisco Mime Troupe
• Various locations; Information, (415) 288-1720

What do you do for your summer vacation? This Tony Award-winning political satire ensemble spends its summer touring Bay Area parks every weekend, starting July 4th. A live band serenades the gathering crowds at 1:30 p.m., and the play begins at 2:00. All of this, meanwhile, is free of charge.

Now, we all know the standard response to that four-letter word in this group's name; but wait, this is different. For one thing, these folks *talk*—and they have a lot to say. SFMT has a definite, left-of-center, political agenda. And they're so good at blending in comedy, pop music, dance—and anything else that's currently hot—that they make politics palat-

able to all audiences. The message comes across through the fun. Hey, as Mr. C already told you: they've won awards. Call them in spring for this year's locations.

Stern Grove Festival
• Sigmund Stern Grove, 19th Avenue at Sloat Blvd., San Francisco; (415) 252-6252

Pick out your spot on the lawn, sniff the aroma of the surrounding eucalyptus and redwood trees, and enjoy some of the best entertainment the city has to offer at this beautiful outdoor amphitheater. How much for this bit of nirvana? Nada! Starting every June, the Stern Grove Festival offers free performances every Sunday afternoon throughout the summer.

Recent shows have featured the San Francisco Ballet, the San Francisco Symphony, the Duke Ellington Orchestra, the Preservation Hall Jazz Band, violinist Isaac Stern, the Pickle Family Circus, the San Francisco Opera, the Kronos Quartet, and so on. With such top-notch entertainment, the festival attracts large crowds of up to 10,000 people; do arrive early.

Shows start at 2:00 p.m. Bring a blanket or something to sit on. If waiting for showtime makes you antsy, you can attend the free talk given at 11 a.m. in the nearby Trocadero Clubhouse ; you can also reserve a picnic table (call ahead), enjoy the lake, or hike the nature trails on the grounds.

Stern Grove prohibits smoking and dogs. And smoking dogs, for that matter. Bench seating is available at the concerts for seniors and disabled patrons.

Along with the festival itself, there are several related events. The **Festival at the DeYoung Museum** brings Stern Grove performers into this Golden Gate Park location with a series of five lecture/demonstrations. Held on Friday afternoons at 1:00 p.m., these highlight the upcoming events at the Grove. Last year's performers included Theatre Flamenco, the San Francisco Ballet, and the

Chitresh Das Indian Dance Group. Tickets are free with museum admission; alone, they cost $5 for adults, $3 for seniors. Information: (415) 750-7645.

Finally, the **Festival at the San Francisco Community Music Center** also offers late afternoon preview performances by Festival artists, free of charge. The center is located at 544 Capp Street, near the Mission BART Station in San Francisco; call (415) 647-6015 for information there.

Summer Festival of Performing Arts

- Golden Gate Park Music Concourse; (415) 474-3914

Enjoy freebie performances of dance, music, drama, and magic, taking place each weekend throughout July, August, and September at the Music Concourse in Golden Gate Park. It's located between the Morrison Plane-

tarium and the de Young Museum. Schedules change annually, so call in the spring for a calendar of the upcoming summer's events.

Union Street Spring Festival

- Union Street (between Gough and Steiner Sts.), San Francisco; (415) 346-4446

This two-day festival in early June has something for everyone. You can watch waiters running up and down hills in the annual Waiter Race, trying to carry full trays across the finish line without any spills; or, show your own moves while a live big band plays, at the swing dance contest. Between events, take in the juried arts and crafts exhibition, featuring works by over 300 local artists. Check the newspapers, or call the number above for a detailed schedule of events.

MOVIES

Everyone complains about the ever-rising cost of going to the movies. There are several ways of getting around this, as Mr. C explains below. In addition to the theaters described here, don't forget that almost every major theater in town offers bargain matinees (usually in the $4 range), which can add up to big savings if you go to the movies often—and if you can go on weekday afternoons or early on weekend days. Otherwise, help yourself to the myriad offerings of the Bay Area's diverse cinema scene:

Castro Theater

- 429 Castro St. (Market St.), San Francisco; (415) 621-6120

The lavish Castro Theater was built in the 1920s, when going to the movies was still a major event; in the age of home video, it continues to make for a special night out. Its original beaux-arts architecture is intact; there are 1,500 seats, a huge screen, and a pipe organ that plays before evening films.

Shows change daily or every other day, with an emphasis on contemporary art films and classic double-fea-

tures. The theater hosts special film festivals throughout the year, including the San Francisco International Film Festival, a Jewish Film Festival, and the Lesbian/Gay Film Festival.

Tickets cost only $3.50 for the Wednesday or weekday matinees. Evenings, tickets go up to $6, but that's still better than first-run megashoeboxes—and the admission price covers both movies on double-feature nights.

Center for Psychological Studies

• 1398 Solano Ave. (Carmel Ave.), Albany; (510) 524-0291

Do you like to hit a cafe after seeing a movie, and analyze it for hours? Here's a rather unusual opportunity. On Friday evenings in this school's auditorium, you can watch a film and then rip it to shreds with the help of a film critic/psychologist. The bill usually offers such symbol-laden classics as *Dr. Jekyll and Mr. Hyde* or Alfred Hitchcock's *Spellbound;* following the screening, the audience is invited to sit around, sip coffee, and discuss what it all means.

Dr. Walter Gorsky, the resident psychologist, introduces each film and leads the discussion. No need to bone up on Freud or Adler to attend (hmm, do you always feel pressured to demonstrate some kind of intellectual prowess in a group setting? Very interesting...). In fact, the center welcomes any member of the public who pays the low $3 price of admission. Feel free to join in, or just listen to all the shrinking.

An added bonus: The school houses an art gallery in the hall adjacent to the screening room. All art on display has deep psychological meanings, of course. What do the pictures say to you? The gallery stays open during the Friday night screenings, and you may even catch a free opening reception.

Cinémathéque

• San Francisco Art Institute, 800 Chestnut St. (Jones St.), San Francisco
• Center for the Arts at Yerba Buena, 701 Mission St. (Third St.), San Francisco
• Information, (415) 558-8129

You won't catch *Rambo* or *Three Men and a Baby* playing here. Cinémathéque specializes in experimental, avant-garde, and underground films with an emphasis on film as a visual art experience. "We show movies in which the director uses film in the way an artist uses paint," says a spokesperson. Although Cinemathéque sometimes shows documentaries, many of the movies seen here offer more in the way of visual beauty than of plot line.

Cinémathéque screens films twice a week. Sunday night showings are held at the San Francisco Art Institute, and Thursday nights take place at the Center for the Arts at Yerba Buena. Admission costs $6.00, but members, seniors, students, and "other-abled" get varying discounts. Inquire by phone or at the box office.

Cole Hall Cinema at UCSF

• 505 Parnassus St. (in the UCSF Medical Center), San Francisco; (415) 476-2542

This is actually a second-run movie theaterone of the very few in the area. Here, courtesy of college activities funding, you can see recent movies that have finished running in the major moviehouses, but haven't yet been released on video. Showings only take place on Thursday and Friday nights at 6:00 p.m. and 8:00 p.m (after all, you wouldn't want those future doctors to miss a night of studying, would you?). Ticket prices are $3.50 for the general public, and $3.00 for students and senior citizens.

Grand Lake Theater

• 3200 Grand Ave. (MacArthur Blvd.), Oakland; (510) 452-3556

Although this theater shows first-run movies at first-run prices, it sure doesn't look like your typical first-run shopping mall cinema. The owner has lovingly restored the building to its 1926 original decor—and then some. The 1,000-seat downstairs theater has become the "Egyptian Room," complete with twinkling stars on the ceiling, full ornamental plaster and hieroglyphics on the walls, and a "cradle of civilization" mystical feel. In the upstairs theater, you'll experience the equally elaborate "Moorish Room." Or, just stand in the lobby to appreciate the Tiffany stained-glass windows, mosaics, and artwork displays.

All of this splendor is combined with state-of-the-art sound and projection systems, along with a mighty

Wurlitzer organ that plays during intermissions. It all makes the $6.50 admission seem more like a bargain. You can save even more by showing up early to catch the $3.50 bargain matinee in the afternoons.

Not far from this is another East Bay movie gem, the **Oaks Theater** in Berkeley. It's located at 1875 Solano Avenue; telephone (510) 526-1836. Both theaters belong to the Renaissance Rialto chain, and similar renovations to the Oaks have already begun. You'll soon find not only an Egyptian room, but a medieval castle room, and an art deco room as well.

The Pacific Film Archive

- University Art Museum, 2621 Durant Ave. (College Ave.), Berkeley; (510) 642-1124

The show changes at the Pacific Film Archive even faster than you can channel-surf. Each night, it's a different movie, "like an ongoing film festival," says the theater.

It seems that virtually *everything* cinematic shows up here eventually, from current Hollywood blockbusters to foreign films and even video art. These are usually arranged into various series, like the recent string of "Banned in the USA" flicks, or the "Classic Mexican Cinema" series.

It's a nice place to watch a flick, too—with 235 seats angled so that nobody can block you, a full-size Cinemascope screen, and a state-of-the-art audio system. Some shows feature live musical accompaniment, or start with an in-person introduction by the film's director.

Tickets cost a hefty $7, seemingly no better than the megaplex around the corner; but that price includes two showsboth the 7:00 and 9:00, each with a different film. The theater schedules some $3.50 matinees as well; and students, seniors, and people with disabilities get in for $3.50 at all times. Stop by for a schedule flyer.

The Paramount Theatre

- 2025 Broadway (20th St.), Oakland; (510) 465-6400

The Paramount is definitely *not* a

MR. CHEAP'S PICKS
Movies

✔ **The Paramount Theater**—A huge old palace that serves up extras like newsreels, cartoons, and games of chance along with the features. Tickets only cost $5, usually for grand-scale classics.

✔ **The Red Vic Movie House**— The only movie house in town with couches to view from. Art flicks and second-run hits.

✔ **The U.C. Theatre**—An exciting and eclectic program, ranging from alternative films to repertory favorites. Best of all, this place serves Ben & Jerry's ice cream.

strip mall, "viewing cubicle" sort of place. Like its Oakland neighbor, the Grand Lake (see listing above), this movie and stage palace features original art-deco decor, a Wurlitzer organ that plays between shows, a screen big enough to do justice to the most elaborate special effects, and other fancy touches. Unlike the Grand, this house remains intact as one gigantic 3,000-seat theater. Why, it's almost as if the show itself doesn't matter; fortunately, these rarely disappoint either.

The Paramount shows classic movies like *Gone With the Wind*—usually preceded by cartoons, previews of old movies, and newsreels from early in the century. Just like the good old days. Before the show, the audience plays "Deco-Win," a raffle-like game with prizes ranging from free dinner at area restaurants to balloon bouquets.

Another custom in the old days was an admission price so low that all you had do was take a pair of returnable soda bottles, redeem them on the way over, and buy your ticket.

Those days, alas, have not returned; still, tickets here are a bargain at $5 apiece. Films are only shown on Friday nights, because the theater hosts the Oakland Ballet and various other live events most nights of the week.

The Red Vic Movie House

- 1727 Haight St. (Cole St.), San Francisco; (415) 668-3994

The Red Vic makes movie-watching almost as cozy as staying at home on the couch. In fact, that's exactly what you *can* sit on here, if you arrive early enough to grab one of those coveted cushy seats. Other homey touches include fresh popcorn served in glass bowls, drinks in real mugs, and fresh-baked cookies from the Cafe Paradiso next door. Perhaps the fun and uniqueness of this place comes from the fact that a local collective has run it for the past 14 years.

The Red Vic shows a little bit of everything, from recent second-run movies to classics to cutting-edge art films. To make things even more interesting, the theater sometimes hosts special events, such as appearances by film directors. Before a recent showing of *High Lonesome*—a film about bluegrass music—a bluegrass band gave a live mini-concert. Nice touch!

For the very best deal, Mr. C advises frequent filmgoers to buy a seven-admission punch card for $25; this works out to a mere $3.57 per show. Don't get out that often? Try a four-admission card for $15, almost as good. Otherwise, tickets cost $5.50 evenings, $4.50 for matinees; hey, that ain't bad itself. Red Vic schedule calendars are available in stores and restaurants all over town.

The Roxie Cinema

- 3117 16th St. (Mission St.), San Francisco; (415) 863-1087

It seems that in the movie house arena—the newer the theater, the smaller the screen and the bigger the price. The Roxie, over 90 years old, is a bit faded but still offers a nice change from the sanitized world of mall movies.

Here you'll find a cutting-edge lineup of first-run European and American art flicks, as well as a repertory of classic movies. Many shows are offered as double features, and film directors frequently show up in person to introduce their films. The Roxie also hosts its own art film festivals.

Recent shows have ranged from *Alien Dream Come True*, billed as "the closest thing to a psychedelic trip," and *Rajneeshpuran: An Experiment to Provoke God*, complete with a discussion by the filmmaker and students of this Eastern religion.

Best ticket buys are the $3 bargain matinees on Wednesdays and weekends. Otherwise, tickets cost $6 for general admission and $2 for seniors.

U.C. Theatre

- 2036 University Ave., Berkeley; (510) 843-6267

This big, beautiful theater just off the Berkeley campus offers two of the best things in life: great movies and Ben & Jerry's ice cream. Not to mention the art gallery in the lobby, the frequent double features, and the fresh-baked cookies for sale at the concession stand.

Older repertory movies, independent and alternative movies, art film premieres, and frequent festivals make up the bill of fare. Recent highlights include The Hong Kong Film Festival, the Cyber Film Festival, the premiere of *The World's Best Commercials*, and the first annual Berkeley Women's Film Festival. For the best bargains, try to make it to the first show of the day, when admission is $3.50. At all other times, tickets cost $6 but remember, that often covers both ends of a double feature.

The UC Cinema belongs to the Landmark chain, which operates five other upscale movie houses in San Francisco, including the **Bridge Theater**, the **Clay Theater**, the **Gateway**, the **Lumiere**, and the **Opera Plaza**. All five offer bargain matinees. You can also save big bucks with their $22 discount card, which gives you five admissions to any of these theaters—bringing prices down to $4.40 a pop.

SECOND-RUN MOVIE THEATERS

Second-run movies are the same Hollywood releases that you see in the shopping malls and downtown cinemas, after they've finished their "first runs" in those major venues. Well before they make their way to pay-per-view and videocassettes, they often show up at some of the theaters listed below. Not only do you get one last chance to see recent hits you may have missed—still on the big screen—but the tickets usually cost less than half of those at the big-deal houses.

AMC Serramonte 6
- 4915 Juniper Serra Blvd. (Serra Center Shopping Plaza), Daly City; (415) 756-6500

All shows $1.75.

The Balboa
- 38 Balboa St. (37th Ave.), San Francisco; (415) 2218184

General admission $5.50; matinees $3.50.

Cole Hall Cinema at UCSF
- UCSF Medical Center, 505 Parnassus St., San Francisco; (415) 4762035

All shows $3.50; students $3.00.

Fairfax Theater
- 9 Broadway, Fairfax; (415) 453-5444

All shows $2.50.

General Cinema Fashion Island Savings Cinema
- 2192 Fashion Island, San Mateo; (415) 341-2270

All shows $1.50.

The Strand
- 1127 Market St. (Seventh St.), San Francisco; (415) 6212227

All seats $2.00; 99¢ matinees.

Tanforan Discount
- 400 Tanforan Park Shopping Center (El Camino Real), San Bruno; (415) 588-0291

Triple feature admission; free refills on popcorn and drinks.

MULTICULTURAL CENTERS

Berkeley Public Library Programs
- 2090 Kittredge St. (Shattuck Ave.), Berkeley; (510) 644-6100

Who says libraries have to be silent places? Not Pat Mullan, who has organized an annual jazz festival here at the Central Reading Room for over five years running. These are more than just a few tunes trotted out on a lazy spring eve. This year's event, entitled "The Year of the Trombone," packed people in for a weekend full of concerts, as did the previous year's "Mainly Monk Festival." It's serious jamming, with a

tad of education tossed in, featuring major local and national-circuit musicians. It's all free, of course, with a limited number of tickets distributed at the door an hour before each concert.

Other BPL programs, all free, are just as ambitious. In recent years, these have included a panel discussion on "Women in Non-Traditional Jobs"; an evening of Native American films; a lecture series on the history of Berkeley, given by the Berkeley Historical Society; readings by the East Bay Women Mystery Writers; workshops on "Drought-Resistant Gardening; and many other diverse happenings. Some events take place at other branches around the city. In all, it's one of the most active libraries you're likely to see; call the number above to find out what's coming up, or stop in to pick up some flyers. Oh, by the way, they've got some books here, too.

Center for the Arts at Yerba Buena
• 701 Mission St. (Third St.), San Francisco; (415) 978- 2787 (ARTS)
"The Center for the Arts will be the Bay Area's answer to the Smithsonian," Mr. C was told by the management here. Still partially under construction, this indoor/outdoor center already boasts three art galleries; a 96-seat multi-media screening room; a huge, totally modular all-purpose forum, with full theatrical lighting and sound capabilities; and a 755-seat theater for music and dramatic performances. All in a convenient SoMa location, near the Civic Center.

By 1995, the center is scheduled to have added an outdoor public performance area, with enough seating for 3,000 people; a sculpture garden; two cafes; and a walk-through waterfall, leading to a memorial dedicated to Dr. Martin Luther King. Also coming in 1995: The brand-new, 200,000 square-foot Museum of Modern Art, with its own galleries, auditorium, restaurant, and research library. Whew!

Currently, the center provides low-cost entertainment and art displays to Bay Area residents. Exhibits and performances highlight works by local and minority artists, with an emphasis on multicultural themes. Recent visual arts showings have included quilts by elder African-American women, a computer-controlled "light show" installation by artist Milton Komisar, and the touring AIDS Memorial Quilt exhibition. Gallery admission is a very reasonable $3; better yet, it's absolutely free from 6 to 9 p.m. on Thursday evenings. Seniors pay only $1 at all times, except

for Thursdays, when they get in free from 11 a.m. to 3 p.m.

Live performances over the past year or so have included the Great Black Music Festival, the Women's Philharmonic, and the Asian Pacific Performing Arts Festival. Tickets for these events vary, depending on the show; but most prices average around $12 apiece. In addition, for people on low or fixed incomes, the center always offers tix reduced to $7 each. If you honestly can't swing the full charge, ask for a lower-priced ticket at the box office.

Fort Mason Center
• Marina Blvd. (Buchanan St.), San Francisco; (415) 441-5705
Score one for the people: Here's a place that swapped guns for culture! Opened in 1977, Fort Mason Center is a converted military warehouse that has been designated as a National Historic Landmark. It now houses galleries, performance spaces, and offices for over fifty arts, environmental, and educational organizations. Each of seven buildings is utilized to the fullest, while three piers are the sites for frequent festivals and expositions. All of this is very conveniently located along the waterfront just west of Fisherman's Wharf.

Established to make the arts accessible to everyone, Fort Mason features free parking and reasonable admission costs. Among some of the extra arts bargains are "pay what you can" performances at the Magic Theatre, one of the country's most respected theater companies; and "Free Museum Day," on the first Wednesday of every month, when all of the center's galleries are open to the public free of charge. Once a month, there is also a free guided tour of the entire center; call Fort Mason's 24-hour recorded information line, (415) 979-3010, for details on upcoming events.

Here is a sampling of the many arts organizations and venues available to the public on the grounds of Fort Mason Center:

Bayfront Theater and Gallery
Book Bay Bookstore
CCSF Fort Mason Art Campus
Cowell Theater
Festival Pavilion
Magic Theatre
Mexican Museum
Museo ItaloAmericano
Performing Arts Workshop
San Francisco Children's Art
   Center
San Francisco Museum of
   Modern Art Rental Gallery
San Francisco African American
   Museum
San Francisco Craft & Folk Art
   Museum
Young Performers Theatre

Plus classes for adults and children in martial arts, performing arts, visual arts, health matters, and natural sciences; readings, lectures, and meetings; cafes; an international travelers' hostel; non-profit agencies; rentable conference facilities; and more.

See listings under "Dance," "Museums," and "Theater" for detailed information on some of these particular organizations; as well as "Books" and "Alternative Lodgings."

New Langton Arts
• 1246 Folsom St. (Eighth St.), San Francisco; (415) 626-5416
In the gritty heart of the SoMa cafe and art scene, New Langton is a pioneer. Begun twenty years ago by a group of gallery owners who wanted to show controversial exhibits that wouldn't be accepted in commercial galleries, NLA has not only hung in there, it has grown. The non-profit center now houses exhibit areas, a video theater, and a concert/performance space in its two-floor building.

The original mission is still very much in evidence here, even as the facility has expanded and the boundaries it used to challenge have blurred. At any given time, you may be able to wander in here and see cutting-edge painting and sculpture, multimedia installations, video programs, literary readings, and avant-garde music concerts. Exhibits change

MR. CHEAP'S PICKS
Multicultural Centers

✔ **Center for the Arts at Yerba Buena**—Relatively new complex of galleries and theaters, complete with rooftop gardens, in the heart of SoMa.

✔ **Fort Mason Center**—Former military base, converted into dozens of performance spaces, galleries, classrooms, and cafes.

monthly. Ticketed events range from $6 to $10, depending on the show; you can also become a member for as little as $20 a year, and get half-price ticket rates. Admission to the galleries, of course, is free. Gallery hours are Wednesday through Saturday from 12 noon to 5:00 p.m.

Whiptail Lizard Lounge
• 4035 18th St. (Castro St.), San Francisco; (415) 267-6979
The Whiptail Lizard Lounge is, in the words of its own newsletter, a "do-it-yourself" lesbian community center. Started by a group of women who are trying to create a lesbian presence in the rather male-oriented Castro, the Whiptail seems to be making progress—with a full slate of events that are usually free or very cheap.

Their programs offer something for everyone. Ongoing monthly activities include a poker and games night, held from 8-11 p.m. on the second Saturday of each month. A "Younger Lesbians Party" happens on the third Saturday, also from 8-11 p.m., and and open-mike performance night takes place every other month or so. Each of these events has admission by donation. Every Sunday from 10 a.m. until noon, you can hang out over coffee and the Sunday papers; and, on the first Sunday of each month, the Whiptail sponsors a potluck dinner.

Have you always wanted to try something new and artistic? The Whiptail recently conducted a "Life Drawing" workshop, and has also formed a women's writing circle. Consider yourself more of a couch potato? Try a Saturday video night, admission $2. And, if all these activities *still* don't offer something that interests you, the Whiptail encourages you to plan your own event. There's just no excuse for not getting off your butt and doing something. The Lounge is drug-, alcohol-, and smoke-free, a great alternative to the high-pressure bar scene. Call or stop in on weekends for a calendar of events.

MUSEUMS

Many San Francisco museums offer free admission one day a month—usually a Tuesday or Thursday. If your boss won't give you the day off simply to enjoy a bargain, consider buying a **Culture Pass**. For only $10, you get one admission to all of the Golden Gate Park museums (the Asian Art Museum, the California Academy of Sciences, the deYoung Museum, plus the Conservatory of Flowers and the Japanese Tea Garden)—a savings of more than 50% off the regular prices at the gate. You can purchase the pass at any of those museums, or by calling (415) 391-2000.

Ansel Adams Center for Photography

- 250 Fourth St. (Folsom St.), San Francisco; (415) 495-7000

This museum's five galleries house the largest collection of photography on the West Coast—everything from point-and-shoot pics to multimedia exhibits incorporating sound and video. You'll find dazzling special shows and a special hall dedicated exclusively to the work of the museum's namesake, Ansel Adams.

Exhibits change every three to four weeks. Recent specials included "Photographers' Images of Their Own Families" (with works by fifty artists); Adams' "Photographs of Water"; and "David Ireland: An Installation Incorporating Light, Film, and Still Photographs."

Admission is free to all on the first Tuesday of each month. Otherwise, tickets cost $4 for adults, $3 for students, $2 for seniors and youth ages 12-17. Children under 12 get in free anytime. The museum is open Tuesday through Sunday from 11:00 a.m. to 5:00 p.m.; evening hours until 8:00 p.m. are added on the first Thursday of every month.

Asian Art Museum

- Tea Garden Drive, Golden Gate Park, San Francisco; (415) 668-8921

The Asian Art Museum houses the largest collection of Asian treasures outside of that continent—over 12,000 objects from 40 nations. Here, you'll see everything from Samurai armor to the oldest known Chinese Buddha anywhere in the world. The museum has vast collections of Chinese jade and Indian Gandhavan sculpture, and similar exotic rarities.

Intriguing special programs frequently add to the permanent exhibits. A few years ago, the Dalai Lama himself created sand mandalas in the museum lobby in conjunction with a show on Tibetan art. The Chinese artist Yani (not to be confused with that new-age king of synthesizer rock music) recently displayed her brush paintings; Tuvan singers from Mongolia performed chants; and a Thai fruit carving expert demonstrated his unique craft. The museum also has an active film program—including private viewings of such major pictures as *The Joy Luck Club*.

See it all for free on the first Wednesday of every month, from 10:00 a.m. to 8:45 p.m. Regular admission costs $5 for adults, $3 for seniors, $2 for youth from 12-17, and nothing for kids. Hours are from 10:00 a.m. to 5:00 p.m., Wednesday through Sunday. You might pay a small extra charge for some special events, but many are free.

California Academy of Sciences

- Concourse Drive, Golden Gate Park, San Francisco; (415) 750-7145

This trio of fun places for all ages includes the **Morrison Planetarium**, the **Natural History Museum**, and the **Steinhart Aquarium**. All three are open 365 days a year from 10:00 a.m. to 5:00 p.m. daily; you'll find lengthier descriptions of each, listed alphabetically throughout this chapter.

Exploratorium

- 3601 Lyon St. (Bay St.), San Francisco; (415) 563-7337

This is the numero uno, happeningest kid's spot in the city—and it's bigtime fun for adults, too. Inside the former Palace of Fine Arts, you'll find more than 650 hands-on science exhibits, including "The Tactile Gallery," where you enter total darkness and use only your sense of touch to guide you through a long tunnel; and "Discernability," which lets you scramble your own television image. The "Light" exhibits let you play with prisms and filters. At "Waves and Resonance," you can move a 400-pound pendulum using only a tiny magnet; while "Weather" lets you play with swirling air and water, or walk through a cloud.

Everywhere you turn, something is spinning, swinging, lighting up, or making a noise. You can even watch museum technicians constructing the Exploratorium's own exhibits, at the Machine Shop. And, each weekend,

new and unusual short films are shown in the McBean Theater, which is free with admission.

Recent additions include displays on virtual reality, computer art, and fun with CD-ROM devices. Also new for spring of '94, the museum has opened "Playspace," a permanent and enclosed activity area for children age four and under with their parents.

Now, with all this to offer, just about any admission price would be a bargain. As it is, admission is $8 for adults, $6 for seniors and students, $4 for kids age six to seventeen, and free for ages five and under. But wait, it gets better. Visit on the first Wednesday of each month, and you can get the whole gang in absolutely free. Hours are Tuesdays through Sundays, 10:00 a.m. to 5:00 p.m. (plus Wednesday evenings until 9:30). The phone number listed above is for speaking to live people; you can also call 561-0360 for recorded information.

Fort Mason Center

- Marina Blvd. (Buchanan St.), San Francisco; (415) 441-5705

So many museums, so little hassle. Park once (no charge!) and you can see them all—four different ethnic collections, plus three other galleries of temporary exhibits. All at this sprawling, National Historic Landmark complex, converted from military use to the arts. On the first Wednesday of every month, admission is free to all of the museums, with hours extended until 8:00 p.m.; and one Saturday afternoon per month, there is a free guided tour of the entire center.

Whenever you visit, pick up one of their great monthly newsletters, filled with articles about new exhibits, a calendar of absolutely every single show, lecture, and meeting going on here, plus all the basic prices/phones/hours info.

The African American Historical and Cultural Society in Building C, telephone (415) 441-0640, features artwork and crafts by artists from both Africa and America. With its atmospheric lighting and vividly colorful displays, there is a hip rhythm and feel to the place, which also has a gift shop filled with more delightful crafts. They also sponsor a youth study group which meets monthly. Open Wednesday through Sunday, 12-5; regular admission is $2 for adults, 50 cents for children.

The Mexican Museum in Building D, telephone (415) 441-0404, presents exhibits of current Latin American artwork, in a variety of media. They also have extensive holdings of Pre-Columbian and folk art. Frequent special events include bilingual storytelling performances. Open Wednesday through Sunday, 12-5; regular admission is $3 for adults, $2 for children and seniors.

The Museo ItaloAmericano in Building C, telephone (415) 673-2200, is a haven for the Bay Area's tightknit Italian community—if Mr. C's recent visit was any indication. A tour group was chattering excitedly in Italian about the paintings on view; yet a glance at the guest register showed local addresses. Exhibits range from the latest in contemporary art from Italy to a history of Italian immigration in California. Open Wednesday through Sunday from 12-5. Regular admission is $2 for adults, free for kids under 12.

The San Francisco Craft and Folk Art Museum in Building A brings in paintings and handcrafts from all over the world. Recent exhibits included a display of traditional festival masks from Bolivia. Open Tuesday through Sunday from 11-5 (opening an hour earlier on Saturday); regular admission is $1 per person.

The San Francisco Museum of Modern Art may be temporarily closed downtown as it moves to new, larger quarters; but they also run a space here (Building A) which can be rented out by local artists for showings of their work. Exhibits change monthly; each begins with a reception, free and open to the public, usually on a Tuesday evening. Have some wine and cheese and culture. Open Tuesday through Saturday, 11:30 a.m. to 5:30 p.m.; free admission.

And then, there are the smaller art galleries spread about the place: **The Bayfront Gallery** and **Cowell Theater Lobby** are open before, during, and after performances in that building, on Pier 2 of the center. And the **Cooks & Company Coffee Gallery**, in Building B, shows current works by students of the Community College of San Francisco, whose "art campus" is located here. It's also a great place to relax over rich coffee and cheap eats. Open daily from 8:00 a.m. to 11:00 p.m.

Fort Mason Center also has a 24-hour recorded information line, which details current exhibits and special events, at (415) 979-3010.

Haas-Lilienthal House

- 2007 Franklin St. (Jackson St.), San Francisco; (415) 441-3004

What was The City really like before The Quake? Not the one we can all remember, but the Big Quake of 1906? Find out by taking a tour of this lovely Victorian home near Pacific Heights. At that time, this house was a mere twenty years old. Miraculously, though nobody knew from earthquake codes in those days, it withstood the disaster.

Today, you can walk through rooms still decorated in that ornate Queen Anne style, seeing period furnishings and artifacts—in guided tours led by docents who can answer practically any question about the era. It's all overseen by the San Francisco Architectural Heritage Foundation. They also run the Heritage Bookstore on the premises, with more to offer fans of Victoriana. The building is only open on Wednesdays and Saturdays from 12-4, and Sundays from 11-5; the last tour begins 45 minutes before closing. Admission is $5 for adults, $3 for seniors and children under 12.

The foundation also sponsors **Pacific Heights walking tours**, pointing out other buildings of the period and special features of the surrounding area. These two-hour strolls take place on Sunday afternoons at 12:30;

meet on the sidewalk outside the house. Prices are the same as the museum admission.

Hearst Museum of Anthropology

- Kroeber Hall, University of California at Berkeley; (510) 642-3681

On a smaller scale than the de Young, the Hearst Museum displays ever-changing exhibits of an anthropological nature. These come from all over the world—and all over the time line. Past exhibits have included artifacts from ancient Egypt and Greece, as well as artwork (textiles, sculpture, jewelry) from Africa, Australia, and Native American cultures. Pictorial essays created by local photographers are also exhibited here. The one permanent display is that of Ishi, the last Yahi Indian—stone tools, arrow heads,and other remnants.

This museum is open Monday through Friday from 10 a.m. to 4:30 p.m. (until 9 p.m. on Thursdays). Weekend hours are 12 noon to 4:30 p.m. Admission is $2.00 for adults, $1.00 for students, and 50¢ for children, except on Thursdays, when everyone gets in free all day.

M.H. de Young Memorial Museum

- Tea Garden Drive, Golden Gate Park, San Francisco; (415) 563-7337

Here's the most wide-ranging art museum in the city, for sure. It's noted, in particular, for its extensive collection of American art. These holdings include works by Winslow Homer, Mary Cassat, James McNeill Whister, and John Singer Sargent.

The de Young also displays works by European masters; ancient art from Egypt, Greece and Rome; rugs and textiles from Central Asia and the Middle East; and a substantial Mexican and Mesoamerican collection.

Recent exhibits include "The Dead Sea Scrolls," "Woodblock Prints" by John Buck, and an exhibit commemorating the 1892 World's Fair held right here in Golden Gate

MR. CHEAP'S PICKS
Museums

- ✔ **Asian Art Museum**—Would you believe they actually *have* all the tea in China? All the china, too. The largest collection of Asian art objects outside of Asia. Next door, the **M.H. de Young Museum** is a similar blockbuster for American art.
- ✔ **California Academy of Sciences**—Dinosaurs, whales, and stars—oh my! It's three museums in one: **The Natural History Museum, the Steinhart Aquarium,** and the **Morrison Planetarium**.
- ✔ **Fort Mason Center**—Ethnic art museums, plus galleries showing works by local artists, all in one sprawling complex that's traded guns for art.

Park. The museum also hosts frequent lectures and demonstrations related to American arts.

Admission is free to all on the first Wednesday of every month, when the museum stays open until 8:45; also on the first Saturday morning of the month, from 10-12 noon. Otherwise, hours are from 10 a.m. until 5:00 p.m. Wednesday through Sunday, and admission costs $5 for adults, $3 for seniors, $2 for youth ages 12-17; children under 12 are admitted free anytime.

Mission Dolores

- 3321 16th St. (Dolores Ave.), San Francisco; (415) 621-8203

Still in use as a church, with masses in English and Spanish, Mission Dolores is the oldest building in all of San Francisco. It's not a museum as such, but the structure dates from 1791 is thus is a vital link with city history. Outside the church is its cemetery, filled with markers for many early San Franciscans—prominent, notorious, and those in between. There is also an area of the cemetery devoted to the native Americans who helped to found the mission. Open daily; admission is free.

Morrison Planetarium

- Concourse Drive, Golden Gate Park, San Francisco; (415) 750-7141

Here's a way to gaze at the stars without catching a chill or getting insect bites. This indoor sky show projects celestial images onto the dome of this round theater. Recent shows have included *Echoes from the Moon*—a replay of the historic Apollo 11 journey—and *A Star Trek Voyage*, which lets you "explore galactic wonders, experience the scorching radiation of an exploding star, and visit the birthplace of suns."

All that for about the price of a trolley ride. Tickets cost either $1.25 or $2.50 depending on the show—quite a bargain for a journey to the farthest reaches of the cosmos. Kids under 17 always get in for $1.25. The first Wednesday of the month is free for all ages. Shows run every day at 2:00 p.m., with several added shows on weekends. The Morrison is open daily from 10-5.

Thursday through Sunday evenings, the tempo picks up quite a bit as the planetarium changes over to its **Laserium** shows. Bursts of color and light dance across the indoor "sky," all to the musical accompaniment of Aerosmith and Pink Floyd (there are some classical music shows, too). It's a distinctly psychedelic experience; bring your headphones to tune in at your own level. Hourlong shows cost a fairly hefty $7, but then, they do have the market cornered in this sort of thing. You do get a dollar off if you come for the earlier (and gentler) 5:00 p.m. show. For 24-hour Laserium recorded information and ticket sales, call (415) 750-7138.

Musée Mécanique

- 1090 Point Lobos Ave., San Francisco; (415) 386-1170

Located around the back of the Cliff House building, overlooking the Pacific near Land's End, this "museum" is a lot of fun for anyone interested in nostalgia. It actually consists of only one kind of mechanical creation—penny arcade machines—room after room of them, tracing the history of these gizmos from the turn of the century to the latest video games. Clearly, this is not so much a museum *per se,* but rather a place for some fanatical collector to show off his neat stuff. Still it is, in a word, unique.

There is no admission fee; you probably won't even see any staff. Just an open doorway—oh so inviting, with organ-grinder music wafting out into the salt air. Also the sounds of "Laughing Sal," a machine which was a fixture at the Playland arcade from 1940 to 1972. Put a quarter in, and the large figure of a woman inside the glass box starts laughing, and laughing, and laughing....

Which is all Sal does. But there are lots of other kinds of machines: Wurlitzer player pianos, including an early Seeburg piano roll "jukebox"; simulated baseball games, the old-fashioned kind, in which you turn a crank to swing a tiny bat and hit a ball past tiny outfielders; dioramas of the wild west ("In the slot put yer dime—See the gulch's gay old time!"); and the ever-popular snapshot photo booths. Some of these are incredibly offbeat, definite museum pieces: "Toothpick Fantasy," for example, is a large diorama of an amusement park—rotating ferris wheels, merry-go-rounds, the works—entirely constructed out of toothpicks by inmates at San Quentin Prison. Guess they had a lot of time on their hands.

All of these machines have been reconfigured, alas, to run off of quarters rather than pennies. Inflation. Basically, the cost of visiting this museum is directly proportional to your curiosity, as in, "Hey—wonder what *this* one does?"

All the way at the rear, technology advances as far as the 70s and 80s (remember "Pong," that primitive video tennis game?). One nod to respectability, at least—or perhaps just sanity—is the sign which reads, "Students not allowed during school hours." See, told you it was a museum. Open weekdays from 11 a.m. to 7 p.m., and from 10 a.m. to 8 p.m.on weekends.

Directly across from the Mécanique, by the way, is a **National Park Service information center**, filled with brochures and photo displays about the Golden Gate National Recreation Area. There is also someone on hand to answer questions about Park Service programs, all of which are free.

Museum of the City of San Francisco

● 2801 Leavenworth St. (Beach St.), San Francisco; (415) 928-0289
On the third floor of the Cannery, right around the corner from Fisherman's Wharf, this small but jam-packed museum is just the thing for a quick overview of San Francisco's brief but exciting history. Or, if you prefer, linger and study the maps, paintings, artifacts, and multi-media displays. These tell the whole story: Spanish missionaries, gold rush boomtown, earthquakes, architecture, all the way up to the present day. Special exhibits add further detail to the permanent collection. Hours are 10 a.m. to 4 p.m., Wednesdays through Sundays; admission is free at all times.

The Natural History Museum

● Concourse Drive, Golden Gate Park, San Francisco; (415) 750-7145
If you haven't had your fill of earthquakes, you can feel the ground rattle beneath your feet at this museum's eight-minute simulated trembler. You even get to choose the magnitude you prefer! Other highlights include a large collection of minerals and gems; insect and African wildlife displays; and, of course, dinosaurs. Can't have a natural history museum without dinosaurs these days.

This is actually the largest natural history museum on the West Coast,

with great special exhibits along with the permanent displays. Recent offerings included a tour stop of the ultra-popular "Star Trek: Federation Science" show; "Birds of a Feather," teaching you how to decode bird language. Meanwhile, the permanent Interactive Science Center gives kids a chance to play with live animals, viewing microscopes, CD-ROM computers, and much more.

Open daily from 10 a.m. to 5 p.m. Come on the first Wednesday of the month to get in for free; otherwise, admission skyrockets to $7 for adults, $4 for youth 12-17 and seniors, $1.50 for kids ages 6-11, and free for those under 5—but these prices also include admission to the Steinhart Aquarium, in the same building (see listing below). You can also get a $2 discount on adult tickets with a BART or MUNI pass.

The Old Mint Museum

● 88 Fifth Street (Mission St.), San Francisco; (415) 744-6830
If you feel you just don't get to see enough dough in your day, this place will make you salivate. The building, opened in 1874 to serve gold rush diggers, has been carefully restored to its original, impressive appearance. The Old Mint contains vaults that once held one-third of the nation's wealth; you can now see gold ingots and rare coins, and view a collection of paintings and sculpture from the old west. You'll also see mining equipment, a fascinating display of early money-making equipment and artifacts, and a film about the gold rush.

If all the talk about money whets your appetite for cash, you can use the minting equipment to stamp out your own coin. Beyond that, ATM cash machines will have to suffice. You won't need to hit one before coming here, though; museum admission is free to all. Making one of those coins will cost you a buck, though. Open from 10:00 a.m. to 4:00 p.m., Monday through Friday. At the time of this writing, early in 1994, the mint was being threatened with permanent closure because of (how's this for irony) lack of funds; call ahead to see if they're up and running.

Palace of the Legion of Honor

• Legion of Honor Drive, San Francisco; (415) 863-3330

High up on a Lincoln Park hill, above Land's End, this majestic building is a direct reproduction of the Palais de la Legion d'Hounneur in Paris. Of course, the United States doesn't actually *have* a Legion of Honor—but we do have this fine museum, which is chock full of French paintings, sculpture, antique furniture, and salons.

Unfortunately, you can't see them until late 1995, as the whole place is currently being renovated for earthquake protection (there's one thing the French don't have). No doubt, there will be a whole new pricing scale when that time arrives, so there's no point in talking about it here. Keep your eyes peeled for *le barrage* of publicity.

The San Francisco Experience

• Pier 39 (Fisherman's Wharf), San Francisco; (415) 982-7550

Have you ever wondered what it would be like to transport yourself back to the excitement of the Gold Rush era, the heyday of cable cars (before they were just a tourist attraction), or the infamous earthquakes that define the experience of life in San Francisco? Hold on to your seats! The San Francisco Experience, a 28-minute multimedia presentation—complete with special effects and props—enables you to do all this without leaving your (rumbling) chair.

Adults and children alike will enjoy this incredible sensory show. In addition, there is an earthquake exhibit in the lobby (no charge) which includes a seismograph and photos of the San Francisco earthquakes of 1906 and 1986. The attraction is open every day from 10:00 a.m. to 8:30 p.m. Admission is $7 for adults, $6 for senior citizens and the military, $4 for youth (ages 5-16), and children under five are admitted for free. *An extra tip from Mr. C*: You can usu-

ally find discount coupons in local newspapers and tourist guides.

San Francisco Maritime National Historical Park

• Hyde St. Pier (Fisherman's Wharf), San Francisco; (415) 929-0202

For a full day of bargain-basement entertainment, put on your Navy bellbottoms and take the kids to Maritime Park. It's located at the western end of Fisherman's Wharf. Here, four big ships are permanantly moored, waiting to be explored—a square-rigger, a pair of 19th-century three-masted schooners, and a friendly old ferry boat. Play around on the poop deck, explore the galleys, turn the wheels, and actually raise the sails, with help from the National Park Service Rangers on board. You can even join in the sea shanty sing-alongs.

On Saturdays, there are puppet shows featuring sailor puppets and rap music (how ship-shape is hip-hop?). Elsewhere in the park, at the end of Polk Street, is the National Maritime Museum, though that's not usually the draw for the typical young Popeye. Mom and Dad will certainly enjoy it, though, with its historical exhibits offering plenty of nautical color.

Admission is free on the first Tuesday of each month, and during the annual "Festival of the Sea," held in late summer. Otherwise, get on board for $3 adults, and $1 for ages 12-17. Kids 11 and under get in free anytime. Open 9:30 a.m. to 5:00 p.m. in winter, 10:00 a.m. to 6:00 p.m. in summer.

San Francisco Museum of Modern Art

• 401 Van Ness Ave. (McAllister St.), San Francisco; (415) 357-4000

All of the great masters of 20th century art are represented at the Museum of Modern Art: Klee, Matisse, Braque, Picasso, Kandinsky, and many others. These holdings go well beyond paintings and sculpture; with an inventory of some 17,000 objects, the museum also houses furniture, architectural models, crafts, photographs, video—even clothing.

For special fun, check out one of the multimedia exhibits. Recent

188

shows included "In the Spirit of Fluxus," a series of experimental performance art and video pieces mixed with two-dimensional art, sculpture, and other objects. Forty artists, many of whom got their start during the far-out 1960s, contributed performances.

Admission is free to all on the first Tuesday of every month, and half price on Thursdays from 5-9 p.m. Otherwise, it's $4 for adults, $2 youth and seniors, and free for kids under 12 at all times. Hours are from 10 a.m. to 5:00 p.m. Tuesday, Wednesday, and Friday; 10:00 a.m. to 9:00 p.m. on Thursday; and 11:00 a.m. to 5:00 p.m. on Saturday and Sunday. Closed Mondays.

Please note: The Museum of Modern Art is moving into brand-new, larger quarters at 151 3rd Street, near Market Street; it is scheduled to close from September 1994 until its reopening at the end of January, 1995. The new facility may well bring new prices, as well.

Steinhart Aquarium
- Concourse Drive, Golden Gate Park, San Francisco; (415) 750-7145

The Steinhart Aquarium contains over 1,000 species of aquatic creatures. No dry, quiet museum this; everyone here is swimming, darting, lurking behind coral, and all those fishy things. You can easily watch them for hours in the "Fish Round-about," a multi-story glass tank. And, at the "Touch Tidepool," you can get up-close-and-personal with your favorite finny species.

Not to be left out are the higher representatives of the food chain—a large array of reptiles and amphibians, penguins, dolphins, and seals. There's also a huge living coral reef display.

Speaking of food, perhaps the most fun of all is feeding time. Fish get fed at 2:00 p.m., penguins at 11:30 a.m. and 4:00 p.m., and seals and dolphins every two hours starting at 10:30 a.m. And when it's feeding time for yourself, you're right in between two restaurant-rich neighborhoods—Sunset, to the south of Golden Gate Park, and Richmond, to the north. The Steinhart is open daily from 10 a.m. to 5 p.m.; admission is free to all on the first Wednesday of each month. Regular admission is $7 for adults, $4 for students and seniors, $1.50 for children ages 6-11; and free for ages 5 and under. These prices also include admission to the Natural History Museum, in the same building (see listing above). Adults can also get $2 off their tickets with a BART or MUNI pass.

Wells Fargo History Museum
- 420 Montgomery St. (California St.), San Francisco; (415) 396-2619

Sit in a real stagecoach and listen to an audio program about travelling overland in the days of the wild west. Use Morse Code to send your own telegraph message. Learn how to prospect for gold, see a map of hot prospecting sites, and check out old-time mining implements. This museum really pans out by immersing you in the fascinating world of the gold rush; best of all, you can do all of this without spending a single nugget. Open Monday to Friday, 9:00 a.m. to 5:00 p.m.

MUSIC

CLASSICAL MUSIC

Berkeley Symphony
- 101 Zellerbach Hall, University of California at Berkeley; (510) 841-2800

For the past 25 years, this orchestra has been offering concerts in Zellerbach Hall on the UC-Berkeley campus. This 90-piece ensemble has a particular emphasis on contemporary American and European composers, such as Olivier Messaien and conductor/composer Pierre Boulez, although there is always one traditional piece—Mozart, Beethoven, *et. al.*—on the bill.

The orchestra is led by Kent Magano, who got his major start here; and now, even though he divides his time between the Halle Orchestra in England and the Opera de Lyons in France, he still returns to conduct the Berkeley Symphony. They present a five concert season, running from September to June. The best ticket deal goes to annual subscribers, but all of their prices are quite reasonable. General admission prices range from $16-$30, with discounts for students and senior citizens bringing the scale down to $12-$23. And in this moderate-sized concert hall (2,000 seats), even balcony seats are close enough to see as well as hear.

Center for the Arts at Yerba Buena

● 701 Mission Street (Third St.), San Francisco; (415) 978-ARTS

Yerba Buena offers low-cost performances in a wonderful, almost-new theater that seats 755 people. The center aims to make cultural events accessible to everyone, so most shows cost only $12 to $15, with $7 tickets available to the "financially challenged," seniors, and students. If you can afford only a $7 ticket, just ask for it: You don't need to prove your destitution, but hey—Mr. C always says that people who can afford to support the arts should do so.

Anyway, among the recent classical music performances here have been concerts by the New Century Chamber Orchestra, the Women's Philharmonic, and a cello recital by David Darling. The center also hosts dance, drama, and video events; see listing under "Multicultural Centers" for more information.

For added fun, check out the center's art museum before the show. You can get in for free on Thursday nights from 6 p.m. to 9 p.m. At other times, admission costs $3. Call for a schedule of upcoming events.

Davies Symphony Hall

● 201 Van Ness Ave. (Grove St.), San Francisco; (415) 431-5400

If you aspire to heights of cultural sophistication, you simply must attend a concert at Louise M. Davies Hall. San Francisco's premier classical music venue hosts over two hundred concerts a year, so you'll have plenty of opportunity to catch a show. Will you be able to afford one? Sure—if you know how to snag a discounted ticket. Regular events, after all, cost at least $22, and that's for the most remote seats in the house. Decent balcony or orchestra seats tend to cost more like $40.

Ah, but you can see the same show as the big-spender patrons for a mere eight bucks! How, you ask? By purchasing a last-minute Center Terrace seat. Just show up at the box office two hours before the concert, with cash in hand. Tickets for these seats are put aside for every show—even for sold-out performances.

The catch, of course, is that you can't reserve ahead. For some events, this can mean waiting in line and hoping for the best. It's worth it, though: These are great seats! You sit on a platform right above the stage, almost on top of the orchestra, looking out on the audience. If you sat any closer to the musicians, they'd ask you to perform.

You can also save money by attending one of the eight annual open rehearsals, held at 8:30 a.m. on performance mornings. These often involve a guest conductor, running through the evening's program, and perhaps working out a few tricky passages with the orchestra. Still, you do get to hear the entire bill. Tickets cost a comparatively cheap $14, and include complimentary coffee and donuts and a lecture on the music. The folks who'll pay top dollar that night won't get those! These tix can be reserved ahead of time, and you should do so, to get the best seats.

And there's more. The Youth Orchestra Series offers another great bargain, with tickets only $20 per person for a season of three concerts featuring the Bay Area's most talented young musicians. Family Concerts is another bargain-priced series, consisting of three matinee concerts for children and parents. Tickets cost $30 for adults and $15 for kids (for all three shows).

If you want to get seriously classical, or classically serious, become a series subscriber; there are several lineups to choose from. You'll still pay at least $21 per ticket, but you get lots of extras, like free pre-concert talks and early-evening chamber music performances, a one-time seat upgrade, two complimentary tickets if you enlist another subscriber, and a newsletter. Most series include six concerts, with tickets starting at $126.

Davies Hall recently underwent extensive renovations, and now receives rave reviews for both outstanding acoustics and high-quality performances. Last season, concerts included guest appearances by Yo-Yo Ma, Itzhak Perlman, John Williams, Bobby McFerrin, and numerous other renowned musicians. With all those concerts, and all those ways to save big bucks, you have no excuse for failing to add a little culture to your life.

Embarcadero Performances at Six
• Three Embarcadero Center (Sacramento St.), San Francisco; (415) 398-6449

The *San Francisco Chronicle* says these concerts "refresh and delight after a particularly hideous day at the office." Even after an adequate or even exhilarating day, you'll find plenty of nourishment for the soul at these 6:00 p.m. concerts, held on Thursdays from November through April.

For one thing, the $6 price of admission leaves enough money in your pocket for dinner later on. Plus, you may have a complimentary glass of wine or mineral water. And then, you can unwind during the one-hour per-

formance. Offerings have ranged from such programs as Tonal Havoc—a recorder ensemble, or Mahal, playing a blend of Middle Eastern, Latin, and Western classical music. Tickets may be purchased at the door, which opens at 5:00 p.m. You can even park for free at the Embarcadero Center Garage (you'll need validation after 5 p.m.). That's worth the price of admission alone!

Grace Cathedral Concert Series
• 1051 Taylor St. (California St.), San Francisco; (415) 445-1309

You know how even schlocky food tastes better at a fancy restaurant? In the same way, all music sounds better in Grace Cathedral. The majesty of the place fills your senses before the concert even starts. And this music ain't schlocky, either.

It's the only Gothic cathedral in San Francisco, filled with beautiful statues, impressive artwork, gorgeous stained glass, and seating for 1,600—in pews and chairs, of course. Arrive early, and you can take a self-guided tour of the place. Or, if you feel like splurging, take the guided tour for $3. Be sure to check out the labyrintha medieval meditation device that guides you around a pattern on the floor. It's modeled after one in a cathedral in France, and stays open only very limited hours (call ahead for visiting times). If you still have some time to kill before the show, go to the gift shop, where you'll find lost of attractive items—from mugs with stained glass patterns to spiritual writings and jewelry.

The concert series (this is about a concert series, remember?) frequently features the cathedral's star attraction, its 7,000-pipe organ-one of the largest on the West Coast. Tickets to organ recitals cost only $6 (why, that's just pennies per pipe!). The Grace Cathedral Men's and Boy's Choirone of three such choral groups in the countryalso presents low-cost performances on a regular basis.

There's about one concert per month here, all year long, and they usually take place on Sunday evenings. Many events feature national and international artists, with considerably higher ticket prices. The Welsh Choir performed in the past year, as did the much-heralded Bulgarian Women's Choir. Tix for these concerts ranged from $19-$35; there are some discounts for students and seniors. Call for a schedule of upcoming concerts.

Noe Valley Ministry

*   1021 Sanchez Street (Elizabeth St.), San Francisco; (415) 282-2317

The Noe Valley Ministry presents a series of chamber music concerts on Sunday afternoons. Most of these concerts feature local musicians, although notables like the Arterius String Quartet have occasionally played here. Tickets cost $8 for adults, and $5 for kids and seniors. See listing under "Folk Music" below for more information.

Noontime Concerts at Old St. Mary's Church

*   660 California Street (Grant Ave.), San Francisco; (415) 982-6666

By noon, as the work day begins to wear on, citizens everywhere have already had enoughdreaming of escape from their prisons of the cubicle, the boss, or housework. If such a day attacks you, find salvation and respite at a free noontime concert at Old Saint Mary's Church, located in the heart of Chinatown. These wonderful half-hour interludes present Bay Area musicians performing classical chamber music with no admission cost (although they invite donations to keep the series going).

The program is entirely different each week, ranging from solo recitals to full orchestras or choral groups. Special concerts commemorate such dates as Bach's birthday in March, Martin Luther King's birthday in January, and the Fourth of July. Concerts take place every Tuesday at 12:30 p.m., year-round. Of course, if you are one of those lucky few who can take an extended lunch break, you'll be perfectly positioned to follow the concert with lunch at one of Mr. C's Chinatown recommendations.

Old First Concerts

*   1751 Sacramento St. (Van Ness Ave.), San Francisco; (415) 474-1608

The Old First Church hosts this year-round concert series, featuring internationally-acclaimed soloists and chamber music troupes at extremely reasonable prices. For just $9, you can hear groups like the Aurora String Quartet or the Camerata Vocale Berlin/Brandenberger; or solo artists like renowned pianist Richard Fields. In addition to its classical music series, the Old First spices up its calendar every few months with special jazz concerts and a variety of ethnic music programs.

The church has good acoustics, and you can see the raised stage from almost anywhere in the house. The 500 seats are, naturally, of the pew variety; it's a good idea to bring a pillow for, er, unencumbered enjoyment. Most concerts take place on Friday nights and Sunday afternoons.

Students and seniors get a $2 discount off the already low prices. You can also save by purchasing a membership, which costs $35 for individuals or $50 for couples; this entitles you to a $4 discount on every ticket, plus two free admissions during the year.

Ratto's Pasta

*   821 Washington St. (Ninth St.), Oakland; 832-6503

As in so many American cities, Oakland's main Italian section sits cheek-by-jowl next to its Chinese district. Ratto's is a large grocery store and restaurant which pretty much anchors the Italian side of the neighborhood (though a Mexican crafts shop is tossed in next door, for good measure). The grocery store, which is reasonably priced if not cheap, seems to have everything in the world—fresh pasta (of course), meats and homemade sausages, imported olive oil, breads, coffee beans, grains, the works.

Next to all this is the restaurant, a huge, bustling room with a lot of old-world charm. Well-worn wooden floors, a handsome service bar with a polished espresso machine, and a stainless steel open kitchen at the far end make Ratto's feel like something out of New York's Little Italy—or the home country itself. It's big, but comfortable.

Now, here's a great deal for opera lovers. Every Friday and Saturday evening, Ratto's serves up fancier food, followed by live opera music. This isn't one of those waiters-doing-a-song-before-dessert things; a four-course meal is served at 6:30, including entrees like lemon-herb chicken with saffron risotto, along with salad, pasta, dessert, and coffee. Then, at 7:30, the show begins—two full hours of opera songs and arias, performed by different professional singers each night. Many of these musicians are working and/or training all around the Bay Area, often young, rising talent ready for the spotlight.

It all adds up to a joyous and passionate evening. And how much for this extravaganza? A very reasonable $22.50 per person, including dinner and the show. Hey, you can spend more than that just to go to some opera houses, and they won't feed you, either. This is a popular attraction; and since it's only offered twice a week, reservations are recommended.

San Francisco Community Music Center
- 544 Capp St. (21st St.), San Francisco; (415) 647-6015

Don't wear your evening wrap and high-brow face here; save it for Davies Hall. At the San Francisco Community Music Center, you can enjoy fine low-cost and free classical music concerts in an informal setting. Most concerts feature performances by students or faculty of this professional music school. The Community Center Orchestra also performs here, as do outside musicians renting the low-cost space. Tickets never go any higher than $8 for adults, and $3 for seniors and kids.

As you can imagine, the center maintains a busy schedule, with about seventy concerts a year. The in-

MR. CHEAP'S PICKS
Classical Music

✔ **Davies Symphony Hall**—Score one of the last-minute Center Terrace tickets at the box office, and you'll have an incredible seat for only $8 in the Bay Area's premier concert hall.

✔ **Embarcadero Performances at Six**—An hour of after-work classical music for $6, including complimentary wine. Plus, you can park for free next door.

✔ **Noontime Concerts**—Get a respite from downtown chaos every Tuesday at 12:30, with free classical music in Old St. Mary's Church. Everything from solo performers to full chamber orchestras.

timate hall holds about 100 people in its orchestra and balcony sections, and is equipped with a nine-foot grand piano. Performances usually take place on Saturday or Sunday evenings, which are often followed by receptions with light snacks. Call for schedule information.

San Francisco Performances
- Various locations; Box office, Sherman-Clay, 141 Kearny St. (Post St.), San Francisco; (415) 392-4400

This organization sponsors five series of concerts each year, taking place at various halls around the city. These include the Chamber Music Series, the Piano Series, the Vocal Series, the Guitar Series, and the Virtuoso Series. Each of these features internationally renowned musicians. Recent performers include such notables as the Tokyo String Quartet, the Alexander String Quartet, pianist Richard Goode, and the Tchaikovsky Trio.

Mr. C found the best deal at Fort

Mason Center, where you can hear the Alexander String Quartet performing the cycle of Beethoven's quartets. These annual Saturday morning performances cost only $10 ($12 at the door), and include a lecture by composer Robert Greenberg, plus free coffee and tea. Other shows cost $20 to $30; but students and seniors can get half-price tickets at the door one hour

before show time, as available.

Performance locations vary; most concerts take place at Symphony Hall, the Cowell Theater at Fort Mason, or the Herbst Theatre at 401 Van Ness. A further tip from Mr. C: Buy tickets in person at the box office downtown, to avoid extra handling charges.

FOLK MUSIC

Ashkenaz
• 1317 San Pablo Ave. (University Ave.), Berkeley; (510) 525-5054
Ashkenaz is a music and dance cafe that serves up hearty portions of rhythm and blues, zydeco, and various world beat genres. In spite of its exotic, Middle Eastern name, the club has the distinct feel of a Texas roadhouse bar—and it's a popular place to dance yourself into a sweaty frenzy. Cover charges generally run $8 to $10 on weekends, a bit pricey; weeknights are more reasonable at $4 to $6, with live music presented six nights a week. There is a full bar, and a menu of snacks and appetizers to fortify yourself for more dancing.

Bands recently featured here—mostly local—include Tocara, with its original pan-Latin dance music; Clint Baker's New Orleans Jazz Band; and Voz Do Brazil, with Brazilian dance music. Fans of old-time jazz will enjoy Gene Gilbeaux and his sixteen-piece swing orchestra. Stop in to pick up a monthly calendar, or check the listings under "World Beat" in the the *Bay Guardian* for show times and cover charges.

Farley's
• 1315 18th St. (Texas St.), San Francisco; (415) 648-1545
This hip cafe at the tippy-top of Potrero Hill has everything a coffeehouse should have: great coffee and tea by the cup, pastries, a well-stocked rack of newspapers and alternative magazines, and plenty of tables to while away an hour or two with all of these. The atmosphere is quiet and relaxed, somewhat different

from the industrial-grunge-rock approach some cafes adopt.

In addition, Farley's hosts a handful of live performances every month. These take place on various evenings, and range from acoustic music to poetry jams to storytelling. There are no admission or cover charges. The cafe walls display works by area artists, featuring someone new each month. These exhibits include a reception evening, again, free and open to the public.

In all, it's one of The City's most happening cafes—a friendly, laid-back place that's well worth the trek if this isn't your usual stomping ground. Stop in for a flyer detailing this month's events.

Freight and Salvage Coffeehouse
• 1111 Addison St. (San Pablo Ave.), Berkeley; (510) 548-1761
For die-hard folk fans, this place is like Hagen-Daaz on a hot summer day. Where else can you hear acoustic music almost every night of the week, with a state-of-the-art sound system and an intimate, old-fashioned coffeehouse ambiance? It's a place even the musicians love. You'll find many of the area's top singer-songwriters, jazz musicians, and world music artists performing here.

You can sit at a table and order great java and sweets. The place nixes evil substances like cigarettes and alcohol (this assumes, of course, that caffeine and sugar are not evil), so you can relax and bask in the music without worrying about your lungs or liver. You also won't have to air the smoke out of your clothes the next day.

For an ultra-cheap deal, catch the Tuesday night open-mike show, hosted by Jim Carter; admission is a mere $2.50. On other nights, tickets range from $6.50 to $12.50 for big-name performers like John Gorka—still a great bargain. Prices stay low because the place is run by a non-profit society. This also means that the staff gets paid next to nothing, so treat your waitron kindly.

You can get tickets through the mail or at the box office. But, if you wait until the last minute and pay at the door, you'll get charged an extra dollar. Doors usually open at 7:30 p.m., with weeknight performances starting at 8:00 p.m. and weekends at 8:30.

Great American Music Hall
- 859 O'Farrell St. (Polk St.), San Francisco; (415) 885-0750

This lovely little theater, with its elaborate ceilings and ornate balconies, makes a great place for hearing the wide range of acoustic, folk, jazz, and country music offered on a regular basis. Down front, a large empty floor space gets set up cafe-style with tables and chairs during acoustic performances. Other times, the floor simply serves as a standing and stomping area.

National acts play here all the time—since it's one of the bigger acoustic venues in town, with 500 seats. Recent performers have included Loudon Wainwright and the Fury Brothers. Tickets run from $5 to $20, with lots of local acts in the very affordable $5 to $7 category. Buy your tickets at the box office or through BASS. The box office opens from noon to 6:00 p.m. Monday through Saturday, and performance evenings until showtime. A full dinner and drinks menu is available during shows.

Java Beach
- 1396 La Playa (Judah St.), San Francisco; (415) 665-5282

The name says it all. Take one of those ultra-hip, downscale-yet-indul-gent SoMa coffeehouses, move it out to the ocean, and you'll have Java Beach. It's a very laid-back place, quiet and mellow by day, just across the highway from the water. Purchase an empty cup at the counter, and name your poison—French Sumatra, Irish Creme, Colombian Supremo, and other caf and decaf varieties. Maybe a piece of pastry or a sandwich to go with it. Then, plop down at a table, or on one of the soft, well-worn couches, and read, play board games, all the coffeehouse cultural activities. Or, sit on one of the park benches outside the door.

The other culture found here is live music, with no cover charge. Schedules change over the long haul, but at the time of this writing, Java Beach offers Irish folk music every Thursday night from 8:00 to 11:00 p.m., and jazz music on Wednesdays from 7:30 to 11.

La Peña
- 3105 Shattuck Ave. (Princeton), Berkeley; (510) 849-2568

A popular spot for Latin-American music, La Peña also hosts a potpouri of other events—from acoustic folk to rap to flamenco dance. It's an informal performance space, with movable seating for 180 people. And, like many other venues in the Berkeley area, La Peña doubles as a restaurant, serving up hot Latin American food to go with the hot sounds.

Tickets for most shows cost between $6 and $12. If you want to eat, entrees range from $4.50 to $10. With prices that low, you can make a night of it—dine here, and then stay for the entertainment—all without going broke. By the way, unlike most other music venues, this one welcomes kids and is wheelchair-accessible.

Live from Redwood
- First Congregational Church, 2501 Harrison St. (27th St.), Oakland; (510) 835-1445

You have to sit in pews and you can't eat or drink on the premises, but don't let that stop you from attending one of the many great concerts in this adventurous series. Actually, "Live from Redwood" consists of two different lineups: one featuring prominent acoustic artists, and the other showcasing new and emerging talent. Both sets of concerts emphasize cultural diversity.

Recent highlights have included "The New Spirituals Project," featuring performances of spirituals commissioned especially for this series. A two-night drumming festival brought in six different percussion acts. Laura Nyro recently performed, as did an a cappella quintet called Vocolot.

Tickets range from $10 to $18, depending on the show; you can save about 10% by buying a series ticket. Not ultra-cheap, perhaps, but it's still no more than the cost of a new CD. Both series run from October through April, with shows taking place on weekends.

Musician's Coffee House
• Mt. Diablo Unitarian Church, 55 Eckley Lane, Walnut Creek; (510) 229-2710

For a transcendent experience in the acoustic realm, head out to hear a show at the Musician's Coffee House. How can you go wrong in a place that offers great music, great refreshments, and a beautiful site out in the country?

The Coffee House features prominent musicians like Richie Havens, Tuck & Patti, and Jesse Colin Young. Ethiopian world-beat star Hanza L. Din has performed here. Warmup acts only do three songs, so you get lots of quality time with your main musical hero. If you arrive early, you can sit out on the patio and tuck into hot entrees like lasagna or enchiladas, with most items priced around just $3. During the show, the Coffee House offers a great array of home-baked goodies—pies, pastries, and cakes.

The music itself is played in the main sanctuary of the church—a comfortable place with chair seating for 300, full carpeting on the floors, and windows on all sides for a light and airy feel. To top it all off, the church

has an excellent sound system.

Performances are scheduled three to four times a month, on weekend nights, from October through May. Tickets cost $9 to $14, depending on the artist. Call for upcoming concerts.

Noe Valley Ministry
• 1021 Sanchez St. (Elizabeth St.), San Francisco; (415) 282-2317

In most cities, folk singers spend a lot their time playing in bars and churches; maybe that's why they have so much angst to sing about. Not so in San Francisco, where church coffeehouses are as rare as kids who love homework. Among the city's places of worship, only this one trades sacraments for singing on a regular basis.

The Noe Valley Ministry offers two music series: acoustic music on Saturday nights, and chamber music on Sunday afternoons. Recent performers include Joan Baez, Hanza L. Din, and Adrian Lig. Ticket prices for these shows range from $9 to $12—a downright bargain. You can buy tickets through the mail or at the nearby Aquarius Records (3961 24th Street).

The chamber music series features mostly local musicians, although notables like the Arterius String Quartet have performed here. Prices for classical concerts are $8 for adults, and $5 for kids and seniors (see listing under "Classical Music," above).

At the acoustic shows, you can buy soft drinks and snacks in an adjoining room. For the higher-brow chamber music performances, the menu includes wine and sweets. An added extra: All performances happen in the on-site art gallery, where you can view works by local painters and sculptors. Call for info on upcoming events.

Ploughshares Concert Series
• Fort Mason Center, Buchanan St. at Marina Blvd., San Francisco; (415) 525-7473

See folk artists like Bill Staines, Utah Phillips, and Gordon Bok, up-close-and-personal, for only $10. The Firehouse concert hall at Fort Mason Center is an intimate room, seating only 125 people; yet it attracts some big-name musicians. You will have to make do with folding chairs, but the cozy setting more than compensates. Plus, you can buy beer, wine, coffee, and sweets as well.

Occasionally, shows get booked into the center's larger Cowell Theatre, nearby. This too is a great place for viewing and listening, with a state-of-the-art sound system, good visibility, and (yes) plush seats.

Ploughshares offers about eight performances a year, with acts ranging from traditional folk to swing to Irish music. Tickets cost $10 for all shows, whether you get them in advance through the mail, or at the door. Call for a schedule of upcoming events.

San Francisco Art Institute Café
• 800 Chestnut St. (Jones St.), 2nd Floor, San Francisco; (415) 749-4567

"We are a unique hidden treasure," the management of this place humbly proclaims. An empty boast? Mr. C thinks not.

First of all, this room—upstairs in the Art Institute's building a few blocks in from Fisherman's Wharf—has huge floor-to-ceiling windows overlooking the bay and the Golden Gate Bridge. Then, there's the food—all made from scratch, yet selling at student prices. You can get soups, sandwiches, salads, and espresso. And, on Thursday nights from 7:00 p.m. to 9:00 p.m, you can enjoy the open-mike show for free. Performers include SFAI students as well as other local musicians; you never know what you're going to get in this mixed bag, but hey—at these prices, who's complaining?

San Francisco Folk Music Club
• Various locations; Information, (415) 661-2217

Hey, all you closet musicianshere's a way to hear good music for free, and at the same time impress other people with your own amazing talents (oh, don't be so modest, now). The San Francisco Folk Music Club sponsors musical get-togethers at different places every other Friday night. Just

---

MR. CHEAP'S PICKS
Folk Music

✔ **Freight and Salvage Coffeehouse**—Great acoustics, coffee-house coziness, and non-profit prices. A favorite stopping place for big acoustic stars on tour.

✔ **Musician's Coffee House**— A place for all the senses—with hot entrees and fresh baked goodies, a beautiful location in a country church, top acts and top acoustics.

✔ **Noe Valley Ministry**—Another church coffeehouse, with a twist: Concerts take place in the chapel's art gallery. Stars like Joan Baez and Hanza L. Din play here, but tickets cost only $12 or less.

---

bring your instrument and do your thing when your turn comes around. In return, listen to your peers strum and sing, exchange tips and information, and enjoy!

For all this fun, you pay only a $5 annual membership fee, which also entitles you to a monthly newsletter giving complete listings of upcoming acoustic music concerts and events. Other club-sponsored happenings include frequent camp-outs in area state parks, and a two-day folk music festival in June (see below).

Don't live in town? Your VW's in the shop again? Don't worry. Check out these similar organizations in outlying areas:

The Marin Folk Music Club— (415) 4560427
The East Bay Folk Music Club— (510) 5264152
The East Bay Pickin' and Fiddlin' Club— (510) 4511122
The Peninsula Folk Music Club—(415) 5920115

Meanwhile, try to get that Beetle fixed in time for the San Francisco Folk Music Club's Annual Folk Festival, which happens every year on the first or second weekend in June. Over sixty acoustic musicians converge at this absolutely free, two-day concert, each delivering a 15-minute set. You won't find any big names on the program, but many of the up-and-coming locals who perform have major talent. Who knows, you may catch one of tomorrow's stars.

Along with the performances, the festival offers a workshop areawhere you can choose from an array of seminars on music, dance, instruments, and more. It all takes place on the campus of John Adams Community College in San Francisco; call (415) 661-2217 for more info.

Tea Spot Café
- 2072 San Pablo Ave. (University Ave.), Berkeley; (510) 848-7376

For low-key, low-cost musical entertainment accompanied by good, cheap food, check out Friday or Saturday nights at the Tea Spot. You can order burgers or a selection of vegetarian items (most under $5), and wash everything down with your drink of choiceespresso, wine, beer, even water.

While you sup, local acoustic musicians perform. The Tea Spot is the spot for an emphasis on female singer-songwriters, although the specific programs vary from week to

week. The cover charge is between $5 and $7, depending on the bill. You don't even have to order food or drinks if you don't want to; there is no minimum and, for that matter, no smoking in this place either.

The Warfield
- 982 Market St. (Sixth St.), San Franciso; (415) 243-8510

With a name like "The Warfield," you might expect to find the Marine Corps Band playing "Marching to Pretoria" here. In fact, this could even happen. The Warfield, you see, hosts an amazingly diverse range of performances, from folk to blues to grunge rock.

It's not exactly a "so intimate you can see the singer's tonsils" kind of venue, with its 2,200 seats and big balcony section. Even so, the Warfield is a pleasant place, an old-time concert hall with an elaborate domed ceiling, gold-leaf trim, and tiered seating that lets you see well from anywhere in the house. There's also a standing room area and a dance floor up front.

Big name performers like Jackson Browne play here, with ticket prices running between $15 and $25not cheap, but sometimes a bargain when compared to other large rock venues of the arena type. If you have any money left over, you can order Mexican food or sandwiches off the food menu and eat at a table while you groove on the music.

JAZZ AND BLUES MUSIC

Blondie's Jazz Club
- 540 Valencia St. (16th St.), San Francisco; (415) 864-2419

Do gentlemen prefer Blondie's? Maybe not, but local jazz musicians sure do. "It's the best place to play in the Bay Area," says Aaron at California Jazz Now, the local paper which follows the jazz scene. "Blondie's features high-class local acts in all styles, it's not high-brow snooty, it's a real jazz club."

Aficionados enjoy the warm, intimate atmosphere (the place seats only fifty), the booths, and the all-jazz juke box. It's a clean place besides, with paintings by local artists displayed on the walls, and two pool tables for further unwinding.

Live jazz is presented on Saturday nights. There's no cover charge and no drink minimum. Recent acts have included such local faves as Jazz on the Line, Ron Graham, and Corner Pocket. By the way, Blondie's doesn't serve food, so fill up (at one of Mr. C's Mission District recommendations, of course) before heading over.

Blues

- 2125 Lombard St. (Fillmore St.), San Francisco; (415) 771-BLUES (2583)

Guess what kind of music this place offers? Blues, of course, every night of the week. Monday nights, it's a jam session with Johnny Nitro and the Doorslammers. Other nights, top-quality local bands play, with some big-name national stars occasionally showing up. Freddy Roulette has played here. So has Kenny Dale-Johnson from Chris Isaaks' band, Jimmy Pugh, and other notable sidemen. Some soul and R&B groups are mixed into the calendar too.

The joint has a dance floor, gold lamé walls, and four huge and slightly outrageous booths upholstered in the best 1950s leopard-skin decor. The club doesn't serve food, but has arrangements with a local delivery service to bring edibles right to your table from area restaurants.

Blues opens up around 8:00 in the evening, and jumps until 2 a.m. There is no cover charge Mondays through Wednesdays; on other nights, cover varies from $3 to $7.

Café Claude

- 7 Claude Lane (Bush St.), San Francisco; (415) 392-3505

Down a narrow alley between Bush and Sutter (near Kearny, one of those "extra" streets), this bistro is indeed trés Francais. Casual, intimate, and immensely popular with those in-the-know, Café Claude attracts an always-interesting crowd of artsy, sophisticated yupsters and international types. Everyone on the wait-staff seems to be authentically French, judging by their accents, which are delightful. They're also friendly, which is less true-to-form; a pleasant surprise.

The restaurant does a brisk business at breakfast, lunch, dinner, and throughout the evening. But then, even the folks who are waiting for tables don't seem to mind; grab your-

self a Pernod and mix in. Two cozy, high-ceilinged rooms include a bar area, exposed beams, and of course, French posters on the walls. If you're in a romantic mood, try for one of the front tables; these are nestled into corners with floor-to-ceiling glass windows which look out over the street. A private nook amidst the din.

The food here is first-rate, and the exotic atmosphere ensures steady evening crowds (see listing under "Restaurants"). Many of the furnishings around the two rooms were shipped piece by piece from France. And, as if the place needed any more reason to pack people in, there is live jazz several evenings a week. A regular rotation of vocalists, trios, quintets, and solo performers add to the scene on Tuesday evenings from 6:30 to 9:30 p.m.; Thursdays and Fridays from 7-10; and on Saturdays from 8-11. Café Claude closes at 10:00 on weeknights, an hour later on weekends, and all day Sunday.

Café du Nord

- 2170 Market St. (Church St.), San Francisco; (415) 861-5016

How can you go wrong in a club with bordello-red walls, a 40-foot hand-carved bar, and live jazz seven nights a week? Crowds pack this Noe Valley club, especially the under-35 crowd; most nights, you won't get seated unless you've made reservations.

Like most area jazz clubs, the establishment doubles as a restaurant, serving dinner Wednesday through Saturday nights. You'll find inexpensive continental food on the menu (linguini, polenta, pizzetas, fresh trout usually priced between $6.50-$8.50). Jazz starts after mealtime, usually about 9:00, and wails until 2:00 a.m. If you arrive after dinner hoping to get a seat, you may be out of luck. Most people sup and then hang onto their seat for the show.

The sounds here range from trad-jazz to Dixieland to Latin and even hip-hop. Recent performers include the Braun Fellinis, Alphabet Soup, and LeMay Smith and the Red Hot

Skillet Lickers. There's a formal stage with a curtain, nine beers on tap, and a pool table. The music cover charge is only $2, if you can get in for just the show; there is no drink minimum.

Cava 555
- 555 Second St. (Brannan St.), San Francisco; (415) 543-CAVA (2282)

At Cava 555, you can hear anything from traditional, straight-ahead jazz to hip-hop, with music almost every night. Regular performers from the local and national circuit include sidemen like Andre Bush, Gregory James, and various members of Herbie Hancock's band.

On weekends, shows start at 9:00 p.m. and go until 1:00 a.m. Mondays through Thursdays, shows start and end earlier. There's no cover Monday through Thursday, but on Friday and Saturday, you pay $3. It's a great deal any night, considering the top-notch quality of the music. On the other hand, food prices don't come in cheap, with entrees starting at about $12. If you must eat, try ordering appetizers, soups, or salads, and be sure to get some of their filling homemade bread, too.

ELEVEN Ristorante + Bar
- 374 11th St. (Harrison St.), San Francisco; (415) 431-3337

Another place that mixes up hot food with cool sounds, the ELEVEN features some of the area's most creative, eclectic jazz every Wednesday and Saturday night. After enjoying a meal of Italian regional cuisine, you can mellow out to the music of performers like the Charlie Hunter Trio, The Groove Shop, and Daria and Nile.

As far as ambiance goes, the name of the place says it all. The ELEVEN is a warehouse transformed into an Italian villa, complete with wrought iron, faux paintings, and swatches of fabric everywhere. No matter where you sit, you have a great view of the band—because they perform in a loft above the bar. Music starts at about 9:00 p.m., and there isn't usually a cover charge.

The food is a bit on the pricey side, with entrees ranging from $9 to $14; but, with or without the chow, there are18 beers on tap—nice. And if you get restless, the six other clubs nearby (including such SoMa faves as Slim's, the Paradise Lounge, and the DNA Lounge) make this a prime area for club-hopping.

Eli's Mile High Club
- 3629 Martin Luther King Jr. Way (MacArthur Blvd.), Oakland; (510) 655-6661

The Jazz and Blues Lovers Guide voted Eli's the "Best Blues Joint in the East Bay." No wonder. The place couldn't be more funky, with its red lights, mismatched chairs, cement floors, and photos of musical greats all over the walls. In fact, many of these legends have played here, from Chuck Berry to James Brown.

Eli's has live blues and dancing every Thursday through Sunday, from 9:00 p.m. to 2:00 a.m. For a fun night out that's really cheap, come in on Sunday—when the cover is only $4, all drinks cost $2.50, and good local musicians jam with the Mile High Blues Band. Other nights, admission costs $6 to hear featured groups like the Key Blues Band or the Bobby Murray Band with Freddy Hughes.

If you work up an appetite on the dance floor, Eli's has pizza, buffalo wings, and other snack foods on the menu. They even have a cash machine on site to help you pay for your meal. There's also a pool table out back (hmm, these two may not be a good mix).

Oakland may scare some people off, but Eli's has taken this into account; the club has its own security staff to watch over your car, and escort you to it, if you wish. So, while you're inside, you can relax and enjoy the music.

Metronome Ballroom
- 1830 17th St. (De Haro St.), San Francisco; (415) 252-9000

Now, here's something different. The Metronome Ballroom is a dance instruction school, mixed in with the art galleries and cafes at the base of

Potrero Hill. They offer classes in everything from fox-trot to hip-hop. And, on weekends, the large wooden dance floor changes from classroom to ballroom; everyone, students and public alike, is welcome to come in and swing. It's a big party, kinda like that prom scene in *Peggy Sue Got Married*—complete with little round tables covered in brightly colored cloths, (recorded) big band music, and snacks.

Friday nights offer a rotation of salsa, swing, waltz, fox-trot, tango, and rumba (two of these per night). Saturdays focus on "West Coast Swing," which the folks here describe as a "fluid, sexy dance." Both nights begin at 7:30 with lessons and a short practice session, followed by the dance party itself from 9:00 to midnight. So, even if you're a rumba rookie, you can get in on the fun. And if you're already a budding Fred or Ginger, you can just show up for the party, for a reduced admission.

Prices for the general public are $10 per person for the entire evening; for the party only, it's $4 on Fridays and $6 on Saturdays (prices are lower for Metronome students). No alcohol is served; there is a concession window with snacks and soft drinks. There is plenty of free on-street parking available.

Olive Oil's
- 295 Francoise Boulevard, Pier 50, San Francisco; (415) 495-3099

It's under the same management as Blondie's (see listing above), but this China Basin club is like a well-to-do cousin. Olive Oil's sits right on the water, with tables available outdoors in good weather. Live jazz is offered on Friday and Saturday nights, and like Blondie's, top local groups play a range of styles from all over the jazz spectrum.

You'll find plenty of parking—a real plus anywhere in town. Local artwork adorns the walls, and an upscale ambiance reigns. Yet, you'll only pay a $5 cover charge to get in for the show; and there's not even a drink minimum.

MR. CHEAP'S PICKS
Jazz and Blues Music

- ✔ **ELEVEN Ristorante + Bar**—Fancy decor, 18 beers on tap, and excellent sightlines make this a very pleasant place indeed. Top local acts perform here with no cover charge.
- ✔ **Eli's Mile High Club**—James Brown and Chuck Berry have both performed here, which tells you what type of place this is: a funky haven for great blues in Oakland. *Ow!*
- ✔ **Pier 23 Cafe**—Cool jazz and a table right on the water; what more could you ask for? Catch some top-notch acts for free here every Tuesday, Wednesday, and Thursday night.
- ✔ **Radio Valencia**—This place is run by a jazz musician, and it shows. Excellent, innovative bands, careful programming of taped music on off nights, and good, cheap food.

Pasand Lounge
- 1875 Union St. (Octavia St.), San Francisco; (415) 922-4498
- 2284 Shattuck Ave. (Bancroft Way), Berkeley; (510) 548-0260.

This long, narrow room in Pacific Heights, which is a not-so-cheap Indian restaurant by day (think of the area, after all) turns into a hot jazz club every night of the week but Monday. It's a cozy place, with exposed wooden rafters, small tables, and a full-length bar running down one side; facing this along the other long wall is the bandstand, where the entertainment is of a raucous, urban style.

At present, the lineup consists of two different backup bands, fronted by a different singer each night. Rhythm and blues, soul, and contemporary jazz-rock sounds easily fill this small club; the high energy is usually matched by the volume, though it's certainly not deafening. And the crowd—a full house, even on the weeknight Mr. C visited—eats it up.

There is never a cover charge for any of this, although there is a two-drink minimum per set (toward the end of the evening, this is less strictly enforced). Beers run about $4; again, not cheap, though not out of line with most clubs. The music starts up around 9:00 on Tuesdays, 8:00 Wednesdays-Saturdays, and at 7:30 on Sundays. Shows usually last until 1:00 or 1:30 in the morning.

Pasand has a second lounge across the bay in Berkeley. This is more of a dance club, where DJ's alternate with a rotation of the same bands and singers from the other branch. Here, the music takes place on Friday and Saturday evenings only, from 8:30 p.m. to about 12:30 a.m. There is a $5 cover charge on Fridays, although it's also ladies' night: women get in free until 11:00 p.m. Saturdays cost $8 for all until 11:00, going up to $10 thereafter. Again, there's a two-drink minimum. This would seem like a college joint, of course, but Pasand does impose a 25-and-up age limit, and requests that men wear coats and ties, while women are asked to "dress to impress." Take that as you see fit, gals.

Pearl's Jazz Club
- 256 Columbus Ave. (Broadway), San Francisco; (415) 291-8255

Pearl's typifies the classic image of the downtown, upscale, sophisticated jazz club which so many people think of. Small tables are wedged into a large room with two levels; the front area is right in front of the band, with a darker, more secluded rear area that's a couple of steps higher (no pun intended, musicians).

Live jazz is offered every night of the week at Pearl's, with no cover charge at all. There is a two-drink-per-set minimum, however, and this is where they get ya. Prices are rather steep, so if you're really on a tight

budget, order carefully. Still, when you add in what this top-notch entertainment would cost you on its own, the evening turns out to be a good deal indeed. A limited food menu is also served until midnight—and savvy City dwellers know that Pearl herself is a longtime Chinatown restaurateur who can whip up good eats as well as good jazz.

The music is definitely worth those prices, whether you hear a piano-based trio, a vocalist and full quintet, or some of the more ethnic groups that play on occasion, such as Latin salsa bands. Most of the bookings, though, consist of straight-ahead traditional jazz—by groups that can be both elegant and powerful. Music begins at 9:00 on weeknights, 9:30 on Fridays and Saturdays, and continues until 1:00 a.m. (1:30 on weekends).

Pier 23 Café
- Pier 23, The Embarcadero (Lombard St.), San Francisco; (415) 362-5125

By day, it looks like just another wooden shack along the waterfront. But appearances can be deceiving! At night, after the real piers have gone to bed, Pier 23 heats up with great food and hot music. Herbie Hancock's band played here recently. So did Ed Kelley, who plays on a recent Pharoah Sanders album. Some nights, the sound changes over to salsa or reggae, and everybody boogies; by 11:00, the joint is packed to capacity with a hip young crowd, all moving in rhythm.

There is no cover charge on Tuesday, Wednesday, and Thursday nights; weekend cover is usually $5 for local bands. Music starts up around 9:30 p.m. or so, after the dinner crowd finishes shoveling down dessert. Food-wise, you can get seafood and ethnic delights, as long as you order before the music starts. Once the show begins, it's drinks only—there's no room for plates.

Radio Valencia
- 1199 Valencia St. (23rd St.), San Francisco; (415) 826-1199

This neat little cafe offers good, cheap food and innovative music. Friday nights, it's piano blues by the Blue Room Boys from 6:30 to 9:00 p.m., with no cover charge. Saturday, acoustic alternative rock bands—like Tarnation and Virginia Dale—can be heard with no cover charge. On Sunday, you'll hear top-notch improvisational jazz for a $5 cover.

Radio Valencia takes its music seriously, even on nights when there's no band. The owner tapes a new program of music for his sound system each day, and puts a card on each table to let you know what's playing. Guess he's a DJ wannabe.

The cafe is open daily from noon to midnight. The menu offers soups, sandwiches, focaccio pizza, and an array of healthy fast foods in the $5 range. There's also espresso, pastries, and six draft beers on tap. Check out the local artwork on the walls—a notch above the usual cafe decor.

Rasselas Jazz Club
- 2801 California St. (Divisadero St.), San Francisco; (415) 567-5010
This large, cabaret-style room (next to, of all things, an Ethiopian restaurant) offers live jazz seven nights a week—with no cover charge on any one of them. With so many evenings to fill, you might guess that there is a wide range of musical styles; and you'd be right. From solo pianists to large bands, the lineup in any given month may include Latin jazz, blues, gospel, South African, and of course, traditional jazz. Monday nights are open-mike jam sessions.

Again, it's a big place, right on the corner of California and Divisidero; floor-to-ceiling plate glass windows line the two sides along each street, while a full bar runs the length of a third wall. The decor is dark and atmospheric, the walls spattered artfully in dark blues and greens. The high ceiling keeps it from getting too smoky—and Mr. C heard a singer during his visit who was raising the roof even higher.

Drinks are, as you'd expect, not as cheap as your corner bar; but they're not as outrageously priced as some nightclubs. Hey, they have to pay the musicians somehow. No minimum is imposed, though, at least on the night Mr. C was there. A limited menu of bar food is available: burgers, sandwiches, the usual. Music plays from 8:00 p.m. to midnight, Sundays through Thursdays; on weekends, enjoy the tunes from 9 p.m. to 1 a.m.

Slow Club
- 2501 Mariposa St. (Hamphire St.), San Francisco; (415) 241-9390
More an eating place than a listening venue, the Slow Club nevertheless books some really interesting experimental jazz. How about a group that plays the saw (that's right, the saw) and southern slide guitar? Or a 15-horn big band? It seems that "anything goes" most accurately describes the music policy here.

You do have to eat dinner here to take in the show, but it's worth it. The food is filling, stick-to-you-ribs stuff like stews, grilled seafood, homemade sausage, and big antipasti. Most items cost under $13, and there's no extra charge for the show. Add it all up, and the dinner-and-music evening is a steal.

As a nightlife area, you might pass this Potrero neighborhood by—with its rather gritty, industrial vibe. Don't let it fool you. Once inside the Slow Club, you'll find a romantic, darkly lit, pleasantly clubby atmosphere.

UP & down Club
- 1151 Folsom St. (Seventh St.), San Francisco; (415) 626-2388
You can dine, dance, groove, and gawk at this multi-faceted club with (as the name implies) an upstairs and a downstairs. The jazz part happens downstairs—fitting, somehow—starting every night at 9:30. Someone from the club likened its atmosphere to "a 1950s jazz club in Paris." If he means it gets smoky and crowded, then he's right. But then, that's fitting, too. And you can catch some great music here, with frequent appearances by such local favorites as the Josh Jones Latin Jazz Ensemble, Alphabet Soup, and the Charlie

Hunter Trio. The club has even released its own CD, featuring UP &
down Club regulars—and it hit #1 on
the charts at KUSF.

If you want some pre-jazz vict-
uals, you won't be disappointed.
Chefs Philippa Spickerman and Rafael Carado are graduates of the California Culinary Academy; yet their
high-class entrees cost only $7 to
$11. Better make reservations for din-
ner, though. In fact, if you want to
see the show, it's a good idea to come
for dinner and stay on. On busy
nights, Thursday through Saturday,
you may not have much chance of
getting seated otherwise.

ROCK AND POP MUSIC

Blake's
• 2367 Telegraph Ave. (Durant Ave.),
  Berkeley; (510) 848-0886
Here's where the under-30 (but over
21, please) crowd congregates to hear
rock, acid jazz, and funk music. Just
off the Berkeley campus, Blake's has
three floors with food, bars, live music
five nights a week, and disco dancing
every Tuesday and Wednesday.

The cover charge stays low, even
on weekends—only $2 to $6—with
students getting in for half-price. On
Tuesdays, everyone gets in free before 10 p.m. Food is also cheap, with
burgers, pasta, barbecue, and Mexican food available until midnight.
And if you like creative frozen
drinks, you're in luck. Specials like
the Chocolate Buzzmeister—a mix of
chocolate, espresso, Jaegermeister,
and ice cream—can make even a
band you don't like more enjoyable.

Bands that play here are the sort
of college-crowd groups that have
names like MCM and the Monster,
the Loved Ones, and the Rat Pack.
These can be heard downstairs in the
dark, appropriately-named Subterranean Room. And, when you've worn
out your dancing shoes (or hi-tops, as
the case may be), you can sit mind-
lessly and watch old cartoons like
Rocky and Bullwinkle or Donald
Duck being projected on a big screen

So, what's UP? Here, you'll find a
bar with a DJ and dancing. Music upstairs leans toward disco, funk, and
classic soul hits. There's usually a
line to get in, so it's best to arrive
early in the evening.

Oh, and as for the gawking part:
Supermodel Christy Turlington owns
this place, and a number of her classy
cohorts can often be found here. If
you like spotting glamorous people,
this is a darn good place to do it. All
this for only $5, the standard cover
charge whether you're headed UP or
down. The club is closed on Sunday,
and no dinner is served on Monday.

while the crowd parties on.

Bottom of the Hill
• 1233 17th St. (Texas St.), San
  Francisco; (415) 626-4455
Potrero, that is. This is a fun and
funky place, with every picture hung
crookedly on the walls and live music until 1:00 a.m., seven nights a
week. Bottom of the Hill features
rock, alternative, and jazz music.
There's room for dancing, if you're
so inspired; and a full food and
drinks menu to keep you going all
night.

For a really great deal, come in on
Sunday between 4:00 and 8:30 p.m.
for the all-you-can-eat barbecue with
live music. There's no cover charge,
and the food costs a ridiculously low
$2 to $3. On other nights, Bottom
serves a variety of good food cheap,
including pastas and salads. A huge
burger with fries is only $3.50. If
weather permits, you can enjoy your
chow outside on the patio, or stay inside at a table near the stage.

The cover charge runs a very reasonable $3 to $4 weeknights, going
up only to $5-$6 on weekends. Hang
out in the pool room, with its big fireplace and works by local artists on
the walls. And if you like jazz, stick
around after the barbecue on Sunday
nights, when Bottom offers mellow
music by candlelight starting at 9:30.

Club DV8

- 540 Howard St. (First St.), San
  Francisco; (415) 957-1730

You thought you were going dancing,
but then you find yourself in a jungle
with waterfalls, or in an Italian villa
filled with strange lights and mirrors.
At Club DV8, dancing is only part of
the fun.

It's the city's biggest disco, covering 40,000 square feet on four floors.
Full-time set designers and entertainment directors ensure an ever-changing, visually dazzling experience.
Each floor has its own theme, atmosphere, and DJ; you'll find go-go dancers and performance artists doing
their thing everywhere. On a recent
evening, an African dance troupe—
complete with native costumes and
drummers—suddenly burst onto the
floor and took over. All in a night's
work for DV8.

The club usually sticks with its
DJs, but live music happens at least
once a month. Performers have included some big-name artists, like
Boy George or Nina Huggins. And, if
you want a break from dancing, the
club offers pool tables, a Caribbean-
theme restaurant with its own live
music, and quieter lounges for talking (nice touch). Check out the Keith
Haring paintings covering an entire
room.

For the best deal, arrive early,
when the club opens up (9:30 on
weeknights, 10:00 Friday, 9:00 Saturday). There's no cover at all during
the first half-hour. If you show up
later, the cover is $3-$5 on
weeknights, and $10 Friday and Sat-
urday. DV8 stays open until 2:00
a.m. weeknights and 4:00 a.m. Fridays and Saturdays.

The DNA Lounge

- 375 11th St. (Harrison St.), San
  Francisco; (415) 626-1409

When all good boys and girls are en-
tering dreamland, the DNA Lounge is
just waking up. It's an after-hours
club, which parties hardy until 4:00
a.m. every night of the week. Live
bands reign "early" in the evening—
from 10:00 p.m. until midnight.

Then, a DJ takes over for dancing until dawn.

The kinds of music played here
runs the gamut, from alternative rock
to hip-hop, jazz, soul, and rhythm &
blues. Recent bands have included
Sonic Brain Jam, Four Non-Blondes,
ABBA (remember them?) with Bjorn
Baby Bjorn, and even the nasty one
himself, Prince.

DNA attracts an alternative crowd
into its gene pool. Consider yourself
warned. There's no seating and no
food, but the place has pinball, pool,
and two bars—including a "Smart
Bar" with protein and vitamin drinks
and coffee concoctions. Admission
ranges from $3-$8 for dance parties,
up to $20 to see those national acts.
You can park all night in the nearby
Costco lot, by the way, for $5.

The Elbo Room

- 647 Valencia St. (17th St.), San
  Francisco; (415) 552-7788

The young and hip rub elbows at the
Elbo Room—a musical hangout for
alternative rockers of all stripes. The
sounds heard here can bend from alternative rock, to hip-hop and rap, to
free-form jazz. Featured bands include lots of well-known local groups
like Alphabet Soup and Slide 5. At
least once a week, there's a night of
dancing to good ol' funk and soul,
with well-known local DJs keeping
things going.

Elbo Room has about twenty beers
on draft—great—but no food. The
place holds about 350 people on its
two floors, each with its own bar. It's
popular and crowded—especially on
weekends. Cover ranges from $2 to
$5 on nights with live music; on danc-
ing nights, just $3 gets you in.

The Endup

- 995 Harrison St. (Sixth St.), San
  Francisco, (415) 543-7700

The Endup was immortalized in Armistead Maupin's *Tales of The City*
as the club where Michael Tolliver
won a dance contest. The Endup is a
bit tamer than Maupin would have
his readers believe, but it is definitely
one of *the* nightspots for gay men
and women on the weekends.

The fun starts on Friday night, when the Endup is home to "Deep"—a theme night which used to be called "Dekadence," and will probably have changed names by time you read this. What won't change is the fun, with DJs cranking out music you can really move to. Cover charge is usually $3 if you go before 11:00 p.m., a few dollars more after. Saturday is the night for "Girlspot" (or, as lesbians in-the-know call it, "G-Spot"), with more high-energy dance music for this particular crowd. If dancing's not your thing, that's okay too; hang out by the fireplace, or get in on a game of pool. Cover charge is usually $5 to $6. And, don't miss the popular "Tea Dance," held on Sundays from 6 a.m. to 11 p.m. The Tea Dance includes, among other things, a mixed-crowd—in every sense of the word.

The Great American Music Hall
- 859 O'Farrell St. (Polk St.), San Francisco; (415) 885-0750

This lovely, intimate little theatre hosts big-name performers like Van Morrison and Al Stewart, as well as acoustic, jazz, and country musicians. Dance bands often appear on weekends, when the tables and chairs get pushed aside and the floor opens up for big-time partying. It isn't exactly a budget place, with tickets for famous acts usually $20 or so, but you can occasionally catch a less renowned performer for $12 to $15. See listing under "Folk," above, for more information.

Johnny Love's
- 1500 Broadway (Polk St.), San Francisco; (415) 931-8021

It's not often that Mr. C comes upon a club that combines live music with low cover charges, and is also one of the hottest spots to see and be seen. Johnny Love's is just such a place. They present live music six nights a week, with a DJ spinning discs on Sundays. The club books high-energy bands in a variety of musical styles, including reggae, funk, and straight-out rock 'n roll. The cover charge is generally $2 to $5 during the week, and a still-reasonable $8 on week-

ends. Occasionally, they'll get a really well-known name, like Clarence Clemons, Chris Isaak, or Mark Allman; on these nights, the cover can go up to $12 or $15. Still not bad. There's never a cover on Sunday nights, and often there isn't one on Mondays or Tuesdays, either.

Before the rock starts up at 9 p.m., Johnny Love's is actually a full restaurant, which features live dinner jazz four nights a week. The menu is a bit on the expensive side, but since the music is included at no charge, it can be a great place for a splurge.

The Kennel Club
- 628 Divisadero St. (Hayes St.), San Francisco; (415) 931-1914

In spite of its name, the Kennel Club is a fun place for music and partying, with lots of world-beat reggae and alternative music on the menu. This is not a sit down and cool-out type of place; the only seating available is on sets of risers against the wall. But for dancing and drinking, you can't go wrong. Kennel has a big dance floor, a huge stage, and holds about 500 people at full capacity.

The program varies from night to night, with a DJ dance party on Saturday. Thursday night is also a dance party called "The Box"—this one for lesbians, with funk and acid jazz on the turntables. Sunday brings in reggae hosted by Dog Wendt, augmented by videos on three large screens.

Live music is usually offered Monday through Wednesday, and occasional Friday nights. Recent featured acts include Heavy Into Jeff and The Last Poets. The cover charge for live music ranges from $3 to $12, depending on the performer. Dance parties cost $5 at the door.

Kimo's
- 1351 Polk St. (Pine St.), San Francisco; (415) 885-4535

With huge windows that look out onto the street, this gay-oriented nightclub is very popular with the "Polk Gulch" crowd. The club offers dancing, drag shows, "bun" contests, and occasional fundraising events.

Cover charges are rarely more than $5. A recent addition to their lineup has been the comedy troupe "Ker-SCHMACKidda," which performs on the last Saturday evening of each month with an admission charge of just $3. Where else in The City can you see live comedy for so little? Kimo's is trying to move more in the direction of a cabaret-style club, so watch for changes in their entertainment fare.

The Paradise Lounge

- 1501 Folsom St. (Eleventh St.), San Francisco; (415) 861-6906

Paradise offers good value for your dancing dollar. The place has three bands every night, a great sound system, and a vast dance floor. Cover charges never go above $7, even when big names like Chris Isaak or Four Non-Blondes play.

For a major deal, come in on Monday night when there's no cover charge at all. You can settle into any of the three lounges in the club, each with its own bar and stage for entertainment. Paradise doesn't serve food, but you can bring something in from the cafe next door if you wish.

Shift gears on the top floor of the Paradise in its beatnik lounge, where poetry readings take place on Sundays and you can order espresso and other coffee drinks (see listing under "Readings and Literary Events"). The Blue Room, downstairs, can hold 500 people and has the club's biggest stage. Watch for new developments; as of this writing, the Paradise plans to expand and add a theater space in the near future.

Paragon

- 3251 Scott St. (Chestnut St.), San Francisco; (415) 922-2456

This upscale restaurant in the Marina, between Chestnut and Lombard, presents live music four nights a week with no cover charge. The menu consists of American bistro food at moderate prices ($15 to $30 for a meal, above Mr. C's usual range; but there are lower-priced items, like boneless breast of chicken with vegetable skewers for $9.95). Its cozy interior

MR. CHEAP'S PICKS
Rock and Pop Music

- ✔ **Club DV8**—A "see and be seen" kind of place, with wild decor and partying until 4:00 a.m. on weekends. No cover at all the first half-hour after the club opens.

- ✔ **DNA Lounge**—Another all-night jam, blending DJs with live acts. Prince has been known to drop in.

- ✔ **The Paradise Lounge**—Three bands a night, three floors, and a cover charge that's cheaper than this book—even for national acts like Chris Isaak. No cover at all Monday nights.

- ✔ **The Paragon**—A more civilized place for yuppie rockers, with good local bands and no cover at all. Big-name acts sometimes play here.

- ✔ **Johnny Love's**—Live bands six nights a week, with modest cover charges. The "in" crowd here knows you don't have to spend a lot to be hip.

features a front room with a bar and a roaring fireplace, and a second room to the rear—all designer-decorated, with mellow lighting. Plus an eclectic blend of artworks by local artists (one room is dominated by a large, Picasso-esque wall mural). In all, the place manages to be both hip and romantic, and definitely for the yuppie set.

Speaking of sets, live bands of all sorts add to the fun on Sunday through Wednesday nights. From 7:30 to 9:30 p.m., a jazz pianist tickles the ivories during dinner. Then, from 9:30 to midnight, this gives way to rock, blues, jazz ensembles, reggae-soca, acoustic—one band was even billed recently as "acousto funkadelia." Interpretations optional. These are local bands, most of which play here (as well as other clubs around the area) on a regular basis throughout the year. Once in a while, bigger-name players like Clarence Clemons may make surprise appearances.

Paragon has a full bar, with no drink minimums or requirements of any kind. You can, of course, skip dinner and just show up for the music. Stop in to pick up an artfully designed monthly calendar.

Rawhide II
- 2280 Seventh St. (Folsom St.), San Francisco; (415) 621-1197

Country and western music is the preferred entertainment at this gay bar/club. There is no cover charge most nights of the week. You do have to pay $5 on Friday and Saturday nights; but that includes *two* drink tickets! And there are more deals to round up. Every night but Sunday, Rawhide II offers free country dance lessons (the actual schedule is from 7-9:30 p.m. Mondays through Thursdays, and from 6:30-8:30 p.m. on Fridays and Saturdays). There is no dress code—feel free to wear your favorite country/western attire and do your best Achy-Breaky.

Another good deal here is Rawhide's "Beer Bust," which takes place on Sundays from 12-6 p.m. Pay just $6.50 for all the Budweiser you can drink. Depending on your capacity—and a pal to drive you back home—that's a lot to lasso.

Slim's
- 333 11th St. (Folsom St.), San Francisco; (415) 255-0333

This SoMa club books big-name national acts five nights a week. It's not strictly rock; blues, alternative, and country acts also play here. Recent shows have included people like John Hiatt, Chris Isaak, and Dave Allen—with ticket prices averaging a reasonable $10 or so. You can enjoy the music from a table in the upstairs balcony, especially good if you plan to dine from Slim's full dinner and appetizer menu; or, just grab a drink, stand with the crowd on the floor downstairs, and enjoy the sounds.

The UP & down Club
- 1151 Folsom St. (Seventh St.), San Francisco; (415) 626-2388

The Up & down Club has one of the more popular discos in the city; in case you're new here, it's the UP side. Owned by supermodel Christy Turlington, the place is frequented by the city's fashionable set; gourmet chefs in the kitchen turn out fancy food at not-outrageous prices.

The upstairs disco features a DJ spinning funk and classic soul hits, for a nightly cover charge of only $5. With its notoriety as a good place for potential stargazing, this is a popular spot, and it can be tough to get in later in the evening—especially on weekends. Isn't it just like Mr. C to rub elbows with the rich and famous for only five bucks? Meanwhile, if you get tired of bopping around on the dance floor, you can also go "down" to the jazz club and restaurant. See listing under "Jazz," above, for more information.

OUTDOORS

Angel Island State Park
- Angel Island, San Francisco Bay; (415) 435-1915

A little bit of heaven in the middle of the Bay, Angel Island offers one square mile of hilly terrain, fantastic 360-degree views from the top of Mount Livermore, and excellent hiking and cycling facilities. The natural beauty alone makes it worth a trip, but Angel Island also has fascinating historic sites to check out.

To get there, take the Angel Island Ferry from Tiburon ($5 round-trip adults, $3 kids, $1 bikesincluding park entrance), or the Red & White Fleet from Fisherman's Wharf in San Francisco ($8 adults, $7 youth, $4 kids). After arriving, you can hike to the top of Mt. Livermore, picnic and lounge on the beach, or enjoy one of the free museum tours.

Angel Island has a colorful history. It has served as a Civil War camp, an immigration station, a quarantine site, a World War I and World War II military base, and a Nike missile base. Remnants of the past dot the island, and you can tour the main points of interest for free.

Start at the immigration station, which earned Angel the nickname "the Ellis Island of the West" from 1910 to 1940. You can see immigrant barracks and detention cells still standing, and watch a multimedia presentation. At the Civil War Camp, you'll see restored military buildings, watch cannons fire, and learn about life at the campthe oldest Civil War site west of the Mississippi. The World War I and II encampments house a visitor's center, a museum, and more original buildings which you can tour.

As you can see, it's easy to spend an entire day on the island; sure enough, the park is open from 8:00 a.m. to sunset year-round. Guided tours, though, are only given on Saturdays and Sundays from May to October.

Berkeley Municipal Rose Garden
• Euclid Avenue and Bayview Place, Berkeley; (510) 644-6530

Want to "cheap out" on Valentine's Day? Bring your date to the Municipal Rose Garden instead of buying a dozen. You'll find over 250 varieties of roses on over 3,000 bushes (but please, don't pick any), all arranged in a lovely amphitheater overlooking the Bay.

Actually, peak season is from May to September, when the flowers are in full bloom. At other times of year, you'll certainly find some flowers, although not as many. The Rose Garden is open from 6:00 a.m. to 10:00 p.m. daily, and there is no admission charge.

Charles Lee Tilden Regional Park
• 2950 Peralta Oaks Ct., Berkeley; (510) 635-0135

Here's a great place for a family outing, with over 2,000 acres available for picnicking, hiking, and swimming in Lake Anza. You'll also find a nature area to explore, with its Environmental Education Center, and a miniature farm complete with livestock. For the kids, there's a merry-go-round, a miniature train, and pony rides. Tilden Park even has its own Botanical Garden, complete with a miniature desert and a Pacific Rain Forest.

The park towers above the city high up on a ridge, with eucalyptus and pine forests as well as several lakes on its grounds. Open 7:00 a.m. to 10:00 p.m. daily. There is no admission charge, but the rides cost either $1 or $2.

Coit Tower
• Telegraph Hill Blvd., San Francisco; (415) 362-0808

At the top of Telegraph Hill, this concrete monument is one of The City's highest and most distinctive monuments. Built in 1933, Coit Tower pays tribute to all the firefighters who battled the flames which threatened to burn San Francisco to the ground after the 1906 earthquake. It's also a prime example of W.P.A. art and architecture, President Roosevelt's public works program which funded artists during the Depression. Check out the wall murals inside, showing those firemen as glorious heroes on an epic scale.

The interior is open to the public, free, from 10 a.m. to 6 p.m. daily; but even after-hours, Coit's parking lot is a popular destination for tourists, couples looking for a bit of romance, and teenagers (generally well-behaved) just hanging out. The lot is a circle at the very end of Telegraph Hill Boulevard, a narrow, winding lane which leads up from Lombard Street in North Beach. The view, day or night, is nothing short of spectacular: almost a perfect 360. From west to east, you can see the Marina District, Fisherman's Wharf, the Embarcadero, the East Bay, both bridges, and—if you walk around to the small park behind the tower—the skyscrapers of downtown. Since this lot is nearly always full, there is a half-hour time limit on parking here—and, usually, a handful of cars waiting at the top of the hill for a spot to open up. Do drive up carefully, as pedestrians also share this narrow road.

Diablo Foothills Regional Park
• Castle Rock Road, Walnut Creek; (510) 837-3145

Nature lovers and rugged Eagle Scout types may not always appreciate the parklands in and around The City, where traffic can still be heard and the skyline hovers nearby. Take heart: Just half an hour's drive from the teeming metropolis, a true wilderness area beckons.

Diablo Foothills is a spread of nearly 1,000 acres, adjoining the 23,000-acre Walnut Creek Open Space/Mt. Diablo State Park area. It's a place of dramatic ridges, mountain peaks, and striking sandstone formations, laced with miles of hiking trails. You may spot golden eagles, hawks, prairie falcons, bobcats, coyote, grey fox, deer, weasels, and more. The park contains a small recreation area within its boundaries, with picnicking, a swimming pool, an archery range, and food concessions. The all-day fee for these amenities is $4 for adults, $3 teens, and $2 kids 6-12. Once you're in, you're on your own.

Filbert Steps
• Filbert St. (Telegraph Hill), San Francisco

Here's one of those neat little features that make The City delightfully unique. Leading down from the Coit Tower (or up to it, depending on your perspective), the Filbert Steps are just that—a series of stairs which replace a part of Filbert Street that's too steep for a roadway. Urban explorers on foot will enjoy walking down from Telegraph Hill Park to the waterfront by way of these graciously carved stone steps. Or up, if a little exercise is desired. Either way, you'll pass all kinds of hidden surprises: sculptures, wall murals, meticulously manicured rose bushes and other flora, and a cafe or two. Not to mention a chance to peek into some affluent Telegraph Hill homes and yards, for a bit of vicarious pleasure.

Looking up and out, of course, you get a fabulous view of the Embarcadero and its piers, the Bay Bridge, the water, and across to Oakland. The path is crisscrossed by quiet streets at the top, graduating to Battery Street and the glitzy new Levi's Plaza at the bottom—where you may wish to pause for some not-so-cheap shopping and refreshment. You'll also pass along Napier Lane, a wooden pathway that is a last vestige of San Francisco's 19th century landscape.

The Golden Gate Bridge
• U.S. Highway 101, San Francisco

There are plenty of great places to get a panoramic view of The City. But few are as thrilling as the Golden Gate Bridge. Energy-hogs traversing back and forth by car have to pay a $3 toll; but walkers, bikers, and joggers can cross to their heart's content (and walk) without spending a dime. And besides, what better way to gain a true appreciation of this feat of engineering magic than to actually stand on it, study it up close, and gaze out to the beauty of the Bay? There is none. If the day isn't too foggy, do bring a camera; the photo ops are unparalleled.

A few things you should know before you attempt to walk across: First of all, it's um, really high. If you are acrophobic, agoraphobic, or hydrophobic, you probably don't belong here. Second, even if you're not afraid of heights, the bridge tends to vibrate (all bridges do, by design) and the cars whizzing past seem awfully close. Finally, be sure to wear warm clothing; it can get very cold and windy up here, even during nice weather.

Japanese Tea Garden
* Tea Garden Drive, Golden Gate Park, San Francisco; (415) 752-1171

This restful and beautifully landscaped oasis—first opened in 1894—offers a winding footpath into another world. Walk over footbridges and pass ponds filled with colorful koi fish (thought to be an unusually clever and trainable species); view waterfalls, pagodas, and statues. This stroll culminates in front of the serenely magnificent, larger-than-life, 18th-century Japanese Buddha—where even the most hardened cynics may feel a twinge of something spiritual.

To complete the experience, pause at the garden teahouse on your way out. For the unusual (but cheap!) price of $2.17, you'll be treated to a cup of Japanese tea and a basket of treats—including sesame cookies, almond cookies, rice crackers, and even a fortune cookie.

Admission costs $2 for adults, $1 for seniors and kids ages 6-12. The garden is open from 9:00 a.m. to 6:00 p.m. daily. The best time to come, by the way, is early in spring, when the cherry trees are in bloom.

Lakeside Park
* Lake Merrit, Oakland; (510) 444-3807

A serene oasis in the middle of Oakland, Lake Merrit offers walking and jogging paths, paddle boat rentals, and tour boat rides (just $1). All amidst the glass-and-steel office towers of the downtown area. At the Lakeside Park Garden Center on Bellevue Avenue and Perkins Street, you can spend hours strolling through the beautiful array of plantings—with Japanese and Polynesian gardens, and sections of cactus, dahlia, fuchsia, chrysanthemums, and palms. There's also an herb garden and a fragrance garden.

MR. CHEAP'S PICKS
Outdoors

✔ **Angel Island State Park**—A place for all moods, Angel Island offers great scenery and rustic-type activities, combined with lots of historic sites to tour. The site of an old immigration station often called "The Ellis Island of the West."

✔ **Golden Gate Bridge**—Few high-priced attractions match the thrill of simply walking across this engineering wonder for free. The views of The City and Marin County are worth overcoming any trepidation.

✔ **The Japanese Tea Garden**—It's beloved by tourists, and for a good reason. A truly lovely oasis, with bridges, waterfalls, and Japanese goodies to sample at the end.

✔ **Land's End Coastal Trail**—Get in your daily constitutional along with breathtaking views. A free walk high above the city's coastline.

✔ **Marin Headlands**—Perhaps the most romantic spot in the Bay Area for parking and viewing the skyline at night. By day, 14,000 acres for hiking and exploring, a stone's throw from The City. Not far away, **Mount Tamalpais** lets you drive all the way up to the top of the world.

✔ **Sea Lions at Pier 39**—Enjoy the beauty of these creatures in their natural habitat. They are free to come and go as they please, and their antics never fail to entertain the constant crowds.

Elsewhere within the park, the Rotary Nature Center has displays of local wildlife year-round. It borders a state wildlife refuge; during the winter months, migrating herons, egrets, and geese congregate here.

No admission is charged for Lakeside Park or the Nature Center. The Garden Center charges $1.50 for parking, and is open from 10 a.m. to 3:00 p.m. weekdays, and 10:00 a.m. to 5:00 p.m. weekends. The Nature Center is open Monday from 12-5, and the rest of the week from 10-5.

Land's End Coastal Trail
• Geary Blvd. (48th Ave.), Lincoln Park, San Francisco; (415) 556-8642

If someone's just told you to take a hike, put on your walking shoes and head over to Land's End. You'll forget all your troubles once you gaze upon the scenic vistas of the Marin Headlands and the Golden Gate Bridge. Plus, the four mile round-trip burns off enough calories to justify an ice cream reward at the end.

To pick up the trail, head down Geary to 48th. Take a right at the end of the street, and look for the trail. It starts near the Cliff House and next to the San Francisco Memorial.

The trail hugs the coastline, following the edge of the cliffs which rise above the ocean. Park benches along the way give you some respite, but the trail does require some exertion. Wear good shoes, and be careful. High winds, slippery rocks, and good ol' macho stupidity have led some hikers to injury.

The trail belongs to the Golden Gate National Recreation Area, and it continues in both directions well beyond Land's End. You'll know it's time to turn around when you reach the exclusive Sea Cliffs area.

Marin Headlands
• Route 101 (near Golden Gate Bridge), San Francisco; (415) 331-1540

Want to feel like you're a million miles from civilization? Head across the bridge to Marin Headlands, where you can get lost in 14,000

acres of hilly wilderness. Only the stunning views of San Francisco and the Golden Gate remind you that urban life hovers nearby.

Marin Headlands offers miles of hiking and biking trails, free camping (make reservations in advance), and a 9,000 acre wildlife preserve. If bucolic beauty isn't your thing, check out the Nike Missile Site. You can take a free tour between 12:30 and 3:30 p.m. the first Sunday of the month, complete with a look at the entire arsenal and a missile-loading demonstration. Not exactly a wholesome family event (unless you want Junior to follow in the footsteps of the Terminator), but interesting to many.

A walk around here in the early evening is a particular pleasure, when you can see the skyline of The City glittering across the water. You may need to battle amorous teens for a parking spot, but the view (of the skyline, that is) will take your breath away. The park opens daily at 9:30 a.m.; closing time for hikers is 4:30, though cars and campers can stay later. There is no admission charge. By the way, there are often special events happening on the weekends— such as bird-watching walks, wildflower walks, crabbing, bike trips, and tours of the old World War II barracks. Call the number above for info.

Mount Tamalpais State Park
• State Route 1, Mill Valley; (415) 388-2070

For a lofty experience close to the city, drive six miles northwest of the Golden Gate Bridge to the base of Mount Tam. Although the mountain measures 2,586 feet above sea level— a modest height by topographical standards—it seems considerably steeper than that because it rises straight up from the ocean.

You can drive all the way to the top and enjoy the beautiful views from the comfort of your bucket seat, but you pay a $5 parking fee at the peak. Hardy souls (or true cheapskates) can avoid the parking charge by hiking all or part of the way up. If you choose to park and hike, you'll find several free places to leave the car along the road. Plenty of great walking and cycling trails are accessible from the parking areas.

Your reward for trudging to the top is a spectacular, 360-degree vista of the entire Bay Area. For the best view, hike an additional half-mile to the top of the fire lookout, and then reward yourself with a treat from the snack bar before heading back down.

Open daily from dawn to dusk. No dogs are allowed on the trails. National Park Service rangers lead guided nature hikes on Saturday and Sunday mornings, departing at 9:30 a.m., free of charge. Most of these are at least four miles long, and only for the rugged. Try to make the trip between March and June, when wildflowers cover the park's 6,000 acres.

Muir Woods National Monument
* State Route 1, Mill Valley; (415) 388-2595

Not far from Mount Tamalpais, Muir Woods is another fine place to escape to when your nerves jangle and you can't get your mind out of hyperdrive. 550 acres of majestic redwood trees in this beautiful forest reserve will bring you back to life in no time.

Only 12 miles north of the Golden Gate Bridge, Muir Woods has no admission charge and offers great trails for hiking and exploring. You'll find trees here up to 367 feet in height, with an average age of 200 years. If these don't help you put your woes in perspective, nothing will. Muir Woods redwoods lack the girth of those more famous sequoias in places further upstate, but they're just as tall and quite awe-inspiring.

The park is open daily from 8:00 a.m. to dusk, with no pets allowed. You can't picnic here either, but a snack bar offers basic provisions.

Point Reyes National Seashore
* State Route 1, Point Reyes, California; Information, (415) 663-1092

About an hour's drive north of the Golden Gate Bridge, Point Reyes stretches out over twenty-five miles,

from Bolinas Point at the southern end to Tomales Bluff, jutting into Bodega Bay, to the north. In all, some 65,000 acres of coastline are brimming with wildlife, nature trails, seashore views, and other urban-escape essentials—with enough to see and do for plenty of return visits.

The area holds a notorious distinction as the epicenter of the 1906 earthquake; hiking along the "Earthquake Trail," you can still see the topographical results of the damage. In fact, there are hundreds of miles' worth of trails, both for walking and horseback riding, as well as four hike-in campground locations. You can't drive up to these truly idyllic spots—and you'll need to get a permit for camping (call the above number for details).

What other treasures await you here? Breathtakingly beautiful beaches, where the ocean crashes against massive rock formations. Walk down the cliffs to get to them, through sand dunes dotted with wildflowers. No swimming here, alas—sharks have been known to hang out here, and the water's too cold anyway. Back on land, there are all kinds of other wildlife...including some 70 species of mammals and 350 types of birds. Not to mention the Point Reyes Morgan Horse Ranch, a replica of a Miwok Indian village, a working dairy ranch, bird observatories, and nature activity programs. Whew!

Admission to the reserve is free. Given all the animals roaming about, pets are not allowed in, except on the North and South Beaches. Visitors are requested to check in at the Bear Valley Visitors Center, near the town of Olema, for a brochure which details the roads, trails, beaches, and other restrictions for using the area.

San Francisco Zoo
* One Zoo Rd. (Sloat Blvd. at 45th Ave.), San Francisco; (415) 753-7061

From the tiniest insects to majestic African elephants, the animal kingdom is well-represented at the San Francisco Zoo, one of the largest in-city zoos in the United States. Pens, houses, and meadows are spread about the grounds, all separated by lush tree landscaping. Say hello to Prince Charles—he of the big paws, not the big ears—one of the world's few white tigers. See fifteen endangered species of monkeys, in reproductions of their natural settings, in at the Doelger Primate Center. On "Penguin Island," the zoo has successfully bred rare Antarctic penguins. And the Children's Zoo offers kids a chance to get close enough to feed all kinds of farmyard animals.

Not to mention "Gorilla World," the Insect Zoo, the Nocturnal Gallery, an aviary, and nature trails, as well as the obligatory kiddie rides, snack bars and patios, gift shops, and more. It's all open from 10:00 a.m. to 5:00 p.m. every day of the year; the Children's Zoo is open from 11-4, and the nature trails—with more opportunities to feed the animals—are only open during the summer, from Tuesdays through Sundays.

Admission is $6.50 for adults, which here means ages 16-65; a bit high, thinks Mr. C—but then, you get so much. Sensibly, though, seniors and youths (age 12-15) cost $3.00, children (age 6-11) cost $1.00, and kids under 6 get in free. The first Wednesday of the month is bargain day, when admission is free to all. Furthermore, you can become a member of the zoo for as little as $35 a year—granting you free admission every day, plus all sorts of other discounts and privileges. Parking is free all the time, in spaces lining the edge of the zoo along Sloat Boulevard.

The Sea Lions at Pier 39
- Pier 39, The Embarcadero, San Francisco

Proving that the best things in life truly *are* free, hundreds of sea lions bathe, bark, and nap in the sun every day on pontoons floating just off Pier 39—entertaining crowds of tourists at the same time. No one is quite sure why these ocean-going mammals started hanging out here a few years ago; for that matter, there's no guarantee that they won't take off someday. But that's the essential beauty of it. Unlike zoos, where you see animals in a replication of their natural habitat, these guys are really in their natural habitat (or at least on the fringe of it). They are free to come and go as they please, and they're not forced to do silly tricks for the audience. Quite frankly, most of them just sleep. National Park Service rangers walk along the docks to make sure no one feeds, teases, or otherwise abuses them; other than that, they're on their own. Signs along Pier 39 direct you toward the sea lions, but you'll probably find them on your own. Just listen for those unmistakable barking sounds.

Strybing Arboretum
- Golden Gate Park, 9th Avenue and Lincoln Way, San Francisco; (415) 661-1316

Travel the world in a mere 70 acres! Strybing Arboretum bombards your senses with the beauty and fragrance of 6,000 different types of plants, collected from every corner of the globe. Here, you'll see one of the world's only "cloud forests," featuring high-altitude species of flora from Central America. There's also a display of unique Malaysian rhododendrons, a self-guiding "Garden of Fragrance" for the visually impaired, a Japanese "Moon Garden," and a "Biblical Garden" featuring plants mentioned—where else?—in the Bible.

The Arboretum is at its very best in the spring, when the magnolias and cherry blossoms make their appearances. Admission is free; hours are from 8:00 a.m. to 4:00 p.m. on weekdays, 10:00 a.m. to 5:00 p.m. on weekends. To get the complete botanical experience in this part of Golden Gate Park, walk across Martin Luther King Drive and visit the Japanese Tea Garden (see listing above).

U.C. Botanical Gardens
- Centennial Drive, University of California at Berkeley; (510) 642-3343

Want to do some floral globetrotting?

These gardens display a variety of plants, flowers, and herbs from all over the world. The gardens are arranged geographically, allowing you to focus on your favorite continent. The vegetation thrives twelve months a year, but of course spring is the time when everything is at its best. A favorite is the Asian rhododendron which reaches full bloom in April. Another popular area is the redwood grove, where you will be dwarfed by the tallest trees on the planet. There is also an extensive "California" section, highlighting the state's diverse array of plant life.

Located on the UC Berkeley campus, the garden's hours are 9 a.m. to 4:45 p.m., with extended hours to 7 p.m. on Wednesdays between Memorial Day and Labor Day. The gardens are closed on Christmas day. There is no admission fee, even for weekend tours, which are given every Saturday and Sunday at 1:30. Fret not if you want a tour on a weekday—private tours can be arranged ahead of time.

READINGS AND LITERARY EVENTS

Poetry is certainly alive and kicking in the Bay Area. Any night of the week, you'll find literary readings in local cafes, bars, and bookstores. And unlike in other cities, these events don't attract a ragged handful of literati. All kinds of people, in fact, are *doing* readings. Mr. C has concluded that 99% of all Bay Area citizens—including infants and canines—write verse.

To find out what's happening on the poetry and literature circuit, pick up a copy of *Poetry Flash*. This monthly newspaper always contains a complete listing of upcoming literary events, reviews of new books, interviews with writers, and other literary stuff—and it's free. You'll find *Poetry Flash* at many bookstores and cafes in the Bay Area.

A Clean, Well-Lighted Place for Books
- 601 Van Ness Ave. (Golden Gate St.), San Francisco; (415) 441-6670
  And other suburban locations

No chance of seeing Papa Hemingway, but where else would you find authors like Art Buchwald, Patti Davis, and Nikki Giovanni talking about their books all in the same month? A Clean, Well-Lighted Place offers an unusually active program of readings by big-name authors.

The store schedules over a dozen readings and signings each month, usually at 7:30 p.m. weeknights. All of these events are free. And they take place in the huge back room—with enough seating for 300 people. Clean, Well-Lighted has two other stores, in Cupertino and Larkspur Landing, which offer frequent literary events of their own.

Black Oak Books
- 1491 Shattuck Ave. (Pine St.), Berkeley; (510) 649-0272

Lots of big-name authors come to Black Oak Books for signings and readings. Al Gore came to promote his environmental book. Susan Sontag and Toni Morrison have appeared here. Unlike the typical small store that accommodates only 50 or so people at once, this shop pushes back its movable shelves and squeezes in more than 300 people for literary events, making it an appealing stop for authors on tour.

About twenty special events happen here each month, usually at 7:30 p.m., and always free. These range from poetry readings to talks about physics, with an occasional musical performance tossed in for good measure (excuse the pun).

The store itself carries new, used, and out-of-print books in a wide range of subject areas. Emerging authors as well as the already-eminent show up. Recent happenings featured April Sinclair, reading from *Coffee Will Make You Black*; Joseph Goldstein, talking about *Insight Meditation: The Practice of Freedom;* and Margaret Atwood, signing *The Robber Bride*.

The Blue Monkey
- 1777 Steiner St. (Sutter St.), San Francisco; (415) 929-7117

This cozy cafe presents two featured poets every Tuesday night at 8:00 p.m., followed by an open-mike reading. Many of the readers here present poetry accompanied by music. If you decide to share some of your verse, there's a five-minute limit.

Come hungry: you can order espresso, beer, wine, pastries, burritos, chili, and other edibles. No admission charge for the readings.

Canessa Park Reading and Talk Series
- 708 Montgomery St. (Columbus Ave.), San Francisco; (415) 553-7798

If you're a big fan of Harlequin Romances, *don't* come to the Canessa Park series. Readings presented here focus on intellectual language arts writing. "Our writers produce the sort of work that appears in *Talisman, Sulphur,* and *Oblique* magazines," says the coordinator. "It's more academic, not like the typical bar or cafe reading series. It's less of a fashion thing here, more serious writing."

Barroom poets, take note. If you want to stop fooling around and see how the pros do prose (and poetry, for that matter), these readings take place on Sunday afternoons at 3:00 p.m. Admission costs $4, and that includes free tea or mineral water. The space also has an art gallery, with paintings and sculptures by local artists on display.

Recent events include Clark Coolidge and Bruce Boone reading

their poetry, a staged reading of a new play, and Robert Bertov talking about his experience as curator of the Robert Duncan estate.

Cody's
- 2454 Telegraph Ave. (Haste St.), Berkeley; (510) 845-7852

Cody's specializes in hard-to-find books on history, political science, and other weighty subjects. With such an emphasis, you might expect all the literary happenings here to be about subjects like "Nihilistic Pre-Marxist Tendencies in Cross-Gender Negotiations." Not! Actually, these guys present as many fun and frivolous events as more sober readings. With over 150,000 titles in stock, the store boasts great fiction, poetry, and music sections, and this is reflected in the type of events scheduled.

Wednesdays and Sundays at 7 p.m. are poetry nights, with an admission charge of just $2. Authors on book tours, meanwhile, can show up almost any night to autograph and read from their newest titles. Some big names have surfaced herelike Donald Johanson, author of *In Search of Human Origins,* and Roddy Doyle, author of *The Commitments.* Recently, Trina Robbins talked about her book, *A Century of Women Cartoonists*, and Jim Cohn delivered a performance of poems from his book *Prairie Falcon*, which was signed for hearing-impaired patrons.

Apart from the weekly poetry readings, other events are free. It all takes place upstairs in a room with seating for sixty; but if you get shut out, you can still hear from anywhere in the store—the authors are miked, and their words literally resound throughout the place.

Easy Going Travel Shop and Bookstore
- 1385 Shattuck Ave. (Rose St.), Berkeley; (510) 843-3533

When earthquakes and the gray of winter make you long for foreign ports in spite of your empty wallet, you should at least make a trip to the Easy Going Travel Shop. Here, you can listen to travel tales and enjoy exotic slide shows as authors discuss their ramblings in faraway lands.

Recent guests have included Pico Iyer reading from *Off the Map*, his book about the world's most obscure places. The editor of the *Consumer Reports Travel Letter* appeared recently to impart travel bargain wisdom, a topic near and dear to Mr. C's heart. Author Tim Cahill read from his *Pecked to Death by Ducks*; and a slide show highlighted cycling tours of Vietnam, the travel destination everyone suddenly seems to be talking about.

Need to know how to pack for three weeks and two climates in a single carry-on bag? Every month, the shop hosts a packing demonstration where you can learn that very sort of thing. This ultra-popular event also packs in lots of people, so show up early for a good seat.

So, if you want to go somewhere exotic—or just look that way—this store can help. All events are free, and usually take place at 7:30 p.m. Call for a schedule. Of course, Easy Going carries a broad array of books, maps, and travel paraphernalia for just about every corner of the globe. And, if even Berkeley is a bit of a hike, you may prefer to visit the store's second location at 1617 Locust Street in Walnut Creek; telephone (510) 947-6660.

Elmwood Café
- 2993 College Ave. (Ashby St.), Berkeley; (415) 848-5050

Along with being a fine place to sip a cup of peppermint tea or cram for a physics final, the Elmwood Café is also a place where you can enjoy the spoken word. The cafe's "Touch of a Poet Series" features several poets reading from their works, presented from 7-9 p.m. on the last two Wednesdays of each month. These performances are grouped into two seasons: "Winter/Spring," runnning from February through June, and "Fall," from September through November.

Each reading includes two featured readers, each locally published

MR. CHEAP'S PICKS
Literary Readings

✔ **Easy Going Travel Shop**—Travel writers share their experiences, plus free extras like slide shows on faraway countries and workshops on the best ways to pack.

✔ **Intersection for the Arts**—Readings for the sake of literature, not just to promote the latest book. There's a stage and theater, poetry and fiction on Tuesdays, and an artist-in-residence each month planning a variety of special events.

✔ **LaVal's Subterranean**—Poetry, Pinter plays, progressive rock, Shakespeare (some things defy alliteration), and pizza, all in a downstairs room under an Italian restaurant in Berkeley. Who says you can't have it all?

✔ **Torsiello Gallery**—Artsy coffee-house atmosphere, Italian pastries, and readings by authors both local and big-time. Free open-mike shows, too.

poets, followed by an open-mike. Their purpose in this venture is to give up-and-coming poets a venue for their work, and to encourage a wider appreciation for poetry in general. All readings are completely free and open to the public. However, you may want to "put some coins in thy purse," to quote the Bard, in order to enjoy the Elmwood's terrific coffees, teas, sandwiches, pastries, and more.

Farley's
- 1315 18th St. (Texas St.), San Francisco; (415) 648-1545

This hip cafe at the tippy-top of Potrero Hill has everything a coffeehouse should have: great coffee and tea by the cup, pastries, a well-stocked rack of newspapers and alternative magazines, and plenty of tables to while away an hour or two with all of these. The atmosphere is quiet and relaxed, somewhat different from the industrial-grunge-rock approach some cafes adopt.

In addition, Farley's hosts a handful of live performances every month. These take place on various evenings, and range from weekly poetry jams to storytelling to acoustic music. There are no admission or cover charges. The cafe walls display works by area artists, featuring someone new each month. These exhibits include a reception evening, again, free and open to the public.

In all, it's one of The City's most happening cafes—a friendly, laid-back place that's well worth the trek if this isn't your usual stomping ground. Stop in for a flyer detailing this month's events.

Intersection for the Arts

- 446 Valencia St. (16th St.), San Francisco; (415) 626-ARTS

This non-profit arts center in the Mission district began sponsoring poetry readings and other things literary in 1975—way back when writers still produced their works by pen and typewriter instead of by mouse and windows. Whichever methods are currently employed, the reading tradition continues, with poetry or fiction every Tuesday night at 8:00 p.m. Recent programs featured Walter Moseley, the detective writer, and poet Wanda Coleman.

The center also hosts a different writer-in-residence each month. Residents offer three nights of readings, workshops, and other activities. Jewelle Gomez, a feminist poet, recently offered a workshop on "Writing about Forbidden Topics" as part of her residency. Nina Iskrenko, a Russian author, spoke on changes in Moscow over the past year, and concluded with a one-night "poetry happening, Moscow-style."

These gatherings take place in the center's 75-seat theatre, complete with a formal stage area. Admission

costs $4. If you show up early, check out the on-site art gallery featuring installation art (works specifically designed to interact with elements in the room). Also, if you like drama, the center frequently hosts new works in progress by up-and-coming playwrights, with tickets usually $10. Call for a schedule.

LaVal's Subterranean

- 1834 Euclid Ave. (Hearst Ave.), Berkeley; (510) 843-5617

This pizza joint (yes, that's right) features a reading by a different Berkeley-area poet every Tuesday night at 8:00 p.m., followed by an open-mike session for others to join in. Shows sometimes get videotaped and shown on local Channel 24. All readings happen downstairs, in the "Subterranean Room," with a stage and seating for 77. You can order Italian food, beer, or wine during the readings.

LaVal's also presents plays in the Subterranean—as often as three nights a week. A resident theater company usually performs scripts by Harold Pinter or David Mamet, but a local Shakespearean company also puts on frequent productions. Tickets cost $6 to $8. Live music (usually rock) follows the plays, with a $4 cover. A little bit of everything!

Modern Times Bookstore

- 888 Valencia St. (20th St.), San Francisco; (415) 282-9246

This left-wing Mission District bookstore carries the latest in social criticism, political commentary, dissident fiction, and more. In addition, the shop hosts an ongoing variety of readings, lectures, and panel discussions. Recent events included Jennifer Harbury reading from her just-published *Bridge of Courage: Life Stories of the Guatemalan Compañeros and Compañeras*; activist and physicist Vandana Shiva with her book *Staying Alive: Women, Ecology, and Development*; and media critic Norman Solomon, speaking about his book *False Hope: The Politics of Illusion in the Clinton Era*.

Events at Modern Times are generally free of charge; some cost just a few dollars. Occasionally, they ask for donations, usually $5 to $10. Modern Times also runs a series called "Jacking In: A Series on Cyberspace Literacy." That's computer networks, for the uninitiated. Recent events in this series have included "Navigating the Internet: A Crash Course" with Eric Theise, and "Playing in the MUDS: Virtual Realities in Text." Both talks had a sliding scale admission fee of $3 to $5.

Nefeli Caffé
- 1854 Euclid Ave. (Hearst Ave.), Berkeley; (510) 841-6374

A few doors down from LaVal's, this upscale coffee and food joint sponsors a weekly reading series on Monday nights at 7:00 p.m. Unlike other venues in the area that offer no distractions from the reading, here you can enjoy good coffee and edibles while listening—certainly a plus if the work doesn't grab you. On the other hand, if it's very good, you may find the waitpeople and patrons cruising the floor a bit annoying.

In any case, the readings are free, with established local poets and fiction writers on the program. You can also enjoy the photography exhibits in the back room, the neighborhood ambiance, and the piped-in jazz before the show.

Speaking of which, the Nefeli also presents live music—usually jazz, or ethnic sounds such as Greek or flamenco—at least once a month. These generally happen on Fridays or Sundays; call or stop by for a current schedule.

Poetry Above Paradise
- 1501 Folsom St. (11th St.), San Francisco (415) 861-6906

In a room above the trendy SoMa rock club, Paradise Lounge, poets read their verse every Sunday night from 8:00 to 10:00 p.m. "*Everyone* has read here," says a spokesman for the program. "Sean Penn, John Doe from the band X, Joyce Young...everyone."

The lineup includes a few featured poets each night: some emerging,

some established. An open-mike usually follows, for the yet-to-emerge. The Paradise also hosts special events, like the recent "Tongues in Time," in which bands *recited* lyrics to their songs.

All readings are free. The room has an excellent sound system, and you can order drinks, including espresso and other coffee concoctions. Paradise serves no food, but you can bring some in from the restaurant next door. Since it's an alcohol-serving establishment, you must be 21 or older to get in.

Polk Street Beans and Cafe
- 1733 Polk St. (Washington St.), San Francisco; (415) 776-9292

Every Thursday night from 8:00-11:00 p.m., this fun and funky hangout has poetry readings. It's an open-mike sort of affair, with up to fifteen readers participating in any one evening. If you worry that the arts are dying, show up and witness this crowd—the place gets packed.

There's no admission charge for the reading. You can buy espresso or other coffee drinks, wine, or beer; also, pastries and specialty sandwiches to feed your body even as you feed your mind. Note that Polk Street also offers live music on occasional Fridays and Saturdays—again, for free (although the unpaid musicians usually pass the hat).

Small Press Traffic
- 3599 24th St. (Guererro St.), San Francisco; (415) 285-8394

This bookstore carries every type of writing, from the experimental to the just plain silly, with an emphasis on small press and self-published work. The program of literary events here reflects the store's eclectic interests, with five different series running at once.

The "Furious Fiction Series" presents flash-fiction (very-short story) writers at 8:00 p.m. on the third Wednesday of the month. A featured author starts the program, followed by an open-mike session. Each participant is limited to four minutes! The "Words and Music Series" combines poetry with live musical accompaniment to back the readers up. This is one of the very latest trends in poetry reading, and it happens on Tuesdays at 8:00 p.m.

"Goddesses We Ain't" features women writing in all styles and genres, presented on the last Thursday of each month at 8:00 p.m. An open-mike follows the featured author, with each reader getting a more generous 15-minute slot.

The "Multicultural Reading Series" takes place on the third Saturday of each month, and is co-sponsored by the well-established Intersection for the Arts (see listing above).

Finally, "Poetry and Prose" presents both local and national writers. Recent authors featured in this series include Peter Money, author of *Minor Roads*, and Sarah Menefee, reading from her *Blood About the Heart*.

You'll find this bookstore a comfy place to hang out and browse while waiting for the reading to start. In a previous incarnation, this was a private apartment, and it still boasts large rooms with picture windows, a kitchen, and a small study. Settle into a stuffed chair with a book, and enjoy some free refreshments after the program.

Torsiello Gallery
- 3363 Grand Ave. (Elwood St.), Oakland; (510) 465-3236

Even if you spend the entire day watching "Love Boat" reruns, you'll feel literary the moment you walk into the Coffee Mill, Oakland's old-est coffeehouse. How can you resist waxing poetical in a place that was specifically designed to be a bohemian hang-out, emulating the best cafes in Greenwich Village and Rome?

Every Thursday night at 7:00 p.m., local poets, fiction writers, and playwrights present their material in the Torsiello art gallery toward the back. It's a lovely and quiet little space, with carpeting and a stage—a real luxury on the readings circuit. Admission costs $3, which should leave enough money in your pocket to order some of the excellent coffee, tea, sandwiches, or Italian pastry for which the Coffee Mill is known.

Authors appearing here range from the unknown to the eminent. On the last Thursday of the month, a free open reading replaces the "featured author" slot. If you want to read some of your own work, just arrive a little early and sign up. Other events—including jazz concerts and chamber music, with admission prices between $5 and $10—are also scheduled frequently. Call or stop in for a calendar of events.

SPORTS AND PLAY

COLLEGE SPORTS

Die-hard sports fanatics know that there is just as much excitement to be found on college campuses as in the professional arenas. (Why do you think so many pro teams have begun using cheerleaders?) What's more, these games often cost far less than the pros; and many schools offer a greater diversity of sports.

Stanford University
- 300 Pasteur Drive, Stanford; (415) 723-4591

If you'd like to catch a good game of baseball or football at below-pro prices, the Stanford University Cardinals (the color, not the bird) are a Division I team in each of those respective sports. Baseball games are played at the Sunken Diamond; while the larger (85,500-seat capacity) Stanford Stadium is the setting for football matchups with such other Pacific-Ten powerhouses like the UCLA Bruins and the USC Trojans.

Ticket prices are very reasonable indeed. For baseball, with a season running from January to June, tix are $4.00. Football games, during September to November, are priced at $20.00-$32.00. There is a student discount for the season pass.

University of California at Berkeley
- University of California at Berkeley, Berkeley; (510) 642-3734

There are more than enough sports played on this campus to entertain even the most ravenous fan—twenty-four, to be exact. Football and basketball, of course, draw the most atttention due to their Division I status. Admission to these contests will cost between $14 and $21, only slightly less expensive than professional teams; however, student rates are available. Many other events, meanwhile, are free or very cheap—such as men's and women's water polo, basketball, and softball. Call the number above for more information and a schedule of upcoming events.

PROFESSIONAL SPORTS

Well, if you must see the big-leaguers only, there are some discount opportunities as well. Here are a few possibilities to try:

Golden State Warriors
- Oakland Coliseum Arena, 66th Ave. (Hegenberger Rd.), Oakland; (510) 638-6300

Basketball has truly become the glamor sport of the '90s (thanks to Jack Nicholson, Nike endorsements, and other factors) with ticket prices to match. At the Oakland Coliseum Arena, home base for the Warriors, there's quite a range of ticket prices indeed; but there is a chance to economize. If you don't need to sit in the courtside seats along "King's Row," you can see a game starting at just $9.50 per seat. The NBA season runs from November through April.

Oakland Athletics
- Oakland Coliseum, 66th Ave. (Hegenberger Rd.), Oakland; (510) 638-0500

The Athletics have had their ups and downs over the last few seasons, but they've brought a lot of excitement to the Bay Area—ever since the Charlie O. Finley era, which added such historic advances to the game as orange baseballs, uniforms with three completely different color combinations, and of course, facial hair. Anyway, tickets to A's games are quite reasonable, with a price range which starts at only $4.50 (going up to $14); better yet, there are additional deals. These include occasional "Half-Price Nights" and discounts on certain seating areas for students, senior citizens, and active military members—enough to make any game a winner.

San Francisco Giants
- Candlestick Park, Jamestown Ave., San Francisco; (415) 467-8000

The San Francisco Giants have re-emerged as a major force in the major leagues—how else can you explain winning over 100 games in a season and not making the playoffs? Of course, now that the divisions have been re-aligned, that 1993 fate seems unlikely to be repeated soon—but then, you never know. That's the beauty of sports. Where were we? Oh yes—ticket prices. These can really swing for the fences, as high as $20 each; but Mr. C reminds you that tix start at the much more down-to-earth price of $5, enough to bring the whole family and still have enough left over for hot dogs. Games begin in April, and continue into October.

San Jose Sharks
• San Jose Arena, 525 W. Santa Clara Way, San Jose; (408) 28-SHARK (287-4275)

One of the newest entries into the ever-expanding National Hockey League (does it seem odd to anybody else for this Canadian ice sport to be played in the balmy climes of Califor-

nia and Florida?), the San Jose Sharks have already become a post-season contender. How much does it cost to see them in their brand-new home, the San Jose Arena? Top-priced seats go for a cool $65.00, but if you don't mind sitting in the top-*located* seats, you'll only have to shell out $14.00. Of course, you may want to bring some binoculars along; otherwise, good luck seeing the puck. The NHL season runs from October through April.

PARTICIPATORY SPORTS

Finally, we come to the kind of sports that require more involvement than drinking beer. The Bay Area is filled with free and inexpensive ways to get out there and play.

Golden Gate Park Sports Facilities
• Golden Gate Park, San Francisco; General information, (415) 556-4283

Next time you're feeling cooped-up (and spent-out), remember that Golden Gate Park is filled with all kinds of free and inexpensive opportunities for participatory sports—from the Fly-Casting Pool to Kezar Stadium events. Plus soccer, tennis, lawn bowling, and of course, Ultimate Frisbee. The area is also a natural (pun intended) for bicycling; and a pair of nearby shops offer bike rentals, which can make for a reasonably priced day's outing. Both located where the Panhandle meets the park, they are **Lincoln Cyclery**, 772 Stanyan Street (at Haight), telephone (415) 221-2415; and **Park Cyclery**, 1856 Haight Street (at Stanyan), telephone (415) 221-3777.

For all you duffers out there, the **Golden Gate Golf Course** is an inexpensive place to tee off—or work on your handicap, out of the limelight. Located near the 47th Avenue entrance from the Richmond, this is a nine-hole, par-27 playing course that's open from dawn to dusk every day of the year. And there's no need to worry about price-gouging pro

shops, ostentatious restaurants, or cart rentals. Just get out there and play. General admission is a way-below-par $8: senior citizens pay only $4; and students pay $3. Valid ID is required for students and seniors. Call (415) 751-8987 for more information.

The City, meanwhile, offers several public golf courses, including the **John McLaren Municipal Golf Course**, also known as **Gleneagles**, in McLaren Park at 2100 Sunnydale Ave., near the Excelsior District; telephone (415) 587-2425. With two nine-hole courses, par 36 each, it's open from sun-up to sun-down daily; the rates are $10.00 for nine holes during the week, $13.00 on the weekends, and $15.00 for eighteen holes during the week, $22.00 on the weekends. The **Lincoln Municipal Golf Course**, in the Richmond, is on Legion of Honor Drive, near the intersection of Clement Street and 34th Avenue; telephone (415) 221-9911. This is an eighteen-hole, par 68 course, open daily from dawn to dusk. Rates are $21.00 during the week, $25.00 on the weekends. Finally, the **Harding Park Municipal Golf Course** on Lake Merced is your chance to play, well, *close* to three other private clubs—with the same idyllic lakefront setting. It's at 2 Harding Boulevard, off of Skyline; telephone (415) 664-4690. The facility offers both a nine-hole, par 32 course and an eighteen hole, par 72; it's open from 6:30 to dusk, and rates are $11.00 for the nine-hole course during the week, $12.00 on the weekends, $24.00 for the eighteen-hole course, $29.00 on the weekends.

Park Bowl
- 1855 Haight St. (Stanyan St.), San Francisco; (415) 826-2695

Here's an inexpensive sport that's often overlooked for good, cheap fun. Park Bowl offers your basic, traditional bowling during the week; each string costs $1.75 per person, plus a $1 shoe rental fee. Can't get a much better fun-per-dollar ratio than that, no matter what your score.

Ah, but this wouldn't be the Haight without some kind of twist—literally and figuratively. On the weekends, Park Bowl becomes the home of "Rock 'n Bowl," an even livelier version of the game. Nightclub lighting, a giant video screen, and 25-inch TVs showing rock videos of all kinds over each alley add a unique backbeat. Will it help your game? Hey, who cares??

Reservations of four or more people are required at R 'n B. Players must also be 21 years old and up, as liquor is served. Rock 'n Bowl's prices are for general admission, and admission policy varies from night to night. On Thursdays, bowl all you want from 9 p.m. to 12:30 a.m for $8. On Fridays, admission is $9 from 10 to 11:30 p.m., and $7 from 11:30 p.m. to 2 a.m. Saturday rates are $10 from 9 to 11:30 p.m., and $7 from 11:30 p.m. to 2 a.m. If you're there for the early shift and they don't need your lane for the late, you can stay on for free.

Billiards Palacade
- 5179 Mission St. (Geneva St.), San Francisco; (415) 585-2331

The game of billiards just barely qualifies for inclusion in a chapter on sports, participatory or otherwise. If nothing else, you at least have to be

---

MR. CHEAP'S PICKS
Sports and Play

✔ **Golden Gate Park**—Anything goes here: cycling, tennis, golf, fly casting, or just plain soaking up the sun.

✔ **Park Bowl**—The "Rock N Bowl" night club twist on this American past-time will knock your socks (and rented shoes) off.

---

on your feet to play, and the consumption of beer is usually involved. Anyway, here's a prime example of one of The City's many billiard halls, located in the Mission District.

The fee for a table at the Palacade is a flat $7 an hour. If this seems at all expensive, don't forget that up to four people can play per game. So you could, for example, get three pals to join in, shoot a couple of hours, and shell out a whopping $3.50 each for the pleasure. Of course, there's always a catch, as in the above-mentioned beverages. In fact, there is a snack bar which racks up sandwiches, tamales, and soft drinks, as well as beer—and it's all reasonably priced.

No one under the age of eighteen is allowed to play pool, but you can still bring the kids in. And wouldn't ya know it, there's a video arcade area to entertain them. Billiards Palacade is closed on Mondays; it's open every other day of the week from 11:30 a.m. until 2:00 a.m.

Family Billiards
- 2807 Geary Blvd. (Wood St.), San Francisco; (415) 931-9115

Like the Billiards Palacade (above), you can bring the whole family down to this billiard parlor—it's got something for everyone. Throw a few quarters in the jukebox and shoot some pool, while your children (and the friends they've begged you to bring along) play the latest video games in the arcade room.

Regular hourly prices are $4.50 for one person, $8 for two, $10 for three, and $12 for four people. But, there is a deal to be found here: If you drop in on Monday, Tuesday, or Wednesday evenings from 5:00 to 9:00, these rates are cut in half. You score even before you start playing! Family Billiards is open Sunday-Thursday 11:30 a.m. to 2:00 a.m.; Friday and Saturday 11:30 a.m. to 4 a.m.; closed Mondays.

THEATER

Here's a little-known way to save money if you like to go to the theater often: **volunteer ushering**. Many professional companies (apart from the Broadway-type downtown houses) need regular folks to help rip tickets, hand out programs, or guide people to their seats. In exchange for your services, you can watch the show for free!

Responsibilities are light. Just dress nicely, arrive a bit early for a few instructions, and then play your role. Once everyone is inside, find a seat for yourself and enjoy the show—you're all done. Ushering can even be a fun cheap date; you'll have a guaranteed conversation starter afterwards. Best of all, you'll save yourself some cash *and* help a theater out at the same time. Call ahead to find out if that new show you've been eyeing uses volunteers, and if so, when they have slots available.

An asterisk following a theater's name below indicates that they do seek volunteer ushers.

Above Brain Wash Theater
- 1126 Folsom St. (Seventh St.), San Francisco; (415) 255-4866

True to its name, this performance space is found upstairs from the popular SoMa laundromat/cafe, the Brain Wash (see listing under "Restaurants"). ABT is not a theater company in itself, but rather a venue frequently rented out by numerous Bay Area experimental troupes. It's a small, flexible, no-frills space; in other words, a long, empty room whose walls have been painted black. Folding chairs can be arranged in various configurations, depending on the play's set design.

And what can you see here? Just about anything, it seems. Recent performances have ranged from Lanford Wilson's emotional drama *Burn This*, featuring Equity actors from the Kudzu Theatre company, to cabaret, standup comedy, staged readings of new plays being developed, gay improvisational theater, storytelling (for grownups), and live music. Shows take place most nights of the week, between various groups; many weekend performances are "late-night" shows. Ticket prices are generally in the $10 range. Call to find out what's on the schedule—you never know what you may get.

American Conservatory Theater
- 405 Geary St. (Mason St.), San Francisco; (415) 749-2ACT (2228)

Since its inception in 1967, ACT has become one of the nation's leaders in what has come to be known as "resident theater"; that is, the idea that you don't have to go to Broadway to see top-notch professional shows. In fact, ACT has won a special Tony Award for its overall work.

Housed in the Geary Theater right downtown in Union Square, the troupe's home was badly damaged during the 1989 earthquake. During the slow but steady repairs, ACT has turned adversity into advantage by expanding into several nearby venues; the **Stage Door Theater** at 420 Mason Street and the **Marines Memorial Theater** at 609 Sutter Street are the two primary spaces, with a few others mustered into service for certain shows.

As a training ground for young actors (Denzel Washington and Winona Ryder are grads), the American Conservatory Theater presents plays and musicals ranging from classics to the very latest works by top playwrights. Tony Kushner's award-winning *Angels in America*, for instance, can be seen in the same season as Shakespeare's *Othello*; raucous comedy, like Moliere's *Scapin*, can alternate with David Mamet's *Oleanna*.

So, can all this be cheap? Well, top ticket prices are approaching $40 (you don't have to go to New York to get those, either). But wait—there are some deals! Students and senior citizens (age 62 and up), with valid ID, can get rush tickets at half-price for any evening performance. Seniors also get a deal on matinees: Any available tix go for $6 each.

Just show up at the theater 90 minutes before curtain time, and pay in cash; one ticket per person. Of course, this only works if tickets are still available for that performance; you take a chance, but it can really be worth it. ACT also offers 20% discounts for groups of fifteen or more people, and 30% discounts for student groups. For more info on all these options, call the main box office at the number above.

Asian American Theater Company*
- 403 Arguello Blvd. (Clement St.), San Francisco; (415) 751-2600

To many San Franciscans, the Richmond means Asian restaurants for days. But there are other kinds of culture from the Far Eastern culture to be sampled here. For over twenty years, the Asian American Theater Company has been producing works

by such well-known playwrights as David Henry Hwang (*M. Butterfly, The Dance and the Railroad*) and Philip Kan Gotanda (*The Avocado Kid*, and the screenplay for *The Wash*), as well as original plays by local writers. The company is a successful mix of community volunteers and professional artists, including Equity actors.

Plays are presented on not one, but three different stages; the main theater is a comfortable auditorium holding about 135 people, with two smaller spaces of a flexible and experimental nature. These two are frequently rented out by other, non-Asian troupes. At present, the recession has hit the AAT hard; the company does not have a set schedule for upcoming shows. Generally, there are one to three new productions each year, with performances Wednesdays through Sundays. Tickets range from $10-$18; discount tix for students and senior citizens are usually $8-$10. Call to find out what's playing next.

The Audium
- 1616 Bush St. (Franklin St.), San Francisco; (415) 771-1616

This is no ordinary theater. It's a theater of sounds only, taking place in a fully darkened room. Since 1975 at this unlikely spot, and for fifteen years before that at other locations, this unique experience has been wowing San Francisco audiences.

The show really begins in the lobby, with isolated sounds peeping out from behind contemporary sculptures. When it's time to enter the theater itself, you walk through a "labyrinth" (to the sounds of a babbling brook) into a semi-darkened room meticulously outfitted with some 200 recessed speakers of every shape and size. They're over your head, under your seat, in front of you, behind you.

The lights dim to total blackness, and the parade of sound begins. Chords and tones from real instruments and electronic keyboards blend with recorded birds, water, trains, brass bands, and more. They dart playfully around the room, whizzing past your head, rumbling the floor, and creating a dazzling sensual experience. By turns, it can be soothing, then startling; many people find that it conjures up moods, emotions, memories.

What is it? A trip through outer space? Through your own mind? You decide—it all depends on what you "bring" to the performance. Composer/performer Stan Shaff, who helped create the Audium with grants from the National Endowment for the Arts, refers to a "geometry of sound." Each show is slightly different, another variation on the experiment, masterfully guided by Shaff—who sits right in there with you, working his magic in the same darkness.

New shows are being developed, to be presented in repertory with Shaff's opus. Currently, performances take place on Friday and Saturday evenings at 8:30 p.m. (latecomers cannot be admitted, for obvious reasons); other nights may have been added to the schedule by the time you read this. Admission is $8, and children under age 18 are not admitted at all. Things can get pretty loud inside, or unsettling, leading to potential disruptions; youngsters aren't always sure what to make of this unusual situation. However, special performances for school groups can be arranged in advance.

Aurora Theater Company*
- 2315 Durant Ave. (Dana St.), Berkeley; (510) 843-4822

In just three years, this professional, Equity troupe has built a strong reputation for itself near the UC campus. In fact, it's located inside the beautiful Berkeley City Club, a landmark building designed by Julia Morgan, architect of the San Simeon mansion. Aurora's cozy theater seats only 67 people; you can definitely leave your opera glasses at home.

The company presents a season of five plays from November through July, with performances on Wednesdays through Sundays; ticket prices are usually $12-$18, and you can save a substantial amount by subscribing. Among the works seen here recently: Harold Pinter's *No Man's Land*; Henrik Ibsen's *Ghosts*; George Bernard Shaw's *How He Lied To Her Husband*; and *Holiday Memories*, a popular Christmas offering adapted from stories by Truman Capote.

Bay Area Intimate Theater
- Various locations; Information, (415) 931-1094

Take in a theatrical performance for only $5—not by showing up at elementary school pageants, but by picking up a discount coupon at any of the ten small theaters which belong to the Bay Area Intimate Theater collective. The theaters in this group are each known for some variety of experimental, improvisational, and educational drama.

Members of the collective include **Exit Theater, Harvest Theater, Open Egg Theater, Tale Spinner, Teatro Mision, Flash Family, California Conservatory Theatre, Theatre Au Naturel, Theater of Yugen,** and **Theater of the Blue Rose**; ask for your free discount coupon at any of these box offices. Once you have it, instead of paying up to $12 per ticket, you can see one show at each venue for the $5 rate. Then, as Karl Malden says, don't leave home without it. Call the number above for more information.

By the way, if progressive theater is your scene, watch local papers for the annual **Bay Area Intimate Theater Fringe Festival** in mid-September. This four-day happening features 30 or more performances *daily* by local, national, and international theater companies, modeled after the famous "Fringe" festival held in Edinburgh, Scotland. Tickets to these shows cost $7 apiece. The festival kicks off at a special stage right in Union Square at noon on the Friday of that week.

Berkeley Repertory Theatre*
- 2025 Addison St. (Shattuck Ave.), Berkeley; (510) 845-4700

Considered one of the Bay Area's premier theater companies, the Berkeley

Rep presents seven shows during its annual September through July season. It's a professional ensemble, with a 400-seat theater, and ticket prices that max out above $30; ah, but wait—Mr. C is on the case.

There are a couple of discount options. For starters, half-price "rush" tickets may be available (unless the performance is sold out) half an hour before curtain; these are offered to students and senior citizens only, with valid ID. For the rest of us, there is hope as well. After opening night, a section of twenty tickets are held aside to be sold at half-price for every Tuesday through Friday performance. These are available to anyone, first-come-first-served; you must buy them in person at the box office, on the day of the show, and pay by cash or check. There is a two-ticket maximum per customer.

Berkeley Rep produces a challenging season of plays from classics to contemporary works. Comedies by Oscar Wilde, and Noël Coward; dramas by Samuel Beckett and Edward Albee; and Bay Area premieres of the latest Off-Broadway hits have all been seen on the BRT stage.

Black Repertory Group*
- 3201 Adeline St. (Alcatraz Ave.), Berkeley; (510) 652-4017

The late Nora Vaughn, founder of the Black Repertory Group, had a vision when she began it in 1964: "We want to be known for more than getting four stars on our plays. We want to pass on our heritage, our pride, our culture." Originally, BRG was little more than the drama program of a Methodist church; over the past thirty years, it has expanded into secular Black themes. It has also grown and changed location, now making its home in a 250-seat theater. The works of such writers as Langston Hughes have graced this stage, as have Charles Fuller's provocative *Don't You Want to Be Free?* and Alice Childress' OBIE Award-winning *Trouble in Mind.* General admission is $10.00, $8.00 for students, $5.00 for seniors and children. Mati-

---

MR. CHEAP'S PICKS
Theater

✔ **The Audium**—Something unusual: theater of sound. An inexpensive, unique experience.

✔ **Magic Theatre**—One of the most prestigious (and adventurous) companies in the country, Magic's prices have risen with its reputation. But they usually offer at least one "Pay-What-You-Can" evening for each production.

✔ **Rush tickets**—Many area troupes offer big discounts to last-minute theatergoers, if seats are available. These include the otherwise high-end **American Conservatory Theater** and the **Berkeley Rep.**

✔ **Tix Bay Area**—This non-profit organization offers two fantastic money-saving options: The Tix booth in Union Square, with day-of-performance discounts, and Tix By Mail, which gets you similar deals in advance.

---

nees are also $5.00. Group rates are available, too—prices vary according to the size. In addition to the five-show season from December through June, BRG provides a variety of workshops, demonstrations, outreach programs, and classes; call for a schedule of events.

Exit Theater
- 156 Eddy St. (Mason St.), San Francisco; (415) 931-1094

This small, experimental theater offers shows every Monday through Saturday, year-round. The program varies from day to day, with staged readings of new scripts on Mondays; "theater of the absurd" on Tuesdays; and an original sketch on Wednesdays. Featured, more polished, performances—usually of new and original works—run Thursday through Saturday.

Recent shows have included *Food from Trash*, a wild play about toxic waste, and *What's for Dinner*, a spoof of TV cooking show hosts. The theater seats about a hundred people—intimate, but not insignificant—and you can order beer, wine, appetizers, or coffee drinks.

For the best deal, says Mr. C, attend on Thursdays; that's when Exit offers a "pay what you can" performance. Name your price (don't be *too* cheap) and you're in. Otherwise, tickets generally cost $5 to $12, depending on the show.

Magic Theatre
- Fort Mason Center, Building D; Buchanan St. at Marina Blvd., San Francisco; (415) 441-8822

From humble beginnings as an experimental troupe, Magic Theatre has grown over the years into one of America's foremost regional theater companies, known as a proving ground for controversial playwrights. These are scripts which may either move on to (or have come here from) Off Broadway and other cutting-edge centers, by such writers as Jon Robin Baitz, Marlane Meyer and Athol Fugard. The Equity actors who work at Magic have performed at many such venues around the country: Joseph Papp's Public Theatre in New York, the Steppenwolf in Chicago, the Berkeley Shakespeare Festival, Yale Rep, and others.

Along with its success on the national scene have come bigger productions, larger budgets—and higher ticket prices. Some of these can rival downtown rates. However, Magic Theatre hasn't forgotten its roots, and remains committed to all audiences, well-to-do and otherwise. For that reason, it offers a "pay what you can" deal for each of its major presentations. At specifically designated performances (usually two or three times during each production, including one matinee) you can literally walk up to the box office and name your price. Some folks offer a dollar for tix that would otherwise cost as much as $20; the friendly folks at the window won't bat an eyelash, and they won't snicker as you walk away with your bargain, either.

Mr. C, a longtime starving artist himself, always believes in supporting the arts; he suggests that you not get *too* stingy on this deal. After all, if it is feasible for you to find some middle ground, you and the theater will both help each other out. Call them, or check newspaper listings to find out which performances feature this special offer. Getting hold of Magic's own newsletter, *Magic News*, will also give you information about post-play discussions, free staged readings of new scripts in development, and in-depth background articles on the playwrights.

Marin Theater Company*
- 397 Miller Ave., Mill Valley; (415) 388-5200

See major shows for a mere pittance just north of The City, at the Marin Theater. Each year, this company presents six shows, ranging from comedies to musicals to serious dramas. Among the offerings have been *Shadowlands* (a big hit on the London stage before the movie version); the comedy *Lend Me a Tenor*; and *The Loman Family Picnic*, a recent off-Broadway piece based on the classic *Death of a Salesman*. Now, you won't see any big-name stars in the leading roles, but this is an Equity troupe (meaning all are union professionals), and the company has a reputation for excellence.

Tickets normally cost $20, rather pricey; ah, but on Tuesdays, all seats go for only $8. Remember, you heard it from Mr. C. That should leave you enough cash to buy fresh-baked cookies, brownies, coffee, or a glass of wine at intermission. Shows run from Tuesday through Saturday at 8:00 p.m., with a Sunday matinee. The theater also presents children's theater performances in the summer; call for a calendar.

Theatre Rhinoceros*

- 2926 16th St. (Mission St.), San Francisco; (415) 861-5079

No, you won't find any rhinoceroses (rhinoceri?) or an other animals from *Wild Kingdom* here; what you will find is a very dedicated, talented and experimental group of actors performing critically-acclaimed plays. Theatre Rhinoceros is the oldest gay and lesbian theater in existence, founded sixteen years ago and priding itself on new and risqué works. Among recent offerings, they premiered *The AIDS Show*, the first of its kind on any stage. The 112-seat main theater presents five shows in its September to June season, with tickets ranging from $12.00 to $18.00. The 57-seat studio has a more open-ended schedule for presenting very new, very unknown productions; tickets here are only $10.00. Call for more information.

Tix Bay Area

- 251 Stockton St. (Geary St.), San Francisco; (415) 433-7827

This is not a theater itself, but rather your way in to many of the area's finest theaters at discounted prices. Tix Bay Area is a booth located in Union Square which sells half-price tickets for shows which have lots of unsold seats on the day of performance. In other words, if you're willing to wait until the last minute (well, last few hours, really), you may be able to save big bucks on a show you want to see that night. These include everything from Broadway tours to smaller, experimental troupes. Half-price tickets have been available for shows at Theater on the Square, Berkeley Rep, American Conservatory Theater, Magic Theater, *Beach Blanket Babylon*, Theater Rhinoceros, "Entree to Murder" mystery-dinner theater, Asian American Theater, and many others. Not to mention dance, opera, and music performances.

A service charge of $1-$3 is added to each ticket; but with top prices in town around $30 and more, you will certainly save a lot. Tix must be purchased in person at the booth, cash only; the booth is open from 11:00 a.m. to 6:00 p.m., Tuesdays through Saturdays (until 7:00 on Friday and Saturday). Any Sunday or Monday shows are offered on Saturday.

In addition to all this, Tix Bay Area is a Ticketmaster outlet, and sells full-price tickets to all the above shows (and more) in advance. They also sell the "Fast Pass," allowing you unlimited travel for a three-day period on all MUNI buses, BART trains, and even cable cars; and the "Culture Pass," giving you discounted admission to many area museums and parks.

TBA's parent non-profit organization, Theater Bay Area, has also just begun a second discount operation, **Tix By Mail**. Designed for Bay Area residents, this is a chance to get similar deals to those offered at the booth—only you can get these in advance, without going downtown. For major commercial shows, these are often preview performances, or balcony seats; still, it's a win-win proposition. You save money, and TBA helps increase audiences for new shows or local ensembles who cannot afford to advertise. It costs you nothing to get on the mailing list, and receive a monthly newsletter highlighting upcoming offers. Just write to:

Tix By Mail
657 Mission St., Suite 402
San Francisco, CA 94105

TBM is a brand-new program, modeled after very successful non-profit mail-order operations in other cities. At the time of this writing, only theaters in San Francisco proper are participating; however—perhaps by the time you read this—the pilot program will have been expanded to include the greater Bay Area and its suburbs.

WALKS AND TOURS

Alcatraz Island

- Golden Gate National Recreation Area; (415) 546-2805

Thinking about a career change to money-laundering? First visit Alcatraz, a former federal penitentiary, and find out just what happens to outlaws—at least, in the days before Whitewater. View the cells that once contained Al Capone, "Machine-Gun" Kelley, and the famous "Bird Man." See the "Control Room," where the baddest thugs were put on ice for a while when they acted up.

Alcatraz was considered "escape-proof," because of the cold, dangerous waters that surround it. Even so, a few celebrated inmates managed to escape before the prison was shut down in 1963; five are still missing. You'll learn all about it on this very complete 2-hour tour.

It all begins with a ferry trip from Pier 41 on Fisherman's Wharf with a slide show and orientation when you arrive on the island. Park rangers then lead you around the prison grounds, and you finish with a self-guided tour through the cell house and museum.

Tours depart every 45 minutes, starting at 9:30 a.m. It pays to reserve ahead of time and to bring good walking shoes; also, to call (415) 546-2700 for advance reservations. The island tour costs nothing, but you have to pay the ferry fare to get there. Ah, they always find a way to get ya. The round-trip (and you *do* want a round-trip) costs $5.75 for adults and $1.25 for kids under 11. For an extra $3, you get an excellent audiocasette tour narrated by former inmates and guards. It's well worth the money if you can swing it—without resorting to any hanky-panky, that is.

Anchor Steam Brewery Tours

- 1705 Mariposa St. (DeHaro St.), San Francisco; (415) 863-8350

Get your brew crew together and take a free tour of one of the most successful independent beer companies in the country. Anchor Steam is a microbrewery, which means they put a lot more time and care into making a lot less beer than anything that ever made Milwaukee famous. The process of turning grains into suds is a rather complex one, and by the time you finish this forty-minute tour, you'll have a newfound appreciation for this potent potable. Oh yes, and there is a complimentary beer tasting at the conclusion.

Tours are given on weekday afternoons by appointment only, and they request that you book at least two weeks in advance; around Christmas and in the summer, the wait can stretch to one month. Fridays tend to fill up early, too—no surprise there.

California Marine Mammal Center

- Marin Headlands, Golden Gate National Recreation Area; (415) 289-7325

This veterinary hospital for injured and stranded wild ocean mammals gives you an unusual chance to observe seals and sea lions up-close. A self-guided tour takes you past displays about the animals. On weekends, volunteer guides lead you around.

You'll hear the animals barking, see them getting therapy, watch them get weighed, see them play with the staff, and perhaps catch them at feeding time. These guys get better treatment than we do at human hospitals! The animal pens and pools are all outside, by the way, so dress accordingly.

Tours are free, but donations are gratefully accepted. CMMC is open

365 days a year, from 10:00 a.m. to 4:00 p.m. daily. In the months between March and August, though, you'll find the largest concentration of animals.

City Guides of San Francisco

• San Francisco Public Library, Civic Center (Larkin and McAllister Sts.), San Francisco; (415) 557-4266

Learn more about the streets of San Francisco, courtesy of the free services of City Guides. You can choose from 18 different walking tours, each focusing on a different area of the city. One walk guides you through the murals in the Mission district. Another focuses on the Victorian architecture of Lafeyette Square. The Cathedral Hill Church tour takes you inside five of the city's oldest churches. The Japantown tour shows you bonsai, flower-arranging, and traditional kimonos. In Pacific Heights, you can view those mansions and consulates up close.

It's an amazing deal, considering that private companies often charge big bucks to tour the same places. Most walks last about an hour, although a few go longer and require some strenuous trudging up and down those hills. Call the City Guides number to get a current schedule and list of departure points.

Federal Reserve Bank Tours

• 101 Market St. (Main St.), San Francisco; (415) 974-3252

Want some free financial advice? Take the hour-long tour offered by the Federal Reserve Bank. You'll start by viewing a video on the Federal Reserve System. Then, you move to the lobby exhibit, full of interactive displays on all things fiscal. One display—a CD-ROM video—lets you play chairman of the Federal Reserve Bank and make monetary policy. Another appoints you president of the United States, and instructs you to set policy on taxation and spending. Not so easy, huh?

After the games, it's time to get down to serious business. The tour goes through the bank itself, showing

you the check clearing department and the cash department, where you'll see federal employees regulating the Bay Area's share of the national cash flow by counting out currency and shredding bills.

This tour won't cost you a single greenback; but you do need to make reservations two weeks in advance. Visits are held each Monday through Thursday at 12:30 p.m. only.

Fort Point National Historic Site

• Marine Drive, San Francisco; (415) 556-1693

Covering 29 acres at the southern end of the Golden Gate Bridge, Fort Point offers spectacular views of both the bridge and the city. Built in 1860, this remains the only fort of its type on the West Coast. It served to defend the Bay from the late 1700s up through World War II.

The thirty-minute tour of the grounds, led by National Park Service Rangers, will show you what life was like for 19th-century soldiers. You'll see cannons, swords, guns, pre-Civil War surgical instruments, jail cells, gunpowder storehouses, and reconstructed soldier's quarters. There is also a short film which tells the history of Fort Point. Be sure to load your Canon (or other camera) for the cannon-loading demonstrations, held twice each day. The fort once held 102 such guns.

Storm the fort Wednesday through Sunday, between 10:00 a.m. and 5:00 p.m. There is no charge for the tour, but for $2.50, history buffs can rent an audio tape that recounts a typical day in the life of a Fort Point soldier during the Civil War.

Glass Elevator Tour

• Various locations; Information, (415) 974-6900

Here's a very different kind of a tour—just right for lazy bums like Mr. C, who don't want to wear down perfectly good shoes trudging up and down hills. This is the eeeeeeasy way to see the city: Just push the button for the top floor, and presto, the city unfolds in front of you.

The San Francisco Convention &

Visitor's Bureau has published a guide to the city's best glass elevators. The Westin St. Francis Hotel in Union Square ranks high, so to speak, with five glass elevators that whiz you up the *outside* of the building to the 32nd floor. From the top, you can see all of downtown, Coit Tower, the Bay Bridge, and the water. Other good rides include the Fairmont Hotel, with a great view of Chinatown and Telegraph Hill; and the Hyatt Regency in the Embarcadero Center.

Call (415) 974-6900 for more information, or stop by the Convention & Visitor's Bureau at 201 Third Street for a free copy of the guide. Tell 'em Mr. Cheap sent you!

Golden Gate Fortune Cookie Company
- 56 Ross Alley (Washington St.), San Francisco; (415) 781-3956

If you believe that some celestial hand determines your fate and then sticks your fortune inside the cookie, you're gonna love this tour. After all, it's been foretold. Watch cookie rounds peeled off of huge griddles and folded into triangles by hand, and then see how those fortunes *really* get inside of cookies.

There are two departments in this company—the, er, obscene fortune group, and the regular fortune team. On either side, the cookies smell delicious, but you'll have to pay $2 to get a sample bag. Well, just think of how many meals you'd have to eat just to get the same number of cookies free. At least the tour itself doesn't cost anything. Open daily from 10:00 a.m. to 8:00 p.m.

Golden Gate Park Tours
- Various locations; Information, (415) 221-1311

On weekends from May through October, you can learn everything you'd ever want to know—plus lots of things you never even thought of—about San Francisco's favorite park. Just take one or more of seven different guided tours, each focusing on the history of a different region of the park. The Strawberry Hill tour takes

you past Stowe Lake and a charming waterfall. The East End tour goes through the fuschia garden and the rhododendron dell. There's also a guided walk through the Japanese Tea Garden (which would otherwise cost you a few bucks), and a tour of all the statues in the park. Tours last about 90 minutes and are absolutely free.

Sponsored by the Department of Parks and Recreation, the tour service also offers occasional walks during the off-season. Call the information line for a current schedule.

Levi-Strauss Factory Tours
- 250 Valencia St. (15th St.), San Francisco; (415) 565-9159

In an old wooden clapboard house in the Mission district, this unique tour shows you how much you've never known about those familiar blue pants. Learn how denim jeans progressed from work clothes for "real men" to high fashion. You'll see mannequins wearing 501s from 1936, and watch classic Levis commercials from the 1950s through the present.

After getting the historical overview, you can tour the cutting and sewing rooms, pass through two laboratories (where, no doubt, they develop all those silly numbers), and see the styling and design department.

Tours are held on Wednesdays only, at 10:30 a.m. and 1:00 p.m., lasting about an hour and a half. Admission is free; sorry, no free samples at the end. It is suggested that you make reservations at least one week in advance.

San Francisco Architectural Heritage Foundation
- 2007 Franklin St. (Jackson St.), San Francisco; (415) 441-3004

This non-profit organization conducts a two-hour walking tour of the Pacific Heights area every Sunday afternoon. The tour focuses on homes and other buildings in this fancy neighborhood which pre-date, and survived, the earthquake of 1906. The tour originates at the Haas-Lilienthal House at the above address, a historic home which you can also tour (see listing under "Museums").

The price of the tour is $5 for adults and $3 for seniors or children under age 12. Meet on the sidewalk outside the Haas-Lilienthal House.

San Francisco By Sea

- Red & White Fleet, Pier 43, Fisherman's Wharf, San Francisco;
- Blue & Gold Fleet, Pier 39, Fisherman's Wharf, San Francisco;
- Golden Gate Ferry, Ferry Building, Embarcadero at Market Street, San Francisco;
- (415) 546-2805 (Red & White); (415) 705-5555 (Blue & Gold)

If you long to view San Francisco from a seal's perspective, prepare to splurge; harbor tours aren't cheap. Mr. C suggests, however, that you can get a relative bargain by taking a *ferry* instead of a cruise.

The Red & White Fleet's commuter ferries, at Pier 43, go to and from both Sausalito and Tiburon, running from early morning through the evening rush hour. Sail past Alcatraz, and see the same city skyline as they see on those pricey harbor tours. The ferry costs $4.50 each way, and if you take the ferry *into* the city, you save parking costs when you arrive. Call for schedule and departure point information.

Cheaper yet, the Blue & Gold Fleet sails to Pier 39 from Oakland and Alameda. You pass right under the Bay Bridge; as you approach, you get great views of Telegraph Hill and Coit Tower. The fare is only $3.50 for adults, $1.50 for kids, and $2.50 for seniors, military, and handicapped persons—including transfers to MUNI buses and free parking in the ferry terminal. Call (510) 522-3300 for schedule information.

Cheapest of all: Take the Golden Gate Ferry's boat to Larkspur, north of Mill Valley. It costs only $2.50 on weekdays, with discounts for kids and seniors, and includes free transfers. Prices go up to $4 for adults on weekends.

If you *must* do a cruise, the Blue & Gold Fleet offers a bay cruise of its own. This is a narrated hour-and-a-

---

MR. CHEAP'S PICKS
Walks and Tours

✔ **Alcatraz Island**—People flock here like birds, and with good reason. A fascinating look at how the bad guys lived, once caught.

✔ **California Marine Mammal Center**—If your kids loved *Free Willy*, you'll love this free chance to get up close and personal with sea mammals.

✔ **City Guides of San Francisco**—Free walking tours of virtually every corner of the city. Sorry, Mr. C can't get you a better deal than that.

✔ **Trips on Tape**—A great way for anti-social or independent types to take a guided tour of The City and beyond, solitary and at any pace. $12.95 gets you a tape that leads you on three days' worth of sightseeing.

---

half of seaborne fun, sailing you under both the Golden Gate Bridge *and* the Bay Bridge, all the way around Alcatraz, and along the waterfront. Adults pay $15, but the fare drops to $7 for kids up to age 18, seniors, and military personnel—not so bad for a leisurely voyage.

Shopper Stopper Discount Shopping Tours

- Various locations; Information, (707) 829-1597

Has Mr. C lost his marbles, recommending a $22 tour? Not really. The $22 you pay to join Shopper Stopper buys you a full-day of on-site instruction in his favorite subject—bargain-hunting. (There is no connection.) It's serious stuff with these folks, too. You'll visit at least six destinations offering incredible prices, and then learn how to get the best deal at each place. You can save hundreds of dollars on future purchases with the wisdom you acquire on this one tour.

The Shopper Stopper bus picks you up at the corner of Market and Grove Streets in downtown San Francisco, on Saturday mornings at 9:40. You'll be taken to visit factories, wholesale distributors, and outlets normally closed to the general public—even places Mr. C can't get you into! Your tour guide teaches you how to buy wholesale, and prepares you for each stop by showing you where to look for the best bargains. On clothing expeditions, you even get tips on color coordinating. As if the proceedings needed any further spicing up, drawings are held for small cash prizes throughout the day. You get a coffee and doughnut break in the morning, and celebrate your purchases with wine and snacks in the afternoon. The tour ends around 4:30 p.m.

So you see, it's a bargain about bargains. Tours vary by season. Best deals are found in January and February, when wholesalers have post-Christmas clearance sales. One recent tour offered a chance to snap up $36 short sets for $4, silk bomber jackets for $19 (normally $69), and hand-knit sweaters for $15. Call for the current schedule of tours. And if there's no distance you won't travel in search of the ultimate treasure, inquire about Shopper Stopper's tours in other cities worldwide.

Takara Sake Tour
• 708 Addison St. (Fourth St.), Berkeley; (510) 540-8250

That's *sake*, as in the Japanese drink. If you're not familiar with these rice and plum wines, or if you think all sake is the same, you should visit the Takara Tasting Room.

Located near the waterfront shopping outlet area in Berkeley, Takara's factory is its California beachhead in the battle to establish sake as a popular drink here in the United States. The company says that its label, Sho Chiku Bai, is the top-selling brand in the U.S. so far. A visit to the factory isn't so much a walking tour as a gustatory one; a tour for the palate through the bigger-than-you-expected world of rice wines.

Upstairs on the second floor, the tasting room is a reproduction of a traditional Japanese ceremonial hall—with a bar. Behind the bar stand hostesses who will tell you about the brew in all its varieties, which you can then sample. Warm sake, chilled sake, milky, sweet, sake for cooking, for dessert—they'll set you up with one small glass after another. And all of this is free!

Now, do be careful. Sake has a slightly higher alcohol content than grape wine (15%). And it is fun to try them all; there really are big differences between the various kinds. Several shots in rapid succession, however, may leave you a bit tipsy. This is probably part of the plan, since they're not giving the stuff away for their health—unless you mean corporate health. Y'see, along with raising sake consciousness in general, the very last bit of the taste tour is a sales pitch. The barmaids just happen to have bottles of each variety right there, in small souvenir sizes, full-size bottles, and by the case. Prices here are no cheaper than at most liquor stores, although you can get a 10% case discount here. So, if you don't mind the hard sell at the end, this can certainly be a fun—and free—diversion on a Berkeley shopping day. Open noon to 6 p.m., seven days.

Transamerica Tower
• 600 Montgomery St. (Washington St.), San Francisco; (415) 983-4000

"The Pyramid," as everyone knows it, has become perhaps one of the most famous skyscraper outlines in the world. Its 48 stories taper to a sharp point some 850 feet off the ground, in an attractive white quartz exterior. But enough about the outside—it's what is *inside* that Mr. C wants to tell you about.

The 27th floor has an observatory which is one of the great places to look out at The City itself. Totally enclosed, this is basically one fabulous picture window. The view is to the north, looking out to North Beach, the Coit Tower, the Bay, Alcatraz Island, and the green hills of Marin County. Between these landmarks, and the antlike movement of cars and people below, the view is endlessly fascinating. You can even get some great camera shots through the glass (Mr. C has done so).

The observatory is free and open to the public during business hours: Monday to Friday, from 8:30 a.m. to 4:30 p.m., except holidays. Back downstairs, the Transamerica lobby offers a small art gallery, with a few hand-picked works by some major international artists and sculptors; and nearby, along the same block, the Transamerica Redwood Park is an oasis of trees and grass in the middle of downtown. It too is open to the public, and is the site of free lunchtime concerts on Fridays from May through September.

Trips on Tape
* 484 Lake Park Ave., Suite 255, Oakland; (510) 653-2553

Here's a unique way to be guided around San Francisco's nooks and crannies. For a mere $12.95, this cassette series leads you on 10 mini-tours of sights both famous and obscure. Even if you think you know the city inside and out, this tape will probably reveal fascinating new facts to you. On various jaunts, you'll find a secret walk hiding actual Gold Rush cottages; discover an artistic tribute to a white poodle near Telegraph Hill; see hang gliders jumping off a cliff; and of course, all of the more famous tourist attractions.

It takes about three days to do everything on the tape—but, being on your own, you can easily pick and choose. Worried about having to hoof it all over town? Relax. The tour makes use of ferries, cable cars, and buses; there's even a driving tour of the wine country.

In fact, if you do decide to venture farther out, Trips on Tape also offers cassettes for Napa Valley, Sonoma Valley, and the Monterey Peninsula. All tapes come with directions and easy mini-maps. The address and phone number above is for the company's office, which you should contact for more details.

RESTAURANTS

For the dining chapters of the book (which many readers consider to be its main course), Mr. C decided not to dig in alphabetically—but rather by geographical area. After all, when you're hungry, you want to eat *now*—no matter how appetizing some place across town may sound. The city has been divided into very broad sections, so that you can just pick up the book and find the cheap choices in your area. Or, the area where you're going to be . . . use this section with the "Entertainment" chapters to plan out a whole day or night on the town!

All of the restaurants in this book are places where you can eat dinner for around $10 per person, not including tax and tip. Lunch prices, of course, can be even lower. Even so, all of these eateries serve filling meals of "real" food, not phony fast food junk.

That $10 figure also does not include alcohol, which is going to be expensive just about anywhere. In fact, many of these places can afford to serve good, cheap food *because* they make their money on the drinks. If you're really tight on cash, you can always nurse one beer or an overpriced soda, eat well, and still come out ahead on the deal.

And check out Mr. Cheap's special "Tip-Free" list for establishments where you can safely save an extra buck or two in that department. These are also noted withan asterisk wherever their full write-ups appear in each chapter. Of course, many of the restaurants in this book offer take-out food, another way to save dough.

Enjoy!

MR. CHEAP'S PICKS
TIP-FREE RESTAURANTS

Yes, the truly budget-conscious can even save an extra buck or two by frequenting some of these restaurants. Mr. C is not suggesting that you sneak out and stiff your waiter; these are places which are self-service or take-out establishments. Here's to 'em.

Berkeley
Bongo Burger, 257
Zona Rosa, 267

Castro
Slider's Diner, 280

Downtown San Francisco
The Bagel, 239
Omar's Café, 246
Slider's Diner, 247

Fisherman's Wharf/Embarcadero
Leon's Bar-B-Q, 299
Omar's Café, 304
Pier 1 Deli, 304

Haight
Taqueria Balazo, 270
Zona Rosa, 271

Mission
Burger Joint, 274

Potrero Hill
Rustico, 278

Oakland
Ike's Rotisserie, 260

Pacific Heights
Amerasian Café, 282
Chestnut Café, 284

Richmond
Eats, 316

SoMa
Brain Wash Café and
Laundromat, 308
Café 180, 309
Java House, 311

DOWNTOWN
including Civic Center and Polk Gulch

The Bagel*
- 1300 Polk St. (Bush St.), San
  Francisco; (415) 441-2212

Walking into the Bagel sorta reminds
Mr. C of a high school cafeteria—
with long, linoleum-topped tables
and brightly colored plastic trays. Unlike school, however, they have
plenty of good, old-style delicatessen
foods to choose from, including
knishes, blintzes, gefilte fish, and
more. Despite the name, the bagels
here are nothing to write home to
New York about, although they aren't
bad.

Other choices will do you far better, though; and the prices are fantastic. Have a nice bowl of chicken
broth with matzo balls for $2.65
($1.45 for a cup); split pea soup is
$1.30 a cup and $2.10 for a bowl. If
you're looking for something a little
more substantial, try a plate of Hun-
garian goulash for $6.35, or roast
chicken for $5.20. Sandwiches fly
out of here (good take-out joint, of
course), especially hot pastrami
($4.40), meat loaf ($3.85), and the
Reuben ($5.40). The standard, if un-
spectacular, deli desserts are offered:
Cheesecake for $1.45, German choco-
late cake for $1.60.

The Bagel has joined the fresh-
squeezed juice craze, bringing not
just the juices but the juice bar right
into the store. Have a glass of OJ
squeezed before your very eyes—the
sweetest, most delicious taste you
can ever experience. These are not exactly cheap—$1.69 for a regular-size
glass, $2.49 for a large—but worth
every penny.

Brother Juniper's Restaurant
- 1065 Sutter St. (Hyde St.), San
  Francisco; (415) 771-8929

Elsewhere in this book, Mr. C has
told you about many thrift shops
benefitting charitable organizations—
where you can save money on
clothes and do some good at the
same time. Well, here's a *restaurant*
where "doing good" meets good
food. All proceeds from Brother Juni·
per's Restaurant benefit the Raphael
House Family Shelter. The shelter is
also supported by the Raphael House
Thrift Shop (see listing under "Shopping: Used Clothing"); all three are
housed in the same Sutter Street
building.

Brother Juniper's Restaurant
serves up delicious breakfast and
lunch dishes. Their hearty eye-openers include the "Decent Breakfast,"
three scrambled eggs with chopped
sausage, sauteed mushrooms, green
onions, tomatoes, and melted cheese,
plus toast, all for just $5.65. For 20¢
more, try the "Spicy Decent Breakfast," in which hot Creole sausage is
substituted. Not only can you get
corned beef hash with an egg and
toast for $5.25, but why not try the
tofu hash: chopped tofu, mushrooms
and green onions sauteed and hashed
with potatoes, with grilled tomatoes
on top, and served with an egg and
toast for $5.35. And, don't miss the
"Benedict Over-Easy" or the yummy
cheese blintzes.

Humbler taste buds will appreciate
BJ's "Simple Breakfasts." Despite
the modest moniker, these offerings
are anything but plain. The French
toast is wonderful, made from the
kitchen's own homemade bread; not
many places serve it up with
whipped butter and real maple syrup,
but this one does—for just $4.25.
The "Abbot's Delight" omelette is
filled with avocado, tomatoes, scallions, sprouts, provolone, and cheddar cheese for $5.65. Plus homemade

pastries including cranberry and bran muffins, banana nut bread, poppyseed cake, and more.

The lunch menu consists mostly of sandwiches, all made on wondrous fresh-baked breads and served with homemade potato salad. Try the "Friar Tuck" ($5.45), with bacon, tuna, avocado, Swiss, and sprouts, on struan bread. All sandwiches are available in half sizes, and for just $4.95 you can get a half-sandwich with soup and a fresh salad. Several homemade soups cost about a dollar for a cup and about two dollars for a bowl. Of course, your lunch wouldn't be complete without sampling one of their desserts, also baked fresh on the premises: Hollywood cheesecake ($2.50), marble cheesecake ($3.25), or Dutch chocolate cake ($1.90).

What's more, all of these lunches are available for take-out. In fact, they have a catering service, which can prepare sandwich trays, salad trays, soups, or pastry and dessert trays. It's a miracle! Brother Juniper's is open for breakfast Monday through Friday from 7 a.m. to 12 noon, and Saturday from 7 a.m. to 12:30 p.m.; and for lunch Monday through Friday from 11:30 a.m. to 2 p.m. only.

Café Claude
* 7 Claude Lane (Bush St.), San Francisco; (415) 392-3505

Down a narrow alley between Bush and Sutter (near Kearny, one of those "extra" streets), this bistro is indeed *trés Francais*. Casual, intimate, and immensely popular with those in-the-know, Café Claude attracts an always-interesting crowd of artsy, sophisticated yupsters and international types. Everyone on the waitstaff seems to be authentically French, judging by their accents, which are delightful. They're also friendly, which is less true-to-form; a pleasant surprise.

You can sit at one of the chic umbrella patio tables which flank the doorway, or press your way up a few steps into the restaurant, which does a brisk business at breakfast, lunch,

dinner, and throughout the evening. But then, even the folks who are waiting for tables don't seem to mind; grab yourself a Pernod and mix in. Two cozy, high-ceilinged rooms include a bar area, exposed beams, and of course, French posters on the walls. If you're in a romantic mood, try for one of the front tables; these are nestled into corners with floor-to-ceiling glass windows which look out over the street. A private nook amidst the din.

Mr. C's resident Francophile comes here often, usually for the lovingly prepared baguette sandwiches. These are filled to overflowing with various meats, plus cornichons, olives, red cabbage, and vinaigrette. Try the smoked chicken baguette, so tender it melts in your mouth. Other varieties include sausage, prosciutto (hey waitaminnit, that's not French), paté (that's more like it), and roast beef. All are priced from $5.50 to $6.25 each. Daily specials get fancier, like duck *rillete*, served with a side salad for $7.25.

Salad entrees are great here too, by the way, like the baked goat cheese salad ($5.50). Add a bowl of onion soup *au gratin* for $4.00. Grilled sandwiches are a French bistro trademark; Mr. C loved his *croque monsieur*, French bread filled with ham and gruyére cheese, then grilled up golden brown. The *croque madame* adds a yummy cheese soufflé topping, and both are around $7.00. At dinner, the menu features such creations as "Merquez sausage with braised narissa vegetables over couscous," a tasty treat for a *trés reasonable* $8.75.

Of course, it wouldn't be Paris without desserts. Chocoate mousse and apple tart are among the usual standouts, along with daily specials like lemon poppyseed pound cake topped with fresh cream, strawberries and blackberries—all for $4.00. Coffee comes served in elegant light blue, gold-rimmed cups and saucers.

So, does Café Claude really belong in Mr. Cheap's book? Well, it certainly does if you're looking for something that is fancier than, say, another taco stand—yet still affordable. Great for a special occasion, or just some exotic fun on a budget.

As if the place needed any more reason to pack people in, there is live jazz several evenings a week (see listing under "Entertainment—Music"). More interesting still, many of the furnishings around the two rooms were shipped piece by piece from France. Café Claude closes at 10:00 on weeknights, an hour later on weekends, and all day Sunday.

Caffé Delle Stelle

- 330 Gough St. (Fell St.), San Francisco; (415) 252-1110

Whether you have important business at City Hall or you're going to hear a concert at Symphony Hall, Caffé Delle Stelle is just steps away with hearty plates of pasta and more. The menu is simple and elegant, yet they manage to throw in a few surprises, all at sensible prices; that makes it a "star" in Mr. C's book.

Appetizers include those oh-so-chic *bruschetta*, garlic toasts topped with fresh tomatoes and basil, for $4.50; and *melanzane e scamorza*, roasted eggplant, smoked mozzarella, and fresh basil, for $6. They also have fresh salads, including *insalata mista*, your basic baby greens, for $4, and *della stella*, with romaine, baby greens, gorgonzola, and walnuts, for $5.

Among the many interesting entrees here are pumpkin and ricotta manicotti cooked with sage in butter ($8.50); *papardelle*, wide ribbons of pasta with lamb, rosemary, onions, and red wine ($8.50); *rustica*, "small ear" pasta with potatoes, sage, fontina cheese, pancetta, and truffle oil ($8.50); and *maile al cartoccio*, pork loin, tomatoes, and herbs cooked—yes—in parchment paper ($10).

Caffé Delle Stelle is open for lunch and dinner from 11 a.m. to 10 p.m., Mondays through Saturdays.

California Culinary Academy

- 625 Polk St. (Turk St.), San Francisco; (415) 771-3500

Only in Mr. Cheap's wildest dreams,

MR. CHEAP'S PICKS
Civic Center

✔ **Caffé Delle Stelle**—Whether you have a big meeting at City Hall or a special date at Symphony Hall, come here for hearty Italian fare—before or after.

✔ **California Culinary Academy**—A gourmet dinner for $9.95? Believe it. Two different restaurants at this school feature the outstanding chefs of tomorrow.

---

you might think, could he find a gourmet dinner for ten bucks. Ah, but it's really possible here at the CCA, one of the country's premier training schools for fine cooking. The Academy Grill Buffet, served Monday through Thursday evenings from 6:00-9:00 p.m., costs $9.95 per person—and it's just one of the several inexpensive gourmet dining options offered by the academy.

Located near the Civic Center, this school is the setting for the successful PBS television show, "Cooking at the Academy"; but these are no TV dinners. The students are supervised by a faculty of chefs from such touted establishments as Stars, Tassajara Bakery, and the Ritz-Carlton Hotel; they're completing a two-year degree program which will land them in similarly high-falutin' restaurants. Yet, you can dine on this classy food for a fraction of what it would cost anywhere else.

There are actually two different restaurants at the CCA. The informal Academy Grill is home to the above-mentioned buffet, where you can choose from a variety of hot and cold items, carved meats, appetizers, and desserts—all for $9.95 . Friday evenings switch to a prime rib buffet

($11.95 per person); luncheons, with inexpensive menu service, are also offered each weekday from 11:30 a.m. to 1:45 p.m. These are the only meals for which no reservations are necessary.

The larger, fancier Careme Room specializes in continental cuisine, with a creative touch. You may find entrees such as grilled loin of swordfish, served with pineapple salsa and plaintain; dry-aged New York steak with tamarind relish; and a spicy orange grilled chicken breast, served with cinnamon couscous and tomatillo guacamole. A three-course meal (appetizer, entree, and dessert) costs $12.95 at lunch and $17.95 at dinner—except on Thursday and Friday evenings, when a buffet dinner is served and the price jumps up to $26.95. An interesting feature of the Careme Room is its glassed-in kitchen, allowing you to watch the master chefs in action.

These prices do not include tax, tip and drinks (both rooms feature a full bar); still, when you consider how much money you're saving on such exquisite food, the CCA remains a fantastic bargain—a relatively inexpensive splurge for that special occasion. There is no dress code, although men tend to wear jackets for the Careme Room.

Reservations *are* required for the Careme; they suggest you try to reserve a week or so in advance. Both restaurants are closed on Saturdays and Sundays. And remember, this is a school; they close for a week or more at spring break, major holidays, and the like. Call the number above and ask for extension 233 to confirm dates and make reservations.

California Pizza & Italian Restaurant
• 1534 California St. (Larkin St.), San Francisco; (415) 775-2525
At CP & I, you'll find a variety of great Italian dinners, including seafood and veal entrees—all, amazingly, under $10. Spaghetti with marinara or alfredo sauce is just $5.75, ravioli with meat sauce is

$6.75 ($1 more with meatballs), and baked lasagna or canneloni is $7.75. Pasta with red or white clam sauce is just $8, same for eggplant parmagiana. All pasta dishes come with bread and a garden salad. Those seafood and veal dishes include dishes like fried prawns, veal scallopini, and veal cutlet Milanese, all priced at $9.65. And all seafood, meat, and poultry entrees come with pasta, bread, and salad, to boot.

California Pizza is most famous, of course, for its pies, which have even won local "best pizza" contests. They are prepared with super-fresh ingredients, like homemade spiced tomato sauce and whole milk mozzarella. Pizzas come in four sizes, starting with the basic small cheese pie for $5.60. Toppings are an additional $1.35 for the first, and about a dollar thereafter. Choose from over twenty such toppings, including surprising stuff like pesto sauce, feta cheese, artichokes, zucchini, sweet corn, jalapeños, and spinach—along with the more traditional pepperoni, mushrooms, and the like. Special combinations are suggested for the creatively-impaired.

They also have a great selection of submarine sandwiches, as well as salads, soups, and desserts. Anything on the menu can be delivered, including their somewhat limited selection of domestic and imported beers and house wines. California Pizza & Italian Restaurant is open from 11 a.m. to 1 a.m., seven days a week.

California Pizza Kitchen
• 438 Geary St. (Powell St.), San Francisco; (415) 563-8911
Not to be confused with the California Pizza and Italian Restaurant in Nob Hill (see listing above), this fast-growing national chain has a lot more to offer than just pizza. The menu ranges from pies to things like potato-leek soup, fresh pastas, lasagna, and Thai chicken. Don't get Mr. C wrong—the pizza's okay, too, especially the rosemary-chicken-potato pie made with white wine and lemon for $8.50 (plenty here for two to

share), and the southwestern burrito pie, topped with lime, black beans, mild chilies, cheddar cheese, tomatillo salsa, sour cream, and white sweet onions (also $8.50). All pies are available without cheese if you wish, and are baked on either traditional or honey-wheat doughs. CPK also makes a point of using no MSG, which is A-OK with Mr. C.

Other entrees include angel hair pasta, penne, or spaghetti, topped with tomato-herb sauce for $5.95, and spinach fettuccine with chicken, tri-color peppers, red onion, and cilantro in a tequila-lime sauce for $8.95. It's a large platter. Desserts are a bit pricey, in the unlikely event that you have room; try sharing a tiramisu ($4.50), Myers' Rum chocolate pecan pie ($3.95), apple crisp ($3.95), or fruit sorbet ($3.50).

Given its Union Square/Theater District location, of course, California Pizza Kitchen makes a good place to stop in after the show for a late-evening nibble—or, just skip the pizza and head straight for those desserts.

Dottie's True Blue Café
- 522 Jones St. (O'Farrell St.), San Francisco; (415) 885-2767

With its checked curtains, counter-and-tables, and fantastic (bottomless) coffee, Dottie's True Blue Café is true to anyone's idea of a classic country breakfast spot—and right in the heart of downtown! Morning specials include "The True Blue Plate," offering two eggs any style with bacon, ham or sausage; home fries; toast or English muffin; and juice, all for $5.95. Can't beat it. "The Southwestern" is a blend of andouille sausage, mushrooms, onions, peppers, and jack cheese in a pancake-style omelette—with home fries, salsa, and tortilla—for $6.75; and "The Alabama Summer," Dottie's pancakes or French toast topped with fresh fruit salad, is $5.75.

Sound like too much, too early? Don't despair, there are plenty of smaller dishes to fill you more simply. Get two eggs with home fries

and toast for $3.75, or an omelette with your choice of filling for $5.25. For an even smaller nibble, try something really different: a hunk of grilled chili-cheddar cornbread with jalapeño jelly ($1.75). Talk about eye-openers. Of course, there are the more standard toasted bagels ($1.25), muffins and scones ($1.50). And finally, if you're the type who can't even muster the energy to chew in the morning, try a fresh fruit smoothie for $3.50 or a low-fat chocolate and banana shake, also $3.50. There's truly something for everyone here at Dottie's.

Lunch is served on weekdays only, from 11:30 a.m. to 2 p.m. This menu includes mostly burgers, sandwiches, and such, priced at $5.75 and up. Try the veggie burgers, or a grilled chicken sandwich on toast with a side order of pasta and pesto. Chili and cornbread is a hearty snack, for just $3.95. Oh, and that coffee is a special house blend of French roast made with a touch of cinnamon. You'll definitely want a refill. Dottie's is open daily from 7:30 a.m. to 2 p.m.

The First Light Café
- 1475 Polk St. (California St.), San Francisco; (415) 928-7566

The First Light Café has a wonderful selection of appetizers, soups, and entrees. Their dinner menu is an ever-changing one, so that you never know what may be offered on any given night. What you do know is that it will be good, creative, and well-priced.

If you like, begin with a soup. Past offerings have included Louisiana gumbo "ya ya" with herb sausage and chicken; Irish stew with lamb meat, cabbage, carrots, and new potatoes; and curried tomato bisque. A small bowl of these costs $3.75, and a large bowl is $6—pricey for soup, perhaps, but these are almost meals in themselves. Salads are generally $4.75 to $5.75, and may include Italian antipasto or a Middle Eastern combo with eggplant, cous-cous, hummus, and pickled vegetables tossed over lettuce.

If you haven't filled up on these starters, dive into one of their exciting entrees. Any night may offer braised shank of lamb ($8.75), chicken scaloppini ($7.75), fettucini in garlic cream sauce with roasted bay scallops ($7.75), red snapper sauteed with Syrian pine nut rice and vegetable knödel ($9.25), or spicy lemon tofu ($6.75). As you can see, this menu scours the globe for a diversity of tastes.

Friday night dinners, now, are something altogether different. It's a prix-fixe meal for just $9.50; you get appetizer, soup, and an entree, served with a basket of homemade breads. This menu changes as well. Some of the recent offerings have included such appetizers as sesame beef meatballs with plum fruit sauce, or vegetarian dumplings with tofu; soups like peanut-chicken chowder with jalapeños, or coconut cream with mushrooms, red curry, and tofu; and entrees like lamb moussaka with Sicilian garlic flan and roasted onions, spicy barbecued Indian chicken with rice pilaf and pineapple kumaki, or vegetarian cauliflower and eggplant curry with black mustard seeds.

Of course, with all these mouthwatering dinner choices, it's easy to forget that First Light also has a substantial breakfast and lunch menu. Breakfast items are served all day and include the famed puff pancake ($3.95), omelettes cooked in white wine and herbs with your choice of ingredients ($5.50), and "A Toast to the French," grilled brioche pastry with sour cream, orange, and nutmeg batter ($2.95). Lunchtime customers rave about the marinated hamburgers ($3.90 to $5.50) and some 25 different combination sandwiches including "Pulitzer's Poultry," an herb chicken filet with tomato and cheese ($5.50), "Painter's Palette," grilled red, green, and yellow peppers with cheese ($5), "Francesca's Fantasy," grilled eggplant with green and red peppers, tomato, and cheese ($5.50), and "Granny's Grill," grilled apple, onion, and cheese ($5). All of First Light's breads and muffins are baked on the premises and their soups are homemade. Mmmmm.

The First Light Café is open Monday through Friday from 6:30 a.m. to 10 p.m., and on Saturday and Sunday from 8 a.m. to 10 p.m.

The Fruit Gallery

- 301 Kearny St. (Bush St.), San Francisco; (415) 362-2216

Despite the name, this is a restaurant, and it's not even limited to produce. In fact, they serve all kinds of meat and vegetarian dishes at super-cheap prices.

The minute you walk into the Fruit Gallery, you'll know you found a good place; it smells wonderful in here. What's cooking? Things like jambalaya made with chicken, prawns, vegetables, and ham, all for a mere $7.65; chicken breast with mango-papaya salsa, served with rice and sauteed vegetables, just $8.75; and tomato and basil fettucine for $6.55.

If you're not hungry enough for a full dinner, FG has a fine assortment of lighter, but no less creative fare. Salad choices, mostly $5-$7, include Chinese chicken salad, Caesar salad, pasta salad with fresh vegetables, and winter spinach salad. Their sandwiches are really great deals—especially since most come with a house salad on the side. You can get a vegetarian sandwich or a walnut tuna sandwich, each on nine-grain bread, for just $5.80. Other offerings include grilled eggplant on sourdough, and the ever-popular tuna melt (each $6.35). And a variety of quesadillas, quiches, and 1/3-pound burgers (whether beef, turkey, or veggie) each go for around six dollars, and all are served with a house salad on the side.

The Fruit Gallery also has "box" breakfasts available for take-out. These include biscuits, scones, breakfast burritos, and scrambled eggs, priced between $2 to $4 each. You can have them delivered, too, for another dollar or so. Call them for more info about delivery areas and charges. The Fruit Gallery is open from 7 a.m.

to 9 p.m., weekdays only; they close at 3 p.m. on Fridays.

The Holding Co. Bar and Grill

- Two Embarcadero Center, Promenade Level, San Francisco; (415) 986-0797

A popular Financial District hangout, the Holding Co. Bar and Grill has a large and loyal following. This is due not only to its extensive bar and beer selection, but also to the creative continental cuisine offered—dishes such as grilled pork tenderloin, Irish lamb stew, jambalaya, and chicken dijonaise. Unfortunately, these dishes aren't particularly cheap. But Mr. C has another reason for including this yuppie haven.

The real bargain here is their happy hour, which takes place every weekday afternoon from 5:00 until the food runs out (usually around 6:30). Holding Co. features one of The City's best hot and cold buffets. It's not vast—two or three choices—but the food is delicious and plentiful. On Mr. C's visit, they had fresh veggies and creamy dip; a warm sausage casserole with a spicy sauce on the side; and a platter of fresh fruit, cheese and crackers. All of this, of course, is free; nurse an overpriced soda, or reasonably priced brew along, and you'll make out like a bandit. Beer specials that day included Anchor Steam and Pete's Wicked Ale, each $3.50 a pint. And, crowded as it can become, the atmosphere remains comfortable and friendly.

And for another good happy hour nibble in this neighborhood, try **Schroeder's** at 234 Front Street (telephone 421-4778). This old-time tavern, not ordinarily a cheap spot, offers a Friday after-work hot buffet of meatballs, roast duck, and a few other treats. Play your (business?) cards right, and for the price of a few drinks, you can get a free dinner out of a good ol' fashioned pub crawl.

Johnny Wok

- 1237 Polk St. (Bush St.), San Francisco; (415) 928-6888

In the area informally known as Polk Gulch, Johnny Wok is well-known for its good food at low prices. If you're looking for a really cheap meal, the lunch specials are particularly hard to beat. Each lunch is served with soup, fried won tons, steamed rice, fresh fruit, and your choice of entree, including eggplant in hot and sour garlic sauce ($3.95), almond or cashew chicken ($4.25), beef with fresh broccoli ($4.50), prawns with lobster sauce ($4.95), and many others.

Not that you'd be disappointed at dinner, either. It's hard to know where to begin on a menu with, literally, hundreds of dishes to choose from. Good ol' sweet and sour pork, for instance, comes in not one, but two versions: There's the original, authentic preparation, in which deep-fried sliced pork is sauteed in a rice wine/vinegar sauce; and then you have "Sweet and Sour Pork a la U.S.," the kind you'll recognize, made with bell peppers, carrots, pineapple, and onion, in the familiar red sauce. Both are just $5.95.

Their vast selection of appetizers includes bon-bon chicken, strips of white meat served with a spicy raw garlic and peanut butter dressing ($4.95); pot stickers ($4.50 for a half-dozen), crispy batter fried prawns ($5.75), and vegetarian egg rolls ($3.50). Soup choices are far from ordinary, with things like shark fin soup ($6.50), seafood velvet soup ($5.25), and minced beef soup ($4.50).

The only dishes that get somewhat more expensive are those with seafood, and even these are fairly reasonable: Hunan exotic prawns are $9.95, and whole rock cod, prepared four different ways, goes for $11.95. Johnny Wok is open seven days a week.

Miz Brown's

- 1356 Polk St. (Pine St.), San Francisco; (415) 771-4221
- 2565 Mission St. (21st St.), San Francisco; (415) 648-6070
- 731 Clement St. (Seventh Ave.), San Francisco; (415) 752-5017

- 3401 California St. (Laurel Village), San Francisco; (415) 752-2039

Miz Brown's is a good ol' fashioned coffee shop, the kind your parents probably took you to—around the age when chicken-in-a-basket and a chocolate milkshake was your idea of a good meal. Now you can continue the tradition, or just satisfy your own comfort food needs, fast and cheap.

Yes, they have fried chicken; it's batter-dipped, crispy, and greasy, served with a pot of honey and an order of soggy fries, all for $6.25. Daily specials, in fact, may consist of combinations like fried chicken and spaghetti with meat sauce for $7.30— good luck finishing. Other dinners include things like chicken fried steak ($5.75) or fish and chips ($6.45), served with a side salad or cup of soup.

The soups are homemade, by the way, and quite tasty. These range from clam chowder to matzoh ball, different choices daily, all $2.75 a bowl or $1.50 a cup. Salads are also available in two sizes, like a chef's salad for $4.60 or $5.65. Sandwiches start with deli-style basics, all under $5, and go up to double deckers (BLT with turkey and fries, $6.25). Burgers start at $3.45, in ten combinations like "mild green chili and Monterey jack" ($5.65). All of these come with French fries, cole slaw, or potato salad.

MB's also has a children's menu. The kiddies will love a "Tiny Tot" burger and fries; you'll love the price, $1.75. And they've recently added a menu of Mexican dishes, such as two tacos (chicken or beef) with rice and beans for $5.25. (Honestly, though, would you go to a place like this for Tex-Mex when there are so many places around the city where you can get the real thing?)

Of course, you have to save room for dessert; hope you like to eat heavy. All the fountain classics are here, from cherry and vanilla cokes to milk shakes and malteds to something called an "Orange Freeze" ($3.15), made with OJ and orange

sherbet. That's more like it. Other desserts include freshly baked pies and homemade rice pudding.

Breakfasts are big here too. The Country Breakfast special will set you up for anything: two eggs, two large pancakes, plus bacon or sausage, all for $6.15. For more dainty appetites, two eggs any style with hash browns and toast are $3.75. Natural, light egg substitutes are available for most orders. Oh, and to return to that nostalgia theme, they have those mini-boxes of cold cereal stacked up on shelves—not to mention individual juke boxes in each booth.

Service is friendly, and the atmosphere is super-casual. One final note: The branch on Clement offers beer and wine, while the Mission Street outpost features a full bar. The others do not serve any liquor. Open well into the evening.

Omar's Café*

- 1 Daniel Burnham Ct. (Post St. at Van Ness Ave.), San Francisco; (415) 673-2423
- Pier 1 Ferry Building (Embarcadero), San Francisco; (415) 834-1173

A fine breakfast and lunch spot, Omar's Café bills itself as "an oasis in a desert of fast food." With their menu of inexpensive deli sandwiches and Middle Eastern specialties, convenient for folks on the run or pausing for a nibble, they may well be right. The fare is certainly more interesting than the usual burger and fries; hitch up your camel and find out.

Everything on the menu is priced under five bucks—good deal already—including deli sandwiches, like a turkey and bacon club or a New York pastrami and Swiss, each $4.95. Add a side order of fresh salad to any of these selections for just 95¢. You can also get a half-sandwich with soup for that same $4.95.

Middle Eastern specialties include a variety of falafel dishes, such as falafel with eggplant, and the rather unusual falafel burrito; both are $4.95, as is a hearty Greek salad with feta cheese. A tabouleh and hummus sandwich goes for $4.75, and a meza plate—a sort of Mediterranean pu-pu platter—is $4.95.

Omar's has a small breakfast menu as well: The big item is filled croissants. Get one with scrambled eggs for $2.95, with ham and cheese for $4.50, or with pastrami, eggs, and cheese for $4.75. As mentioned above, these are real-ingredient alternatives to those attempts at breakfast sandwiches cranked out by fast-food McChains. Omar's also serves up bagels with cream cheese for $1.75, along with an assortment of pastries and other quick grabs. Kind of a downer: The Embarcadero branch is tucked inside a foyer, open only on the side facing the parking lot. A rather unfortunate fate for a waterfront location.

Slider's Diner*

- 1204 Sutter St. (Polk St.), San Francisco; (415) 885-3288
- 449 Castro St. (Market St.), San Francisco; (415) 431-3288

Slide into this fun and funky little diner, where you can get wonderful burgers at equally wonderful prices. What makes their burgers so wonderful? Well, they have an in-house butcher, so beef patties are ground fresh daily using only 100% USDA choice chuck. Order your burger at the counter; when it arrives, dress it however you please at the self-serve condiment bar. A plain six-ounce burger is $3.25, while an eight-ouncer is $3.75. You can add cheese for an extra quarter; they also have some special combinations like bacon cheese ($4.75), avocado cheese ($4.95), and chili cheese ($5.50).

Of course, you don't *have* to be a burger fan to find something you like here, though it helps. You can also get fried chicken, with fries and a salad, for $4.95. There are sandwiches, too, like rib-eye steak with grilled onions and mushrooms ($5.25) and Italian chicken with grilled onions and peppers ($4.95), along with old faves like grilled cheese. Another big item here is hot

---

MR. CHEAP'S PICKS
Downtown

- ✔ **The Fruit Gallery**—Who says cheap food can't be healthy? More than just fruit, this downtown eatery has a menu full of nutritious vegetarian and meat dishes.
- ✔ **The Holding Co. Bar and Grill**—A favorite hangout for the downtown office crowd, especially during the happy hour buffet—one of the best around.
- ✔ **The Square**—As in Union. Cheap and filling Chinese food, within steps of the theater district. Plus live piano music at no charge.
- ✔ **Sushi Bune**—Cheap sushi? Well, it's *moderately* priced, done to perfection, and close to Union Square. Good enough.

---

dogs; a plain 1/4-lb. dog is $2.95. Add cheese for $3.25, and chili for $3.95. For something a little different, try a Louisiana link—hot stuff—for $2.95. A side order of fries is $1.50, a bit pricey; but they're hot, golden, and plentiful. Other side orders include soups, salads, chili, and Buffalo wings. Of course, it wouldn't be a diner if it didn't have floats and shakes! When it comes to diner atmosphere, though, Slider's offers plenty of modern-day style. Chrome counters, black and white tile floors, and black vinyl stools clash with MTV videos on the built-in television screens. Call it "neo-diner."

Spuntino

- 524 Van Ness Ave. (McAllister St.), San Francisco; (415) 861-7772

Conveniently located near City Hall, the Museum of Modern Art, Symphony Hall, and more, Spuntino is a great place to fulfill your dining desires on the way to or from tending to your artistic desires. Whether you're looking for a heaping plate of pasta, a quick sandwich, or a little *dolci,* you'll find it at Spuntino.

Hearty pasta dishes (pastas are made fresh right here), are $7 to $10, depending on ingredients. Specialties include rigatone with Italian sausage, tomato sauce, onions, and saffron ($7.95), fettucini al pesto ($8.95), and linguine with seafood, garlic, olive oil, hot pepper, and parsley ($9.95). They also bake up a variety of thin-crust pizzas in their wood fire oven. Try the "Quattro Stagione" pizza with proscuitto, mushrooms, arugula, olives, tomato sauce, and mozzarella for $8.50; or "Salsiccia" with sausage and hot salami for $8.25.

Spuntino also offers panini, those neatly grilled Italian sandwiches—including the "Spuntino" with roasted chicken, roasted peppers, watercress, and caper-mayonnaise on toscano bread ($6.95). Others include the "Tacchino," filled with smoked turkey, Swiss cheese, lettuce, tomato, onion, and mayonnaise on a baguette (also $6.95) and "Tasca Vegetariana" with baked eggplant, smoked mozzarella, mushrooms, tomato, and garlic on pizza bread ($7.25). All panini are served with a green salad.

Speaking of which, folks looking for a light meal shouldn't miss Spuntino's selection of soups and salads. Try a cold pasta salad for $4.95, or a fresh, leafy spinach salad for $5.50. Or, go for a combination of soup, salad, and housebaked bread—a light and healthy repaste—for $5.25.

Whatever you decide on, don't skip dessert! These are as reasonably priced as they are sinfully decadent. A wedge of cheesecake, with fruit on top, is $2.95; and tiramisu is just $3.95. Other treats include pecan torte ($2.95) and chocolate truffle cake ($3.95). These may just be meals in themselves!

The Square Bar and Restaurant

- 400 Geary St. (Mason St.), 2nd Floor, San Francisco; (415) 776-8699

Looking for something quick and inexpensive on your way to the theater? The Square is conveniently located right in the middle of the downtown theater district. It can be difficult to find good low-priced meals this close to all the action. And, even if you don't have tickets to the latest smash hit, give this place a try anyway. The design, with its art deco decor, is quite elegant; adding to the refined atmosphere is The Square's piano bar, where someone tickles the ivories every Tuesday through Saturday from 9:30 p.m. until 2:00 in the morning. No extra charge for the live music.

The menu leans toward the Oriental, though not exclusively. Appetizers include pot stickers and egg rolls, but also fried calamari as well. There is a good selection of soups, such as spinach with bean curd, hot and sour, and won ton.

They have what seems like a limitless selection of entrees, all priced at a reasonable $7 to $10. Choices like almond chicken, garlic chicken, sweet and sour pork, shrimp with snow peas, and beef with broccoli are always good bets. If you like your food hot and spicy, try the Hunan chicken, hot braised squid, sizzling garlic prawns, garlic braised eggplant, or Mongolian lamb. They also have a several varieties of fried rice and chow mein. And all just a block from the restaurant's namesake, Union Square.

The Stardust Café

- 1305 Polk St. (Bush St.), San Francisco; (415) 931-1004

This little cafe is, in every way, intended as an *homage* to Marilyn Monroe. Her image is plastered to every wall. The chrome-and-turquoise seats, and black-and-white linoleum floor, harken back to a day when *Some Like It Hot* was playing at the local theater. Certainly, the low prices on basic American diner fare will make you feel like you've stepped back a few decades.

Stardust's basic hamburger is just $2.84 (why this particular number? Who knows). All other burgers—including "The Californian" with avocado and Monterey jack cheese, the "Maui Wowi" with pineapple and bacon, or the "Italian Stallion" with black olives and mozzarella, are $3.54. Same price for plenty of other sandwiches, like the barbecue beef sandwich or the "Jaws" (a.k.a. tuna salad). Or, try the chicken Marseilles sandwich—grilled chicken breast topped with mushrooms, American cheese, and grilled in lemon juice and white wine. That's about as exotic as you'll ever see in a place like this. Of course, none of these would be complete without a heap of fries for $1.19 or onion rings for $1.69. For a complete All-American meal, get the "Stardust Special," which includes the basic burger, fries, and a small soda for $3.19.

The Stardust also has a delicious, if limited, breakfast menu. The big draw is "The Stardust Breakfast Special": Two eggs, two pancakes, and two pieces of bacon or sausage, for $2.98. French toast is especially yummy here, too. Open Mondays through Fridays from 6 a.m. to 11 p.m., Saturdays and Sundays from 7 a.m. to 11 p.m.

Sun's Café
- 652B Polk St. (Eddy St.), San Francisco; (415) 776-9595

Located in that rather tough area, the Tenderloin, Sun's Café is nevertheless a dependable choice for your basic breakfast and lunch favorites at great low prices. In fact, the menu choices barely break five bucks. It's a small place of only a half-dozen tables or so; the interior is bright and cozy, with a very friendly staff. The neighborhood, just above the Civic Center, is okay by day; and the appropriately named Sun's isn't open at night anyhow.

Start your day off right with two eggs, any style, plus ham, sausage, or bacon for $4.15. A muffin sandwich,

with ham or bacon, makes a great "on-the-go" breakfast and it will fit nicely into your budget, too, at just $2.65 (and better than the McChain variety). Omelettes are a good deal, starting at $3.85. For a dollar more, have one filled with mushrooms and cheese; all come with hash browns and toast. The French toast ($3.25), meanwhile, is quite good. A stack of three pancakes is just $3.15, and you can get two pancakes with bacon, ham, or sausage for $3.35.

The lunch menu is also chock-full of quick bargains. Get a hamburger—with fries!—for $3.15. Sure, they're not hand-rolled patties, but it's not that kind of a place. You can make it an avocado burger for $3.85, and a double cheeseburger for $4.85. Deli sandwiches are only $3.50, including turkey, ham, tuna salad, and vegetarian (with cream cheese, tofu, avocado, and walnuts). A chef's salad, with egg, avocado, cheese, turkey, and ham, tops out the menu at $5.25. Sun's Café is open Monday through Saturday, from 7 a.m. to 3 p.m. only.

Sushi Bune
- 389 Geary St. (Mason St.), San Francisco; (415) 781-5111

What a fun concept: a sushi boat! At this Union Square eatery, the sushi bar is a long oval with the chefs standing in the center, preparing fish which they gently arrange on small trays. These trays are then placed onto a track filled with water; and so, as you sit on the outside of this oval, lovely plates of sushi float past you. Pick up whatever strikes your fancy.

Each plate holds two pieces of sushi, or six sushi rolls. Depending on the fish itself, plates are priced at $1.50 (California rolls, for instance), $1.95 (yellowtail), $2.50 (tuna, salmon), and so on, up to $3.50. The crab, in particular, is superb. Prices are indicated by the design of the plate; when you're finished, the staff figures your bill by counting the various empty plates up—sort of like a Japanese dim sum.

Full dinners are available as well, including sashimi platters ($11), various tempura dinners (around $10), and the like. These prices include a bowl of miso soup, salad, rice, and tea. Among the appetizers, meat-filled pot stickers are light and tasty (another nod to dim sum?); you get eight for $4.50. Be warned: If you stay with the little boats instead, it *sounds* cheaper, but these can really add up. It's so tempting to try "just one more" as the boats waft past you (pretty smart concept, eh?).

Even so, you can eat very well here in the range of $10-$15 per person, which places Sushi Bune at the upper end of Mr. C's scale—but still a reasonable tab for an expensive cuisine. It's important to note that all of the fish is extremely fresh; Mr. C's sushi expert points out that this is the most important factor for sushi and sashimi. Sure, you can spend less at other places, but you won't get this kind of quality. She herself first learned of the restaurant based on a recommendation from a Japanese friend, always a good sign.

Thai Bar-B-Q
- 730 Van Ness Ave. (Turk St.), San Francisco; (415) 441-1640
- 1958 Shattuck Ave. (University Ave.), Berkeley; (510) 549-1958

San Francisco Bar-B-Q
- 1328 18th St. (Texas St.), San Francisco; (415) 431-8956

It may sound like chicken and ribs, but this is one (actually, three) of The City's great Asian barbecue-and-noodle houses. These small, family-style joints serve up great, freshly-prepared food, cheap.

The menu may be bland ("Bar-B-Q Chicken Dinner $5.75, Bar-B-Q Lamb Dinner $7.75, Bar-B-Q Scallops Dinner $8.25. . ."), but hey, we're not looking for creativity here. What you will get are huge portions of hot food at prices that go no higher than $8.75. And that's for a complete dinner, with rice, salad, and bread on the side.

Mr. C opted for one of the "Noodles" entrees, which offer a similar array of choices served in a large bowl on a bed of egg noodles. He enjoyed the tasty, if not super-spicy, Thai pork sausage ($5.50); as with all noodle dishes, this combo was garnished with lettuce and ground peanuts over the top,and far too many noodles to finish.

Other interesting choices include duck, prawns, veal, salmon steak, and oysters. Most of these are available as full entrees, noodle dishes, or appetizer plates. And that's about it, folks. You can add a salad, topped with meat ($5.25); or a bowl of beef noodle soup ($3.25). There are a few beers and wines, including Singha beer and Anchor Steam (each $2.75). House wines are $1.75 a glass. Seating, by the way, is ultra-informal, at long tables side-by-side with your fellow diners. Chances are, working on this wonderful food, you'll hardly look up enough to notice.

Tommy's Joynt
- 1101 Geary Blvd. (Van Ness Ave.), San Francisco; (415) 775-4216

Brace yourself before walking in here—Tommy's may not be a joy to the faint of heart or delicate of stomach. It's a wild scene: a combination cafeteria and pub which can get pretty rowdy at times. But it's always fun, and never dull. The food and liquor counters line opposite walls, separated by long tables with plastic red-checked cloths; the place is all set up for industrial-strength eating. Meanwhile, every available inch of those walls—not to mention the ceiling—is filled with beer signs, wacky sayings, nostalgic advertisements, and yard sale junk ranging from frying pans to ski poles to a giant candy cane. Tommy's is a trip, man.

The food? It's um, hearty—and cheap. Full dinners rarely cost more than $6, with a selection that changes (very little) daily. That price can get you a plate heaped with turkey, pastrami, or beef cut off of the roast as you order—plus mashed potatoes or cooked vegetables, salad or beans, and bread. Other daily specials may include braised lamb shanks, spareribs, or baked calamari. Oh, and buffalo stew. You heard right; they're proud of it here, and it's the real thing, served over rice for $5.65. A bowl of buffalo chili is $4.65.

And then there are "lighter" sandwich items which cost even less, like Polish sausage and sauerkraut ($3.85), a sloppy joe overflowing with barbecued turkey ($3.65), and something else Mr. C had never tried before: beer and bean soup ($1.60 for a bowl). Tasty, all right, though you won't have to worry about driving home.

Speaking of beers though: If you're not driving, there are some great ones to try here. Dozens and dozens, in fact—something from just about every beer producing country in the world. Fuller's from England, Guinness from Ireland, Asahi from Japan, Russkoye from Russia, Aass from Norway (think Tonya knocked back a few of these?), Red Stripe from Jamaica, and many more, all one price—$2.50. Many of these same beers are on tap as well, with a rotating selection offered in $1.50 and $2 drafts all the time. There is a full bar actually, along with hot beverages like "coffee expresso" (their spelling).

There are smaller, individual tables toward the back, if you can get one. Tommy's does a lively business well into the evening, especially late at night as other dining options dwindle. Can you think of anything better to eat as a midnight snack than this stuff?

Tumbleweed Café
- 1245 Van Ness Ave. (Sutter St.), San Francisco; (415) 474-0200

Walking into the Tumbleweed Café, you may feel like Michael J. Fox in *Back to the Future* (the first one, not those retread sequels). The decor is right out of the 1950s, with chrome-and-turquoise vinyl seats and formica-topped tables. The walls are adorned with bits of tumbleweed (what did you expect?) and old Coke ads. But it's not just the decor that will make you feel like you're in another decade: The prices almost seem to come from yesteryear, too.

MR. CHEAP'S PICKS
Polk Gulch

✔ **Brother Juniper's Restaurant**—Not only do you get a delicious meal, you help out folks in need. This restaurant is owned and operated by The Raphael House for the Homeless.

✔ **First Light Cafe**—From the first light to the last, this cafe offers a menu of eclectic and filling foods, reasonably priced.

✔ **Tommy's Joynt**—Divey, kitschy bar atmosphere, with a cafeteria-style lineup of heavy, heavy foods.

✔ **Tumbleweed Café**—A 1950s-style diner serving up huge portions of Tex-Mex. Sounds strange? Just roll with it.

The menu is an encyclopedia of traditional American diner food, things like hot meatloaf sandwiches and beef brisket. The Tumbleweed serves a number of blue-plate specials for lunch and dinner, all nicely priced under $10. Try their turkey dinner with mashed potatoes, vegetables, and cranberry sauce ($7.95), chicken picatta with rice and vegetables ($7.95), or a New York steak with baked potato and vegetables ($8.95). All of these are served with warm cornbread and a choice of soup or salad. Their soups, by the way, are dee-*lish*. Mr. C really enjoyed the chicken and pasta soup, with big chunks of real chicken and hearty pasta rounds.

Hamburgers are ground fresh each day, right in the kitchen, and grilled over an oakwood-fired barbecue. The basic version is just $3.95! Some of the more interesting variations include the Tumbleweed burger, topped with green chili, onions, and jack cheese, for $4.95; and the San Francisco burger, with bacon, guacamole, and a choice of cheese, for $5.50. You can add potato salad, French fries, or a side salad for an additional 95¢.

Other sandwiches include things like grilled spicy chicken breast for $5.95, or the "Special Tumbleweed Sandwich" with roasted pork, grilled onions, and melted jalapeño jack for $5.50, as well as cold deli sandwiches. Tumbleweed also has a great selection of meal-sized salads. Choose from specialties like chicken caesar salad ($6.50) and Oriental chicken salad ($5.95).

Old meets new at dishes like the brie burger or the blackened meatloaf; not to mention a variety of Tex-Mex specialties such as chili and quesadillas. These make meals that are good, filling, and very cheap. The chili is made daily with fine-grade chopped beef, sweet and hot peppers, freshly ground spices, and beans—topped with cheddar cheese and onions. It comes served with warm cornbread for just $2.95 a cup, $3.95 a bowl, and $5.95 for "Texas-size." Quesadillas, just $3.95 to $4.95, are served with guacamole, sour cream, and salsa fresca.

Breakfast fans will find early-morning nirvana here. Along with the usual standbys, you'll find such novelties as banana-pecan pancakes ($3.75), cinnamon-nut-raisin French toast ($3.95), and a California scramble with avocado, tomato, and jack cheese ($5.95). Plus more than a dozen different omelettes. For something really different, try a shrimp and broccoli omelette, topped with Hollandaise sauce, for $6.95. All in all, if you love these comfort foods as much as Mr. C, you'll be glad this diner exists in the present.

Vic's Place
- 44 Belden St. (Pine St.), San Francisco; (415) 981-5222

Belden Street is one of those cozy little side alleys downtown, this one running between Pine Street and Bush Street, about half a block up

from Kearny. This prime location makes Vic's a perfect place for business-crowd lunch. It's actually a bar which, like many, serves up hearty portions of pub food at low prices. Unlike other pubs, however, they serve lunch only, with the kitchen closing around 2:30 in the afternoon.

Vic's is a burger place—and there are plenty to choose from. Try the "Financial Burger" ($5.45), topped with cream cheese and walnuts; an "Acapulco Burger" with guacamole, lettuce, tomato, and pineapple ($5.45); or the ominous-sounding-but-really-harmless "Rosemary's Baby Burger," topped with peanut butter, crisp bacon, guava jelly, and fresh spinach leaf ($5.40). Obviously, some of the offerings are not for the faint of heart. All burgers are a one-third of a pound of choice beef, and they're served with French fries.

Don't want a burger? Try the filet of chicken breast sandwich, garnished with spinach and tomato. They also have a choice of salads for the nutrition-conscious. And then, there's a regular line-up of daily specials. On Mondays enjoy fettucine al Vittorio ($5.30); on Wednesdays, try eggplant parmigiana and pasta ($5.60); and on Thursdays, it's corned beef and cabbage (also $5.60). All specials come with a side salad.

Oh yeah, and don't leave without sampling one of Vic's desserts, including cheesecake for $2.95 or carrot cake for $1.75. Lunch is served on weekdays only.

Victor's Pizzeria and Restaurant
- 1411 Polk St. (Pine St.), San Francisco; (415) 885-1660

Part of that burgeoning section of Polk Street known as Polk Gulch, Victor's is a little storefront restaurant serving a variety of delicious Italian specialties. With just about twelve tables, Victor's offers a cozy and relaxed atmosphere. While it may be ultra-casual, with prices to match, the food here is every bit as good as you'll find in chi-chi North Beach *trattorias*.

There is quite a selection of pastas

and sauces, all made fresh on the premises. Choose from fettucine, linguine, cappelini, spaghetti, or rigatoni; top it with marinara, bolognese, mushroom, Alfredo, pesto, and more. A heaping plate costs just $8.50; add meatballs or Italian sausage for another $1.50. And these all come with soup or salad, as well as homemade bread and butter. They also have a great selection of stuffed pastas, all for just $8.95, including cannelloni, lasagna, tortellini, and ravioli.

Victor's meat entrees and specialties get a little pricey, some a tad above Mr. C's usual limit, but not unreasonably so. Veal fans should try the picatta or scallopini for $10.95. If you prefer chicken, the Milanese ($9.95) is *molto bene*. And again, those prices include a side vegetable, pasta, homemade bread, and soup or salad. Specialties, all $9.50, include gnocchi pesto, linguini with red or white clam sauce, and angel hair puttanesca.

Of course, they also have pizzas, starting from just $6.95 for a twelve-inch size. There are over twenty toppings to choose from, including spinach, jalapeños, fresh garlic, baby clams, and pesto. Calzones start at $5.95 for the "mini" size. All of their dishes, and especially the pizzas and calzones, are available for take-out. Victor's Pizzeria and Restaurant is open Sunday through Thursday from 11 a.m. to 11:30 p.m., and Friday and Saturday until 12:30 a.m.

Village Café
- 1426 Polk St. (California St.), San Francisco; (415) 771-9598

With soups, salads, burgers, and sandwiches, this is your traditional working man's (okay, person's) downtown coffee shop. They also serve breakfast all day—always a good sign, says Mr. C.

Salad selections range from a simple house salad for just $1.85 to chef's salad ($4.95) and breast of chicken salad ($5.25). Sandwiches include grilled veggie and cheese ($3.75), turkey club ($4.75), and an "ABC" burger—that's avocado, bacon, and cheese ($4.95). All of these sandwiches come with your choice of homemade potato salad or French fries.

Hungrier diners will want to go straight to the main courses. These include fried chicken with fresh vegetables and French fries ($6.95), grilled pork chops ($6.95), and grilled beef liver with onions ($5.25). Seafood entrees include fish and chips ($7.95) and deep-fried prawns or scallops with French fries ($7.95). All entrees are served with soup or salad, choice of boiled red potato, home fries or rice, fresh vegetables, and warm French bread—quite a deal, in all.

Don't forget about breakfast! Some patrons consider this to be the best meal of the day here (see one customer's "Ode to Home Fries" on the takeout menu). Order up a New York steak and two eggs for $6.95, corned beef hash and two eggs for $5.50, or just two eggs any style for $2.75. All of these come with home fries and toast. They also have lots of interesting omelettes, such as chili bean and cheese ($4.95, again with those poetic home fries and toast).

Strictly a breakfast and lunch kind of place, the Village Café is open Monday through Friday from 7 a.m. to 3:30 p.m., Saturday and Sunday 7 a.m. to 4 p.m.

Wing Lum Café
- 1150 Polk St. (Sutter St.), San Francisco; (415) 771-6888

Mr. C walked through these doors based on a strong recommendation, only to discover the restaurant had changed hands. Nevertheless, since it still looked like a good place, he sat down and tried it anyway. Guess what? The new version is good, too. It's an attractive restaurant with big storefront windows; in this rather gritty neighborhood, that means you can sit at the front and enjoy free entertainment all through your meal.

Start off with an appetizer, like deep-fried squid ($5.75), pot stickers ($3.50), or fried won tons ($2.95). They also have some more unusual soups than the standard fare, including such varieties as winter melon soup ($4.25) and seaweed soup ($3.95).

Most of Wing Lum's entrees are priced under $7, including many of their seafood dishes; even such normally-expensive choices as Szechwan prawns, shrimp with snow peas, crab meat with mushrooms, jade scallops, and squid with salted greens. Chicken and beef dishes are also good here, served in large portions; these include things like lemon chicken, crispy duck, Mongolian beef, and mixed vegetables with

pork. There are also plenty of vegetarian dishes including Chinese greens, hot and spicy eggplant, and Szechwan-style bean cakes.

And then there are the super-cheap chow mein, noodle, and rice dishes—most under $5. Mr. C enjoyed an order of good ol' beef chow mein ($4.25); other good choices are Singapore rice noodles ($4.95) and Hunan kung pao chicken over rice ($4.50). Wing Lum Café is open Monday through Saturday from 11 a.m. to 10 p.m., and Sunday from 4 p.m. to 10 p.m.

EAST BAY
Berkeley, Oakland

¡Ay Caramba!
• 1901 University Ave. (MLK Dr.), Berkeley; (510) 843-1298

Along with a great name and a great sign, ¡Ay Caramba! has a super selection of Mexican food at low prices. Nothing on the menu goes for more than seven dollars and change, and most items are a lot less. This is especially welcome in area so heavily populated with cash-starved college students.

Most of the menu is a game of mix-and-match. Pick what you like: burritos (rolled up with beans, brown rice, lettuce, and salsa); tacos (with beans, salsa, and cilantro); or tostados (with beans, lettuce, guacamole, sour cream, and salsa). Then, choose your fillings, from the roster of beef, fish, chicken, squid, or vegetables, and *olé*! None of these options is more than $5.50—with the tostados at the high end, tacos at the low end ($3 to $4), and burritos in the middle ($4 to $5).

Full entrees are a little more expensive, but still very cheap—considering how much you get for your dough. A platter of chicken enchiladas is $6.50, with rice and beans; *chiles capones*, two mild ancho chili

peppers filled with cheese and cilantro and baked in a light tomato sauce, are also $6.50; and *pollo con octzingo mole*, chicken in a Oaxaca style sauce of roasted chilies, fruit, nuts, and unsweetened Mexican chocolate, is just $7.15. These choices are both delicious and exotic—certainly far beyond your standard south-of-the-border fare—yet, they don't require *mucho dinero*.

Meanwhile, if you're just looking for a simple snack to enjoy with friends, you'll find that here, too. Nachos, covered with melted cheese, beans, guacamole, sour cream, and salsa, are just $4.15. Or, stick with guacamole and chips ($3.85) or salsa and chips ($1.95). A respectable college-area hangout, though not an all-nighter, Caramba is open until 9:30 p.m. on weeknights, and until 10:00 on weekends.

Barney's Gourmet Hamburgers
• 1591 Solano Ave. (Peralta St.), Berkeley; (510) 526-8185
• 5819 College Ave. (Ghabod St.), Oakland; (510) 601-0444
• 4162 Piedmont Ave. (41st St.), Oakland; (510) 655-7180

- 3344 Steiner St. (Lombard St.), San Francisco; (415) 563-0307
- 4138 24th St. (Castro St.), San Francisco; (415) 282-7770

Big is the operative word at Barney's. This growing chain of attractive, yuppie restaurants is getting big, with locations all around the Bay Area. They serve up a big menu of big, juicy burgers—plus a few other things. The prices, however, are not as big as you'd expect. Which makes Barney's big with Mr. C.

Those burgers include six-ounce, freshly rolled beef and eight-ounce, boneless chicken breast sandwiches. The basic Barney burger (can you sense an alliteration overload coming?) is just $3.95; add cheese for another fifty cents, and/or fries for $1.75. Or, step up to the Big Barney Burger, a half-pounder, for $4.95, and a larger order of fries for $2.25; still not bad at all. By the way, they do up a nifty order of spicy curly fries for $3.25, too.

Meanwhile, there are no less than twenty-two variations of burgers (big is the word, remember). Try the pizza burger ($4.75), or perhaps the Popeye burger ($4.95), topped with sauteed spinach and feta cheese. The Maui Waui ($5.25) is glazed with teriyaki sauce, and served with pineapple and Canadian (?) bacon. And the Russian burger ($4.95) adds layers of sour cream, scallions, and sauteed mushrooms, served on dark rye bread instead of a roll.

Most of these are also available on chicken sandwiches as well, usually a dollar more. And don't forget the tofu patty burgers, for the health-conscious crowd. Plus soups and salads, club sandwiches, and—at the Oakland branches only, for some reason—weekend breakfast entrees of omelettes and other egg plates. Forget parking at the Marina location, by the way. All branches are open for lunch and dinner seven days a week (though not past 10 p.m., except in summer), and offer efficient take-out service as well.

Bette's Ocean View Diner
- 1807 4th St. (Hearst St.), Berkeley; (510) 644-3230

The first thing that strikes you about Bette's Ocean View Diner is that it has no view of the ocean. Or even the bay, for that matter. In fact, this popular Berkeley restaurant and take-out deli has no view whatsoever, unless you count people-watching. *That* you can do in abundance, especially at weekend brunch, when you may wait as long as an hour for a table. Bette's is located smack in the heart of Berkeley's outlet shopping district, and yups by the carful spend the day browsing and eating and reading the paper.

The food will be worth the wait. If you can't get in right away, you can do just fine by popping into the bakery/deli shop to grab a homemade scone or a muffin and some fine, dark coffee, pulling a free copy of the *East Bay Express* out of the sidewalk box, and basking in the California sunshine until your name is called. Benches and tables are provided for this purpose. Of course—to paraphrase John Lennon—if the sun don't come, you get your tan from standing in the California rain.

Anyway, once you're in, Bette's is a *nouvelle* twist on the traditional New York diner. Instead of pancakes, they serve up apple pancake soufflés ($7.25), which are both monstrous and scrumptious. A recent brunch special was a frittata made with Kalamata olives, feta cheese, leeks, and potatoes, all rolled together for $6.75. Same price for a combination plate of scrapple, poached eggs and grilled tomatoes—sort of like yuppie soul food.

Weekdays offer breakfast and lunch only; basic deli-style sandwiches are a bit pricey at $6-$8, but they are hugely stuffed (so that you will be, too) and come with homemade potato salad or cole slaw. Slightly fancier is the sauteed chicken sandwich ($7.50), served on a baguette with jack cheese, black beans and salsa. Homemade soups and chili are usually $2.50-$3.50. And chili dogs are just $4.95.

Daily lunch specials, generally $7.75 each, may be as simple as pot roast over noodles, or as complex as turkey scallopini with sweet potato fritters and cranberry-horseradish relish. You sure won't find *that* back at the ol' corner coffee shop (we're not in Queens anymore, Toto. . .).

Blake's

- 2367 Telegraph Ave. (Durant Ave.), Berkeley; (510) 848-0886

This hip restaurant/bar is immensely popular with Cal students, due in part to the fact that they mix live rock bands in with plenty of cheap food (see listing under "Entertainment: Music"). Like so many bars Mr. C has covered—and he's covered quite a few in his time—Blake's makes their money on drinks, so they can afford to "underprice" the food.

All of the items on the menu here stay under $8, with many priced far lower. You can get a big, juicy 1/3-lb. burger, with salad or French fries, for a mere $4.75. Perfect for the traditional student budget as well as the traditional student diet. Try such variants as the Mexican burger, topped with jack cheese and salsa for $5.25; or a Texas burger with barbecue sauce and cheddar cheese for $5.25. They have lots of other big sandwiches, too, from barbecued beef ($5.95), to a vegetarian garden burger ($4.95)—which neatly encapsulates the entire Berkeley culinary spectrum. All of these are served with a side salad and French fries.

Blake's entrees are a steal! Have a plate of linguine marinara for $4.45 or vegetarian lasagna for $5.45, both served with salad and bread. Rustle up a top sirloin steak, with baked potato, a side vegetable, and bread, all for $7.50. Barbecued chicken with salad and bread goes for $5.95, and vegetarian tamales with black bean chili, rice, and salsa are just $4.95.

Being such a regular hangout, Blake's has a large lineup of snacks, appetizers, and side orders. A plate of vegetarian nachos with beans, jack and cheddar cheeses, sour cream, sliced jalapeños, olives, and fresh salsa will keep the gang busy (and less poor) for $4. Mr. C and his companion really enjoyed a serving of Cajun popcorn shrimp ($4.95) and the 7" mini-pizza ($3.95), a perfect pair for sharing. Other big hits include potato skins ($4.95), mozzarella cheese sticks ($3.95), and stuffed jalapeños ($4.95).

The atmosphere is boisterous and lively, especially in the basement where they run movies and other forms of visual accompaniments on a big screen. Blake's is open from 11 a.m. to 1:15 p.m. everyday, good for late-night hanging; it's located right in the middle of a busy stretch of clothing, book, and music stores just off the campus—you can't miss it.

The Blue Nile

- 2525 Telegraph Ave. (Dwight Way), Berkeley; (510) 540-6777

The Blue Nile has received numerous accolades for its authentic Ethiopian cuisine—read 'em in the window. Like so many ethnic foods, Ethiopian cooking is delicious, filling. . .and cheap! Besides, this off-campus restaurant is just plain different, with its North African decor, dim lighting, and beads hanging all over the place—a kind of low-rent exotic.

For those who've never had Ethiopian food, this will be a really fun experience. Like many Asian and Indian dishes, these specialties consist mainly of diced meats and vegetables cooked into a spicy stew. The difference lies in the spices themselves, and the combinations of ingredients. A bigger difference is that, rather than using a fork or chopsticks, Ethiopian food is eaten with your hands; using *injera*, a kind of crêpe-like bread, to pick up portions of the stews. The wait staff is extremely friendly and helpful, if you need any kinds of explanations.

Dinner entrees range in price from $6.25 to $7.45, and lunch plates from $4.85 to $5.45, for smaller portions. Many of these are vegetarian dishes, such as *yemisir wat*, a spicy lentil and vegetable stew, and *gomen wat*, mustard greens steamed in special sauce with vegetables. Meat dishes include *doro wat*, a very hot and spicy chicken dish; *ve-beg alecha*, a mild lamb dish; and *ye siga wat*, which is a hot and spicy beef stew. There are also combination plates, which let you sample a few different dishes; the vegetarian combo ($6.95), for example, consists of lentils, split peas, mustard greens, rice, injera, and *kinche*, a bulgur (cracked wheat grain) soup. Or, choose any three meat dishes for $7.45.

It's all delicious and hearty stuff, perfect for student budgets, as well as anyone looking for something unique.

Bongo Burger*
- 1839 Euclid Ave. (Hearst St.), Berkeley; (510) 540-9573
- 2505 Dwight Way (Telegraph Ave.), Berkeley; (510) 549-9147

Colleges were invented to support this kind of hangout. Both north and south of UCal, Bongo beats the drums for quick, greasy, cheap eats with a Mediterranean slant.

Burgers range from the standard ($2.75) to a Persian burger ($3.45) made with ground, marinated lamb instead of beef. A chicken breast sandwich is $3.50; a ground lamb shish kebab, served in a slice of pita bread, is a mere $1.80. And, inexplicably, Polish sausages and hot dogs have worked their way onto the menu as well. Add fries or onion rings for under a buck.

All of these are charcoal grilled, and certainly tasty—if a bit carcinogenic. They are also available in dinner platter form ($3.95-$4.95), adding a salad (greens or tabouli), pita bread and tahini sauce. Or, go for the more traditional falafel sandwich ($1.50/small, $2.55/large) or falafel platter ($3.25). That's about it, except for basic eggs and and cheese omelettes, offered any morning until noon. You won't even have to leave a tip—can't get much cheaper than that!

Brothers' Bagels
- 1469 Shattuck Ave. (Pine St.), Berkeley; (510) 649-9422
- 1281 Gilman St. (Santa Fe St.), Berkeley; (510) 524-3104

MR. CHEAP'S PICKS
Berkeley

✔ **Bette's Ocean View Diner**— The only view is of the waves of people waiting for tables—and the amply portioned, beautifully done comfort food.

✔ **Blake's**—A popular student hangout, for both yummy eats and raucous entertainment.

✔ **The Blue Nile**—Authentic Ethiopian food in the heart of Berkeley—go figure! Choose from a wide a range of meat and veggie dishes, from spicy to mild.

✔ **Fat Apple's**—Wonderful waffles and other breakfast items make this a first choice for Cal students with visiting 'rents.

✔ **Long Life Vegi House**—Right outside the U-Cal campus, this family-style Chinese restaurant serves up vegetable, seafood, and tofu dishes at rock-bottom prices.

✔ **Tea Spot Café**—In the boonies of Berkeley, this menu full of comfort foods and inexpensive entertainment is worth seeking out.

✔ **Zachary's Pizza**—Stuffed pizzas get rave reviews from the press; low prices get rave reviews from Mr. C.

- 4301 Piedmont Ave. (John St.), Oakland; (510) 654-5211

Transplanted New Yorkers know that it's virtually impossible to find a decent bagel west of the Hudson River. Now, Mr. C won't promise you that Brothers' Bagels are as good as those at Katz's on the Lower East Side, but then, Katz's has gone downhill anyway. These bagels, at least, are quite good, very fresh, and cheap! They're made the traditional New York way, by boiling the bagel in pure water before it is baked. Choose from plain, salt, egg sesame, onion, garlic, pumpernickel, whole wheat sesame or plain, and cinnamon raisin. They also have a variety of specialty bagels including "Seed City" (didn't the Beach Boys sing an ode to this one?), cranberry, pumpkin, and even green olive. Hey, some folks dig 'em. Anyhow, they're all just 50¢ each or $5.35 for a baker's dozen.

But, what's a bagel without a little *shmear*? Have your choice of bagel with plain cream cheese ($1.50), cream cheese mixed with fruit preserves ($1.85—that sure ain't New York), or lox ($1.95). If you need something a little more substantial to nosh on, you can get a bagel with New York Nova trim lox and cream cheese ($3.95), Atlantic Nova sliced lox and cream cheese ($5.65), or smoked whitefish spread ($2.95), each served with sliced tomato and red onion.

But Brothers' is more than just a bakery. They also have a choice of vegetarian and meat sandwiches, all made to order. Try old favorites like roast beef ($4.25) or hot pastrami and cheese ($4.25); or something a little more trendy, like a tofu burger or garden blend burger, each served on a nine-grain bun for $3.95. All sandwiches include sliced tomato, red onion, and a *nice slice a' pickle*. Sorry, Mr. C (from New York himself, originally) got nostalgic for a minute there.

Brothers' Bagels also sells their cream cheeses and blended spreads, including lox by the pound. And could this be a chic Left Coast deli without an espresso bar and some sweet pastry? 'Course not. They're open seven days a week.

Café de Bordeaux
- 326 Seventh St. (Harrison St.), Oakland; (510) 891-2338

How about it—a continental restaurant in Oakland's Chinatown. What's more, it's one of the least expensive

such places you're ever likely to see—with full dinners like scallops and shrimps in white wine sauce, prawns provençale, chicken Dijon, and veal marsala, all at or under $10. And those prices *include* soup or salad, vegetables, rice, and coffee or tea!

It's all served up in a comfortable setting that is elegant in a simple way—with linen tablecloths, muted lighting, and quick, friendly service. Mr. C supped on a large grilled swordfish steak ($9.95) that was quite good; his companion loved the chicken teriyaki ($8.50), made with strips of fresh chicken breast. There are also several pasta dishes, such as spinach fettucine with shrimps in pesto sauce ($9.50). Most of the three dozen dinner entrees are priced from $8.50-$9.95; don't forget, that's for a full meal.

Appetizers range from escargots ($5.25—and if you're surprised to hear Mr. Cheap talking about a menu item like that, you're not alone!) to a crock of French onion soup *au gratin* ($3.75)—but of course. By the way, there is a small but serviceable children's menu (Bordeaux Burger and fries, $4.50), and soft drinks, to complement the select red and white wines.

Believe it or not, this is a Chinese-owned establishment, and there are a few Asian items on the menu—more at lunch than at dinner. Rice plates, for example (all $4.95), include chicken curry and chicken with mushrooms and vegetables. Most of the dinner entrees are available at lunch for about a dollar less, too. Open seven days a week, until 9:30 p.m.

Café Rocco
- 1131 Folsom St. (Seventh St.), San Francisco, (415) 554-0522

Café Rocco, just four blocks from Moscone Convention Center, serves up pasta, sandwiches, and Italian meals at great low prices. Its convenient location makes it a great spot for lunch while poking around all those great SoMa shops. Rocco's is primarily a lunch spot, open seven days a week until 3 p.m.; but they do serve dinner on the weekends (Thursday, Friday, and Saturday) until 10 p.m.

The daytime menu focuses on the three "S's" of light eating: sandwiches, soups, and salads. Sandwiches, served on sourdough bread with French fries, include such choices as Italian sausage with grilled peppers and onions, and marinated grilled chicken breast, each $6.95. Soups include minestrone and pastina soups, $2.25 for a cup and $3.95 for a bowl. Specialty salads include calamari salad for $5.95 and marinated chicken salad for $7.25.

Pasta dishes, available anytime, include linguini with clams in red or white sauce for $9.25, pasta primavera for $8.50, and pasta with meat balls for $7.95. If you don't want a full, dinner-sized entree, side orders are available. Pasta with marinara or meat sauce ($3.95), ravioli with the same choices ($4.95), and ravioli pesto ($5.95) are just some of your options here.

Dinner selections (most of which are also available at lunch time, actually) are more expensive, but still fit comfortably into Mr. C's price range. The ones that go a few cents over his usual $10 limit are mainly seafood dishes—which are always more expensive anyway. Even so, calamari sauté over linguini is a relative bargain at $10.25. Other hot entrees include grilled marinated chicken breast ($8.25), roast beef ($9.75), and eggplant parmigiana ($9.25). All of these are served with pasta or vegetables.

Edy's Family Restaurant and Ice Cream Fountain

• 2201 Shattuck Ave. (Allston Way), Berkeley; (510) 843-3096

Edy's is a Berkeley tradition; has been for nearly seventy years. Let's just say they've served their share of Cal students over the years. It's a fairly large restaurant, which still manages to feel nice and cozy—especially with its menu well-stocked with comfort foods, and waitresses who call you "honey."

They have a number of good, cheap dinner selections like veal parmigiana and filet of sole (each $7.95), fried chicken ($6.95), and deep-fried jumbo prawns ($9.95). They also have Greek dinners, including baked half-chicken ($7.95), chicken shish kebab ($10.95), and fried calamari ($6.95). All dinners include soup or salad; choice of potato, rice or spaghetti; vegetables; and bread and butter. In other words, this is a good place to stuff yourself before cramming for that exam. Pasta dishes are truly budget-conscious, including spaghetti ($5.95) and ravioli ($6.95). These are topped with Edy's homemade Italian meat sauce, and served with garlic bread plus soup or salad.

Edy's is also a popular stop for breakfast or lunch. Breakfast is served all day (nice!) and includes the usual offerings, with a few unusual choices tossed in—like linguica and eggs ($4.95). Omelettes also offer some new tantalizing varieties like the "Greek" (with feta cheese, green onions, and tomatoes) and "Pacific" (shrimp, mushrooms, green onions, bell peppers, and Swiss cheese), each $5.95. Lunches mainly offer your basic hot and cold sandwiches, most priced at around $4.50, plus burgers and salads. Daily specials may add veal cutlet, liver with onions and bacon, and ground round steak. They're all just $5.95 and come with potatoes or rice, vegetables, and bread and butter.

Desserts, run the same international gamut as the rest of the menu: baklava, New York cheesecake, rice pudding. But don't forget, this is a true, old-fashioned fountain; Edy's has an amazing selection of ice cream specialties like the "Monte Cristo," vanilla and toasted almond ice cream covered with caramel sauce and cashew nuts, then topped with whipped cream and a cherry, all for $3.75. The "English Toffee" is similar but topped with toffee candy ($3.95); and the "Five by Five," is no less than five scoops of ice cream, thick marshmallow sauce, sliced bananas, nuts, whipped cream and a cherry, served with a *pitcher* of hot fudge ($4.95). Who needs dinner?

Open until 11 p.m. Sunday-Friday, 'til midnight on Saturday.

Fat Apple's
* 1346 Martin Luther King, Jr. Way (Rose St.), Berkeley; (510) 526-2260

This neighborhood place is popular with all sorts of Berkeley types—students, families, anyone who happens to drop by. It's a friendly, casual spot, with a menu of simple favorites and a bakery on the premises. On weekends especially, when brunch is served from 7 a.m. until 2 p.m., the line often extends out the door at peak times.

Breakfasts, indeed, are scrumptious. Corned beef hash, with a pair of fried eggs and your choice of toast or a homemade croissant, is $6.00. Buttermilk waffles, light and tasty, are just $2.75; you can top them with extras like blueberry sauce, walnuts, yogurt, or strawberries and real whipped cream. Or, try the whole wheat pancake special ($4.25), served with one egg and bacon or ham—or, even better, delicious apple-chicken sausage. Good coffee, too, along with fresh baked scones, muffins, and cheese puffs.

For lunch or dinner, again, it's the can't-miss basics. Burgers, with one-third of a pound of fresh meat, start at $4.50; or, go for a homemade meatloaf sandwich ($5.50), turkey and pasta salad ($4.00 small, $7.00 large), grilled chicken breast with potato, and soup or salad ($8), or a bowl of homemade chili ($4.50). There are also several vegetarian entrees, including vegetable polenta lasagna ($7.50), made without eggs or cream; and baked tofu salad ($7) over brown rice.

A limited selection of beers and wines are available, all from $2.00 and up; plus espresso, cappuccino, and the like. Dinner is served until 11:00 p.m. nightly.

Ike's Rotisserie*
* 3859 Piedmont Ave. (MacArthur St.), Oakland; (510) 450-0453

Here's a good example of the kind of quick, easy, filling eatery that all cities can offer—yet never have enough of. Ike's is an attractive counter-and-tables joint, run with a personal touch, serving Middle Eastern cuisine. It's cozy, freshly painted, and decorated with framed photographs of survivors of the 1988 earthquake in Armenia. These were taken by owner Ike Aykanian himself, and are not as somber as they sound—cute portraits of large-eyed children and so forth.

Anyway, back to the food. It's good and cheap. Take out a falafel sandwich for $3.00, or have a seat and a half-chicken dinner straight from the rotisserie for just $3.75. It's served in a garlic sauce, with picked vegetables and pita or lavash bread. Even a whole, rotisseried chicken—get ready—is only $6.75. And it's moist and tasty.

Other platters, which come with two side dishes (lentil soup, hummus, cracked wheat, etc.) and the above extras, include things like falafel ($4.25) and chicken or beef shawarma ($5.75). Imagine getting a whole dinner, enough to satisfy an average-sized appetite, at these prices—and, if you need more, it's inexpensive enough to add more of those salads and side dishes.

A few beers and wines are available, none higher than $2.25; you may wish to try the "Middle Eastern Yogurt Soda" ($1.25), but Mr. C declined. For dessert, baklava (what else?) is just a dollar a slice. Convenient to this neighborhood shopping district, Ike's is open for lunch and dinner every day but Sunday.

La Méditerranée
* 2936 College Ave. (Ashby Ave.), Berkeley; (510) 540-7773

Fans of Middle Eastern food will also be happy to find La Méditerranée (if they haven't already), where Greek and Mediterranean specialties are served at prices as low as sea level itself. Start with an appetizer of hummus, baba ghanoush, tabouleh, or stuffed grape leaves, each $4.95, or one of the many different soups and salads.

LM's house specialties include the *Levant* sandwich—cream cheese, herbs, cucumbers, lettuce, feta cheese, and tomato, rolled up in Levantine bread ($7.80); *lule kebab*, lean ground lamb baked with parsley, spices, onions, and tomatoes, served over rice pilaf ($9.00); Lebanese *kibbeh*, a mix of ground lamb and cracked wheat, seasoned and baked with pine nuts (also $9.00); and pomegranate chicken—drumsticks marinated in pomegranate sauce, baked with wild herbs, and served over rice ($8.45).

All of these specialties are served with your choice of a green salad, Armenian potato salad, or a cup of soup. La Méditerranée also has a number of fillo dough specialties, all handrolled, including cheese *karni*, chicken *cilicia*, Levantine meat tarts, and Greek spinach and feta pies, each $8.70. Again, these dishes are served with a choice of salads or soup.

Finish off your meal with a traditional Middle Eastern dessert, such as *datil armandra*—dates and nuts rolled in fillo dough, and served warm with whipped cream. Baklava, cheese cake, chocolate mousse and more are all reasonably priced from $3 to $4. Be sure to sip a cup of strong Turkish coffee with them. As the menu says, *Anoush Ella!* (May it be sweet!).

Long Life Vegi House

• 2129 University Ave. (Shattuck Ave.), Berkeley; (510) 845-6072
Ask any Chinese food fan in Berkeley for a recommendation, and they're likely to rave about this large but homey place just off campus. So have most major newspapers and magazines in the area, whose reviews are posted in the window. Why? Probably because the food is so delicious, healthy, and best of all, cheap.

LLVH serves a completely vegetarian menu—that is, if seafood fits your definition of vegetarian—using traditional styles and all natural ingredients (i.e., no MSG, o.k.?). What all this leaves is still a vast ocean of choices, such as eggplant in a zesty garlic sauce, and braised tofu with black mushrooms and greens (each $5.75, as are practically all the vegetable and tofu dishes). And, if you love the nuts in cashew chicken, try another house special, Long Life Mixed Nuts ($6.50), served again in a spicy garlic sauce. Noodle dishes are super bargains: Tan-tan noodles are just yummy in a peanut sauce, while vegetables over crispy noodles is another good deal. Add a big bowl of egg drop and corn soup, and you've got a whole meal. All of these are priced at $3.95.

There are also the sometimes-successful tofu copies of meats here, in entrees like Vegi-chicken with string beans ($6.50), served in a black bean sauce, and broccoli Vegi-beef ($5.50). Whether or not you find these to be worthy substitutes, you cannot deny that they are less expensive (and less artery-clogging) than the real things.

Still, Mr. C suggests staying with the *undeniably* real things, like the real vegetable dishes, and the seafood, although it's a bit more expensive. Most of these are $7.75 and $8.75, still quite reasonable. Szechuan prawns, an LLVH specialty, are served in a light, but spicy tomato sauce; oysters in black bean sauce, with onions and peppers, is another good bet.

Long Life has several permanent specials which will add years to your wallet, such as complete "Family Dinner" meals from $7.50 per person, and a variety of rice plate lunch specials from $3.65—for soup, a spring roll, and an entree from the main menu served over brown rice. Unlike other Chinese restaurants, lunch specials are available from 11:30 a.m. to 3 p.m. *seven days* a week. Dim Sum is added on the weekends, same hours.

Mel's Drive-In

- 2240 Shattuck Ave. (Bancroft Way), Berkeley; (510) 540-6351
- 2165 Lombard St. (Fillmore St.), San Francisco; (415) 921-3039
- 3355 Geary Blvd. (Stanyan St.), San Francisco; (415) 387-2244

Mel's Drive-In is an authentic 1950s-style diner, complete with those paper soda-jerk hats, bobby sox and saddle shoes, oldies music on the juke box, and plenty of good, cheap food. Mel's menu features an eclectic mix of diner classics, like meat loaf and chicken pot pie, along with truly 90s cuisine like gourmet turkey burgers and California fruit salad.

Predictably, burgers are a big item here. Their choice ground chuck has no additives or preservatives and is delivered fresh daily. Try "The Famous Melburger," a third of a pound of beef served on a sesame seed bun with lettuce, tomato, Bermuda onions, mayonnaise, and pickle chips, for just $4.50. Make it a half-pounder for just 75¢ more. The true bargain in this department is the "Big Mel Combination Plate," a half-pound burger, great French fries, and a tossed green salad for $6.50. People who are looking for healthier choices may want to go for the gourmet ground turkey burger ($5.95) instead. It's a ground turkey patty served on a whole wheat bun with cole slaw, potato salad, or French fries. Go all out with the "Turkel Burgel," topped with two strips of bacon, cheddar cheese, and thousand-island dressing for $6.95 (so much for health food).

Mel's has plenty of other sandwiches, like the fried egg sandwich for $3.95 and a fresh turkey breast sandwich for $5.95. Don't miss the charbroiled chicken sandwiches: The "American Graffiti" (named, as you may know, because Mel's in L.A. was featured in that rock 'n roll classic) has sauteed mushrooms, Swiss cheese, and fries for $6.75. Did Mr. C mention the hot dogs? Or, the salads? The choices are enough to make you dizzy!

Dinner blue-plates are also cheap in price, but not in portions. "Mel's

Spring Chicken," crispy fried chicken with coleslaw and fries ($7.45), "Grandma's Turkey Meat Loaf" with cranberry sauce, lumpy mashed potatoes, homemade gravy, and vegetables ($7.95), or broiled pork chops with grilled onions, potatoes, and veggies ($7.95) are just a few of the myriad choices.

Mel's is also a popular breakfast stop. The menu includes pancakes, French toast, and waffles, hash and eggs, omelettes, and more. And, Mr. C couldn't leave off without telling you about Mel's tantalizing ice cream fountain and other desserts—pies, chocolate fudge cake, and cheesecake, not to mention shakes, malts, sundaes, floats, vanilla Cokes, and more. Just go already!

Petrouchka

- 2930 College Ave. (Ashby Ave.), Berkeley; (510) 848-7860

Petrouchka, only a half-dozen blocks or so from the Berkeley campus, serves up hearty Russian specialties, along with more Westernized vegetarian dishes, too. If you think of Russian food as just beef stroganoff (which they have, of course; flambéed with brandy, or sautéed with mushrooms and onions in rich sour cream sauce, each for $9.95) then you are in for a surprise.

Meat dishes are a bit on the pricey side; a few rise a dollar or two over Mr. C's usual limit, but still quite reasonable. Try salmon *shpinatom*, salmon wrapped in spinach and served in a flaky, buttery pastry for $10.95; *golubtsy*, cabbage leaves stuffed with ground beef and brown rice and served with tomato sauce and sour cream for $8.95; or Manchurian *shashlyk*, a kind of kebab made with chicken marinated in fresh ginger, soy, lemon, garlic, and honey, for $11.95. All entrees come with side orders of cracked wheat pilaf, fresh vegetables, and red cabbage.

Vegetarian specialties are more reasonably priced, and as mentioned above, they offer something a little out of the ordinary—at least for Russian cuisine, which is already unusual for many folks. Featured items include *peretz Petrouchka*, a green bell pepper stuffed with brown rice, mushrooms, carrots, raisins, pine nuts, and olives, and topped with tomato sauce and sour cream, for $8.95; and a tofu version of the Manchurian *shashlyk* for $9.25. There are even dishes from further afield, such as the Greek specialty *moussaka*—layers of eggplant, tomato sauce, and cheese baked with a topping of bechamel sauce and black olives, for $8.95.

Don't miss Petrouchka's rich desserts; these are as traditionally heavy as you'd expect. Specialties include *charlotte malakoff*, a combination of chocolate, ground almonds, and Grand Marnier, served with seasonal fruit puree for $3.75; chocolate mousse, made with a recipe that includes espresso coffee and brandy, for $2.95; and the aptly named "Chocolate Decadence," a rich confection of chocolate baked wtih egg yolks and served with that fruit puree, again for $3.75.

Pirro's

• 2283 Shattuck Ave. (Bancroft Way), Berkeley; (510) 849-1273

Berkeley residents don't have to trek all the way over to San Francisco's North Beach to get good Italian food—not when they have Pirro's, just a short walk from Cal. Whether you're looking for lunch entrees, a sandwich, a pizza to enjoy with friends, or a full dinner, Pirro's has you covered.

Lunch entrees are very reasonably priced indeed; you can get spaghetti and meatballs, ravioli, spinach fettucine with clam sauce, or lasagna, all between $4.10 and $4.50. These are served with French bread, and are available any time of the day. Sandwiches are also a bargain. Hamburgers start from a mere $2.90 (cheeseburgers from $3.05); a meatball and mozzarella sandwich is $3.10. Choose from all kinds of cheeses and breads on those sandwiches, along with a selection of soups and salads.

Looking for the quintessential

MR. CHEAP'S PICKS
Oakland

✔ **Café de Bordeaux**—Sure, it's in Chinatown East; but these folks run a continental bistro with lunches and dinners that are classy and low-priced.

✔ **Ratto's**—Old-World Italian lunches in a big, bright room; plus moderately priced dinner/opera packages on weekends.

American meal, anytime of the day? It's pizza! Solo diners will appreciate Pirro's nine-inch, individual pizza, just $4.30 for the basic cheese pie. Add mushrooms, salami, Italian sausage, or pepperoni for only 40¢ each (try to find *these* prices in The City). Health-conscious? Try the vegetarian special, with mushrooms, bell pepper, onions, and fresh tomatoes for $5.60. They also make pizzas on French bread, again from $4.30.

Pirro's dinner menu includes plenty of traditional favorites. For the best value, order a full dinner, which includes minestrone soup or salad, French bread, and ice cream for dessert. Specialties include meat or vegetarian lasagna or cannelloni, each $10.70; ravioli, $9.60; and spinach fettucine with marinara sauce, $9.20. If you prefer a la carte, knock $3 off these prices.

All items on the menu are also available as take-out—perfect for late nights spent cramming for mid-terms. Pirro's is open Monday through Thursday from 11 a.m. to 11:30 p.m., Friday until midnight; Saturday from 11:30 a.m. to midnight, and Sunday from 4:30 to 10:30 p.m. only.

Pollo's

• 100 Berkeley Square (Addison St.), Berkeley; (510) 486-8027

Barely a stone's throw from UC-

Berkeley, Pollo's puts together an interesting and tasty array of international foods for breakfast, lunch, or dinner. These go well beyond the joint's namesake (that's *chicken*, son), all with prices that will fit into any student's or visitor's budget.

This is also a great place to meet up with the gang because almost everyone will find something to enjoy. Barbecued chicken, of course, is the specialty of the house; a quarter-chicken is just $4.10, while a half-bird goes for a still-reasonable $5.99. But the menu also stretches to include Middle Eastern standards, like gyros ($3.69); Mexican favorites, like burritos ($2.75 to $3.79); as well as good ol' American basics—burgers for $2.29, grilled cheese sandwiches for $2.45, and BLTs for $3.50. This is a snack food hangout, with such things as nacho platters for just $2.99 to $3.99.

Stop in for breakfast, quick and cheap. Several varieties of omelettes are priced from $3.69 to $4.45. Or, you can get two eggs with home fries, toast, and jam, and bacon or sausage, all for $3.99.

Ratto's Pasta
• 821 Washington St. (Ninth St.), Oakland; 832-6503

As in so many American cities, Oakland's main Italian section sits cheek-by-jowl next to its Chinese district. Ratto's is a large grocery store and restaurant which pretty much anchors the Italian side of the neighborhood (though a Mexican crafts shop is tossed in next door, for good measure). The grocery store, which is reasonably priced if not cheap, seems to have everything in the world—fresh pasta (of course), meats and homemade sausages, imported olive oil, breads, coffee beans, grains, the works.

Next to all this is the restaurant, a huge, bustling room with a lot of old-world charm. Well-worn wooden floors, a handsome service bar with a polished espresso machine, and a stainless steel open kitchen at the far end make Ratto's feel like something out of New York's Little Italy—or

the home country itself. It's big, but comfortable.

There are two unique opportunities to enjoy all of this, both of which also happen to be easy on the budget as well. Lunches, served on weekdays, are offered cafeteria-style. A variety of homemade pasta dishes are priced around $3.50 to $5.00 for a heaping plate. Add a glass of house wine for $2.00, and you have hearty, simple elegance. There are freshly made desserts too, along with the above-mentioned espresso.

Now, here's another great deal. Every Friday and Saturday evening, Ratto's serves up fancier food, followed by live opera music. This isn't one of those waiters-doing-a-song-before-dessert things; a four-course meal is served at 6:30, including entrees like lemon-herb chicken with saffron risotto, along with salad, pasta, dessert, and coffee. Then, at 7:30, the show begins—two full hours of opera songs and arias, performed by different professional singers each night. Many of these are working and/or training all around the Bay Area, often young, rising talent ready for the spotlight.

It all adds up to a joyous and passionate evening. And how much for this extravaganza? A very reasonable $22.50 per person, including dinner and the show. Hey, you can spend more than that just to go to some opera houses, and they won't feed you, either. This is a popular attraction; and since it's only offered twice a week, reservations are recommended.

Taiwan Restaurant
• 2071 University Ave. (Shattuck Ave.), Berkeley; (510) 845-1456

Much like language, food is an ever-changing, fluid art form that is strongly influenced when it "migrates" through other regions. The Taiwan Restaurant specializes in the Taiwanese versions of dishes from Beijing, Szechwan, Canton, Hunan, and Manchuria. They also offer a selection of Taiwan's native dishes for (in their words) "those who feel adventurous."

Adventurous souls will certainly not lack for dishes to thrill their taste buds. Try squid with celery for $4.75, fresh red snapper filet in red or white wine sauce for $6.50, or wok-fried oysters in black soybean sauce for $5.95. They also offer a variety of Taiwanese soups, like "Petals of Pork" soup ($4.50), or fish ball soup ($4.75).

If you prefer something a bit more familiar, try their regional Chinese dishes. Appetizers include spring rolls ($3.50) and fried spareribs ($5.50) along with the usual assortment of soups. Regular customers rave about Taiwan's dumplings; you'll find them under "Rice & Noodles." Six steamed dumplings, with meat or vegetable fillings, are just $3.05.

House specialty dishes are all nice and cheap, and you're sure to see many of your favorites on the list. If you like seafood, go for the spiced prawns ($6.95), red snapper in lemon sauce ($6.50), or sauteed scallops ($7.50). Meat dishes include pork with pickled greens ($5.95), lemon chicken ($5.95), and Mongolian lamb ($5.95). Vegetarians are not forgotten either—choose from over twenty different meatless dishes, including basil with eggplant ($4.50), vegetable chow mein ($3.75), or wok-fried spinach with garlic ($4.50).

The Taiwan Restaurant also has one of *the* best lunch specials around. For just $2.86—that's right folks, $2.86—you'll get the soup of the day, steamed rice, and an entree from such choices as cashew chicken, mandarin beef, pork with bean sprouts, vegetables deluxe, or broccoli chicken. And for $3.88, you can move up to things like spiced prawns. Just off the Berkeley campus, this is a classic place for student budgets.

Tea Spot Café
• 2072 San Pablo Ave. (University Ave.), Berkeley; (510) 848-7376
In the boonies of Berkeley, but worth seeking out, is the Tea Spot Café. They describe themselves as serving "comfort food for the discriminating palate." With their varied selections of breakfast and lunch dishes, and a revolving menu of dinner creations, this is a pretty apt description.

Breakfast is definitely the big thing here, available until noon on weekdays, and all day on the weekends (yeah!). You could go with the traditional two eggs any style for $4.35 (ho hum), but why, when they offer such wonderful alternatives? Try the Mexican scramble—eggs scrambled with scallions, corn chips, green chilis, jack and cheddar cheeses, and salsa, all for $5.75; or the tofu scramble, same price, marinated tofu sauteed with spinach, scallions, and tomatoes.

They also have interesting omelette choices, such as the Southwestern—filled with turkey sausage, scallions, tomatoes, and jack cheese, with sour cream and salsa on the side ($7.25). All of the egg breakfasts come with home fries and toast.

Folks who have a sweet tooth will want to try one of the "from the griddle" offerings like buttermilk pancakes; but again, for something different, try the banana walnut pancakes, made with fresh sliced bananas and walnuts thrown right into the batter, for $4.25. For an extra dollar, try sour cherry syrup, real maple syrup, or pomegranate molasses as a topping. On the weekends, breakfasts get even more offbeat: Blueberry rice griddle cakes ($5.25), and banana fritters ($4.25).

Lunch choices are mostly sandwiches and burgers, but they do throw in some salads, soup, and chili, too. As with the breakfasts, these sandwiches are anything but boring. Specialty sandwiches include blackened chicken ($5.75), grilled eggplant ($4.75), and pesto grilled cheese ($5.25). Along with the basic hamburger, they also have turkey and tofu burgers. All sandwiches are served with cole slaw and pickles.

Dinner is only served Thursday through Saturday evenings, and the menu is different every night. Some entrees recently presented were apricot pinon chicken ($8.25), stir-fry vegetables over brown rice ($6.50), and grilled sesame tofu steaks ($7.25). Interesting appetizers, too, such as grilled polenta and chicken satay, along with a choice of salads.

The Tea Spot Café is also a great place to hang out and hear local musicians (See listing under "Entertainment: Music"). They're open Tuesday through Saturday from 8 a.m. to 2:30 p.m. and Sunday, for brunch only, until 2 p.m. Dinner is served Thursday through Saturday from 5:30 p.m. to 9:00 p.m.

Thai Bar-B-Q
- 1958 Shattuck Ave. (University Ave.), Berkeley; (510) 549-1958
- 730 Van Ness Ave. (Turk St.), San Francisco; (415) 441-1640

San Francisco Bar-B-Q
- 1328 18th St. (Texas St.), San Francisco; (415) 431-8956

It may sound like chicken and ribs, but this is one (actually, three) of The City's great Asian barbecue-and-noodle houses. These small, family-style joints serve up great, freshly-prepared food, cheap.

The menu may be bland ("Bar-B-Q Chicken Dinner $5.75, Bar-B-Q Lamb Dinner $7.75, Bar-B-Q Scallops Dinner $8.25. . ."), but hey, we're not looking for creativity here. What you will get are huge portions of hot food at prices that go no higher than $8.75. And that's for a complete dinner, with rice, salad, and bread on the side.

Mr. C opted for one of the "Noodles" entrees, which offer a similar array of choices served in a large bowl on a bed of egg noodles. He enjoyed the tasty, if not super-spicy, Thai pork sausage ($5.50); as with all noodle dishes, this combo was garnished with lettuce and ground peanuts over the top,and far too many noodles to finish.

Other interesting choices include duck, prawns, veal, salmon steak, and oysters. Most of these are available as full entrees, noodle dishes, or appetizer plates. And that's about it, folks. You can add a salad, topped with

meat ($5.25); or a bowl of beef noodle soup ($3.25). There are a few beers and wines, including Singha beer and Anchor Steam (each $2.75). House wines are $1.75 a glass. Seating, by the way, is ultra-informal, at long tables side-by-side with your fellow diners. Chances are, working on this wonderful food, you'll hardly look up enough to notice.

Zachary's Pizza
- 5801 College Ave. (Oak Grove St.), Berkeley; (510) 655-6385
- 1853 Solano Ave. (Alameda Ave.), Berkeley; (510) 525-5950

Zachary's Pizza has been proclaimed the "Best pizza in the Bay Area" in both the San Francisco *Focus* magazine and the *East Bay Express* reader's polls. It has gotten positively gushing write-ups in the *Chronicle*, *Examiner*, *California* magazine, and the *Contra Costa Times*.

What's all the fuss about? Their "stuffed pizza," that's what. If you're thinking that this must be like a calzone or a deep dish pizza, guess again. And try one. Basically, it involves a thin layer of dough baked in a deep pan, which is literally stuffed with cheese, spices, and whatever ingredients you choose; it's then covered with another thin layer of dough, which melts into the cheese as the pie bakes. Finally, it is topped with mildly spicy tomato sauce. The only downside to this yummy invention is, of course, the 30 to 40 minutes' cooking time. And, since this is such a popular place, sometimes the wait for a table is even longer. In short, you can invest a whole evening on one of these pizzas. Fortunately, time—not money—is the heaviest investment you'll make.

Now, would Mr. C be of any use to you if he didn't suggest a few ways around this dilemma? If you do have time to spare, order a salad while you're waiting. Zachary's offers a house salad for $2.59 or a spinach salad for $3.39, with a homemade vinaigrette or mustard-French dressing. Another approach: Order your pizza while you're waiting in line for your table, so the pie is ready, or close to it, when you sit down. A third solution is to order a half-baked pizza, which you can then take home and finish baking at your leisure. In fact, you can take home an uncooked pizza (or two or three. . .) and keep it in the fridge for those "what'll I serve the guys?" emergencies.

A small stuffed pizza, 10 inches in diameter, is ideal for two people and costs $9.20, plus a few dollars extra for more ingredients. Bigger sizes, for four to five people, range up to top prices around $18.99. If you're having trouble deciding how to fill your pizza, the restaurant lists a few favorite combinations to inspire you. Zachary's pride and joy, the spinach and mushroom stuffed pizza, has the unusual price of $11.13 (small). One of *Focus* magazine's Gold Medal judges proclaimed "It's better than mom's lasagna." (Didn't know magazines *had* mothers.)

Zachary's also has a regular thin crust pizza which, though it hasn't won the kudos of its big brother, uses the same homemade dough and spicy tomato sauce. A small thin pizza serves one or two people, and starts at $5.55 for a plain cheese pie. Since these are smaller, they only take about 20 minutes to cook. Special combinations can be ordered either stuffed, starting at $12.50, or thin, from $8.85. These include such delicious and unique creations as chicken pizza, made with baked chicken breast, mushrooms, and a fresh basil/garlic/tomato sauce; and Mexican chorizo pizza, with chorizo sausage, jack cheese, and mild diced green chilies.

Along with great food, Zachary's is a fun place to eat—an upscale, yet still affordable hangout where students meet yuppies. The restaurant is festooned with street signs of famous Chicago avenues, the city that invented deep dish pizza; clever pictures adorn the walls, showing pies

as Picasso, Van Gogh, and other artists might have portrayed them. Zachary's is open seven days.

Zona Rosa*
- 2366 Telegraph Ave. (Durant St.), Berkeley; (510) 649-0292
- 1797 Haight St. (Shrader St.), San Francisco; (415) 668-7717

Sure, there are only about a zillion burrito-stand restaurants in the Bay Area. Well, Zona Rosa is consistently one of the more popular examples, as crowds will attest. Why? Could it be the fact that they make a slavish point of using only fresh ingredients ("everything except tortillas is made from scratch")? Ingredients that include no preservatives, chemicals, or MSG? No lard, and only vegetable oil? Could be. Or, maybe it's just that everything is delicious, filling, and cheap. Hey, that's all Mr. C needs to hear.

Your basic burrito, made with diced steak or chicken ("grilled in your view") and served with rice and beans, costs $3.45. A larger version is available for just $4.20. Add salsa or guacamole for another 45 cents. Can't beat that! Simple, tortilla and cheese quesadillas are a mere $1.60, with the same additions offered. Nachos con Carne (that being beef or chicken) are $4.99, which is about as much as you can spend on one platter in here; that price will also get you a combo plate, with your choice of any two kinds of tacos or enchiladas, plus rice, beans and salad. Fill up!

There are also several all-vegetarian entrees, right down to the non-dairy cheese which can be substituted if you prefer. Whatever you get, they'll prepare it for you quickly at the front counter; Zona Rosa is a grab-a-tray and find-a-seat kind of place. Don't forget the lunchtime special, offered until 2:00—an enchilada or taco, rice, beans, salad, and soda, all for $3.99. In the evenings, ZR serves until 10 p.m. only.

HAIGHT-ASHBURY
including the Haight, Cole Valley

Café Paradiso
- 1725 Haight St. (Cole St.), San
  Francisco; (415) 221-5244

This place almost seems out of
place amidst the hard-rocking joints
at this end of the Haight; a cozy,
laid-back, romantically lit bar and
restaurant, located next door to the
Red Vic Movie House. Certainly
makes a nice alternative. And although the food matches the upscale
atmosphere, the prices do not. The
menu offers a little bit of everything—from Tex-Mex to crêpes,
from snacks to full dinners.

Start off with appetizers like sourdough bread with roasted garlic and
pesto ($2.95), nachos topped with
homemade vegetarian chili ($3.95),
or the soup of the day ($1.95 a cup,
$3.95 a bowl). During Mr. C's visit,
this was a tasty corn bisque.

Salads and sandwiches include
Greek salads filled with the works;
these come in sizes labeled "huge"
($7.50) and "medium" ($5.25). Sandwiches continue the Middle East-
ern/healthy theme, like hummus,
grilled chicken, or the Paradiso
($4.95), a veggie burger made from
rice, nuts, eggs, cheese, fresh vegetables, and herbs. All sandwiches give
you a choice of great breads from the
Tassajara Bakery—French sourdough, five-grain, potato, onion dill.

Full entrees, which come with
bread and a side salad, take the "comfort food" route. They range from turkey pot pie ($7.50) to macaroni and
cheese—but *please*, it's not just *any*
mac. This one's made with sun-dried
tomatoes, sauteed mushrooms, and
bechamel sauce, all for $6.95. Or, try
one of the ever-changing daily specials, such as crêpes Dijon (also
$6.95), filled with vegetables, spin-
ach, and three different cheeses. Try

to save room for the great homemade
desserts, too.

All of these are available from
lunch through 10:00 p.m. on
weeknights; an hour later on weekends. But wait, there's more. Sad to
say, this is one of the few Haight restaurants serving food any later than
that; on Thursdays, Fridays and Saturdays, at least. A separate late-night
menu is served until 12:30 a.m.,
made up primarily of the appetizers
and desserts from the regular fare.
Again, while the rest of the street is
settling down for the night, this can
be quite a relaxing scene: small, can-
dlelit tables, artistic murals on the
walls, and a long, fully stocked bar.

Ganges Restaurant
- 775 Frederick St. (Willard St.), San
  Francisco; (415) 661-7290

This restaurant near the Cole Valley
area is inexpensive cuisine to the
power of two: it's Indian and vegetarian. Low-priced as it is, the atmosphere is quite elegant—with a decor
of natural wood and burgundy velvet
and mellow lighting. A host will
greet you; sit at regular tables, or opt
for the rear section with traditional
Eastern seating on floor cushions.

As to the food itself, there are also
a few options: choose from four different dinner combinations, or go a la
carte. Either way, you'll see several
curries of the day, selected from over
a dozen possibilities. These include
such yummy blends as baked bananas stuffed with coconut, cilantro,
and green chilies; zucchini mixed
with garbanzo bean flour and a spicy
peanut sauce; kofta, or vegetarian
meatballs, with spices, onions, nuts,
and sour cream; and many others.
Not all of these are necessarily hot
and spicy—mater paneer, for exam-

ple, is a mild casserole of peas and farmer's cheese.

Anyway, you get to fit one of these into the dinner combinations. For $12.50, you can have the works: an appetizer, papadum (a spicy, crisp bread), your curry, vegetables on the side, saffron rice, flat (soft) bread, and an Indian dessert. For $11.50, you can skip the appetizer course; for $9.50 and $8.50, you can have still smaller versions of the deal. If you choose to dine a la carte, there is still an $8.50 minimum per person; but there is a wider selection of appetizers ($1.50 to $4) and side dishes ($3-$4.50), with the curries priced at $5.50 each.

It's all delicious. Add a 22-ounce glass of Taj Mahal beer for $4.25, or a domestic brew ($1.75); wines by the glass or carafe are also served; as are various teas (try the *chai*, a spiced tea sweetened with milk and honey, $1.50). Desserts (most $2.50) are traditional Indian style creations, from rice pudding to *shreekhand*, a blend of yogurt and sour cream mixed with saffron and nuts.

Take-out orders are welcomed. The Ganges is open for dinner only, Tuesdays through Saturdays from 5-10 p.m. On Friday evenings, usually from 7-9 p.m., live tablas music adds to the exotic fun.

Kan Zaman
- 1793 Haight St. (Shrader St.), San Francisco; (415) 751-9656

A meal at Kan Zaman is like a trip to a faraway land—much farther than just the end of the Haight. The restaurant features traditional Middle Eastern food at very reasonable prices. All of the cheap and wonderful favorites are here, gathered into *maza*, sort of a sampler platter. Cold maza plates include things like hummus, tabouleh, and baba ganoush. Hot mazas include falafel, meat pies, stuffed grape leaves, and spicy sausage.

Mazas can be ordered a la carte, or in combinations. Individual cold mazas are about $2 or so; hot items range from $2.25 to $4.50. Three

---

MR. CHEAP'S PICKS
The Haight

- ✔ **Kan Zaman**—A truly Middle Eastern setting to go with the Middle Eastern menu. Sit on pillows in the front window so you can people-watch as you munch falafel.
- ✔ **Mad Dog in the Fog**—A rah-ther authentic English tavern, highlighting The City's Victorian connection. Darts, unusual beers, and cheap pub food.
- ✔ **Zona Rosa**—Perhaps the best quality among the Bay Area's many burrito joints.

---

combination plates are on the main menu: The "basic maza," with two cold items and one hot item of your choice, for $6.95; the "basic maza plus," with three cold and and two hot items, for $9.75; and the "total maza," with four cold and three hot items, for $14.50. All of these are served with pita bread. The larger combinations are fun and cheap eats for groups; mix and match your favorites, or sample a variety of tastes.

Not everything must be ordered in this way. Falafel and kebab (chicken or beef) sandwiches are $3.25 and $3.95, respectively. Also, Kan Zaman has recently expanded into breakfast offerings. Again, these take the form of platters, like the "Casablanca Brunch," which includes hard boiled eggs, feta cheese, zatar bread with olive oil, and home fries (are those Middle Eastern?) for $4.75; and "Sunrise in Old Jerusalem," with timeria, strawberries, and fruit for $3.95.

Kan Zaman has a number of interesting drink possibilities, at any time of day. Strong blends of Arabic tea and coffee, as well as warm, spiced wine are a few of the more unusual offerings. They also have sweets like biscotti, baklava, rice pudding, and more for $1.50 to $2. And, while we're on the subject of indulgences: If you smoke, you may want to try their flavored tobacco in authentic *shee sha* pipes, also called *hookahs*. Waiters will bring the pipes to your table, clean and ready to smoke, and they will give you pointers if you're new to this particular method.

At Kan Zaman you will truly feel as if you've stepped into another country, even another century. Along with regular tables, you can sit on plush floor pillows; the entire room is decorated with woven rugs, copper pots, and other Middle Eastern touches. Late in the evening, genuine belly dancing adds to the (literally) exotic atmosphere. Glimpse it all before going in, if you wish, through the large windows at the front.

Mad Dog in the Fog
- 530 Haight St. (Fillmore St.), San Francisco; (415) 626-7279

Here's Mr. Cheap's choice along the gritty restaurant/bar stretch of the lower Haight. Mad Dog is perhaps the closest thing in The City to an authentic English pub (Mr. C knows and loves the real thing). It's a bustling, lively place for a pint and a game of darts, with over a dozen fine beers on tap—including Guinness *and* Murphy's Irish Stout, Blackthorn Cider, and Fuller's E.S.B. (extra special bitters—a sweet and heavy brew, definitely *not* for the light beer crowd). There are many more varieties in bottles for the beer connoisseur. Most are priced at $3 a pint, which is not unreasonable a' tall.

What makes the place even more authentic is the food. Like any good pub, cheap eats are both made possible by—and an attraction for—the bar. All the English classics are here, along with a few San Fran stringers mixed in for that trans-Atlantic feel. Bangers and mash, which may sound naughty but is just British for sausage and potatoes, is $5 and includes baked beans on the side. Same price for a chicken pastie (meat pie),

served hot with beans and a salad on the side; or, have one filled with sausage and chopped egg, or cooked veggies (that California twist).

Mr. C enjoyed a big, hearty plate of Shepherd's Pie ($6), again with sides of beans and salad; the Ploughman's Lunch, same price, is available for both lunch and dinner. It's a cold platter of cheeses, salad, vegetables, and bread, served with what the English call "a packet of crisps"; that's potato chips to the average American. Out of place, but hardly out of line, are such dinners as chicken curry over rice, and Jamaican jerk chicken with mashed potatoes, each $6.

These are all available daily from the pub's opening time of 11:30 a.m. to 9:30 p.m. during the week; and until 5:30 p.m. Friday and Saturday, 7:30 p.m. Sunday. The bar's too busy at the other times, and that's where you place your order. Find a table, and someone from the kitchen will eventually find you with the food. Those homemade pasties, by the way, are always available until 1:00 a.m.— for those who don't believe that Guinness is "a meal in itself."

Mr. C has some extra deals to report on: Monday's happy hour stretches from 11:30 a.m. to 6:00 p.m., when you can get a free drink with any meal. Pints are also reduced from $3 to $2.25, and pitchers from $11 to $8. Also, Mad Dog hosts live jazz and rock bands on Sunday evenings from 9-11, with no cover charge; same deal for an open-mike night on Tuesdays from 8-10, featuring acoustic music acts.

Taqueria Balazo*
- 1654 Haight St. (Cole St.), San Francisco; (415) 864-8608

Funky, colorful lighting—almost like the scenery for some futuristic video—and a rock beat set this place apart from the many other taco stands around town. That, and the darkly humorous imagery of skeletons and such, borrowed from the Mexican "Day of the Dead" holiday.

Don't worry, though; you don't have to be a rock 'n roller in a studded collar to eat here (though it probably helps). As to the menu itself, well, it's your basic Mex—but cheap. Tacos, filled with chicken or pork, are just 95¢ each. Same price for a simple cheese quesadilla. Burritos, whether chicken, pork, or steak, go for $2.95 on a plate with rice and beans, salsa and chips. Of course, if you *are* a Deadhead, you may want to order Jerry's Burrito ($3.75), filled with "tender cactus" (yep), beans, goat cheese, and rice.

There are, in fact, several vegetarian and seafood dishes here, including tacos stuffed with sautéed vegetables. And, for something that is definitely different, try a tostada de Ceviche—snapper marinated in lime juice—just $1.50.

There are beers in the refrigerator case, as well as imported fruit drinks like mango and papaya. Seating is limited, but there are some tables here. Many people seem to order something at the counter and continue their stroll along the Haight, munching away.

Zona Rosa*
- 1797 Haight St. (Shrader St.), San Francisco; (415) 668-7717
- 2366 Telegraph Ave. (Durant St.), Berkeley; (510) 649-0292

Sure, there are only about a zillion burrito-stand restaurants in the Bay Area. Well, Zona Rosa is consistently one of the more popular examples, as crowds will attest. Why? Could it be

the fact that they make a slavish point of using only fresh ingredients ("everything except tortillas is made from scratch")? Ingredients that include no preservatives, chemicals, or MSG? No lard, and only vegetable oil? Could be. Or, maybe it's just that everything is delicious, filling, and cheap. Hey, that's all Mr. C needs to hear.

Your basic burrito, made with diced steak or chicken ("grilled in your view") and served with rice and beans, costs $3.45. A larger version is available for just $4.20. Add salsa or guacamole for another 45 cents. Can't beat that! Simple, tortilla and cheese quesadillas are a mere $1.60, with the same additions offered. Nachos con Carne (that being beef or chicken) are $4.99, which is about as much as you can spend on one platter in here; that price will also get you a combo plate, with your choice of any two kinds of tacos or enchiladas, plus rice, beans and salad. Fill up!

There are also several all-vegetarian entrees, right down to the non-dairy cheese which can be substituted if you prefer. Whatever you get, they'll prepare it for you quickly at the front counter; Zona Rosa is a grab-a-tray and find-a-seat kind of place. Don't forget the lunchtime special, offered until 2:00—an enchilada or taco, rice, beans, salad, and soda, all for $3.99. In the evenings, ZR serves until 10 p.m. only.

MISSION AREA
including the Castro, Noe Valley, Potrero Hill

Asimakopoulos Café
- 288 Connecticut St. (18th St.), San Francisco; (415) 552-8789

If you can just pronounce the name of this place, you're doing well already. It's one of the many delightful discoveries tucked way up at the top

of Potrero Hill—a refined, yet relaxed, restaurant serving elegant food at reasonable prices.

The name also tells us, of course, that the cuisine here is Greek; but this is no gyros shack. Several complete dinners start just above ten dollars; these are served with fresh vegetables perfectly cooked *al dente*, your choice of soup or salad (Mr. C recommends the chicken rice soup, in a creamy lemon base) and, of course, warm pita bread.

Among the lower priced entrees, moussaka is a classic, and beautifully done: layers of eggplant and ground beef with a custard sauce baked over the top. The chef spikes the meat with cinnamon, a twist Mr. C had never encountered before; it's beautiful. Spanakopita is another Greek favorite, in which spinach and feta cheese are baked inside flaky phyllo dough. Kota lemoni is grilled marinated chicken, with a lemon and herb tang to it, served with rice pilaf. Each of these, as full dinners, is priced at $11.50. Other choices range up to $16 or so, along with fresh fish, at market prices; each is available a la carte, for $2 less (but see how much extra you get for those two bucks!).

A fun budget choice, or as a great idea for sharing, is the hot appetizer plate ($9.75). This includes several of the phyllo-and-fillings items, meatballs seasoned with mint, locanico sausage flavored with orange, as well as hummus and pita bread. Or, try the souvlaki ($8 for two skewers, $2.25 each additional), wonderfully tasty grilled lamb, pork, and chicken, served with fried potatoes.

Have a bottle of Anchor Steam for $2.50 (they probably walked these over from the brewery, a few blocks away), or a glass of house wine for $2.75. Authentic Greek wines are on hand as well. The setting is light and open; works by area artists hang on cream-colored walls. Ceiling fans turn slowly overhead. There is a central counter, and natural wood tables.

As you can probably tell, Asimakopoulos is the sort of place Mr. C loves to find: slightly above his usual price range, yet way above his accustomed dining experience. Still, it's not outrageously priced; the place fills up even on weeknights, clearly with a neighborhood crowd of regulars who find it a comforting end to the work day. And, for those who prefer to unwind at home, there's also the **Kali Orexi Deli** just around the side at 1518 18th St.; telephone (415) 552-8794. Here, the same kitchen turns out soups, salads, sandwiches, and a handful of main entrees to go. Both operations are open seven days a week.

Aux Delices

- 1002 Potrero Ave. (22nd St.), San Francisco; (415) 285-3196
- 2327 Polk St. (Green St.), San Francisco; (415) 928-4977

Aux Delices has received rave reviews from *San Francisco Focus*, which declared it the best restaurant in the Russian Hill area, and *San Francisco Magazine*, which said this is "the finest Vietnamese cuisine in The City." Their combination of Vietnamese and French influences is certainly winning raves with the critics, and their low prices win similar raves from Mr. C.

Unlike many Viet houses which cook up soups and stews, Aux Delices works more in the entree manner of other Asian restaurants. They have several vegetarian dishes, all for $5.95, including mixed mushrooms with tender greens, bean curd with black mushrooms, and vegetables with house curry. Pork, chicken, and beef dishes, meanwhile, are just as plentiful and cheap. Try a plate of "Singing Chicken with Ginger" ($6.95), pork with broccoli or asparagus ($6.50), a stuffed half-chicken with gravy ($7.95, or a whole one for just $15), and beef with vegetables in spicy sauce ($6.95).

Seafood dishes are also very well-priced. Sweet and sour shrimp is a real bargain at $6.50, about as low a price for those craved crustaceans as you're likely to find anywhere (much less at a restaurant with so many accolades). Squid with vegetables ($6.95) are another good deal; and don't miss AD's pan-fried catfish ($7) and sauteed red snapper ($7.95).

Finish off your meal with such traditional Indochinese treats as custard or fried bananas. This branch of Aux Delices is open for lunch only, week-

days from 11 a.m. to 2:30 p.m. The
Polk Street location is open for dinner everyday from 5 p.m. to 10 p.m.

Barney's Gourmet Hamburgers

- 4138 24th St. (Castro St.), San
  Francisco; (415) 282-7770
- 3344 Steiner St. (Lombard St.),
  San Francisco; (415) 563-0307
- 1591 Solano Ave. (Peralta St.),
  Berkeley; (510) 526-8185
- 5819 College Ave. (Ghabod St.),
  Oakland; (510) 601-0444
- 4162 Piedmont Ave. (41st St.),
  Oakland; (510) 655-7180

Big is the operative word at Barney's.
This growing chain of attractive, yuppie restaurants is getting big, with locations all around the Bay Area. They
serve up a big menu of big, juicy burgers—plus a few other things. The
prices, however, are not as big as
you'd expect. Which makes Barney's
big with Mr. C.

Those burgers include six-ounce,
freshly rolled beef and eight-ounce,
boneless chicken breast sandwiches.
The basic Barney burger (can you
sense an alliteration overload coming?) is just $3.95; add cheese for an-
other fifty cents, and/or fries for
$1.75. Or, step up to the Big Barney
Burger, a half-pounder, for $4.95, and
a larger order of fries for $2.25; still
not bad at all. By the way, they do up
a nifty order of spicy curly fries for
$3.25, too.

Meanwhile, there are no less than
twenty-two variations of burgers (big
is the word, remember). Try the pizza
burger ($4.75), or perhaps the Popeye
burger ($4.95), topped with sauteed
spinach and feta cheese. The Maui
Waui ($5.25) is glazed with teriyaki
sauce, and served with pineapple and
Canadian (?) bacon. And the Russian
burger ($4.95) adds layers of sour
cream, scallions, and sauteed mushrooms, served on dark rye bread instead of a roll.

Most of these are also available on
chicken sandwiches as well, usually a
dollar more. And don't forget the tofu
patty burgers, for the health-conscious crowd. Plus soups and salads,
club sandwiches, and—at the Oak-

MR. CHEAP'S PICKS
The Mission

✔ **Pauline's Pizza Pie**—Thin
crust, "eccentric" toppings, and
upscale surroundings in the
up-and-coming Mission.

✔ **Ti-Couz**—Another example of
the Mission's trendier
side—French crêpes. As much
fun to watch as to eat.

---

land branches only, for some reason—
weekend breakfast entrees of omelettes and other egg plates. Forget
parking at the Marina location, by the
way. All branches are open for lunch
and dinner seven days a week
(though not past 10 p.m., except in
summer), and offer efficient take-out
service as well.

Bottom of the Hill

- 1233 17th St. (Texas St.), San
  Francisco; (415) 626-4455

Potrero, that is. This is a fun and
funky place, with every picture hung
crookedly on the walls and live music until 1:00 a.m., seven nights a
week. Bottom of the Hill features
rock, alternative, and jazz music.
There's room for dancing, if you're
so inspired; and a full food and
drinks menu to keep you going all
night.

For a really great deal, come in on
Sunday between 4:00 and 8:30 p.m.
for the all-you-can-eat barbecue with
live music. There's no cover charge,
and the food costs a ridiculously low
$2 to $3. On other nights, Bottom
serves a variety of good food cheap,
including pastas and salads. A huge
burger with fries is only $3.50. If
weather permits, you can enjoy your
chow outside on the patio, or stay inside at a table near the stage.

The cover charge runs a very reasonable $3 to $4 weeknights, going
up only to $5-$6 on weekends. Hang

out in the pool room, with its big fireplace and works by local artists on the walls. And if you like jazz, stick around after the barbecue on Sunday nights, when Bottom offers mellow music by candlelight starting at 9:30.

Burger Joint*
• 807 Valencia St. (19th St.), San Francisco; (415) 824-3494

The Burger Joint is part of the funky, artsy Mission scene; the sort of place where you can get a side of neon with your burger and fries. Everything here is quick and cheap; in fact, you have a choice of exactly four items. These are: 1. A basic hamburger, served on a toasted bun with mayo, lettuce, tomato, red onion, pickles, and French fries, for $4.75 (add cheese for an extra 20¢). 2. A garden burger, the vegetarian version, for $4.45, served on a toasted sprouted whole wheat bun with the same accoutrements. 3. An all-beef hot dog, just $2.75, served on a steamed bun. 4. French fries all by themselves (cooked in peanut oil, slightly healthier than usual deep-frying); a small order for $1.50, or a large for $2.50.

And that's all, folks. Well, there are a bunch of beverages to wash these down; in fact, they actually have more in the way of drinks than food, including sodas, several flavors of Calistoga water, and iced tea, plus milk shakes and root beer floats. What could go better with a hot dog?

The Burger Joint manages to be retro and up-to-the-minute at the same time. The neon accents and booth seating make it an upscale dining experience for this area, sort of a combination of hip fast food. They're open from 11 a.m. to 11 p.m. every day.

Dusit Thai Restaurant
• 3221 Mission St. (29th St.), San Francisco; (415) 826-4639

This restaurant is quite a find, mixed in with basic working-class neighborhood stores in the heart of the Mission/Noe Valley area. Yet a clipping from the Examiner, one of several great reviews posted in the window,

calls Dusit "dollar for dollar, probably the best food deal in San Francisco." These folks must be doing something right.

A peek inside the heavy wooden front door furthers the "oasis" idea. The narrow storefront dining room is elegantly done up with linen tablecloths and napkins, on small tables neatly lined up along both walls. It's a family-run place, and a polite, friendly hostess immediately comes to greet you. Service is definitely as important here as the food itself.

Speaking of which, the extensive (and *not* expensive) menu lists over one hundred items, with something for every taste in Thai cuisine. Meats, seafood, vegetarian dishes, curries, noodles...they're all here. Start off with an order of spring rolls ($4.25), deep-fried and crispy; or one of several soups, most of which are $2.95, such as bean thread soup—ultra-thin noodles, chicken, tiny shrimps, and vegetables in a tasty broth.

Curry dishes allow you to mix and match sauces and meats; the kitchen is also perfectly willing to heat up or tone down the spices to your desires. Beef, chicken and pork entrees are mostly in the $6-$8 range. Among the more interesting choices are *nuer toa-hu* ($6.25), spicy marinated beef sauteed with peppers, garlic, basil, and tofu, in a black bean sauce; *karee kai* ($6.25), a chicken dish in a mild yellow curry, with onions, zucchini, tomatoes, potatoes, and peanuts; and *moo yang* ($6.50), thin slices of pork which are broiled in a combination of spices and honey and served with chili sauce. It's these complex blendings of spicy and sweet that makes the food here so wonderful.

Seafood dishes are about a dollar higher, but still reasonable; vegetarian entrees are a bit lower, most at $5.95. And of course, if you are among the many who judge such a restaurant by its pad Thai ($6.25), you'll be very happy here indeed.

Lunches, by the way, are even better bargains; Dusit offers another fifty or sixty lunch platters, most of which are $5.25, all culled from the main dinner menu. Combination rice plates, at $6.25, come topped with things like barbecued beef and chicken in a sweet and sour sauce, and seafood curry. These are available weekdays only, between 11:30 a.m. and 2:30 p.m. No lunch is served on weekends; and the restaurant is closed all day Tuesday. Dinner hours are 5-10 p.m., six nights a week.

Goat Hill Pizzeria
- 300 Connecticut St. (18th St.), San Francisco; (415) 641-1440

So that's what Potrero means! Actually, Mr. C's trusty *Español/Ingles* dictionary defines a *potrero* as a stud farm, but we won't go any further with this exploration. Instead, Mr. C urges you to explore this yummy restaurant all the way up at the top of the hill. Not only does it serve what many feel to be among the best pizza in the city, but for big appetites, GHP offers a Monday night bargain that just can't be beat.

That's right, folks—every Monday from 5:00-9:30 p.m., just $7 per person gets you all the pizza you can eat, along with all the trips to the salad bar you wish. And there's no skimping, either. The busy open kitchen (you'll pass it on your way to the dining room) cranks out pies of every sort, topped with all your favorites on a crunchy sourdough crust. One variety after another is brought to each table around the room; pick whichever you like, as long as you want. Whatta deal.

Of course, Goat Hill is open every night (lunch too), and they do make a few other things besides pizza. Try a bowl of their homemade vegetable minestrone and garlic bread for $3.50, a platter of ravioli in meat sauce for $7.75 (with meatballs, $9.50), or vegetarian lasagne made with artichoke hearts, spinach, and four cheeses for $8.50. Half-orders are available on all pastas ($4.50-$5.75). Pizza toppings, by the way, range from the usual (salami, green onions, black olives) to the unusual (ham and pineapple, linguica and feta

cheese, pesto and sun-dried tomatoes).

Plus hot sandwiches, chef's salads, and more. Beers and wines are available too; beer by the bottle, on tap (from $1.75), or in pitchers, and wines by the glass (from $2.50), carafe, or liter. It's a mellow place, with plenty of room, traditional red-checked tablecloths and a friendly staff. Open until 9:30 every night; Fridays and Saturdays 'til 10:30.

Miz Brown's
- 2585 Mission St. (21st St.), San Francisco; (415) 648-6070
- 1356 Polk St. (Pine St.), San Francisco; (415) 771-4221
- 731 Clement St. (Seventh Ave.), San Francisco; (415) 752-5017
- 3401 California St. (Laurel Village), San Francisco; (415) 752-2039

Miz Brown's is a good ol' fashioned coffee shop, the kind your parents probably took you to—around the age when chicken-in-a-basket and a chocolate milkshake was your idea of a good meal. Now you can continue the tradition, or just satisfy your own comfort food needs, fast and cheap.

Yes, they have fried chicken; it's batter-dipped, crispy, and greasy, served with a pot of honey and an order of soggy fries, all for $6.25. Daily specials, in fact, may consist of combinations like fried chicken and spaghetti with meat sauce for $7.30—good luck finishing. Other dinners include things like chicken fried steak ($5.75) or fish and chips ($6.45), served with a side salad or cup of soup.

The soups are homemade, by the way, and quite tasty. These range from clam chowder to matzoh ball, different choices daily, all $2.75 a bowl or $1.50 a cup. Salads are also available in two sizes, like a chef's salad for $4.60 or $5.65. Sandwiches start with deli-style basics, all under $5, and go up to double deckers (BLT with turkey and fries, $6.25). Burgers start at $3.45, in ten combinations like "mild green chili and Monterey jack" ($5.65). All of these come with French fries, cole slaw, or potato salad.

MB's also has a children's menu. The kiddies will love a "Tiny Tot" burger and fries; you'll love the price, $1.75. And they've recently added a menu of Mexican dishes, such as two tacos (chicken or beef) with rice and beans for $5.25. (Honestly, though, would you go to a place like this for Tex-Mex when there are so many places around the city where you can get the real thing?)

Of course, you have to save room for dessert; hope you like to eat heavy. All the fountain classics are here, from cherry and vanilla cokes to milk shakes and malteds to something called an "Orange Freeze" ($3.15), made with OJ and orange sherbet. That's more like it. Other desserts include freshly baked pies and homemade rice pudding.

Breakfasts are big here too. The Country Breakfast special will set you up for anything: two eggs, two large pancakes, plus bacon or sausage, all for $6.15. For more dainty appetites, two eggs any style with hash browns and toast are $3.75. Natural, light egg substitutes are available for most orders. Oh, and to return to that nostalgia theme, they have those mini-boxes of cold cereal stacked up on shelves—not to mention individual juke boxes in each booth.

Service is friendly, and the atmosphere is super-casual. One final note: The branch on Clement offers beer and wine, while the Mission Street outpost features a full bar. The others do not serve any liquor. Open well into the evening.

The Patio Café
- 531 Castro St. (18th St.), San Francisco; (415) 621-4640

Of all the restaurants Mr. C has visited, the Patio Café is one his favorites for atmosphere. The rough-hewn wooden floors, tables, and chairs, surrounded by huge tropical plants, gives the place a laid-back atmosphere that is at once lush and rustic. Combine this with its prime location in the Castro (which is becoming more upscale every second), and

you'll understand why Mr. C decided to include it, despite the fact that a few of the dinner entrees go above Mr. C's usual limit of $10.

Enough of the Patio's entrees stay near or under that boundary; plates like spaghettini Roma with tomato, garlic, basil, and capers ($6.95), Chinese ginger chicken ($8.75), All-American meatloaf ($7.95), and Cajun corn-crusted red snapper ($8.95). And, as you can see, the choices are as varied as the countries of the globe itself.

If you're not quite hungry enough for a full meal, try one of their great sandwiches or meal-sized salads. These healthy and filling offerings include a Caesar salad with parmesan and anchovies for $6.50 (or $8.75 with grilled chicken breast over the top); and warm spinach salad with bacon, mushrooms, and feta cheese for $7.95. Meanwhile, a grilled half-pound burger with French fries is just $5.25; add 50¢ more for your choice of Swiss, cheddar, or jack cheese. Vegetarians aren't left out, either. Try the grilled vegi-burger with French fries for $5. They also have several grilled chicken breast sandwiches, including one with jack cheese, guacamole, salsa, and sour cream for $6.95.

Early risers are sure to enjoy the Patio's breakfast menu. Super-cheap weekday breakfast deals will really open your eyes: How about two eggs with bacon or sausage, home fries, and toast or muffin for $2.95, and French toast (or pancakes) with scrambled eggs, home fries, and bacon or sausage for $3.75. These specials are only available Monday through Friday from 8 a.m. to 11 a.m.

Other breakfast specialties include eggs Benedict or eggs Patio (with sauteed spinach and mushrooms in place of the Canadian bacon), each $6.95. The Patio Scramble combines eggs with fennel sausage, mushrooms, spinach, and feta cheese for $6.75. And ten varieties of omelettes include a three-bean chili omelette for $6.25, or the North Beach omelette with sauteed ham, ricotta, and pesto for $6.75. Definitely different.

Pauline's Pizza Pie

• 260 Valencia St. (15th St.), San
  Francisco; (415) 552-2050

There's no peril with *this* Pauline. No
danger of a pizza dinner that's anything less than superb. Pizza is just
about all you can get here, in fact;
but don't go thinking that Pauline's
has anything to do with grabbing a
slice at your corner pie shop. With its
gentrified approach to the Mission
District—waitservice, tablecloths
with place settings, and limited hours
(5-10 p.m., Tuesdays through Saturdays only)—there *must* be something
special about the place.

And it must be the pizza. It's incredible, even just to look at: thin
dough, baked to a crunchy, dark
brown around the edges, and what
they call "eccentric" toppings
(French chevre cheese, pancetta, artichoke hearts, double-smoked ham,
and the like). Hey, how about a Cajun pizza? They call it the "Louisiana
Andouille," and it arrives topped
with andouille sausage, fontina
cheese, bell peppers and onions.
Pesto pizza is a truly yuppie concoc-
tion, in which those pine nuts are
combined with garlic and basil. And
there are always nightly specials to
ask about.

If all this is getting a bit fancy for
your tastes, you can design your own
pies using more traditional toppings.
Cheese pizzas with one topping start
at $10, and these range only up to
$15.25 for extra large; special combi-
nations take the price up to about
$20, but this mega-size will feed four
people, which works out very reasonably indeed. In a sense, bigger is actually cheaper, and you definitely get a
better value if you bring some friends
along.

The "eccentric" toppings mentioned above depend, says the menu,
on the "eccentricity of seasons, sup-
pliers, and chef." These will also add
a few more bucks to the price of your
pie; again, if you're sharing with
even one person, your food bill
shouldn't go over ten bucks each.

Of course, there are other niceties
to add to the meal. A full-size basic

MR. CHEAP'S PICKS
The Castro & Noe Valley

✔ **Dusit Thai**—A classy Noe
  Valley storefront, and by all
  accounts one of the best dining
  bargains in The City.

✔ **The Patio Café**—Great
  atmosphere and reasonably-
  priced food, big in both quality
  and quantity.

✔ **Pozole**—It can be difficult to
  find cheap eats in the
  fashionable Castro, but this
  little restaurant offers authentic
  Latin food at authentically low
  prices.

---

green salad is a bit up there at $5.65,
but then it's "grown and hand-picked
by California certified organic farmers." House wines are available at a
reasonable $2.25 a glass, up to $8 for
a full carafe; beers start under $2. On
the other side of the meal, if you
have room, homemade chocolate
mousse and Graffeo's coffee await
you.

In all, Pauline's offers a pizza pie
that actually makes for a fine dinner
out. And a popular one, at that—tables can be tough to get at this cozy,
intimate restaurant, which only accepts reservations for large groups.

Pozole

• 2337 Market St. (Castro St.), San
  Francisco; (415) 626-2666

Pozole, in the heart of the Castro,
serves up a hearty selection of Latin
American dishes. Similar to Mexican
food (in fact you'll find quesadillas
and burritos on their menu), Latin
American cuisine maintains its own
unique style and flavor.

Try the dish for which this restaurant is named: "Pozole" ($3.50), a
combination of hominy, roasted chilies, sweet peppers, garlic, and citrus
in a tomato chicken broth; or en-

salada do Brazil ($3.95), made with baby greens, hearts of palm, red onions, and cucumber topped of by a lime-mezcal-chili pepper vinaigrette. All of the dishes here are unusual—even ones that at first may seem familiar. For example, the Californiano burrito is no ordinary one: It's filled with tender cactus, pasilla peppers, tomatoes, and roasted garlic in a tomatillo-lime sauce, served with black beans and Mayan rice ($5.50). And the quesadilla Cancun has cactus, smoked tomatoes, rock shrimp, and roasted garlic, served with three salsas ($6.95).

In fact, *nothing* here costs more than $6.95, which suits Mr. C just fine. That includes entrees like "Chicken Tamale del Salvador," corn masa, chicken, and olives in a light tomato-garlic lime sauce, sour cream, and salsa, served with a side order of black beans, all for $5.95; and "Pollo de la Plaza," boneless chicken in a sauce made from bitter orange, chipotle, dried apricots, smoked dried chiles and other flavors. It's served with pozole rice and black beans for $6.95. Don't miss the "Empanadas Arcangel," two crispy pastry shells stuffed with carrots, raisins, red onions, celery, potatoes, and cheese. They're served with black beans and Mexican salad for $5.95.

Who knows? After dinner, perhaps you'll find a Spanish film playing at the Castro moviehouse around the corner.

Rustico*

- 300 DeHaro St. (16th St.), San Francisco; (415) 252-0180

Amidst the art students and furniture design crowd who spend much of their days at the foot of Potrero Hill sits this off-kilter building which houses, among other things, a couple of charming cafes. Trendy without being too overpriced, they are casual places to relax over coffee and pastry or a full meal. Rustico clearly derives its name from the energetic young Italian chef who presides over its pastas, sandwiches, and other hearty creations.

It's a cross between a tradtional restaurant setup and a takeout place, in which you place your order at the counter and find a seat among the natural wood butcher-block tables. But, when your food is ready, relax—they'll bring it to you. The menu is also a sort of mix-and-match affair, offering numerous combinations at fixed prices. Choose from a variety of daily pasta dishes, plus one of several cold salads from romaine to tuna, for $5.75; add a bowl of hearty soup for another buck. Mr. C loved the vegetarian lasagna, served with a hunk of fresh crusty bread; black bean soup; and very fresh Caesar salad, whipped up on the spot. Herb roasted chicken was another delicious entree choice. For lighter appetites, go with a soup and salad combo, just $4.95.

Rustico also specializes in whole wheat crust pizzas, which are a bit pricier, though they are packed with ingredients. The basic, Margherita, starts at $9.95 for a small (enough for two not-too-hungry people) and goes up to $14.95 for the large (enough to feed the whole art class). Other varieties come with toppings like roasted eggplant, sauteed spinach, calamata olives, marinated broccoli...y'know, designer pizza. Yummy, and okay if you're sharing. Or, get a hefty slice for $3.25. Panini sandwiches ($5-$6) are also good deals.

This is also a good place for breakfast; two poached eggs and a bagel are $4.50, or try a vegetable frittata for $3.50. Espresso is just a dollar, and caffe latte is $1.75. Later in the day, you can sip one of these with something sinfully rich from the dessert case—like a peanut butter brownie or pecan pie—while chatting with a companion or just reading the paper. It's one of urban life's many pleasures. Rustico is open daily until 9:00 p.m., except on Sundays, until 4:00.

Sally's Upstairs

- 300 DeHaro St. (16th St.), San Francisco; (415) 626-3354

Upstairs from Rustico (and from

Sally's own pastry shop) is a more full-service, sit-down restaurant—all in the same building, the funky one with the railroad car along one side. Sally's Upstairs is a bright, airy sort of place, with hanging plants, a lunch counter, and small tables. The food has a natural, health-conscious slant; lots of vegetarian dishes, though not exclusively.

In fact, the menu ranges all over the place, from baba ghanoush sandwiches to jambalaya. Have a complete roast half chicken dinner for $7.50, with brown rice, a homemade biscuit, and steamed vegetables or a side salad. The jambalaya ($6.25), a mix of Andouille sausage, Black Forest ham, chicken, peppers, and rice, comes with salad and "three vegetable corn bread." And the "La Bamba" burrito ($5.95) combines chicken, guacamole, black bean chili, sour cream, and salsa.

Can they do so many styles well? Sure can. And, for smaller appetites or nibbling, basic sandwiches and burritos start around $4. Perhaps a Caesar salad, made with sun-dried tomatoes and new potatoes ($4.25 small, $6.25 large). Or, tea and pastries—available in low-fat preparations—from Sally's bakery. They also serve fresh-squeezed fruit juices, from organic apple juice to "Roger Rabbit," which blends carrots, spinach, and cilantro into a zippy cocktail ($2.25 for an eight-ounce glass).

For the less health-henpecked, beers and wines are available too; plus Spinelli coffees (though you can have your latte made with soy milk!). Sally's also exhibits works by local artists on its walls; these usually run for a month or so at a time, and have opening receptions to which the public is invited free of charge. The restaurant is open from 8 a.m. to 8 p.m. daily.

San Francisco Bar-B-Q
- 1328 18th St. (Texas St.), San Francisco; (415) 431-8956

Thai Bar-B-Q
- 730 Van Ness Ave. (Turk St.), San Francisco; (415) 441-1640

MR. CHEAP'S PICKS
Potrero Hill

✔ **Goat Hill Pizza**—Way up at the top of the hill, some say this pizza is tops in town. Ascend on Monday nights, for the all-you-can-eat salad and slices deal.

✔ **Rustico**—Mix-and-match pastas, salads, and soups—plus coffees and pastries. Good place to stop in while furniture shopping at the bottom of the hill.

- 1958 Shattuck Ave. (University Ave.), Berkeley; (510) 549-1958

It may sound like chicken and ribs, but this is one (actually, three) of The City's great Asian barbecue-and-noodle houses. These small, family-style joints serve up great, freshly-prepared food, cheap.

The menu may be bland ("Bar-B-Q Chicken Dinner $5.75, Bar-B-Q Lamb Dinner $7.75, Bar-B-Q Scallops Dinner $8.25. . ."), but hey, we're not looking for creativity here. What you will get are huge portions of hot food at prices that go no higher than $8.75. And that's for a complete dinner, with rice, salad, and bread on the side.

Mr. C opted for one of the "Noodles" entrees, which offer a similar array of choices served in a large bowl on a bed of egg noodles. He enjoyed the tasty, if not super-spicy, Thai pork sausage ($5.50); as with all noodle dishes, this combo was garnished with lettuce and ground peanuts over the top, and far too many noodles to finish.

Other interesting choices include duck, prawns, veal, salmon steak, and oysters. Most of these are available as full entrees, noodle dishes, or appetizer plates. And that's about it, folks.

You can add a salad, topped with meat ($5.25); or a bowl of beef noodle soup ($3.25). There are a few beers and wines, including Singha beer and Anchor Steam (each $2.75). House wines are $1.75 a glass. Seating, by the way, is ultra-informal, at long tables side-by-side with your fellow diners. Chances are, working on this wonderful food, you'll hardly look up enough to notice.

Slider's Diner*
- 449 Castro St. (Market St.), San Francisco; (415) 431-3288
- 1204 Sutter St. (Polk St.), San Francisco; (415) 885-3288

Slide into this fun and funky little diner, where you can get wonderful burgers at equally wonderful prices. What makes their burgers so wonderful? Well, they have an in-house butcher, so beef patties are ground fresh daily using only 100% USDA choice chuck. Order your burger at the counter; when it arrives, dress it however you please at the self-serve condiment bar. A plain six-ounce burger is $3.25, while an eight-ouncer is $3.75. You can add cheese for an extra quarter; they also have some special combinations like bacon cheese ($4.75), avocado cheese ($4.95), and chili cheese ($5.50).

Of course, you don't *have* to be a burger fan to find something you like here, though it helps. You can also get fried chicken, with fries and a salad, for $4.95. There are sandwiches, too, like rib-eye steak with grilled onions and mushrooms ($5.25) and Italian chicken with grilled onions and peppers ($4.95), along with old faves like grilled cheese. Another big item here is hot dogs; a plain 1/4-lb. dog is $2.95. Add cheese for $3.25, and chili for $3.95. For something a little different, try a Louisiana link—hot stuff—for $2.95. A side order of fries is $1.50, a bit pricey; but they're hot, golden, and plentiful. Other side orders include soups, salads, chili, and Buffalo wings. Of course, it wouldn't be a diner if it didn't have floats and shakes! When it comes to diner at-

mosphere, though, Slider's offers plenty of modern-day style. Chrome counters, black and white tile floors, and black vinyl stools clash with MTV videos on the built-in television screens. Call it "neo-diner."

Taqueria La Cumbre
- 515 Valencia St. (16th St.), San Francisco; (415) 863-8205

You want good Chinese food? Go to Chinatown. Italian food? Head over to North Beach. When it's Mexican food you're after, there's no question—the Mission is the place to be. After all, if you throw a rock in any direction there, chances are you'll hit a taco house (please don't try this; just take Mr. C's word for it). Taqueria La Cumbre is one of the area's best.

And they have a lot more than just tacos. Taqueria La Cumbre cooks up a number of traditional meats, including carne asada (steak), pollo asada (broiled chicken), chicken in red herb sauce, chili Colorado (steak in chili), and even such delicacies as pork stomach and beef tongue. All of these are available as full dinner plates, with rice, beans, salad, and tortillas, for $7.00; or inside of tacos, served with rice and beans for $1.80; or in burritos, with rice and beans for $2.50. You can also get deluxe burritos ($3.70) and deluxe tacos ($2.60), which come with rice, beans, cheese, sour cream, and guacamole. For vegetarians, there's a special dinner plate of cheese, rice, beans, salad, and tortillas—just $5.00. Vegetarian burritos are $2.30 (regular) and $3.70 (deluxe).

Even if you go for a small taco or such, you can fill out a meal by ordering some side dishes. Guacamole and chips go for $2, salsa and chips just $1. You can also get larger sizes, to take home for a meal or for your next party. Rice, beans, guac, and all those meat preparations are all sold by the pint and half-pint.

The Tavern on 16th
- 2007 16th St. (Utah St.), San Francisco; (415) 626-2626

In the shadow of the elevated Route 101, cut off somewhat from the trendier part of lower Potrero Hill, sits this very cozy, friendly, working-class bar. On a limited schedule, the Tavern also serves up hearty, inexpensive food with the brews.

It's a large, surprisingly bright and airy place by day, with a separate dining area a few steps above the bar. White tablecloths at lunchtime give the room a further bit of sprucing. Meanwhile, you can dine on a hefty platter of pot roast and mashed potatoes for just $7.95; same price for pork chops and potatoes, or the daily pasta special. If you want something smaller, a Tavern burger and French fries go for $5.75; or, for a fancier touch, try the rare roast beef sandwich with watercress and horseradish cream; it's served with fries for $6.75.

It almost seems as though this is a bar with an identity crisis. There are soups and salads, too, as well as standard bar appetizers. Daily entree specials such as glazed ham steak, osso bucco with polenta, and prime rib. Even the Irish classic of corned beef, cabbage and boiled potatoes.

Lunch is served on weekdays only, from 11:00 a.m. to 3:00 p.m.; dinners are added on Wednesday through Saturday nights only, from 5:30 to 10:00. Check out the daily happy hours from 3-5 p.m., when you can find deals like Pabst Blue Ribbon drafts for just $1.50 a pint. Now, *that's* the stuff of a working-class hero.

3-J's Deli & Cafe

- 3853 24th St. (Sanchez St.), San Francisco; (415) 282-1213

Walking up and down the hills of Noe Valley can really help you work up an appetite. With deli sandwiches, Middle Eastern specialties, and Philly-style cheese steaks, 3-J's Deli & Cafe is a great place to refuel.

Deli sandwiches are just $3.75, including corned beef, pastrami, roast beef, and tuna salad, and come on your choice of bread with lettuce, tomato, onion, mayonnaise, and mustard. "Gourmet" sandwiches, like prosciutto or the Reuben, are $4.50. Salad lovers can choose from chef

salad, Greek salad, or a stuffed avocado for $4.95, or the cold salad plate for $4.25.

3-J's has a selection of terrific hamburgers. The basic variety is just $4.50; "Joe's Burger," topped with sauteed onions, mushrooms, peppers, and provolone cheese, is $5.95; and the avocado burger is just $5.25. Several varieties of Philly-style cheese steaks start at $3.95, served on an Italian roll with melted provolone cheese. 3-J's also has chicken breast and fish filet sandwiches, each served with fries or salad, for $5.50.

They also have a bunch of Middle Eastern specialties, like a falafel sandwich for $3.50, gyros for $3.95, and shish kebab served in a pita with hummus, tahini, lettuce, and tomato for $4.95. Italian specialties include a meatball sandwich for $3.95, an Italian sausage sandwich for $3.95, and chicken or fish parmesan for $4.95.

3-J's is also a great place to get your day started off right. Get two eggs any style with toast and home fries for $2.75; add sausage or bacon for $3.75; make it Italian sausage or Canadian bacon for $3.95. Omelettes are also popular. An Italian style omelette, with provolone and tomato sauce, is $3.95. Pancakes and French toast are just $2.50 and eggs Benedict is $5.95. Breakfast is served until 11:30 a.m. on weekdays, and until 2 p.m. on Saturday and Sunday.

Ti-Couz

- 3108 16th St. (Valencia St.), San Francisco; (415) 25-CREPE (252-7373)

Ah, the rustic farms of Brittany, in the northwest of France. The simple meals, hearty peasant wines, boisterous company, all in the heart of. . .the Mission? *Mais oui.* This fabulously popular *crêperie* is so boisterous, in fact, that it has just doubled its size by taking over the shop next door—and it's still packed. Yet a meal here—hip and classy as it is—can still be very reasonably priced.

It certainly is different, and makes a fun night out. Ti-Couz, by the way, means "the old house"; indeed, its exterior looks much like a French chateau, complete with one of those wooden front doors that's split into an upper and lower half. Inside, the restaurant is also split, into two long, narrow rooms of booths and counter seating. Mr. C and his companion thought they were "settling" for the latter, in order to avoid an hour's wait; but this turned out to be a piece of good luck.

Y'see, this unique food really is the show here. At the counters, you get to watch the crêpes being made all night, and it's a mesmerizing art. You'd hardly think that such delicate creations could be cranked out at the non-stop pace the customers demand; but the concentration and skills of the gourmet chefs are intense. One after another, a precise portion of buckwheat batter is ladled onto the round hotplate; carefully spread to the exact same diameter with a wooden device like a Vegas *croupier's* stick; the filling of diced meat, seafood, vegetables, or fruits is tossed on; and, at just the right moment, it's all folded up and then decorated with a zig-zag of *crème fraiche*. Rarely do they break one; if so, it won't be served.

The menu itself can be a bit confusing, with basic choices and addins listed individually: sausage with basil butter, smoked salmon with scallions, and so on. Combinations are also suggested, such as scallop and tomato or ratatouille and cheese. Mr. C

was frankly advised by the waitress to ignore the menu's instructions to order an appetizer crêpe with dinner; indeed, the main course crêpe was large and satisfying. Besides, let's face it—this is just a (yummy) diversion on the way to the dessert crêpes.

Mmmm, dessert. There are just as many possible combinations here: sweet crepes filled with things like caramel, white chocolate, bananas, berries (in season), or Nutella, that sinfully rich chocolate-hazelnut spread found in gourmet shops. Go for the Grand Marnier *flambée*; the pear, ice cream, and chocolate; or again, mix and match to your heart's (and sweet tooth's) content.

The prices all but the most basic, unadorned crepes, whether dinner or dessert, start around $4-$5; nearly everyone adds at least one ingredient, usually another $1.50 or $2. Of course, the more creative you get, the more expensive the crepes become; but you can do very well for yourself for around Mr. C's $10 per person goal. Other additions include fresh green salads from $3; beers and house wines, also from about $3; or, you can sip a glass of cider, Kir, or champagne—which seems appropriate to the party-like atmosphere. You get a lot for your money at Ti-Couz, well beyond the food. Open for lunch and dinner, seven days a week; be prepared for a wait on busy nights, as reservations are not taken in advance.

NORTH AREA
including Hayes Valley, Japantown, Marina District, Pacific Heights, Western Addition

Amerasian Café*

● 2165 Union St. (Fillmore St.), San Francisco; (415) 563-9638

Cheap eats on Union Street? Hey, Mr. C can find inexpensive food *anywhere*. It seems that even yuppies can overdose on overpriced food once in

a while, and this place is clearly a popular alternative to the chi-chi bistros—especially at lunchtime, for folks who work in the area.

The Amerasian Café is a small, eat-in-or-take-out kind of place, where you order at the counter and take your tray to one of the handful of tables. It's all done up quite handsomely, though, in keeping with the rest of the neighborhood: a gleaming black tiled floor, real marble-top tables, nice ambiance. A significant part of that atmosphere, by the way, are the wonderful aromas that hit you as soon as you walk in the door.

"Where chopsticks meet steak," proclaims the menu, in attempting to describe the eclectic mix of freshly prepared foods. What that really means is that they've taken a predominantly Chinese/Japanese/Korean lineup, and added things like salads, soups, eggs, and burgers. To be honest, the Asian dishes seem far more enticing than the "Amer-" side. Go for some good ol' sweet and sour chicken ($5.25), served neatly on a platter with boiled rice. Or, for that matter, try almond chicken, garlic, Korean BBQ....and you have the same choices for beef and seafood dishes. All are in the $5-$6 range (seafood items are mostly $6.95), and you do get quite a heaping portion. For another buck, you can substitute brown rice.

In fact, there are quite a lot of options for the health-conscious crowd. Whether you prefer meatless burgers ($4.80), vegetable tempura ($4.95), broccoli and tofu with rice ($5.25), or vegetable and tofu udon noodle soup ($4.50), there are enough choices here for the carnivore and vegetarian alike to go for weeks without repeating entrees. Three-egg omelettes, served with home fries and wheat toast, offer you a choice of nearly twenty different fillings. Interestingly, a one-ingredient version costs $4.75, while you can put in any two ingredients for—surprise—$4.75. Well now, that's a bargain right there!

Of course, it wouldn't be Union Street without coffees, espressos, lattes, and the like. Also fresh juices, juice shakes, and even a few beers and wines. The cafe is open for lunch and dinner seven days a week—until 7:00 p.m. on Sundays, and to 10:00 p.m. all other evenings.

MR. CHEAP'S PICK
Hayes Valley

✔ **Suppenküche**—The atmosphere is minimalist and trendy, the food is hearty, and the beer is plentiful. What more could you ask for?

Barney's Gourmet Hamburgers
- 3344 Steiner St. (Lombard St.), San Francisco; (415) 563-0307
- 4138 24th St. (Castro St.), San Francisco; (415) 282-7770
- 1591 Solano Ave. (Peralta St.), Berkeley; (510)526-8185
- 5819 College Ave. (Ghabod St.), Oakland; (510) 601-0444
- 4162 Piedmont Ave. (41st St.), Oakland; (510) 655-7180

Big is the operative word at Barney's. This growing chain of attractive, yuppie restaurants is getting big, with locations all around the Bay Area. They serve up a big menu of big, juicy burgers—plus a few other things. The prices, however, are not as big as you'd expect. Which makes Barney's big with Mr. C.

Those burgers include six-ounce, freshly rolled beef and eight-ounce, boneless chicken breast sandwiches. The basic Barney burger (can you sense an alliteration overload coming?) is just $3.95; add cheese for another fifty cents, and/or fries for $1.75. Or, step up to the Big Barney Burger, a half-pounder, for $4.95, and a larger order of fries for $2.25; still not bad at all. By the way, they do up a nifty order of spicy curly fries for $3.25, too.

Meanwhile, there are no less than twenty-two variations of burgers (big is the word, remember). Try the pizza burger ($4.75), or perhaps the Popeye burger ($4.95), topped with sauteed spinach and feta cheese. The Maui Waui ($5.25) is glazed with teriyaki sauce, and served with pineapple and

Canadian (?) bacon. And the Russian burger ($4.95) adds layers of sour cream, scallions, and sauteed mushrooms, served on dark rye bread instead of a roll.

Most of these are also available on chicken sandwiches as well, usually a dollar more. And don't forget the tofu patty burgers, for the health-conscious crowd. Plus soups and salads, club sandwiches, and—at the Oakland branches only, for some reason—weekend breakfast entrees of omelettes and other egg plates. Forget parking at the Marina location, by the way. All branches are open for lunch and dinner seven days a week (though not past 10 p.m., except in summer), and offer efficient take-out service as well.

Chestnut Café*
- 2016 Fillmore St. (Pine St.), San Francisco; (415) 922-6510

Here's an inexpensive, cafeteria-style deli that makes a pleasant alternative to the more trendy dining choices in the Pacific Heights area. Chestnut Café is a lively, bustling breakfast and lunch spot, with a well-stocked salad bar (small size $2.50, large $3.80) homemade soups ($1.80 a bowl) and super-cheap eye-opener specials. How about two eggs any style, with ham or bacon, and toast, all for $3.49? Fine indeed. Add a double cappuccino for $1.50, or fresh house coffee for just 75 cents a cup—take *that*, Starbucks!

The sandwich menu is basic, but long, with just about everything under $4. It's even arranged alphabetically: avocado, avocado & bacon, avocado & cheese, avocado & cream cheese....you get the idea. Not to mention fresh roast turkey, meatloaf, seafood salads, BLTs, and the like. Daily specials offer combinations such as soup and a sandwich for as little as $3.85.

Basically, that's about it; for between-boutique nibbling, Chestnut also offers fresh-squeezed juices and "health smoothies," as well as a tempting variety of freshly baked pastries. A daytime kind of place, the

cafe closes at 5:30 p.m. on weekdays, and 5:00 on weekends.

Chestnut Street Grill
- 2231 Chestnut St. (Pierce St.), San Francisco; (415) 922-5558

Chestnut Street is to the Marina district what Union Street is to Pacific Heights. It's lined with trendy, yuppie cafes and boutiques, plus a movie theater or two. For those who wish to hob-nob with the hoi-polloi, but on a lighter budget, Mr. C has found this friendly, relaxed tavern with a menu that's as easy to afford as it is unique.

Sandwiches are the house specialty. But wait—this is no sub shop. There are 123—count 'em, 123—different combinations, piled high on fresh sourdough bread, all priced between $3.50 and $5.75. And that doesn't even include fourteen hamburger variations, plus another half-dozen hot dog choices.

In true neighborhood pub style, nearly all of these are named for the regular patrons who perfected each particular stack. Thus, you can order the "Laurie Dahl & Sue Andrews" ($4.95), made with salami, ham, Swiss cheese, raw onions, lettuce, and tomatoes. Or, for the same price, the "Tom Fitzgerald," in which Swiss cheese is melted over roast pork and sliced tomato. For heartier appetites, the "Max Blackwood" ($5.25) combines knockwurst, Provolone, fried onions, and baked beans on a French roll.

Looking for something healthier? The "Mike Riordan" ($4.95) blends shrimp salad, alfalfa sprouts, avocado, and tomato on whole-grain bread. And then, there's the just-plain-kooky, like the "Humm-Baby" ($3.95), combining cucumbers, Swiss cheese, sprouts, and anchovies. Evidently, no one would lay personal claim to this one.

You can add tradtional bar sides to any of these—from Buffalo wings ($3.95) to great, crispy steak fries or onion rings ($2.50). Six-ounce burgers are mostly in the $5-$6 range, with salads and omelettes a bit higher. And there are full dinners each evening, like chicken teriyaki ($9.95) or pork chops ($10.75), all served with salad, rolls, and a side vegetable. Still, to paraphrase a well-worn saying: When in Rome, order the sandwiches. Most of the cheerfully satisfied patrons who filled every table on Mr. C's visit were doing so.

Interestingly, even though this is a tavern, there were quite a few families present in the early evening. It is a bright, handsome restaurant, with a dining room semi-separated from the bar area. It is a full bar, with a good variety of bottled beers as well. These are not as cheap as they could be (though not outrageous); it is the liquor, of course, which makes the cheap food possible. In all, you certainly get a great deal in a delightful setting. Open for lunch and dinner seven days, including weekends until midnight.

Doidge's

● 2217 Union St. (Fillmore St.), San Francisco; (415) 921-2149

For over twenty years, this cozy eatery has been a landmark in Pacific Heights, if not the city in general. How many breakfast joints do you know of that take reservations? That's how hot this spot always is, especially on weekends. Doidge himself presides over the scene from behind the cash register at the front counter; you may be relegated to a seat here if you haven't booked ahead. In the adjoining room, which feels kind of like a sunny Victorian parlor, there are ten or so tables filled with happy customers.

Needless to say, breakfast (and weekend brunch) are the peak meals, when folks feast on large platters—call them *nouvelle* homestyle. These are primarily egg dishes, as well as pancakes and sandwiches, soups and salads. The prices are not exactly cheap, in and of themselves; but then, the place is in demand—and don't forget where you are! Considering the size and quality of the portions, you certainly get good value for the money—while staying around the $10 per person mark, as Mr. C always tries to do.

Most of the egg dishes are in the $6-$8 range, like eggs Benedict ($7.75) in a homemade Hollandaise sauce. Many of the important elements at Doidge's are homemade, such as the fantastic poppyseed toast that comes with these entrees (plus great home fries). Omelettes start at $6, but they're big, and made with fresh ingredients like avocado, spicy Italian sausage, and mushrooms sauteed in butter. For something a little different, try the breakfast casserole ($7.50), a tasty mix of sausage, potatoes, onions and tomatoes, baked with cheese and topped with a poached egg.

Sandwiches, all around $6, range from a "chuckburger" with mushrooms to a BLT with cheese to avocado, cream cheese and tomato, all on that terrific bread. These also come with your choice of homemade soup, a green salad, cottage cheese, or home fries.

It's good stuff, and perfect with a side of boutique browsing along Union Street (though Mr. C can hardly recommend spending any cash in *those* places). Do plan ahead, if you can, by making reservations, unless you're in such a relaxed mood that you don't mind waiting up to an hour for a table. Doidge's opens up at 8:00 a.m. daily; "last seating" is at 1:45 in the afternoon on weekdays, and 2:45 on weekends.

MR. CHEAP'S PICK
Marina District

✔ **Chestnut Street Grill**—Sandwiches and sandwiches and sandwiches and. . . you get the idea. All in an upscale pub setting and an expensive neighborhood.

Food Inc.
• 2800 California St. (Divisadero St.), San Francisco; (415) 928-3728

Food Inc. calls itself a "gastro-nomia," and it is indeed a delight for several of the senses. A combination shop and cafe, it appeals to people who have expensive tastes, but per-haps not the wallets to match. It cer-tainly offers some wonderfully prepared dishes at affordable prices—especially for Pacific Heights.

Opera music greets you on the sound system as you walk into the cozy cafe. A half-dozen small tables line the front windows, faced by a long glass-case counter where you place your order. At either end of the room, shelves line the walls from floor to ceiling, stocked with wines, cheeses, and packaged gourmet foods from around the world.

Primarily a breakfast and lunch place (although they serve until 9:00 p.m.), you can give your day a real jump-start with large cup—more like a small bowl—of cappuccino or latte provençale, each under $2. Several other yummy beverages include mo-cha latte, white hot chocolate, and a variety of teas. If you can make room on the table, add an "oeuf croquette" with toast and bacon ($3.25), or their high-toned version of the Egg McMuffin, made with Black Forest ham on focaccia bread ($3.65). Lots of great breads, biscotti, soups and quiches ("mini-quiche" Lorraine, $2.85).

Moving on into the day, Food Inc. is the epitome of a fancy salad and sandwich shop. Mr. C's companion, who eats here frequently, considers the salad Niçoise ($5.75) to be one of the biggest and best anywhere in The City—and she's sampled a few. Warm chevre salad, same price, is an-other fine option; while the pasta salad ($4.75) offers you a choice from several daily varieties, along with a mixed greens salad. On the hot side, that same price gets you a plate with two types of pasta and a hunk of fresh bread; and there are four kinds of individual pizza, each $4.50, such as pesto and marinated mozzarella.

In between are the sandwiches, in-cluding eggplant on onion focaccia—topped with artichoke hearts, parmesan cheese, and sun-dried toma-toes, and a dollop of fontina cheese melted over it all—for just $4.95. Ten more choices are all around five bucks each. And then, there are daily hot specials, like vegetarian lasagna or polenta casserole, usually $5.95 or thereabouts.

A good selection of beers and wines are offered; have a glass of vino for $2.75, or select a bottle (rea-sonably priced, plus a $3 corkage fee). And of course, all of the foods at Food Inc. are available for take-out.

Frankie's Bohemian Café
• 1862 Divisadero St. (California St.), San Francisco; (415) 921-4725

There really is a Frankie at this cafe, and he really is from Bohemia, that famous and far-flung corner of the Czech Republic. Most nights, you'll find this energetic host pulling 22-ounce drafts (!) from behind the bar. Opened in the summer of 1992, Frankie's has been a real success story—the place is packed, loud, and smoky in the evenings, when the trendy young set comes in to wolf down huge burgers, plates of pasta, and a uniquely East European dish called *brambory*.

This item is described on the hand-written menu in Frankie's fractured (and charming) English: "Shredded fresh potato and zucchini, spices and herbs...baked shortly on drop of vir-gin olive oil, 10 inches big potato cake like..." The idea is that this be-comes the base for one of seven dif-ferent toppings, which are cooked right on the pancake. The vegetarian brambory ($7.95) adds grilled and marinated eggplant, artichoke, baby carrots and olives; the Bohemian ($9.95) tops it with grilled tiger shrimp and mushrooms in teriyaki sauce.

Some of these prices come peril-ously close to Mr. C's limits, but only the heartiest of appetites will be able to finish one of these off. Especially if you've gorged yourself first on the basket of fresh Italian bread that's brought out to each table with a dipping plate of not just olive oil, but olive oil with fresh minced garlic. Mmmm.

Burgers, as noted above, are a popular staple here. Again, there are several varieties to choose from, most priced at $5.95 or $6.95 ("All burgers are coming with homemade fresh cut French fries, lettuce, tomato, onion and pickle on side"). These range from your basic cheeseburger (Swiss, American, cheddar, jack) to a vegetarian burger with beans instead of fries, a turkey burger, and even a swordfish steak burger topped with pesto ($7.95). All are done up big and juicy; among the curious items found in the front window is a framed endorsement from an organization called AmHEATS—the American Hamburger Evaluation and Testing Society, of course.

Then there are pastas with chicken or fresh fish mixed in ("...limited selection of fish to make sure we sell it, not freeze it. Tomorrow we get new one!"). Also salads, soups, steaks, all priced under $10 each—a very cosmopolitan menu indeed. And to wash it all down, there are those gigantic beers: Sierra Nevada, Full Sail, Guinness, Red Hook, Newcastle, and more...all on tap, and all $3.50 for 22 ounces. A couple of wines are also available. It is worth noting, though, that Frankie's does not have a full bar, and this leads to a substantial thinning of the crowd by about 9 p.m. Depending upon your view, this either makes the tiny cafe less interesting or more comfortable; during the early evening, getting a table in here can be almost as difficult as keeping smoke out of your contact lenses.

The Good Earth
- 1865 Post St. (Fillmore St.), San Francisco; (415) 771-0151
  And other suburban locations

The Good Earth caters to those who want healthy food, but don't want to work *too* hard at it. Sure, there are tofu dishes, but there's plenty of good

ol' carnivorous fare as well. The surroundings, meanwhile, are as spartan as a Nob Hill living room. Call it yupscale health food.

Nevertheless, Good Earth has a variety of soups, salads, sandwiches, and dinner entrees that are great tasting and healthy. And despite a location in the heart of Japantown, this restaurant even serves up burgers and Mexican specialties, (not to mention hefty desserts) that are good for you.

Sandwiches are served on tengrain bread with a side salad; these include such choices as cashew chicken ($5.95), the "Good Earth Vegetarian" with cheddar and jack cheese, cucumbers, tomato, sprouts, pickles, lettuce, and mayonnaise ($5.25), and almond tuna ($5.95). Mexican specialties include a vegetarian tostada ($6.55), vegetarian burrito ($5.65), and soft tacos with chicken or tofu ($6.55). And, would you believe, healthy burgers? Have either an additive-free beef burger or a vegetarian "Planet Burger," each $5.75, served with lettuce, tomato, pickle, and a side salad. Add cheese, cheddar or jack for an additional 50¢.

Entrees are more expensive, but still fall comfortably within Mr. C's means. Pasta dishes are very popular, including Chinese chicken pasta for $8.75, vegetarian lasagna for $8.25, and pasta primavera for $7.95. These all come with your choice of salad or one of their soups of the day. Specialty entrees venture into such items as ginger trout served with rice and vegetables ($9.45), Malaysian cashew chicken stir-fry with rice ($9.45), and "Magic Eggplant Casserole" ($6.95). What's magical about it? Perhaps the fact that it sounds like something you'd whip up out of leftovers, yet it's delicious.

Good Earth has a full bar, including a cocktail area, and lots of fine wines at reasonable prices. And don't miss their fabulous desserts. Most are around $2.50—such a deal!—including carrot cake, apple pie, and pecan pie. Can this stuff really be healthy? Well, after you've been so good *all through* dinner...

Leon's Bar-B-Q
- 1911 Fillmore St. (Bush St.), San Francisco; (415) 922-2436
- 2800 Leavenworth St. (Fisherman's Wharf), San Francisco; no phone
- 2800 Sloat Blvd. (46th Ave.), San Francisco; (415) 681-3071

Soul food in Pacific Heights? Leon's feels a lot more like a diner in the deep South, with good, greasy ribs, spicy jambalaya, and homemade sweet potato pie. Service is, well, let's just say laid-back. But the food is worth it.

Lunch plates, served all day, are great bargains. A whole slew of entrees are all priced at $6.40, including pork ribs, half roast chicken, hot link sausages, and more. These come with cornbread, plus your choice of baked beans, potato salad, cole slaw, fries, or even spaghetti. That jambalaya ($4.95) will make your eyes water. And the barbecued smoked turkey sandwich, served on a roll with a side order for $5.95, is a tasty, messy treat.

Dinners offer similar choices, in larger portions or paired together; beef ribs for $10.95, ribs and hot links for $13.50, baby back ribs and chicken for $13.95. These all come with two side orders, as well. Or, try 'em all with a sampler plate ($14.95) of chicken, links, ribs, sliced beef, corn muffins, beans, potato salad—a little bit of everything. Wash these down with one of a half-dozen bottled beers; and, if you have room, send it all home with one of those pies—including chocolate pecan pie and peach cobbler, all $2.75 a slice.

Basic stuff, but definitely the real thing. Leon's Fisherman's Wharf branch, at the Anchorage, isn't a restaurant, just a take-out stand, which closes in the evenings. The other joints are open until 10 p.m. daily; the Parkside location is across the street from the San Francisco Zoo.

Mel's Drive-In
- 2165 Lombard St. (Fillmore St.), San Francisco; (415) 921-3039
- 3355 Geary Blvd. (Stanyan St.), San Francisco; (415) 387-2244
- 2240 Shattuck Ave. (Bancroft Way), Berkeley; (510) 540-6351

Mel's Drive-In is an authentic 1950s-style diner, complete with those paper soda-jerk hats, bobby sox and saddle shoes, oldies music on the juke box, and plenty of good, cheap food. Mel's menu features an eclectic mix of diner classics, like meat loaf and chicken pot pie, along with truly 90s cuisine like gourmet turkey burgers and California fruit salad.

Predictably, burgers are a big item here. Their choice ground chuck has no additives or preservatives and is delivered fresh daily. Try "The Famous Melburger," a third of a pound of beef served on a sesame seed bun with lettuce, tomato, Bermuda onions, mayonnaise, and pickle chips, for just $4.50. Make it a half-pounder for just 75¢ more. The true bargain in this department is the "Big Mel Combination Plate," a half-pound burger, great French fries, and a tossed green salad for $6.50. People who are looking for healthier choices may want to go for the gourmet ground turkey burger ($5.95) instead. It's a ground turkey patty served on a whole wheat bun with cole slaw, potato salad, or French fries. Go all out with the "Turkel Burgel," topped with two strips of bacon, cheddar cheese, and thousand-island dressing for $6.95 (so much for health food).

Mel's has plenty of other sandwiches, like the fried egg sandwich for $3.95 and a fresh turkey breast sandwich for $5.95. Don't miss the charbroiled chicken sandwiches: The "American Graffiti" (named, as you may know, because Mel's in L.A. was featured in that rock 'n roll classic) has sauteed mushrooms, Swiss cheese, and fries for $6.75. Did Mr. C mention the hot dogs? Or, the salads? The choices are enough to make you dizzy!

Dinner blue-plates are also cheap in price, but not in portions. "Mel's Spring Chicken," crispy fried chicken with coleslaw and fries ($7.45), "Grandma's Turkey Meat Loaf" with cranberry sauce, lumpy mashed potatoes, homemade gravy, and vegetables ($7.95), or broiled pork chops with grilled onions, potatoes, and veggies ($7.95) are just a few of the myriad choices.

Mel's is also a popular breakfast stop. The menu includes pancakes, French toast, and waffles, hash and eggs, omelettes, and more. And, Mr. C couldn't leave off without telling you about Mel's tantalizing ice cream fountain and other desserts—pies, chocolate fudge cake, and cheesecake, not to mention shakes, malts, sundaes, floats, vanilla Cokes, and more. Just go already!

Mi Burrito
- 2408 California St. (Fillmore St.), San Francisco; (415) 563-3509

It can be difficult to find good, cheap food in Pacific Heights. Mi Burrito, which has been serving the Bay Area since 1975, is a relatively new addition to this chic neighborhood, bringing with it good renditions of standard Mexican fare. Burritos (naturally), tacos, enchiladas, and more can be found here, quick and cheap; few items, with the exception of seafood dishes, are more than $8.

Dinner plates are the best deal—they include beans, rice, and salad with each entree. Six bucks gets you a plate of chile rellenos, enchiladas, or tamales; for a dollar more, have beef tacos, chicken tamales, or cheese enchiladas. "Especiales de la Casa" include things like carne asada ($7.95) and chicken fajitas ($7.95), also served with rice and beans.

Going a la carte is even less expensive. Burritos are filled with diced tomatoes, beans, and onions, plus your choice of roast pork ($3.60), grilled steak ($4.75), or melted jack cheese ($3.55). A vegetarian burrito, with jack and cheddar cheese, sour cream, guacamole, rice, beans, lettuce, and salsa, is $4.75. Crisp and soft tacos come in several varieties, ranging in price from $2.50 to $4.50. Lighter appetites will appreciate MB's soup offerings, like chicken with fresh vegetables ($3.95) and menudo, a Mexican tripe soup (not the really bad 1980s pop band), for $4.95. With

---

MR. CHEAP'S PICK
Japantown

✔ **Mifune**—Inside the mall. Inexpensive, filling noodles and soups.

---

any of these simpler offerings, you can always add side orders like beans or rice for $1.50, chips for $1, and tortillas for 75¢. Open from 11 a.m. to 10 p.m. Monday through Saturday, and 11 a.m. to 9:30 p.m. on Sunday.

Mifune
- 1732 Post St. (Buchanan St.), San Francisco; (415) 922-0337

One of several eateries tucked inside the Kintetsu Mall—the landmark structure in Japantown—Mifune has been run by the Miwa family for over fifty years. Like most Japanese restaurants, the food here is quick, healthy, and inexpensive.

The setting is traditional and the seating is in booths; Mifune is a popular lunch spot. Appetizers include such treats as a plate of California rolls ($3.80) or vegetable tempura ($5). Follow these immediately (and the service is indeed fast) with a deep bowl of hot noodles in broth, several varieties of which are priced between $4-$6. Choose *soba* (white flour) or *udon* (buckwheat) noodles, along with additions like chicken, beef and egg, or others. Believe Mr. C, one of these bowls can be a meal in itself.

Cold noodle dishes are served with a dipping sauce, diced green onions and hot mustard; *Yamakake* ($6) consists of grated potato over soba noodles. Dinners, served after 4:00 p.m., add things like *Daimyo* ($9.30) to the menu—a dish of hot noodles, sashimi, and salad. Sip a cup of warm *sake* or have a bottle of Kirin beer, each $2.25; or enjoy the pot of green tea brought to every table.

Right across the hall is another Japantown fave, **Isobune** (telephone 563-1030), which does for sushi what Mifune does for noodles. As soon as you enter, a dazzling sight greets you: a completely round dining counter and serving area, separated by a moat of gushing water. On this fast-moving stream float tiny platters of sushi, in dozens of varieties. Grab anything you like, as much as you want, and your bill will be tallied up at the end of your meal. Most plates have two pieces each, and cost between $1.20 and $2.15. It's fresh, unique, and touristy—but hey, it works.

Original Henry's
• 3339 Steiner St. (Chestnut St.), San Francisco; (415) 673-4407

It is easy to become lulled into thinking that North Beach is the only place to get Italian food. Well, that's just not so. Original Henry's in the Marina District has a fantastic selection of Italian dishes at prices far lower than you'll see at many of its North Beach counterparts.

Begin your food odyssey with one of their many interesting appetizers like fried eggplant ($3.95), escargots ($3.95), or fried calamari ($5.95). Those with a fairly light appetite may want to try one of the many pasta dishes, like baked lasagna ($6.95), spaghetti with meat balls ($6.95), linguini with baby clams ($6.95), or eggplant parmigiana, prepared with or without meat ($6.95). All pasta dishes are served with salad and French bread and butter.

Folks with a heartier appetite will want to try one of the full-size entrees. Veal and seafood dishes are a bit pricier but still very reasonable; try veal scaloppini or veal marsala (each $8.95), sauteed scallops or fresh rainbow trout (each $9.95). Other specialties include chicken cacciatore ($7.95), roast chicken ($6.95), and pork chops parmigiana ($7.95). Even steak dinners are great deals here: just $9.95 for a fourteen-ounce T-bone, and $8.95 for a New York steak. All entrees are served with bread and butter and your choice of

vegetables, spaghetti, or rigatoni, and soup or salad.

Original Henry's also serves a variety of French bread sandwiches, filled with things like Italian sausages for $4.95, and eggplant for $3.95. There are a few salads to choose from too, as well as soups, including minestrone, clam chowder, and cream of potato-leek, just $2 to $2.50 a bowl.

Original Henry's also has a breakfast menu and the most expensive item on it—steak and eggs—is just $5.95. Choose from a variety of omelettes for $3.95 each, indulge your sweet tooth with pancakes or French toast for $2.95, or go a little fancy with eggs Benedict or eggs Florentina for $4.25 each.

Powell's Place
• 511 Hayes St. (Octavia St.), San Francisco; (415) 863-1404

This soul food restaurant is one of the city's better secrets; now that the Hayes Valley is catching on—after many years as a dangerous area, avoided by most—this may not be a secret much longer. Powell's combines a simple, counter-and-tables front room with two other dining rooms which offer a bit of Southern formality. The front room is decorated with framed photographs of great jazz and soul musicians; many more are represented in the jukebox beneath them, ranging from Count Basie to the Rev. Al Green to Patti Labelle. The dining rooms offer linen tablecloths and napkins. Wherever you eat it, the food is first-rate.

The day starts off with hearty breakfasts (and you can get 'em until 3:00 in the afternoon), most of which are under $5. Two eggs with hash browns or grits, and a homemade biscuit, are joined by bacon ($4.25), smoked sausage ($4.75), or a beef pattie ($4.25). A country ham omelette is $3.75. At lunch, try a pork chop sandwich for $4.75; same price for a barbecued rib sandwich. Add a cup of pinto bean soup for $1.75.

For lunch or dinner, the specialty of the house is, of course, southern fried chicken. Order it up by the piece: A breast is $1.45, drumsticks are $1.00, and so on...or have it as part of a full dinner for $8.00, which includes corn muffins and your choice of two side dishes (greens, black-eye peas, mashed potatoes and gravy, etc.).

In fact, there is a daily rotation of dinners with these choices: Monday offers barbecued ribs ($9.50), "smothered" pork chops ($8.75), meatloaf ($8), and several other entrees. On Tuesday, beef short ribs ($8.75) joins the list, while ox tails ($8) drops off, and the others just move around. Actually, the daily menus don't change much at all; there are about a dozen great dishes here, most of which are usually available. Well, that's the south for you; it's not known for fast moves. No problem.

Sanppo
- 1702 Post St. (Buchanan St.), San Francisco; (415) 346-3486

Here's a good choice among Japantown's many offerings—a comfortable, well-appointed restaurant with a diverse menu. Soups, sushi, tempura...they've got a bit of everything, in an attractive wood-paneled setting complete with potted indoor trees. A bit touristy, but that's to be expected in this neighborhood. Oh, and the food's good, too.

Mr. C recommends one of the *donburi*, a complete meal in one bowl for about seven bucks. These are hearty servings, indeed. Try oyakodon ($6.50), which combines chicken, vegetables and scrambled eggs over rice, topped with soy sauce. Or the donburi special ($7.25), beef teriyaki and tempura over rice. The other really cheap way to go is the variety of noodle soups, all around $6-$7 and hard to finish; okame ($5.95), buckwheat noodles and fish cakes in broth, is a good bet.

Speaking of tempura, there are several of these lightly fried dishes to choose from; the combination plate ($8.50) includes fish, chicken, prawns and vegetables. As one of the main entrees, this meal includes a

---

MR. CHEAP'S PICK
Pacific Heights

✔ **Frankie's Bohemian Café**— A boisterous bar where big burgers and old-world delicacies meet beside even bigger draft beers.

---

bowl of miso soup, white rice, and green tea. Other main choices range from tori nabe ($7.95), chicken, vegetables, eggs, and tofu cooked in a tasty broth; roast pork ($7.75), sauteed with veggies; sliced beef and eggplant in a snappy ginger sauce ($8.25); salmon teriyaki ($8.95), and many others.

And, on the subject of seafood, there are over a dozen sushi, sashimi, and maki plates, starting from as low as $6.25. The temaki sushi platter ($10.95) is a sure crowd-pleaser, allowing you to "roll your own" from tuna, shrimp and crabmeat, along with avocado and cucumber. This can also make a good snack for two. The same is true for the half-dozen combination platters, like tempura, sashimi and gyoza (fried pork dumplings); at $13.25, it's a bit over Mr. C's usual limit, but this again includes soup, salad, rice, and tea. Mmmm.

Suppenküche
- 601 Hayes St. (Laguna St.), San Francisco; (415) 252-9289

Suppenküche, a relatively new restaurant in the up-and-coming Hayes Valley, serves up huge portions of hearty German food—a cuisine not often found in The City—accompanied by steins of hearty German beer. Yet, this bistro gives old-world foods a trendy new turn. Minimalism is the style here. The room is lit by candles and you'll sit on natural wood benches at simple, unfinished tables. When it's busy, which it frequently is, the place gets kind of noisy; but that only lends it more of that beer hall feel.

True to its name, soup lovers have lots of delectable choices here. Gemüsecreme Suppe, a vegetable cream soup, is just $3.50 a bowl; Frische Erbsensuppe, fresh pea soup, is also $3.50, or $5.50 with sausage tossed in. Those with lighter appetites may want to try the mixed salad, "German style," for $4.50; or the same with chicken salad added ($6.00).

Main courses, again, are sort of "nouvelle Bavarian"—if there is such a term. These consist of appetizers and entrees like Grüne Sauce mit Röstkartoffeln, sour cream herb sauce with roast potatoes ($6.50); Lauchkechen mit fischer Tomatensauce, which is puff pastry topped with leeks, Gouda cheese, and fresh tomato sauce ($7.50); or Bratwurst mit Rotkohl und Kartoffelbrei, fresh bratwurst with red cabbage and mashed potatoes ($9.00).

There is a good wine list to accompany all this, with wines from Germany, Alsace, Austria, Tuscany, and our own backyard. The beer choices are all from Germany, with eight brews on tap and many more in bottles. These change periodically, but you may find brands like Spaten, Heppeweitzer, Bitburger, and others rarely found on this side of the world. The knowledgeable wait staff is extremely friendly, and will be happy to explain any of the food and drink offerings you may request.

And don't miss dessert. Choose between Hausgemachter Apfelstrudel mit Schlagrahm, homemade apple strudel with whipped cream, for $3.50; or Rotweinbirne mit Fruchtpurree und Vanilleis, poached pear in red wine with fruit puree and vanilla ice cream, all together for $4. Mmmm....

There are more substantial, and more expensive, entrees; along with the bar tab, and perhaps dessert, Suppenküche can add up to be a not-so-inexpensive dinner. But then, it's a hot new sort of place, in a hot area. Still, careful cheapsters can enjoy this scene without setting the budget back too much. Food is served until 10 p.m. only.

NORTHEAST AREA
including Chinatown, Fisherman's Wharf, Nob Hill, North Beach, and Russian Hill

Alcatraz Bar and Grill
• Pier 39, San Francisco; (415) 434-1818

Pier 39 is probably the best-known tourist spot in The City. Because of the abundance of tourists, just about everything around the pier area is expensive, from the T-shirt shops to (definitely) the restaurants. Sure, there are plenty of snack shops and fast-food joints, but any place where you can get a sit-down meal without spending a fortune is a real find.

It is for this reason that Mr. C has decided to include the Alcatraz Bar and Grill, despite the fact that the dinner entrees go a few dollars over Mr. C's usual $10 limit. It's such a fun restaurant—surrounded by many other more expensive places—that it's a relative bargain if you really want the experience of dining in the Fisherman's Wharf area.

They really take the Alcatraz theme to the hilt here. The whole restaurant is painted gray, and you can even take pictures in a mock prison cell. The adjacent retail store is full of Alcatraz souvenirs, which are anything but cheap (in price, anyway). More authentic prison paraphernalia is on view in display cases. Meanwhile, many of the restaurant's tables face huge windows with a clear view of Alcatraz—assuming it's a clear day, of course.

Begin your meal with appetizers, or, as the folks here call them, "The Preliminary Hearings." Bread and water is available for a dollar; but Mr. C suggests going with something a little more substantial, like chips and guacamole with pico de Gallo salsa ($5.95), potato skins with bacon, cheese, and sour cream ($4.95), or "popcorn" calamari, breaded and fried ($5.95). Among the dinner entrees, try Pelican Island pasta, angel hair pasta topped with bay shrimp, fresh basil and chopped tomato, for $10.95. "On the Bay" is a sauté of fresh salmon, cod, and prawns in a white wine, garlic, and herb cream sauce, served over rice, for $13.95. And a ten-ounce New York steak served with French fries is $12.95. All dinner entrees include clam chowder; or you can do some time at the salad bar.

Alcatraz does have a lunch menu as well. Though the prices are lower than at dinner, they aren't anything to write home about—or a bargain-hunting book, for that matter. Most sandwiches are priced at $6.95 and burgers at $7.95 (again, remember where you are). A better deal is the "Early Birdman Special" (get it?) served every weekday from 4:30 p.m. to 6 p.m. In this plea bargain, $10.95 gets you salad or clam chowder, fresh pan-fried snapper or New York steak, rice and fresh vegetables, plus ice cream for dessert.

Otherwise, when it comes to dessert, don't try to escape without sampling one of AB & G's yummy and heavy confections. Try a slice of mud pie ($2.95), New York style cheesecake ($2.25), or Ma Barker's brownie sundae ($2.95). After one of these, you're free to go—but you won't be able to get far.

Aux Delices
- 2327 Polk St. (Green St.), San Francisco; (415) 928-4977

- 1002 Potrero Ave. (22nd St.), San Francisco; (415) 285-3196

Aux Delices has received rave reviews from *San Francisco Focus*, which declared it the best restaurant in the Russian Hill area, and *San Francisco Magazine*, which said this is "the finest Vietnamese cuisine in The City." Their combination of Vietnamese and French influences is certainly winning raves with the critics, and their low prices win similar raves from Mr. C.

Unlike many Viet houses which cook up soups and stews, Aux Delices works more in the entree manner of other Asian restaurants. They have several vegetarian dishes, all for $5.95, including mixed mushrooms with tender greens, bean curd with black mushrooms, and vegetables with house curry. Pork, chicken, and beef dishes, meanwhile, are just as plentiful and cheap. Try a plate of "Singing Chicken with Ginger" ($6.95), pork with broccoli or asparagus ($6.50), a stuffed half-chicken with gravy ($7.95, or a whole one for just $15), and beef with vegetables in spicy sauce ($6.95).

Seafood dishes are also very well-priced. Sweet and sour shrimp is a real bargain at $6.50, about as low a price for those craved crustaceans as you're likely to find anywhere (much less at a restaurant with so many accolades). Squid with vegetables ($6.95) are another good deal; and don't miss AD's pan-fried catfish ($7.00) and sauteed red snapper ($7.95).

Finish off your meal with such traditional Indochinese treats as custard or fried bananas. This branch of Aux Delices is open for dinner from 5 p.m. to 10 p.m. The Potrero Avenue location is open for lunch only, weekdays from 11 a.m. to 2:30 p.m.

Bocce Café
- 478 Green St. (Grant St.), San Francisco, (415) 981-2044

The Bocce Café has, without question, the best seating in San Francisco. Along with the regular wooden chairs, many of the tables have booth-type bench seats covered with soft, smooshy pillows. If you've come here after a day spent walking up and down the hills of The City, you may just want to sink into this cozy upholstery and disappear. But then you'd miss all the great food.

For such a large, showy restaurant, the Bocce Café serves up delicious Italian specialties at amazingly low prices. Start off with a bowl of minestrone soup ($2.95) or bruschetta ($1.75); other appetizers, priced at $5.95, include fancy treats like carpaccio, fried calamari, and mussels bordelaise. Small salads, from Caesar to grilled chicken or chêvre, are just $3.75.

The bulk of the menu divides into long lists of entrees which are all priced at either $5.95 or $6.95 (with daily specials that get a little pricier). For $5.95, choose from such pasta dishes as linguine, penne, and spaghetti, paired up with your choice of sauce—Alfredo, pesto, sauteed eggplant marinara, carbonara, and more. The same price covers alternatives like the "Bocce cheeseburger" or a chicken teriyaki sandwich, both served with French fries; but hey, when in Rome. . .

Entrees under the $6.95 banner include some fancier specialties, like linguine with fresh mussels, or fettucine in sauteed calamari marinara, along with familiar favorites like lasagna and eggplant parmigiana. Several individual-sized pizzas are also $6.95, in such combinations as roasted eggplant and minced garlic, or oregano, garlic, and basil. You can also get a pizza made on focaccia bread, topped with roasted eggplant, bell peppers, and onions.

If you still have room left after one of these huge meals, desserts are a bit less expensive here than in many North Beach cafes. You may prefer to sit over an espresso, or a liqueur from the large, handsome bar. The restaurant itself is a large, high-ceilinged room, done in natural woods and decorated with various cooking accoutrements, giving it all a bright, Mediterranean feel. Outside,

through a set of double doors, there is a garden with patio tables; and, yes, a bocce court. Valet parking is available here. It isn't something Mr. C would do, but this of course can be a real asset in such a car-congested district.

The Buena Vista Café
- 2765 Hyde St. (Beach St.), San Francisco; (415) 474-5044

When you get this close to touristy areas like Ghirardelli Square, Fisherman's Wharf, and the cable car turnaround, it's very difficult to find good, cheap food. But, as Mr. C always says, where there is a bar filled with people imbibing over-priced drinks, you'll often find some delicious, *under*-priced food.

Hence, his inclusion of the Buena Vista Café—which claims to be *the* bar where Stanton Delaplane introduced Irish coffee to the United States. The cafe also declares itself the "oldest and busiest" bar in San Francisco. Well, try to disprove them! Located just steps from some of The City's top attractions, the Buena Vista serves up big portions of good, old-fashioned pub fare. Entrees here are real bargains. Try fried chicken or hamburger steak, each of which comes with French fries, vegetables, green salad, and sourdough bread, for $7.99. A little bit more expensive, but still very reasonable, are seafood entrees like prawns or Eastern scallops, same sides, for $9.95.

Then there are the big sandwiches and burgers; for something a little different, try the cheddar burger, topped with sauteed onions, cheddar cheese, and bacon bits ($5.75). Other interesting sandwich offerings include the Reuben grill, which combines grilled corned beef, Monterey jack cheese, and sauerkraut on rye bread for $5.95. All sandwiches come with potatoes or cole slaw.

Unlike most bars, Buena Vista also has a breakfast menu which is served all day. Perhaps this is a nod to folks who had too many of those Irish coffees the night before? Breakfasts are actually more expensive than the lunch and dinner foods, but many of them—like steak and eggs—could just as easily *be* dinner! You'll find the usuals here, along with house creations like the "JLK Special," an omelette filled with bacon bits, onion, green peppers, and mushrooms for $6.29; or the "Jim Ruffolo Breakfast" of scrambled eggs, a bowl of chili, and onion garnish for the same price. All breakfasts come with fresh hash brown potatoes and toast.

The Buena Vista opens its doors at 9 a.m. on weekdays, an hour earlier on weekends; they're open until 2 a.m. every night, though food is served until 9:30 p.m. only.

Caffé Greco

* 423 Columbus Ave. (Green St.), San Francisco; (415) 397-6261

Caffé Greco is a very happening North Beach hangout. Patrons sit and play chess, sip espresso, or just watch the world stroll by the storefront windows. It's also one of the better spots in this cafe-rich neighborhood to get sandwiches, salads, sweets, and other nibbles.

Focaccia sandwiches are good and cheap: get one with provolone, lettuce, and roasted peppers for $4.95, or one with proscuitto, fresh mozzarella, and roasted peppers for a dollar more, among the half-dozen choices. These are also available in a smaller, open-face style, with the same choices of ingredients, for $3.25 each. Other types of sandwiches are also available and just as reasonably priced, like a croissant with provolone and tomato for $4.75. Or, if your appetite is a bit lighter still, try a salad, like the Greco green salad ($5.95) of mixed greens, tomato, mozzarella cheese, roasted peppers, and calamata olives.

Really, though, a cafe is a cafe, and folks with a sweet tooth will not be disappointed here. Greco has a fine assortment of not-overpriced pastries, including tiramisu for $3.75 and cannoli, with a chocolate and fruit filling, for $2.98. Even their coffee drinks, usually the highest-priced items at these trendy cafes, are reasonable. A single espresso costs

MR. CHEAP'S PICKS
Chinatown

✔ **House of Nanking**—Dive doesn't even begin to describe the ambience here, but the food is fresh and without flaw. Ask anyone waiting to get in.

✔ **The Pot Sticker**—The name says it all: A great selection of pot stickers, including steamed, fried, with meat, or without. Of course, they also have a full menu of wonderful Mandarin specialties.

$1.30; a double is $1.90. Caffe lattes are $1.90 single, $2.65 double. And you may be just as satisfied with a cup of the rich house coffee, just $1 for a small, $1.50 for a large. Caffé Greco also has a selection of wines and beers. Open late, from 7 a.m. to 11 p.m. weekdays, 8 a.m. to 11 p.m. on weekends.

Caffé Viva

* 318 Columbus Ave. (Grant Ave.), San Francisco; (415) 392-5700

This cute North Beach bistro has huge windows looking out onto the street, making it an ideal spot to sip coffee and watch all the hip and trendy people stroll by. It's also a great place to get a sandwich, most of which are priced under $5. The house specialty is the "Hot Toasted"—prosciutto cotto and mozzarella cheese between two slices of sourdough bread, toasted in their European rack toaster, just $3.97.

Other good bets include the grilled chicken sandwich with pesto, housespread, roasted peppers, red onions, and fresh organic greens; and organic tofu with housespread, pesto, roasted pepper, fresh fennel, red onion, and greens. Both are priced at $4.66. And if you're wondering what "housespread" is, it's Viva's own blend of sun-dried tomatoes, extra virgin olive oil, and herbs.

Caffé Viva also has, of course, a fabulous selection of sweets. A huge glass case is filled with traditional Italian and other European goodies, including tiramisu and lemon tarts. Of course this wouldn't be a true North Beach cafe if they didn't have plenty of espresso, cappuccino, caffe latte, and the like. Open late into the evening.

Capp's Corner
● 1600 Powell St. (Green St.), San Francisco; (415) 989-2589

A legend in North Beach, don't even think about trying to get into Capp's on a Saturday night without a reservation. Besides great food at fantastic prices, this restaurant is loads of fun. The room is dominated by a huge bar; behind it, the lively, outgoing bartenders hold court with banter that covers everything from current events to movies. The entire wait staff is just as friendly.

Despite the pub-like atmosphere, this is very much a family restaurant. In fact, the dinners here are served family-style, which is what makes it such an incredible bargain. The concept is simple. There is one list of entrees for $10.50, and another list of entrees for $12.50. All of these include minestrone soup, salad, pasta, vegetables, and dessert. Soups are served in a huge tureen, and salads in a large bowl, for everyone at the table to share—and there is plenty for everyone.

Entrees for $10.50 include meat or cheese ravioli, steamed mussels and clams with linguine, and pasta primavera. The higher-priced entrees include leg of lamb, calamari steak, fresh fish of the day, eggplant parmigiana, and baked veal cannelloni. Anyone with a lighter appetite can have just the soup, salad, pasta of the day, and dessert, all together for only $8.50. Whatta deal! They also have a kids' dinner, for children under twelve, which includes soup, pasta of the day, a smaller-size main entree, and dessert (again, $8.50).

Capp's Corner is open for lunch, on Mondays through Fridays from 11:30 a.m. to 2:30 p.m. only. Most of the choices are priced at $8.50 (do you see a pattern here?), including fresh fish, roast garlic half-chicken, eggplant parmigiana, and roast pork loin. Daily specials may add things like corned beef and cabbage, braised short ribs, and risotto with clams. All lunches are served with soup or salad, pasta, and spumoni for dessert. Is it any wonder this place is so hard to get into? For that matter, after you've stuffed yourself silly, it may be even harder to get out.

Gold Spike Restaurant
● 527 Columbus Ave. (Green St.), San Francisco; (415) 421-4591

Finding a place to eat in North Beach is *never* a problem; finding a good one that you can afford may be more challenging. If you're panning around here, there are a few gems mixed in—and the Gold Spike is definitely paydirt. You want authentic North Beach atmosphere? This cafe is small and funky, with background music that changes from big band jazz to opera in a beat. You're sure to notice the decor of dollar bills taped to the ceiling; when Mr. C inquired about these, the waiter simply replied, "Italian overhead." Most importantly, they serve huge portions of really great Italian food and you won't need too much gold to pay for it.

Now, there are a couple of different ways you can approach dining at the Gold Spike. You could go a la carte: Entrees, served with fresh vegetables and pasta, are just $9.95. Choose from Italian pot roast, roasted half-chicken, chicken marsala, eggplant parmigiana, sauteed calamari or chicken livers, and many others. Only one entree—caciucco, an Italian seafood stew with crabs, clams, calamari, and prawns—goes out of Mr. C's price range at $12.95.

But why skimp when, for just three bucks more, you can have a six-course family-style dinner? That's right—tack $3 onto any of the above entrees, and you'll get antipasto, minestrone, green salad, pasta (ravioli or rigatoni), and dessert. What a feast. Not to mention a great deal—it would cost you almost $3 to add just *one* of the those extras to the price of an entree!

If your appetite is a little lighter, try a pasta dish. Ravioli, rigatoni, and spaghetti are all priced between $7.50 and $8.95, in a red sauce with or without meat. If you prefer pesto, it's an additional $1.95. Seafood pasta dishes, with various combinations of shellfish, are a little pricier at $10.95 to $11.95.

The Gold Spike is open 5 p.m. to 10 p.m. weekdays and 5 p.m. to 10:30 p.m. Friday and Saturday. They're closed on Wednesdays.

Golden Flower Vietnamese Restaurant
- 667 Jackson St. (Grant Ave.), San Francisco; (415) 433-6469

This is a small restaurant in Chinatown that illustrates the growing diversity of Asian restaurants in that neighborhood. Space is very tight in here, so during the lunch rush they will very likely seat you at a table with other diners. Think of it as cafeteria-style and go with the flow.

The specialty here is *pho*, or noodle soup. This is what the crowds come to feast on at lunch time. And feast they do—the portions are huge. For $3.50 you get a large, steaming bowl of soup with rare steak and beef balls, or with well-done flank, brisket, tendon, and tripe. Don't be fooled into thinking these soups aren't filling; they are so chock-full of meats and noodles that they are meals in themselves. No need to be a carnivore, by the way. If red meat's not your game, try the *hu tieu tom cua*, or seafood noodle soup. $3.95 gets you a bowl filled with shrimp, calamari, fish ball, crab meat, and rice or egg noodles. Chicken noodle soup ($3.50) is another good bet.

Golden Flower has more than just soup, though. Some of their dishes (chow mein, for instance) are very similar to their Chinese counterparts. Try beef, pork, or chicken chow mein, served with egg noodles, for

---

MR. CHEAP'S PICKS
Fisherman's Wharf

- ✔ **Alcatraz Bar and Grill**—You won't need to rob a bank to chow down here; one of the cheapest menus on touristy Pier 39.
- ✔ **Little Rio Café and Pizzeria**—Yummy pizzas and other Brazilian specialties at south-of-the-border prices.

---

just $4.50. Mr. C particularly liked chicken with snow peas, also $4.50. In fact, that same price will buy you any of several specialty dishes here, including Kung-po chicken, cashew chicken, beef with broccoli, or sweet and sour pork. Seafood dishes are also quite reasonable. Sizzling shrimp with vegetables, cashew prawns, or spicy curried calamari are each $4.75. The more daring diner may want to try fresh catfish in a clay pot of broth, just $5.50.

Golden Flower serves lunch and dinner everyday from 9:30 a.m. to 9:30 p.m.

House of Nanking
- 919 Kearny St. (Pacific St.), San Francisco; (415) 421-1429

House of Nanking is, quite possibly, *the* best Chinese restaurant in San Francisco. Don't take Mr. C's word for it: ask anyone in the throng of people waiting outside to get a seat. Even with Chinese restaurants by the dozens all around it (HON is well-situated on the border between Chinatown and North Beach, where Columbus crosses Kearny), the lines of people waiting to get in here has got to tell you something.

Mr. C should warn you, however: These people are lining up for the food, and not for the atmosphere. House of Nanking is small and plain, with a counter and maybe four or five tables; yet they pack in as many people as they can. If you sit at the counter, you'll likely be asked to move over a spot to accomodate a couple who've just squeezed inside the door. It's all part of the fun, loud, boisterous atmosphere that is Nanking. Mr. C thinks this is fine; but he admits it is not the place to go for a quiet, romantic dinner—Brandy Ho's, next door, is a better bet for atmosphere.

Okay, 'nuff said about character. Once you get a spot, begin with an appetizer or soup. Soups are $3.75 for a bowl; try the house special, Nanking fish soup. Mr. C loved the pot stickers, which he watched one of the cooks cut and fill right in front of him; and, at just $3 for six dumplings, these are a super bargain. In fact, the best seats in the house are at the counter, where you can really watch the show—cooks whirring about, all chopping, filling, frying, and sauteeing.

Entrees are similarly low-priced and the portions are huge. Chicken filet with Tsing-Tao beer sauce is, as they say in New York, "to die for." At just $4.95, with steamed rice, it's also a great deal. Same for the kung pao chicken, ma-po bean curd, and twice-cooked pork. Beef dishes, including Nanking beef, Hunan beef, and others, are a mere $5.25 each. The only dishes that are even a bit expensive (barely) are the seafood selections—and they're only a buck or two more. Try the kung pao squid ($5.50), prawns with Tsing-Tao beer sauce ($6.95), and Nanking scallops ($7.95). Bargain veggie dishes include dry braised string beans, eggplant Szechuan style, and sizzling rice with assorted vegetables, all just $4.95.

House of Nanking is open Monday through Friday from 11 a.m. to 10 p.m., Saturday noon to 10 p.m., and Sunday from 4 p.m. to 10 p.m.

Il Pollaio
● 555 Columbus Ave. (Union St.), San Francisco; (415) 362-7727

If you immediately think of spaghetti when you think of Italian cooking, Il Pollaio will change that notion. This place serves up heaping portions of char-broiled chicken and meats, in a cozy North Beach storefront. They only have about a dozen or so tables, so it can get pretty tough to snag one, especially on weekend nights; fortunately, everything on the menu is available for take-out. These offerings are a wonderful alternative to the usual fast foods.

The big deal here is chicken. A whole prepared chicken costs only $7.80 (!) and a half-chicken is $4.25. You can also get a half-chicken with a choice of salad (green, cole slaw, or beans) for $6.25. Side orders include soup, French fries (which are the big, delicious, steak-sized sort), and marinated eggplant.

Il Pollaio does cook up some other meats, including veal, T-bone steak, pork chops and ribs—and even rabbit. Or, perhaps you'll enjoy a plate of two Italian sausages, with a choice of salad, for $4.85; or an Il Pollaio hamburger with French fries for $5.45.

If you still have room after one of these hefty dinners, try some of the mouth-watering desserts like flan, cheesecake, chocolate mousse cake, or almond torte, all just $2. The restaurant has an extensive wine list that includes vintages from Italy, California, Argentina, and Chile. All in all, Il Pollaio is one of the best deals—and least-known—in North Beach.

King Tin Restaurant
● 826 Washington St. (Grant Ave.), San Francisco; (415) 982-8228

Remember, all the good restaurants in Chinatown are not always on the main drags—many can be found on hilly sidestreets. The King Tin Restaurant is located in the very heart of Chinatown, just steps from plenty of cheap import stores and kitschy souvenir shops. King Tin may not offer much in the way of ambiance, but it has plenty to offer in the way of good and inexpensive food.

This place was recommended to Mr. C by a particularly friendly clerk in one of those shops, definitely a good sign; most of the diners during a busy lunchtime visit were Asian, and very little English could be found among the clientele or the staff. Difficult as that can make the ordering, this too is often a plus for authentic Oriental meals.

Begin your dining adventure with an appetizer. Mr. C and his companion enjoyed a plate of classic pot stickers (six for $4), fried up nice and crisp on the bottom. The restaurant also makes a number of tasty soups, including hot and sour soup ($5.50) and shredded duck and vermicelli in soup ($4.50). If those prices look high to you, they're not—considering that these soups, in large bowls packed to overflowing with noodles and meat, can easily be meals in themselves.

The vast menu of entrees is varied and well-priced. Mr. C's companion raved about the kung pao chicken ($6.00)—again, a gigantic plate of meat and shredded vegetables, again, too much to finish. Other specialties include almond chicken ($6.00), sauteed mixed seafood ($8.00), mu shu pork ($6.50), and a mixed vegetables platter ($7.00). They also have a number of barbecue dishes, and serve a highly recommended dim sum brunch on weekends.

Leon's Bar-B-Q*
- 2800 Leavenworth St. (Fisherman's Wharf), San Francisco; no phone
- 1911 Fillmore St. (Bush St.), San Francisco; (415) 922-2436
- 2800 Sloat Blvd. (46th Ave.), San Francisco; (415) 681-3071

Soul food at Fisherman's Wharf? Uh huh! This branch of Leon's, at the Anchorage, isn't a sit-down restaurant, but rather a take-out stand—but it serves up the same good, greasy ribs, spicy jambalaya, and homemade sweet potato pie as its cousins. Service is, well, let's just say laid-back. But the food is worth it.

Lunch plates, served all day, are great bargains. A whole slew of entrees are all priced at $6.40, including

pork ribs, half roast chicken, hot link sausages, and more. These come with cornbread, plus your choice of baked beans, potato salad, cole slaw, fries, or even spaghetti. That jambalaya ($4.95) will make your eyes water. And the barbecued smoked turkey sandwich, served on a roll with a side order for $5.95, is a tasty, messy treat.

Dinners offer similar choices, in larger portions or paired together; beef ribs for $10.95, ribs and hot links for $13.50, baby back ribs and chicken for $13.95. These all come with two side orders, as well. Or, try 'em all with a sampler plate ($14.95) of chicken, links, ribs, sliced beef, corn muffins, beans, potato salad—a little bit of everything. Wash these down with one of a half-dozen bottled beers; and, if you have room, send it all home with one of those pies—including chocolate pecan pie and peach cobbler, all $2.75 a slice.

Basic stuff, but definitely the real thing. Leon's closes up shop here in the evenings, but the other joints are open until 10 p.m. daily; the Parkside location is across the street from the San Francisco Zoo.

Little John's Italian Food
- 2065 Polk St. (Broadway), San Francisco; (415) 929-1890

The name says it all. Little John's serves delicious Italian food at really great prices. There are so many dishes to choose from, it's hard to know where to begin. More than twenty pasta choices, most of which are $6.95, include spaghetti marinara, eggplant parmigiana, rigatoni or linguini vongole, and tortellini with meat sauce. All their veal dishes, including marsala and scaloppini, are just $8.95. Most of the chicken dishes, including cacciatore and parmigiana, are just $7.95. Even the seafood dishes—like fresh clams with linguini, fried prawns, or cioppino—manage to stay just under $10.

Little John's is also a great place for a quick sandwich. Get a roast chicken sandwich for just $3.50, or try sweet Italian sausage for $3.95. They also have several kinds of cheese steak sandwiches, just $3.75 to $4.25 for a small, $6 to $6.95 for a large. Choose from interesting varieties like barbecue steak or pizza cheese steak, or just go with your basic Philly. They even have a "no cheese" choice.

Little John's also has a breakfast menu, with a few offerings that go beyond the "same old"—including eggs Florentine and eggs Benedict, each high in calories but low in price ($4.95). A variety of omelettes, including mushroom and cheese, provençale, and five-herb, are just $3.95; and your basic stack o' pancakes is $2.99.

Situated right next to Johnny Love's, a popular entertainment spot (see listing under "Entertainment: Music"), Little John's is a good spot for a bite to eat before hitting the dance floor.

Little Rio Café and Pizzeria
• 2721 Hyde St. (Beach St.), San Francisco; (415) 441-3344

In the tourist-trap-laden area of Ghirardelli Square and Fisherman's Wharf, Little Rio Café and Pizzeria is one of the few restaurants where you won't have to choose between the dinner tab and, say, a week's lodging. The pizzas are wonderful and come in a number of mouth-watering combinations. What's more, they come in five, count 'em, *five* sizes. These range from extra-small, an eight-inch diameter perfect for single diners, to the extra-large seventeen-incher, which can comfortably feed a family of four. The extra-small starts at $6.35 for a plain cheese pie, and goes up to $7-$10 with one to four toppings. Then, there are the special house combinations (running $8-$10 in extra-small), including the "Ipanema," topped with ham, pineapple, and bacon; the "Brazilian," with olive oil, hearts of palm, chopped tomatoes, and oregano; and the "Romana," with Italian olives, capers, and chopped tomatoes. Meat combinations are more expensive, like the "Little Rio," with sausage, salami, pepperoni, mushroom, and tomato,

and the "Gaúcha," with hamburger, Canadian bacon, pepperoni, salami, sausage, and fresh garlic.

Don't care for pizza? Don't despair; there are plenty of other goodies on this menu to keep you happy. Brazilian specialties include *bife acebolado*, beef (marinated overnight with spices) which is sauteed with fresh onions, and served with rice, beans, and corn; and *frango assado*, baked chicken served with rice or potatoes and a house vinaigrette. All of the Brazilian specialties are around $9, reasonable indeed; half-orders are also available for $6.50, and you can even substitute a green salad for rice and beans. They also have a number of pasta dishes to choose from, including fettucine with mushrooms ($8.50), fettucine with meatless sauce ($7.50), and meat ravioli ($7.80). Sandwiches, all around $4, are available too.

Little Rio offers an impressive selection of beers from around the world, and their prices on hot drinks such as espresso, latté, and cappuccino won't keep you up at night, either. The restaurant is open seven days a week, from 12 noon to 10 p.m.

Magic Lamp Café
• 900 Beach St. (Ghirardelli Square), San Francisco; (415) 885-6500

If your three wishes are cheap food, cheap food, and cheap food, you'll feel like you've found your genie in this Lamp. Located in touristy Ghirardelli Square, the cafe serves up good-sized portions of Middle Eastern cuisine. Whether your looking for a quick snack, or need a full meal to replenish yourself after a day of sightseeing, you'll find it here.

Hungry folks will probably want to try a platter, such as the shawerma—marinated slices of lamb served over hummus, with onions, tahini, and pita bread ($5.25). Or, perhaps the mussaka platter, sliced eggplant stuffed with spiced beef, onion and pine nuts served over rice, with tzatziki and pita ($5.75). They also have two entree-sized salads, Greek and chicken breast, for $4.95

each. If you want something a little more familiar, try the barbecued chicken: It's just $6.75 for a whole bird (!) or $3.75 for a half, and each comes with pita bread and garlic sauce.

Folks with lighter appetites may want to stick with sandwiches. Along with Middle Eastern specialties like kefta kebab ($5.95), falafel ($3.95), and the ever-popular gyro ($3.95), the Magic Lamp also has American standbys like turkey ($4.25), roast beef ($4.25), or prosciutto ($4.95). If sandwiches don't tickle your fancy, how about a pizza? Try the Armenian pizza, made with spiced beef, onion, tomato, and melted mozzarella cheese—or a Greek pizza, with feta cheese, onion, tomato, olive oil, olives, and bell peppers—each in an individual size for just $2.95. Or, try their selection of salads, like tabouleh, tahini, or hummos.

The Magic Lamp also has a small breakfast menu that includes feta cheese on pita bread, and musabaha, which is hummos and whole garbanzo beans mixed with tahini sauce, garlic, lemon, olive oil, and served wtih pita bread and tomato. All are priced around $3.50.

Mario's Bohemian Cigar Store Café

• 566 Columbus Ave. (Union St.), San Francisco; (415) 362-0536

This tiny storefront restaurant, barely bigger than the bar that dominates the room, is nevertheless a North Beach legend. The food is wonderful and cheap and the atmosphere can't be beat. Neighborhood folk hang out here, talking long into the night over coffee, drinks, and wonderful focaccia sandwiches.

Half a dozen focaccias are priced between $5 and $6; and they are hearty portions indeed. Some of these specialties include chicken, breaded and fried with Swiss cheese, and topped with a light marinara sauce; meatballs with Swiss cheese, sliced onions, and marinara; and the frittata, which is eggs, sauteed zucchini, garlic, onions and herbs, Swiss cheese

---

MR. CHEAP'S PICKS
North Beach

✔ **Bocce Cafe**—The comfy seats are wonderful enough to bring you here, but it's the trendy atmosphere and inexpensive Italian food that really bring in the crowds.

✔ **Capp's Corner**—Gigantic portions of pasta and more—served family-style. They'll fill you up without emptying your wallet.

✔ **The Gold Spike Restaurant**—Fun and funky North Beach cafe atmosphere, without the trendy North Beach cafe prices.

✔ **Il Pollaio**—Italian food isn't *just* spaghetti, y'know. This small, storefront eatery specializes in Italian-style roast chicken with all the trimmings.

✔ **Mario's Bohemian Cigar Store Café**—Mario's is more than a cafe, it's an institution. "People-watching" may be tops on the menu, but the focaccia sandwiches and other Italian specialties are not far behind.

✔ **North Beach Pizza**—These guys make pizza delivery into a high-tech science, but they still put plenty of heart and soul into all their wonderful meals.

---

and marinara. They also have veggie and eggplant varieties for you noncarnivores.

But there's more here than just sandwiches. Mario's also serves several hot dinners, like cannelloni filled with roasted veal and chicken, fresh spinach, and ricotta cheese, with light marinara and mozzarella over the top, all for $7.75. On Thursdays, they make a polenta and sausage stew, sauteed in white wine, garlic, onions and herbs, served with light marinara sauce for $7.75. And there's also pizza, a 12" thin crust variety with mozzarella cheese, onions, green bell peppers, marinated sweet red bell peppers, Italian herbs, Italian salami, and ham, $7.50 for an individual pie.

Don't leave without trying their pastries, especially Mario's Bohemian biscotti and tiramisu. Mario's is open until midnight Monday-Saturday and 'til 11 p.m. on Sunday, with food served until closing.

Mo's

● 1322 Grant Ave. (Vallejo St.), San Francisco; (415) 788-3779

The burgers are big at this North Beach storefront—in size and in popularity. You can watch them cooking in the window, turning and dripping on a grill over open flames. And there's more to meet (or meat) the eye than just beef; chicken breast, Polish sausage and eggplant are among the juicy options. Pick your patty, and then build from there with about a dozen toppings—including roasted jalapeños, mushrooms sauteed in garlic, and apple-smoked bacon.

The basic burger starts at $4.50, with lettuce, tomato, and red onion; or, for the same price, try the lamb burger—ground beef and lamb mixed with onion and spices, and topped with jalapeño mayonnaise. An eggplant parmigiana sandwich is $5; chili dogs are $4.50. Add some French fries for $1.25; for more fun, try the chili cheese fries for $3.50.

And that's about it. It's a small, but fun, menu, which pretty well describes the restaurant itself. Beverages range from sodas and coffees to beer, wine, and root beer floats. It's a hoppin' little place, serving until 10:30 p.m. on weeknights, an hour later on weekends. Makes a nice alternative if you find yourself pasta'd out in North Beach.

Mu Ping

● 1545 Polk St. (Sacramento St.), San Francisco; (415) 928-1379

Mu Ping is well-known for its seafood, offering over thirty different entrees. They have some of the lowest seafood prices around, too. Try the prawns with chili sauce ($7.50), braised tofu with shrimp or crab meat ($7.50), and scallops with garlic sauce ($8.00).

Don't like seafood? No problem—there are still plenty of dishes to satisfy your palate. Mu Ping has several poultry specialties too, like snow white chicken ($5.95) and crispy half-duck ($8.50). If you like beef or pork, Mr. C recommends that you try beef with sa-cha sauce ($6.25) and shredded pork in mandarin sauce ($5.95). For vegetarians, they have a large selection of veggie and tofu dishes as well. Not to mention seaweed egg flower soup, $3.50, and crab meat with asparagus soup for $4.50.

Mu Ping offers over 25 "business" lunch specials, which give you soup, a spring roll, steamed rice, and fresh fruit, along with your main entree. These may include sweet and sour pork, chicken with assorted vegetables, broccoli with oyster sauce, and prawns with lobster sauce, and all of them are priced under $4 for the whole a deal. Mu Ping is open seven days a week.

Nob Hill Noshery

● 1400 Pacific Ave. (Hyde St.), San Francisco; (415) 928-6674

You wouldn't expect a restaurant in such a ritzy neighborhood to have such low prices on their *nosh* (snacks, that is), sandwiches, and full dinners—but they do. This place has a surprisingly laid-back atmosphere, with patrons kicking back in window seats as they munch on nachos supreme ($3.95), dry salami with cheese ($3.95), or baked brie with French bread ($3.95). Big spenders may choose the paté and cheese platter for $5.95. Add an order of Dutch crunch bread for a dollar, or a plate of *dolmas* (stuffed grape leaves) for just $1.95.

Want more than just a snack? They have a slew of sandwiches, all prepared with lettuce, tomato, onion, bean sprouts, mustard, mayonnaise, and a deli salad, on a variety of breads. Try mortadella with pistachios, or fresh vegetables and cheese, each $3.95. Have a Black Forest ham sandwich, or something hot like a reuben, for $5.95. For a dollar more, there's the "Noshery Brie-Ami," hot pastrami and brie on a French roll. They also have salads, including deli salads by the pound.

Moving on up the "filling" ladder, most main entrees are $6.95, including half of a spit-roasted chicken, vegetarian lasagna with salad, old-fashioned meat loaf, and pasta with meatballs. All come with rice or potato (except pasta dishes, natch) and bread and butter. Even cheaper is the daily quiche special, just $5.95 with a dinner salad.

And let us not overlook NHNC's selection of breakfast and brunch items, served all day. Get three scrambled eggs with toast or a bagel for $3.95. Add two bucks, and you can add ham, sausage, or bacon. A breakfast burrito, vegetarian or with meat, is just $3.95 again with toast or a bagel. Those with smaller appetites can choose from bagels, croissants, pastries, and cereals.

Nosh away at the Nob Hill Noshery Cafe seven days (and evenings) a week.

North Beach Pizza
- 1499 Grant Ave. (Union St.), San Francisco; (415) 433-2444

North Beach Pizza takes its pizza delivery *very* seriously. Their vans are equipped with hot ovens and radio communication to get you your pizza hot and fresh. They also bring hot peppers, parmesan cheese, napkins, and paper plates to your door, free upon request. Their order-taking system is completely computerized (you can even order by fax, at 433-7217); all this gives NBP strong claim as San Francisco's fastest free delivery service.

So, what is it that they're rushing out to you, anyway? Well, their pizzas, which they also claim are The City's most-awarded pies, are made

---

MR. CHEAP'S PICKS
Russian Hill & Nob Hill

✔ **Polk St. Beans and Café—** A funky cafe brewing up coffee, food, and entertainment—all cheap!

✔ **Rendezvous Café—**Retro-style entrees (and prices) in a new-fashioned setting.

✔ **Aux Delices—**Their formal, stylish Vietnamese dishes have won rave reviews in several Bay Area publications. The Polk location serves dinner only; the one on Potrero Avenue just serves lunch.

---

with whole milk mozzarella cheese, hand spun dough, their very own sauce, and super-fresh toppings. Whatever they're doing, it sure is good. A small, plain six-slice pizza costs $6.26, and additional toppings are just under $1 each. Choose from pepperoni, fresh mushrooms, spinach, pineapple, zucchini, jalapeño peppers, pesto, and many others. They also have a number of house special combinations: Try the "Coit Tower Special," with mushroom, sausage, salami, pepperoni, and cheese ($9.81, small); "Verdi's Special," with fresh spinach, pesto, onions, and feta cheese ($11.31); or the "Bianca Special," with cream sauce, broccoli, onion, mushrooms, zucchini, and cheese (also $11.31). Don't understand those odd prices, but hey, they're cheap.

If you're not a pizza fan, don't despair. NBP has a whole menu full of pasta dishes and meat entrees to satisfy any taste (these can all be delivered, too). Pasta dishes are available a la carte or as dinners, for an additional $1.10, which adds a cup of minestrone soup or a side salad, and bread. There are more than a dozen dishes to choose from, including cannelloni ($7.60), vegetarian lasagna ($7.60), eggplant parmigiana ($6.90), and ravioli ($7.50). Slightly more expensive, but still very reasonable, are their dinners like veal Milanese, pan-fried in lemon butter sauce ($9); chicken cacciatore ($7.85); and calamari, fried in garlic and butter sauce ($7.95). Again, an extra $1.10 gets you a full meal, with vegetables, spaghetti in meat sauce, bread and butter, and minestrone soup or salad.

Finally, for lunchers, or those with a small appetite, they have a great selection of submarine sandwiches, each $3.50 to $3.75. These are served on a crusty, crunchy French roll with sliced tomatoes, lettuce, and the special house sauce. Choose from hamburger, meat ball parmigiana, Italian sausage, pizza sub (with salami, pepperoni, and mozzarella), or ham and cheese. They also have salads, including a chef's salad for $4.25 or antipasto salad for $5.20.

The restaurant, comfortably done up in modern-style booths, also serves beer, wine, and soft drinks. North Beach Pizza is open daily from 11 a.m. to 1 a.m., Friday and Saturday until 3 a.m.

Omar's Café*
- Pier 1 Ferry Building (Embarcadero), San Francisco; (415) 834-1173
- 1 Daniel Burnham Ct. (Post St. at Van Ness St.), San Francisco; (415) 673-2423

A fine breakfast and lunch spot, Omar's Café bills itself as "an oasis in a desert of fast food." With their menu of inexpensive deli sandwiches and Middle Eastern specialties, convenient for folks on the run or pausing for a nibble, they may well be right. The fare is certainly more interesting than the usual burger and fries; hitch up your camel and find out.

Everything on the menu is priced under five bucks—good deal already—including deli sandwiches, like a turkey and bacon club or a New York pastrami and Swiss, each $4.95. Add a side order of fresh salad

to any of these selections for just 95¢. You can also get a half-sandwich with soup for that same $4.95.

Middle Eastern specialties include a variety of falafel dishes, such as falafel with eggplant, and the rather unusual falafel burrito; both are $4.95, as is a hearty Greek salad with feta cheese. A tabouleh and hummus sandwich goes for $4.75, and a meza plate—a sort of Mediterranean pu-pu platter—is $4.95.

Omar's has a small breakfast menu as well: The big item is filled croissants. Get one with scrambled eggs for $2.95, with ham and cheese for $4.50, or with pastrami, eggs, and cheese for $4.75. As mentioned above, these are real-ingredient alternatives to those attempts at breakfast sandwiches cranked out by fast-food McChains. Omar's also serves up bagels with cream cheese for $1.75, along with an assortment of pastries and other quick grabs. Kind of a downer: The Embarcadero branch is tucked inside a foyer, open only on the side facing the parking lot. A rather unfortunate fate for a waterfront location.

Pier 1 Deli*
- Pier 1 (Embarcadero), San Francisco; (415) 982-3686

Just along the block from Omar's, here is another cool spot for a hot bite to eat. Pier 1 Deli is little more than your basic greasy spoon; but, transported to the waterfront—and unlike Omar's, with an actual view—this can be a delightful place for a quick nibble.

Breakfast is served all day, and it sure is cheap enough: Two eggs, with hash browns and toast, are $2.95. A stack of pancakes is $2.55. A cup of caffe latte is $1.10, and a cappuccino is just 90 cents—try to match *that* in North Beach.

At lunchtime, try one of their homemade soups, like clam chowder, usually $1.10 for a cup or $1.85 for a bowl; homemade chili is $1.45 and $2.35, respectively. Follow these with a grilled chicken sandwich ($3.75), hot Polish sausage ($2.95), or gyros ($3.25). A quarter-pound cheeseburger is $3.45; same price for a chef's salad.

Bottled beers and wine coolers are available from the refrigerator cases at one side of the rather dingy interior (Mr. C prefers to think of this as dockside atmosphere). But, when the weather's nice, you can also sit outside on the wooden deck patio. Pier 1 Deli is open bright and early on weekdays, from 6 a.m. to 6 p.m.; on Saturdays from 9-4; and it's closed on Sundays.

Polk St. Beans and Café
- 1733 Polk St. (Washington St.), San Francisco; (415) 776-9292

Polk Street (the cafe, if not always the area) is a fine place to hang out, sip cappuccino, and leaf through, say, a volume of verse. It's also a great place to have freshly made hot and cold sandwiches, vegetarian specialty sandwiches, salads, assorted soups and the like.

Hot sandwiches are just $4.95. Try the "North Beach," brimming with ham, salami, and provolone on focaccia bread; the "Patsy," with pastrami and Swiss cheese on focaccia; or the "Golden Gate Great," with turkey, bacon, avocado, lettuce, and tomato, all on a croissant. Cold sandwiches are even cheaper. A smoked ham or pastrami sandwich is $3.75, "dolphin-friendly" tuna salad is $3.95, and egg salad is just $2.95.

Veggie sandwiches include the "New Yorker," an open-face sandwich with cream cheese, sliced apples, raisins, and nuts, with melted jack cheese over the top ($4.50); "Vegetarian's Special" with olive-garlic cream cheese, cucumbers, sprouts, tomato, onion, and sunflower seeds on wheat bread ($3.95); and the "French Tomato," toasted French sourdough spread with special dressing, topped with provolone and tomato ($3.75). All sandwiches are served with a fresh side salad.

Breakfast at Polk St. Beans is also very cheap. For $4.25, you can get an egg burrito or an egg croissant. For just $2.95, you can have steamed eggs with toast, granola topped with

fresh fruit, or hot raisin-apple-walnut oatmeal. Assorted bread stuffs, including muffins, croissants, scones, and bagels are all $1.50 or less. And you must try the toasted focaccia bread, $1.25 a piece.

Polk St. Beans and Café also hosts open-mike poetry readings and occasional live bands (see listing under "Entertainment: Poetry and Literary Events"), all in a totally smoke-free environment. They open every day at 8 a.m. and close at 9 p.m. on Sunday, Monday, and Wednesday, 7 p.m. on Tuesday, and at 11 p.m. Thursday-Saturday.

The Pot Sticker
- 150 Waverly Place (Grant Ave.), San Francisco; (415) 397-9985

The Pot Sticker certainly lives up to its name, offering a goodly variety of these Oriental appetizers—fried, steamed, or boiled, with meat or without, all for just a few dollars each. They're served up hot, fresh, and delicious.

The Pot Sticker is popular with local folk, probably because its out-of-the way location keeps it from being too overrun by out-of-towners. Waverly Place is one of those marvelous little side streets, almost like alleys, laced through downtown; this one is off of Grant Avenue, the main Chinatown thoroughfare. The PS atmosphere can be described alternately as "unpretentious" or "seedy," depending on your outlook. The point is, the food is wonderful, so who gives a hoot about the decor?

Besides its namesake, the restaurant serves up lots of other tasty appetizers. Try fried prawns ($2.75), a green onion pancake ($1.95), or fried spareribs ($2.25). If you can't decide between all these tempting offerings, then you probably want the combination plate: A pot sticker, a spring roll, sesame chicken, fried won ton, and fried spareribs, all for $5.95. There is also a selection of soups, including vegetarian hot and sour, sizzling rice, won ton, and—for the truly adventurous—seaweed soup, all $3.50 to $4.25 per bowl.

What? You're still hungry? Move on to full-size dinner entrees. Beef and chicken dishes are all around $6.50, including Szechwan or Mongolian beef, General Tsao's chicken, and orange chicken. Pork dishes are also very popular, especially at $5.55 to $6.25, including mandarin pork, sweet and sour pork, and sliced pork with mushrooms.

Seafood is a bit pricier, but still reasonable at $7.25 to $7.95, including princess squid, Hunan prawns, and scallops with hot garlic sauce. Vegetarians are not left out at Pot Sticker either; in fact, veggie dishes are of course the cheapest, most $4.95. Try Hunan braised eggplant, hot bean curd, and sauteed broccoli.

Luncheon specials are just $3.50 to $4.95 each. These are smaller versions of many of the popular dishes above, along with "twice-cooked pork," Hunan crispy chicken, and shrimp with green peas. The Pot Sticker is open everyday from 11:30 a.m. to 9:45 p.m.

Rendezvous Café

• 1760 Polk St. (Washington St.), San Francisco; (415) 292-4033

The Rendezvous Café is a funky, off-beat restaurant with interesting artwork and a pile of *SF Weekly* and *Bay Guardian* newspapers to give it that appropriately artsy feel. This atmosphere is not merely derived from hot-looking decorations and alternative rags, however; the food is priced low enough so that artists (and anyone on a similar budget) can actually afford to eat here.

The Rendezvous has a selection of dinner entrees which include broiled halibut steak served with rice for just $7.95; fried chicken, with French fries or mashed potatoes, for $6.95; sirloin steak, same sides, for $7.95; or ravioli with meat sauce and a slice of sourdough garlic bread for just $5.50. Mr. C enjoyed teriyaki chicken and rice ($6.95), tasty indeed. Even the seafood entrees are reasonably priced. You can get fish and chips for just $6.95 or sauteed seafood, which includes scallops,

prawns, and fish fillets with mushrooms, broccoli, tomato basil, and garlic, for just $8.50. All dinner entrees are served with a vegetable and come with a choice of soup or dinner salad.

If your tastes run a little simpler (or your wallet's even thinner), choose from a number of sandwich options. Do you love burgers? They've got 'em, handmade patties of fresh 100% ground chuck beef, served with lettuce, tomato, onion, and pickle. A 1/3-pound hamburger is just $3.25, a dollar more for a half-pounder. Cheeseburgers are just $3.50 ($4.50 for the half-pound). Specialty burgers, $3.95 to $4.95, include mushroom and cheese, teriyaki, and bacon and cheese. Add French fries to any burger for 75¢ more. Health-conscious folks may want to try a vegetarian burger or a turkey burger, each served with fries (okay, so it's not *completely* healthy), $4.25 each. Other sandwiches run the gamut from basics like a BLT to more unusual offerings like a tofu club with a mildly spicy peanut sauce. All of these range from $3.25 to $5.25, and come with lettuce, tomatoes, pickle, and homemade coleslaw. Choose from multi-grain, whole wheat, sourdough, rye, or white bread.

The Rendezvous also has an extensive breakfast menu. For something a little different, try some crêpes, with your choice of filling and served with home fries, for $3.95 to $4.95. Fillings include scrambled eggs with ham, cheese, or vegetables. They have a variety of omelettes too, including "Popeye's Delight" with spinach, tomato, and jack cheese ($5.50), and the house special with onion, bell pepper, mushroom, ham, and avocado ($5.75). If your sweet tooth wakes up early in the morning, try buttermilk pancakes (stack of four, $2.95) or French toast ($3.25).

The Rendezvous Café serves breakfast from 7 a.m. to 2 p.m. daily. Dinner entrees and sandwiches are served from 11:30 a.m. until 10 p.m. daily.

Steps of Rome
- 348 Columbus Ave. (Broadway), San Francisco; (415) 397-0435

The Steps of Rome is perhaps one of the trendiest of all those Italian *pasticcerias* in North Beach. Among other things, this means that a double espresso is $1.90 and a double latte is $2.55! What then, is Mr. C doing here? Well, much like a bar that charges heavily for its drinks and offers cheap food to compensate (and keep you drinking), the food at Steps of Rome is not as outrageously priced as the hot beverages. And for an added bonus, you get all the hipness this crowd can deliver.

Steps offers a number of good pasta dishes, including lasagna, pasta alla cara (mushrooms, spinach, zucchini, tomatoes, and cream sauce), pasta alla vodka (Italian bacon, vodka, tomatoes, and cream), and pasta al sugo di agnello (lamb, mushrooms, garlic, and tomatoes). All of these creations are a mere $5.95 each, served with bread and butter. Their fresh salads are extra, alas, but for just $4.75 you can choose from several salads and antipasti (with names like "Insalata di Piazza di Spagna"). That still brings your food bill to just over $10.

If you're not in the mood for pasta, they have a number of grilled panini sandwiches. These are served on focaccia bread, with choices like prosciutto, mozzarella, and eggplant ($5.95), ham and Swiss ($4.75), and bruschetta ($4.95).

Steps of Rome has a number of absolutely yummy desserts. These, of course, will put you as far off your budget as your diet—but they're worth it. If you want to splurge a bit, Mr. C says to go for the amaretto cheesecake, $3.50, or the ever-popular tiramisu, $3.75.

Szechwan of San Francisco
- 2209 Polk St. (Vallejo St.), San Francisco; (415) 474-8282

Szechwan of San Francisco serves this authentic Chinese cuisine at authentically low prices; several newspaper writeups in the window attest to their popularity. Their dining room, meanwhile, is quite elegant— with calla lily arrangements and beautiful lamps hanging from the ceiling. This is a good place to impress a date without the threat of having to wash dishes later in the evening.

Start off your culinary experience with an appetizer. These include good ol' steamed dumplings, four for $3; shrimp toast, $3.25; and spring rolls, two for $3. Soups, mostly $5 a bowl, cover such basics as won ton, hot and sour, and sizzling rice.

House specialties, like sesame beef, sliced leg of lamb, Szechwan lotus chicken, and chung-king prawns, can be ordered a la carte or as full dinners. That means you also get the soup of the day, a spring roll, steamed rice, and ice cream for dessert. Prices range from $7.95 to $12.75 for a la carte servings and $11.95 to $16.75 for dinners; seafood dishes, like "Ocean Party" (lobsters, scallops, and prawns) make up the more expensive end of the scale.

Beyond the specialties they have some wonderful poultry, seafood, pork, beef and lamb, and vegetable dishes. These include sliced chicken with fresh mushrooms ($8.25), shrimp with ginger sauce ($7.95), sweet and sour pork ($7.25), Mongolian beef ($7.95), and jade bean curd ($5.95).

Szechwan also has some great lunch specials that are super-cheap. For $4.75 to $5.50, you can get vegetarian's delight, cashew chicken, shrimp with garlic sauce, and more, all served with an egg roll and steamed rice. Szechwan serves lunch Monday through Saturday from noon to 2 p.m., and is open for dinner from 5 p.m. to 10:30 p.m. every day.

Tai Chi Restaurant
- 2031 Polk St. (Pacific St.), San Francisco; (415) 441-6758

Tai Chi (the restaurant, not the movement exercise) is not much to look at in terms of decor; if truth be told, it's sorta grungy. But Mr. C sometimes prefers good, cheap food to fancy accoutrements, and this Polk Gulch establishment is just such a place.

Tai Chi is very popular for lunch. That's because they have some of the cheapest lunch specials around—and the portions are huge, too. Priced at $3.75, these come with soup, steamed rice, and "fruit salad." Now, their fruit salad is nothing more than a small dish of cut oranges, but they were very fresh and sweet. Aside from that minor marketing fib, everthing else is excellent. Besides, would you really *want* the canned, syrupy stuff which usually passes for fruit salad in many restaurants? Thought not.

Anyway, you can choose from over twenty dishes including snow peas with beef, sweet and sour shrimp, mixed vegetables, hot spicy eggplant, and more. Mr. C tried the Hunan chicken; the portion was huge (the vegetables, in particular, were huge), and it was all very tasty. So was the soup of the day, hot and sour—and there are six varieties of won ton soup alone.

Similarly, TC's dinner entrees are very cheap, even by Chinese restaurant standards. You can find plenty of dishes for under $6 each, including Szechuan beef and cashew chicken. Most of the seafood dishes stay under $7—practically unheard-of—including shrimp with broccoli, kung pao squid, and shrimp with black mushrooms. Noodle and rice dishes are even less, as you'd expect; but let's face it, nothing will break your bank here.

SOMA
South of Market Street

Brain Wash Café and Laundromat*
- 1122 Folsom St. (Seventh St.), San Francisco; (415) 861-FOOD (3663)

In Mr. C's humble opinion, here's one of the best ideas to come down the pike in a long time. Take a laundromat—not the most convivial place, see—and combine it with a cafe and bar, so that desperate city dwellers, down to their last clean shirts, can relax over food and beverages during the spin cycle. Pure genius!

Just *offering* food would be welcome enough; but the fare at the Brain Wash is actually terrific. It's all home-cooked, hearty, and not over-priced—considering the industrial-grunge-meets-yuppie surroundings. You certainly won't forget you're in SoMa, with BW's warehouse feel, splashes of paint on the walls, and tiny cafe tables.

Occasional specials notwithstanding, nothing here goes much over seven bucks. They have lots of creative sandwiches, including a Southwestern chicken sandwich ($6.95), a vegetarian hummus sandwich ($4.50), and a falafel sandwich ($4.95). All sandwiches are served with pasta salad on the side; substitute French fries or a garden salad for an additional 75¢. They also have burgers, each of which is a half-pound of fresh beef (or the vegetarian equivalent, if you prefer) and is served with fries. Try "The Burger of Doom," topped with grilled onions, mushrooms, and mozzarella or the "Right-on Cay-jon Burger," a pan-blackened burger with jalapeños aioli, onions, and bell peppers, all topped with melted cheese. Both are $6.95.

"International" specialties include a marinated lemon-herb chicken breast, garnished with Greek olives and steamed vegetables, and served with fries for $6.95; vegetable stir-fry in a spicy peanut sauce over steamed rice for $5.95; and the "Brain Wash Super Vegetarian Burrito" stuffed with black beans, rice, cilantro salsa, and topped with melted cheese and sour cream for $5.45. Folks with lighter appetites can also go for salads, soups, or chili.

The Brain Wash also has a wonderful breakfast menu, perfect for brunch with your weekend chores. Get two eggs, any style, for $3.75; make it $4.95 with ham, bacon, or sausage. They also offer a number of different omelettes, most around $5. The griddle menu includes "Wash-Day Blues," fresh blueberry pancakes for $4.75; and, on the weekends, orange French toast (mmmm. . .) for $3.95. Breakfast is served Monday through Friday from 8:30 to 11 a.m., and from 8 a.m. to 1 p.m. on weekends. The Brain Wash is open seven days a week, from 7:30 a.m. to 11 p.m., for all your internal and external needs.

And, for your cultural needs, live bands add to the way-hip atmosphere every Wednesday and Friday night at 9 p.m. the focus is on progressive rock 'n roll, from local bands. If you're a spoken word fan, come enjoy poetry readings every Saturday at 8:30 p.m. There is no cover charge for music or poetry in the cafe. But there's more! Upstairs, the "Above Brain Wash" Theater presents a busy schedule of performance art, drama, and cabaret, at very modest ticket prices—which is usually where the modesty ends (see listing under "Entertainment: Theater").

Café 180*
- 180 Howard St. (Main St.), San Francisco; (415) 442-1800

It's tricky to find good, cheap lunch spots so close to the hustle and bustle of downtown. Café 180 is nothing fancy, to be sure; they feature hot and cold sandwiches, a salad bar, and the like. Still, it's a serviceable shop for grabbing a quick lunch on the go. And, because it is so close to a number of office buildings, it's very popular for take-out.

Food at Café 180 is served cafeteria-style, so no tip is required—another cost-saver. It is also, as you can probably imagine, no-frills. This isn't

---

MR. CHEAP'S PICKS
SoMa

✔ **Brain Wash Café and Laundromat**—Yes, a cafe and laundromat in one, what a smart idea! Relax over good eats while your skivvies run through the spin cycle.

✔ **Hamburger Mary's**—This raucous hippie hangout has great burgers and your usual greasy-spoon offerings—with some healthy twists.

✔ **Hanno's Bar and Grill**—At lunchtime, some of the best burgers ever, at super-cheap bar-food prices.

✔ **Max's Diner Bakery and Bar**—Old-fashioned portions at old-fashioned prices! It may not be NYC, but it comes darn close.

---

the place to take an important client. It's more the kind of place to go with your co-workers and gossip about the boss.

Deli sandwiches are just a few bucks each. Get avocado, cucumber, and cheese for $3.25, up to a triple-decker club for $3.95. Hot sandwiches are similarly priced: Try the meatloaf ($3.55), tuna and cheese melt ($3.55), hot Italian sausage ($3.25), or a chili dog ($2.95). Speaking of which, you can get a cup of their "famous" chili for $1.85 or a bowl for $2.75. Soups are $1.55 and $2.15, respectively.

Check out the well-stocked salad bar, charging 25¢ per ounce. Why, you could get a pound of the stuff for just $2! There's plenty of greens, vegetables, and fresh fruits to choose from, along with bread and butter at no extra charge. For those looking for a *really* quick lunch, they have a number of health shakes, including the high protein shake, the "Liquid

Lunch," and the "Sunflower Special," all $1.95.

Café 180 makes an equally fine pre-office breakfast place. You can get a basic scrambled eggs and toast plate for a super-cheap $1.79. They also have all sorts of omelettes, plus a selection of bagels, croissants, and other pastries at the register for those in a real hurry. Café 180 opens bright and early at 6:00 a.m., serving until 4:00 p.m., weekdays only.

Flower Market Café
● 698 Brannan St. (Sixth St.), San Francisco; (415) 495-7162

Where else could this place be, but the Flower Market? If you're looking for blooming bargains, be sure to read about some of the wholesalers here who sell to the public (in the "Flowers and Plants" chapter). Meanwhile, if the bustling crowds make you work up an appetite, this cafe is a fine place to wet your whistle or fill your tummy for breakfast or lunch. It's big, clean, and just as busy as the market itself.

Flower Market Café serves up the basics, from big, three-egg omelettes (starting at $5.75, with red potatoes and French bread) to hamburgers, sandwiches and salads. The burgers, one-third of a pound of freshly rolled meat, start at just $5, with lettuce, tomato and Bermuda onion; thick steak fries, too. A spinach salad platter, with mushrooms, bacon, eggs, onions, and honey-mustard dressing, is $6.75. Sandwiches are mighty tall, and served on several kinds of great fresh bread.

But it's with the daily specials that things get interesting. You may find things like banana pancakes ($4), or chicken apple sausage with eggs, potatoes and toast ($5.65). Give 'em a try. Breakfast, by the way, is served all day long—the mark of a good diner. Of course, that's only until 2:30 in the afternoon, when the frantic pace finally slows down and the cafe closes. But then, it opens at 6:00 in the morning (5:00 a.m. on Wednesdays and Fridays; closed all day Sunday). By mid-afternoon, the

coffee-fueled staff could probably do with a nap.

Hamburger Mary's
● 1582 Folsom St. (12th St.), San Francisco; (415) 626-5767

SoMa landmark, Sixties landmark, Hamburger Mary's is loud in every sense of the word. The music is loud, the decor is loud, the orange and yellow lighting is loud. And cluttered. The walls and ceilings are covered with every manner of kitsch, including old-time advertisements, lunchboxes, globes, beads, statuettes of the Virgin Mary (hence the name?), and more. It's a wild bar scene, as well as a fun place to eat.

The menu itself offers an eclectic mix from health food (tofu burgers) to junk food (good ol' burgers and fries). But even the junk food is deceiving, since the burgers are served on nine-grain bread and the fries are fried in cholestrol-free Canola oil. What's the deal? A biker bar that blasts Pearl Jam at top volume doesn't seem like a place for wholesome food—but it is.

Any way you look at it, the food here is good and cheap, and that's all that counts in Mr. C's book. The Mary Burger is their "humble beginner," and at just $5.75 for 1/3-pound of beef on nine-grain bread served with fries, it's anything but humble. Add avocado spread or bacon for $6.95; bacon and cheese for $7.95. By the way, if you don't want French fries—which are terrific—you can get home fries, cole slaw, or cottage cheese instead.

All you vegetarian-types should just skip right to the section of the menu marked, appropriately, "Meatless." Here you'll find the Tofu Mary (no preservatives, no cholesterol, no dairy or animal products, no *nuthin'*) for $5.95, and the Tofu Mary with cheese for $6.95. Add avocado for $1.95 or mushrooms for $1.25. Or, try an avocado, lettuce, and tomato sandwich, cold or hot off the grill, for $6.25.

There are plenty of traditional sandwiches, too, like the charbroiled chicken breast sandwich ($6.95). For something a bit out of the ordinary, give the fresh snapper sandwich ($5.95) a try. Dinners are a bit more expensive, but not unreasonable; especially since they come with soup, cole slaw, or salad, and your choice of potato or cottage cheese. Catch a fresh broiled snapper for $7.95, teriyaki chicken for $8.50, or a charbroiled sirloin steak dinner for $9.25. Don't miss the great desserts, including carrot cake, cream cheese pie, or chocolate cake.

Hamburger Mary's also has a great breakfast menu, which is available any time of day—always a good sign. Try a "fantasy" omelette: Start with a three egg omelette for $3.95, and add your fantasy ingredients, ranging from 75¢ for onions or sprouts to $2.95 for crab. Most are an additional $1.25 or so, including mushrooms, peppers, cheddar cheese, and salsa. Needless to say, which and how many ingredients you add will determine the price you pay for your fantasy. Omelettes come with home fried potatoes, as well as banana bread or nine-grain toast. Those who like to start off with something sugary in the morning will want to know about Hawaiian toast ($4.25)—Hawaiian sweet bread dipped in egg batter and grilled, for an offbeat variation on French toast. It's served with a choice of maple syrup, honey, orange marmalade, or strawberry preserves.

Hamburger Mary's is open Tuesday through Thursday from 11:30 a.m. to 1 a.m., Friday from 11:30 a.m. to 2:30 a.m., Saturday 10 a.m. to 2:30 a.m., and Sunday 10 a.m. to 1 a.m.

Hanno's Bar & Grill
- 431 Natoma St. (Howard St.), San Francisco; (415) 982-1837

Hanno's Bar & Grill, known to SoMa insiders as Hanno's in the Alley, is your basic neighborhood dive. This means that they serve good, hearty food at low prices, to go along with the booze. The place, hidden away between Mission and Howard, has a sort of warehouse feel—exposed

brick walls, ceiling beams. Yet it has a certain refinement, too, with white linen tablecloths and fresh carnations on each table during breakfast and lunch.

Hanno's claims to have the "best burgers anywhere around." Fortunately, the food is better than their grammar. These burgers are fresh, hand-formed patties perfectly designed to fit on a large hunk of French bread. All of their burgers, served with hot, hand-cut fries, are just $4.50 each; that includes the mushroom burger and patty melt. The only exception is "Hanno's Special Burger" ($4.95), with sauteed mushrooms and cheese.

There are several hefty deli sandwiches to choose from as well. Choose from roast beef ($4.75), hot pastrami ($4.50), Philly cheese steak ($5.50), or tuna ($3.95), all served with potato salad or French fries. Add a green salad for $2.00, or a bowl of the day's soup for $1.50; large salads, topped with things like warm chicken breast, are often on the menu too.

Along with its lunches of burgers and brews, Hanno's also serves breakfast with its eye-openers. Rustle up two eggs, any style—with toast and cottage potatoes—for $1.99; pancakes with a choice of bacon, sausage, or ham, also $1.99; or a Denver omelette for $3.50. Food is served on weekdays only; breakfast from 7 a.m. to 11 a.m., and lunch from 11 a.m. to 2 p.m. No dinner is served.

The Java House*
- Pier 40, The Embarcadero (Townsend St.), San Francisco; (415) 495-7260

Can't get much cheaper than this, folks. Or more character for your dollar. If you're wandering around the waterfront, below the Bay Bridge, this can be a fun place to stop in for an early breakfast or lunch—provided you like greasy-spoons, which Mr. C definitely does.

But, look: Java House offers you the same romantic view as any fancy-shmancy, high-priced, waterfront restaurant—in this case, sailboats quietly bobbing up and down in the South Beach Marina—but nothing on the menu tops four bucks. Beat *that*, Fog City.

Sure, the menu consists mostly of sandwiches, burgers, and eggs, but you're missing the point. What's interesting about Java House is its dockside ambiance. The place has been running here since 1912, making it one of the area's oldest eateries. It's a simple wooden-shack structure, run by a friendly Greek couple, at least one of whom is can usually be found behind the counter. Place your order here, find a table, and pick up your food when it's called out.

Authentic working-class style is part of Java's charm. It's a style that appeals to construction workers and our men in blue, along with men in shirtsleeves and ties (business women, too, don't worry). Are these folks looking for chevre and sun-dried tomatoes? No, thank you. Go for a hearty three-egg cheese omelette, served with toast and home fries for $3.05; make it ham and cheese for another dollar. And, of course, they've got good java.

A stack of pancakes is $3.75, though it'll be just that, a bare stack; yet, you can get the eggs and hotcakes plate for $3.50. Go figure. Meanwhile, sandwiches are also around three bucks: roast beef, chicken salad, crabmeat, liverwurst, hot pastrami, BLT. . . you name it, they've got it. Soups are a dollar a cup, or just $1.65 a bowl: minestrone, split-pea, New England clam chowder, and more. Other lunch options include six-ounce burgers ($2.75), Polish sausage ($2.45), and chili dogs ($2.95).

You get the idea. With all the yuppie condo development going on in this quiet (but waking up) corner of SoMa, here's hoping the Java House sticks around. It really is good to the last drop.

Max's Diner Bakery and Bar
- 311 Third St. (Folsom St.), San Francisco; (415) 546-6297

One of the many slogans posted at Max's Diner's states that "this is a bad place for a diet and a good place for a diet." How so? Because their menu has plenty of low-fat dishes, lean turkey sandwiches and burgers and such—but then they expect you to blow it on the most gargantuan, sinful desserts in The City. Max's Diner is a fun 1950s-style diner with plenty of booths, a great staff, and Ike-era music and decor (neither of which is too loud).

You'll find a number of touches here which tell you that service is a high priority. Sodas come with free refills. Each table has three kinds of mustard: sweet-hot, Dijon, and deli, not to mention ketchup, A-1 steak sauce, Lea & Perrins Worcestershire sauce, and tabasco. They even give you Bazooka bubble gum with your check.

But, what about the food? It's just as high-class. Mr. C really enjoyed his tall New York pastrami on rye (you can almost hear the screaming cabbies), especially appreciative of the fact that the bread wasn't soggy; it goes for $7.50. Sandwiches are served with potato salad, but you may substitute French fries (they don't mind—*that's* not like NY!) which were hot, fresh, and delicious. Max's also has combination sandwiches like turkey, corned beef, pastrami, and cole slaw ($8.95). They have all kinds of burgers, including turkey, lamb, and good, old-fashioned beef, as well as grilled sandwiches on sourdough bread. Most of these range from $6 to $8.

There are also plenty of low-priced entrees, though a few go out of Mr. C's price range. Low-fat entrees give you their calorie and fat information on the menu (so you'll know how far you can splurge at dessert). Local red snapper with vegetables and potatoes is a good catch at $8.95; red Roma tomatoes served on angel-hair pasta with garlic, capers, and sweet basil is $7.95; turkey breast with cranberry sauce for just $5.95 is another best bet. And, don't miss their "Salary Savers" including meatloaf for $6.95, pot roast for

$7.50, and roast turkey for $5.95, all served with mashed potatoes and a vegetable.

Max's breakfast roster is somewhat limited, especially in comparison to the rest of the menu; but these items are available all day, one of Mr. C's most important diner criteria.

Don't forget those mega-desserts. These are not, strictly speaking, cheap; but with rich, gooey sauces shipped in from New York, who can resist? Ice cream treats include a "Rocky Road Brownie" topped with ice cream, hot fudge, and marshmallow ($4.50), and the macaroon crumble with hot fudge, creamy marshmallow, and coconut macaroon all over ($4.95). They also have cakes, pies, and brownies. Try the Snickers cheesecake ($4.95), "Niagara Falls" cake with its waves of chocolate and buttercream ($4.25), or good old-fashioned apple pie ($3.50). Well, Max did say, "this is a bad place for a diet." In fact, the word "diet" shouldn't even be used here.

Near the Civic Center, you'll also find **Max's Opera Cafe** at 601 Van Ness Avenue; telephone (415) 771-7300. Part of a ritzy complex of movies, dining and shopping, most of the entrees at this branch are a bit more expensive than their SoMa counterparts. Still, they do have relatively inexpensive sandwiches and those incredible desserts—as well as aria-singing waiters.

Parc Place
- 160 Spear St. (Mission St.), San Francisco; (415) 957-9818

It's difficult to find inexpensive restaurants this close to the Financial District. Parc Place has a menu that is stocked (get it?) with salads, sandwiches, full entrees, and more, all at very reasonable prices. Actually, Mr. C doesn't recommend this as a particularly cheap *lunch* spot; but for dinner, it's a winner.

Those salads and sandwiches go far from the norm. Try the lemon beef salad ($7.50); chicken salad chinoise ($6.75) and walnut prawn salad ($7.50) are also good bets. Sandwiches include a Cajun sausage sandwich and a croissant club, each $6.75. You can also get a half sandwich with a green salad and a cup of soup for $5.95—definitely a good deal.

Parc's full-size entrees will make your mouth water. Try scallops sauteed in lemon butter and wine, finished with a dill mornay sauce, for $9.75; beef scallopini marsala for $8.75; and chicken sauté, also $8.75. The menu tops out at $11.25, with the New York steak *au poivre*. Pasta dishes are an even better deal. Try calamari Siciliano ($7.95), chicken fettucini ($7.95) or Cajun pasta ($8.95). A true business area haunt, Parc Place is only open from 11 a.m. until 7 p.m. every day.

Zeke's Diamond Bar and Grill
- 600 Third St. (Brannan St.), San Francisco; (415) 392-5311

After a full day of prowling the outlets and factory stores packed so densely into this part of SoMa, what do you really want to do? Eat, right? Well, Zeke's Diamond Bar and Grill ain't much on atmosphere, but it does have an interesting menu of inexpensive food. Located just steps from the fabulous Six-Sixty Center, what could be more convenient?

The menu is quite small, but the offerings are yummy enough to make up for this lack of breadth. Sandwiches are always a good bet. They offer the Diamond Burger ($5.95), grilled chicken ($6.25), and the 49'er Dog, a frankfurter grilled with cheese and onions and smothered with Zeke's chili ($4.95). All of these are served with French fries and cole slaw.

Entrees include Franceschi pasta, a spaghetti dish served with robust tomato meat sauce and grilled eggplant, for $7.50; fettucini di jeffio, pasta with sundried tomatoes, asparagus tips and mushrooms in a light brie cream sauce, also $7.50; and lamb stew for $5.95. They also have a few appetizers and salads for those who just need a light snack to re-fortify themselves for more bargain hunting!

WEST AREA
including the Parkside, the Richmond, Sunset

Angkor Wat
- 4217 Geary Blvd. (Sixth Ave.), San
  Francisco; (415) 221-7887

Angkor Wat has received rave reviews from the *San Francisco Chronicle* and the *San Francisco Examiner*, and *San Francisco Focus* has rated it the best Cambodian restaurant every year since 1987. What's more, on Friday and Saturday nights, performances by the Cambodian Classical Ballet at 7:30 p.m. and 9:30 p.m. accompany the food. There is no extra charge for the entertainment (Mr. C's favorite words), but it does get very crowded; it's best to make reservations. When you're not enjoying the ballet, you can gaze at the bas-relief wall carving that is a reproduction of the Angkor Wat Temple, one of the seven wonders of the ancient world.

Don't forget about the food! Appetizers here are nice and cheap, just $2.95 for Cambodian style crépes or prawn rolls, and soups. They have dozens of similarly inexpensive entrees, such as *baksei laak khlouwn*, marinated chicken with spicy red curry, yams, carrots, string beans, potatoes, and coconut, for $8.95; *sach ko kroeung aing*, marinated sliced beef with ground peanuts and spices, charbroiled on brochettes, for $9.95; and lamb curry, also $9.95. Seafood dishes are a little more expensive, but still quite reasonable. Try a swordfish kebab ($10.95), pan-fried catfish simmered in a tangy lime sauce ($9.95), and scallop brochettes ($10.95).

Angkor Wat also has a full vegetarian menu with more appetizers, soups, and entrees. Not only are these dishes healthy, but they tend to be cheaper than dishes with meat. Get mixed vegetables stir-fried in olive oil for $5.95, baked eggplant in a garlic-lime sauce for $5.95, or vegetable curry for $6.95. Veggie appetizers include grilled stuffed mushrooms for $3.50 and papaya salad for $2.95. This truly is one of the standouts among Richmond's many Asian restaurants; it's open seven days a week, for lunch from 11 a.m. to 2:30 p.m., and for dinner from 5-10 p.m. (to 10:30 on weekends).

Bill's Place
- 2315 Clement St. (25th Ave.), San
  Francisco; (415) 221-5262

Bill knows burgers. The menu at this good, though slightly down-at-the-heels, diner is heavily weighted toward heavy hamburgers—two dozen varieties, all freshly ground and pattied daily on the premises. The basic burger will only set you back $3.95; but why not try one of the "Celebrity Burgers," like the "Letterman" ($4.90), made with avocado and alfalfa sprouts—do we really think Dave goes for this?—or "Carl Payne's Cable Car Burger" ($4.70), topped with lettuce, tomato and a fried egg.

Getting more elaborate, the "Carol Doda" ($6.20) enters the realm of artwork: named for the (in)famous topless dancer, this features two patties—yes, side by side—each topped with an olive. "In Honor of Red Skelton" ($5.40) is a similarly creative rendition of the clown's face. And your mother told you it was bad to play with your food! Finally, "The Works" tops a cheeseburger with bacon, avocado, mushrooms, and sprouts, all on a French roll for $6.95. Each of these (except for the basic) includes terrific hand-cut French fries, too.

Those who don't eat red meat won't be left out—there are half a dozen varieties of chicken burgers, using whole chicken breasts ($5-$6), as well as tuna melts, grilled cheese sandwiches, even peanut butter and jelly. Plus hot dogs, homemade soups, and omelettes. All of the comfort food groups are well-represented at Bill's.

Speaking of which, leave us not forget the fountain. Dreyer's ice cream, in a dozen flavors, is the prime ingredient in a host of sodas, shakes, sundaes, and a la mode desserts. Enjoy 'em at the counter, at a booth, or, when the weather's nice, on the patio out back.

Bill's also has a liquor license, with a basic selection of beers and wines available. It's definitely a hangout type of place, nothing fancy or trendy, but clearly with a number of regulars. It's been here for over three decades, and by the look of them, so have some of the customers.

Cheers Café
- 127 Clement St. (3rd Ave.), San Francisco; (415) 387-6966

The beginning of Clement has been undergoing something of a renaissance, and Cheers is a good example—a bistro which manages to be upscale without being too overpriced. The interior is light and airy, with linen tablecloths, (recorded) jazz music, and waiters in formal attire.

The menu, though, is mostly informal: eggs, salads, sandwiches, pastas, and pizzas, all given a nouvelle turn—with a handful of more expensive meat entrees as well. Stick with things like smoked Gouda cheese, Black Forest ham, and sun-dried tomatoes on French bread ($5.95), with a green salad on the side; an avocado, jack cheese, and sour cream omelette ($5.50), served with home fries and bread; seafood cannelloni, filled with shrimp, crabmeat, mushrooms, and shallots in a sherry cream sauce, served with salad and a baguette ($7.50); and individual-sized pizzas. Most of these are $8.50, topped with such combinations as prosciutto and wild mushrooms or chevre, sun-dried tomatoes and spinach. Or, create your own.

MR. CHEAP'S PICKS
The Richmond

✔ **Angkor Wat**—Any place that combines cheap food with cheap entertainment is truly a find. This Cambodian restaurant serves great food with free weekend performances of traditional Asian ballet.

✔ **Mescolanza**—If you think you have to go to North Beach to get great Italian food, think again. This place has a magnificent selection of continental dishes at moderate prices.

If you thought the Richmond was solely devoted to greasy spoons and inexpensive ethnic restaurants, Cheers will be a pleasant surprise. It's not the cheapest place in the neighborhood, but you can certainly have quite an elegant meal here without blowing your budget. Good place for weekend brunch too, by the way, which is served until 3:00 p.m.

Cleopatra
- 1755 Noriega St. (25th Ave.), San Francisco; (415) 753-5005

The western half of The City truly seems to have every single foreign and domestic cuisine represented at least once. Noriega Street may be lined with Asian storefronts, but here's a fine alternative option: Middle Eastern. Cleopatra is a large, comfortable Sunset shop, wrapping around a corner not far from the reservoir. Its appearance takes on the look of the imperial English tea rooms that found their way into that ancient region (the Middle East, that is).

Inside, the restaurant divides into a small front room with simple tables, dominated by a take-out deli counter, and a larger dining room. The folks here are friendly, and will be happy to help you through the intricacies of the menu. The food itself, meanwhile, is good and cheap.

Several kinds of hot sandwiches are all priced under $5—and they're a handful. Souvlaki is Mr. C's favorite—ground beef or chicken, mixed with spices, marinated, and slow-cooked on a spit—it comes in a pita pocket with a house blended sauce, all for $4.80. Same price for a hot, juicy lamb shish-kebab sandwich. And falafel (which Mr. C sometimes refers to as "veggie McNuggets") sandwiches are just $3.90.

For a more formal meal, start off with an appetizer of grape leaves stuffed with ground meat and rice, flavored with lemon juice ($3), spinach turnovers in flaky dough ($4.50), or fool m'dammas ($4.25), a casserole made with fava beans. If you're here with a large enough group, the mezza plate gives you a choice of five different appetizers for $20; it sounds like a lot, but there's plenty for everyone.

Then, you can move on to such dinners as the shawarma plate, slices of marinated beef in a zesty tahina sauce, just $6.95; a baked half-chicken platter with vegetables for $8.25; and kebab dinners featuring beef, lamb, chicken, and even prawns, all between $7.50 and $8.95. For the total experience, be sure to finish off with a slice of baklava and a cup of Turkish coffee—but be warned, it's strong stuff.

Eats*

- 50 Clement St. (Second Ave.), San Francisco; (415) 752-8837

Down the block and across from Cheers, this is a more casual place to start off a day of shopping around the consignment shops in the Richmond—especially since it's located near the beginning of Clement. Eats is a classic breakfast and lunch place, with self-service and cozy surroundings dominated by plants and ceiling fans. It's sort of a cross between a cafeteria and a luncheonette parlor.

Turkey seems to be the specialty

of the house; they bake up whole birds here daily, most of which winds up on the turkey plate ($5). Real meat is topped with homemade gravy, with mashed potatoes, stuffing, and cooked vegetables on the side. For an extra fifty cents, you can have all white meat.

Giant-sized sandwiches, including grilled chicken, meatloaf, and the like, are priced between $4-$6. Freshly rolled one-third-pound burgers start from $3.75. Big salad platters here, too; Mr. C enjoyed the teriyaki chicken salad plate ($4.95), in which hot, tasty chicken was piled atop a huge salad of fresh greens, sprouts, onions, tomatoes, red peppers, pickles, and sliced hard-boiled eggs. Add soup and fresh bread for another fifty cents—in varieties like turkey vegetable (of course) or cream of asparagus.

Breakfast, served from 7:00 a.m. daily (except Sundays, when there is a separate brunch menu from 8:30 to 3:00), includes three-egg omelettes with many unusual fillings (black bean omelette, $4.50). Or, if even these aren't hearty enough to start your day, go for the "Omelette Cake"—a four-layer affair with your choice of various fillings, all for $4.95. Breakfast is served through the day, but there are usually specials from 7-11 in the morning, like two eggs, toast and orange juice for $2.95. Dinner is not served here; there are no Eats after 3 p.m.

Leon's Bar-B-Q

- 2800 Sloat Blvd. (46th Ave.), San Francisco; (415) 681-3071
- 1911 Fillmore St. (Bush St.), San Francisco; (415) 922-2436
- 2800 Leavenworth St. (Fisherman's Wharf), San Francisco; no phone

Looking for cheap eats after a day at the zoo? How 'bout some soul food. Leon's feels like a diner in the deep South, with good, greasy ribs, spicy jambalaya, and homemade sweet potato pie. Service is, well, let's just say laid-back. But the food is worth it.

Lunch plates, served all day, are

great bargains. A whole slew of entrees are all priced at $6.40, including pork ribs, half roast chicken, hot link sausages, and more. These come with cornbread, plus your choice of baked beans, potato salad, cole slaw, fries, or even spaghetti. That jambalaya ($4.95) will make your eyes water. And the barbecued smoked turkey sandwich, served on a roll with a side order for $5.95, is a tasty, messy treat.

Dinners offer similar choices, in larger portions or paired together; beef ribs for $10.95, ribs and hot links for $13.50, baby back ribs and chicken for $13.95. These all come with two side orders, as well. Or, try 'em all with a sampler plate ($14.95) of chicken, links, ribs, sliced beef, corn muffins, beans, potato salad—a little bit of everything. Wash these down with one of a half-dozen bottled beers; and, if you have room, send it all home with one of those pies—including chocolate pecan pie and peach cobbler, all $2.75 a slice.

Basic stuff, but definitely the real thing. Leon's Fisherman's Wharf branch, at the Anchorage, isn't a restaurant, just a take-out stand, which closes in the evenings. The other joints are open until 10 p.m. daily.

Little Beijing Restaurant
- 1316 Noriega St. (20th Ave.), San Francisco; (415) 681-6012

There is little to distinguish Little Beijing from any of the hundreds of Chinese storefront restaurants in the Richmond and Sunset areas; it's small and cozy, with just a handful of tables and a half-hearted attempt at decor. So, Mr. C, why this place above the others? Because locals choose it above the others, that's why.

The food is hearty and wonderful, and on any given day or night (except Mondays, when it's closed), the place is packed. Nothing special—it's just good, that's all. And cheap. The menu is *anything* but small; with more than 150 items, it still mentions that "our chef will take special orders from you, even if it is not on the menu." Can there be something they've left out? Chicken dishes

alone include mu shi, sweet and sour, lemon, Kung Pao, Hunan, curry, and a dozen more—most of which only cost $4.95. Same thing with beef (most are $5.25), lamb, and pork. There are more than forty seafood entrees, all under $8 except for whole-fish platters.

And we haven't even touched the appetizers and soups, an omission you shouldn't repeat. Then, there are the dinner specials for groups: For as little as $6.95 per person, they'll cover any size group from two on up. The more people in your party, the more different dishes they'll add. For $7.25 each, two diners can get pot stickers, hot and sour soup, sizzling pork and rice, and Hunan chicken; add a person, they'll add Mongolian beef. Add a fourth, they'll toss in braised shrimp. You get the idea.

Lunch specials, meanwhile, offer forty plates taken from the main menu, each served with rice, soup, and tea; they'll fill you up for a mere $2.95 to $3.75. Try to beat that; on second thought, don't. Take-out and free delivery ($10 minimum) are also available, and they make good options during peak dinner hours, when it can be impossible to get a table.

Little Paris Sandwich Shop
- 444 Clement St. (Sixth Ave.), San Francisco; (415) 221-6028

No, it's not a cafe on Left Bank; more like a greasy spoon in Saigon. There's nothing fancy beyond the name at this little storefront Vietnamese kitchen, where you can sit at formica tables or get take-out at the counter. The food's not fancy either, but it is dependable—and you certainly get a lot for a little.

A plate of lemon grass chicken or pork, served over rice, costs $4.00. An order of "spareribs with rice stick" is just $3.25. A bowl of beef and rice stick soup, at $3.75, is almost too big to finish. Everything is made up fast, kind of like an Asian McDonald's—only a bit more healthy.

Not to say that Viet food doesn't have its heavier side. Mr. C ordered a sandwich of barbecued pork, served on a French roll and filled with shredded carrots, bok choy, onions, and celery. It was messy, but delicious—and only $2.00. Egg rolls are just 50¢ each; and you can also get packages of spring rolls to take home and heat up yourself. Hey, it's not chic, but it is quick. In this bustling Richmond neighborhood, that can count for a lot.

Louis' Restaurant

• 902 Point Lobos Ave., San Francisco; (415) 387-6330

Headed out to see the Seal Rocks? Looking for a dining alternative to the touristy Cliff House? Walk a few yards up and around the bend, and you can't miss Louis', a diner which clearly fills that niche. Louis' is nothing more than a classic greasy spoon (the kind of joint Mr. C prefers anyway). Yet it commands the same dramatic ocean view as the Cliff House, at prices that aren't nearly so fancy.

Of course, the food ain't fancy either, but it's all good, hearty basics. A burger goes for $4.95, with French fries. The BLT, though made with sourdough bread, is a bit pricey at $6.25; but don't forget, this *is* a tourist attraction we're talking about. You're going to pay *something* for that; just not as much here.

Breakfast is served all day. A simple cheese omelette, with fries, is $5.85; the Sutro, named for the baths which once occupied the spot just below, combines turkey, ham, Monterey jack cheese, and fries for $6.85. Or, enjoy a plate of good ol' waffles for $3.45.

Louis' even looks like a traditional diner that's been transplanted from somewhere in town and wedged into the hill. Its windows, facing the Pacific, are large and sunny (well, on a good day, that is). Try to get the corner booth, and you'll almost feel like you're having a meal in midair. They keep fairly traditional diner hours, too: from 6:30 a.m. to 4:30 p.m., Mondays through Thursdays, and until 7:00 p.m. Fridays through Sundays. If you've brought the kiddies, you can have lots of budget-priced fun by eating here, and perhaps visiting the nearby Musée Mécanique or taking no-charge hikes along the Lands End Coastal Trail (see listings under "Museums" and "Walks and Tours," respectively, in the "Entertainment" section).

Lucky Garden Restaurant

• 1125 Clement St. (12th Ave.), San Francisco; (415) 668-0938

Nothing to look at from the outside, Lucky Garden will be a lucky break for you if you venture inside. This tip was given to Mr. C by an acquaintance who works just down the block, and swears by it for good, cheap eats. The large menu combines Chinese and Vietnamese foods, specializing also in vegetarian meals; it's a clean, simple, family-run kind of establishment. What more could you want?

Mr. C recommends, as he often does, the Viet side of the menu. Nearly two dozen soup combinations are all priced from $3.75 to $4.75. Take your pick—rare steak and well-done brisket, seafood and egg noodles, barbecued pork and rice—any one of these can be a great meal in itself. Or, add an appetizer: six potstickers, whether meat-filled or vegetarian, are just $3.25.

Most of the traditional Chinese entrees are easily a dollar or two less than you usually find. All of the beef dishes, like Mongolian or beef and broccoli, are $5.75. Lemon chicken is $5.95. Barbecued pork chow mein (or chow fun) is a deal at $3.95. Even the seafood dishes rarely go above $6.50, including prawns in lobster sauce and sauteed scallops.

From 11 a.m. to 3 p.m. on weekdays, Lucky Garden offers the ever-popular lunch specials. Nearly thirty options are a mere $3.50 or $3.95: crispy duck, beef curry, sweet and sour pork, prawns and broccoli, and lots more. All of these come with soup and salad. Dinner specials offer varied, complete meals for groups, priced from $7.25 to $9.95 per person. You get quite a lot, plenty for all.

Meanwhile, just about the entire menu—appetizers, soups, entrees—is duplicated in vegetarian versions of the same things. Many of these are made with tofu substitutes; all are made with no MSG. As you'd expect, these entrees are not only healthier, they're cheaper! None of the fifty or more entrees tops $5.50. Go ahead—stuff yourself, guilt-free. And there's not even a *chance* you'll have to wash dishes when the bill arrives.

The restaurant is open seven days a week, and offers free delivery on orders over $15.

Mel's Drive-In

- 3355 Geary Blvd. (Stanyan St.), San Francisco; (415) 387-2244
- 2165 Lombard St. (Fillmore St.), San Francisco; (415) 921-3039
- 2240 Shattuck Ave. (Bancroft Way), Berkeley; (510) 540-6351

Mel's Drive-In is an authentic 1950s-style diner, complete with those paper soda-jerk hats, bobby sox and saddle shoes, oldies music on the juke box, and plenty of good, cheap food. Mel's menu features an eclectic mix of diner classics, like meat loaf and chicken pot pie, along with truly 90s cuisine like gourmet turkey burgers and California fruit salad.

Predictably, burgers are a big item here. Their choice ground chuck has no additives or preservatives and is delivered fresh daily. Try "The Famous Melburger," a third of a pound of beef served on a sesame seed bun with lettuce, tomato, Bermuda onions, mayonnaise, and pickle chips, for just $4.50. Make it a half-pounder for just 75¢ more. The true bargain in this department is the "Big Mel Combination Plate," a half-pound burger, great French fries, and a tossed green salad for $6.50. People who are looking for healthier choices may want to go for the gourmet ground turkey burger ($5.95) instead. It's a ground turkey patty served on a whole wheat bun with cole slaw, potato salad, or French fries. Go all out with the "Turkel Burgel," topped with two strips of bacon, cheddar cheese, and thousand-island dressing for $6.95 (so much for health food).

Mel's has plenty of other sandwiches, like the fried egg sandwich for $3.95 and a fresh turkey breast sandwich for $5.95. Don't miss the charbroiled chicken sandwiches: The "American Graffiti" (named, as you may know, because Mel's in L.A. was featured in that rock 'n roll classic) has sauteed mushrooms, Swiss cheese, and fries for $6.75. Did Mr. C mention the hot dogs? Or, the salads? The choices are enough to make you dizzy!

Dinner blue-plates are also cheap in price, but not in portions. "Mel's Spring Chicken," crispy fried chicken with coleslaw and fries ($7.45), "Grandma's Turkey Meat Loaf" with cranberry sauce, lumpy mashed potatoes, homemade gravy, and vegetables ($7.95), or broiled pork chops with grilled onions, potatoes, and veggies ($7.95) are just a few of the myriad choices.

Mel's is also a popular breakfast stop. The menu includes pancakes, French toast, and waffles, hash and eggs, omelettes, and more. And, Mr. C couldn't leave off without telling you about Mel's tantalizing ice cream fountain and other desserts—pies, chocolate fudge cake, and cheesecake, not to mention shakes, malts, sundaes, floats, vanilla Cokes, and more. Just go already!

Mescolanza

- 2221 Clement St. (24th Ave.), San Francisco; (415) 668-2221

If you think you have to go all the way to North Beach to get good Italian food—or if you think that all Richmond has to offer are cheap Oriental restaurants—guess again. Mescolanza has been named as one of the top ten Italian restaurants in the Bay Area by the *San Francisco Chronicle*, and it has received rave reviews from *San Francisco Focus* and "Ask the Critics" as well. What's more, being in a lower-rent area than North Beach, the prices here are far below those of other restaurants that aren't nearly as good.

The pasta dishes are the real bargain here. Try a plate of spinach tortellini al prosciutto for $8.25; gnocchi lucchese or fettucine with pesto, each $7.75; linguine with clam sauce, also $8.25; and ravioli verdura for $8.50. Meat entrees go a few dollars over Mr. C's normal limit, but you certainly won't find these to be over-priced. Tender veal marsala, for example, is $11.00; and pollo arrosto—roasted chicken to you and me—is just $10.75.

Mescolanza's pizzetas, mini-piz-zas for one, are also a big hit. These are prepared in over a half-dozen va-rieties, all of which are priced at $7.75. Try "Pizzetta Mediterraneo," topped with tomatoes, mozzarella, an-chovies, capers, garlic, and oregano; "Pizzetta Frutti di Mare," with toma-toes, mozzarellla, clams, shrimp, and garlic; and "Pizzetta Melanzane," with tomatoes, mozzarella, eggplant, and pesto on top. The restaurant is open every evening from 4:30 p.m. to 10 p.m.

Miz Brown's

- 731 Clement St. (Seventh Ave.), San Francisco; (415) 752-5017
- 3401 California St. (Laurel Village), San Francisco; (415) 752-2039
- 1356 Polk St. (Pine St.), San Francisco; (415) 771-4221
- 2585 Mission St. (21st St.), San Francisco; (415) 648-6070

Miz Brown's is a good ol' fashioned coffee shop, the kind your parents probably took you to—around the age when chicken-in-a-basket and a chocolate milkshake was your idea of a good meal. Now you can continue the tradition, or just satisfy your own comfort food needs, fast and cheap.

Yes, they have fried chicken; it's batter-dipped, crispy, and greasy, served with a pot of honey and an or-der of soggy fries, all for $6.25. Daily specials, in fact, may consist of combinations like fried chicken and spaghetti with meat sauce for $7.30—good luck finishing. Other dinners in-clude things like chicken fried steak ($5.75) or fish and chips ($6.45), served with a side salad or cup of soup.

The soups are homemade, by the way, and quite tasty. These range from clam chowder to matzoh ball, different choices daily, all $2.75 a bowl or $1.50 a cup. Salads are also available in two sizes, like a chef's salad for $4.60 or $5.65. Sandwiches start with deli-style basics, all under $5, and go up to double deckers (BLT with turkey and fries, $6.25). Burgers start at $3.45, in ten combina-tions like "mild green chili and Mon-terey jack" ($5.65). All of these come with French fries, cole slaw, or potato salad.

MB's also has a children's menu. The kiddies will love a "Tiny Tot" burger and fries; you'll love the price, $1.75. And they've recently added a menu of Mexican dishes, such as two tacos (chicken or beef) with rice and beans for $5.25. (Hon-estly, though, would you go to a place like this for Tex-Mex when there are so many places around the city where you can get the real thing?)

Of course, you have to save room for dessert; hope you like to eat heavy. All the fountain classics are here, from cherry and vanilla cokes to milk shakes and malteds to some-thing called an "Orange Freeze" ($3.15), made with OJ and orange sherbet. That's more like it. Other desserts include freshly baked pies and homemade rice pudding.

Breakfasts are big here too. The Country Breakfast special will set you up for anything: two eggs, two large pancakes, plus bacon or sau-sage, all for $6.15. For more dainty appetites, two eggs any style with hash browns and toast are $3.75. Natural, light egg substitutes are available for most orders. Oh, and to return to that nostalgia theme, they have those mini-boxes of cold cereal stacked up on shelves—not to men-tion individual juke boxes in each booth.

Service is friendly, and the atmos-phere is super-casual. One final note: The branch on Clement offers beer and wine, while the Mission Street outpost features a full bar. The others do not serve any liquor. Open well into the evening.

Pat O'Shea's Mad Hatter

- 3848 Geary Blvd. (Third Ave.),
  San Francisco; (415) 752-3148

Pat O'Shea's is your typical sports saloon—multiple TV screens showing several different games, a full bar, pool tables. They also have what every sports bar worth its salt (peanuts) should have: cheap, hearty food. Obviously, you're not going to find a seven-course gourmet meal here; the menu consists mostly of good-sized appetizers, sandwiches, and burgers.

Appetizers are just the thing for sharing with friends as you whoop it up over college hoops, another 49ers triumph, or World Cup soccer. Try the delicious Thai chicken wings, served with a spicy dipping sauce, for $5.50; or nachos, with salsa fresca, sour cream, refried beans, cheddar cheese, and chorizo, for $5.95. This could also be a meal in itself.

O'Shea's also features hearty burgers and sandwiches. The classic 1/3-lb. beef burger, with lettuce, tomato, and onion, is served with homemade French fries for just $5.50; add another 50¢ for jack, Swiss, or cheddar cheese. The mushroom burger and the Western bacon-cheddar burger are rather pricey at $8.00 and $8.50 respectively, but they are loaded with goodies. A better deal is the old-fashioned beef hot dog with chopped fresh tomatoes and sweet red onions ($3.50) or the grilled smoked hot link sausage sandwich with barbecue sauce and peppers ($5). Other sandwiches include a grilled chicken sandwich ($5.50) and a tuna salad sandwich on whole wheat ($4.50).

O'Shea's has pizza, too—though it's actually from **Nizario's**, just down the block at 3840 Geary Boulevard (telephone 752-7777). It's not the cheapest pizza Mr. C has ever found, $6 to $9 for a 12" pie depending on toppings; but it isn't completely outrageous and you can always get slices. They do have plenty of toppings to choose from, including feta cheese, jalapeños, pineapple, pesto, and more, and they have a number of special house combinations.

What goes better with burgers and pizza than beer? They certainly have plenty to choose from, many on tap, and the prices aren't bad. Get domestic pints for $2.50, just $3 for microbrew varieties like Pete's Wicked Ale, Samuel Adams, Red Hook, and Dry Draft Cider. Imports like Harp and Guinness go for $4 a pint. The Mad Hatter stays up until 2 a.m. seven days a week.

Tennessee Grill

- 1128 Taraval St. (22nd Ave.), San
  Francisco; (415) 664-7834

Just below McCoppin Square, this is Mr. C's pick in the Parkside area—a genuine, old-fashioned coffee shop and grill with lots of good, greasy-spoon atmosphere. It's open for breakfast, lunch, and dinner (until 9:00 p.m.) every day. There are two rooms, one with a long counter for those who like to watch the grill action, and a larger, bright room with booths and tables. And the place has a liquor license, with draft beer for $1.50 and cheap chablis for $1.20 a glass. Can't even beat that by staying home.

The food, meanwhile, is good and hearty. Give your day a start you won't soon forget, with a breakfast of chuck steak and eggs ($5.95, with a half-pound of meat). Or, get one egg, two hotcakes, and three strips of bacon, all for $2.50. For lunch, good bets include a steak sandwich and fries ($4.85), fried half-chicken with two vegetables ($4.70), and Tennessee's salad bar, with its all-you-can-eat deal for a healthy $3.50. All the usual sandwiches are here too, from burgers to grilled cheese to BLT.

Dinner offers bigger portions of much the same stuff. Main entrees, all priced between $5.50 and $7.95, all include soup or salad, potato, vegetables, and bread. Go for some grilled pork chops with apple sauce, chicken fried steak, or broiled lamb chops. The "chef's special" is steak and prawns for $7.35; but this is clearly not a seafood kind of place. When in Rome, you know. . .

There are also reduced-price entrees for senior citizens, and for children age 12 and under. Desserts are strictly the basics—pie, cheesecake, jello—does anybody still consider this a dessert? As Mr. C noted, this is an old-fashioned eatery. Hey, it's all part of the charm.

Ton Kiang

- 3148 Geary Blvd. (Spruce St.), San Francisco; (415) 752-4440
- 5821 Geary Blvd. (22nd Ave.), San Francisco; (415) 387-8273

This pair of Chinese restaurants brings something different to the Richmond: affordable elegance. They're not as cheap as their traditional neighborhood counterparts, but then, they don't look it either, making good choices for a fancier Oriental dining experience that still won't break the bank.

Ton Kiang specializes in what's known as Hakka cooking, a lesser-known alternative to your basic Cantonese and Szechuan. In particular, this refers to a selection of stews which are served up in traditional-styled clay pots, all of which are priced between $6.50 and $9.00.

These include such varieties as cod fillets with tofu, beef brisket, spiced eggplant, and bean thread with prawns. Each is swimming in broth, with vegetables and rice—and if you think it won't be enough for a meal, just try to finish one.

Meanwhile, Ton Kiang has plenty of the more standard entrees, most of which are reasonably priced—and you do get a lot of beautifully prepared food on each plate. Kung pao chicken with peanuts is $6.50, for example; so is mu shu pork. The large menu is skewed toward seafood, including several kinds of fillet and whole fish entrees, as available; fresh lobster and crab dishes; and sixteen different preparations of prawn.

Tofu, fried rice, and vegetarian dishes offer an even less expensive option; most of these are in the $5 to $6 range. Ton Kiang also offers fantastic and extensive dim sum, served until 3:00 p.m. every day of the week. All in bright, modern surroundings—and definitely geared to large groups, with banquet facilities upstairs at the western branch.

HOTELS AND LODGING

Always on the lookout for a bargain, Mr. C has tried to wade through the tricky waters of the hotel biz to find rooms where you can stay for well under $100 a night. In fact, many offer rooms for under $60 a night. These waters are tricky because hotel rates ebb and flow. And don't forget that taxes are always going to be added on top of any quoted price. Here, then, are the results of this not-necessarily scientific survey.

Two important tips: First of all, you should always, *always* ask about discounts. No hotel room ever has only one price. Take advantage of any discounts you can—including corporate, AAA, military, American Association of Retired Persons, and others. Furthermore, if you're going to be in town long enough, ask about weekly rates.

Finally, if you can at all, be sure to make reservations—and make them *early*. San Francisco gets a lot of convention and business crowds. This also means that many rooms are empty come Friday, so you can get great weekend package deals at almost any hotel in the city. Even ritzier places may run under $100 a night with one of these specials.

HOTELS AND MOTELS

The Allison Hotel
- 417 Stockton St. (Sutter St.), San Francisco; (415) 986-8737

Located just a block north of Union Square, the Allison Hotel was recently acquired by new management, and has been completely renovated. That makes it a rare find: an old-time, residential hotel which looks modern and also caters to the budget traveler.

Seven stories means that you can get some sunny rooms here, even in the middle of downtown. The rooms are small, but the beds are new and comfy, the bathrooms have modern fixtures and plumbing, and the color TVs have cable and remote controls. Rates start as low as $30 a night for a single with a shared bathroom down the hall; add ten dollars for a small private bathroom. Doubles start at $35 with a shared bath, $45 with private bath. All of these rates go up by ten dollars more during the prime summer months, but still, they're hard to beat.

Larger rooms, for three or four people, are available; even these go no higher than $75 a night. The Allison also offers weekly rates, starting from as low as $200 a week. Parking is always tough anywhere downtown, and the hotel does not have its own facilities—but it does happen to be located right in front of the Stockton-Sutter Garage, one of The City's true *parking* bargains. Hourly rates are super-cheap, much lower than any other garage or lot; and you can park in here overnight (from 7:00 p.m. to 7:00 a.m.) for a fixed price of $3.

Beach Motel
- 4211 Judah St. (47th Ave.), San Francisco; (415) 681-6618

The Sunset area, close to the wide-open Pacific, is a natural spot for a cluster of motels, some of which are not terribly expensive, depending on the time of your stay. Like the motel strip along Lombard Street in the Marina, many of these places seem virtually identical: run by husband-wife teams (i.e., short-staffed), often run-down, some in the process of gradual renovation. Basically, these are inexpensive, no-frills places to rest your head at night in a really beautiful location. After all, the beach is just across the highway, and many of the rooms overlook the water.

The Beach Motel is one of the nicer examples among these establishments. A room with a queen-size bed goes for as little as $40 a night in the off-season (generally speaking, November through April). Weekly rates are available from about $210, very good indeed. All rooms offer color TV with cable, including HBO; direct-dial telephones; kitchenette rooms are also available. And there is free parking on the premises, no small consideration either.

Unlike downtown hotels which cater to the business crowd, and which sometimes offer weekend discount deals, the weekends are of course more expensive at places like this one. And all rates go up during the summer season. Hey, it's the beach. Also in this neighborhood, check out the **Oceanview Motel** at 4340 Judah Street; telephone (415) 661-2300. It's nearly identical in every way.

Brady Acres
- 649 Jones St. (Post St.), San Francisco; (415) 929-8033 or (800) 6-BRADY-6

Sure, it sounds like a tale of two sitcoms, but. . . .Travelers on an extended stay in San Francisco want all the creature comforts of home; Brady Acres comes pretty close. Each of the 25 rooms is equipped with a microwave oven, refrigerator, coffee maker, and toaster. They even come with all the kitchen stuff you might need, like china, flatware, and glasses; and most rooms include a wet bar with a bar sink. Every room also has a cassette player and a color TV. What's more, each room has its own *private* telephone line, from which you can make unlimited free local phone calls, as well as its own answering machine for your messages. And, in the basement, you'll find a coin-operated washer and dryer with free laundry soap. This is beginning to feel more and more like home!

Now, can all this comfort be cheap? Yes! Brady Acres has affordable weekly rates: $300 to $390 in the summer (May through September) and $250 to $300 in the winter (October through April). That can be as little as $35 a night. Daily rates are reasonable, too: $50 to $55 for a single, and $60 to $65 for a double.

Brady Acres is conveniently located downtown, just blocks away from the Civic Center, Union Square, Chinatown, and more. As an added bonus, proprietor Deborah Brady is a native San Franciscan (O rare!) who is more than happy to share her in-depth knowledge of The City with you any time.

Campus Motel
- 1619 University Ave. (California St.), Berkeley; (510) 841-3844

The Campus Motel is not only low on rates, but it's long on history, too. Bought by a woman in 1952, she, along with her family, has owned and operated it ever since. As you can probably imagine, it wasn't all that common for women in the 1950s to buy and run hotels, but she did it—and those looking for inexpensive lodging in Berkeley are much the better for it.

Rooms here generally go for $45 to $50 a night, depending on occupancy, rising by about $5 during peak season, roughly the last two weeks of May (graduation time, naturally). The motel is conveniently located just five blocks from UC, and each room includes cable television, direct-dial phones, and free coffee in the morning. The Campus Motel also provides free parking—a big plus anywhere in the Bay Area. In addition to standard motel-type rooms, there are a few larger suites available; one with three double beds ($75 a night) and one with two twin beds and a double ($65 a night). Another one offers a kitchenette *and* two double beds ($65 to $75 a night); it's great for when the whole family wants to come visit. Who knows? With all this comfort, they may not want to leave!

The Herbert Hotel
- 161 Powell St. (O'Farrell St.), San Francisco; (415) 362-1600

It can be difficult to find inexpensive hotels in the heart of downtown, but here's another one. The Herbert Hotel is a block from Union Square, right near the start of the Powell Street cable car lines. Now, Mr. C must tell you, this ain't exactly the Four Seasons Clift (where many celebrities stay when in The City); but for those of us who aren't on an expense account—heck, even if you are—these prices more than make up for any shortcomings in the luxury department.

As with many hotels in San Francisco, the cheapest rates are for rooms with a shared bath, just down the hall. Such rooms at the Herbert go for a mere $25 a night. Bargain *city*! Rooms with a private bath are still very reasonable at just $30 a night—go ahead, live a little. Weekly rates are offered here, as available: $90 for a shared bath, $105 to $130 for a room with a private bath. The more expensive rooms, of course, are those facing the street; most popular with the tourists. The Herbert is a clean, safe hotel and in a perfect location for sightseeing—in fact, the San Francisco Visitor Information Center is also nearby, around the corner.

The Hotel David
- 480 Geary St. (Taylor St.), San Francisco, (415) 771-1600 or (800) 524-1888

Hotel David calls itself a "bed and

breakfast," since you get a free breakfast each morning of your stay. But
hold on a minute! Unlike some B &
Bs, where "breakfast" may mean muffins and coffee, the David serves up a
sumptuous, scrumptious, prepared-to-
order culinary odyssey. In their dining room, choose anything from their
renowned menu of ethnic (primarily
Jewish) delicacies—blintzes, potato
pancakes, omelettes, bagels, French
toast made from challah bread, and
more. It's all included in the price of
your room, which nevertheless remains quite reasonable. You even get
25% off anything from the lunch and
dinner menus. And, if you book two
or more nights here, they will transport you via shuttle bus from SFO airport to the door of the hotel, at no
charge. Such a deal!

The Hotel David offers comfortable rooms with direct-dial telephones, color TVs, radios, and
hot-towel racks. The rooms are good-
sized and feature "sleep-ease" mattresses. Two floors of the building are
reserved for non-smokers. The hotel
is located right on Theatre Row, close
to Union Square, the cable cars, and
other tourist attractions. The rates are
as uniform as the quality: Singles
cost $69, doubles $89, all year round.

The Hotel Durant
• 2600 Durant Ave. (Telegraph Ave.),
  Berkeley; (510) 845-8981 or (800)
  238-7268
Just a block from UC-Berkeley, The
Hotel Durant features rooms with private baths and rates which include a
continental breakfast. Rooms start
from about $87 for a single and $97
for a double; even with the school so
close by, prices remain pretty constant throughout the year. Be sure to
ask about discounts for which you
may be eligible, including AAA, corporate, and anything to do with the
university. The Hotel Durant is an old
classic built in 1920, and rates also include in-house parking.

The Durant also has its own restaurant, **Henry's Publick House**; telephone (510) 845-8981. It's an
elegant, English-style pub serving

hearty American fare. Why this trans-
Atlantic mixup? Who knows. Prices
here are not, strictly speaking, cheap
(entrees range from $5.95 to $12.95),
but they certainly won't break the
bank. And if you're not loaded, the
area is—with inexpensive restaurants, that is, many of which are profiled elsewhere in this book.

For similar accommodations and
prices, you may also want to take a
look at the nearby **Hotel Shattuck**,
located at 2086 Allston Way (Shattuck Ave.); telephone (510) 845-
7300. Toll-free numbers are (800)
742-8882 in California, and (800)
237-5359 outside the state. The Shattuck offers low winter rates ($69 for
a single; $79 for a double), and their
summer rates are very competitive
($90 for a double; $100 for a double).
Both the Shattuck and the Durant
charge a fee for parking.

The Leland Hotel
• 1315 Polk St. (Bush St.), San
  Francisco; (415) 441-5141
The Leland is a very affordable in-
town hotel located in the area affec-
tionately referred to as "Polk Gulch."
It's a district in-between the ritzy
neighborhoods of Nob Hill on one
side, and Pacific Heights on the
other—in more ways than one. The
gulch bears no visible relation to
either hill, but it is near many good
restaurants and within a quick walk
of many of The City's top attractions.
MUNI buses stop nearby, ready to
take you to Fisherman's Wharf, Union Square, SoMa, and points beyond.

And, while this area is just north
of the notorious Tenderloin, the hotel
does maintain 24-hour security. The
staff is extremely helpful and very
friendly; messages are efficiently delivered, and visitors must check in before being allowed upstairs. The
Leland is also gay-owned and operated, though not overtly so; it's by no
means a restriction on the clientele.

This is one of The City's many
older, residential hotels, and a very
well-kept one. Rates run from a super-
cheap $35 a night up to $68 a night.
That bottom rate involves sharing a

hallway bathroom; studios, outfitted with private baths and small kitchenettes, are just $58 for one person, $68 for two. Weekly rates for studios ($200 per week) are also available. Kitchenettes have dishware and cookware provided. The rooms are quite comfy, especially good for an extended visit. Rooms facing Polk Street are bright and sunny in the morning, with plenty of windows offering views of the always-entertaining street scene. Unfortunately, that same activity can make these rooms noisy at night. There are some studios which face the quieter side street.

Lombard Plaza Motel
- 2026 Lombard St. (Webster St.), San Francisco; (415) 921-2444

Looking at the stretch of motels along Lombard Street in the Marina District will make you feel as though you've left The City entirely, and instead landed at some boardwalk honky-tonk resort area. Still, this is easily the highest concentration of low-priced lodging anywhere in San Francisco. It's a mix of well-known budget chains and independents, most offering the same set of amenities, including free parking lots (a very attractive feature if you've brought or rented some wheels).

The Lombard Plaza is one of the nicest of the bunch, with its long, low structure, hanging planters and trelliswork, and natural wood decks—again, kind of like a beach motel without the beach. It's a husband-and-wife-run operation, and they clearly put lots of care into the place, which has been recently renovated. The rooms Mr. C checked were small and cozy, but they had brand-new carpeting, totally modern bathroom fixtures, handsome wooden wardrobe closets, color TV with cable, and those cute little refrigerator-microwave oven units made for such establishments. You also get direct-dial telephones in each room.

Rates start as low as $35 a night for a single room, and $59 for a double; prices go quite a bit higher during peak summer months. Suites are

MR. CHEAP'S PICKS
Hotels and Motels

✔ **Brady Acres**—A tale of two sitcoms? This may be in the heart of downtown, but it sure isn't priced like it— especially when you consider all the amenities included.

✔ **The Leland Hotel**—On wild and wacky Polk Street, this residential hotel has a variety of rooms, and rates, to fit any budget.

✔ **The Lombard Plaza Motel**—One of the lowest on the low-priced Lombard strip—yet nicely furnished, run with a personal touch, and a block from chic Chestnut Street.

available as well. The folks here were even offering discount coupons for breakfast at some of the many casual eateries nearby, a definite cost-cutter.

Among some of the other low-priced motels in this bargain neighborhood, Mr. C found the best mix of low rates and decent rooms at **Econo Lodge**, 2505 Lombard Street, telephone (415) 921-2505 or (800) 424-4777, which has also been recently taken over and modernized; and the **Lanai Friendship Inn** at 2361 Lombard Street, telephone (415) 931-7810, offering a large number of rooms (some renovated) and low weekly rates. Finally, the **Van Ness Motel** at 2850 Van Ness Avenue, telephone (415) 776-3220, offers similarly low prices in a nicer location. It's at the corner of chic Chestnut Street, which somehow manages to co-exist with the more garish Lombard Street just a block away.

Ramada Limited
- 240 Seventh St. (Folsom St.), San Francisco; (415) 861-6469 or (800) 544-0502

Mr. C doesn't usually devote much ink to big-name chains, only because he figures that most folks already know about these places. But the Ramada Limited deserves some mention, being located in the alternative and trendy SoMa district. Just recently taken over (and formerly known as the Yerba Buena Inn), it's a local motel with some major amenities. Parking, for one. The place has not only a small lot on the premises, but a garage across the street—definitely a premium anywhere *near* downtown. Color TV with cable, laundry facilities, and coffee available all day in the lobby are just a few more of the, um, perks.

Meanwhile, all the rooms are being renovated even as this book goes to print. For that reason, there's not much point in quoting prices, which of course are bound to rise; still, Mr. C expects that this will be one of the less expensive, nicely appointed motels in this lively, funky part of town. Call or check them out for current rates.

The Temple Hotel
- 469 Pine St. (Kearny St.), San Francisco; (415) 781-2565

Here's another long-time, residential and transient downtown hotel, located near the Financial District and just below Chinatown. Sure, the place is old, and the elevator is one of those cage types you see in black-and-white movies. But the simple rooms have been kept up nicely, with plenty of modern touches—such as color TVs (no cable) and new, coordinated linens and drapes. Everything is spotlessly clean, tended to with daily maid service.

Certainly, you get as much as you could expect for such low rates in a desireable part of town. Daily rates for a room with a shared bath down the hall are $30 a night for a single, and $35 double; rooms with a private bath only cost $10 per night more. And here's the part Mr. C really likes: a discount! Stay for three or four days, and 10% will be deducted from your bill. A five or six-day stay gets you 15% off, and rates by the week are 20% below the standard prices. That means you can spend a week here for as little as $168, or $24 a night. Good deal.

ALTERNATIVE LODGING

If you seek something different from the standard hotel or motel, the Bay Area has plenty of unique options—mainly, bed and breakfasts, and hostels. B&B's generally cost more than hotels, but they also give you more; hostels cost far less. In either case, the establishments described below are all great values.

For those who've never stayed in a hostel, Mr. C would like to offer a little primer. Hostels provide a safe, secure place to sleep and bathe, often in dorm-like settings, at *extremely* low prices. What you give up is privacy, chi-chi amenities, and, in some cases, a certain amount of come-and-go freedom. Hostels are often affiliated with tightly-knit national or international organizations, which set up strict guidelines and quality standards. You have to be in by a specified hour; you may also have to stay out during the middle of the day, when the staff takes care of housecleaning.

Unaffiliated hostels can be a bit dodgy; usually they have fewer rules and more freedoms, and many don't have a curfew or lockout period. You may not feel as certain of what you're getting into, given the fact that many of these are run by—and cater to—a freewheeling crowd of world travelers; but most are just fine, and very friendly. Do be sure to inquire about security measures.

American Youth Hostel at Union Square

- 312 Mason St. (O'Farrell St.), San Francisco; (415) 788-5604

This particular establishment is indeed affiliated with Hostelling International-American Youth Hostels, the big daddy of the bunch. It's a standard dormitory-style hostel with shared bathrooms and kitchen facilities. It is open 24 hours, with no lockout or curfew—quite unusual. And, being smack-dab in the heart of downtown makes the place convenient to many of The City's biggest attractions.

The rates here are $14 a night for AYH members, $17 a night for nonmembers. You can spend that same extra three bucks and become a member, by the way, in case you plan to continue hosteling in the future. Hostelling International also has affiliated hostels up and down the coast in Montara, Pescadero, Sausalito, and Point Reyes.

Fort Mason International Hostel

- Fort Mason Center (Bldg. #240), Marina Blvd. at Buchanan St., San Francisco; (415) 771-7277

Fort Mason International Hostel offers a bit of both ends of the hostel spectrum. It is affiliated with Hostelling International-American Youth Hostels, and there is a lockout period from 11 a.m. to 3 p.m.; however, there is no night-time curfew. Best of all, the rate is just $13 per night, and half-price for children under 17 accompanied by a guardian. You'll be charged the same prices whether or not you're a member of HI-AYH, but you should note that they require a picture identification for admittance.

The hostel, one of the largest around, has a total of 150 beds. Family rooms are available upon request

for parents with children (it's wise to call in advance). Bathrooms are shared, with separate facilities for men and women, of course. There is a fully-outfitted kitchen, where you can store and prepare your own food—another cost-cutting feature popular with hostelers.

It's all housed in a former barracks building in Fort Mason Center, once a military warehouse facility, now a premier arts complex and a National Historic Landmark. Theaters, galleries, cafes, and a bookstore are among the several dozen organizations sharing the grounds with this hostel. The Marina itself is a short, picturesque stroll away, with the Golden Gate Bridge looming in the distance. In the opposite direction, you have the Fisherman's Wharf area. For price *or* location, this hostel is hard to beat; together, it's an incredible deal.

The Globe Hostel

- 10 Hallam Place (Folsom St.), San Francisco; (415) 431-0540

The Globe Hostel is affiliated with Interclub, an independent chain of hostels catering to international travelers. In fact, you have to *prove* you're an international traveler to stay here. The result, though, is that you'll get to meet exciting and interesting people from all over the world.

The Globe also differs from many other hostels in that they offer more hotel-like accommodations. You can get private rooms for about $36 per night, for two people; $12 more for each additional person. Private rooms can be reserved in advance, but only by advance payment. To stay in one of the shared rooms, which hold up to five guests, you'll pay just $12 a night or $70 a week. Rates can even go as low as $10 per night in the off-season. Can you believe it?

Each room has its own bathroom,

MR. CHEAP'S PICKS
Alternative Lodging

✔ **The Globe Hostel**—If you're an international traveler—and you can prove it— you'll find cheap accommodations and plenty of other travelers to keep you company.

✔ **Pacific Tradewinds Guest House**—A little more like a traditional hostel, but still with plenty of flexibilty. Not to mention the free sock wash!

so the number of people with whom you're sharing the facilities will be considerably lower than at most hostels. They also offer a bar, pool table, cafe, TV lounge, sun roof, free coffee, and more. Two cats roam around to keep you company, and there are plenty of common areas where you can meet and mingle with your fellow travelers. And all of this is in a hip SoMa location, surrounded by great clubs and hangouts—many of which are profiled in this book. Since there is no lockout or curfew imposed by the hostel, you can enjoy as much of that nightlife as you can stand; especially with all the money you'll save by staying here instead of a hotel.

Gramma's Rose Garden Inn
• 2740 Telegraph Ave. (Stuart St.), Berkeley; (510) 549-2145

Gramma's Rose Garden Inn is comprised of two turn-of-the-century mansions, along with three newer buildings, entirely surrounded by English rose gardens. The prices here are bit higher than many of the other places Mr. C has reviewed; many rooms go up to $145 a night, but some start as low as $85. This isn't as unreasonable as it may sound to dyed-in-the-wool cheapsters, considering how much you get for your

money. All rooms have private baths, phones, and televisions; some of the higher priced rooms have fireplaces, decks, porches, and/or scenic views. All rates include a full breakfast; wine and cheese in the evening; plus coffee, tea, and homemade cookies available all day. Sundays feature a full brunch, also included in the price of the room.

Located just a few blocks from UC-Berkeley, Gramma's Rose Garden Inn is the place to book when Mom and Dad want to turn a school-year visit into an honest-to-goodness vacation getaway.

Grand Central Hostel
• 1412 Market St. (Tenth St.), San Francisco; (415) 703-9988

Grand Central Hostel is an independent, unaffiliated hostel in a superb downtown location near the Civic Center. Even so, they have some of the lowest rates around: Shared room and bath accommodations are just $9 per night in the winter and $15 per night in the summer. Some private rooms are available as well, at just $18 per night for a single and $27 per night for a double. These are first-come, first-serve so you can't reserve them in advance.

These rates include free breakfast, as well as free coffee and tea during the day. There is a kitchen for cooking your own meals; TV rooms for something to watch while you're eating; and an exercise room to work the calories back off. Plus a fax machine (sign of the times), bike storage, and laundry facilities. There is no lockout period or curfew here, so you are free to come and go as you please. Rooms are designated for smokers and non-smokers; weekly rates are available.

Pacific Tradewinds Guest House
• 680 Sacramento St. (Kearny St.), San Francisco; (415) 433-7970

This is a small dormitory-style hostel in the heart of Chinatown. They have 29 beds on two floors, with a bathroom on each level. Rates are just $12 per night; and, if you stay a week, you'll get the seventh night free! There's no curfew, but they do lock the doors at midnight—if you want to stay out later, you can arrange to get night keys. The hostel is closed from 12 noon to 4 p.m. for cleaning, but. . . the folks here are flexible. You're not "locked-out" *per se*; you can drop things off or pick stuff up—as long as you stay out of their way. There is a kitchen for guest use, as well as a laundry service for just $2; drop off your laundry and they will wash, dry, and fold it. This is starting to sound better than living at home with Mom and Dad!

But, before you decide to move in forever: Pacific Tradewinds tries to restrict its facilities to international travelers and students. If you're not from outside the U.S., or a student on vacation, they will try to steer you toward other accommodations.

Oh, and then there's the free sock wash. What on earth is *that*?? you ask. Well, it seems the proprietors noticed that, after a day of running around San Francisco (especially in the summertime), the one thing visitors really wanted was clean socks. So, they began to gather people at about 8 p.m. to have a sock wash. Neat idea, huh? They don't do it all the time—only when people are interested—but y'know, this is the kind of group bonding experience that you just won't find at the Hilton. Go ahead. Ask *them*.

The Red Victorian Bed and Breakfast Inn

- 1665 Haight St. (Cole St.), San Francisco; (415) 864-1978

The Red Victorian Bed and Breakfast Inn, better known to locals as the "Red Vic," is owned and operated by a longtime Haight artist. The result is a hotel filled with various theme rooms; you can spend a night in the "The Summer of Love Room" or the "The Japanese Tea Garden Room." Many do not have private baths, but don't worry—the shared bathrooms have themes of their own, like the "Aquarium" bath and the "Starlight" bath. These rooms, of course, are the bargains here; they go for $65 to $90 a night. Rooms with private baths start at $95 a night, going up to $135—for the "Peacock Suite," with its king-size canopy bed and a bathtub with a moon window looking into a sitting room. Not for the frugally-inclined, unless of course they've saved so much money by using this book that they can afford to splurge.

All prices include a continental breakfast of bagels, granola, fruit, coffee, and various teas. There is a meditation room, and the folks here will even lend you meditation tapes if you wish. The Red Vic has a homey atmosphere for days—this definitely ain't the Holiday Inn. And of course, the second you step outside, you're right there in the middle of perhaps the liveliest scene in all of San Francisco—The Haight. 'Nuff said.

The Red Victorian is also home to the Global Village Hospitality Center, a store filled with clothes, jewelry, and gifts from around the world. It's not necessarily cheap, but it's fun. Down the block, the Red Vic Movie House presents offbeat films at bargain prices (see listing under "Entertainment: Movies").

ALPHABETICAL INDEX